Belgium & Luxembourg

Bruges, Ghent &
Northwest Belgium
p83

Antwerp &
Northeast Belgium
p142

Brussels
p34

Wallonia
p183

Luxembourg
p243

D0965033

Mark Elliott, Catherine Le Nevez, Helena Smith,
Regis St Louis, Benedict Walker

Contents

GALERIES ST-HUBERT, BRUSSELS P38

ALEKSEI VELIZHANIN / SHUTTERSTOCK ©

BRABO FOUNTAIN, ANTWERP P145

MISTERVLAD / HUTTERSTOCK ©

Contents

CHÂTEAU DE VIANDEN, VIANDEN P261

UNDERSTAND

SURVIVAL GUIDE

SPECIAL FEATURES

Welcome to Belgium & Luxembourg

Bruges canals, Antwerp fashion, Luxembourg bubbles, Trappist beers, chocolate and chips, belfries and castles, crazy carnivals... These two small countries certainly punch above their weight.

Unexpected Riches

As well as historic town cores and a bounty of Unesco sites, discover stalactite-filled caves, post-industrial heritage, forest-edged kayaking rivers, rural châteaux and sandy North Sea beaches. Cutting-edge museums and finely endowed galleries unveil the complex history of what has been a crucible of European art, from the Flemish Primitives, through Rubens' voluptuous nymphs and art nouveau's sinuous curves to bizarre surrealism, comic strips and 21st-century fashion. And in spring, don't miss some of the world's weirdest carnivals lubricated by some of the planet's finest beers.

Battle Scars

Since at least Roman times, what we now call Belgium and Luxembourg have regularly fallen in the path of invaders, not least in the last two centuries. A lion statue atop a conical artificial hill overlooks the world-famous Waterloo battlefield where Napoleon was finally defeated. Seemingly endless rows of white gravestones in Flanders fields commemorate four years of WWI hell. And haunting museums honour those who died in WWII, notably during the devastating 'Battle of the Bulge', Hitler's last-ditch counter-attack in Luxembourg and the Ardennes.

Town & Country

With magical market squares, belfries, canals and step-gabled houses, most of Belgium's 'art' cities lie in predominantly flat, Dutch-speaking Flanders. These places are close together and seamlessly interconnected by regular public transport. In contrast, much of hilly, French-speaking Wallonia is profoundly rural, so it's useful to have your own wheels to reach the activity-packed holiday spots of the Ardennes. Luxembourg falls somewhere between the two: beyond its compact, sophisticated capital lie many pretty castle villages that are rural yet relatively accessible.

Chips, Chocolate & Beer

Luxembourg is a gourmet's paradise while Belgium's remarkable range of comestible specialities goes far beyond the country's diminutive size. Brussels and Liège compete over what constitutes the perfect waffle, while countless speciality shops sell sublime chocolates. Jumbo mussels are served with crispy, twice-fried frites that you'll only call 'French' fries at your peril. Brewing is an almost mystical art in Belgium with a dazzling rainbow of different styles, most notably the six great Trappist beers, created within active monasteries. Meanwhile Luxembourg maintains its own celebratory mood with an ever-flowing supply of local Moselle bubbly.

Why I Love Belgium & Luxembourg

by Mark Elliott, Writer

As a school child, some of my most vivid travel memories were of Luxembourg's Clervaux castle rising spookily through the mist. And of Brussels' baffling Atomium that seemed to be related more to my chemistry lessons than to practical architecture. Later, living 15 years in Belgium, I came to realise that the country's love of surrealism goes deeper than Magritte's pipe or the orange-lobbing Gilles at Binche carnival, creating a self-deprecating humour in people for whom their country's very creation sometimes still seems like an 1830 geopolitical joke.

For more about our writers, see p320

Above: Brussels, p34

Belgium & Luxembourg

Bruges
Postcard-perfect canals, medieval masterpieces (p85)

Antwerp
Fashion, nightlife and Rubens (p144)

Ghent
Beautifully real, with Van Eyck's best (p128)

Ypres
Poignant WWI memories, amazing regeneration (p116)

Brussels
Art nouveau, comics and the Grand Place (p34)

Binche
The world's weirdest Mardi Gras? (p195)

NORTH SEA

Bergen op Zoom

Goes

Vlissingen

Zeebrugge
Blankenberge
De Haan
Knokke-Heist
Boudewijn Kanaal
Lissewege
Lillo

Ostend
Bruges
Eeklo
Leopold Kanaal

St-Niklaas
Lokeren
Antwerp
Boechout
Lier

Koksijde
De Panne
Oostduinkerke
Nieuwpoort
Veurne
Diksmuide
Torhout

Dunkirk
Esen

Calais

Westvleteren

Poperinge

Ghent
Breendonk
Boom
Willebroek

St Martens Latem
Dendermonde
Mechelen

WEST-VLAANDEREN
Roeselare
Lije
OOST-VLAANDEREN
Aalst
Meise

Ypres
Kortrijk
Oudenaarde
BRUSSELS

Menen
WALLONIA
Mouscron
Geraardsbergen
Ninove
Halle
Tervuren

Tourcoing
Roubaix
Ronse
Dender
Waterloo
Wavre

Lille
Louvain-la-Neuve

Béthune
Tournai
Ath
HAINAUT
Nivelles
Villers-la-Ville

Pipaix
Leuze
Le Roeulx
Canal Charleroi-Bruxelles

Lens
Mons
La Louvière

Douai
Valenciennes
Cuesmes
Binche
Charleroi

FRANCE
Arras
Borinage
Sambre

Beaumont

Amiens
Péronne
Philippeville
Botte de Hainaut
Mariembourg

St-Quentin
Chimay
Couvin

ELEVATION
450m
300m
150m
75m
0

Charleville-Mézières

Laon

Compiègne

Soissons

Creil

0 50 km
0 25 miles

Reims

NORTH SEA

51°N

N 0 ——— 50 km
0 ——— 25 miles

• Oss
• Kleve
's-Hertogenbosch
Wesel •

Lier
Moats, green ramparts and
enchanting *begijnhoven* (p167)

Helmond •

Herne

Gelsenkirchen •
• Breda
• Tilburg

Baarle-
Hertog

Essen •
Bochum

Eindhoven •

NETHERLANDS
Venlo •

Duisburg •

• Hoogstraten

Krefeld •

Oostmalle •
• Turnhout

Antwerpen Turnhout

Düsseldorf •
Wuppertal

ANTWERPEN
Achel •

Mönchengladbach •

Herentals •
• Mol

• Weert

Solingen

Herentals

Roermond •

Albert Kanaal

LIMBURG
Maaseik •

Leverkusen •

Aarschot Diest •
Nationaal Park
Hoge Kempen

Rillaar •
Scherpenheuvel
Genk • Sittard •

Kessel-Lo •
Hasselt • Maasmechelen

Leuven
VLAAMS-
BRABANT
Bilzen •

• Cologne

• Tienen
Sint Tongeren •
Maastricht

Hoegaarden •
Truiden • Lanaye

• Aachen
Düren •

Hannut •
Rutten •

Waremme •

Bonn •

• Gembloux
Seraing • Liège •
• Eupen

Namur •
Marche-
les-Dames
Verviers

Han-sur-Lesse
Classic, if commercial,
cave experience (p213)

LIEGE
Remouchamps •

NAMUR
Spa •
Haute Fagnes
Nature Reserve

GERMANY

Francorchamps •
Malmedy •

• Godinne
Coo •
Stavelot •

Dinant •
Trois
Ponts •
St Vith •

Anseremme •
Marche-en-
Famenne

Villers-
sur-Lesse
Jemelle •

Han-sur-
Lesse
Champlon Wemperhardt •

La Roche-en-Ardenne •

St-Hubert •

Clervaux •

Redu •
Transinne •
Bastogne •

• Libramont

• Vianden
Bitburg •

Neufchâteau •
Diekirch •

Bouillon
Crusader castle and
kayaks (p216)

Ettelbrück
Martelange •

Müllerthal
Echternach •

Gutland

Sure

Mersch •
LUXEMBOURG
• Trier

Florenville •
Arlon •
LUXEMBOURG
CITY
• Wasserbillig

• Virton
Petange •
Ehnen •

Esch-sur-
Alzette
Schengen •
Remich •

Luxembourg City
Old-town charm across
a stunning gorge (p245)

• Thionville
• Saarlouis

Homburg •

Belgium & Luxembourg's
Top 15

Bruges

1 Laced with canals and full of evocative step-gabled houses, Bruges (p85) is the ultimate picture-postcard tourist destination. Of course, that's all too well known and the city is often overrun, but come midweek in February you may have it largely to yourself. Year-round you can escape the crowds and carriage rides by dipping into some of Bruges' majestic art collections. The Groeningemuseum is hard to beat, offering a potted history of Belgian art, with an outstanding selection of works by the Flemish Primitives.

Brussels' Grand Place

2 Brussels' heart beats in the Grand Place (p38) – the most theatrically beautiful medieval square in Europe. It is ringed by gold-trimmed, gabled guild-houses and flanked by the 15th-century Gothic town hall. The cobblestones were laid in the 12th century, when the square was used as a marketplace; the names of the surrounding lanes evoke herbs, cheese and poultry. And indeed the Grand Place still hosts a flower market, as well as Christmas stalls, concerts and – every two years – a dazzlingly colourful 'carpet' of flower petals.

YASONYA / SHUTTERSTOCK ©

CAPTUREPB / SHUTTERSTOCK ©

KOBBY DAGAN / SHUTTERSTOCK ©

© CLAUDE LEE SADIK, USED WITH PERMISSION OF BENOIT NIHANT

Carnival Capers

3 If your neighbours' idea of a good time is to dress up in barrel costumes jingling with little bells, don spooky masks and ostrich-feather hats and then go throwing oranges at passers-by, you might wonder about their sanity. Then again you might just be living in Binche. That's the town whose unique Mardi Gras carnival (p196) has long been so indulgent it gave the English language the term 'binge'. Belgium's carnival season stretches way beyond Shrove Tuesday with other unique twists, especially in Stavelot, Malmedy and Aalst. Carnaval de Binche (p196)

Chocolate

4 In 1857 Swiss confectioner Jean Neuhaus opened a sweet shop (p80) in Brussels' glorious Galeries St-Hubert – it's still there. But it was in 1912 that Neuhaus' son was credited with creating that most Belgian of morsels, the praline, by filling a chocolate shell with a flavoured centre. Belgian chocolates remain world-beaters due to the local insistence on 100% cocoa butter, and every town has its selection of *chocolatier* shops: hushed, hallowed temples where glove-handed assistants patiently load up *ballotin* boxes with your individual selection. Chocolate maker, Benoit Nihant (p232)

Flemish Primitives

5 Western representational art was transformed in the 15th century by Bruges-based painters, notably by the Van Eyck brothers, whose mastery of oil paints allowed them to simulate reality and paint faces that expressed emotional states. This development was aided by Flanders' economy, which meant that the time was ripe for mercantile sponsors to commission secular works as well as religious works full of hidden messages... Does Ghent's *Mystic Lamb* (p129) really hold secret clues to a mysterious Jesus legacy? *The Adoration of the Mystic Lamb* (p129)

Belfries & Begijnhoven

6 When Unesco contemplated Belgium's magnificent smorgasbord of medieval architecture, it was clearly too overwhelming to decide what should go on the World Heritage list. So a whole range was selected. This includes 33 belfries (churchlike clock towers built as symbols of civic freedoms), fine examples of which are found in Tournai, Bruges and St-Truiden. Also included were around 20 beautiful *begijnhoven*: enclosed urban villages that were a form of 'convent lite'. It's hard to beat those of Lier (p167), Turnhout, Diest and Kortrijk. *Begijnhoven*, Kortrijk (p123)

Castles

7 Get ready for an overload of spectacular castles. Antwerp and Ghent both have medieval ones right in their city centres. For ruins, Larochette, Bourscheid and Beaufort are hard to beat, while the Ardennes town of Bouillon (p217) is dominated by the remains of a castle that was sold to fund a crusade. French-style *châteaux* include Modave and riverside Freÿr. Then there are vast, dour but powerfully brooding fortress-citadels at Namur, Huy and Dinant that retained military importance well into the 20th century. Château de Bourscheid (p260)

Antwerp Art & Fashion

8 Fashion-focused Antwerp (p144) has it all. Its skyline is still dominated by one of the lowlands' most magnificent stone steeples and its medieval house-museums are stuffed with works by its most famous 17th-century resident, Pieter Paul Rubens. It's also a modern city that's famed for its port and diamond trade, offering state-of-the-art museums, vibrant nightlife and an edgy design scene: it's hard to think of anywhere else in the world with so many big-name boutiques, designer consignment shops and *brocante* dealers, all packed into a compact city centre.

HANS-PETER MERTEN / GETTY IMAGES ©

Belgian Beer

9 Ordering in a classic Belgian beer-pub might require you to trawl through a book-fat menu of over 200 choices. Each brew is served in its own special, occasionally outlandish, glass. Exports of Hoegaarden, Leffe and Stella Artois have long brought mainstream Belgian brewing (p283) into bars worldwide, but what really excites are the strong, abbey-brewed Trappists, locally crafted dark ales, crisp golden Tripels and, for the adventurous, a range of sharp, spontaneously fermented lambics, often made more palatable by blending or by flavouring with soft fruit.

Art Cities

10 If you love the medieval appeal of Bruges but want to be a little more original, a great choice is Ghent (p128). This historic city has its share of canalside splendour but also delights with a great arts scene and has a grittier charm that many visitors find refreshing. Or try Mechelen – it's overloaded with splendid churches, and the grand central square is graced with a fanciful town-hall complex that's only topped for sheer flamboyance by the statue-adorned equivalent in Leuven, Belgium's great university city.

Ghent (p128)

TWIN DESIGN / SHUTTERSTOCK ©

FREDERIC COLLIN / GETTY IMAGES ©

WILLEQUET MANUEL / SHUTTERSTOCK ©

Caves of the Ardennes

11 You don't need to be a daring speleologist to explore some of northern Europe's most awesome cave systems, hollowed out beneath the rolling countryside of the Belgian Ardennes. The best known, at Han-sur-Lesse (p213), even starts with a train ride, while at Remouchamps you float part of the way on an underground river. For all-round cave credentials, it's Hotton and Rochefort that really impress. Once you're caved out, the region offers gentle kayaking amid pretty valleys and plenty of hiking in forests between castles and grey-stone villages. *Grottes de Han (p213), Han-sur-Lesse*

Luxembourg City

12 No it's not just banks and Eurocrats. Wealthy Luxembourg City (p245) is one of Europe's most underestimated capitals, with a fine range of museums and galleries and a brilliant dining scene. But most impressive is the town centre's spectacular setting, straddling a deep-cut river gorge whose defences were the settlement's original *raison d'être*. Come on a summer weekend when accommodation prices drop, the streets are often full of music and there's an ample flow of the local bubbly.

Flanders Fields

13 Flanders' fields around Ypres (Ieper), once known for potato and hop production, became synonymous with senseless death in the wake of WWI's trench warfare. A century on, the area remains dotted with movingly manicured graveyards, white memorial crosses bearing silent witness in seemingly endless rows. Museums across the region vividly evoke the context and conditions that everyday soldiers endured. The beautiful central squares of Diksmuide and Ypres (p116), both architectural wonders in themselves, seem all the more astonishing when you realise they were totally rebuilt after WWI obliteration. *Wooden trench from WWI, Ypres (Ieper; p116)*

Art Nouveau

14 Swirls and technical daring are the almost organic hallmarks of art nouveau, an early-20th-century architectural style of which Belgian cities retain some world-beating examples. When star architect Victor Horta designed his own Brussels house, he combined engineering innovation with artistry to create a masterpiece. Across town, the Musée des Instruments de Musique occupies another superb example: the Old England building (p44). In Antwerp there are several further scatterings of art nouveau gems in the Zurenborg and 't Zuid districts. Musée Horta (p49), Brussels

Cartoon Culture

15 Few Belgian homes lack a collection of *bande dessinée* (cartoon strip) albums. As with *manga* in Japan, these are considered a major art-form, often referred to locally as the 'ninth art' (cinema being considered the eighth). Of the many prominent Belgian cartoonists, the best-known internationally is Hergé (the creator of Tintin), who's celebrated with a fine museum in Louvain-la-Neuve. Brussels also has a comic-strip museum (p45) and a whole series of house-ends painted with *bande dessinée* tableaux, as have other Belgian cities. Musée Hergé (p199)

Need to Know

For more information, see Survival Guide (p291)

Currency
Euro (€)

Language
Dutch (Flanders), French (Wallonia), both (Brussels), German (Eastern Cantons), Luxembourgish, French and German (Luxembourg).

Visas
EU citizens can stay indefinitely; many other nationals can enter visa-free for up to 90 days.

Money
Credit cards are widely accepted. ATMs are very prevalent.

Mobile Phones
Most EU mobile phone contracts allow customers to use roaming data in Belgium and Luxembourg as though they were in their home country. For non-EU visitors, the cheapest and most practical solution is usually to purchase a local SIM card for your GSM phone, assuming it's not blocked by your home network.

Time
Central European Time (GMT/UTC plus one hour)

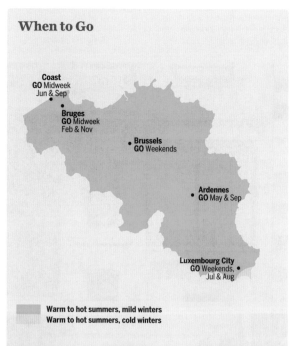

When to Go

Coast
GO Midweek Jun & Sep

Bruges
GO Midweek Feb & Nov

Brussels
GO Weekends

Ardennes
GO May & Sep

Luxembourg City
GO Weekends, Jul & Aug

Warm to hot summers, mild winters
Warm to hot summers, cold winters

High Season
(Jul–Aug)

➡ Warm weather, many outdoor activities and festivals.

➡ Hotels get overloaded in the Ardennes, Bruges and coastal towns but are cheaper in Brussels and Luxembourg City.

Shoulder Season
(May, Jun & Sep)

➡ Pleasant weather reasonably likely but rush-hour traffic jams return.

➡ Crowds are thinner; prices might fall slightly but most tourist facilities still open.

➡ Luxembourg wine festivals in early autumn.

Low Season
(Oct–Mar)

➡ Weather often cold and wet.

➡ Hotels cheaper, but some attractions close.

➡ From start of Lent there are numerous superbly colourful carnivals.

➡ Bruges is at its quietest in February.

Useful Websites

Visit Brussels (https://visit.brussels/en) The capital region.

Visit Wallonia (www.walloniabelgiumtourism.co.uk) Tourism website for Wallonia.

Visit Flanders (www.visitflanders.com) Tourist information on Flanders.

Visit Luxembourg (www.visitluxembourg.com) Tourist information on the Grand Duchy.

Lonely Planet (www.lonelyplanet.com/belgium) Destination information, hotel bookings, traveller forum and more.

SNCB (www.belgiantrain.be) Trains in Belgium.

Mobilitéit (www.mobiliteit.lu) Countrywide information on all forms of Luxembourg public transport.

Important Numbers

Emergency	☑112
Country codes (Belgium/ Luxembourg)	☑32/352
International access code	☑00
Police (Belgium/ Luxembourg)	☑101/113

Exchange Rates

Australia	A$1	€0.64
Canada	C$1	€0.64
Japan	¥100	€0.77
New Zealand	NZ$1	€0.58
UK	UK£1	€1.13
US	US$1	€0.86

For current exchange rates, see www.xe.com.

Daily Costs

Budget: Less than €100

➡ Dorm bed including breakfast: €22–30

➡ Midweek lunch: €10–15

➡ Train ticket: €10

➡ Museum entry: €5–15

➡ Beer: €2–4

➡ Short-hop city bike hire: €2

Midrange: €100–250

➡ Double room at B&B or midrange hotel: €60–140

➡ Car hire per day: €20–30

➡ Two-course meal with wine for two: €80–110

Top End: More than €250

➡ Double room at better hotel or top B&B: €140–200

➡ Cocktails: €9–20

➡ Degustation meal with wine for two: €180–350

Opening Hours

Many sights, especially museums, close on Mondays. Restaurants normally close one or two full days per week. Opening hours for shops, bars and cafes vary widely.

Banks 8.30am–3.30pm or later Monday to Friday, some also Saturday morning. However, few banks exchange money and ATMs are open 24 hours.

Bars 10am–1am, but hours very flexible. Often open later on Friday and Saturday nights.

Restaurants noon–2pm and 7pm–9.30pm

Shops 10am–6.30pm Monday to Saturday, to 5pm in Luxembourg. Sunday opening limited.

Arriving in Belgium & Luxembourg

Brussels Airport There are several trains an hour (4.40am to 12.30am) to central Brussels (€8.50, 20 minutes) and two to Leuven (€8.80, 15 minutes).

Bruxelles-Midi station Take any east-bound train to Bruxelles-Central station (3 minutes, 4.45am to 12.15am) rather than walking into central Brussels.

Charleroi ('Brussels-South') Airport Two or three buses per hour run to to Brussels (around €15, 4.30am to midnight, 55 minutes). Flibco (www.flibco.com) offers connections to Luxembourg, Bruges and Ghent. Or buy a combo ticket allowing a TEC bus ride to Charleroi-Sud train station (20 minutes) plus a rail connection to your destination.

Luxembourg Airport Buses (€2) into Luxembourg City run from 5.30am to 11pm every 10 minutes Monday to Friday, every 20 minutes on Saturday and every 30 minutes on Sunday. A new tram service should start in 2021.

Getting Around

Train A good network of trains makes public transport the best way to reach northern Belgium's car-averse cities.

Bus Buses are important in rural Wallonia and Luxembourg, often used in conjunction with trains rather than in competition.

Car In Belgium's less populous south, public transport can be sparse: away from the jammed motorways, having your own wheels makes a lot of sense.

Bicycle Cycling is a local passion, rentals are easy and cycle paths common.

For much more on **getting around**, see p299

First Time Belgium & Luxembourg

For more information, see Survival Guide (p291)

Checklist

➡ Check the validity of your passport and whether you need a visa.

➡ Download offline maps for your smartphone.

➡ Print necessary boarding passes and car-hire receipts.

➡ Organise travel insurance.

➡ Consider joining Hostelling International.

➡ Investigate phone roaming charges, ensuring that your phone is unlocked if you plan to use a local SIM card on arrival.

➡ Make advance reservations for popular and/or high-end restaurants.

What to Pack

➡ Passport and driving licence

➡ European adaptor plug

➡ USB hub or multi-plug

➡ A phrasebook

➡ Padlock for hostel lockers

➡ Student card if relevant

➡ Corkscrew (packed it in your checked baggage for flights) as screwtop wine bottles are rare

Top Tips for Your Trip

➡ You can save a lot of money on accommodation by visiting tourist towns midweek and larger 'business' cities at weekends.

➡ Don't assume that all hotels will have air-conditioning or 24-hour reception. For B&Bs, arrange arrival times in advance.

➡ Rush-hour traffic jams can be painful around big cities. But take smaller country roads in rural areas and you'll discover some charming scenery; distances are short anyway.

➡ Sip slowly: Belgian beers can pack quite a punch.

➡ Bicycle-hire options make train-bike combinations an appealing way to visit the country.

➡ Lunch options are typically simpler but much cheaper than dinners in the same restaurant, though top dining establishments rarely open till evening.

What to Wear

Antwerp is a major fashion centre, yet even in its upmarket boutiques you can see the Belgian love of understatement. In a male business context, a blazer and slacks are likely to be more appropriate than a tailored suit, which might be considered stuffy. Smart casual is the norm for going out to restaurants. In winter it's worth bringing heavy clothes when things can feel much colder than the temperature suggests due to the pervading damp. Conversely, in summer humidity can make conditions feel surprisingly hot, and air-conditioning is rare.

Sleeping

➡ High season (May to September) sees fewer accommodation options available, particularly on the weekends.

➡ The Ardennes gets very crowded in July and August.

➡ Look out for business hotels in places such as Brussels, Liège and Mechelen as they may drop their rates during weekends.

➡ Breakfast is often included in hotel rates.

➡ Quoted prices usually include national taxes but many towns also add a small city tourist tax.

Money

➡ Chip-and-PIN credit cards are widely accepted, but some places stipulate cash only.

➡ Occasionally only one or two international cards are accepted (typically MasterCard and/or Visa).

➡ ATMs are common but exchange offices rare. Banks don't usually offer exchange for non-account holders.

➡ For last-minute bookings with smaller hotels and B&Bs, try phoning direct rather than using online services.

➡ Some cities have one day a month with free entrance to municipal museums.

Bargaining

Gentle haggling is common in markets, but in all other instances you're expected to pay the stated price.

Tipping

Restaurants, bars and hairdressers Tipping is not required: personnel receive living wages and all charges are included within stated prices. If service was quite exceptional, you could show appreciation, but even then 10% would seem generous.

Tourist-oriented locations Unaware foreigners regularly leave disproportionate tips leading to a certain expectation from staff but tipping is still not obligatory.

Upmarket hotels A tip of €0.50 to €2.50 is common for door staff and porters.

Taxis In Belgium tipping drivers is not required. In Luxembourg rounding up is common by up to 10%. Airport taxi drivers might hint (or even state outright) that a tip is appropriate but that's a gentle scam. Don't be bullied.

Language

In Flanders it's polite to know some basic Dutch greetings...and of course the term *'pintje'* for ordering beer, but so many locals speak great English that it's almost embarrassing to try much more. In Wallonia, a grasp of French will prove more important. If you learnt French in France, be prepared for a few little differences. However, don't think it's clever to speak French in Flanders: English will generally be better understood and better appreciated. In Luxembourg, a few words of Luxembourgish will impress those who speak it but that's by no means every resident.

Etiquette

Say hello, wave goodbye When entering a shop or arriving at a cash desk, it's polite to offer a cheery greeting to staff. When you leave, say thank you and good day/good evening.

Giving gifts When visiting someone's home, it's appropriate to bring wine, flowers or chocolates – choose the brand carefully!

Liberal or conservative? Local ideas about political correctness might not match your own. Don't jump too quickly to conclusions. A lighter-hearted approach to serious issues is common, and underneath, many attitudes are very liberal.

Greetings Men and women alike greet each other with a handshake; close friends exchange three skimmed kisses on the cheek (starting with the right cheek).

Punctuality Being punctual is expected whether for meetings, appointments or restaurant reservations.

If You Like...

Castles

Belgium and Luxembourg are remarkably overendowed with fortifications: from grand châteaux to rugged stone ruins to pre-WWI fortresses.

Château de Modave This indulgent château is lavishly furnished and set on a cliff edge. (p225)

Château de Bouillon The medieval castle that was sold to fund a crusade. (p217)

Château de Bourscheid Luxembourg's largest and most dramatic castle ruin. (p260)

Crupet Quaint castle house in a supercute village with a reputation for good-value trout meals. (p211)

Château de Vianden Magnificently restored castle that dominates Luxembourg's most appealing country town. (p261)

Château de Belœil Country palace whose formal gardens help it compete for the moniker of 'Belgium's Versailles'. (p191)

Citadelle de Namur Citadel-fortress whose structure is functional and brooding but unquestionably impressive. (p205)

Fort de Huy A stark, indomitable fortress within which WWII Nazis imprisoned writer PG Wodehouse, among others. (p224)

Gravensteen A medieval castle plumb in the middle of Ghent. (p129)

Chimay A royal castle close to a cute square that's perfect for sipping the eponymous Trappist brew. (p203)

Surreal Belgium

Brussels' Underpants Museum may have closed, but a veritable treasure trove of surrealism remains. Indeed Belgium's marvellous sense of the absurd could be dated back to the sheer improbability of its 1830 creation.

Musée Magritte The world's largest collection of the surrealist pioneer's paintings and drawings. (p44)

Verbeke Foundation Taking conceptual art to its most extraordinary outer limits. (p165)

La Ducasse Recreating the battle of St George in Mons' central square. (p193)

Goupil le Fol Enter an alternative universe in search of fruit wine. (p71)

Retsin's Lucifernum A Bruges vampire invites you home. (p101)

Le Pot au Lait Even before you start drinking, this amazing Liège bar's trippy interior will have your head spinning. (p231)

Atomium A building designed like a schoolchild's chemistry-set model of a carbon lattice. (p59)

'King of Liars' Seat The 'throne' on which the best prevaricator is crowned during Namur's fun-filled Fêtes de Wallonie. (p207)

Mannekin Pis As if one peeing boy statue weren't enough, Geraardsbergen sports the 'other' one. (p127)

Baarle-Hertog Ponder the absurdity the world's craziest border. (p166)

Festval Outremeuse Part of Liège declares 'independence' then goes into jocular spasms of drunken delirium. (p228)

Industrial Heritage

The region has often been at the forefront of European technological advances. Inspired visitor attractions bring alive everything from medieval Mosan metalwork to 21st-century wind energy.

Blégny Mine Have your senses bombarded with the subterranean sights and sounds of a 20th-century coal mine. (p234)

Museum Plantin-Moretus The world's oldest surviving printing works is a work of art in itself. (p145)

Val St-Lambert The Belgian glassware that took the world by storm a century ago. (p229)

Speelkaartmuseum Discover the huge scale of machines once required to make playing cards. (p165)

Le Bois du Cazier Climb a slag heap in archetypal postindustrial Charleroi. (p200)

Canals of the Borinage Remarkable ship-lifts, old and new. (p194)

Centre Touristique de la Laine et de la Mode A fascinating textile museum. (p233)

Antwerp Port Vibrant, ugly and thrillingly vast. (p153)

Spa Monopole Bottling the spring water that turned Spa into Europe's original spa. (p236)

Outdoor Action

If you want to get out into the fresh air, a wide range of outdoor delights await.

Bouillon Attractive centre from which to kayak some of the prettiest rivers of southern Belgium. (p216)

Coo This tiny Ardennes village is well equipped for drop-in visitors with an array of outdoor-sports options. (p237)

Belgian Coast Swimming is an option on Belgium's sandy coastline, though it can get chilly! (p103)

FDHW This remarkable route near Hasselt crosses 'through' a lake at eye level. (p179)

Müllerthal Trails Walking Luxembourg's pretty micro-canyons (p259)

Durbuy A rustic setting with lots of outdoor fun. (p223)

Skiing Test out the cross-country trails of the misty Hautes Fagnes. (p241)

Parc d'Aventure Tree Climber Fly through the forest on zip lines above Vianden. (p262)

Belfries & Begijnhoven

Oh yes, Bruges is gorgeous. But it's by no means the only place with a magical medieval centre and pretty urban canals. Another 16 Flemish towns have beautiful *begijnhoven* (enclosed semi-religious subvillages) with special gems at Diest, Kortrijk and Turnhout. And over 30 Belgian cities have historic belfry towers that are Unesco-listed.

Ghent Canalside scenery, three *begijnhoven* and a city-centre castle that once tried to intimidate the rebellious townsfolk. (p128)

Lier Compact, canal-ringed beauty with a lovely *begijnhof* and a fanciful clock tower. (p167)

Tournai Belgium's oldest belfry, a beautiful main square and a superb Romanesque cathedral. (p186)

Mechelen Belgium's religious capital is overloaded with fine churches. (p168)

Ypres The Ieper Lakenhalle is arguably Belgium's most glorious single building, yet astonishingly it's a post-WWI rebuild. (p116)

Sint-Truiden Three towers for the price of one. (p180)

Thuin Slate spires and baubles towering above the town's 'hanging gardens'. (p201)

Going Underground

Beneath the limestone Ardennes, several spectacular caverns and underground waterways have been made accessible for the non-speleologically adept. And there are several constructed tunnel-systems to explore if that's your thing.

Grotte de Lorette The Lorette caves are remarkable for their depth, stalactite spaghetti and carbonate concretions; lots of steps. (p214)

Grottes de Hotton Superb natural grottoes and a fabulously vertical subterranean chasm, with smaller crowds than most Ardennes caves. (p223)

Grottes de Han Accessible caves with some of Belgium's greatest stalactites. (p213)

Les Grottes du Remouchamps This cave-complex tour ends with a memorable underground river ride. (p238)

Namur Souterrains Explore the astounding network of tunnels beneath Namur's gigantic citadel-fortress. (p205)

Bock Casemates A honeycomb of of defensive passages beneath the heart of Luxembourg City. (p245)

Het Ruihuis See Antwerp from below, discovering the historic sewers by boat ride or guided walk. (p147)

Phillipeville Souterrains Ten kilometres of subterranean tunnels form an unexpected labyrinth beneath this former French military enclave. (p202)

Silex's Drop a few metres into a hole from which flints for prehistoric tools were once mined at one of the world's most unlikely Unesco World Heritage sites. (p193)

Month by Month

January

Days are short, cold and often grey but snow might lay just long enough for an Ardennes ski weekend.

🏃 Ski Time

Belgium has no Alpine mountains but when enough snow falls on the Ardennes modest slopes, the perilous E411 (over)fills with day-tripping skiers making a beeline for the handful of little hillside pistes in the Haute Fagnes. (p241)

February

Damp, foggy or sparkling if cold, early February is one time you might have beautiful Bruges largely to yourself...until the start of the Carnival holiday, that is.

🎭 Carnival

Orange-lobbing Gilles lead one of the world's oddest carnivals in Binche on Shrove Tuesday (Mardi Gras), a day that might fall in February or March. The Sunday before, Malmédy's carnival climaxes with the parade of the masked *Haguètes*, and the next day Eupen's Rosenmontag is joyously colourful.

March

March could host a late carnival or an early Easter. Either way there's still bound to be plenty of pageantry and Lenten shenanigans.

🎭 Burning of Winter

The Spirit of Winter is ceremonially cremated on the first Sunday of Lent, both with bonfires in Belgian village fields and cruciform fires on hillsides in Luxembourg where the day's called *Buergsonndeg*.

🎭 Laetare

Sinister Pinocchio-like *Blanc Moussis* stuff confetti down women's clothes, dangle smelly dried herrings in people's hair and beat bystanders with dried pigs' bladders. It's all part of Stavelot's unique Laetare carnival (www.laetare-stavelot.be), culminating on the fourth Saturday of Lent.

April

Spring arrives with a day of practical jokes. At Easter children seek out eggs in their gardens, deposited there not by Easter bunnies but by the 'Bells of Rome'.

🎭 Penitents' Procession

After dusk on Good Friday, Lessines turns off the city lights as eerie figures in monks' habits and medieval conical hoods parade moodily around town carrying flaming torches. The procession dates back to 1475.

🏃 On Your Bike

Three of Belgium's most important cycling races take place in April, including the one-day classic Ronde van Vlaanderen (Tour of Flanders; www.rvv.be), famed for its classic steep climbs on rough cobbled lanes.

👁 Serres Royales

The glorious royal greenhouses at Laeken (Brussels) open to the public for three weeks.

May

May starts with old-fashioned chivalry as Belgian men present female friends or colleagues with a delicate sprig of Lily of the Valley.

☆ Hanswijk Procession

Part religious tableau, part medieval pageant, the Sunday before Ascension see thousands dress up to thank the Virgin Mary for sparing Mechelen from the plague back in 1272.

☆ Zinneke Parade

This thoroughly contemporary one-day multicultural parade is held every even-numbered year, designed to bridge social divides and expose Brussels' zanier side (www.zinneke.org).

☆ Heilig-Bloedprocessie

On Ascension Day, Bruges' biggest folklore event sees the parading around town of an enormously revered reliquary supposedly containing a few drops of Christ's blood.

☆ Belgian Pride

From tiny radical beginnings in Ghent (1978), Belgian Pride has gone through numerous iterations. Now based in Brussels, it involves a rainbow parade that attracts up to 100,000 people in mid-May.

☆ Sprinprozession

Echternach pilgrims celebrate the town's Anglo-Saxon founding father with handkerchief dances on Whit Tuesday morning.

☆ Brussels Jazz Weekend

Three fabulous evenings of free, nonstop jazz, blues and zydeco concerts on the last weekend of the month, all over Brussels.

☆ Ducasse de Mons (Le Doudou)

On Trinity Sunday (eight weeks after Easter Sunday), a golden 'coach' of relics parades through town, then Mons goes completely nuts as St George fights the dragon on the Grand Place.

June

A great travelling month with long, long days and mild weather but the full-on holiday season is yet to hit the Ardennes. However, some rural hotels and restaurants take a two-week pre-peak rest.

☆ Kattenstoet

Ypres' cat festival (www.kattenstoet.be) sees furry feline toys flung about while giant cats parade through the street. It's held every third year (next in 2021) on the second Sunday of June.

☉ Waterloo Battle Re-enactments

On the weekend nearest 18 June, Waterloo celebrates the anniversary of the 1815 battle with re-enactments by costumed 'soldiers'.

☆ Luxembourg National Day

Luxembourg City becomes one giant party zone on 22 June, culminating in a major firework display. Next day there's a military parade.

☆ Couleur Café

This three-day festival (www.couleurcafe.be) brings world-music concerts, workshops, ethnic-dining opportunities and over 75,000 people to Brussels' Atomium area at the end of June.

July

Schools close and Belgians begin their lengthy holidays: suddenly beach and Ardennes hotels are full. Across the region it's party time with a smorgasbord of summer festivals.

☆ Wiltz Festival

An impressive month-long theatre, jazz and music festival in the château grounds at Wiltz (www.festivalwiltz.online.lu).

☆ Ommegang

It costs nothing to watch Brussels' biggest medieval-style procession (www.ommegang.be) wind around town from the Sablon. But book tickets ahead to witness the lavish finale on the illuminated Grand Place. It's on the first Thursday of July.

☆ Rock Werchter

The four-day Belgian equivalent of Glastonbury or Roskilde rocks fields north of Leuven (www.rockwerchter.be). Accommodation fills up all across eastern Flanders.

☆ Les Francofolies

In the first week of July, Spa hosts one of Belgium's biggest French-language cultural festivals (www.francofolies.be), notable for attracting some of the biggest names in *chanson*.

☆ Tomorrowland

Tomorrowland is the world's largest annual electronic music festival, held annually in the appropriately named town of Boom, 16km south of Antwerp on the last two weekends of July.

De Gentse Feesten

This fabulously raucous 10-day festival (www.gentse feesten.be) transforms the heart of Ghent into a youthful party of music and street theatre, with packed streets and merry drinking.

Belgian National Day

Brussels celebrates Belgium's 1830 declaration of independence with a large military parade in the morning, brass bands on the Place de Jeu de Bal around 7pm, then fireworks at 11pm.

☆ Luxembourg Jazz & Blues Rallye

The Grund and Clausen areas of Luxembourg City party all night to a fine array of free concerts.

Boetprocessie

Held in Veurne since 1644, this solemn street parade (www.boetprocessie.be) sees hundreds of biblically costumed players illustrate 40 scenes from Jesus' life, death and resurrection interspersed with masked 'penitents' in brown monk-style robes, some carrying heavy wooden crosses. Last Sunday of July.

🏃 Tour de Wallonie

For five days, professional cyclists race across Wallonia (www.trworg.be), heading west to east in even years, reversing the route in odd years.

August

Belgium's two-month summer holiday continues with the beach towns of Flanders and activity villages of the Ardennes at peak capacity. Lots of festivals add to the fun.

☆ Festival Musica Antiqua

This week-long festival of medieval music (www. mafestival.be) takes place in Bruges in the first week of August.

☆ La Nuit du Livre

Redu's book-fest on the first Saturday of August is accompanied by music and midnight fireworks.

☆ Folk Dranouter

One of Europe's most important folk-music festivals (www.folkdranouter.be) is held on the first weekend of August at Dranouter, a small town 12km southwest of Ypres.

Meyboom

On 9 August this merrily low-key Brussels' folkloric procession (www.mey boom.be) ends with the planting of a 'tree of joy', as has happened since 1308. Symbolically the tree must be raised (just) before 5pm to ensure the rights of the ancient guilds.

St-Rochus-Verlichting

In Aarschot, electric lamps are extinguished from dusk to midnight on 15 August, replaced by flickering lines of candles along window sills and footpaths and accompanied by folk dances and brass bands.

Festival Outremeuse

A week of raucously drunken celebrations in Liège's 'Republic of Outremeuse' (www.tchantches.eu) culminates on 15 August when sermons are read in full Walloon dialect, then everyone gets tipsy on *pékèt* (gin).

Golden Tree Pageant

Every five years in mid to late August, Bruges lays on this grandiose procession (www.goudenboomstoet.be) celebrating the 1468 marriage of Charles the Bold to Margaret of York. Next in 2022.

Giants' Procession

On August's fourth weekend, Ath holds a series of parades featuring enormous Unesco-listed models with biblical and folkloric connections. One such giant, Goliath (Gouyasse), has his trousers 'burnt' on Friday night, gets married on Saturday, then fights David.

◉ Flower Carpet

On even-numbered years, Brussels' Grand Place is decorated with half a million begonia petals that create the effect of a giant 'carpet' (www.flowercarpet. brussels).

September

Back to work...and those depressingly snail-paced rush-hour traffic jams rematerialise on the main city ring roads. However, the weather is often lovely while accommodation in rural getaways is no longer overstretched.

🏎 Belgian Grand Prix

Formula 1 comes to Spa-Francorchamps (www.belgium-grand-prix.com) in late August/early September; expect full occupancy at every hotel in eastern Wallonia and beyond.

◉ Heritage Days

The second weekend of September sees Flanders' Open Monumentendag (www.openmonumentendag.be) and Wallonia's Journées du Patrimoine (www.journeesdupatrimoine.be). Both open a selection of monuments to the public, many of which are not otherwise accessible. A week later Brussels follows suit.

🎋 Combat de l'Échasse d'Or

On the third Sunday of September, Namur's weeklong Fêtes de Wallonie (www.fetesdewallonie.be) culminates in this jousting competition between two teams of stilt-walkers dressed in medieval garb.

October

As temperatures cool, days get shorter and trees develop a pretty autumnal blush. Many a restaurant finds space on its menu for boar, venison and other forms of game.

🎋 Nocturne des Coteaux

Liège comes alive at dusk on the first Saturday of October with 20,000 candles forming beautiful patterns on the city's vertiginous stairway, Montagne de Bueren.

🍷 Hasseltse Jeneverfeesten

The most celebrated moment in Hasselt's famous gin festival (www.jeneverfeesten.be) comes at 3pm when the little Borrelmanneke Fountain briefly pours forth *jenever* (gin) instead of water. Third weekend of October.

November

Christmas markets begin making the rounds of many a town square. These typically come with nativity scenes that sometimes have living characters rather than mannequins... right down to a bemused baby in the manger.

🎋 All Saints' Day

The first of November *(Allerheiligen/Toussaint)* is the day that Belgian families take flowers to the graves of deceased relatives.

☆ Ars Musica

This respected festival of contemporary classical music (www.arsmusica.be) is held in late November every even-numbered year at various Brussels venues.

December

Belgian kids get presents twice over, not just on 24–25 December but also on 6 December from red-coated, bushy-bearded Sinterklaas/St-Nicholas. A speciality for the day is fancily shaped *speculaas/speculoos* (cinnamon-flavoured gingerbread).

Itineraries

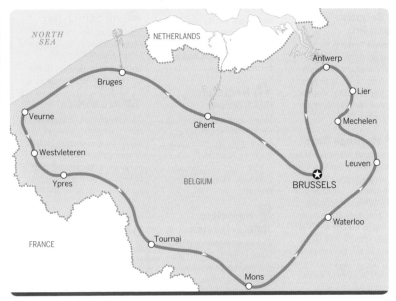

Belgium's Greatest Hits

Taking in nearly a dozen of Belgium's top destinations in two weeks is likely to be an exhausting but unforgettable experience.

You will of course admire the Grand Place in **Brussels**, explore gloriously multifaceted **Ghent** and visit idyllic, ever-popular **Bruges**. Then add a day in **Ypres** with its magnificent cloth hall and moving WWI history; if you're driving, get there by swinging through lovable **Veurne** and beer-grail **Westvleteren** en route.

Tournai is well worth a brief stop to admire its magnificent Romanesque cathedral, then head to historic **Mons** with its excellent portfolio of museums. Looping back towards Brussels, the **Waterloo** battle site is a major draw, if slightly fiddly to reach by public transport. Or keep going northeast to **Leuven** – brew-home of Stella Artois and Leffe – with its splendid town hall and mind-blowing square full of student bars.

Before giving in to the irresistible pull of amazing **Antwerp**, do stop in underrated **Mechelen**, Belgium's spiritual heart. And don't miss lovely **Lier**, a gem of a town with a loop of canal, an extensive central square, a plethora of old houses, a Unesco-listed *begijnhof* and a remarkable astronomical clock speckled with planets and dials.

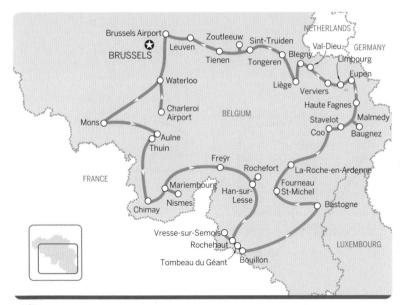

Dawdling on the Back Roads

This driving trip takes in some of Belgium's more off-beat cities and its most charming rural corners. Starting from the airport in either Brussels or Charleroi, pick up a rental car and drive via Napoleon's **Waterloo** to museum-rich **Mons**, which was Europe's cultural capital back in 2015. Continue via **Aulne** abbey ruins and the 'hanging gardens' of **Thuin** to spend two nights in or around the pretty little castle town of **Chimay**, famed for its beer. Tootle on along the pretty lanes to **Mariembourg** and very attractive **Nismes**, possibly taking the steam train. Visit the splendid gardens of **Freÿr** and the fabulous caves at **Han-sur-Lesse** or less commercial versions at **Rochefort**, which is home to another Trappist brewery and some fine local accommodation. From Rochefort drive down to **Bouillon** with its looming Crusader castle ruin, and kayak along some of Belgium's loveliest wooded valleys around **Vresse-sur-Semois**. Follow the Semois Valley in both directions enjoying the panoramas at **Rochehaut** and **Tombeau du Géant**.

Head northeast to visit the excellent war museum at **Bastogne**, then cut across through thick forests via St-Hubert and the impressive open-air museum of **Fourneau St-Michel** to **La Roche-en-Ardenne**, with its castle ghost and sad but fascinating WWII history. Famed for its long-nosed carnival characters, attractive **Stavelot** makes a good base for outdoor activities organised at nearby **Coo**. Or sleep in cathedral-town **Malmedy** and visit the WWII museum at **Baugnez** before making a day-hike on the **Hautes Fagnes**. Stop for coffee and pastries in **Eupen**, Belgium's only really Germanic city, or for a beer in delightful little **Limbourg** en route to underrated **Verviers**, a once-grand city with an excellent new chocolate museum. Lovely country lanes lead on to beautiful **Val-Dieu** monastery and nearby **Blegny**, where you can descend into Belgium's last accessible coal mine. After a dose of boistrous, big-city action in sprawling **Liège** comes quieter, appealing **Tongeren**, Belgium's 'oldest' town and then the Roman road to attractive **Sint-Truiden**. Wander the pretty Haspengouw lanes and peruse the remarkable church in **Zoutleeuw** plus more Roman remnants in **Tienen** before spending your last night in the lively student city of **Leuven**.

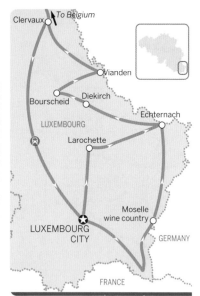

5 DAYS — Lovable Luxembourg

Little Luxembourg makes an unexpectedly complete destination. Accommodation prices in Luxembourg City fall dramatically at weekends, while midweek is better for the rural castle villages, with smaller crowds and less traffic on the country lanes.

Arrive in **Luxembourg City** on Friday afternoon to make the most of the city's nightlife, particularly at Rives de Clausen within a former brewery. Buy a Luxembourg Card on Saturday if you're planning to see all of the main museums, or just stroll the city ramparts and gorges. On Monday strike out for **Echternach**, either via **Larochette** or through the **Moselle wine country**. Hike in the Müllerthal micro-canyons then head to **Diekirch** to learn about Luxembourg's WWII history at the country's national military museum. Consider visiting **Bourscheid** to admire one of the Grand Duchy's most impressive medieval castle ruins and its 17th-century neighbour. Head to **Vianden**, whose restored fortress looms above the town, reached by a chairlift. Travel on to pretty **Clervaux**, whose castle contains Edward Steichen's World Heritage–listed photography exhibition *Family of Man,* then continue to Liège in Belgium or return to Luxembourg City.

7 DAYS — Belgian Beer Tour

You could claim cultural motivations for touring Belgium's monasteries and historic towns, pretending that you're only tasting the local brews out of politeness along the way. But do sign up a patient designated driver – some of these magnificent monster-brews tip the scales at 10% or more.

Start in **Brussels** by paying respects at L'Arbre d'Or, the brewers' guild building on the Grand Place. Learn about lambics at Cantillon brewery, then let beer teach you local history at Het Anker in **Mechelen**.

While exploring the hop-growing region of western Flanders, the ultimate beer pilgrimage is to Sint-Sixtus Abbey at **Westvleteren**, home to the rarest of Trappist brews. Compare it with a St-Bernardus Tripel sipped in nearby **Watou**.

Time your arrival at **Pipaix** to coincide with a visit to the steam brewery. Then continue into the rural Botte du Hainaut area, home to legendary **Chimay** Trappist beer, and the Fagnes brewery at **Mariembourg**.

Belgium's southeast holds a brewery-monastery at **Orval** and **Achouffe**. Heading back to Brussels, visit **Val-Dieu** brew-abbey and try some white beer at **Hoegaarden**.

Plan Your Trip
Travel with Children

From spooky rambles through candlelit castles to high-tech space simulators and splashing about on beaches and rivers, Belgium and Luxembourg have plenty to thrill and inspire beyond the sheer magic of historic chocolate-box cityscapes. And most museums make a point of offering special activities aimed at a younger audience.

Children's Highlights

Theme- & Activity-Parks

Very helpfully, several of Belgium's best theme parks have been installed near enough to other major sites so that one parent might slope off to enjoy a different kind of attraction while the rest of the family is busily soaking up the fun rides.

Pairi Daiza (p192) An incredible array of wildlife lives amid beautifully designed gardens, Chinese temples, African villages and other striking recreations.

Lacs de l'Eau d'Heure (p202) An activity-filled outdoor area featuring the impressive Natura Parc.

Plopsaland (p112) The biggest theme park on the coast is tucked back off the beach strip at De Panne. Related Plopsa Coo in the Ardennes is smaller but prettier, with plenty nearby for adults.

Domaine Provincial de Chevetogne (p215) Imaginative playgrounds, a petting zoo, forested areas, minigolf and lakeside fun.

Educational Activities

The difference between educational attractions and theme parks is increasingly blurred as the best install simulators and full-sense experiences. Many museums are designed in large part with children in mind, and include interactive activities

Best Regions for Kids

Rural Wallonia
The array of summer sports activities goes well beyond the archetypal kayaking weekend, offering something for kids of all ages, with Durbuy and Coo especially well set up.

Bruges
Adding to its beauty, Bruges excites the less historically minded with museums of chips and chocolate.

The Coast
Even if it's too cold to swim, children can ride *kwistax* (pedal carts) along the promenade and visit crazy sandcastles.

Ghent
Magical townscapes inspire, while plenty of interactive museums have kid-friendly activities.

Antwerp
The city is very much a grown-ups' town, but the zoo (p149) will keep kids engrossed, museums cater well for tweens, and teens love the shopping.

Brussels
After gazing at the unforgettable Atomium (p59), particularly child-friendly attractions include Train World (p43), puppet shows at Toone (p78), dino-discovery at Musée des Sciences Naturelles (p52), miniature architecture at Mini Europe (p60) and cartoon characters at Centre Belge de la Bande Dessinée (p45).

and workshops. It's well worth looking at the websites of the various museums or sights before going, as some activities might operate only on certain days of the week. Naturally a lot will be in local languages, but many are tactile and intuitive, so an adventurous child is likely to enjoy them, and most tour leaders speak excellent English. Even non-child-specific museums tend to have a toddlers' zone equipped with relevant play activities.

Technopolis (p171) Mechelen's cutting-edge science-experience museum constantly adds new educational delights.

Euro Space Center (p214) A major interactive experience, though be aware that it's awkward to reach without a car.

Musée des Sciences Naturelles (p52) Meet a family of real dinosaurs.

Earth Explorer (p107) Lets rip in Ostend with earthquakes and storms, then goes on to explain them.

Train World (p43) This cracking new Brussels diversion for children and adults offers hands-on exploration of historic locomotives.

Natur Musée (p248) Stuffed animals, preserved insects and more life-size dinosaurs reside at this Luxembourg City museum.

Outdoor Excitement

Château de Bouillon (p217) This wonderfully evocative Crusader ruin is likely to inspire young minds, especially during the birds of prey show. The site is all the more special if you visit on a summer's night by the light of burning torches.

Han-sur-Lesse (p213) Younger kids might find the cave visit a little long, but there's the fun of starting out by train. With the 'safari' and various other minor attractions, it all adds up to a fine day out.

Outdoor Freizeit (p258) Older kids will enjoy canoeing and kayaking on Luxembourg's Sûre river.

Durbuy (p223) Belgium's smallest 'town' is brilliantly set up with activities to keep the whole family active, while a few kilometres away in Barvaux there's also the summer fun of a great cornfield labyrinth.

Planning

Entrance Fees

Many attractions are free for those under 26 (or in some instances 21), which can make a big difference if you're planning to visit a number of museums. Otherwise there are usually discounted children's tickets for those aged 12 years or under.

Accommodation & Eating

Hotels don't usually charge for toddlers, while many will provide an extra bed for children for around €15 (though it's very variable). A great idea for bigger families is to rent a self-catering *gîte* to use as a base. Rentals are usually per week. Many mid-range restaurants have a small selection of simpler dishes and/or smaller portions for children. If you need a high chair, it's worth calling ahead to check availability.

Babies

Baby cots are available on request in many B&Bs, hotels and even some hostels, but it's worth reserving ahead as they're often limited.

Breastfeeding in public is acceptable, though not commonly seen.

Transport

Train travel in Belgium is free for under-12s when accompanied by an adult if the journey starts after 9am. Luxembourg is more generous, with public transport free countrywide for those aged 20 and younger.

In cars, children under 12 must sit in the back and those under 1.35m tall must use a child's safety seat: for car-rental and taxis book well ahead if these are required.

Further Information

For all-round information and advice, check out Lonely Planet's *Travel with Children*.

For Luxembourg, www.livres.maison moderne.lu/familyguide is a remarkably detailed resource.

Regions at a Glance

Brussels

Architecture
Beer
Music

Art Nouveau Trail

Victor Horta was Brussels' master architect, his buildings characteristically austere from the outside but light-filled symphonies of curved wood and stained glass within. Take a neighbourhood walk to find other gorgeously ornamented art nouveau houses.

Spontaneous Success

Brussels' unique contribution to brewing is the spontaneously fermented lambic. But if that's too off-the-wall for your taste buds, the capital's opulent old *cafés* and hip new minimal bars are sure to offer something that will wow your senses.

Jazz Heaven

Brussels is mad about jazz. The Jazz Weekend is a highlight in May's festival program, but year-round you can enjoy great live music in venues from basement bars to sit-down restaurants and jazz clubs.

p34

Bruges, Ghent & Northwest Belgium

Medieval Towns
Beer
Battlefields

Step-Gabled Delights

Whether prettily preserved like Bruges, Veurne and Damme, reconstructed like Diksmuide and Ypres, or a vibrant mixture like Ghent, there are few places in Northern Europe that thrust so much medieval-style architecture in your face.

Heavenly Hops

The hops that flavour virtually all great Belgian beers are cultivated around Poperinge, an area that is, not surprisingly, the epicentre of great local brewing and home to the almost mystical Trappist wonder, Westvleteren 12.

Flanders Fields

WWI cemeteries are movingly beautiful throughout the region, with battlefield tours, war museums and trench sites in special concentrations around Ypres, whose whole centre was meticulously rebuilt after the war.

p83

Antwerp & Northeast Belgium

Architecture
Beer
Galleries

Beguiling Buildings

For architectural inspiration take in the *begijnhoven* of Diest, Lier and Turnhout, the cathedrals at Antwerp and Mechelen, the belfries of Hoogstraten and Tienen, and the city halls of Leuven, Mechelen and Zoutleeuw.

Rainbow of Ales

Westmalle and Achel are this region's Trappist brews, but Het Anker's Mechelen-brewed range is arguably as fine. International exports Leffe and Stella Artois come from Leuven, and Hoegaarden makes the classic White Beer.

Rubens & More

Galleries in Lier, Leuven, Mechelen and Antwerp are all impressively endowed with great artworks. There's a very wide range to peruse from contemporary to old masters, but in Antwerp, especially, much revolves around Rubens who spent most of his life here.

p142

Wallonia

Festivals
Castles
Caves

Folklore Overload

Fantastical festivals feature orange-lobbing Gilles at Binche, Pinocchio-esque Blanc Moussis in Stavelot, pincer-wielding Haguètes at Malmedy, George re-slaying the Dragon at Mons and pointy-hatted penitents parading eerily through torch-lit Lessines.

Fortify Yourself

From the medieval ruins of Bouillon and La Roche to the latter-day fortress of Huy and Namur, via splendid châteaux like Modave and Belœil, Wallonia has a castle for all seasons.

Cavern Country

Han, Hotton, Remouchamps or Rochefort? These four superb cave systems are distinctly different, so why not visit them all while touring Wallonia's pretty hill country? Just be prepared for plenty of steps and dress appropriately for temperatures of around 10–12°C.

p183

Luxembourg

City
Castles
Wine

Capital Class

One of Europe's more underrated capitals, Luxembourg City has a gloriously dramatic clifftop-and-valley setting and backs up its scenic impact with interesting museums, great dining and a lively bar scene.

Fortress Fiesta

The nation is studded with spectacular castles, often picturesquely set in idyllic wooded countryside. Looming Vianden contrasts brilliantly with ruined Bourscheid or Beaufort. Hollenfels' castle houses a hostel, while Bourglinster's hosts two fabulous restaurants.

Bubbling Over

Sipping fine fizzy wines amid the immaculately groomed hillside vineyards of the Moselle Valley is all the more enjoyable with the region's handy bicycle-hire scheme. Many wineries have tours and tastings, and there is a whole series of harvest festivals to celebrate the gathering of the grapes.

p243

On the Road

Bruges, Ghent & Northwest Belgium
p83

Antwerp & Northeast Belgium
p142

Brussels
p34

Wallonia
p183

Luxembourg
p243

Brussels

POP 1.2 MILLION; LANGUAGES: FRENCH & DUTCH

Best Places to Eat

➡ Comme Chez Soi (p68)

➡ L'Idiot du Village (p68)

➡ Mer du Nord (p65)

➡ SAN in Brussels (p65)

Best Places to Stay

➡ Chambres d'Hôtes du Vaudeville (p62)

➡ Hôtel Métropole (p63)

➡ Villa Botanique Guesthouse (p64)

➡ Vintage Hotel (p64)

➡ Hôtel Le Dixseptième (p63)

Why Go?

Belgium's fascinating capital, and the administrative capital of the EU, Brussels is historical yet hip, bureaucratic yet bizarre, self-confident yet unshowy, and multicultural to its roots. These contrasts are multilayered – Francophone alongside Flemish, and Eurocrats cheek-by-jowl with immigrants. And all this plays out in a cityscape that swings from majestic to quirky to rundown and back again. Organic art nouveau facades face off against 1960s concrete disgraces, and regal 19th-century mansions contrast with the brutal glass of the EU's Gotham City. This whole maelstrom swirls out from Brussels' medieval core, where the Grand Place is surely one of the world's most beautiful squares.

One constant is the quality of everyday life, with a *café/bar* scene that could keep you drunk for years. But Brussels doesn't go out of its way to impress. The citizens' humorous, deadpan outlook on life is often just as surreal as the canvases of one-time resident Magritte.

Driving Distances (km)

	Brussels	Antwerp	Liège	Bruges	Arlon
Antwerp	47				
Liège	90	115			
Bruges	115	113	205		
Arlon	187	236	140	283	
Ostend	140	138	230	25	300

History

From a marshy outpost of Charlemagne's empire, Brussels grew to city status in the 13th century and, via dynastic struggles and rebellions, became the capital of an independent state. From being the centre of a brutal colonial regime that oppressed the Congo to becoming the headquarters of both NATO and the EU, the story of the city is troubled, tangled and fascinating.

Foundations

According to legend, St-Géry built a chapel on a swampy Senne (Zenne) River island in AD 695. The settlement that grew around it became known as Bruocsella (from *bruoc*, marsh, and *sella*, dwelling) by 979 when Charles, Duke of Lorraine, moved here from Cambrai. He built a fort on St-Géry island amid flowering irises, which have since become the city's symbol. By 1100 Bruocsella was a walled settlement and capital of the Duchy of Brabant. In 1355 the Count of Flanders invaded and seized Brussels. However, a year later, Brussels citizens, led by Everard 't Serclaes, ejected the Flemish. 't Serclaes went on to become a prominent local leader fighting for ever more civic privileges, a stance that finally saw him assassinated in 1388. This caused a furore in Brussels, whose townsfolk blamed the lord of Gaasbeek and took revenge by burning down his castle. Today, an anachronistic statue of 't Serclaes' corpse (at Grand Place 8) is still considered a potent source of luck.

Booming Brussels

Meanwhile, the cloth trade was booming. By the 15th century, prosperous markets filled the streets around the Grand Place, selling products for which some are still named: Rue au Beurre (Butter St), Rue des Bouchers (Butchers' St) etc. The city's increasingly wealthy merchant guilds established their headquarters on the Grand Place, where medieval tournaments and public executions took place in the shadow of a towering Hôtel de Ville.

From 1519 Brussels came to international prominence as capital of Charles Quint's vast Habsburg Empire. But Charles' future successor, the fanatically Catholic Philip II of Spain, was unimpressed with the lowlanders' growing interest in Protestantism. His Spanish Inquisition resulted in thousands of executions, including those of anti-Spanish Counts Egmont and Hoorn in front of the Maison du Roi.

The City Under Siege

In 1695, Louis XIV's French army under Marshal De Villeroy bombarded Brussels for 36 hours, hoping to divert Dutch attention from its attempts to regain Namur. This was truly catastrophic. Around 4000 houses were destroyed, around a third of the city was reduced to rubble and damage is thought to have been in the order of €5 billion in today's terms. The Grand Place was virtually obliterated, though miraculously the Hôtel de Ville survived relatively intact. And within five years most of the square's guildhalls were rebuilt, making them even more impressive than they'd been before.

Austrian rule in the 18th century fostered urban development, with the construction of grand squares such as Place Royale. Many of the Upper Town's architectural gems were built during this time and in the brief eras of French and Dutch rule that followed. In 1830 Brussels proved the unlikely starting point of the curious 1830 'operatic' revolt that led Belgium to entirely unexpected independence.

The Congo & Postwar Brussels

In the early 1800s Brussels was home to around 100,000 people. However, the city grew enormously in both population and stature during the next century, greatly funded by Wallonia's industrial revolution along with King Léopold II's plunder of the Congo. While an estimated 10 million people were killed in the Congo, Brussels lavished on itself some of Europe's finest belle époque and art nouveau buildings.

Unlike much of the country, Brussels survived both world wars comparatively unscathed. The city underlined a new era of postwar optimism by hosting the 1958 World's Fair in the shadow of the Atomium. Brussels' growth was further boosted when it became the headquarters of NATO and the EEC (later EU). However, in the city's pursuit of progress and modernism, much fine architecture was torn down to make way for mediocre concrete office buildings, a form of architectural vandalism that's now widely known as Brusselisation. A stint as Cultural Capital of Europe in 2000 finally gave the city the push it needed to start properly protecting heritage buildings and sprucing up neglected neighbourhoods.

Brussels Highlights

❶ Grand Place
(p38) Strolling round or drinking on Europe's most gorgeous square.

❷ Old England Building (p44) Admiring one of Brussels' finest art nouveau creations while perusing a mesmerising music museum.

❸ Musées Royaux des Beaux-Arts (p44) Seeing everything from Magritte's bowler hat to Breughel's falling Icarus in this palace of visual art.

❹ Atomium (p59) Pondering one of the world's oddest 20th-century builldings

❺ House of European History (p53) Getting to grips with the whole continent's story at this hi-tech and impressive new museum.

❻ Musée Art & Histoire (p53) Browsing everything from Roman mosaics to antique sleds in the museums flanking Brussels' very own Arc de Triomphe.

❼ A l'Imaige de Nostre-Dame (p72) Delving into tiny medieval alleys around the Bourse to discover Brussels' magical, secret drinking holes.

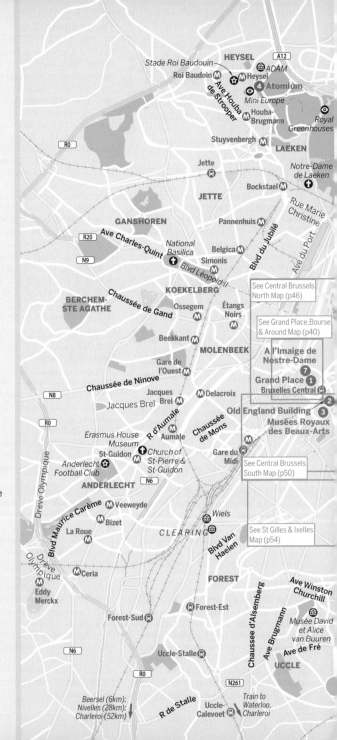

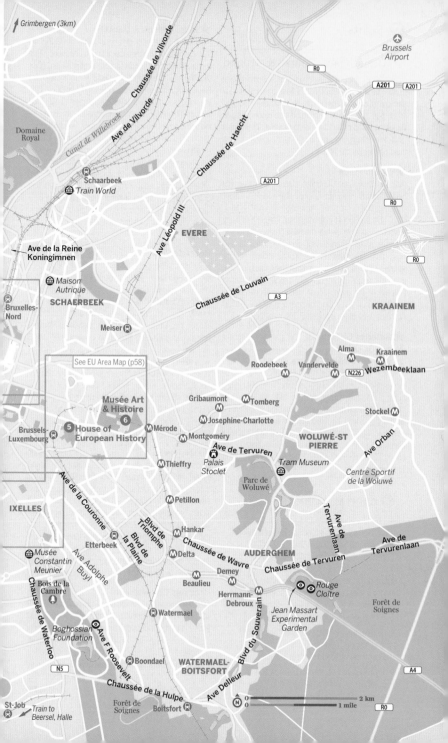

◉ Sights

◉ Grand Place, Bourse & Around

From the spectacular historic centrepiece of the Grand Place, there's lots to explore in the cobbled streets of the Îlot Sacré (once an island in the Senne), around the neoclassical **Bourse** (Map p40; Place de la Bourse; 🚇 Bourse) (stock exchange) and in revitalised St-Géry, also formerly an island.

★ Grand Place   SQUARE
(Map p40; Ⓜ Gare Centrale) Brussels' magnificent Grand Place is one of the world's most unforgettable urban ensembles. Oddly hidden, the enclosed cobblestone square is only revealed as you enter on foot from one of six narrow side alleys: Rue des Harengs is the best first approach. The focal point is the spired 15th-century city hall, but each of the antique guildhalls (mostly 1697–1705) has a charm of its own. Most are unashamed exhibitionists, with fine baroque gables, gilded statues and elaborate guild symbols.

★ Galeries St-Hubert   ARCHITECTURE
(Map p40; ☑ 02-545 09 90; www.grsh.be; Rue du Maré aux Herbes; Ⓜ Gare Centrale) When opened in 1847 by King Léopold I, the glorious Galeries St-Hubert formed Europe's very first shopping arcade. Many enticing shops lie behind its neoclassical glassed-in arches flanked by marble pilasters. Several eclectic *cafés* spill tables onto the gallery terrace, safe from rain beneath the glass roof. The arcade is off Rue du Marché aux Herbes.

ℹ CAPITAL SAVINGS

➡ The cheapest way to see a bunch of top sites is with the **BrusselsCard** (www.brusselscard.be; 24/48/72hr €26/34/42). The card gets you into 40 museums and provides free city transport plus discounts for other attractions and some shops and restaurants. It's available through the tourist offices, STIB agencies and larger museums.

➡ On the first Wednesday afternoon of each month, most of Brussels' major museums are free to enter.

➡ The Arsène50 office (p76) at the tourist office offers heavily discounted tickets for cultural events.

★ Musée Mode & Dentelle   MUSEUM
(Fashion & Lace Museum; Map p40; ☑ 02-213 44 50; www.costumeandlacemuseum.brussels; Rue de la Violette 12; adult/child/BrusselsCard €8/free/free; ☺ 10am-5pm Tue-Sun; Ⓜ Gare Centrale) Lace making has been one of Flanders' finest crafts since the 16th century. While *kloskant* (bobbin lace) originated in Bruges, *naaldkant* (needlepoint lace) was developed in Italy but was predominantly made in Brussels. This excellent museum reveals lace's applications for underwear and outerwear over the centuries, as well as displaying other luxury textiles in beautifully presented exhibitions. There's a new focus here on Belgium's ahead-of-the-curve fashion industry, with changing exhibitions of contemporary textiles.

Hôtel de Ville   HISTORIC BUILDING
(City Hall; Map p40; ☑ visitors office 02-279 43 47; Grand Place; guided tours €5; ☺ tours 3pm Wed year-round, 10am & 2pm Sun Apr-Sep; Ⓜ Gare Centrale) Laboriously built between 1444 and 1480, the splendid, slightly asymmetrical Hôtel de Ville was almost the only building on the Grand Place to escape the 1695 French bombardment – ironic considering it was their primary target. The stone facade is replete with Gothic gargoyles and reliefs. Its intricate tower soars 96m, topped by a gilded statue of St-Michel, Brussels' patron saint. For 45-minute guided tours, go to the tourist office 40 minutes before the departure time to buy tickets.

Maison du Roi   HISTORIC BUILDING
(Musée de la Ville de Bruxelles; Map p40; Grand Place; Ⓜ Gare Centrale) This fanciful feast of neo-Gothic arches, verdigris statues and mini-spires is bigger, darker and nearly 200 years younger than the surrounding guildhalls. Once a medieval bread market, the current masterpiece is an 1873 rebuild and nowadays houses the Brussels City Museum. Don't miss Pieter Bruegel the Elder's 1567 *Cortège de Noces* (Wedding Procession).

Brussels City Museum   MUSEUM
(Musée de la Ville de Bruxelles; Map p40; ☑ 02-279 43 50; www.museedelavilledebruxelles.be; Grand Place; adult/concession/BrusselsCard €8/6/free; ☺ 10am-5pm Tue-Sun, to 8pm Thu; Ⓜ Gare Centrale, 🚇 Bourse) Old maps, architectural relics and paintings give a historical overview of the city. Don't miss Pieter Bruegel the Elder's 1567 *Cortège de Noces* (Wedding Procession).

Fondation Jacques Brel MUSEUM
(Map p40; ☑02-511 10 20; www.jacquesbrel.be; Place de la Vieille Halle aux Blés 11; adult/student €5/3.50, walk with audioguide €8, walk & museum €10; ⊙noon-6pm Tue-Sat, plus Mon Aug; Ⓜ Gare Centrale) *Chansonnier* Jacques Brel (1929–78) made his debut in 1952 at a cabaret in his native Belgium and shot to fame in Paris, where he was a contemporary of Édith Piaf and co, though his songs continued to hark back to the bleak 'flat land' of his native country. At the time of writing, the museum was being redeveloped, with the audio walking tour still available.

Manneken Pis MONUMENT
(Map p40; cnr Rue de l'Étuve & Rue du Chêne; Ⓜ Gare Centrale) Rue Charles Buls – Brussels' most unashamedly touristy shopping street, lined with chocolate and trinket shops – leads the hordes three blocks from the Grand Place to the Manneken Pis. This fountain-statue of a little boy taking a leak is comically tiny and a perversely perfect national symbol for surreal Belgium. Most of the time the statue's nakedness is hidden beneath a costume relevant to an anniversary, national day or local event: his ever-growing wardrobe is displayed at the Maison du Roi.

Rue des Bouchers STREET
(Map p40; Ⓜ De Brouckère) Uniquely colourful Rue and Petite Rue des Bouchers are a pair of narrow alleys jam-packed with pavement tables, pyramids of lemons and iced displays of fish and crustaceans. It's all gloriously photogenic, but think twice before eating here, as the food standards are generally poor. Don't miss peeping inside marionette theatre Toone (p78) and, nearby, into the wonderful, age-old biscuit shop Dandoy (Map p40; ☑02-511 03 26; www.maisondandoy.com; Rue au Beurre 31; snacks from €6; ⊙9.30am-7pm Mon-Sat, 10.30am-7pm Sun; ☺Bourse), full of splendid moulds for *speculaas/speculoos* (traditional spiced biscuit) figures.

Église St-Nicolas CHURCH
(Map p40; Rue au Beurre 1; ⊙8am-6.30pm Mon-Fri, 9am-6pm Sat, to 7.30pm Sun; ☺Bourse) Near the Bourse, this pint-sized church is as old as Brussels itself. What really makes it notable is its virtual invisibility – the exterior is almost totally encrusted with shops. Appropriately enough, it's dedicated to the patron saint of merchants.

OTHER PISSERS

The inexplicably famous Manneken Pis has a much younger squatting little 'sister', 20th-century **Jeanneke Pis** (Map p40; Impasse de la Fidélité; Ⓜ Gare Centrale), and there's also **Zinneke** (Map p40; cnr Rue des Chartreux & Rue du Vieux Marché aux Grains; ☺Bourse), a mongrel dog standing with cocked (if dry) leg as though to show his contempt for the surrounding Fashion District.

Statue of Everard 't Serclaes STATUE
(Map p40; Rue Charles Buls; Ⓜ De Brouckère) A 1902 statue of city hero Everard 't Serclaes depicts his reclining corpse. A contemporary 'tradition' claims that rubbing the statue will bring you good luck. It's on the wall of L'Etoile, the Grand Place's smallest house, in the arcaded alley beside the Hôtel de Ville.

Musée de la Brasserie MUSEUM
(Map p40; ☑02-511 49 87; www.beerparadise.be; Grand Place 10; €5; ⊙10am-5pm daily Apr-Nov, noon-5p°m Sat & Sun Dec-Mar; Ⓜ Gare Centrale, ☺Bourse) Brussels' brewery museum is authentic in the sense that it occupies the basement of the brewers' guildhall and has some 18th-century brewing equipment. But visitors are often disappointed because it's small and no actual brewing takes place (though you do get a beer at the end). To see a real brewery in action, head to the Musée Bruxellois de la Gueuze at the Cantillon Brewery (p58).

⊙ Ste-Catherine

It's hard to imagine today, but fishing boats once sailed up the now-invisible River Senne, mooring in the heart of Ste-Catherine, which for centuries was a major fish market. Although the river has been covered over since 1870, the area's reputation for fish persists and the main reason you're likely to visit is to choose from the numerous well-regarded seafood outlets and restaurants around Place Ste-Catherine.

★Argos GALLERY
(Map p46; ☑02-229 00 03; www.argosarts.org; Rue du Chantier 13; €6; ⊙11am-6pm Wed-Fri; Ⓜ Yser) A not-for-profit gallery in a former banana warehouse, founded in 1989 to promote video art that engages with politics. In addition to temporary video exhibits, the media library stores 5000 films, dating from

Grand Place, Bourse & Around

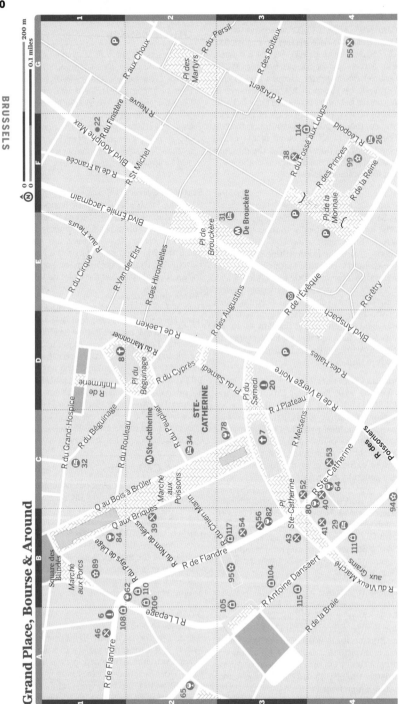

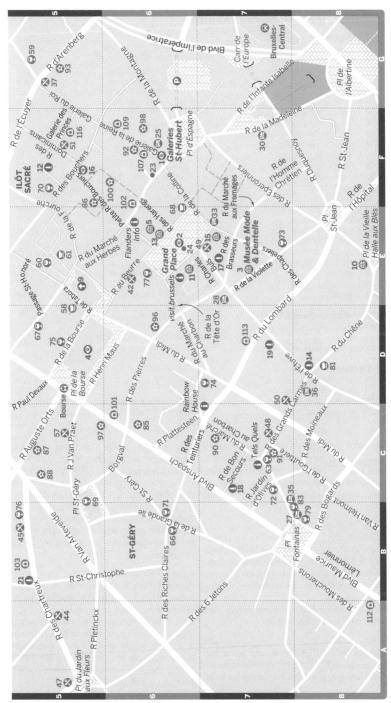

Grand Place, Bourse & Around

the 1960s to today. A bookshop features works about experimental cinema and cultural studies, and a bar serves coffee, wine and Ricard. The now quiet street the gallery sits on was once a hub of the boat-building industry.

Église St-Jean-Baptiste
au Béguinage   CHURCH
(Map p40; Place du Béguinage; Ⓜ Ste-Catherine) This soaring 1657 Flemish baroque masterpiece was designed by Luc Fayd'Herbe, a student of Rubens. It's often cited as Belgium's most beautiful church and has become something of a temporary refuge and work space for asylum seekers.

MIMA   MUSEUM
(Map p46; ☑ 0472 61 03 51; www.mimamuseum.eu; Quai du Hainaut 39; adult/concession/BrusselsCard €9.5/7.5/free; ☉ 10am-6pm Wed-Sun; Ⓜ Comte de Flandre) On the banks of the Brussels Canal, the engaged and engaging Millennium Iconoclast Museum of Art (MIMA) showcases contemporary art with a permanent collection that includes works from outsider artist Daniel Johnston and cinematographer Nicolas Karakatsanis. Founded in 2016, Kanal also hosts several temporary exhibitions throughout the year on topics such as protest art.

Église Ste-Catherine   CHURCH
(Map p40; Place Ste-Catherine; Ⓜ Ste-Catherine) Église Ste-Catherine must be one of the only religious buildings that positively encourages folks to urinate on its walls (there's a 'pissoir' on its northwestern flank). Inside is a black statue of the Virgin and Child that Protestants once hurled into the Senne (1744); the statue was found 'miraculously' floating on a chunk of turf.

Pigeon Soldat Memorial MONUMENT
(Map p46; Ⓜ Ste-Catherine) This monument commemorates the carrier pigeons of WWI.

Tour Noire TOWER
(Map p40; Place du Samedi; Ⓜ Ste-Catherine) Boxed in on three sides and incongruously dwarfed by the back of a Novotel Hotel, this tower is an ivy-draped remnant of Brussels' original city wall.

○ Schaerbeek

Much of the area around the Gare du Nord (Bruxelles-Nord) is seedy but further north, Schaerbeek features a wonderful old town hall, classic train station and a lively, diverse vibe.

★ **Train World** MUSEUM
(🕿 02-224 74 98; www.trainworld.be; Place Princesse Elisabeth 5; adult/concession/BrusselsCard

€12/9/free; ⊙ 10am-5pm Tue-Sun; 🚊 58, 59, 🚊 7, 92, 🚆 Schaerbeek) Wonderful old engines gleam in the low light of this imaginative and beautiful museum, which is located in the renovated 1887 Schaerbeek station. Exhibits include *Le Belge*, the country's first locomotive.

You can climb on board the engines, wander into a historic station cottage and walk over a railway bridge. A train simulator is an added bonus.

Halles de Schaerbeek ARTS CENTRE
(Map p46; 🕿 02-218 21 07; www.halles.be; Rue Royale Ste-Marie 22; 🚊 92, 93) This arts centre was a 1901 former food market, and is a great example of glass and wrought-iron industrial architecture. It has been restored as a cultural centre and performance space.

☉ Cathedral Area

★ **Old England Building** HISTORIC BUILDING
(Map p50; Rue Montagne de la Cour 2; Ⓜ Gare Centrale, Parc) This 1899 former department store is an art nouveau showpiece with a black facade aswirl with wrought iron and arched windows. The building contains the groundbreaking **MIM** (Musée des Instruments de Musique; 🖉 02-545 01 30; www.mim.be; adult/concession €10/8; ☉ 9.30am-5pm Tue-Fri, 10am-5pm Sat & Sun) music museum, a celebration of music in all its forms, as well as a repository for more than 2000 historic instruments. The emphasis is very much on listening, with auditory experiences around every corner, from shepherds' bagpipes and Chinese carillons to harpsichords. Don't miss the **rooftop café** (🖉 02-502 95 08; www.mim. be/the-restaurant; meals €12-16; ☉ 10am-4.30pm, closed Mon) for a superb city panorama.

★ **Musées Royaux des Beaux-Arts** GALLERY
(Royal Museums of Fine Arts; Map p50; 🖉 02-508 32 11; www.fine-arts-museum.be; Rue de la Régence 3; adult/6-25yr/BrusselsCard €10/3/free, with Magritte Museum €15; ☉ 10am-5pm Tue-Fri, 11am-6pm Sat & Sun; Ⓜ Gare Centrale, Parc) This prestigious museum incorporates the **Musée d'Art Ancien** (ancient art); the **Musée d'Art Moderne** (modern art), with works by surrealist Paul Delvaux and fauvist Rik Wouters; and the purpose-built Musée Magritte. The 15th-century Flemish Primitives are wonderfully represented in the Musée d'Art Ancien: there's Rogier Van der Weyden's *Pietà* with its hallucinatory sky, Hans Memling's refined portraits, and the richly textured *Madonna with Saints* by the anonymous artist known as Master of the Legend of St Lucy.

Musée Magritte GALLERY
(Map p50; 🖉 02-508 32 11; www.musee-magritte-museum.be; Rue de la Régence 3; adult/under 26yr/BrusselsCard €10/3/free; ☉ 10am-5pm Tue-Fri, 11am-6pm Sat & Sun; Ⓜ Gare Centrale, Parc) The beautifully presented Magritte Museum holds the world's largest collection of the surrealist pioneer's paintings and drawings. Watch his style develop from colourful Braque-style cubism in 1920 through a Dali-esque phase and a late-1940s period of Kandinsky-like brushwork to his trademark bowler hats of the 1960s. Regular screenings of a 50-minute documentary provide insights into the artist's unconventionally conventional life.

Cathédrale des Sts-Michel & Gudule CHURCH
(Map p46; www.cathedralisbruxellensis.be; Place Ste-Gudule; admission free, treasury €1, crypt €3; ☉ 7.30am-6pm Mon-Fri, 3.30am-3.30pm Sat, 2-6pm Sun; Ⓜ Gare Centrale) Host to coronations and royal weddings, Brussels' grand, twin-towered cathedral bears at least some resemblance to Paris' Notre Dame. Begun in 1226, construction took 300 years. Stained-glass windows flood the soaring nave with light, while column-saints brandish gilded tools. An enormous wooden pulpit by Antwerp artist Hendrik Verbruggen sees Adam and Eve driven out of Eden by skeletons. To climb the cathedral towers (€5; 10am on the second Saturday of each month), sign up a day or two ahead. The treasury is open shorter hours and the crypt by appointment only.

Jewish Museum MUSEUM
(Map p50; 🖉 02-512 19 63; www.aejm.org/members/jewish-museum-of-belgium; Rue des Minimes 21; €8; ☉ 10am-5pm Tue-Sat; Ⓜ Louise) The Jewish Museum hosts good temporary photography exhibits and a permanent collection relating to Jewish life in Belgium and beyond, with a section on the Holocaust. The museum was hit by a terrorist attack in 2014 that killed four people; there is stringent security on arrival and the building is protected by armed guards.

Bibliothèque Royale LIBRARY
(Map p50; www.kbr.be/en; Blvd de l'Empereur 4; ☉ 9am-7pm Mon-Fri, to 5pm Sat) The city's modern library is a beautifully designed space, containing a small museum about books and printing, and a top-floor cafeteria.

Église Notre-Dame de la Chapelle CHURCH
(Map p50; Place de la Chapelle; ☉ 9am-7pm Jun-Sep, to 6pm Oct-May; 🚊 Anneessens) **FREE** Brussels' oldest surviving church now curiously incorporates the decapitated tower of the 1134 original as the central section of a bigger Gothic edifice. Behind the palm-tree pulpit, look on the wall above a carved confessional to find a small memorial to 'Petro Brevgello'; ie the artist Pieter Bruegel the Elder, who once lived in the nearby Marolles.

Statue of Godefroid (Godefroy) de Bouillon STATUE
(Map p50; Ⓜ Gare Centrale, Parc) The bold equestrian statue at the centre of Place Royale depicts Godefroid (Godefroy) de Bouillon, the crusader knight who briefly became the first European 'king' of Jerusalem in 1099.

Coudenberg   ARCHAEOLOGICAL SITE
(Map p50; www.coudenberg.com; adult/under 26yr/BrusselsCard €7/6/free; ⏰9.30am-5pm Tue-Fri, 10am-6pm Sat & Sun; Ⓜ Parc) Coudenberg Hill (now Place Royale) was the site of Brussels' original 12th-century castle. Over several centuries this was transformed into one of Europe's most elegant and powerful palaces, most notably as the 16th-century residence of Holy Roman Emperor Charles V. Around the palace, courtiers and nobles in turn built fine mansions. The vast complex was destroyed in a catastrophic 1731 fire, but beneath street level the basic structure of the palace's long-hidden lower storeys remains.

Whole stretches of the medieval street layout are now discernible for those wanting a subterranean archaeological excursion. The visit starts at **Musée BELvue** (⏰070 500 45 54; www.belvue.be; Place des Palais 7; adult/concession €7/6; ⏰for groups with reservation 9.30am-5pm Mon, to 5pm Tue-Fri, 10am-6pm Sat & Sun), itself an interesting audio-guided museum of Belgian history since independence, situated in a former royal residence.

Palais Royal   PALACE
(Map p50; ☑02-551 20 20; www.monarchy.be; Place des Palais; ⏰10.30am-4.30pm Tue-Sun late Jul-early Sep; Ⓜ Parc) **FREE** These days Belgium's royal family lives at Laeken, but this sturdy 19th-century palace remains its 'official' residence. One unique room has had its ceiling iridescently clad with the wing cases of 1.4 million Thai jewel beetles by conceptual artist Jan Fabre. You'll also see contemporary royal portraits. It's only open to visitors in summer.

★**Centre Belge de la Bande Dessinée**   MUSEUM
(Belgian Comic Strip Centre; Map p46; ☑02-219 19 80; www.comicscenter.net; Rue des Sables 20; adult/concession €10/7; ⏰10am-6pm; Ⓜ Rogier) This centre offers a definitive and enjoyable overview of the country's vibrant comic-strip culture. Even if you're not excited by the 'ninth art', do peep inside the superb 1906 art nouveau building, a Victor Horta classic built as a fabric store with a wrought-iron superstructure and a glass roof. You don't have to pay an entrance fee to enjoy the central hallway or to drink a coffee at the attached cafe.

COMIC-STRIP MURALS

Dozens of comic-strip murals enliven Brussels' alleys and thoroughfares, with more added year after year. Some favourites:

Tibet & Duchateau (Map p40; Rue du Bon Secours 9; 🚇Bourse) Very effectively depicts a life-sized figure teetering towards a *trompe l'œil* window.

Josephine Baker (Map p50; Rue des Capucins 9; Ⓜ Porte de Hal) One of the most distinctive Marolles murals, in which slinky chanteuse Josephine, with a leopard on a lead, shakes hands with a rotund monk. Behind, both in the mural and in real life, is the looming dome of the Palais de Justice. Baker performed in Brussels in the 1920s and '30s, and famously kept a leopard as a pet.

Tintin (Map p40; Rue de l'Étuve; 🚇Bourse) The most renowned Belgian fictional character.

Peeping Policeman (Map p50; Rue Haute; Ⓜ Louise) This Hergé character uses the terrace end brilliantly for a little spying.

Cubitus (Map p40; Rue de Flandre; Ⓜ Ste-Catherine) A tetchy-looking Manneken Pis gazes up at his pediment, from which he has been displaced by a grinning, peeing bear.

FC de Kampioenen (Map p46; Rue du Canal; Ⓜ Ste-Catherine) This bright, dynamic mural features not a football club but a parade of characters based on a TV series that ran from 1990 to 2011.

Sacrifice mural (Map p46; Blvd Barthélémy; Ⓜ Ste-Catherine) In 2016 and 2017 an anonymous new series emerged, depicting male and female genitalia and a graphic scene of child sacrifice inspired by a Caravaggio painting. Another image, of a flayed body hanging upside down, appears to be by the same artist, and is based on 17th-century painting *The Corpses of the Brothers De Witt* by Jan de Baen. The images are raw, without clear cartoony outlines, and their subtext is political corruption, familial violence and sexual hypocrisy... Brussels street art just got a whole lot edgier.

Central Brussels North

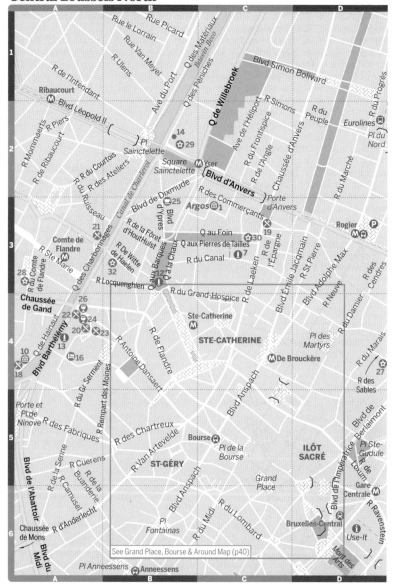

Right opposite in a former newspaper office, the free **Marc Sleen Museum** (Map p46; ☑ 02-219 19 80; www.marc-sleen.be; Rue des Sables 33-35; ⊙ 11am-1pm & 2-6pm Tue-Sun) celebrates the creator of long-running comic-book character Nibbs.

National Bank of Belgium Museum   MUSEUM
(Map p46; ☑ 02-221 22 06; www.nbbmuseum.be; Blvd de Berlaimont 3; ⊙ 10am-5pm Mon-Fri; Ⓜ Gare Centrale) FREE Unexpectedly absorbing, the renovated National Bank of

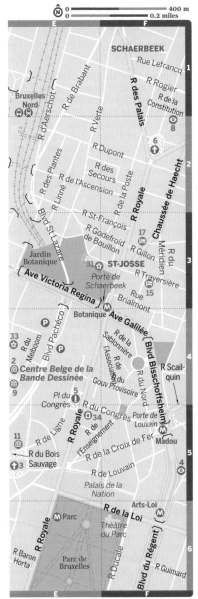

Belgium Museum is far more than just a coin collection. It houses well-presented exhibits that trace the very concept of money all the way from cowrie shells to credit cards.

Église Ste-Marie CHURCH
(Map p46; Place de la Reine; 🚊 92, 93) Looking east along Rue Royale, your gaze is unavoidably drawn to this very distinctive octagonal 19th-century church in neo-Byzantine style,

BRUXELLOIS

The old Marolles-Brussels dialect, Brux-ellois, is a curious mixture of French, Dutch and Walloon, with elements of Spanish and Yiddish thrown in: you can hear it at the charming puppet shows at the Théâtre Royal de Toone (p78), which hosts performances in Bruxellois.

These days very few people beyond Place du Jeu-de-Balle actually speak the full dialect. Nonetheless, certain Bruxellois words are used, consciously or otherwise, to punctuate local French, whether for comic effect or because no better words exist. Here are some classic examples that hint at the playful Bruxellois character:

➡ *blèter* – to snivel, complain

➡ *froucheleir* – man with wandering hands

➡ *in stoemelings* – sneakily, on the quiet

➡ *papzak* – fatso

➡ *zatlap* – habitual drunkard

➡ *zieverair* – time-waster, idiot

replete with buttresses and a star-studded central cupola.

Colonne du Congrès MONUMENT
(Map p46; Place du Congrès; M Madou) Brussels' 25m-tall version of Nelson's Column is an 1850s monolith topped by a gilded statue of King Léopold I. It commemorates the Belgian constitution of 1831. The four female figures around its base represent the four constitutionally upheld freedoms of religion, association, education and the press. The last of these encouraged Victor Hugo, Karl Marx and others to visit Belgium back when such freedoms were much more restricted in other parts of Europe. Between two bronze lions, an eternal flame honours Belgian victims of the two world wars.

◎ Sablon & Marolles

Brussels' once resolutely working-class Marolles quarter has partly shed its proletarian image with a clutch of intimate restaurants and funky interior-design shops along the main streets, Rue Haute and Rue Blaes. Nonetheless, pockets of original Bruxellois character can still be found, notably around the Place du Jeu-de-Balle. At a few of the enjoyable downmarket *cafés* here you might

overhear people speaking in the earthy Bruxellois dialect, and at least one stall still sells the traditional street food: snails. Note that, despite the name, Jeu-de-Balle (aka *balle-pelotte*) is no longer played here.

★**Église Notre-Dame du Sablon** CHURCH
(Map p50; Rue de la Régence; ⊙ 9am-6.30pm Mon-Fri, 10am-6.30pm Sat & Sun; M Porte de Namur) The Sablon's large, flamboyantly Gothic church started life as the 1304 archers' guild chapel. A century later it had to be massively enlarged to cope with droves of pilgrims attracted by the supposed healing powers of its Madonna statue. The statue was procured in 1348 by means of an audacious theft from an Antwerp church – apparently by a vision-motivated husband-and-wife team in a rowing boat. It has long since gone, but a boat behind the pulpit commemorates the curious affair.

Place du Petit Sablon PARK
(Map p50; M Porte de Namur) About 200m uphill from Place du Grand Sablon, this charming little garden is ringed by 48 bronze statuettes representing the medieval guilds. Standing huddled on a fountain plinth like two actors from a Shakespearean drama are Counts Egmont and Hoorn, popular city leaders who were beheaded in the Grand Place in 1568 for defying Spanish rule. The site of Egmont's grand former residence lies behind.

Palais de Justice HISTORIC BUILDING
(Map p50; Place Poelaert; M Louise, ☐ 92, 94) Larger than St Peter's in Rome, this 2.6-hectare complex of law courts was the world's biggest building when it was constructed (1866–83). While the labyrinthine complex is undoubtedly forbidding, it is not easy to secure. Indeed, in several high-profile cases criminals have absconded from its precincts. Behind the building a terrace offers wide panoramas over the Brussels rooftops, with the Atomium and Koekelberg Basilica the stars of the skyline show. A glass elevator (Map p50; Place Breughel, Rue de l'Epée; ⊙ 7.30am-11.45pm; M Louise) FREE leads down to the earthy Marolles district.

Designed to evoke the temples of the Egyptian pharaohs, the Palais de Justice was sited on the hill dominating the working-class Marolles as an intimidating symbol of law and order. When its architect, Joseph Poelaert, went insane and died during its construction, legends promptly suggested he'd been struck down by the witchcraft of the numerous Marolles residents evicted to make way for the building. The term *ski-even* (twisted) *architekt* remains a characteristic insult in the old Bruxellois dialect.

Porte de Hal   HISTORIC BUILDING
(Map p50; www.kmkg-mrah.be; Blvd du Midi; adult/concession/child/BrusselsCard €7/5/3/ free; ☉9.30am-5pm Tue-Fri, 10am-5pm Sat & Sun, last entry 4.15pm; Ⓜ Porte de Hal) For centuries Brussels was surrounded by a grand 8km fortress wall. It was partly demolished in the 1790s, then removed altogether on Napoleon's orders in 1810. Well, almost. In fact, a few isolated parts survived, including the Porte de Hal, one of the seven very imposing 14th-century gatehouse towers, which the French preserved for use as a military prison. The Porte de Hal was converted into a museum in 1847 and romantically embellished with statuary, windows and neo-Gothic turrets thereafter.

Today an audioguide leads you round its decent little city-history museum and exhibition of armour, and you can climb to the 6th-storey battlements.

◉ St-Gilles & Ixelles (Elsene)

Brussels' inner-southern suburbs are most interesting for their *cafés,* restaurants and residential architectural gems, most of which you can only see from the outside.

★**St-Gilles Town Hall**   HISTORIC BUILDING
(Maison Communale de St-Gilles; Map p54; ☑02-536 02 11; www.stgilles.irisnet.be; Place Maurice van Meenen; ☉8am-noon daily & 3-6pm Tue-Sun; Ⓜ Horta) One of Brussels' overlooked architectural wonders, this splendid Napoleon III–style palace sports a soaring brick belfry dotted with gilt statuary. Try to see the wedding-hall ceiling, painted by Belgian symbolist artist Fernand Khnopff.

★**Musée Horta**   MUSEUM
(Map p54; ☑02-543 04 90; www.hortamuseum.be; Rue Américaine 25; adult/child €10/3; ☉2-5.30pm Tue-Sun; Ⓜ Horta, 🚃91, 92) The typically austere exterior doesn't give much away, but Victor Horta's former home (designed and built 1898–1901) is an art nouveau jewel. The stairwell is the structural triumph of the house: follow the playful knots and curlicues of the banister, which become more exuberant as you ascend, ending at a tangle of swirls and glass lamps at the skylight, glazed with plain and citrus-coloured glass.

★**Flagey**   NOTABLE BUILDING
(Map p54; www.flagey.be; Place Flagey; 🚃81, 82) This marvellous 1938 'liner' building originally conceived as the national radio building, is now the centre of an up-and-coming nightlife area. With its distinctive round 'periscope' tower, it's an art deco classic that hosts a hip cafe, a cinema and various music venues.

Musée Constantin Meunier   MUSEUM
(☑02-648 44 49; www.fine-arts-museum.be/en/museums/musee-meunier-museum; Rue de l'Abbaye 59; ☉10am-noon & 1-5pm Tue-Fri; 🚃93, 94) **FREE** This intimate museum occupies an Ixelles town house that was the last home

---

ST-GILLES TO IXELLES, AN ARCHITECTURAL STROLL

Starting up Ave Paul Dejaer from Metro Horta, notice the the colourfully refurbished **art nouveau house** (Map p54; Ave Paul Dejaer 9) across the road from a lovely, old fashioned charcuterie store. There's another behind the splendid St-Gilles Town Hall at **Rue du Savoie 66** (Map p54), from which you can walk south towards then east alongside **St-Gilles Prison** (Map p54; Ave Ducpétiaux) whose crenellated facade imitates a Crusader fortress. Continue along Ave Ducpétiaux, where houses **18–24** (Map p54) are further art nouveau classics, to the Musée Horta (p49). Further northeast, admire the big circular window of **Rue Africaine 92** (Map p54), the 1935, art deco **Église des Augustins** (Map p54; Place de l'Altitude Cent; ☉11am-6pm) concrete church, and *sgraffito*-topped **Rue Faider 83** (Map p54), before passing the 1893 **Hotel Tassel** (Map p54; Rue Paul-Émile Janson 6), Victor Horta's first truly art nouveau house-design. A year later Horta created nearby Hotel Solvay (p57), a masterpiece commissioned by a family of soft-drink manufacturers who gave him free rein. To appreciate its intricacies you'll need to get inside on a pre-booked ARAU tour (p60). Finish your stroll at the **Étangs d'Ixelles** (Map p54), a pair of lakes flanked by fine mansions, and perhaps a drink at the 1938 art deco classic Flagey, with its hip cafe and periscope tower.

Central Brussels South

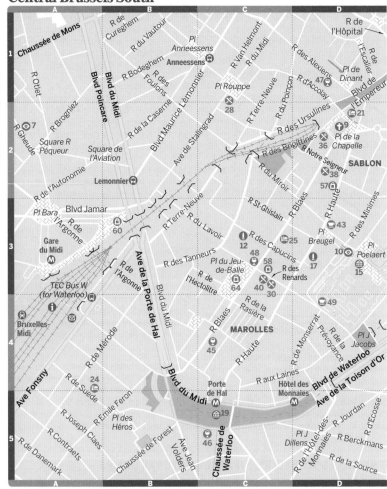

and studio of Brussels-born artist Constantin Meunier (1831–1905) and presents a substantial collection of his later works. Meunier is best known for emotive sculptures and social-realist paintings, including larger-than-life bronzes depicting muscular miners from Hainaut, dock workers from Antwerp and men reaping fields.

Musée d'Art Fantastique MUSEUM
(Map p54; ☑ 0475 41 29 18; www.fantastic-museum.be; Rue Américaine 7; €6; ⊙ 2-5pm Sat & Sun May-Sep; Ⓜ Horta) In what seems an outwardly typical Ixelles town house, this museum

hits you with jumbled rooms full of cyborg body parts, Terminator heads and vampire cocoons, then lets you electrocute a troll.

⊙ Matongé

Taking its name from a Kinshasa square, Matongé is home to Brussels' African community, though the compact area also encompasses a much wider ethnic mix. Like parts of Kinshasa, the architecture has its share of tired old 1960s concrete, but even the dreary **Galerie d'Ixelles** (Map p50; Ⓜ Porte de Namur) comes to life with African

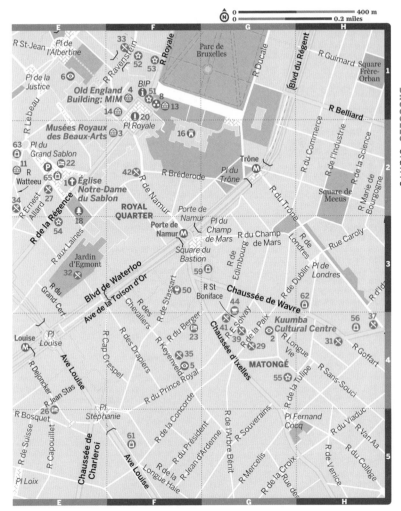

hairstylists, bars and a Congolese CD/DVD outlet. The **Kuumba Cultural Centre** (Map p50; ☎ 02-503 57 30; www.kuumba.be; Rue de la Paix 35; ⊙ 2pm-midnight Tue-Sat; Ⓜ Porte de Namur) organises tours of the district, plus excellent events featuring Congolese bands, dance workshops and food.

◉ EU Quarter & Cinqantenaire

Along the thundering thoroughfares Rue de la Loi and Rue Belliard, tragically bland office blocks are packed so close together they form dark concrete canyons. To the east, EU office buildings cut a brutally modern gash through a once-attractive neighbourhood behind Bruxelles-Luxembourg station. But it's not all horror. The EU area also has lovely gardens, fountains and some fine art nouveau houses, notably around Sq Marie-Louise.

Then there's the Cinquantenaire, a triumphal arch reminiscent of Paris' Arc de Triomphe. It was designed to celebrate Belgium's 50th anniversary (*cinquantenaire*) in 1880 but took so long to build that by that date only a temporary plaster version was standing. The full beast wasn't completed until 1905. In summer, the arcade forms

Central Brussels South

the curious backdrop to a drive-in cinema screen, while around it are several grand-scale museums. To climb to the top of the arch, enter via the free Army Museum (p54).

★ **Musée des Sciences Naturelles** MUSEUM
(Map p58; ☎ 02-627 42 11; www.naturalsciences.be; Rue Vautier 29; adult/concession/child/Brussels Card €7/6/4.50/free; ⏱ 9.30am-5pm Tue-Fri, 10am-6pm Sat & Sun; ⊒ 38) Thought-provoking and highly interactive, this museum has far more than the usual selection of stuffed animals. But the undoubted highlight is a unique 'family' of iguanodons – 10m-high

dinosaurs found in a Hainaut coal mine in 1878. A computer simulation shows the mudslide that might have covered them, sand-boxes allow you to play dino hunter and multilingual videos give a wonderfully nuanced debate on recent palaeontology.

The bus here departs from next to Gare Centrale in the direction of Homborch, stopping at De Meeus on Rue du Luxembourg.

★ **Parc du Cinquantenaire** PARK
(Map p58; Rue de la Loi & Rue Belliard; Ⓜ Mérode) Parc du Cinquantenaire was built during Léopold II's reign. It's best known for its

cluster of museums – art, history, military and motor vehicles – which house an incredible 350,000 artefacts. The Royal Art and History Museums in the southern wing of the Cinquantenaire buildings are full of antiquities. Autoworld, in the northern building, has a huge collection of vintage cars. There is also the massive Arcade du Cinquantenaire, a triumphal arch built in 1880 to celebrate 50 years of Belgian independence.

★ **Musée Art & Histoire** MUSEUM
(Map p58; ☑ 02-741 73 01; www.kmkg-mrah.be; Parc du Cinquantenaire 10; adult/child/Brussels Card €10/4/free; ⊙ 9.30am-5pm Tue-Fri, from 10am Sat & Sun; Ⓜ Mérode) This rich collection ranges from ancient Egyptian sarcophagi and Meso-American masks to icons to wooden bicycles. Decide what you want to see before coming or the sheer scope can prove overwhelming. Visually attractive spaces include the medieval stone carvings set around a neo-Gothic cloister and the soaring Corinthian columns (convincing fibreglass props) that bring atmosphere to an original AD 420 mosaic from Roman Syria. Labelling is in French and Dutch, so the English-language audioguide (€3) is worth considering.

House of European History MUSEUM
(HoEH; Map p58; http://historia-europa.ep.eu; Rue Belliard 135; ⊙ 1-6pm Mon, 9am-6pm Tue-Fri, 10am-6pm Sat & Sun; ☑ 21,27,59,60,80) FREE Housed in the beautifully renovated Eastman Building in Parc Léopold, this airy, elegant new museum takes you into some dark corners of European history, from war and destruction to the biggest peace project ever endeavoured. There are detours from this tumultuous path for Dutch tulips, English football and European cuisine, this last described in disappointingly broadbrush terms. The highly (perhaps overly) interactive experience takes about 1½ hours, with permanent and temporary exhibitions that you can roam through in 24 languages.

Maison Cauchie NOTABLE BUILDING
(Map p58; ☑ 02-733 86 84; www.cauchie.be; Rue des Francs 5; adult/child €7/free; ⊙ 10am-1pm & 2-5.30pm 1st Sat & Sun of each month; Ⓜ Mérode) Built in 1905, this stunning house was the home of architect and painter Paul Cauchie (1875–1952), and its *sgraffito* facade, adorned with graceful female figures, is one of the most beautiful in Brussels. It looks like a Klimt painting transformed into architecture. A petition saved the house from

GREEN BRUSSELS

A great way to get off the beaten track in Brussels and discover the leafier fringes is to walk or cycle the **Promenade Verte** (www.promenade-verte.be), a 60km circuit divided into seven easy 5km to 10km sections. The route takes in the verdant Forêt de Soignes and surprisingly rustic parts of Uccle, as well as traversing more industrial landscapes.

demolition in 1971, and since 1975 it has been a protected monument. If you can't time a visit to meet the limited opening hours, the facade alone definitely warrants a visit.

EU Parliament NOTABLE BUILDING
(Map p58; ☑ 02-284 34 57; www.europarl.europa.eu; Rue Wiertz 43; ⊙ tours 10am & 3pm Mon-Thu, 10am Fri; ☑ 38, Ⓜ Trône) FREE Inside this decidedly dated blue-glass building (completed only just over a decade ago) political junkies can sit in on a parliamentary session in the huge debating chamber known as the hemicycle, or tour it when parliament's not sitting. Tours of the complex are via multilingual headphones.

The visitor centre **Parlamentarium** (www.europarl.europa.eu/visiting/en/brussels/parlamentarium; Rue Wiertz 60; ⊙ 1-6pm Mon, 9-6pm Tue-Fri, 10am-6pm Sat & Sun) FREE has longer hours, an interactive floor map allowing you to tour the EU, profiles of parliament members, a discussion room and a one-hour scavenger hunt designed to interest kids.

Maison St-Cyr HOUSE
(Map p58; Sq Ambiorix 11; Ⓜ Schuman) The haunting facade of this narrow building is an extravagance of knotted and twisted ironwork. It was built in 1903 for painter Léonard St-Cyr by Gustave Strauven (1878–1919), who worked as an apprentice to Horta and also built art nouveau houses in Schaerbeek.

Square Marie-Louise SQUARE
(Map p58; off Ave Palmerston; Ⓜ Maelbeek) You can feed the ducks in the pretty tree-lined pond surrounded by greenery and a smattering of art nouveau architecture.

Charlier Museum HOUSE
(Map p46; ☑ 02-220 26 91; www.charliermuseum.be; Ave des Arts 16; adult/concession/BrusselsCard €5/4/free; ⊙ noon-5pm Mon-Thu, 10am-1pm Fri; Ⓜ Madou) A lesser sight on the Horta trail,

St-Gilles & Ixelles

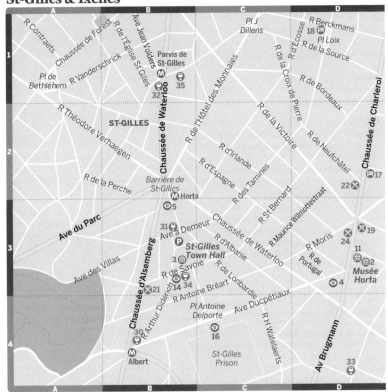

this grand private house was remodelled and extended by the architect in 1893. It displays a rather stuffy collection of mid- to late-19th-century paintings and sculpture.

Berlaymont Building   NOTABLE BUILDING
(Map p58; Rue de la Loi 200; M Schuman) The European Commission, the EU's sprawling bureaucracy, centres on the vast, four-winged Berlaymont building. Built in 1967, it's striking but by no means beautiful, despite a billion-euro rebuild between 1991 and 2004 that removed asbestos-tainted construction materials. Information panels dotted around the building give insight into the history of this neighbourhood and Brussels' international role. The building is not open to the public.

Musée Antoine Wiertz   MUSEUM
(Map p58; ☑ 02-648 17 18; info@fine-arts-museum. be; Rue Vautier 62; ☉ 10am-noon & 1-5pm Tue-Fri,

plus alternate weekends; ☑ 34, 80, ฿ Trône, Maelbeek) FREE If you're into the shocking or nasty, this museum may appeal. Antoine Wiertz (1806–65) was a Brussels artist bent on painting giant religious canvases depicting hell and other frenzied subjects. The building was Wiertz' home and studio and was also once the residence of noted Flemish writer Hendrik Conscience.

Musée Royal de l'Armée
et d'Histoire Militaire   MUSEUM
(Royal Museum of the Armed Forces & of Military History; Map p58; ☑ 02-737 78 11; www.klm-mra.be; Parc du Cinquantenaire 3; ☉ 10am-6pm Tue-Sun; M Mérode) FREE Extensive displays of weaponry, uniforms, vehicles, warships, paintings and documentation dating from the medieval period through to Belgian independence and the world wars. You can climb to the top of the arch or take the lift for sweeping city views.

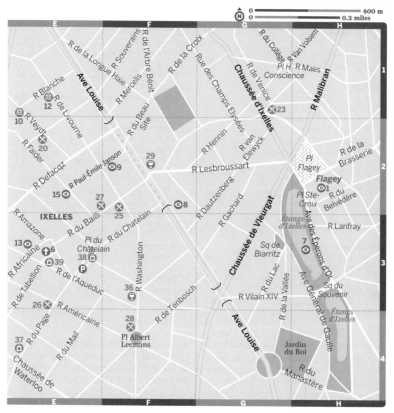

Tervuren

A 20-minute ride on tram 44 from Montgoméry metro station follows beautiful tree-lined Ave de Tervuren east past opulent embassy villas, the lovely parkland ponds of Woluwé and through the northern reaches of the leafy Forêt de Soignes. Sit on the right (south) side to spot the 1911 **Palais Stoclet** (Woluwe-Saint-Pierre 1150), whose radically geometric exterior is an early premonition of art deco: the architect was instructed to produce a Gesamtkunstwerk ('total work of art'). The building is closed to the public, but its dazzling interiors feature work by Klimt and Khnopff.

Africa Museum   MUSEUM
(☑02-769 52 11; www.africamuseum.be/en/home; Leuvensesteenweg 13, Tervuren; adult €12, concessions free–€8; 🚋44) Due to reopen in late 2018 after five years of restoration, the revived Africa Museum looks set to be a big draw, and a world away from its earlier dusty colonial incarnation. The exhibits are predominately from former Belgian colony the Congo, and include some beautiful musical instruments, masquerade masks and artfully carved pot lids. Resident artists and a digital project give the space a contemporary focus.

Tram Museum   MUSEUM
(☑02-515 31 08; https://trammuseum.brussels; Ave de Tervueren 364; adult/concession/BrusselsCard €12/10/free; 🚋 Tram Museum) Volunteer-run museum with some lovely old trams, which you can clamber onto. Pay a little extra for a ride on a historic vehicle.

Forêt de Soignes

Directly south of Tervuren, **Forêt de Soignes** (Zoniënwoud; www.foret-de-soignes.be) 🏃 is a botanical cathedral of glorious towering

St-Gilles & Ixelles

beech trees stretching almost to Waterloo. The forest was planted by proto-Belgium's 18th-century Austrian rulers, with oaks added later by the French, to provide timber for future naval ships. By the time those trees had matured, however, shipbuilders preferred metal, so the trees went uncut. Today the result is a delightful regional park with hundreds of kilometres of cycling, horse-riding and walking paths. Tucked into the forest fringes are the **Jean Massart Experimental Garden** (www.ulb.ac.be/musees/jmassart; Waversesteenweg 1850, Auderghem; €3; ⊙9am-5pm Mon-Fri; ☐41, 72, Ⓜ5, ☐94) ✈ FREE, a wonderful collection of 300 medicinal plants, and **Rouge Cloître** (☑02-660 55 97; www.rouge-cloitre.be; Rue de Rouge-Cloître 4; ⊙2-5pm Wed-Sun; ☐34, 72, ☐5), an education-focused arts centre occupying a rural 14th-century abbey.

◎ Uccle (Ukkel) & Forest

Uccle is an affluent, middle-class *commune,* though you'd hardly think so from a first glance at the graffiti-tagged station Uccle-Stalle, which is closer to the gritty, post-industrial inner-suburb of Forest.

Musée David et Alice van Buuren   MUSEUM
(☑02-343 48 51; www.museumvanbuuren.com; Ave Léo Errera 41; adult/senior/student/child €10/8/5/free, garden only €5/4/2.50/free; ⊙2-5.30pm; ☐60, ☐3, 4, 7) In a 1928 art deco showpiece house you'll find this exquisite museum, where five rooms are crammed with sublime furnishings, stained glass and top-quality paintings covering five centuries of art. Also notable are more than 30 works by van Buuren's talented symbolist protégé, Van de Woestyne, and a Vincent van Gogh sketch for the latter's classic *Peeling Potatoes.*

Wiels   GALLERY
(☑02-340 00 50; www.wiels.org; Ave Van Volxemlaan 354; adult/concession/BrusselsCard €10/7/free, Wed evening free; ⊙noon-6pm Wed-Sun; ☐82) It's well off the usual tourist track in a run-down inner-city *commune,* but this converted brewery building located towards Bruxelles-Midi houses the capital's new centre for contemporary art and photography exhibitions. In the downstairs cafe the old tiled walls and copper vats have been retained.

Nearby, **C L E A R I N G** (☑02-644 49 11; www.c-l-e-a-r-i-n-g.com; Ave Van Volxem 311; ⊙10am-6pm Tue-Sat) FREE is another contemporary gallery showing the work of young artists.

Boghossian Foundation HOUSE
(Villa Empain; ☑02-627 52 30; www.villaempain.
com; Ave Franklin Roosevelt 67; adult/concession
€8/4; ⊙11am-6pm Tue-Sun; ☐71, ☐25, 94) Architecture fans should take the trip to this
striking, symmetrical, 1930s villa, which
combines austere design with gorgeously
opulent materials: marble, polished granite
and gleaming bronze. Built for the 21-year-
old Baron Louis Empain, the building was
requisitioned by the Nazis during the war
and abandoned in the 1990s. The art foundation that restored and now runs the villa
stages themed exhibitions, displaying work
by artists such as De Chirico, Joseph Beuys,
Jeff Koons and Andy Warhol.

It's on the edge of the lovely **Bois de la
Cambre** (☐92, 93), an 1862 park with lawns
and a cafe-restaurant on an island in an artificial lake.

⊙ Alsemburg &
Southwest Brussels

Beyond the city's official boundaries, tucked
into Brussels' southwestern periphery, are
several lambic-brewing suburban villages
and a couple of delightful castle ruins.

★Museumtuin Kasteel
van Gaasbeek CASTLE
(☑02-531 01 30; www.kasteelvangaasbeek.be;
Kasteelstraat 40, Lennik; adult/concession €10/8;
⊙8am-8pm Apr-Nov, to 5pm Nov-Apr) Originally built to guard the medieval Brabant–
Flanders border, 14km southwest of Brussels,
angry locals burnt down this castle in 1388 in
response to the murder of Everard 't Serclaes,
the man credited with restoring Brussels
from Flemish occupation. Rebuilt soon
afterwards, the majority of the property

today is the result of an extensive 1897 renovation. Set among manicured 17th-century
gardens, it houses a lavishly furnished museum that showcases elements of the many
historical eras its walls have witnessed.

Take bus 142 from Erasmus metro station.

Kasteel van Beersel CASTLE
(☑02-359 16 46; www.visitbeersel.be; Lotsestraat
65, Beersel; adult/child €3/1; ⊙11am-5pm Tue-Sun
Mar–mid-Nov, Sat & Sun only winter, closed Jan)
The 1310 Kasteel van Beersel is the closest
medieval castle to Brussels. From the outside it's a beauty – the picture-perfect brick
towers, rebuilt in 1498, are topped off with
17th-century roofs and rise proudly above a
tree-ringed moat. Inside it's an empty shell;
the building was used as a cotton factory in
the 19th century.

The castle is handily close to the west
Brussels ring motorway (junction 19). By
train from Brussels, you'll need to change at
Halle, from where services run three times
an hour to Beersel station, adjacent to the
castle. Halle's interesting historical centre is
worth a quick look while you're in transit.

De Lambiek MUSEUM
(☑02-359 16 36; www.delambiek.be; Gemeen-
veldstraat 1, Alsemberg; adult/child €3/1; ⊙11am-
5pm Wed-Sat, from 2pm Sun) This showpiece
attraction is for fans of the Brussels area's
trademark *gueuze* and lambic beers. The De
Lambiek visitors centre explains the beers'
qualities and production methods, then
offers a tasting of a range of speciality brews
that can prove hard to find anywhere else.
Alsemberg is a 40-minute drive from Brussels. By public transport, take a train to Halle
and then change to a bus for Alsemberg.

BRUSSELS' ART NOUVEAU MASTERPIECES

Brussels excels in art nouveau architecture. In the city centre, don't miss the Old England
Building (p44). Many other top examples are scattered fairly widely, but there are decent
concentrations of fine facades in St-Gilles and Ixelles, where a classic art nouveau house,
the former home of maestro architect Victor Horta, hosts an eponymous museum (p49).
Near the Cinquantenaire monument, the loveliest of all art nouveau town houses is the
Maison Cauchie (p53), while Horta aficionados should head to Schaerbeek to see his
first major commission: **Maison Autrique** (☑02-215 66 00; www.autrique.be; Chaussée de
Haecht 266; adult/senior/concession €7/5/3; ⊙noon-5.30pm Wed-Sun; ☐92, 93). The famous
Palais Stoclet (p55), now Unesco listed, is not open to visitors.

Excellent Atelier de Recherche et d'Action Urbaines (p60) tours can get you into some
normally closed gems, including the **Hôtel Solvay** (Map p54; Ave Louise 224; Ⓜ Louise)
and **Hôtel Van Eetvelde** (Map p58; Ave Palmerston 2-4; Ⓜ Schuman), whose facades
barely hint at the wonders within.

BRUSSELS SIGHTS

EU Quarter & Around

0 — 400 m
0 — 0.2 miles

Anderlecht

Now best known for its **football club** (http://rsca.be; Van den Stock Stadium, Ave Théo Verbeeck 2; ⊙10am-6pm Tue, Wed & Fri, 2-8pm Thu, 10am-2pm Sat; MSt-Guidon), the rather bleak suburb of Anderlecht was once a pretty rural getaway. Hints of that character are still somewhat in evidence near metro St Guidon, notably around the *café*-ringed square Place de la Vaillance, where several 1920s buildings have pseudo-medieval facades.

Erasmus House Museum MUSEUM
(☑02-521 13 83; www.erasmushouse.museum; Rue du Chapitre 31; €1.25; ⊙10am-6pm Tue-Sun, begijnhof closed noon-2pm; MSt-Guidon) Anderlecht was still a country village when world-famous humanist Erasmus came to 'play at farming' in 1521. The lovely brick home where he stayed for five months is now an appealing museum tucked behind the near-

by 16th-century Gothic **Church of St-Pierre and St-Guidon** (⊙9am-noon daily & 2-5.30pm Thu-Tue). It's furnished with fine artworks, including several Flemish Primitive paintings, and contains some priceless manuscripts. There's a 'philosophy garden' behind the museum, and the entry fee also allows access to Belgium's smallest *begijnhof*.

Cantillon Brewery BREWERY
(Musée Bruxellois de la Gueuze; Map p50; ☑02-520 28 91; www.cantillon.be; Rue Gheude 56; €9.50; ⊙10am-5pm Mon, Tue & Thu-Sat; MClemenceau) Beer lovers shouldn't miss this living brewery-museum. Atmospheric and family run, it's Brussels' last operating lambic brewery and still uses much of the original 19th-century equipment. After hearing a brief explanation, visitors take a self-guided tour, including the barrel rooms where the beers mature for up to three years in chestnut wine casks. The entry fee includes two taster glasses of Cantillon's startlingly acidic brews.

EU Quarter & Around

BRUSSELS SIGHTS

Expect to see plenty of cobwebs, as spiders are considered friends of lambic's spontaneous fermentation process, which occurs in a vast, shallow copper tub in the attic room.

Koekelberg

National Basilica CHURCH
(Basilique Nationale du Sacré-Cœur; ☏ 02-421 16 69; www.basilicakoekelberg.be; Koekelberg Hill; ⊙9am-5pm May-Sep, 10am-4pm Oct-Apr; Ⓜ Elisabeth) FREE Ghastly but gigantic, this is the world's fifth-largest church and the world's largest art-deco building. When construction started in 1905 (to celebrate Belgium's 75th anniversary), a truly magnificent feast of neo-Gothic spires was planned. However, WWI left state finances impoverished, so a 1925 redesign shaved off most of the intricate details. The lumpy result, finally completed in 1969, has some attractive stained glass but is predominantly a white elephant of dull brown brick and green copperwork.

Take the lift (adult/BrusselsCard €5/3) to a 53m-high panorama balcony for sweeping views, including an interesting perspective on the Atomium.

Heysel & Laeken

North Brussels' Heysel district developed as the base for international trade fairs and is home to the national stadium, **Stade Roi Baudouin** (☏ 02-479 36 54; www.prosportevent. be; Ave de Marathon 135; Ⓜ Heysel), and the astonishing Atomium. En route from the centre you'll pass through Laeken whose trio of palaces are residences for the Belgian royals, though the only section that is open to the public is the set of 1873 **Royal Greenhouses** (Serres Royales; ☏ 02-551 20 20; www.monarchy. be; Ave du Parc Royal 61; €2; ⊙late Apr-early May; 🚃 4, 23) containing many rare tropical species. Directly north are exotic 1905 buildings in the style of a Chinese pavilion and a Japanese pagoda, both part of a museum of far-eastern antiquities that is currently closed for long-term restoration.

Belgian royals are laid to rest in the crypt of the triple-spired church of **Notre-Dame de Laeken** (☏ 02-479 2362; www.ndlaeken-olv-laken.be; Parvis Notre-Dame; ⊙2-5pm Tue-Sun Jan-Nov; 🚃 53 from Metro Bockstael).

Atomium MONUMENT
(☏ 02-475 47 75; www.atomium.be; Av de l'Atomium; adult/teen/child €15/8/free; ⊙10am-6pm; Ⓜ Heysel, 🚃 51) The space-age Atomium looms 102m over north Brussels' suburbia, resembling a steel alien from a '60s Hollywood movie. It consists of nine house-sized metallic balls linked by steel tube-columns containing escalators and lifts. The balls are arranged like a school chemistry set to represent iron atoms in their crystal lattice... except these are 165 billion times bigger. It

was built as a symbol of postwar progress for the 1958 World's Fair and became an architectural icon, receiving a makeover in 2006.

At night the spheres sparkle magically, and the panorama-level restaurant reopens at 7pm (except during midsummer), putting starched cloths on its functional tables and serving decent dinners with a view. Dinner guests don't pay the tower entrance fee, but reservations are essential.

ADAM MUSEUM
(Art & Design Atomium Museum; ☑02-669 49 29; http://adamuseum.be; Place de Belgique 1; adult/ concession/BrusselsCard €4/3/free; ⊙10am-6pm; Ⓜ Heysel, ☒51) Worth seeing in combination with the Atomium, ADAM features a surprisingly intriguing collection of classic plastic: the 1965 Universale, which was the first plastic chair; enduringly popular stackable Vignelli tableware, designed in 1964; late-'60s inflatable furniture; and much, much more. The museum celebrates the affordable, democratic and playful side of plastic, but is a little light on the environmental impact of the stuff. A regular contemporary-design event – Design Generations – showcases the work of Belgian designers across all disciplines.

Mini Europe AMUSEMENT PARK
(www.minieurope.com; Ave de Bouchout 10; adult/ child €15.50/11.50, with Atomium €27.50/18; ⊙10am-5pm Apr-Jun & Sep-Dec, 9.30am-8pm Jul & Aug; Ⓜ Heysel) Want to fool your friends that you saw all of Europe? Easy. Just photograph the dozens of 1:25-scale models of the continent's top monuments at Mini Europe. On certain midsummer Saturday nights it stays open till midnight, with firework displays at 10.30pm.

ⓘ INSIDE INFORMATION

A great way of exploring a specific area or indulging in a passion for anything from *gueuze* beers to Belgian politics is to contact **Brussels Greeters** (https://visit.brussels/en/sites/greeters) two weeks before your trip. You fill in a simple online form and the coordinator sets you up with up to six other visitors and a local, who will take you to relevant sights in the city, usually with stops for coffee and lunch along the way (trips take two to four hours). There is no charge for the service, and tips are not accepted.

◉ Grimbergen

Briefly its own principality during the 18th century, Grimbergen has a superb central **basilica** (Kerkplein 1; ⊙7am-7pm) sharing a small square with a series of historic houses signed in Gothic scripts. A short stroll south, the leafy Prinsenbos park leads to castle ruins sitting inaccessibly in their moat, and a museum of rural craft in the castle's former outbuildings. Just northeast of the centre are a couple of charming watermills linked by a lovely seemingly rural footpath. Although technically outside Brussels, Grimbergen is less than a 15-minute detour from the Atomium if you're driving.

☞ Tours

Groovy Brussels Bike Tours CYCLING
(Map p40; ☑0484 89 89 36; www.groovybrussels. com/brussels-bike-tour; tour incl bicycle rental €29; ⊙10am daily Apr-Oct, plus 2pm weekends; Ⓜ Gare Centrale) Many first-time visitors love this tour for the ride and for the beer and *frites* stops along the way (food and drink cost extra). Tours start from the Grand Place and take 3½ hours; the maximum group size is 12. The outfit also offers chocolate and beer walking tours.

Brussels by Water BOATING
(Map p46; ☑02-201 10 50; www.brusselsbywater. be; Quai des Péniches 2b; trips from €10; Ⓜ Ribaucourt) Brussels' canals offer an interesting perspective of the capital.

★ARAU CULTURAL
(Atelier de Recherche et d'Action Urbaines; Map p40; ☑02-219 33 45; www.arau.org; Blvd Adolphe Max 55; tours €10-20; ⊙Apr–mid-Dec; Ⓜ De Brouckère) Get up close and personal with a wide variety of Brussels' architecture with this resident-run heritage-conservation group, which runs a program of coach tours (€20) and walking tours (€10) taking you into buildings that are often otherwise off limits. Bookings can be made online through the Brussels tourist office.

Brussels City Tours TOURS
(Map p40; ☑02-513 77 44; www.brussels-city-tours. com; Rue du Marché aux Herbes; adult/concession/ child €29/26/15; ⊙10am; Ⓜ Gare Centrale) These three-hour tours cover everything from the Atomium to the EU, and include some lovely art nouveau houses. You kick off with a walking tour of the Grand Place and are then transported by coach.

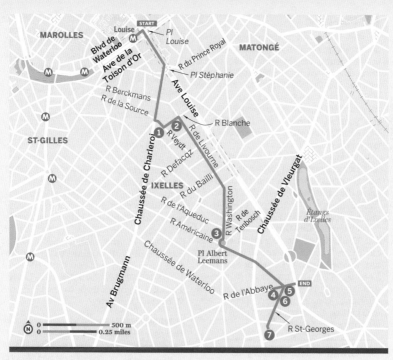

🏃 City Walk
Contemporary Galleries of Ixelles

START LOUISE METRO STATION
END ABBAYE TRAM STOP, AVE LOUISE
LENGTH 3KM; THREE HOURS

Brussels is a contemporary-art hot spot, with international galleries shifting their operations to Ixelles. This walk takes under an hour, but we've allowed two extra hours for seeing the exhibits and lunching.

Head down Ave Louise, take a right onto Chausée de Charleroi, then a left onto Rue Veydt. Here you come to **1 La Patinoire Royale** (Rue Veydt 15), once a skating rink and now home to Galerie Valérie Bach. This hall now hosts art and photography exhibitions.

Head down Rue Blanche and turn right into Rue de Livourne, where you'll find **2 Rudolphe Jansen** (Rue de Livourne 35), a funky white space that has hosted over 100 shows. Its focus has traditionally been photography, but has widened to other media.

From here, continue to join Rue Washington; at no 50 look out for a art nouveau town house built by Ernest Blerot. Stop for lunch at corner restaurant **3 Ötap** (Pl Albert Leemans).

Cross the roundabout, ringed with tall plane trees, and head down Rue Americaine before turning right onto Rue de l'Abbaye, where you'll reach a cluster of galleries.

4 Almine Rech (Rue de l'Abbaye 20) is owned by Picasso's grandson's wife, who has represented Jeff Koons and Julian Schnabel. A few steps away is **5 Messen De Clerq** (Rue de l'Abbaye 2a), which hosts edition sales of artists such as Marina Abramović and Anish Kapoor.

Nearby on Rue St-Georges sits **6 Xavier Hufkens** (Rue St-Georges 6), a stylish two-floor space. Willem de Kooning and Tracey Emin are among its stable of artists.

Continue along Rue St-Georges till you reach a brutalist concrete pavilion sitting under a tower block. There's another branch of Xavier Hufkens here, and also **7 Hopstreet** (Rue St-Georges 109), its name picked out in neon. There are generally some weird and wonderful artistic assemblages here.

To end your tour, return up Rue St-Georges to Rue de l'Abbaye. Turn right to Ave Louise, and catch a tram back to the metro stop.

🛏 Sleeping

Brussels has a vast range of accommodation. If you're on a short break, try to stay in the centre, ideally around the Grand Place or perhaps in nearby Ste-Catherine, which is less frenetic. Otherwise, areas like St-Gilles offer a more 'local' experience and the chance to explore some beautiful streets and squares. There's a good network of B&Bs and guesthouses, which can compare favourably to hostel beds.

With much of Brussels' accommodation scene aimed squarely at Eurocrats and business travellers, many midrange and top-end hotels drop their rates dramatically at weekends. Shop around and check carefully for internet deals, especially on chain hotels.

For camping, **Ciel Ouvert** (Map p58; 🖉 02-640 79 67; https://cielouvertcamping.wordpress.com/about; Chaussée de Wavre 203; large tent/small tent/person €14/7/7; ⊘ reception 8am-11pm Jul & Aug; ⓡ Bruxelles-Luxembourg) is a basic, summer-only place hidden in the garden of Etterbeek's church of St-Sacrement. Otherwise options are way out of town, eg in pretty Grimbergen.

🏛 Grand Place, St-Géry & Ste-Catherine

★ Chambres d'Hôtes du Vaudeville
B&B **€€**

(Map p40; 🖉 0484 59 46 69; www.theatreduvaudeville.be; Galerie de la Reine 11; d from €120; 🛜; ⓡ Bruxelles Central) 🛇 This classy B&B has an incredible location right within the gorgeous (if reverberant) Galeries St-Hubert (p38). Delectable decor styles include African, modernist and 'Madame Loulou' (with 1920s nude sketches). Larger front rooms have claw-foot bathtubs and *galerie* views, but can be noisy with clatter that continues all night. Get keys via the Café du Vaudeville, where breakfast is included. Vaudeville's unique house beer is provided free in the minibar.

Druum
B&B **€€**

(Map p46; 🖉 0472 05 42 40; www.druum.be; Rue du Houblon 63; s/d €105/115; 🛜; ⓡ 51) Brussels' most stylish B&B appeared after the owners gave artists carte blanche to rework the six bedrooms. Now this former pipe factory is a quirky homage to apartment-style living with incredible one-offs like a gigantic concrete bed for four and the cassette tapes of former studio recordings found in the stripped-back HS63 room.

Hotel Café Pacific
HOTEL **€€**

(Map p40; 🖉 02-213 00 80; www.hotelcafepacific.com; Rue Antoine Dansaert 57; s/d from €69/99; 🛜; ⓡ Bourse) The hip design look here is all you'd expect from this Fashion District address, though the reception is just a desk attached to a revamped *café*. Most rooms come with high-powered showers and large but subtle black-and-white nudes above the bed. Fabrics by Mia Zia, toiletries by Bvlgari.

Downtown-BXL
B&B **€€**

(Map p40; 🖉 0475 29 07 21; www.downtownbxl.com; Rue du Marché au Charbon 118-120; d €109-119; 🛜; ⓡ Anneessens) Near the capital's gay district, this B&B is superbly located if you're dancing the night away. From the communal breakfast table and help-yourself coffee bar, a classic staircase winds up to good-value rooms featuring zebra-striped cushions and Warhol Marilyn prints. One room features a round bed. Adjacent **Casa-BXL** (Map p40; 🖉 0475 29 07 21; Rue du Marché au Charbon 16; d €109-119) offers three rooms in a more Moroccan-Asian style.

Hôtel Noga
HOTEL **€€**

(Map p40; 🖉 02-218 67 63; www.nogahotel.com; Rue du Béguinage 38; s weekday/weekend from €95/65, d €130/85; ✳@🛜; Ⓜ Ste-Catherine) This very welcoming family hotel established in 1958 uses model yachts to give the lobby and piano room a certain nautical feel. Sepia photos of Belgian royalty, along with historic bellows, top hats and assorted random kitsch, lead up to variously decorated rooms that are neat and clean without particular luxury. Wi-fi is free for the first hour.

Hôtel Welcome
BOUTIQUE HOTEL **€€**

(Map p40; 🖉 02-219 95 46; www.hotelwelcome.com; Rue du Peuplier 1; d €89-210; ⊜✳; Ⓜ Ste-Catherine) The wooden-panelled reception area does nothing to prepare guests for the full-colour decor in each uniquely designed room transporting you to, say, Tahiti, Congo, Cuba or Zanzibar.

Hotel Residence Le Quinze
HOTEL **€€**

(Map p40; 🖉 02-546 09 10; www.hotel-le-quinze-grand-place.be; Grand Place 15; d from €98, with view €148; 🛜; Ⓜ Gare Centrale) With a location right on the fabulous Grand Place, Le Quinze offers recently revamped, budget-boutique-hotel decor. Views from the front rooms are truly breathtaking, but bear in mind that you'll also share the sounds of a square that remains alive with activity (and occasional full-scale rock concerts) till the wee hours.

La Vieille Lanterne
B&B **€€**

(Map p40; ☑ 02-512 74 94; www.lavieillelanterne.
be; Rue des Grands Carmes 29; s €78-95, d €84-115;
☎; 🏠 Anneessens) Look out at the Manneken
Pis from the window of Room 5 in this neat,
unsophisticated, six-room B&B-style 'hotel',
accessed by steep spiral stairs from an archetypal gift shop. Check in before 10pm.

★ Hôtel Métropole
HOTEL **€€€**

(Map p40; ☑ 02-217 23 00, reservations 02-214 24
24; www.metropolehotel.com; Place de Brouckère
31; d €170-350, weekend rates from €130; ❄ ✱ ☎;
Ⓜ De Brouckère) This 1895 showpiece has a
sumptuous French Renaissance–style foyer with marble walls, coffered ceiling and
beautifully etched stained-glass back windows. The *café* is indulgent and the bar
(with frequent live music) features recently
'rediscovered' murals by a student of Horta.
One of the lifts is an 1895 original.

Rooms have been redecorated in styles
varying from art deco to 'Venetian baroque'.
Much of the furniture is restored from 1930s
originals.

★ Hôtel Le Dixseptième
BOUTIQUE HOTEL **€€€**

(Map p40; ☑ 02-517 17 17; www.ledixseptieme.be;
Rue de la Madeleine 25; d €130-190, ste €200-370;
✱ ☎; 🏠 Bruxelles Central) A hushed magnif-
icence greets you in this alluring boutique
hotel, partly occupying the former 17th-
century residence of the Spanish ambas-
sador. The coffee-cream breakfast room
retains original cherub reliefs. Spacious executive suites come with four-poster beds.
Across a tiny enclosed courtyard-garden in
the cheaper rear section, the Creuz Suite
has its bathroom tucked curiously into a
14th-century vaulted basement. Lifts stop
between floors, so you'll need to deal with
some stairs.

Hôtel Amigo
HOTEL **€€€**

(Map p40; ☑ 02-547 47 47; www.roccoforte
hotels.com/hotels-and-resorts/hotel-amigo; Rue
de l'Amigo 1-3; d weekend/summer/weekday from
€180/200/320, ste from €1300; ❄ ✱ @ ☎;
🏠 Bruxelles Central) Let faultlessly polite
besuited staff usher you into central Brussels' top address. Behind a classical Flemish
facade lies a stone-flagged reception area
worn smooth by centuries of footsteps.
Stylishly designed rooms have an airy and
imaginative vibe, with art deco touches, surreal carved 'fruit' elements and art ranging
from signed Goosens caricatures to Magritte
prints and framed Tintin figurines.

WORTH A TRIP

MEISE BOTANIC GARDEN
....

Belgium's national botanic garden **Plan-
etuin Meise** (Botanic Garden Meise; ☑ 02-
260 09 20; www.br.fgov.be; Bouchout Domain,
Nieuwelaan 38; adult/senior/concession
€7/6/3.50; ⊙ 9.30am-5pm) is located in
the village of Meise, 12km north of Brussels. Home to 18,000 plant species, it's
based around two lakes and includes the
Kasteel van Boechout, a moated castle
that Léopold II gave to his sister, Princess
Charlotte, after her own at Tervuren burnt
down in 1879. The park's most prized
orchids, carnivorous plants and famous
giant Amazonian water lilies are housed in
the Plantenpaleis (Plant Palace), a series
of 13 connecting greenhouses.

DeLijn buses 250 and 251 run every
15 minutes from Bruxelles-Nord (35
minutes) via Bockstael metro station
(20 minutes).

Dominican
BUSINESS HOTEL **€€€**

(Map p40; ☑ 02-203 08 08; www.thedominican.be;
Rue Léopold 9; d weekday/weekend from €185/120;
✱ @ ☎; Ⓜ De Brouckère) Combining classic
elegance with understated modern chic, this
excellent top-end palace occupies the site of
a former abbey right behind La Monnaie.
It's hard to beat for style, and the location
is wonderfully central, albeit in an area suffering from rather patchy architecture and
atmosphere.

🛏 Royal Quarter, Marolles & Midi

HI Hostel John Bruegel
HOSTEL **€**

(Map p50; ☑ 02-511 04 36; www.jeugdherbergen.
be/en/brussels; Rue du St-Esprit 2; dm/tw adult
€23.90/64, youth €21.60/60; ⊙ lockout 10am-
2pm, curfew 1am-7am; ❄ @ ☎; Ⓜ Louise) Superbly central but somewhat institutional
with limited communal space. The attic singles are a cut above singles at other hostels.
Internet costs €2 per hour, lockers €1.50.
There's a 10% discount for HI members.
Free wi-fi.

Hotel NH Collection Brussels Grand Sablon
BUSINESS HOTEL **€€**

(Map p50; ☑ 02-518 11 00; www.nh-hotels.com/
hotel/nh-collection-brussels-grand-sablon; Rue
Bodenbroek; d from €105; ☎; Ⓜ Porte du Namur)
With a wonderful location right on the

Sablon, this modern hotel has a neutral business feel, but it's impeccably quiet and comfortable. It has a brasserie restaurant and an in-house gym. Great location for the museums and Sablon Antiques Market (p78).

Room Brussels   B&B €€

(Map p50; 📞 0494 53 69 35; www.theroom-brussels .com; Rue Blaes 130; d from €65; 📶; Ⓜ Louise) Not the most stylish option in town, but it's cosy, quiet and very centrally located, and has welcoming hosts. A bargain for the area.

L'Art de la Fugue   B&B €€

(Map p50; 📞 0478 69 59 44; www.lartdelafugue. com; Rue de Suede 38; d from €95; Ⓜ Gare du Midi) If your taste is for opulence rather than minimalism, this could be the place for you. Rooms are done out in rich colours and piled with carvings, throws, mirrors and antiques. It's very convenient for Eurostar arrivals, as it's only a short stroll from the Gare du Midi.

🛏 Botanique

Centre Vincent van Gogh   HOSTEL €

(Map p46; 📞 02-217 01 58; www.chab.be; Rue Traversière 8; dm €22-26, s/tw/tr €35/60/90; @📶; Ⓜ Botanique) The lobby bar and pool-table verandah are unusually hip for a hostel, but rooms are less glamorous and, from some, reaching the toilets means crossing the garden courtyard. No membership is required, but you have to be under 35 unless in a group.

★ Villa Botanique
Guesthouse   GUESTHOUSE €

(Map p46; 📞 0496 59 93 79; http://villabotanique guesthouse.be; Chaussée de Haecht 31; dm €30, d €60; 📶; Ⓜ Botanique) This idiosyncratic, warmly friendly venture is housed in an im-

pressive 1830s mansion near the botanical gardens and has a mix of dorms and private rooms. Guests connect with each other over a simple breakfast (included in the price) at a long table in the dining room. A kitchen in which guests can self-cater overlooks a spacious communal garden.

There are three private rooms: a double, twin and single.

🛏 St-Gilles & Ixelles

★ TheBedToBe   B&B

(📞 0496 55 96 26; http://thebedtobe.be/home; Rue Léon Cuissez 27; d from €105; 📶; 🚊 59) Three rooms and a one-bedroom apartment, impeccably done out in a minimal style with a hint of Japan in the paper lanterns and deep baths, plus a dash of mid-century chic. The lovely host serves fresh bread and croissants for breakfast. To encourage sociability there are no TVs.

★ Vintage Hotel   HOTEL €€

(Map p50; 📞 02-533 99 80; www.vintagehotel.be; Rue Dejoncker 45; d from €65, caravan from €135; 📶; Ⓜ Louise) Stylish, modern option near Ave Louise but situated on a quiet courtyard, where a 1958 Airstream caravan provides an urban 'glamping' experience – it's kitted out with bed, TV, shower and loo, a little table and a couple of chairs. In the converted mansion building, the focus is on 20th-century design in primary colours. Online discounts available.

Jardin Secret   BOUTIQUE HOTEL €€

(Map p50; 📞 02-510 83 49; https://jardinsecret hotel.be; Rue du Berger 22; d €79-115; Ⓜ Porte de Namur) A lovely secret indeed in the lively St-Boniface neighbourhood. This is a tranquil garden hideaway in a modern building, tucked away from the street in a Japanese-style courtyard. You enter via a plant shop; there is greenery in the rooms too, which are otherwise furnished in earthy tones with natural fabrics. Double and family rooms available.

Jam Hotel   BOUTIQUE HOTEL €€

(Map p54; 📞 02-537 17 87; www.jamhotel.be; Chaussée de Charleroi 132; d €55-115; ⊘ 5pm-midnight Mon-Sun; 📶🏊; 🚊 92, 97) Jam takes the city's penchant for distressed concrete and runs with it, throwing in primary colours, a funky rooftop bar, a street-edge plunge pool and industrial-chic rooms. The rooftop bar is a cosy drinking lair with furry chairs, a warming open fire and knockout views across the capital. It also serves the daintiest gin and tonic in the city.

Pantone   HOTEL €€

(Map p54; ☑ 02-541 48 98; www.pantonehotel.com; Place Loix 1; d from €59; Ⓜ Hotel des Monnaies) An eye-popping array of Pantone colours greets you here, from the turquoise pushbike at reception to moulded-plastic chairs to lime-green bedrooms – all with refreshing swaths of white, too. Modern, stylish and functional, as well as surprisingly affordable.

EU Quarter

★ **Nest Brussels**   B&B €€

(Map p58; ☑ 0488 38 80 29; http://bb-the-nest. hotelsbrussels.net/en; Rue Wayenberg 24; d €80-110; ☎; ☐ 38, Ⓜ Porte de Namur) Beautifully tasteful B&B with subtly coloured Turkish carpets, ikat cushions and Moroccan tiles. Run by a young family, it offers great value in the EU district, and a personal atmosphere. Three rooms; a simple breakfast is provided.

Living in Brûsel   B&B €€

(Map p58; ☑ 0497 57 24 27; www.livinginbrusel. be; Ave de la Chasse 132; d from €135; ☎; Ⓜ Thieffry) Styling itself an urban B&B, this place is set in a large stone town house built in 1913, and has five spacious and quietly stylish rooms plus a handy elevator. Breakfast pastries and cakes are homemade.

✗ Eating

If money is no object, check out one of Brussels' dozen Michelin-starred restaurants. Even with a plutonium credit card you may need reservations weeks in advance for mythic Comme Chez Soi (p68). Also central is **Sea Grill** (Map p40; ☑ 02-212 08 00; www. seagrill.be; Radisson SAS Royal Hotel Brussels, Rue du Fossé aux Loups 47; ⊘ noon-2pm & 7-10pm, closed mid-Jul–mid-Aug; ☎; Ⓜ De Brouckère), superb for fish though unatmospherically located in a business hotel, while unusual Korean-French **SAN in Brussels** (Map p40; ☑ 02-318 19 19; http://sanbxl.be/en; Rue de Flandre 19; lunch €28, dinner €65; ⊘ noon-2pm & 7-10pm Tue-Sat; ☎; Ⓜ Ste-Catherine) is fun and funky. A classic, if you don't mind the lengthy taxi ride, is Pascal Devalkeneer's **Chalet de la Forêt** (www.lechaletdelaforet.be; Dreve de Lorraine 43; mains from €64; ⊘ noon-2.30pm & 7-10pm Mon-Fri; ☐ B43), set amid towering beeches in the Forêt de Soignes.

✗ Grand Place, St-Gery & Ste-Catherine

Directly around the Grand Place, places can be attractive but underwhelming, and you should be especially careful to check prices on the quaint but touristy Rue and Petite Rue des Bouchers. The streets around Place St-Géry offer a small line-up of great-value Asian eateries. For fish and seafood, Ste-Catherine restaurants are highly regarded, or save money eating at stand-and-snack at tables outside **Mer-du-Nord** (Noordzee; Map p40; www.vis handelnoordzee.be; Rue Ste-Catherine 45; items from €7; ⊘ 8am-6pm Tue-Fri, to 5pm Sat), a fishmonger with takeaway window that cooks sublime scampi, not deep fried but soaked in herb dressing. Nearby, **Charli** (Map p40; ☑ 02-513 63 32; http://charliboulangerie.com/en; Rue Ste-Catherine 34; items from €1.50; ⊘ 7.30am-7pm Mon-Sat, 8am-1.30pm Sun) ✎ is a fabulous little bakery and the 1902 **Cremerie de Linkebeek** (Map p40; ☑ 02-512 35 10; Rue du Vieux Marché aux Grains 4; items from €5; ⊘ 9am-3pm Mon, to 6pm Tue-Sat) is arguably the city's best cheese and sandwich shop.

★ **Arcadi**   BRASSERIE €

(Map p40; ☑ 02-511 33 43; www.arcadicafe.be; Rue d'Arenberg 1b; mains €10-15; ⊘ 8am-11.45pm Tue-Fri, from 7.30am Sat, from 9am Sun; Ⓜ Gare Centrale) The jars of preserves, beautiful cakes and fruit tarts at this classic and charming bistro entice plenty of Brussels residents, as do well-priced meals such as lasagne and steak, all served nonstop by courteous staff. With a nice location on the edge of the Galeries St-Hubert, this is a great spot for an indulgent, creamy hot chocolate.

Nona   PIZZA €

(Map p40; ☑ 02-324 78 79; www.nonalife.com; Rue Ste-Catherine 17-19; pizzas €7-14; ⊘ noon-10pm Sun-Wed, noon-11pm Thu-Sat; Ⓜ Ste-Catherine) ✎ With a striped monochrome awning, marbled counter and Neapolitan slow-rising-dough pizzas, Nona is a slice of *bella vita* in Brussels. Barring Italian tomatoes and olive oil, the ingredients are Belgian and mostly organic, including the *mozzarella di bufala*. Try pizzas featuring pumpkin and bacon, or gorgonzola, pear and pine nuts, or perhaps the vegetarian 'From Dries with Love'.

Fin de Siècle   BELGIAN €

(Map p40; Rue des Chartreux 9; mains €12-20; ⊘ bar 4.30pm-1am, kitchen 6pm-12.30am; ☐ Bourse) From *carbonade* (beer-based hotpot) and *kriek* (cherry beer) chicken to mezzes and tandoori chicken, the food is as eclectic as the decor in this low-lit cult place. Tables are rough, music constant and ceilings purple. There's no phone, no bookings and no sign on the door, but the customers keep coming.

Yi Chan
ASIAN €

(Map p40; ☑02-502 87 66; https://en-gb.face book.com/yichanbrussels; Rue Jules Van Praet 13; dim sum for 4 €16; ⊘ noon-3pm & 6-11.30pm Mon & Wed-Fri, noon-midnight Sat & Sun; ☑ Bourse) A modest and friendly family-run restaurant and cocktail bar, decked out with an arch of plastic cherry blossom. The homemade dim sum hits the spot; otherwise the dishes are Vietnamese style.

De Markten
CAFE €

(Map p40; ☑02-512 34 25; www.demarkten.be; Rue du Vieux Marché aux Grains 5; 2 skewers €8, mains €14.50, soups & salads €4-5; ⊘9am-8pm Mon-Thu, to 5pm Fri, to 1pm Sat; Ⓜ Ste-Catherine) This Flemish community centre on Oude Graanmarkt square features lectures, workshops and an eponymous cafe with one of the city's best terraces. Run by Joris Lens, chef of the former AUB.SVP restaurant, it offers honest, locally sourced food such as satay (meat skewers) from his native Limburg, and craft beers.

Den Teepot
VEGAN €

(Map p40; Rue des Chartreux 66; mains from €8; ⊘noon-2pm Mon-Sat; ☎☑; ☑Bourse) A macrobiotic, veggie lunch place located above a mustard-yellow 'bio' shop. Bright decor with murals adorning the walls.

Le Phare du Kanaal
CAFE €

(Map p46; ☑02-410 06 84; www.lepharedukanaal. com; Quai des Charbonnages 40; mains €10-20; ⊘9am-8pm Mon-Fri, 10am-6pm Sat; Ⓜ Comte de Flandre) Overlooking the canal, cosy Le Phare du Kanaal specialises in healthy seasonal nibbles like homemade granola, sweet potato soup with cumin, and scrumptious homemade desserts, including a killer caramelised orange pie.

★ MOK
VEGETARIAN €

(Map p46; ☑02-513 57 87; www.mokcoffee.be; Rue Antoine Dansaert 196; mains €10-20; ⊘8.30am-6pm Mon-Fri, 10am-6pm Sat & Sun; ☑; Ⓜ Comte de Flandre) MOK serves some of the capital's best coffee and offers a wide range of vegan-inspired recipes prepared by Josefien Smets – think crispy tofu and pickled cucumber sandwiches or the legendary avocado toast. A big picture window looks out onto Rue Dansaert.

Le Cercle des Voyageurs
BRASSERIE €€

(Map p40; ☑02-514 39 49; www.lecercledes voyageurs.com; Rue des Grands Carmes 18; mains €15-21; ⊘11am-midnight; ☎; ☑Bourse, Anneessens) Delightful bistro featuring globes, an antique-map ceiling and a travel library. If your date's late, flick through an old *National Geographic* in your colonial leather chair. The global brasserie food is pretty good, and there are documentary screenings and free live music: piano jazz on Tuesday and experimental on Thursday. Other gigs in the cave have a small entrance fee.

Henri
FUSION €€

(Map p40; ☑02-218 00 08; www.restohenri.be; Rue de Flandre 113; mains €17-24; ⊘noon-2pm Tue-Fri & 6-10pm Tue-Sat; Ⓜ Ste-Catherine) In an airy white space on this street to watch, Henri concocts tangy fusion dishes such as tuna with ginger, soy and lime, artichokes with scampi, lime and olive tapenade, or Argentine fillet steak in parsley. It has an astute wine list and staff who know their stuff.

Flamingo
BRASSERIE €€

(Map p46; ☑02-219 77 47; Rue de Laeken 177; mains €15-25; ⊘8am-1am Mon-Thu, to 2am Fri, 10am-2am Sat, to 11pm Sun; Ⓜ Yser) An all-day brasserie from restaurant designer Frederic Nicolay – the man behind Grand Central (p69), BarBeton (p73) and **Kumiko** (Map p46; ☑0473 36 94 81; www.kumiko.be/en; Rue d'Alost 7; mains €10-20; ⊘8am-11.30pm Mon-Thu, to 1.30am Fri & Sat, 10am-10.30pm Sun; ☎; ☑86, ☑51) – Flamingo gets busy at lunchtime as diners share *gyozas* (dumplings), slurp ramen and devour juicy burgers served between colourful buns. The relaxed restaurant sells a wide range of beers and hosts the occasional live concert.

Oficina
BELGIAN €€

(Map p46; ☑0472 04 95 30; http://oficina-brussels.be; Rue d'Alost 16; mains €10-30; ⊘noon-2.30pm & 6-10pm Mon-Fri, 6-10pm Sat; ☑51) This little corner restaurant designed by Frederic Nicolay focuses on seasonal and organic produce and offers a minimalist but quality menu on its blackboard. Concrete walls and tiled floors give it an industrial edge, while vintage school chairs and bohemian flower arrangements soften the atmosphere. Come for its €10 daily special – think burrata with roasted fennel and green salad.

Brasserie Horta CAFE €€
(Map p46; www.brasseriehorta.be; Rue des Sables 20; mains €14-18; ⊘noon-3pm Tue-Sun; Ⓜ Rogier) An attractive place serving salads and Belgian standards.

Belga Queen Brussels BELGIAN €€
(Map p40; ☑02-217 21 87; www.belgaqueen.be; Rue du Fossé aux Loups 32; mains €18-25, weekday lunch €16; ⊘noon-2.30pm & 7pm-midnight; Ⓜ De Brouckère) Belgian cuisine is given a chic, modern twist within a magnificent, if reverberant, 19th-century bank building. Classical stained-glass ceilings and marble columns are hidden behind an indecently hip oyster counter and wide-ranging beer and cocktail bar (open noon till late). In the former bank vaults beneath, there's a cigar lounge that morphs into a nightclub after 10pm Wednesday to Saturday.

Kokob ETHIOPIAN €€
(Map p40; ☑02-511 19 50; www.kokob.be; Rue des Grands Carmes 10; menus per person from €20; ⊘6-11pm Mon-Thu, noon-3pm & 6-11pm Fri-Sun; Ⓖ Annessens, Bourse) A warmly lit Ethiopian bar/restaurant/cultural centre at the bottom of Rue des Grands Carmes, where dishes are best shared and eaten from and with pancake-like *injera* – it's a place to visit in a group rather than on your own. Traditional coffee ceremonies are held on Wednesday evening and noon to 3pm Sunday.

Viva M'Boma BELGIAN €€
(Map p40; ☑02-512 15 93; www.vivamboma.be; Rue de Flandre 17; mains €15-21; ⊘noon-2.30pm & 7-10pm Thu-Sat, noon-2pm Mon & Tue; Ⓜ Ste-Catherine) Hefty Belgian classics are served in a long, narrow bistro entirely walled in gleaming white tiles like the butchers' shop it once was. Stuffed sheep's and pig's heads meet and greet.

In 't Spinnekopke BELGIAN €€
(Map p40; ☑02-511 86 95; www.spinnekopke. be; Place du Jardin aux Fleurs 1; mains €15-25; ⊘noon-2.30pm & 7-10.30pm Mon-Fri, 7-10.30pm Sat; Ⓖ Bourse) This age-old classic occupies an atmospheric 17th-century whitewashed cottage, with a summer terrace spilling onto the revamped square. Bruxellois specialities and meats cooked in beer-based sauces are authentic but hardly a bargain, and some of the tables feel a tad cramped.

Bij den Boer SEAFOOD €€
(Map p40; ☑02-512 61 22; www.bijdenboer. com; Quai aux Briques 60; mains €15-28, menu

€29.50; ⊘noon-2.30pm & 6-10.30pm Mon-Sat; Ⓜ Ste-Catherine) Convivial fish restaurant, with mirror-panelled walls, model yachts, sensible prices and a jolly ambience. The wine of the month is €20 a bottle.

La Maison du Cygne BELGIAN €€€
(Map p40; ☑02-511 82 44; www.lamaisondu cygne.com; Rue Charles Buls 2; mains €38-65, menus from €65; ⊘noon-2pm & 7-10pm Mon-Fri, 7-10pm Sat; Ⓜ Gare Centrale) Gastronomic Belgo-French seasonal cuisine is served in this sophisticated restaurant on the 2nd floor of a classic 17th-century guildhall. Book way ahead to score one of the few tables with a Grand Place view. For something slightly less formal, try its 1st-floor **Bistrot du Cygne** (Map p40; www.be; Rue Charles Buls 2; mains €15-27; ⊘noon-10.30pm; Ⓜ Gare Centrale).

L'Ogenblik FRENCH €€€
(Map p40; ☑02-511 61 51; www.ogenblik.be; Galerie des Princes 1; mains €25-33; ⊘noon-2.30pm & 6.30pm-midnight Mon-Sat; Ⓖ Bourse) It may be only a stone's throw from Rue des Bouchers, but this timeless bistro with its lace curtains, resident cat, marble-topped tables and magnificent wrought-iron lamp feels a world away. It has been producing French classics for more than 30 years, and the expertise shows. Worth the price for a special meal in the heart of town.

Cathedral Area

★**Laurent Gerbaud** CAFE €
(Map p50; ☑02-511 16 02; www.chocolatsgerbaud. be; Rue Ravenstein 2; snacks from €5; ⊘7.30am-7.30pm; Ⓜ Parc) A bright and welcoming cafe with big picture windows that's perfect for lunch, coffee or hot chocolate if you're between museums. Don't leave without trying the wonderful chocolates, which count as healthy eating in the world of Belgian chocs because they have no alcohol, additives or added sugar. Friendly owner Laurent also runs chocolate-tasting and -making sessions.

Sablon & Marolles

This is an area of extremes eating-wise: on the Sablon you'll often be paying a hefty premium for being seen in the 'right' place, though there are exceptions, while for really cheap food and drink try any *café* on Place du Jeu-de-Balle.

★ **Claire Fontaine**   DELI €

(Map p50; ☑ 02-512 24 10; Rue Ernest Allard 3; snacks from €6; ☺ 11am-7pm Tue-Sat; Ⓜ Porte de Namur) Just off Place du Grand Sablon, this is a tiny but atmospheric tile-floored *épicerie*, fragrant with spices and home-cooked dishes – there's a small kitchen at the back. It's perfect for a nutritious and filling takeaway sandwich or quiche, or you can stock up on oils, wine and boxes of *pain d'épices* (spiced biscuits).

★ **TICH**   VEGAN €

(Map p50; ☑ 02-503 83 30; www.tich.cool; Rue de Namur 25; mains €8-9, desserts €2-4; ☺ 9am-6pm Mon-Fri, 10am-6.30pm Sat & Sun; ☑; 🚇 Royale) 🍃 A vegan canteen-cum-concept store, TICH sells organic groceries and vegetarian-friendly cookbooks alongside its açai bowls, cold-pressed juices and avocado on toast topped with fennel and pickled red onions. It even does its own brand of cotton sweaters among its promising, ecofriendly fashion range.

Le Perroquet   CAFE €

(Map p50; ☑ 02-512 99 22; Rue Watteeu 31; light meals €9-15; ☺ noon-11.30pm; Ⓜ Porte de Namur) Perfect for a drink, but also good for a simple bite (think salads and variations on croque-monsieurs), this art nouveau cafe with its stained glass, marble tables and timber panelling is an atmospheric, inexpensive stop in an area that's light on such places. Popular with expats.

Het Warmwater   CAFE €

(Map p50; www.hetwarmwater.be; Rue des Renards 25; snacks from €5; ☺ 10am-6pm Thu-Sun; ☑; Ⓜ Louise) Endearing and friendly little daytime cafe with stencilled teapots and art collages on the walls. The food – *croque-monsieurs*, salads, cheese and meat platters, and quiches – is simple but satisfying.

Bel Mundo   BRASSERIE €

(Map p46; ☑ 02-669 08 45; www.facebook.com/belmundo; Quai du Hainaut 41-43; mains €10-15; ☺ noon-2.30pm Mon-Wed, to 2.30pm & 6-9pm Thu & Fri; 🚇 51) 🍃 As Brussels' most sustainable restaurant, Bel Mundo makes scrumptious, affordable dishes using seasonal vegetables from its organic backyard garden and unsold supermarket items in a bid for zero food waste. The furniture is made of recycled pallets, crafted in the carpentry workshop, and the friendly staff were previously unemployed long term. Expect soups, seasonal salads and pasta dishes.

Les Brigittines   FRENCH, BELGIAN €€

(Map p50; ☑ 02-512 68 91; www.lesbrigittines.com; Place de la Chapelle 5; mains €16-24; ☺ noon-2.30pm & 7-10.30pm Mon-Fri, noon-2.30pm & 7-11pm Sat; 🔊; Ⓜ Louise) Offering grown-up eating in a muted belle époque dining room, Les Brigittines dishes up traditional French and Belgian food. Its classic (and very meaty) dishes include veal cheek, pigs' trotters and steak tartare. Staff are knowledgeable about local beer and artisanal wines, and can advise on pairing these with your food.

La Fabrique   CAFE €€

(Map p50; ☑ 02-513 99 48; www.lafabriqueresto.be; Blvd de Waterloo 44; mains €20-30; ☺ 11am-4pm Tue-Fri, 10.30am-3.30pm Sat & Sun; Ⓜ Louise) This superbly restored orangery in Parc d'Egmont has huge windows that allow the sunlight to glaze the tables. During the week, it sells healthy lunches like artichoke salad with cheese croquettes and a devilish *suikertaart* (sugar tart). Its gargantuan weekend brunch buffet includes roasted pumpkin, ricotta and spinach ravioli, smoked salmon with dill and all manner of eggs.

Restobières   BELGIAN €€

(Map p50; ☑ 02-502 72 51; www.restobieres.eu; Rue des Renards 9; mains €12-24, menus €15-38; ☺ noon-3pm & 7-11pm Tue-Sun; Ⓜ Louise) Beer-based twists on typical Belgian meals are served in a delightful if slightly cramped restaurant. The walls are plastered with bottles, grinders and countless antique souvenir biscuit tins featuring Belgian royalty. Try the *carbonade* (beer-based hotpot) or *lapin aux pruneaux* (rabbit with prunes).

★ **L'Idiot du Village**   BELGIAN €€€

(Map p50; ☑ 0487 11 52 18; www.lidiotduvillage.be; Rue Notre Seigneur 19; mains around €30; ☺ noon-2pm & 7.30-11pm Wed-Fri, 7.17-10.30pm Tue & Sat; Ⓜ Louise) Booking ahead is essential to secure a table at this colourful, cosy restaurant, secluded on a little side street near the Place du Jeu-de-Balle flea market. Dishes are rich and aromatic and portions plentiful considering the cachet of the place.

✕ **Place Roupe**

★ **Comme Chez Soi**   FRENCH €€€

(Map p50; www.commechezsoi.be; Place Rouppe 23; mains from €49; ☺ 7-9pm Tue & Wed, noon-1.30pm & 7-9pm Thu-Sat; 🚇 Anneessens) The name evokes cooking just like 'at home', but unless you have a personal chef crafting North Sea lobster salad with black truffles and potatoes, sole fillets with Riesling and shrimp mousseline or perhaps spicy lacquered pigeon breast with wild rice, it's nothing of the sort. This is extraordinary food from master chef Pierre Wynants' son-in-law, Lionel Rigolet.

EU Quarter

There's plenty of fine dining for Eurocrats but visitors might prefer to queue for frites at **Maison Antoine** (Map p58; ☑ 02-230 54 56; www.maisonantoine.be; Place Jourdan; chips €2.60-3; ⊙ 11.30am-1am Sun-Thu, to 2am Fri & Sat; M Schuman), a classic little *fritkot* (takeaway chip kiosk) that's been frying since 1948. Its reputation as 'Brussels' best' is self-perpetuating and many *cafés* on the surrounding square, including beautifully wrought-iron-fronted **L'Autobus** (Map p58; ☑ 02-230 63 16; Place Jourdan; M Schuman), allow *frite* eaters to sit and snack so long as they buy a drink. For great ice cream in a dizzying variety of flavours head to **Capoue** (Map p58; ☑ 02-705 37 10; www.capoue.com; Ave des Celtes 36; ⊙ 1-10pm; M Mérode).

Grand Central   BUFFET €
(Map p58; www.legrandcentral.com; Rue Belliard 190; mains €12; ⊙ 9am-midnight Mon-Fri, 10am-midnight Sat, to 7.30pm Sun; M Schuman) Spread out across two floors, this huge bar-restaurant packs the crowds in with its buffet lunches and dinners. Expect slow-roasted aubergines, tomatoes with white beans and all manner of healthy salads to accompany ribs and steaks that have been cooked on a wood-fired grill, along with fresh fish. The on-site barista is something of a coffee Picasso too.

Domenica   ITALIAN €
(Map p58; ☑ 02-657 30 67; www.domenica. eu.com; Rue de Trèves 32/b; mains €3.50-€8.50; ⊙ 8am-7pm Mon-Fri; ☐ 12, 21, 22, 27, M Trône) Selling honest, ethically sourced lunches to a predominantly Eurocrat crowd, Domenica holds up its values of quality and sustainability with homemade lasagne, stunning truffle pizzas made from 24-hour slow-rise doughs, and a small selection of vegan chocolates. Gourmets should fill their grocery baskets with creamy balls of Pugliese burrata and bottles of organic wine.

Ixelles

There's a lot of choice around Ixelles, with some elegant and hip new options. In the Matongé, inexpensive African, Pakistani, South American, Italian and Franco-Belgian eateries are located side by side along Rue Longue Vie and are liberally scattered on Chaussée de Wavre. Meanwhile, one block southwest, St-Boniface is an island of decidedly trendier bistros and coffee shops.

★ Saint-Boniface   FRENCH, BASQUE €
(Map p50; ☑ 02-511 53 66; www.saintboniface.be; Rue St-Boniface 9; mains €12-17; ⊙ noon-2.30pm & 7-10pm Mon-Fri; M Porte de Namur) An enchanting old-world restaurant near the eponymous old church featuring gingham tablecloths, walls jammed with framed pictures, and authentic dishes from France's southwestern and Basque regions, notably *cassoulet*, Périgord duck, foie gras and *andouillette* (strongly flavoured tripe sausage – very much an acquired taste).

Comptoir Rodin   CAFE €
(☑ 02-203 00 14; www.comptoir-rodin.be; Ave Auguste Rodin 8; lunch bowls €11; ⊙ 7.30am-6pm Mon-Fri, 10.30am-5pm Sat & Sun; ☑; ☐ 81) ⬗ A small bronze replica of Rodin's *The Thinker* welcomes visitors to this hidden canteen, which was once a military hospital. Refurbished with sleek concrete floors, bare brick walls and mismatched furniture, Comptoir Rodin and its verandah hosts lunches that are worth musing over – try the aubergine toast or the meatball bowls. Plenty of veggie, vegan and gluten-free options.

Knees to Chin   VIETNAMESE €
(Map p54; ☑ 02-644 18 11; www.kneestochin.com; Rue de Livourne 125; mains €10-15; ⊙ 11.30am-9pm Mon-Sat; ☐ 93, 94) Behind the turquoise-tiled facade of Knees to Chin is an emporium of delicious Vietnamese rice-paper rolls. The menu is seasonal, so expect anything from caramelised paprika and coconut omelette to crispy bacon and Peking duck. Mix and match the rolls with fresh homemade sauces, but don't miss the heavenly steamed *bánh bao* (stuffed steamed bun).

L'Horloge du Sud   AFRICAN €
(Map p50; www.horlogedusud.be; Rue du Trône 141; mains from €12; ⊙ 11am-3pm & 6pm-midnight Mon-Fri, 6pm-midnight Sat; M Porte de Namur) A Matongé institution, the exterior here is distinguished by a large clock – hence the name. It has a Senegalese owner and serves all types of African food to a mixed European and African crowd as well as homemade *bissap* (hibiscus) juice. There's often live music.

King Kong
PERUVIAN €

(Map p54; ☑02-537 01 96; www.kingkong.me; Chaussée de Charleroi 227; mains €8-22; ⊗noon-2.30pm & 7-10pm; 🚇 Janson) Sea-bass ceviche, quinoa burgers and pulled-pork sandwiches are among the Peruvian-inspired street food sold at this jungle-like restaurant, where hanging plants and rattan chairs give a tropical atmosphere. Accompany everything with yuca (cassava) fries, and save room for *alfajor* (a *dulce de leche*–filled biscuit).

Fika
CAFE €

(Map p50; ☑02-502 88 85; Rue de la Paix 17; mains €5-10; ⊗8am-6pm Tue-Fri, 9am-7pm Sat & Sun; 🚇71) Fika serves Swedish pastries such as *Kanelbullar* (cinnamon fluffy pastries) and *Havreflarn* (oat-flake biscuit with chocolate), along with quality coffee from La Capitale in a soothing and minimalist Scandinavian interior.

Le Framboisier
ICE CREAM €

(Map p54; ☑02-647 51 44; www.leframboisierdoré. be; Rue du Bailli 35; ⊗1-7pm; 🚇 Louise) Imaginatively flavoured ice cream to take away or, in summer, eat in the garden. Sorbets, including some made from Cantillon beers, are the house specialities.

Ballekes
BELGIAN €

(Map p54; www.ballekes.be; Chaussée de Charleroi 174; mains €10-20; ⊗6.30-10pm Mon, noon-2.30pm & 6.30-10.30pm Tue-Thu, noon-3.30pm & 6.30-10.30pm Sat, 6.30-10pm Sun; 🚇92, 97) Honouring the meatball recipes of their grandmas, Florence and Thibaut roll out four different kinds of *boulette* at Ballekes (beef, pork, chicken or quinoa) and slather them with decadent toppings like a rich *Brusseleir* (tomato sauce) or a hardcore Trappist beer sauce. Wash them all down with a brew from the Brussels Beer Project.

★ Bouchery
FRENCH €€

(☑02-332 37 74; www.bouchery-restaurant.be; Chaussée d'Alsemberg 812a; veg lunch buffets €18, 4-course menus €58; ⊗noon-2pm & 7-11pm Mon-Fri, 7-11pm Sat; 📷; 🚇Globe) 🌿 Using locally sourced and organic ingredients, award-winning chef Damien Bouchéry puts his own twist on French cooking with veal tartare and grilled nectarines, and chickpea fries, among the delicate dishes to grace the four- to eight-course evening menus. Almost everything is homemade, from the bread and butter to the lacto-fermented goods. Weekday lunches are a vegetarian buffet.

★ Kitchen 151
MIDDLE EASTERN €€

(Map p50; ☑02-512 49 29; www.kitchen.onefive one.be; Chaussée de Wavre 145; mains €15-30; ⊗6-10pm Mon-Sat & 11.30am-3pm Sat; 🚇34, 38, 80, 95) Standing at a culinary crossroads, Kitchen 151 offers a whole world of flavours from the Middle East. Drag thick, fluffy pitas through velvety hummus, or gorge on a veggie burger made with pumpkin, Portobello mushrooms, tahini and almonds. If you're sharing a mezze, be sure to try the smoky baba ganoush.

L'Ultime Atome
BELGIAN €€

(Map p50; ☑02-513 13 67; www.ultimeatome.be; Rue St-Boniface 14; mains €11-19; ⊗8.30am-1am Mon-Fri, 10am-1am Sat & Sun; 🚇Porte de Namur) This cavernous brasserie has curious train-wheel decor enlivening the pale wooden panelling of an otherwise classic cafe. A youthful crowd keeps things buzzing day and night, and the nonstop kitchen turns out great-value meals, including cheesy endives, tagines and mussels (€17).

Café des Spoors
FRENCH €€

(Map p54; ☑02-534 13 03; www.cafedesspores.be; Chaussée d'Alsemberg 103; menus from €26; ⊗7-11pm Mon-Sat; 🚇3, 4, 51) Mushroom fans will be in heaven at this homage to *funghi*: dine on black chanterelle, black trumpet, truffles and more. The dark-coloured decor mimics the mushroom. An eccentric winner.

Bistro Madame
MEDITERRANEAN €€

(Map p54; ☑02-259 26 27; bistromadamebxl@ gmail.com; Rue Veydt 41; mains €13-20; ⊗noon-2pm & 7-10pm Tue-Fri, 7-10pm Sat; 🚇92, 97) A carefully curated seasonal menu and stunning terrazzo bar make this Italian-inspired restaurant the perfect setting for an *aperitivo* or a tête-à-tête dinner. Sit within dark-green walls and choose mussels au gratin with rocket (arugula) pesto or choose sea bream with mango chutney. Accompany with natural wines.

Hinterland
CAFE €€

(Map p54; ☑02-537 97 47; www.hntrlnd.be/en; Chaussée de Charleroi 179; pancakes €9; ⊗8am-7pm Mon-Fri, 9am-7pm Sat & Sun; 📷; 🚇92, 97) 🌿 This cosy, hard-to-leave cafe is a sanctuary of healthy organic breakfasts (think açai bowls and matcha chia puddings), homemade vegan lunches and sustainable packaging.

Les Brassins
BELGIAN €€

(Map p50; ☑02-512 69 99; www.lesbrassins.be; Rue Keyenveld 36; mains €13.50-23; ⊗noon-3pm

& 6-11pm Mon-Fri, noon-midnight Sat, to 11pm Sun; M Louise) On a quiet, unpromising backstreet, this unpretentious brasserie is decorated with old enamel brewery adverts and serves reliable, well-priced Belgian home-cooked classics such as *carbonade* (beer-based hotpot), *filet américain* and *boulettes* (meatballs), accompanied by perfect *frites* or *stoemp* (mashed potatoes with root vegetables) and washed down by an excellent range of Belgian beers. No credit cards.

Nearby, film buffs might be curious to walk past a private house that was **Audrey Hepburn's childhood home** (Map p50; Rue Keyenveld 46; M Louise).

La Quincaillerie
SEAFOOD €€

(Map p54; ☑ 02-533 98 33; www.quincaillerie.be; Rue du Page 45; mains €19-38; ⊙ noon-2.30pm Mon-Sat, 7pm-midnight daily; M Horta) A Victorian stairway and station-style clock dominate this brasserie-restaurant. Wooden box-drawers, gleaming copperware and a green wrought-iron interior date from its days as an upmarket ironmonger's shop. Upper-level seating is a bit squashy but offers unusual views down upon other diners. Menus are multilingual and food standards reliable.

★ÖTAP
MEZZE €€€

(Map p54; ☑ 0472 75 47 38; http://ötap.com; Place Albert Leemans 10; mains €30-50; ⊙ 5-11pm Tue-Sat; ☑ 38) ÖTAP chef Paul-Antoine Bertin serves small seasonal plates with natural wines and expertly presented cocktails. Expect anything from Iberico ham rolls to smoky, stuffed courgette flowers and warm Breton artichokes with a mustard dip. In warm weather there's street seating outside the attractive whitewashed building.

Hortense & Humus
VEGETARIAN €€€

(Map p54; ☑ 0479 54 44 87; hortense.cocktails@gmail.com; Rue de Vergnies 2; mains €20-45; ⊙ noon-2.30pm & 6pm-12.30am Wed-Sat, noon-8pm Sun; ☑; ☑ 71) With a Sistine Chapel–style ceiling and gold trimmed furniture, H&H is a real treat that serves haute vegetarian cuisine such as salt-crust baked swede with roasted Jerusalem artichoke and shiitake mushrooms, and chestnut cake topped with poached pears. Most of the herbs and vegetables are grown in the garden, and the rest is locally sourced.

🍸 Drinking & Nightlife

Cafe or *café*? Brussels has plenty of the former, serving coffee of every variety and day-time snacks. *Cafés,* though, are more particular: essentially drinking places, these are Belgium's equivalent of the British pub, and nearly every street in the centre has at least one marvellously atmospheric example. Styles vary from showy art nouveau places and medieval survivors around the Bourse to hip options in St-Géry and Ixelles.

🍷 Grand Place & Around

If you want to drink on the glorious Grand Place, the 'secret' upper room of **Chaloupe d'Or** (Map p40; ☑ 02-511 41 61; https://chaloupedor.be/en; Grand Place 24; ⊙ 11am-1am; M Gare Centrale) makes for a wonderful vantage point (when open) and the **Roy d'Espagne** (Map p40; ☑ 02-513 08 07; www.roydespagne.be; Grand Place 1; ⊙ 9.30am-1am; M Gare Centrale) is another delight – yes those are inflated dried pigs' bladders above your head. But you can save up to 50% on drinks by walking just a block or two further.

La Fleur en Papier Doré
BROWN CAFE

(Map p50; ☑ 02-511 16 59; www.goudblommekeinpapier.be; Rue des Alexiens 53; ⊙ 11am-midnight Tue-Sat, to 7pm Sun; ☑ Bruxelles Central) The nicotine-stained walls of this tiny cafe, adored by artists and locals, are covered with writings and art by Magritte and his surrealist pals, some of which were reputedly traded for free drinks. *'Ceci n'est pas un musée',* quips a sign on the door reminding visitors to buy a drink and not just look around.

★Goupil le Fol
BAR

(Map p40; ☑ 02-511 13 96; www.goupillefol.com; Rue de la Violette 22; ⊙ 4pm-2am; M Gare Centrale) Overwhelming weirdness hits you as you acid-trip your way through this sensory overload of rambling passageways, ragged old sofas and inexplicable beverages mostly based on madly fruit-flavoured wines (no beer is served). Unmissable.

Via Via Café
BAR

(Map p40; www.viavia.world/en/belgium/brussels; Quai aux Briques 74; ⊙ 3pm-midnight Mon, to 1am Tue-Thu, to 2.30am Fri, 2pm-2.30am Sat, to midnight Sun; M Ste-Catherine) Rub shoulders with a Flemish crowd at this industrial cafe, with brick and concrete floors, away from the nearby touristy hot spots. Try local beers such as those from Brussels Beer Project (p72), or a homemade soft. The large open bar room is stocked with boardgames and guidebooks, and there's another bar and events space upstairs.

★ Toone BAR

(Map p40; Petite Rue des Bouchers; beer from €2.50; ⊙ noon-midnight Tue-Sun; Ⓜ Gare Centrale) At the home to Brussels' classic puppet theatre (p78), this cosy timber-framed bar serves beers and basic snacks.

Brussels Beer Project BREWERY

(Map p46; ☑ 02-502 28 56; www.beerproject. be; Rue Antoine Dansaert 188; ⊙ 2-10pm Thu-Sat; ☒ 51) With sumptuous beers and a constant flow of new brews taste-tested by the public, this micro-brewery and bar is one of the most innovative players in Brussels' beer scene. Classic BPP brews like the Delta IPA and Grosse Bertha wheat beer are on sale in the taproom, with brewery tours available.

Moeder Lambic Fontainas BEER HALL

(Map p40; www.moederlambic.com; Place Fontainas 8; ⊙ 11am-1am Sun-Thu, to 2am Fri & Sat; ☒ Anneessens, Bourse) At last count, Moeder was serving 46 artisanal beers. The setting is contemporary rather than old world: walls are bare brick and hung with photos, and booths are backed with concrete. It dishes up great quiches and cheese and meat platters. The mood is upbeat and the music loud.

Poechenellekelder CAFE

(Map p40; Rue du Chêne 5; ⊙ 11am-1am Tue-Sun; ☒ Bruxelles Central) Despite facing Brussels' kitsch central, this is a surprisingly appealing *café* full of genuine old puppets. It offers a great selection of fairly priced beers, including Oerbier and *gueuze* (a type of lambic beer) on tap.

À la Mort Subite BROWN CAFE

(Map p40; ☑ 02-513 13 18; www.alamortsubite.com; Rue Montagne aux Herbes Potagères 7; ⊙ 11am-1am Mon-Sat, noon-midnight Sun; Ⓜ Gare Centrale) An absolute classic unchanged since 1928, with lined-up wooden tables, arched mirror panels and entertainingly brusque service.

Damejeanne CAFE

(Map p46; ☑ 0488 69 96 19; www.facebook.com/ damejeannecafe; Blvd d'Ypres 33; ⊙ 11am-midnight Tue-Thu, 11am-1am Fri & Sat; ☒ 51) With sleek bare bricks, exposed concrete and a beautiful tiled floor, this light-filled *aperitivo* bar also serves moreish snacks to soak up the booze. Try the comforting pasta au gratin or the prosciutto ham with honeydew and figs.

Délirium Café PUB

(Map p40; www.deliriumcafe.be; Impasse de la Fidélité 4a; ⊙ 10am-4am Mon-Sat, to 2am Sun; Ⓜ Gare Centrale) This *café's* barrel tables, beer-tray ceilings and over 2000 world beers were already impressive. Now they've added a rum garden, a tap house and the Floris Bar (from 8pm), serving hundreds of *jenevers* (gins), vodkas and absinthes.

Métropole Café CAFE

(Hotel Métropole; Map p40; www.metropolehotel. com; Place de Brouckère 31; beer/coffee/waffles from €4/4/8; 🛜; Ⓜ De Brouckère) The magnificently ornate belle époque interior easily justifies the hefty drink prices, though, curiously, a large number of punters still decide to sit on its comparatively unappealing street terrace.

Au Soleil BAR

(Map p40; ☑ 02-513 34 30; Rue du Marché au Charbon 86; ⊙ 10.30am-late; ☒ Bourse) This old clothes shop has been converted into a shabby-chic bar with good beats and surprisingly inexpensive drinks given its status as a favourite for poseurs in shades.

Celtica BAR

(Map p40; www.celticpubs.com/celtica; Rue de Marché aux Poulets 55; ☒ Bourse) Lewd, loud, central and – most importantly – cheap: just €1 for a beer.

🍷 Bourse

If you do nothing else in Brussels, visit at least a couple of these close-packed yet easily overlooked gems around the Bourse (p38), Belgium's 1873 stock-exchange building with its sculpture-adorned neoclassical facade that was partly created by Rodin, then a young apprentice.

★ A l'Imaige de Nostre-Dame PUB

(Map p40; Rue du Marché aux Herbes 8; ⊙ noon-midnight Mon-Fri, 3pm-1am Sat, 4-10.30pm Sun; ☒ Bourse) Down a tiny hidden alley from Rue du Marché aux Herbes 5, Nostre-Dame has an almost medieval feel but retains a genuine local vibe. A magical old *café...* except for the toilets.

★ Le Cirio PUB

(Map p40; ☑ 02-512 13 95; Rue de la Bourse 18; ⊙ 10am-midnight; ☒ Bourse) This sumptuous 1886 *grand café* dazzles with polished brasswork and aproned waiters, yet prices aren't exorbitant and coiffured *mesdames* with small dogs still dilute the gaggles of tourists. The house speciality is a half-and-half mix of still and sparkling wines.

Au Bon Vieux Temps   CAFE
(Map p40; ☑02-217 26 26; Impasse St-Nicolas;
☉11am-midnight; ⓜBourse) Duck beneath the
statue of the bishop, then tunnel through the
centuries to this lushly panelled 1695 gem.
You'll find fireplaces, fascinating characters
and even Westvleteren 12 on the menu.

À la Bécasse   CAFE
(Map p40; ☑02-511 00 06; www.alabecasse.com;
Rue de Tabora 11; ☉11am-midnight, to 1am Fri &
Sat; ⓜGare Centrale) Almost hidden down a
body-wide alley-tunnel, the Bécasse has long
rows of tables that give it a certain Bruege-
lesque quality, even though it's 'only' been
operating since 1877. The unusual speciality
is *panaché*, a jug of Timmermans lambic
mixed with fruit beer or faro to make it more
palatable. It's not to everyone's taste.

🍷 St-Gery & Ste-Catherine

Monk   BAR
(Map p40; ☑02-511 75 11; www.monk.be; Rue
Ste-Catherine 42; ☉11am-2am Mon-Sat, 2pm-2am
Sun; ⓜSte-Catherine) Dark wood, a piano
and opal lights set the mood of this classic
Belgian pub. Mostly attended by Flemish lo-
cals, Monk serves a wide array of reasonably
priced draught and bottled beers.

BarBeton   BAR
(Map p40; ☑02-513 83 63; www.barbeton.be;
Rue Antoine Dansaert 114; ☉10am-midnight; 🛜;
ⓜSte-Catherine) Typical of the new array of
hip but relaxed Brussels bars, BarBeton has
a tiled floor and wood furnishings. It's good
for an early breakfast, and there's a lavish
€15 brunch on Sunday. Cocktail happy hour
is 7pm to 8pm Thursday, there's an *aperitivo* buffet from 6pm to 8pm Friday, and DJs
play from 10pm till late on Saturday.

Floréo   PUB
(Map p40; ☑02-514 39 05; https://en-gb.face
book.com/LeCafeFloreo; Rue des Riches Claires 19;
drinks from €1.80, wraps/mains €6/12; ☉11am-
late; ⓜBourse) Big windows and a 1920s and
'30s charm make this intimate *café* a particularly relaxing place to read the newspapers (provided in several languages) by day.
On weekend evenings things heat up around
10pm with a DJ perched on the wooden spiral stairs. There's also a soul-funk jam session on Thursday night around 9.30pm.

Walvis   BAR
(Map p46; ☑02-219 95 32; www.cafewalvis.be; Rue
Antoine Dansaert; ☉11am-2am Mon-Thu & Sun, to

4am Fri & Sat; 🛜; ⓜSte-Catherine) Sounds from
soul to punk to progressive rock (live, DJs or
just through the speakers) play at this uber-
cool bar, where entry's free, the atmosphere
buzzes and the staff are great.

Au Laboureur   PUB
(Map p40; Rue de Flandre 108; beer €1.60;
☉9.30am-10pm; ⓜSte-Catherine) Amid surrounding trendiness, this refreshingly unpretentious corner bar still attracts crusty
beer-nursing locals with unfeasibly long
moustaches. Hurry before it gentrifies.

Booze'n'Blues   BAR
(Map p40; Rue des Riches Claires 20; beer from €2;
☉4pm-late; ⓜBourse) Cramped and rough,
Booze'n'Blues features a mannequin torso,
an old jukebox and an extended bar panelled like a choir stall. Unpredictable, entertainingly grouchy staff.

Roskam   BAR
(Map p40; ☑02-503 51 54; www.cafe-roskam.
be; Rue de Flandre 9; ☉4pm-2am, to 4am Fri;
ⓜSte-Catherine) Navy tiles and a stylised
horse-head sign identify this bar and music
venue, a small and welcoming neighbourhood place that hosts great Sunday-night
jazz concerts.

Bar des Amis BAR

(Map p40; www.bardesamis.be; Rue Ste-Catherine 30; ⊙5pm-late Sun-Thu, 3pm-late Fri & Sat; 🛜; Ⓜ️Ste-Catherine) A great bar to kick-start a night out, right in the centre of the vibrant Ste-Catherine area. The cosy atmosphere is enhanced by vintage items on the walls.

Club des Halles CLUB

(Map p40; 📞02-289 26 60; www.cafedeshalles.be; Pl St-Géry 1; ⊙10am-midnight; 🚇Bourse) Popular city-centre club in the vaulted cellars beneath the buzzing Café des Halles.

Madame Moustache CLUB

(Map p40; www.madamemoustache.be; Quai au Bois à Brûler 5-7; ⊙9pm-4am Tue-Sun; Ⓜ️Ste-Catherine) A cute Ste-Catherine club with a retro, burlesque feel, it hosts funk all-nighters and swing nights, plus garage and DJ sets.

Fontainas Bar BAR

(Map p40; 📞02-503 31 12; Rue du Marché au Charbon 91; ⊙10am-late Mon-Fri, 11am-late Sat & Sun; 🚇Bourse) The ripped black-vinyl seats, '60s tables and light fittings, and cracked tiles of this loud and gay-friendly bar provide the backdrop for locals reading newspapers by day, until the party starts at night.

🍷 Royal Quarter

Le Marseillais du Jeu de Balle BAR

(Map p50; 📞02-503 00 83; www.facebook.com/lemarseillaisdujeudeballe; Rue Blaes 163; ⊙10am-11pm; Ⓜ️Porte de Hal, 🚇Lemmonier) This traditional corner bar is a much-loved old stager on the square. It serves baguettes and beers, but the speciality is pastis: an anise-flavoured spirit.

L'Inattendu CAFE

(Map p50; Rue de Wynants 13; beers €1.70-3, mains €8-15.50; ⊙9am-11pm Mon-Thu, to 5am Fri; Ⓜ️Louise) As unexpected as the name suggests, this is one classic little wood-panelled café-bistro tourists and locals have largely overlooked. Basic, traditional pub meals are served, including *stoemp* (€9.50) and *waterzooi* (cream-based stew; €12).

Fuse CLUB

(Map p50; www.fuse.be; Rue Blaes 208; cover €5-12; ⊙11pm-7am Sat; Ⓜ️Porte de Hal) The Marolles club that 'invented' European techno still crams up to 2000 people onto its two dance floors. Once a month it also hosts epic gay night La Démence, a hugely popular rave that attracts men from all over Europe and beyond.

Brasserie Ploegmans CAFE

(Map p50; https://ploegmans.wordpress.com; Rue Haute 148; mains €13.50-18.50; ⊙noon-2.30pm Tue-Fri & 6-10pm Tue-Sat, closed Aug; Ⓜ️Louise) This classic local hostelry with old-fashioned mirror-panelled seats and 1927 chequerboard flooring is well regarded for its typical Bruxellois meals.

🍷 St-Gilles, Ixelles & Uccle

★Maison du Peuple BAR

(Map p54; www.maison-du-peuple.be; Parvis de St-Gilles 37a; ⊙8.30am-1am, to 3am Sat & Sun; 🛜; Ⓜ️Parvis de St-Gilles) This 19th-century building faces out onto the market square of Parvis de St-Gilles. A combined *café*, bar and exhibition space, its scruffy-cool decor, with exposed light bulbs and bare-brick walls, marks it out as one of the hippest destinations in the area. Regular club nights.

★Brasserie de la Renaissance PUB

(Map p54; 📞02-534 82 60; Ave Paul Dejaer 39; ⊙9am-midnight; Ⓜ️Horta) This grand *café* has a high-ceilinged room whose walls sport an ornate load of gilt stucco tracery. Despite the grandeur, drinks are cheap and the food (Portuguese, Italian and Belgo-French) is an amazing bargain.

★Comptoir Florian TEAHOUSE

(Map p50; 📞02-513 91 03; www.comptoirflorian.be; Rue St-Boniface 17; coffee/tea €2.50/4.50; ⊙11am-8pm Tue-Sat; Ⓜ️Porte de Namur) Two tiny, super-cosy tasting rooms behind a tea-trading store offer six bean types for its coffees, and 200 teas, served in an eclectic range of pots. The teahouse has a classic curved-wood and tiled interior.

★Chez Moeder Lambic BROWN CAFE

(Map p54; 📞02-544 16 99; www.moederlambic.com; Rue de Savoie 68; ⊙4pm-3am; Ⓜ️Horta) An institution. Behind windows plastered with beer stickers, this tattered, quirky old *café* is the ultimate beer spot in Brussels. Sample some of its hundreds of brews while flipping through the collection of dog-eared comics.

Brasserie Verschueren PUB

(Map p54; Parvis de St-Gilles 11-13; ⊙8am-1am; Ⓜ️Parvis de St-Gilles) A characterful and enjoyably down-at-heel art nouveau *café*, with geometric floor tiling, a handsome wooden bar, stained glass and vintage light fittings. Check out the scoreboard with coloured slats representing Belgian football teams. Very affordable, simple food is served.

Chez Franz
BAR

(Map p54; ☑02-347 42 12; http://chezfranz.com; Ave du Haut-Pont 30; ☺8am-midnight Mon-Thu, to 1am Fri, 10am-1am Sat, to midnight Sun; 🚋Ma Campagne) An emporium of nocturnal activities such as gigs, and of apéritifs featuring deli cuts and cheese platters, Chez Franz is a locals' bar. The beers are generous and there's a selection from the Brussels Beer Project brewery. Try a biodynamic Italian wine or a French grenache.

Jester
BROWN CAFE

(Map p50; www.facebook.com/JesterBrussels; Ave de la Porte de Hal 4; ☺7pm-midnight; Ⓜ Porte de Hal) Jester is a self-proclaimed brown *café*, with a minimalist stained glass window looking out onto the medieval Porte de Hal. The interior stylishly combines wooden furnishings with wall panels decorated with geometric gold pyramids in relief. They serve pizza and dumplings, but the real draw here is the live music – mainly acoustic jazz.

Bar du Matin
BAR

(Map p54; ☑02-537 71 59; http://bardumatin. blogspot.com; Chaussée d'Alsemberg 172; ☺8am-1am Sun-Thu, to 2am Fri & Sat; 🛜; Ⓜ Albert) This trendy bar sits on a corner, the noisy road screened by beech trees. There's a great beer menu and '60s decor with an aluminium bar, wood columns and softly flattering light.

Alice Cocktail Bar
COCKTAIL BAR

(Map p54; ☑02-647 70 44; www.rougetomate. be; Ave Louise 190; cocktails €10-14; ☺6pm-1am Mon-Thu, to 2am Fri & Sat; 🚋54, 81, 93, 91) Cocktail mixologists bewitch with their concoctions at this converted 19th-century town house above the Michelin-starred Rouge Tomate restaurant. Elegantly renovated into a 1940s-style lounge, Jean-Luc Moerman's photography and a grand piano set the mood at this upmarket address.

Spirito Brussels
CLUB

(Map p50; ☑0483 58 06 97; www.spiritobrussels. com; Rue de Stassart 18; €15; ☺11pm-6am Fri & Sat; Ⓜ Porte de Namur) The name refers to the former function of the building: an Anglican church. The decor is still very much intact, but it's now lit in shades of violet and orange. There's a lounge, three different bars and a massive dance floor. Spirito promise to keep the faith, with hip-hop and R&B.

Tarzan
WINE BAR

(Map p54; ☑02-538 65 80; Rue Washington 59; ☺5-11pm Mon-Fri, 3-11pm Sat, to 10pm Sun; 🚋93, 94) 🍃 Welcome to the natural wine emporium, where legendary nights begin. Have a punk rosé, a glass of bubbly or a more rock-and-roll wine featured on the wall board. Food-wise, expect equally exquisite little dishes (€10 to €25) to share, like homemade hummus or beetroot laced with avocado mash

LGBT BRUSSELS

The compact but thriving Rainbow Quarter centres on Rue du Marché au Charbon. Here you'll find a dozen gay-oriented *cafés* – try **Stammbar** (Map p40; http://stammbar.be; Rue du Marché au Charbon 114; ☺9pm-1am Mon-Sat, to 3am Sun; 🚋Anneessens) – and two LGBT information centres/bars, the thriving and multilingual **Rainbow House** (Map p40; ☑02-503 59 90; www.rainbowhouse.be; Rue du Marché au Charbon 42; ☺6.30-10.30pm Wed-Sat; 🚋Anneessens) and Francophone **Tels Quels** (Map p40; ☑02-512 32 34; www.telsquels.be; Rue du Marché au Charbon 81; ☺from 5pm Sun-Tue, Thu & Fri, from 2pm Wed & Sat; 🚋Anneessens), which runs phone helpline **Telégal** (☑02-502 07 00; open 8pm to midnight).

Belgian Gay & Lesbian Pride (www.pride.be; ☺May) culminates in this area with a vast all-night party. The **Festival du Film Gay & Lesbien de Bruxelles** (www.fglb.org; ☺late Jan/early Feb.) runs for 10 days in late January and Cinéma Nova runs occasional **Pink Screen Weeks** (www.gdac.org).

La Démence, is a huge international rave party held at Fuse. It's only on once a month; check the website for dates. **Chez Maman** (Map p40; ☑02-502 86 96; www.chez-maman.be; Rue des Grands Carmes 12; ☺from 10pm Fri & Sat; 🚋Anneessens) is the capital's most beloved transvestite show, while new burlesque venue **Cabaret Mademoiselle** (p77) also hosts transvestite nights and club nights. Try also established and stylish *café* **Le Belgica** (Map p40; www.lebelgica.be; Rue du Marché au Charbon 32; ☺10pm-3am Thu-Sun; 🚋Bourse).

Handily central gay-friendly accommodation includes Downtown-BXL (p62), which is well placed for the nightlife area.

Green Lab   COCKTAIL BAR
(⌨0475 36 54 85; www.greenlab.bar; Ave Louise
520; ⊙4pm-2am Mon-Thu, to 3am Fri & Sat, to midnight Sun; 🚃93, 94) Lovers of the green fairy
will revel in absinthe shots (up to 89.9% alcohol!) and other botanical potions in this
bar dedicated to Van Gogh's favourite drink.
If you'd rather keep your ears intact, opt for a
Kimerud gin and tonic with elderflower and
grapefruit. The menu includes cheese platters and homemade beef jerky.

🍷 EU Quarter & Etterbeek

OR Coffee   COFFEE
(Map p58; ⌨09-336 37 36; www.orcoffee.be; Place
Jourdan 13; ⊙8am-5pm Mon-Fri, from 9am Sat &
Sun; 🙴; 🚃59, 60) Coffee geeks rejoice: this
speciality espresso bar, which roasts its own
beans, also serves some of the best caffeine
in the city. Among sofas, blackboards and
unwieldy greenery, the owners host cup-
pings (coffee tastings) and workshops.

Guinguette Maurice   BEER GARDEN
(Map p58; ⌨0492 50 62 85; www.facebook.
com/GuinguetteMaurice; Parc du Cinquantenaire;
⊙10am-11pm Mon-Sun; 🚃22) Each summer,
a series of *guinguettes* (temporary kiosks)
pops up around the parks of Brussels. Shaded
Guinguette Maurice is a lovely spot for beer,
fresh lemonade and the odd yoga lesson.

La Terrasse   PUB
(Map p58; ⌨02-732 28 51; www.brasseriela
terrasse.be; Ave des Celtes 1; beers €2.40-4.50,
mains €9.90-18; ⊙8am-midnight Mon-Sat,
10am-midnight Sun; Ⓜ️Mérode) Handy for the
Cinquantenaire, this wood-panelled classic
café has a tree-shaded terrace and makes
an ideal refreshment stop after a hard day's
museuming. Snacks, pancakes, ice creams,
breakfasts (from €3.90) and decent pub
meals are all available at various times. Try
sampling the 'beer of the month'.

Piola Libri   BAR
(Map p58; ⌨02-736 93 91; www.piolalibri.be; Rue
Franklin 66; ⊙noon-8pm Mon-Fri, to 6pm Sat, closed
Aug; 🙴; Ⓜ️Schuman) Italian Eurocrats relax
after work on sofas, at pavement tables or
in the tiny back garden and enjoy free tapas-style snacks with chilled white wines at
this convivial bookshop-*café*-bar. It has an
eclectic program of readings and DJ nights.

Kitty O'Shea's   PUB
(Map p58; Blvd Charlemagne 42; ⊙noon-1am;
Ⓜ️Schuman) Friendly Irish pub near the
European Commission that's great for beer,
sport and socialising.

☆ Entertainment

For extensive listings, check www.agenda.
be, English-language magazine *Bulletin*
(www.thebulletin.be/category/culture) and
the *Word* (http://thewordmagazine.com/
neighbourhood-life), which has excellent
suggestions for the weekend. For discounted arts, music and cinema tickets, head to
Arsène50 (Map p50; www.arsene50.be; Rue Royale 2; ⊙12.30-5pm; Ⓜ️Parc).

Cinema

★Cinéma Galeries   CINEMA
(Map p40; ⌨02-514 74 98; www.arenberg.be;
Galerie de la Reine 26; 🚃Bourse) Inside the
graceful glassed-over Galeries St-Hubert,
this art deco beauty concentrates on foreign
and art-house films. An authentic Brussels
movie experience.

Cinema Nova   CINEMA
(Map p40; ⌨02-511 24 77; www.nova-cinema.
org; Rue Arenberg 3; Ⓜ️Gare Centrale) The ultimate in alternative cinema, Nova shows
off-beat international movies that are more
thought-provoking than entertaining (subtitles will be French/Dutch), and there's a
brilliantly rough student-style bar.

Actor's Studio   CINEMA
(Map p40; ⌨02-512 16 96; www.actorsstudio.cine
news.be; Petite Rue des Bouchers 16; 🚃Bourse)
This intimate three-screen cinema, a little
hard to locate just off touristy Petite Rue
des Bouchers, shows art-house flicks as well
as some mainstream reruns, and has a tiny
bar. Try to catch a movie here – it's one of
the city's indie treasures and the tickets are
cheaper than in the big movie houses.

Palace Cinema   CINEMA
(Map p40; ⌨02-503 57 96; www.cinema-palace.be;
Blvd Anspach 85; €8.75; 🚃Bourse) An impressive
1905 picture palace and music hall reinvent-
ed: this is the city's oldest cinema, housed in
a fine art nouveau building. For part of its
history the place was a nightclub. The angu-
lar lobby incorporates rough-hewn concrete
pillars and a ceiling hung with wacky lamps,
while the four screens show a mixture of art-
house and mainstream movies.

★Cinematek   CINEMA
(Map p50; ⌨02-507 83 70; www.cinematheque.be;
Rue Baron Horta 9; Ⓜ️Gare Centrale) In a wing
of the BOZAR cultural centre, the modern

and stylish Cinematek includes a little museum where you can browse archives and memorabilia. The real highlight, though, is the program of silent films screened nearly every day at the cinema, with live piano accompaniment. There's also an impressive program of art-house movies.

Live Music & Cabaret

Major international artists are most likely to play **Forest National** (☑02-340 22 11; www.forestnational.be; Ave du Globe 36; 🚇81) or the somewhat smaller, more central **AB** (Ancienne Belgique; Map p40; ☑02-548 24 84; www.abconcerts.be; Blvd Anspach 110; 🚇Bourse).

Art Base   LIVE MUSIC
(Map p46; ☑02-217 29 20; www.art-base.be; Rue des Sables 29; ⊘Fri & Sat; Ⓜ️Rogier) One of the best little venues in town for music fans with eclectic tastes. It resembles someone's living room, but the programming is first rate, and it's worth taking a punt on Greek *rebetiko*, Indian classical music, Argentine guitar or whatever else is playing.

Cabaret Mademoiselle   CABARET
(Map p40; ☑0474 58 57 61; www.cabaretmademoiselle.be; Rue du Marché au Charbon 53; ⊘7pm-late Wed-Sat; 🚇Bourse) `FREE` Burlesque and brassy, Cabaret Mademoiselle is a new venue that combines drag, circus and comedy, served up with some first-rate Belgian beers.

Brass'Art   WORLD MUSIC
(Map p46; ☑0486 03 79 56; https://en-gb.facebook.com/brassartdigitaalcafe; Place Communale 28, Molenbeek; snacks from €3; ⊘8am-10pm Mon-Sat, 10am-6pm Sun; 🔊; Ⓜ️Comte de Flandre) 🌱 Sitting on the long Place Communale in the predominately Arab and African Molenbeek district, this simple and hugely inviting bar-*café* is run by volunteers. The #refugeeswelcome sign on the door sets the tone; inside you can enjoy bargain pancakes and Moroccan mint tea. It's best in the evening, though, when African musicians play and jam together and the dancing starts.

Théâtre du Vaudeville   THEATRE
(Map p40; ☑02-512 57 45; www.theatreduvaudeville.be; Galeries St-Hubert, Galerie de la Reine 13-15; Ⓜ️Gare Centrale) Cabarets, concerts and various theatre productions take place at this old theatre within the Galeries St-Hubert. Program leaflets are available in the foyer inside the arcade.

Beursschouwburg   LIVE MUSIC
(Map p40; ☑02-513 82 90; www.beursschouwburg.be; Rue Auguste Orts 22; ⊘exhibition area 10am-6pm Mon-Sat, cafe 7.30pm-late Thu-Sun, closed summer; 🚇Bourse) Offers a diverse mix of music including rock, jazz, rap and disco.

Flagey   LIVE MUSIC
(Map p54; www.flagey.be; Place Flagey; 🚇81, 82) Ixelles' stylish flagship venue in an art deco liner-esque building has several concert halls and an eclectic music policy.

Le Botanique   ARTS CENTRE
(Map p46; ☑02-218 79 35; Rue Royale 236; ⊘11am-6pm Mon-Fri, noon-6pm Sat & Sun; Ⓜ️Botanique) Cultural centre, exhibition hall and concert venue with an 1826 glass verandah. Overlooks the botanical gardens.

Jazz & Blues

★**L'Archiduc**   JAZZ
(Map p40; ☑02-512 0652; www.archiduc.net; Rue Antoine Dansaert 6; ⊘4pm-5am; 🚇Bourse) This intimate, split-level art deco bar has been playing jazz since 1937. It's an unusual two-tiered circular space that can get incredibly packed but remains convivial. You might need to ring the doorbell. Saturday concerts (5pm) are free; Sunday brings in international talent and admission charges vary.

★**Music Village**   JAZZ
(Map p40; ☑02-513 13 45; www.themusicvillage.com; Rue des Pierres 50; cover €7.50-20; ⊘from 7.30pm Wed-Sat; 🚇Bourse) A 100-seat jazz venue housed in two 17th-century buildings with dinner (not compulsory) available from 7pm and concerts starting at 8.30pm or 9pm at weekends. The performers squeeze onto a small podium that's visible from any seat.

★**Sounds Jazz Club**   JAZZ
(Map p50; ☑02-512 92 50; www.soundsjazzclub.be; Rue de la Tulipe 28; ⊘8pm-4am Mon-Sat; Ⓜ️Porte de Namur) A small and unassuming but immensely popular Ixelles venue, Sounds has concerts most nights, with styles varying from modern to big band to salsa. The website has links to artists' web pages.

Bizon   BLUES
(Map p40; ☑02-502 46 99; www.cafebizon.com; Rue du Pont de la Carpe 7; ⊘4pm-late, from 6pm Sat & Sun; 🚇Bourse) A happening grunge bar in St-Géry featuring home-grown live blues, a range of beers and a selection of *jenevers* (gin). Located on a street of lively *café*-bars.

Jazz Station
JAZZ

(Map p58; ☎02-733 13 78; www.jazzstation.be; Chaussée de Louvain 193a; ☺exhibitions 11am-7pm Wed-Sat, concerts 6pm Sat & 8.30pm some week-nights; Ⓜ Madou) An appealing venue in an 1885 former station. There are also exhibitions, a multimedia jazz archive and practice rooms, where you can listen in on musicians honing their art.

☆ Classical Music

★ BOZAR
LIVE MUSIC

(Map p50; www.bozar.be; Palais des Beaux-Arts, Rue Ravenstein 23; Ⓜ Gare Centrale) This celebrated classical-music space is home to the National Orchestra and Philharmonic Society. From the outside, the Horta-designed 1928 art deco building is bold rather than enticing, but Henri Le Bœuf Hall is considered to be one of the five best venues in the world for acoustic quality. BOZAR also hosts major art and science exhibitions.

Conservatoire Royal de Musique
CLASSICAL MUSIC

(Royal Music Conservatory; Map p50; ☎02-511 04 27; www.conservatoire.be; Rue de la Régence 30; Ⓜ Porte de Namur) Classical-music venue for student performances.

☆ Theatre & Dance

★ Théâtre Royal de Toone
THEATRE

(Map p40; ☎02-511 71 37; www.toone.be; Petite Rue des Bouchers 21; adult/child €10/7; ☺typically 8.30pm Thu & 4pm Sat; Ⓜ Gare Centrale) Eight generations of the Toone family have staged classic puppet productions in the Bruxellois dialect at this endearing marionette theatre, a highlight of any visit to Brussels. Shows are aimed at adults, but kids love them too.

Rosas
DANCE

(☎02-344 55 98; www.rosas.be; Van Volxemlaan 164; ☒32, 82, 97) This Brussels-based company built around choreographer Anne Teresa De Keersmaeker strikes a winning balance between traditional and avant-garde dance. When not globetrotting it typically performs at La Monnaie (p78) or **Kaaitheater** (Map p46; ☎02-201 59 59; www.kaaitheater.be; Sq Sainctelette 20; Ⓜ Yser).

Le Lac
ARTS CENTRE

(Map p46; ☎02-582 58 41; www.lelac.info; Rue de Witte de Haelen 36; €7; Ⓜ Ste-Catherine, ☒51) This vast two-tier artists' studio opens onto the street and hosts ad hoc exhibitions and events. It sells beers and snacks, and you can look at the art work. Concerts happen in the street outside in summer, such as Moroccan *gnaoua* trance musicians performing against the surreal backdrop of the castellated Petit-Château, formerly barracks and now a migrant centre.

Théâtre La Montagne Magique
THEATRE

(Map p46; ☎02 210 15 90; https://lamontagne magique.be; Rue du Marais 57; Ⓜ Botanique) Productions aimed at kids and teens, as well as workshops for aspiring actors.

Bronks Youth Theatre
THEATRE

(Map p40; ☎02-219 75 54; www.bronks.be; Rue de Marché aux Porcs 15; Ⓜ Ste-Catherine) Offers theatre, mime and workshops for toddlers and children most weekends.

Théâtre Royal de la Monnaie/Koninklijke Muntschouwburg
PERFORMING ARTS

(Map p40; ☎02-229 13 72; www.lamonnaie.be; Place de la Monnaie; Ⓜ De Brouckère) Belgium was born when an opera at this grand venue inspired the 1830 revolution). Nowadays it primarily hosts contemporary dance, and classic and new operas.

Koninklijke Vlaamse Schouwburg
THEATRE

(Map p46; ☎02-210 11 12; www.kvs.be; Rue de Laeken 146; Ⓜ Yser) Behind a restored Renaissance facade, the state-of-the-art Royal Flemish Theatre mounts edgy dance and theatre productions, occasionally in English.

Maison de la Bellone
CONCERT VENUE

(Map p40; ☎02-513 33 33; www.bellone.be; Rue de Flandre 46; Ⓜ Ste-Catherine) The glass-vaulted courtyard of this 18th-century stunner is used for occasional concerts.

Shopping

Beer and chocolate are two of the big shopping draws for visitors. But Brussels is also great for fashion, from funky vintage stores and alternative designer boutiques on and around Rue Antoine Dansaert to the chic boutiques of Ave Louise. Two worthwhile shopping experiences are the early morning **Jeu-de-Balle Flea Market** (Map p50; www.marcheauxpuces.be; Place du Jeu-de-Balle; ☺6am-2pm Mon-Fri, to 3pm Sat & Sun; Ⓜ Porte de Hal, ☒Lemonnier), and the vast multicultural Sunday market round **Gare du Midi** (Marché du Midi; Map p50; ☺7am-1pm Sun; Ⓜ Gare du Midi). Other classic Brussels markets include the weekend **Sablon Antiques Market** (Map p50; www.sablon-antiques-market.com; Place

BRUSSELS' FASHION DISTRICT

You don't have to be a fashion hound to enjoy the quirky facades, shops and idiosyncrasies of the compact area that neatly divides St-Géry and Ste-Catherine. Heading northwest from the Bourse, you'll pass the magnificent wrought-iron frontage of the Beursschouwburg (p77), a cultural centre built in 1885 as a grand brasserie.

Head to Rue des Chartreux to admire the art nouveau ironwork over the entrance to classic café **Le Greenwich** (Map p40; 🖉 02-511 41 67; www.greenwich-cafe.be; Rue des Chartreux 7; drinks from €2.50, croque/spaghetti €5/10; ⏰ 11am-10pm; 🚇 Bourse) and admire the vintage bounty of clothes store **Gabriele** (Map p40; 🖉 02-512 67 43; www.gabrielevintage. com; Rue des Chartreux 27; ⏰ 1-7pm Mon & Tue, 11am-7pm Wed-Sat; 🚇 Bourse). Look out for a typically Brussels-style piece of street humour, the statue of cocked-legged dog Zinneke ('Mongrel').

Heading west up Rue Antoine Dansaert towards the canal, you'll see increasing numbers of Moroccan shops and cafes among cutting-edge bars and chi-chi boutiques. Hip but not unduly daunting to enter, **Stijl** (Map p40; 🖉 02-512 03 13; www.stijl. be; Rue Antoine Dansaert 74; ⏰ 10.30am-6.30pm Mon-Sat; Ⓜ Ste-Catherine) stocks Antwerp Six classics (Ann Demeulemeester, Dries Van Noten) but also features clothes for both sexes by up-to-the-minute designers (Haider Ackermann, Gustavo Lins, Raf Simons etc) with prices clearly labelled. Designer-eyewear specialist **Hoet** (Map p40; https:// hoet.be/en/home; Rue Antoine Dansaert 97; ⏰ 10.30am-6.30pm Tue-Sat; Ⓜ Ste-Catherine) has an extraordinary line in silver-filigree eyeshades and the shop facade's Parisian-style gables are worth admiring. **ICON** (Map p40; 🖉 02-502 71 51; www.icon-shop.be; Place du Nouveau Marché aux Grains 5; ⏰ 10.30am-6.30pm Mon-Sat; 🚇 Dansaert) stocks high-class prêt-à-porter, with an avant-garde selection of Belgian designers, including Valentine Witmeur Lab and the transgressive Filles à Papa. Down an alley lies stylish bookshop **Passa Porta** (Map p40; www.passaporta.be; Rue Antoine Dansaert 46; ⏰ 11am-7pm Tue-Sat, noon-6pm Sun; 🚇 Bourse).

Along Rue Léon Lepage, you'll find another cluster of fashion stores, including feminine but edgy **Just In Case** (Map p40; www.justincase.be; Rue Léon Lepage 63; ⏰ 11am-7pm Tue-Sat; Ⓜ Ste-Catherine), while on Rue de Flandre there's a style-conscious branch of **Oxfam** (Map p40; 🖉 02-522 40 70; Rue de Flandre 104; ⏰ 11am-6pm Mon-Sat; Ⓜ Ste-Catherine), hip eco-fashion store **Wonderloop** (Map p40; www.wonderloop.be; Rue de Flandre 35; ⏰ 11am-7pm Tue-Sat; Ⓜ Ste-Catherine) 🏷 and the artful white-on-white boutique of **Martin Margiela** (Map p40; www.maisonmargiela.com; Rue de Flandre 114; ⏰ 11am-7pm Mon-Sat; Ⓜ Ste-Catherine), often tagged the Antwerp Six's unofficial seventh member.

---

du Grand Sablon; ⏰ 9am-6pm Sat, to 2pm Sun; Ⓜ Porte de Namur), and the Wednesday afternoon foodie-fest on **Pl du Châtelain** (Map p54; ⏰ afternoon Wed; Ⓜ Louise).

**Manufacture Belge
de Dentelles**   ARTS & CRAFTS
(Map p40; 🖉 02-511 44 77; www.mbd.be; Galerie de la Reine 6-8; ⏰ 9.30am-6pm Mon-Sat, 10am-4pm Sun; Ⓜ Gare Centrale) Excellent stock of antique lace, and staff who love the stuff.

De Biertempel   DRINKS
(Map p40; 🖉 02-502 19 06; http://biertempel.wix-site.com/debiertempel; Rue du Marché aux Herbes 56b; ⏰ 9.30am-7pm; 🚇 Bourse) As its name states, this shop is a temple to beer, stocking upwards of 700 brews along with matching glasses and other booze-related merchandise. For more ordinary beers and for bulk

purchases, make like the locals and go to the supermarket.

Belge une fois   ARTS & CRAFTS
(Map p50; 🖉 02-503 85 41; www.belgeunefois.com; Rue Haute 89; ⏰ 11am-6pm Wed-Sat, 1-6pm Sun; 🚇 92, 93) Belge une fois is a concept store selling creations by the eponymous designers' collective. It also sells artefacts, accessories and light fixtures by other Belgian designers. Expect everything from simple postcards and concrete cacti holders to large photography prints.

Foxhole Vintage Marolles   VINTAGE
(Map p50; 🖉 0477 20 53 36; https://foxhole vintage.com; Rue des Renards 6; ⏰ 10am-6.30pm Thu-Sun; Ⓜ Louise) Vintage and used clothing are given a hip twist within a lovely sloping alley in the heart of the Marolles. Stylishly

arranged by colour, the selection includes belts, bags, shoes and sunglasses. There's a section for men, often including army jackets and denim.

Kure
FASHION & ACCESSORIES

(Map p50; ☑ 02-503 81 13; www.kure.be; Ave Louise 78; ☺ 10.30am-7pm Mon-Fri, 10am-7pm Sat, 12.30-5pm Sun; ☐ 93, 94) A temple of affordable fashion, Kure sells cute jumpsuits by Can Pep Rey and Second Female, soft cardigans by Designers Remix and second-skin leather pants by Anine Bing. Out the back, souvenir hunters will find ceramics, scented candles and local cuberdon sweets.

Beermania
DRINKS

(Map p50; ☑ 02-512 17 88; www.beermania.be; Chaussée de Wavre 174; ☺ 11am-9pm Mon-Sat; Ⓜ Porte de Namur) Complete with a tasting *café*, international delivery service and online sales.

Rose
GIFTS & SOUVENIRS

(Map p54; ☑ 02-534 98 08; www.rosebleu.be; Rue de l'Aqueduc 56-58; ☺ 10.30am-6pm Mon, to 6.30pm Tue-Sat; ☐ 81) Forget Ali Baba's cave; Rose is an embarrassment of homeware riches, from pineapple lamps and hand-embroidered Macon & Lesquoy pins to leather birthday cards and Unicorn-scented room-fragrance sprays.

Lulu
HOMEWARES

(Map p54; ☑ 02-537 25 03; www.lulustore.eu; Rue du Page 101; ☺ 8am-7pm Tue-Sat, to 5pm Sun; ☐ 92) This former garage is now a concept store selling ceramic cacti holders, handmade

Italian sunglasses and minimal Scandinavian furniture pieces. Its small corner cafe serves a mean quiche and good coffee too.

ⓘ Information

MEDICAL SERVICES

Community Help Service (☑ 02-648 40 14; www.chsbelgium.org) English-speaking crisis helpline. Can also help find English-speaking doctors, dentists and other health professionals.

Hôpital St-Pierre (☑ 02-535 31 11; www. stpierre-bru.be; Rue Haute 290-322; ☺ emergency 24hr, consultation 8am-5pm; Ⓜ Louise) Central hospital offering emergency assistance.

MONEY

Find exchange facilities near the Bourse, at Bruxelles-Midi station and at Brussels Airport.

POST

Gare du Midi (Map p50; Ave Fonsny 1e; ☺ 7am-7pm Mon-Fri, 10am-3pm Sat; Ⓜ Gare du Midi, Ⓡ Bruxelles-Midi)

Ste-Catherine (Map p40; Blvd Anspach 1; ☺ 8am-6pm Mon-Fri, 10.30am-4pm Sat; Ⓜ De Brouckère)

TOURIST INFORMATION

BIP (Map p50; ☑ 02-563 63 99; http://bip. brussels/en; Rue Royale 2-4; ☺ 9.30am-5.30pm Mon-Fri, 10am-6pm Sat & Sun; Ⓜ Parc) Helpful Brussels area tourist office.

Flanders Info (Map p40; ☑ 02-504 03 00; www.visitflanders.com; Rue du Marché aux Herbes 61; ☺ 9am-6pm Mon-Sat, 10am-5pm Sun; 🛜; Ⓡ Bourse) The low down on the Flanders region.

CHOC-SHOPPING

You can't go wrong with great-value pralines from Leonidas but for chocolate connoisseurs willing to pay almost three times the price, there are some fine alternatives:

Pierre Marcolini (Map p50; ☑ 02-512 43 14; www.marcolini.be; Rue des Minimes 1; ☺ 10am-7pm Sun-Thu, to 6pm Fri & Sat; Ⓜ Porte de Namur) Rare chocolate beans, experimental flavours (eg tea) and suave designer black-box packaging. The chain's dozen Brusssels locations include the Eurostar departures hall.

Mary (Map p46; ☑ 02-217 45 00; www.mary.be; Rue Royale 73; ☺ 10am-6pm Mon-Sat; Ⓜ Madou) Supplies artisanal pralines to Belgium's royals plus the occasional US president.

Neuhaus (Map p40; ☑ 02-512 63 59; www.neuhaus.be; Galerie de la Reine 25; ☺ 10am-8pm Mon-Sat, to 7pm Sun; Ⓜ Gare Centrale) For stained-glass windows and sumptuous displays visit the stunning flagship shop of Belgium's original chocolate house – established 1857.

Planète Chocolat (Map p40; ☑ 02-511 07 55; www.planetechocolat.be; Rue du Lombard 24; ☺ 11am-6pm Mon & Sun, 10.30am-6.30pm Tue-Sat; Ⓡ Bourse) Both moulds and chocolates are made on-site. At 4pm Saturday and Sunday there are praline-making demonstrations explaining chocolate's development, culminating in a chance for visitors to create their own chocolates.

Tourist Information Booth (Map p50; ☺8am-8pm; Ⓜ Gare du Midi) Handy information booth if you're at Gare du Midi.

Use-It (Map p46; ☑ 02-218 39 06; www.brussels.use-it.travel; Galerie Ravenstein 17; ☺10am-6pm Mon-Sat; ☏; Ⓜ Gare Central) Very welcoming youth-oriented office with a list of nightly events, great maps and a free city tour.

visit.brussels (Map p40; ☑ 02-513 89 40; Hôtel de Ville, Grand Place; ☺9am-6pm; Ⓡ Bourse) High-quality information and handouts, with an additional office on Rue Royale, where you'll also find the Arsène50 desk, which provides great discounts on theatres, gigs etc.

❶ Getting There & Away

AIR

Brussels Airport (https://www.brussels airport.be/en) is 14km northeast of the city centre. The arrivals hall (Level 2) has currency exchange, ATMs, car-rental agencies and tourist info. Level 1 has a train station; Level 0 a bus terminus and luggage lockers.

Bus

Eurolines (Map p46; ☑ 02-274 13 50; www.eurolines.be; Rue du Progrès 80; Ⓜ Gare du Nord) and **FlixBus** (www.flixbus.co.uk) operate services to London, Amsterdam, Paris and other international destinations from Bruxelles-Nord.

TEC Bus W (for Waterloo) (Map p50; 🚌W)

Car

Major car-rental companies have offices at Gare du Midi and Brussels Airport, but rentals from their downtown premises usually cost less.

Avis (☑ 02-537 12 80; www.avis.be; Rue Américaine 145; ☺8am-5pm Mon-Fri, to noon Sat; 🚌93, 94)

Budget (☑ 02-537 12 80; www.budget.be; Rue Americaine 145; ☺8am-5pm Mon-Fri, to noon Sat; 🚌93, 94)

Train

Bruxelles-Midi (Gare du Midi; luggage office per article per day €4, luggage lockers per 24hr small/large €3/4; ☺luggage office 6am-9pm; Ⓜ Gare du Midi, Ⓡ Bruxelles-Midi) is the main station for international connections: the Eurostar, TGV and Thalys high-speed trains (with prebooking compulsory) stop here. Most other mainline trains stop in quick succession at Bruxelles-Midi, **Bruxelles-Central** (Gare Centrale) and, except for Amsterdam trains, also at **Bruxelles-Nord** (Gare du Nord). Information offices at all three stations open early morning to late evening. For all enquiries, consult www.belgiantrain.be/en or call 02-555 2555.

BOOKS & COMICS

Passa Porta (p79) A meeting point for literary types in the city.

Librebook (Map p50; ☑ 0479 33 09 84; https://librebook.eu/en; Chaussée de Wavre 128; ☺1-7pm Wed, Thu & Sat, to 8pm Fri; Ⓜ Porte du Namur) Great events and featured authors from around the world.

Sterling Books (Map p40; ☑ 02-223 62 23; www.sterlingbooks.be; Rue du Fossé aux Loups 23; ☺10am-7pm Mon-Sat, noon-6.30pm Sun; Ⓜ De Brouckère) Has strong English-language sections.

Tropismes (Map p40; ☑ 02-512 88 52; http://tropismes.com; Galerie des Princes 11; ☺11am-6.30pm Mon, 10am-6.30pm Tue-Thu, 10am-7.30pm Fri, 10.30am-7pm Sat, 1.30-6.30pm Sun; Ⓜ Gare Centrale) Gorgeous bookshop in the swish Galerie des Princes.

Brüsel (Map p40; www.brusel.com; Blvd Anspach 100; ☺10.30am-6.30pm Mon-Sat, from noon Sun; Ⓡ Bourse) Chic comic-book shop with English translations available.

Pêle-Mêle (Map p40; ☑ 02-548 78 00; https://pele-mele.be/bruxelles; Blvd Maurice Lemonnier 55; ☺10am-6.30pm; Ⓜ Anneessens) Secondhand bookshop with a huge stock, much in English, plus an upstairs cafe.

❶ Getting Around

TO/FROM THE AIRPORT

Airport City Express (tickets €9; ☺5.30am-12.20am) trains run four times hourly between Brussels Airport and the city's three main train stations, Bruxelles-Nord (15 minutes), Bruxelles-Central (€10, 20 minutes) and Bruxelles-Midi (25 minutes).

Express bus 12 links the airport to the city via Nato HQ and Schuman metro station (prepurchased/bought aboard €4/5). It should take around 30 minutes, but allow much more time at rush hour. After 8pm on weekends, the slower route 21 is substituted. See www.stib.be for the rather complex timetables.

An airport taxi to central Brussels costs around €40 (some accept credit cards), but once you're stuck in rush-hour traffic you'll probably wish you'd taken the train.

BICYCLE

Bicycles can be carried on the metro and trams except during rush hour (7am to 9am and 4pm to 6.30pm Monday to Friday).

Rental

Villo! (☑ 078-05 11 10; http://en.villo.be; subscription day/week €1.60/8.20) is a system of 180 automated stations for short-term bicycle rental (under 30/30/60/90/120min free/€0.50/1/1.50/2). First you need a subscription (day/week/year €1.60/8.20/32.60), then charges accumulate and are debited from your credit/bank card. When making stops, the idea is to return the bike to the nearest station and take a new one when continuing. Failure to return the bicycle or to follow the rules could cost you €150.

For longer bike hires, try **FietsPunt/PointVelo** (☑ 02-513 04 09; www.cyclo.org; Carrefour de l'Europe 2; per day/week €15/45; ◷ 7am-7pm Mon-Fri; ℞ Bruxelles-Central), which is also a cycle-repair shop. You'll need ID and credit card or a €150 deposit. The shop is somewhat hidden: look left as you leave Bruxelles-Central station via the daytime-only Madeleine exit. Another rental option is **Maison des Cyclistes** (☑ 02-502 73 55; www.provelo.be; Rue de Londres 15; ◷ noon-6pm Mon-Fri, 10am-6pm Sat & Sun Apr-Oct; Ⓜ Trone), which also offers tours.

CAR

Street parking requires meter payment when signs say *betalend parkeren/stationnement payant* (usually 9am to 1pm and 2pm to 7pm Monday to Saturday).

PUBLIC TRANSPORT

STIB/MIVB (www.stib-mivb.be) runs the integrated bus-tram-metro system with services from about 6am to midnight. After midnight, it's taxi only except on Friday/Saturday and Saturday/Sunday nights, when Noctis night-bus routes operate twice hourly from midnight to 3am, most starting from Place de Brouckère. Normal tickets and travel cards are valid.

Tickets

Tickets are valid for one hour and are sold at metro stations, at STIB/MIVB kiosks, at newsagents and on buses and trams. Single-/five-/10-journey STIB/MIVB tickets cost €2.10/8/14 including transfers. Unlimited one-day passes cost €6. Note that airport buses are excluded, and slightly higher 'jump' fares apply if you want to connect to city routes operated by De Lijn (Flanders bus), TEC (Wallonia bus) or SNCB/NMBS (rail). Children under six travel free.

Tickets must be validated, before travel, in machines located at the entrance to metro platforms or inside buses and trams. Unvalidated tickets incur fines of €55. Random checks are made.

Brussels airport sells one-day passes and the **BrusselsCard** (www.brusselscard.be; 24/48/72hr €26/34/42).

Metro

Metro stations are marked with a white 'M' on a blue background. Lines 1A (northwest–southeast) and 1B (northeast–southwest) share the same central stretch, including useful stops at Bruxelles-Central, Ste-Catherine and Schuman (for the EU area). Line 2 basically follows the Petit Ring. Don't expect London-style frequency: trains only run every 10 to 15 minutes. While you wait there's often artwork to peruse. Highlights include the following:

Bourse Paul Delvaux' *Nos vieux trams bruxellois* depicts old trams in the capital.

Horta Relics from Horta's Maison du Peuple have been integrated into the foyer.

Porte de Hal Old trams and futuristic vehicles merge in scenes mirroring the comic strips of artist François Schuiten.

Stockel Features life-sized murals of Tintin and pals.

Tram, Premetro & Bus

The complex transport web has no central hub, so grab a free STIB/MIVB transport map before going too far. Underground *premetro* trams link Brussels-Nord and Brussels-Midi via the Bourse, travelling beneath the boulevard known consecutively as Adolphe Max/Anspach/Maurice Lemonnier.

ROLLERBLADES

Belgium is perhaps unique in having special road rules for 'rollers' (those on rollerblades or rollerskates). On Friday evenings from June to September certain major city streets give temporary right of way to rollers from 7pm (see www.belgiumrollers.com).

TAXI

Official taxis can be identified by white, yellow and blue triangular stands on the car roof. They charge €2.40 pick-up plus €1.80/2.70 per kilometre within/outside the Brussels region. There's a €2 supplement between 10pm and 6am. Waiting costs €30 per hour. Taxes and tips are officially included in the meter price, so you should ignore requests for extra service charges. Taxis wait near the three central train stations, outside Hôtel Amigo, near the Grand Place and at Place Stéphanie on Ave Louise.

To call a cab, try **Taxis Bleus** (☑ 02-268 00 00; www.taxisbleus.be), **Taxis Verts** (☑ 02-349 49 49; www.taxisverts.be) or, for disabled/wheelchair-bound visitors, **Taxi Hendriks** (☑ 02-752 98 00; www.hendriks.be).

Bruges, Ghent & Northwest Belgium

Best Places to Eat

➡ De Stove (p97)

➡ Den Gouden Harynck (p98)

➡ 't Hemelrijck (p128)

➡ Holy Food Market (p138)

➡ Restaurant Pegasus (p116)

➡ Moment! (p105)

Best Places to Stay

➡ 1898 The Post (p137)

➡ Hotel Messeyne (p124)

➡ Manoir Carpe Diem (p105)

➡ Guesthouse Nuit Blanche (p95)

➡ Main Street Hotel (p119)

➡ Treck Hostel (p136)

Why Go?

This chapter covers East Flanders (Oost-Vlaanderen) and West Flanders (West-Vlaanderen), though just to confuse visitors, these two provinces only comprise only around half of the total Flemish region that covers the whole of northern Belgium. The top highlights here are a series of enticing cities featuring fabulous medieval marketplaces, cobbled streets, belfries and *begijnhoven*. It's beautiful Bruges that usually steals the show with its atmospheric, picture-perfect waterways lined with step-gabled houses. But wonderful Ghent has photogenic canals of its own, a central castle and a grittier, more 'real' atmosphere enlivened by a big student population.

Buffer your explorations with the dunes and beaches of the Belgian Coast, the thought-provoking WWI sites and cemeteries of Ypres Salient, the hop fields and breweries around Poperinge and the hilly landscapes of the 'Flemish Ardennes' around Geraardsbergen. It doesn't take long to understand why folks keep falling for Flanders.

Driving Distances (km)

	Poperinge	Kortrijk	Ypres	Ghent
Kortrijk	42			
Ypres	12	28		
Ghent	92	48	76	
Bruges	83	44	57	55

Bruges, Ghent & Northwest Belgium Highlights

1 Belfort (p87) Gazing in awe at the vista when you climb Bruges' 83m-high belfry.

2 In Flanders Fields Museum (p116) Appreciating the destruction and horrors of war in Ypres.

3 Mystic Lamb (p129) Marvelling at Ghent's 1432 altarpiece, one of the world's earliest-known oil paintings.

4 National Hopmuseum (p115) Gaining insight into Belgium's obsession with beer in Poperinge.

5 Ostend (p106) Cheering on the regeneration of this rebounding port city where Marvin Gaye wrote his last hit.

6 Biking (p103) Cycling along Noorweegse Kaai from Bruges to Damme.

7 Church of our Lady (p127) Ascending the Muur – Geraardsbergen's famously steep cobbled rise – to this delightful chapel.

8 IJzertoren (p114) Refreshing your perspective from this incongruous tower of peace in Diksmuide.

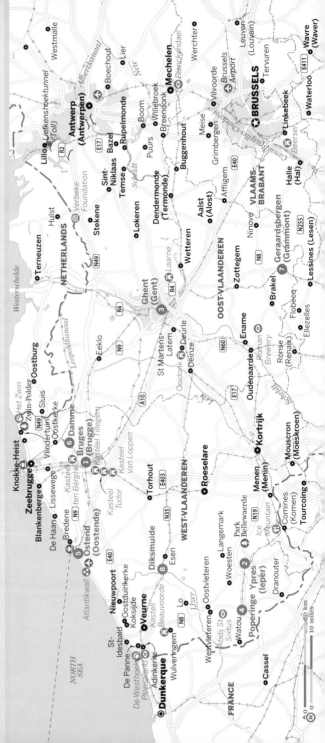

BRUGES

POP 118,284

If you set out to design a fairy-tale medieval town, it would be hard to improve on central Bruges (Brugge in Dutch), one of Europe's best preserved cities. Picturesque cobbled lanes and dreamy canals link photogenic market squares lined with soaring towers, historical churches and lane after lane of old whitewashed almshouses.

For many the secret is already out; during the busy summer months, you'll be sharing Bruges' magic with a constant stream of tourists in the medieval core.

To really enjoy Bruges, stay one or two nights – day trippers miss out on the city's stunning nocturnal floodlighting – and try to visit midweek to avoid weekend crowds.

The best times to visit are in spring, when daffodils carpet the tranquil courtyard of the historic begijnhof (p93) retreat, or outside of Christmas in winter, when you'll have the magnificent, if icy, town almost all to yourself.

History

The fortress around which Bruges grew was originally constructed by Baldwin Iron Arm, first Count of Flanders, just beyond the head of a long sea channel called the Zwin. As with other Flemish cities, Bruges' medieval prosperity came from trading and manufacturing textiles from high-quality English wool. Trade came via the Zwin and a linking waterway from nearby Damme village. Thirteenth-century traders meeting at the Bruges house of a certain Van de Burse (Vlamingenstraat 35) were the first to formalise stock trading; to this day stock exchanges are still called *bourses* in many languages. By 1301, Bruges' citizens were already so wealthy that French King Philip the Fair's wife, Joanna of Navarre, claimed: 'I thought I alone was queen, but I see that I have 600 rivals here.'

Despite occasional rebellions, Bruges' zenith came in the 14th century. As a key member of the Hanseatic League (a powerful association of northern European trading cities), international trading houses set up shop here, and ships laden with exotic goods from all over Europe and beyond docked at the Minnewater.

Prosperity continued under the dukes of Burgundy, especially Philip the Good (r 1419–67), who arrived in 1430 to marry Isabella of Portugal. Bruges grew fat and at one point the population ballooned to 200,000, double that of London. Flemish art blossomed and the city's artists, known as the Flemish Primitives, perfected paintings that were anything but primitive.

However, the guildsmen's relationships with their distant overlords was tense. A dynastic conflict between the French and Habsburg empires in 1482 caused rising taxes and restrictions of the guildsmen's privileges. This in turn sparked a decade of disastrous revolts. At one point in 1488, presumptuous Bruges townsmen even dared to imprison the Habsburg heir, Maximilian of Austria, for four months on a site that's now the Craenenburg Café (Markt 16). The Habsburgs took furious retribution, with Bruges forced to demolish its city walls. While on paper the 'Liberty of Bruges' remained as a powerful autonomous district, traders sensed the city's coming demise. The Hanseatic League moved from Bruges to Antwerp and many merchants followed. But most devastating of all, the Zwin gradually silted up so Bruges lost all access to the sea. Despite attempts to build another canal, the city's economic lifeline was gone and the town was left full of abandoned houses, deserted streets and empty canals. Bruges slept for 400 years.

THE BRUGES MATINS, 1302

The precocious wealth and independent-mindedness of Bruges' medieval guildsmen brought political tensions with their French overlords. In 1302, when guildsmen refused to pay a new round of taxes, the French sent in a 2000-strong army to garrison the town. Undeterred, Pieter De Coninck, dean of the Guild of Weavers, and Jan Breydel, dean of the Guild of Butchers, led a revolt that would go down in Flanders' history books as the 'Bruges Matins' (Brugse Metten). Early in the morning on 18 May, guildsmen crept into town and murdered anyone who could not correctly pronounce the hard-to-say Dutch phrase *'schild en vriend'* (shield and friend). This revolt sparked a widespread Flemish rebellion. A short-term Flemish victory six weeks later at the Battle of the Golden Spurs (p124) near Kortrijk gave medieval Flanders a very short-lived moment of independence.

Bruges

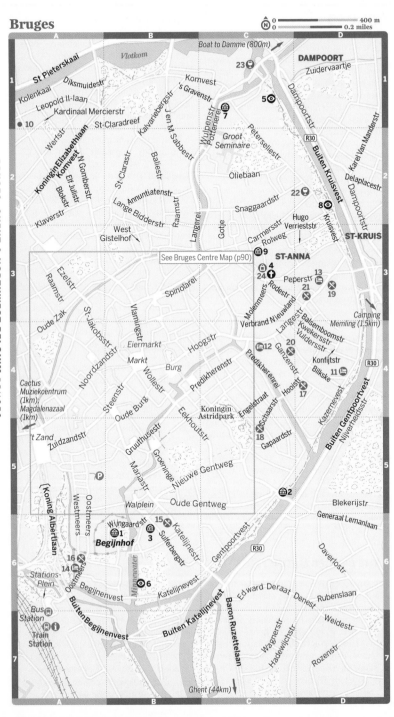

Bruges

The city slowly emerged from its slumber in the early 19th century as war tourists passed through en route to the Waterloo battlefield. In 1892 Belgian writer and poet Georges Rodenbach published *Bruges-la-Morte* (Bruges the Dead), a novel that beguilingly described the town's forlorn air and alerted well-heeled tourists to its preserved charm. Curious wealthy visitors brought much-needed money into Bruges, and ever since the town has worked hard at renovations and embellishments to maintain its reputation as one of the world's most perfectly preserved medieval time capsules.

Antique Bruges escaped both world wars relatively unscathed and now lives largely off tourism. However, beyond the cute central area, greater Bruges includes a newer sprawl where vibrant manufacturing industries produce glass, electrical goods and chemicals, much of it exported via the 20th-century port of Zeebrugge ('Sea Bruges') to which Bruges has been linked since 1907 by the Boudewijnkanaal (Baudouin canal).

⊙ Sights

Old-town Bruges is neatly encased by an oval-shaped moat that follows the city's medieval fortifications. Though the walls are gone, four of the nine 14th-century gates still stand. The city centre is an ambler's dream, its sights sprinkled within leisurely walking distance of its compact centre. The train station (p102) sits about 1.5km south of the central square (Markt); buses shuttle regularly between the two, but it's a lovely walk via Minnewater (p93).

⊙ Markt

Flanked by medieval-style step-gabled buildings, Markt (Map p90) is Bruges' nerve centre, a splendid open market square where horse-drawn carriages clatter between open-air restaurants and camera-clicking tourists, all watched over by a verdigris-green statue of Pieter De Coninck and Jan Breydel, the leaders of the Bruges Matins revolt. The buildings aren't always quite as medieval as they look, but together they create a fabulous scene; even the neo-Gothic former post office building is architecturally magnificent.

★**Belfort**   HISTORIC BUILDING
(Belfry; Map p90; ☑050 44 87 43; www.visit bruges.be/nl/belfort; Markt 7; adult/child €12/10; ⊙9.30am-6pm) Towering 83m above the square like a gigantic medieval rocket is this fabulous 13th-century belfry. There's relatively little to see inside, but it's worth the mildly claustrophobic 366-step climb for the fine views. Look out through wide-gauge chicken wire for panoramas across the spires and red-tiled rooftops towards the wind turbines and giant cranes of Zeebrugge. Visitor numbers are limited to 70 at once, which can cause queues at peak times.

The belfry's 47-bell carillon is still played manually on a changing schedule (typically Wednesdays and weekends). Timings are posted on a signboard in front of the

13th-century **Markt Hallen** (Map p90; ☑ 050 44 87 43; Markt 7), the former market halls, where occasional exhibitions and fairs are hosted.

Museum-Gallery

XPO Salvador Dali GALLERY

(Map p90; ☑ 050 33 83 44; www.dali-interart.be; Markt 7; adult/child €10/8; ☉ 10am-6pm) Located within the Belfort (p87), this small gallery has one of the largest private collections of work (primarily sketches, painting and sculpture) of the great surrealist artist. It also hosts visiting exhibitions and works.

Historium MUSEUM

(Map p90; ☑ 050 27 03 11; www.historium.be; Markt; adult/child €14/7.50; ☉ 10am-6pm) The Historium occupies a neo-Gothic building on the northern side of the Markt (p87). The immersive one-hour audio and video tour aims to take you back to medieval Bruges: a fictional love story gives narrative structure, and you can nose around Van Eyck's studio, among other pseudo-historic experiences.

Historium isn't heavy with facts, but it aims to provide a solid starting point for those just beginning to investigate the long and complex history of this medieval city.

Historium's most recent inclusion is a new virtual reality experience of time travel; the ticket price including this is a flat €17.50.

◉ Burg

One short block east lies the less theatrical but still enchanting, tree-filled square called Burg (Map p90). That has been Bruges' administrative hub for centuries. Its southern flank incorporates three superb interlinked facades that glow with gilded detail.

Stadhuis HISTORIC BUILDING

(City Hall; Map p90; ☑ 050 44 87 43; www.visit bruges.be/en/stadhuis-city-hall; Burg 12; adult/concession/under 18yr €6/5/free; ☉ 9.30am-5pm) The beautiful 1420 stadhuis features a fanciful facade that's second only to Leuven's (p174) for exquisitely turreted Gothic excess. Inside, an audioguide explains numerous portraits in somewhat excessive detail before leading you upstairs to the astonishing **Gotische Zaal** (Map p90; ☑ 050 44 87 43; www.visitbruges.be/nl/stadhuis; Burg 12; adult/concession €4/3; ☉ 9.30am-5pm) (Gothic Hall). The exterior is smothered with replica statues of the counts and countesses of Flanders, the originals having been torn down in 1792 by

French soldiers. Entrance includes admission to the Gotische Zaal and Brugse Vrije.

Basiliek van het Heilig Bloed CHURCH

(Basilica of the Holy Blood; Map p90; ☑ 050 33 67 92; www.holyblood.com; Burg 13; €2; ☉ 9.30am-noon & 2-5pm, closed Wed afternoons mid-Nov–Mar) The western end of the stadhuis (p88) morphs into the Basiliek van het Heilig Bloed. The basilica takes its name from a phial supposedly containing a few drops of Christ's blood that was brought here after the 12th-century Crusades. The right-hand door leads upstairs to a colourfully adorned chapel where the relic is hidden behind a flamboyant silver tabernacle and brought out for pious veneration at 2pm daily.

Also upstairs is the basilica's one-room treasury, where you'll see the jewel-studded reliquary in which the phial is mounted on Ascension Day for Bruges' biggest annual parade, the Heilig-Bloedprocessie (p94). Downstairs, entered via a different door, is the basilica's contrasting bare-stone 12th-century Romanesque chapel, a meditative place that's almost devoid of decoration.

Brugse Vrije HISTORIC BUILDING

(Liberty of Bruges; Map p90; ☑ 050 44 87 11; Burg 11a; €6; ☉ 9.30am-noon & 1.30-5pm) Eye-catching with its early baroque gables, gilt highlights and golden statuettes, this was once the seat of the 'Liberty of Bruges', the large autonomous territory and administrative body that ruled from Bruges (1121–1794). Much of the building is still used for city offices, but you can visit the former aldermen's room, the **Renaissancezaal**, to admire its remarkable 1531 carved chimney piece. Admission also includes entry to the stadhuis.

Above a black-marble fireplace and alabaster frieze, an incredibly detailed oak carving depicts a sword-waving Emperor Charles V. Charles is flanked by his grandfathers, Ferdinand of Aragon and Maximilian of Austria, both of whom sport extremely flattering codpieces.

◉ Central Canal Area

★ **Groeningemuseum** GALLERY

(Map p90; ☑ 050 44 87 11; www.visitbruges.be/en/groeningemuseum-groeninge-museum; Dijver 12; adult/concession/under 18yr €12/10/free; ☉ 9.30am-5pm Tue-Sun) Bruges' most celebrated art gallery boasts an astonishingly rich collection that's strong in superb Flemish Primitive and Renaissance works, depicting the conspicuous wealth of the city with glittering realistic artistry. Meditative works include Jan Van Eyck's radiant masterpiece *Madonna with Canon Van der Paele* (1436) and the *Madonna Crowned by Angels* (1482) by the Master of the Embroidered Foliage, where the rich fabric of the Madonna's robe meets the 'real' foliage at her feet with exquisite detail.

★ **Museum Sint-Janshospitaal** MUSEUM
(Memlingmuseum; Map p90; ☎ 050 44 87 43; www.visitbruges.be/en/sint-janshospitaal-saint-johns-hospital; Mariastraat 38; adult/concession/under 18yr €12/10/free; ☉ 9.30am-5pm Tue-Sun) In the restored chapel of a 12th-century hospital building with superb timber beamwork, this museum shows various torturous-looking medical implements, hospital sedan chairs and a gruesome 1679 painting of an anatomy class. But it's much better known for its six masterpieces by 15th-century artist Hans Memling, including the enchanting reliquary of St Ursula. This gilded oak reliquary looks like a miniature Gothic cathedral, painted with scenes from the life of St Ursula, including highly realistic Cologne cityscapes.

Onze-Lieve-Vrouwekerk CHURCH
(Church of Our Lady; Map p90; Mariastraat; adult/concession/under 18yr €6/5/free; ☉ 9.30am-5pm Mon-Sat, from 1.30pm Sun) **FREE** Dominating its surrounds, this 13th-century church was reopened in 2015 after extensive renovations. Its enormous 115m spire is unmissable throughout much of the city. Inside, it's best known for Michelangelo's serenely contemplative 1504 *Madonna and Child* statue, the only such work by Michelangelo to leave Italy during the artist's lifetime. Look out also for the *Adoration of the Shepherds* by Pieter Pourbus.

In the church's apse, the treasury section displays some splendid 15th- and 16th-century artworks plus the fine stone-and-bronze tombs of Charles the Bold (Karel de Stoute) and his daughter, Mary of Burgundy, whose pivotal marriage dragged the Low Countries into the Habsburg empire with far-reaching consequences.

Brouwerij De Halve Maan BREWERY
(Map p90; ☎ 050 33 26 97; www.halvemaan.be; Walplein 26; ☉ 10.30am-6pm, closed mid-Jan) **FREE** Founded in 1856, though there has been a brewery on the site since 1564, this is the last family *brouwerij* (brewhouse)

LINGER & LEARN

Bruges vies to keep tourists in town a little longer by offering slick, multisensory museums on some of Belgium's best-known industries:

Brewing – **The Beer Experience** (Map p90; ☎ 050 69 92 29; www.bruges-beermuseum.com; Breidelstraat 3; with/without 3 tastings €12/8; ☉ 10am-6pm)

Chocolate making – **Choco-Story** (Map p90; ☎ 050 61 22 37; www.choco-story.be; Wijnzakstraat 2, Sint-Jansplein; adult/child €8/5; ☉ 10am-5pm) – last praline demonstration at 4.45pm

Chip frying – **Frietmuseum** (Map p90; ☎ 050 34 01 50; www.frietmuseum.be; Vlamingstraat 33; adult/concession/child €7/6/5; ☉ 10am-5pm, closed Christmas to mid-Jan)

Diamond cutting – **Diamantmuseum** (Diamond Museum; Map p90; ☎ 050 34 20 56; www.diamondmuseum.be; Katelijnestraat 43; adult/senior/student €8/7/7, combined ticket with Choco-Story €14; ☉ 10.30am-5.30pm) – polishing demonstrations at 12.15pm and 3.15pm cost €3 extra.

in central Bruges. Multilingual 45-minute guided visits (€8; 11am to 4pm, to 5pm Saturday) depart on the hour. These include a tasting but can sometimes be rather crowded. Alternatively, you can simply sip one of their excellent *Brugse Zot* (Bruges Fool, 7%) or *Straffe Hendrik* (Strong Henry, 9%) beers in the appealing brewery *café*.

Arentshuis GALLERY
(Map p90; ☎ 050 44 87 11; Dijver 16; adult/concession/child €4/3/free; ☉ 9.30am-5pm Tue-Sun) This stately 18th-century patrician house displays the powerful paintings and dark-hued etchings of Frank Brangwyn (1867–1956), a Bruges-born artist of Welsh parentage. His images of WWI – he was an official war artist – are particularly powerful. Admission is free with your Groeningemuseum ticket.

Hof Arents PARK
(Map p90; ☉ 7am-10pm Apr-Sep, to 9pm Oct-Mar) Behind the Arentshuis, Hof Arents is a charming little park where a hump-backed pedestrian bridge, **St-Bonifacius-brug** (Map p90), crosses the canal for idyllic views. Nicknamed Lovers' Bridge, it's where many a Bruges citizen steals their first kiss.

Bruges Centre

BRUGES, GHENT & NORTHWEST BELGIUM

N
200 m
0.1 miles

Markt

Burg

Belfort

Peperstr
De Damhouderstr
Langestr
Molenmeers
Predikherenstr
St-Annarei Verversdijk
Hoogstr
Groenerei
Blekersstr
Sint-str
Hoornstr
Boomgaardstr
Kandelaarstr
Peerdenstr
Hertsbergestr
Meestr
Braambergstr
Steenhouwersdijk
Vismarkt
Krom Genthof
Golden Handrei
Oosterlingenplein
Torenbrug
Spinolarei
Spiegelrei
Jan Van Eyckplein
Koningstr
Engelsestr
St-Maartensplein
Ridderstr
St-Jansstr
St-Walburgastr
Twijnstr
Kelkstr
Mallebergplaats
Burgstr
Breidelstr
Blinde Ezelstr
Genthof
Woensdagmarkt
Biskajersplein
Spanjaardstr
Rode Haanstr
Academiestr
Wijnzakstr
B Ostenstr
Wapenmakersstr
St-Janssstr
St-Jansplein
Philipstockstr
Garre
Kipstr
Kraanrei
Kraanplein
Cordoeaniersstr
Ieperstr
Vlamingstr
Stadsschouwburg Bus Stop
Ejermarkt
Geernaartstr
Kortewinkel
Augustijnenrei
Jan Miraelstr
St-Jorisstr
Pieter Pourbusstr
Grauwwerkersstr
Naaldenstr
Kuipersstr
J Van Oostr
A Willaertstr
Niklaasstr
Desparsstr
St-Amandsstr
Kleine St-Amandsstr
Geldmuntstr
Zakske
Ezelstr
St-Jakobsstr
Boterhuis
Pandreitje
Palmstr
Muntplein
Muntpoort
Prinsenhof
Ontvangersstr
Geerwijnstr
Moerstr
Siedestr
Groenestr
Raamstr
Rozendal
Leeuwstr
Oude Zak
Beenhouwersstr
Potterierei
Steenhouwersdijk
Braambergstr

Markt (Historium) InfoKantoor

Sights and numbered points:
60, 69, 24, 25, 36, 29, 35, 74, 26, 54, 48, 9, 20, 7, 2, 23, 1, 15, 58, 53, 4, 18, 64, 57, 17, 11, 67, 73, 72, 78, 80, 40, 43, 59, 70, 63, 47, 30, 42

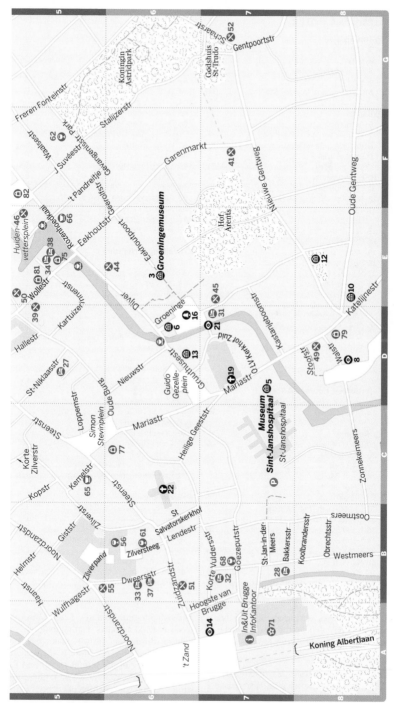

Koning Albertlaan

Bruges Centre

◎ Top Sights

◎ Sights

◎ Activities, Courses & Tours

◎ Sleeping

◎ Eating

◎ Drinking & Nightlife

◎ Entertainment

◎ Shopping

Privileged guests staying at the Guesthouse Nuit Blanche (p95) get the moonlit scene all to themselves once the park has closed.

Lumina Domestica　　　　　　MUSEUM
(Domestic Lamp Museum; Map p90; ☑ 050 61 22 37; www.luminadomestica.be; Wijnzakstraat 2, Sint-Jansplein; adult/child €7/5; ☺10am-5pm)

The enlightening Domestic Lamp Museum has over 6500 artefacts relating to domestic lighting throughout history, making it the largest collection of its kind. It sheds light on the history of the humble lamp and illuminates one's awareness about the consumption and conservation of energy.

St-Salvatorskathedraal CATHEDRAL
(Map p90; ☑ 050 33 68 41; Sint-Salvatorskoor-
straat 8; treasury adult/child €2/1; ⊙ 2-5.45pm
Mon, 9am-noon & 2-5.45pm Tue-Fri, 9am-noon
& 2-3.30pm Sat & Sun, treasury 2-5pm Sun-Fri)
Stacked sub-towers top the massive central
tower of 13th-century St Saviour's Cathedral.
In daylight the construction looks somewhat
dour, but once floodlit at night, it takes on
a mesmerising fascination. The cathedral's
interior is vastly high but feels oddly plain
despite a selection of antique tapestries. Beneath the tower, a glass floor reveals some
painted graves, and there's a passingly interesting **treasury** displaying 15th-century
brasses and a 1559 triptych by Dirk Bouts.

Gruuthusemuseum MUSEUM
(Map p90; ☑ 050 44 87 43; Dijver 17; adult/conces-
sion €8/6; ⊙ 9.30am-5pm Tue-Sun) The museum takes its name from the flower-and-herb
mixture *(gruut)* that used to flavour beer
before the cultivation of hops. The romantic heraldic entrance in a courtyard of ivy-
covered walls and dreaming spires is arguably
more interesting than the rambling, somewhat unsatisfying decorative-arts exhibits
within. The unusual view from the upstairs
oratory window into the treasury-apse of the
Onze-Lieve-Vrouwekerk (p89) is worth a look.
The museum is closed for major renovations;
it's scheduled to reopen in August 2019.

Godshuis St-Jozef &
De Meulenaere HISTORIC BUILDING
(Map p90; Nieuwe Gentweg 24; ⊙ 10am-4pm)
FREE The Godshuis St-Jozef and De Meu-
lenaere almshouses offer one of the city's
best oases of calm; enter via the green door.

Huis Ter Beurze NOTABLE BUILDING
(Former Stock Exchange; Map p90; ☑ 050 33 33
83; Vlamingstraat 35) It's believed that the
world's first stock exchange began in and
around this 13th-century house. It's not
open to the public, but the space is used for
special events and functions.

◎ Begijnhof Area

This idyllic area backs onto **Minnewater**
(Map p86), now known in English as the
'Lake of Love' but originally a dock during
Bruges' medieval heyday.

★**Begijnhof** HISTORIC BUILDING
(Map p86; Wijngaardstraat; ⊙ 6.30am-6.30pm)
FREE Bruges' delightful *begijnhof* dates
from the 13th century. Despite the hordes

of summer tourists, remains a remarkably
tranquil haven. Outside the 1776 gateway
bridge lies a tempting (if predictably tourist-
priced) array of terraced restaurants, lace
shops and waffle peddlers. Just inside the
main entrance, Ten Wijngaarde is an endearing little four-room museum.

Godshuis de Vos HISTORIC BUILDING
(Map p86; Noordstraat 2-8) Historical almshouse built in 1713.

Gentpoort HISTORIC BUILDING
(Map p86; ☑ 050 44 87 11; www.visitbruges.be/en/
gentpoort-gate-of-ghent; Gentpoortvest; adult/child/
under 18yr €4/3/free; ⊙ 9.30am-12.30pm & 1.30-
5pm) One of Bruges' four remaining city gates
now houses a local history museum.

◎ St-Anna & Dampoort Areas

Jeruzalemkerk CHURCH
(Map p86; ☑ 050 33 88 83; www.adornes.org/en;
Peperstraat 3; adult/concession €7/3.50; ⊙ church
& museum 10am-5pm Mon-Sat) Within the
so-called **Adornesdomein** estate is one of
Bruges' oddest churches, the 15th-century
Jeruzalemkerk, built by the Adornes family.
Supposedly based upon Jerusalem's Church
of the Holy Sepulchre, it's a macabre monument with a gruesome altarpiece covered in
skull motifs and an effigy of Christ's corpse
tucked away in the rear mini-chapel. The entry price includes admission to a small museum occupying several of the estate's pretty
almshouses.

The estate, dating from 1429, remains in
the ownership of the Adornes family. The
Count and Countess Maximilien de Limburg
Stirum are the seventeenth generation of descendants of Anselm Adornes, whose heart
is enshrined in a black-marble tomb in the
church – presumably the only remains that
were able to be returned to Bruges after he
was murdered in Scotland in 1483.

Kantcentrum MUSEUM
(Lace Centre; Map p86; ☑ 050 33 00 72; http://
kantcentrum.eu; Balstraat 16; adult/child €5/4;
⊙ 10am-5pm) The Kantcentrum displays a
collection of lace in a row of interlinked old
cottages. In the afternoons (2pm to 5pm)
you can watch bobbin lace being made by
informal gatherings of experienced lace-
makers and their students who gather to
chat and work here. Once you've seen how
intricate the process is, you'll swiftly understand why handmade lace is so expensive; a
small piece costs €10.

DON'T MISS

ALL ABOARD: BRUGES BY WATER

The must-do activity in Bruges is to see the city by water on 30-minute **canal boat tours** (adult/child €8/4; ⊙10am-6pm Mar–mid-Nov) that depart roughly every 20 minutes from jetties south of the Burg, notably Rozenhoedkaai and Dijver. Regulated by the city, all operators do the same loop for the same price and boats are all of similar quality. You might need to queue for up to 15 minutes.

Also popular, if over-rated, is riding the paddle-steamer **Lamme Goedzak** (☑050 28 86 10; www.bootdamme-brugge.be; Noorweegse Kaai 31; adult/child one-way €8.50/6, return €10.50/9.50; ⊙10am-5pm Easter–mid-Oct) to Damme, a lazy 35-minute canal trip departing every two hours from a point 800m northwest of Dampoort (bus 4 from the Markt).

OLV-ter-Potterie   MUSEUM
(Our Lady of the Pottery; Map p86; ☑050 44 87 43; www.visitbruges.be/en/onze-lieve-vrouw-ter-potterie-our-lady-of-the-pottery; Potterierei 79; adult/concession/under 18yr €6/5/free; ⊙9.30am-12.30pm & 1.30-5pm) Admission to this small historical church-hospital complex is free with a St-Janshospitaal (p89) museum ticket. Ring the bell to gain entry and you'll find fine 15th- to 16th-century art. The lushly baroque church section houses the reliquary of St-Idesbaldus and a polychrome wooden relief of Mary breastfeeding baby Jesus. In more prudish later centuries, the Virgin's nipple received a lacy camouflage, rendering the scene bizarrely impractical.

Volkskundemuseum   MUSEUM
(Museum of Folk Life; Map p86; ☑050 44 87 43; www.visitbruges.be/en/volkskundemuseum-folklore-museum; Balstraat 43; adult/concession/under 18yr €6/5/free; ⊙9.30am-5pm Tue-Sun) This appealing Museum of Folk Life presents visitors with 18 themed tableaux illustrating Flemish life in times gone by – a 1930s sweets shop, a hatter's workshop, a traditional kitchen and more. The museum is a static affair, but it's in an attractive *godshuis* (almshouse), and the time-warp museum *café* De Zwarte Kat (p98) has a fine selection of beer. Temporary exhibits upstairs are often worth a look. Traditional lollies are made here on the first and third Thursday of the month.

Koeleweimolen   WINDMILL
(Map p86; ☑050 44 87 43; Kruisvest 11; adult/concession €3/2; ⊙9.30am-12.30pm & 1.30-5pm Tue-Sun Jul & Aug) In the 13th century, Bruges' great walls were dotted with *molens* (windmills) where cereals were ground into flour – at one time 25 ringed the city. Today, four stand on the eastern banks and can be visited. This one, dating from the 1760s, was moved to its present location in 1996 and still functions as a mill. The other is the

18th-century **St-Janshuismolen** (Map p86; ☑050 44 87 43; Kruisvest 3; adult/concession/under 18 €4/3/free; ⊙9.30am-12.30pm & 1.30-5pm Tue-Sun May-Sep), still in its original location. Each houses a small museum.

🧭 Tours

Half-hour **horse-carriage tours** depart from the Markt and include a brief pit stop at the *begijnhof*. In summer, jumping aboard around 6pm means quieter streets and hopefully you'll see Bruges' buildings glowing golden in the sun's late rays. The price (€50 for up to five people) is set by the city; attempts at haggling won't go down well. Conversely, don't pay a cent more.

For highly lauded 'free' (ie tips only) **walking tours**, sign up online with **Legends** (Map p90; ☑0472 26 87 15; www.legendstours.be/walking-tours-bruges; Markt) **FREE** then look for the red umbrella on Markt at the alotted time. They also offer pub crawls and tours.

Quasimundo   CYCLING
(Map p90; ☑050 33 07 75; www.quasimundo.eu; Predikherenstraat 28; adult/student €28/26; ⊙Mar-Oct) Guided bicycle tours around Bruges (2½ hours, morning) or via Damme to the Dutch border (four hours, afternoons). Bike rental included. Book ahead.

Quasimodo   BUS
(Map p86; ☑050 37 04 70; www.quasimodo.be; Veldmaarschalk Fochstraat 69; under/over 26yr €55/65) Quasimodo runs minibus Triple Treat tours that visit a selection of castles plus the fascinating WWII coastal defences near Ostend. Its Flanders Fields tour visits the Ypres Salient.

✪ Festivals & Events

The main folkloric festivals are the **Heilig-Bloedprocessie** (www.holyblood.com; ⊙Ascension Day), and every fifth year, the

Pageant of the Golden Tree (Gouden Booms-toet), next due in 2022.

🛏 Sleeping

🛏 Central Bruges

Hostel Lybeer HOSTEL **€**
(Map p90; ☑ 050 33 43 55; www.hostellybeer.com; Korte Vuldersstraat 31; dm from €26, s/d without bathroom €42/74; @ 🛜) The Lybeer once had plenty of tatty edginess to it, but has recently been tastefully renovated. It's handily central in a typical Bruges terraced house and has a large and convivial sitting and dining room.

★B&B Dieltiens B&B **€€**
(Map p90; ☑ 050 33 42 94; www.bedandbreakfast bruges.be; Waalsestraat 40; s/d/tr from €70/80/90; 🛜) Old and new art fills this lovingly restored classical mansion, which remains an appealing real home run by charming musician hosts. Superbly central yet quiet. It also operates a holiday flat (from €75 per night) nearby in a 17th-century house.

Baert B&B B&B **€€**
(Map p90; ☑ 050 33 05 30; www.bedandbreakfast brugge.be; Westmeers 28; s/d from €80/90; 🛜) In a 1613 former stable, this is one of very few places in Bruges where you'll get a private canal-side terrace (flower-decked, though not on the loveliest canal section). Floral rooms have bathrooms across the landing; bathrobes are provided. A big breakfast spread is served in an enclosed glass verandah; extras include a welcome drink and a pack of chocolates.

★B&B SintNik B&B **€€**
(Map p90; ☑ 050 61 03 08; www.sintnik.be; St-Niklaasstraat 18; s/d from €125/135; 🛜) Room 1 has a claw-foot bath and antique glass panel, but it's the other two rooms' remarkable Pisa-like belfry views that make this welcoming B&B so special and popular.

Hotel Bla Bla HOTEL **€€**
(Map p90; ☑ 050 33 90 14; www.hotelblabla.com; Dweersstraat 24; s/d incl breakfast from €85/95; 🛜) A shuttered and step-gabled building given an elegant makeover, with parquet floors, modern artworks and soothingly pale rooms. Excellent buffet breakfast.

Hotel Patritius HOTEL **€€**
(Map p90; ☑ 050 33 84 54; www.hotelpatritius.be; Riddersstraat 11; r incl breakfast from €98; P ❄ 🛜)

Enter this proud 1830s townhouse through the carriageway and past a bar-lounge. Up the historical spiral staircase, 16 guest rooms vary in size and style; some have exposed beams, others are mildly chintzy and some are renovated in a bolder style (albeit with oddly kitschy dog portraiture). There's a decent breakfast and pretty garden. Parking costs extra.

Passage Bruges HOSTEL **€€**
(Map p90; ☑ 050 34 02 32; www.passagebruges.com; Dweersstraat 26-28; d/tr from €64/98; 🛜) This small private hostel has spartan but stylish, large and well-priced private rooms (no dorms). Rooms have shared bathrooms. Its located above its namesake **Gran Kaffee De Passage** (Map p90; mains €10-18; ⊙ 5-11pm Tue-Thu & Sun, noon-11pm Fri & Sat), an invitingly old-fashioned cafe-restaurant.

B&B Setola B&B **€€**
(Map p90; ☑ 050 33 49 77; www.bedandbreakfast-bruges.com; St-Walburgastraat 12; d from €75; ➔🛜) Pleasant and very central, with three neat and attractive pine-floored rooms arranged around a guest kitchen. The Orange Room has A-frame beams and two ladder-accessible extra beds.

Hotel Bourgoensch Hof HOTEL **€€**
(Map p90; ☑ 050 33 16 45; www.belforthotels.com; Wollestraat 39; standard/canal-view from €125/150; 🛜) This historical hotel with recently updated rooms boasts a central location and one of the most spectacular canal views in Bruges.

★Guesthouse Nuit Blanche B&B **€€€**
(Map p90; ☑ 0494 40 04 47; www.bb-nuitblanche.com; Groeninge 2; d from €185; P ❄ 🛜) Pay what you like, nowhere else in Bruges can get you a more romantic location than this fabulous B&B, which started life as a 15th-century tannery. It oozes history, retaining original Gothic fireplaces, stained-glass roundels and some historical furniture, while bathrooms and beds are luxury-hotel standard.

Room rates cover the bottle of bubbly in your minibar. Drink it in the fabulous canal-side garden or on 'Lovers' Bridge' in Hof Arents (p89), to which the guesthouse has a unique private entrance.

★Relais Bourgondisch Cruyce BOUTIQUE HOTEL **€€€**
(Map p90; ☑ 050 33 79 26; www.relaisbourgondisch cruyce.be; Wollestraat 41-47; d from €245; P ❄ 🛜) This luxurious little boutique hotel occupies

a part-timbered medieval house that's been tastefully updated and graced with art, antiques, Persian carpets and fresh orchids. A special delight is relaxing in the canal-side lounge while envious tourists cruise past on their barge tours.

Most of the 16 rooms are somewhat small but full of designer fittings, including top-quality Vispring beds, Ralph Lauren fabrics and (in some) Philippe Starck bathrooms.

Côté Canal-Huyze Hertsberge　B&B €€€
(Map p90; ☎050 33 35 42; www.brugesbedandbreakfast.be; Hertsbergestraat 8; d from €165; ☺☎) Very spacious and oozing good taste, this late-17th-century house has a gorgeous period salon decked out with antiques and sepia photos of the charming owner's great-great-grandparents (who moved in here in 1901). The four guest rooms are comfortably grand, each with at least partial views of the tranquil little canal-side garden.

Dukes' Palace　LUXURY HOTEL €€€
(Map p90; ☎050 44 78 88; www.hoteldukespalace.com; Prinsenhof 8; d from €143; P☎⛲) This large-scale five-star hotel is imposingly tall with a Disneyesque turret. It partly occupies the Prinsenhof building, Bruges' 15th-century royal palace where Phillip III of Burgundy created the chivalric Order of the Golden Fleece in 1430. It was largely rebuilt in 2008 – some guest rooms retain historical elements, and the decor creates a timeless feel.

Number 11　B&B €€€
(Map p90; ☎050 33 06 75; www.number11.be; Peerdenstraat 11; d from €150; ☎) Featuring the distinctive ceramic works of Martine Bossuyt, pralines on the pillow, and logoed linens, this top-notch artistic B&B feels like an intimate boutique hotel. There's a private salon and courtyard garden for the handful of guests.

🛏 Beginhof Area

't Keizershof　HOTEL €
(Map p86; ☎050 33 87 28; www.hotelkeizershof.be; Oostmeers 126; s/d incl breakfast from €45/50; P☎) Remarkably tasteful and well kept for this price, this hotel's seven simple rooms with shared bathrooms are above a former brasserie-cafe decorated with old radios (now used as the breakfast room). Free parking.

🛏 St-Anna & Dampoort Areas

Bauhaus　HOSTEL €
(St Christopher's Hostel; Map p86; ☎050 34 10 93; www.bauhaus.be; Langestraat 133-137; dm/d from €21/39; @☎) One of Belgium's most popular hang-outs for young travellers, this backpacker village incorporates a hostel, apartments, a nightclub, internet cafe and a little chill-out room that's well hidden behind the reception and laundrette section at Langestraat 145. Simple and slightly cramped dorms are operated with key cards; hotel-section double rooms have private shower cubicles. Bike hire is also available.

Smarter 'pod' dorms have better bunks with curtains and reading lamps. Take bus 6 or 16 from the train station (p102).

B&B Yasmine　B&B €€
(Map p86; ☎050 68 70 32; www.gallery-yasmine.be; Langestraat 30-32; s/d €85/95; ☎) The amazing location, budget prices and warm welcome at this self-styled gallery and B&B make it a winner. The super-generous breakfast includes pancakes.

B&B Marjan Degraeve　B&B €€
(Map p86; ☎050 34 57 11; www.bedandbreakfastmarjandegraeve.be; Kazernevest 32; s/d from €55/65; ⊙closed Feb; P☺☎) Two remarkably eccentric guest rooms with private bathrooms are overloaded with religious trinkets and all manner of arty bits and pieces. The house has a pleasant if slightly out-of-centre location. Bicycle rental is available and you'll find homemade wine and beer in your in-room fridge. Parking is available (€8).

🛏 Around Bruges

Camping Memling　CAMPGROUND €
(☎050 35 58 45; www.campingmemling.be; Veltemweg 109; sites €26-32; ⊙year-round; ☎) Quiet campground in St-Kruis where pitch prices assume two adults. Get off bus 11 at Vossensteert and walk back 400m towards Bruges.

✖ Eating

✖ Central Bruges

★**Den Gouden Karpel**　SEAFOOD €
(Map p90; ☎050 33 33 89; www.dengoudenkarpel.be; Vismarkt 9-11; dishes from €4; ⊙11am-6pm Tue-Sat) Take away or eat in, this sleek little *café/bar* is a great location for a jumpingly fresh

seafood lunch, right by the **fish market** (Map p90; Vismarkt; ⊘7am-1pm Tue-Fri). Crab sandwiches, smoked salmon salads, shrimp croquettes and oysters are on the menu.

Soup
SOUP €

(Map p90; Hallestraat 4; soups from €6.50; ⊘11am-3.30pm Thu-Tue) As the name suggests, Soup does soup well – it's a great little find for a healthy, hearty meal that's quick and easy and won't break the bank.

Marco Polo Noodle Bar
NOODLES €

(Map p90; ✎050 73 42 85; www.marco-polo-noodles.com; Katelijnestraat 29; noodle soups €9-14; ⊘noon-3.30pm & 5-9.30pm) You can't beat this always-cramped little noodle bar for its wide range of Asian flavours, from pho to ramen and dumplings too. Great value. It's just outside the centre.

Patisserie Schaeverbeke
PASTRIES €

(Map p90; ✎050 33 31 82; www.schaeverbeke.be; Schaarstraat 2; pastries from €2; ⊘7.30am-7pm Fri-Wed) This splendid little patisserie is piled with creamy fruity cakes, croissants and fresh fragrant bread.

Happy House
CHINESE €

(Map p90; ✎050 33 65 31; Geldmuntstraat 30; dishes €6-18; ⊘noon-8pm) If you're travelling on a budget and don't mind eating al fresco, this tidy takeaway joint has decent-sized portions of westernised Chinese dishes at non-tourist-trap prices. There are a few stools and a counter inside, but no real seating.

★ Lieven
BELGIAN €€

(Map p90; ✎050 68 09 75; www.etenbijlieven.be; Philipstockstraat 45; mains €22-34; ⊘noon-10pm Tue-Sun) You'll need to book ahead for a table at this extremely popular, excellent-value Belgian bistro. It works wonders with local ingredients, and is recognised by its peers from around the country. Simple food done well in a trendy but relaxed environment.

★ De Stove
INTERNATIONAL €€

(Map p90; ✎050 33 78 35; www.restaurantdestove. be; Kleine St-Amandsstraat 4; menu without/with wine €51/69; ⊘7-9pm Fri-Tue, plus noon-1.30pm Sun) Having just 20 seats keeps this gem intimate. Fish caught daily is the house speciality, but the monthly changing menu also includes the likes of wild boar fillet on oyster mushrooms. Everything, from the bread to the ice cream, is homemade. Despite perennially rave reviews, this calm one-room family restaurant remains friendly, reliable and inventive, without a hint of tourist-tweeness.

That's Toast
BREAKFAST €

(Map p90; ✎050 68 82 27; Dweersstraat 4; breakfasts €6-18; ⊘8.30am-4pm Wed-Sun) Bruges' best breakfast restaurant has already gained a following with locals and visitors for its all-day breakfasts including everything from eggs and waffles to tea and toast.

Bistro Arthies
BISTRO €€

(Map p90; ✎050 33 43 13; www.arthies.be; Wollestraat 10; mains €17-24; ⊘noon-10pm Wed-Mon; ✎) Managed by Arthies – an interior designer who looks like a dashingly gothic Billy Connolly. He uses a projected clock, giant black flower bowls and stylishly wacky lamps to create an ambience that's eccentric yet fashion-conscious. Meals are hearty; the menu features beef (steak and stew), pork (ribs and ham hock), chicken, fish and vegetarian options.

Opus Latino
TAPAS €€

(Map p90; ✎050 33 97 46; Burg 15; tapas €5-12, pasta €11-18; ⊘11am-10pm) Modernist *café* with weather-worn terrace tables right at the waterside, where a canal dead-ends beside a Buddha-head fountain. Access is via the easily missed shopping passage that links Wollestraat to Burg (p88), emerging near the Basilica of the Holy Blood (p88). Serves tapas, pastas and pizzas, as well as more substantial fare.

IN BRUGES

'Maybe that's what hell is – the entire rest of eternity spent in Bruges.' The city hit the big screen when the 2008 Sundance Film Festival premiered the action-comedy *In Bruges*. Written and directed by Irish playwright Martin McDonagh, it stars Colin Farrell and Brendan Gleeson, who play hitmen ordered by their boss (Ralph Fiennes) to hide out in Bruges during the pre-Christmas frenzy. The tagline 'Shoot first, sightsee later' gives you an idea of the plot – made more bizarre by encounters with a string of surreal Felliniesque characters. It's peppered with hilariously obscene, aggressive and un-PC invective about the quaintly pretty city which, to their credit, the people of Bruges seem to find as funny as everyone else.

BRUGES, GHENT & NORTHWEST BELGIUM BRUGES

De Bottelier
MEDITERRANEAN €€

(Map p90; ☑ 050 33 18 60; www.debottelier.com; St-Jakobsstraat 63; mains €15-23; ☺noon-10pm Tue-Fri, 7-10pm Sat) Decorated with hats and old clocks, this adorable little restaurant sits above a wine shop overlooking a delightful canal-side garden. Diners are predominantly local. Reservations are wise.

't Gulden Vlies
BELGIAN €€

(Map p90; ☑ 050 33 47 09; www.tguldenvlies. be; Mallebergplaats 17; mains €14-28; ☺7-11pm Wed-Sat) Intimate late-night restaurant with old-fashioned decor and good-value Belgian cuisine.

Chagall
BELGIAN €€

(Map p90; ☑ 050 33 61 12; www.restaurantchagall. be; St-Amandsstraat 40; mains €20-29; ☺noon-9pm Thu-Tue) Checked olive banquettes, candles, an upright piano and shelves cluttered with knick-knacks make you feel like you're dining in a family home. Seafood, including several variations on eel, is Chagall's forte, but it also does daily meat specials and good deals on two- and three-course menus.

Den Gouden Harynck
INTERNATIONAL €€€

(Map p90; ☑ 050 33 76 37; www.goudenharynck. be; Groeninge 25; set lunch menu €45, midweek dinner €65, surprise menu €95; ☺noon-1.30pm & 7-8.30pm Tue-Fri, 7-8.30pm Sat) Behind an ivy-clad facade, this uncluttered Michelin-starred restaurant garners consistent praise and won't hurt the purse quite as se-

---

ⓘ LATE NIGHT, EARLY MORNING

If your stomach demands more than just chips or a kebab after 11pm, try the effortlessly elegant, open-kitchened restaurant **Christophe** (Map p90; ☑ 050 34 48 92; www.christophe-brugge.be; Garenmarkt 34; mains €19-32; ☺6pm-1am Thu-Mon), which serves until 1am.

Most of the restaurants that line the Markt (p87) offer breakfasts with a view from €8, but check carefully what's included before sitting down. If you just want coffee and a croissant, the cheapest deal is at chain bakery **Panos** (Map p90; Zuidzandstraat 29; pastries & sandwiches €2-7; ☺7am-6.30pm Mon-Sat, 11am-6.30pm Sun); its Zuidzandstraat branch opens early, has plenty of seating and, unlike many other Bruges bakeries, doesn't charge extra for eating in.

---

verely as certain better-known competitors. Its lovely location is both central and secluded. Exquisite dishes might include noisettes of venison topped with lardo and quince purée, or seed-crusted fillet of bream.

★Den Dyver
BELGIAN €€€

(Map p90; ☑ 050 33 60 69; www.dyver.be; Dijver 5; mains €23-47, tasting menu €45; ☺noon-2pm & 6.30-9.30pm Fri-Mon) Den Dyver is a pioneer of fine beer dining where you match the brew you drink with the one the chef used to create the sauce on your plate. This is no pub: beers come in wine glasses served on starched tablecloths in an atmosphere of Burgundian grandeur. The lunch menu includes *amuse-bouche,* nibbles and coffee.

Begijnhof Area

De Bron
VEGETARIAN €

(Map p86; ☑ 050 33 45 26; Katelijnestraat 82; snacks from €6; ☺11.45am-2pm Mon-Fri; 🖉) By the time this glass-roofed restaurant's doors open, a queue has usually formed outside, full of diners keen to get vegetarian fare direct from *de bron* (the source). Dishes are available in small, medium and large, and there are some delicious soups, such as pumpkin. Vegans are catered for on request.

★De Stoepa
BISTRO €€

(Map p86; ☑ 050 33 04 54; www.stoepa.be; Oostmeers 124; mains €12-26; ☺noon-2pm & 6pm-midnight Tue-Sat, noon-3pm & 6-11pm Sun) A gem of a place in a peaceful residential setting. It's got a slightly hippie/Buddhist ambience; oriental statues, terracotta-coloured walls, a metal stove and wooden floors and furniture give a homey but stylish feel. Best of all is the leafy terrace garden. Tuck into the upmarket bistro-style food.

St-Anna & Dampoort Areas

De Zwarte Kat
CAFE €

(Map p86; ☑ 050 44 87 43; Balstraat 43; light meals €7-12; ☺11.45am-2pm) This homely little *café* belonging to the Volkskundemuseum (p94) is a quaint spot for a light lunch, local beer or coffee and cake.

★Pomperlut
BELGIAN €€

(Map p86; ☑ 050 70 86 26; www.pomperlut.be; Minderbroedersstraat 26; mains €14-22; ☺6am-10pm Tue-Sat) Opposite the lovely Koningin Astridpark, with a fine outdoor terrace and a cosy dark-wooded interior, this popular bistro serves traditional Belgian food and beer. It has particularly friendly, welcoming staff.

Pro Deo
BELGIAN €€

(Map p86; ☑ 050 33 73 55; www.bistroprodeo.be; Langestraat 161; mains €17-29; ⏰ 11.45am-1.45pm & 6-9.30pm Tue-Fri, 6-10pm Sat) A snug and romantic restaurant in a 16th-century white-washed gabled building. The couple that owns it brings a personal touch, and serves up superb Belgian dishes such as *stoofvlees* (traditional stew).

In 't Nieuwe Museum
CAFE €€

(Map p86; ☑ 050 33 12 80; www.nieuw-museum.com; Hooistraat 42; mains €17-26; ⏰ 6-11pm Fri-Tue, plus 12.30-2.30pm Sun) So called because of the museum-like collection of brewery plaques, money boxes and other mementos of *café* life adorning the walls, this fami-ly-owned local favourite serves succulent meat cooked in a 17th-century open-fire oven. Specials include veggie burgers, eel dishes, ribs, steaks and creamy *vispannetje* (fish casserole).

Resto Ganzespel
BELGIAN €€

(Map p86; ☑ 050 33 12 33; www.ganzespel.be; Ganzenstraat 37; mains €12-21; ⏰ 6.30-10pm Sat & Sun) Providing a truly intimate eating experience in a lovely old gabled building, the owner serves classic Belgian dishes such as meatballs and *kalfsblanket* (veal in a creamy sauce), as well as pasta dishes. Upstairs are three idiosyncratic B&B guest rooms (doubles €55 to €85), one with a musical shower.

Sans Cravate
FRENCH €€€

(Map p86; ☑ 050 67 83 10; www.sanscravate.be; Langestraat 159; mains €38-42, menus €58-89; ⏰ noon-2pm & 7-9.30pm Tue-Fri, 7-9.30pm Sat) Bare brick walls, a modern fireplace and striking contemporary ceramics form a stage for this open-kitchened 'cooking theatre' that prides itself on its gastronomic French cuisine and fresh ingredients.

🍷 Drinking & Nightlife

★ Herberg Vlissinghe
CAFE

(Map p90; ☑ 050 34 37 37; www.cafevlissinghe.be; Blekerstraat 2; ⏰ 11am-10pm Wed-Sat, to 7pm Sun) Luminaries have frequented Bruges' oldest pub for 500 years; local legend has it that Rubens once painted an imitation coin on the table here and then did a runner. The interior is gorgeously preserved with wood panelling and a wood-burning stove, but in summer the best seats are in the shady garden where you can play boules.

Nice snacks such as croques, soup, and cheese and meat platters are available.

★ De Garre
PUB

(Map p90; ☑ 050 34 10 29; www.degarre.be; Garre 1; ⏰ noon-midnight Sun-Thu, noon-12.30am Fri, 11am-12.30am Sat) Try its Garre draught beer, which comes with a thick floral head in a glass that's almost a brandy balloon; the pub will only serve you three of these as they're 11% alcohol. The hidden two-floor *estaminet* (tavern) also stocks dozens of other fine Belgian brews, including the remarkable Stru-ise Pannepot (€3.50).

★ L'Estaminet
BROWN CAFE

(Map p90; ☑ 050 33 09 16; www.estaminet-brug-ge.be/en; Park 5; ⏰ noon-late) With its dark-timber beams, low lighting, convivial clat-ter and park setting, L'Estaminet scarcely seems to have changed since it opened in 1900. It's primarily a drinking spot, but also serves time-honoured dishes such as spa-ghetti bolognese with a baked cheese crust (€10). Summer sees its loyal local following flow out onto the front terrace.

't Klein Venetie
CAFE

(Map p90; ☑ 0475 72 52 25; www.kleinvenetie.be; Braambergstraat 1; ⏰ noon-midnight) Don't miss the superb canal view from outside this popular cafe. With the belfry (p93) towering above a perfect gaggle of medieval house-fronts, the view is lovely any time, but it's especially compelling at dusk as the flood-lights come on.

Rose Red
BAR

(Map p90; ☑ 050 33 90 51; www.cordoeanier.be/en/rosered.php; Cordoeaniersstraat 16; ⏰ 11am-11pm Tue-Sun) Outstanding beers from 50 of the best breweries in Belgium, served by charming and informative staff in this pink-hued and rose-scattered bar. There are five to six beers on tap and 150 bottles, or you can taste four beers for €10.

Snack on tapas-style dishes, including cheese produced by the Trappist monks of Chimay (from €3.50).

Merveilleux Tearoom
CAFE

(Map p90; ☑ 050 61 02 09; www.merveilleux.eu; Muntpoort 8; ⏰ 10am-6pm) An elegant marble-floored tearoom on a cobbled passage near the Markt (p87). Coffee comes with a dain-ty homemade biscuit and sometimes a little glass of strawberry ice cream or chocolate mousse. Pretty cakes and tea are on offer too. Mains €15 to €24; high tea €11.

Entrenous CLUB
(Map p86; ☑ 050 34 10 93; Langestraat 145; ⊗ 10pm-late Fri & Sat) A real nightclub in the centre of the city. A very youthful crowd packs out the DJ nights, gigs and after-parties.

De Republiek COCKTAIL BAR
(Map p90; ☑ 050 73 47 64; http://republiekbrugge. be; St-Jakobsstraat 36; ⊗ noon-1am Wed-Sun, from 5pm Mon-Tue) Set around a courtyard comprising characterful brick buildings, this big buzzing space is super-popular with Bruggelingen (Bruges locals). DJs hit the decks on Friday and Saturday nights. There's a long cocktail list, plus a range of well-priced meals (including vegetarian options) available until midnight.

't Brugs Beertje CAFE
(Map p90; ☑ 050 33 96 16; www.brugsbeertje.be; Kemelstraat 5; ⊗ 4pm-midnight Mon, Thu & Sun, to 1am Fri & Sat) Legendary throughout Bruges, Belgium and beyond for its hundreds of Belgian brews, this cosy *bruin café* (brown cafe) is filled with old advertising posters and locals who are part of the furniture. It's one of those perfect beer-bars with smoke-yellowed walls, enamel signs, hop-sprig ceilings and knowledgeable staff to help you choose from a book full of brews.

Du Phare TAVERNA
(Map p86; ☑ 050 34 35 90; www.duphare.be; Sasplein 2; ⊗ bar 11.30am-late, kitchen 11.30am-3pm & 6pm-midnight, closed Tue) Tucked into the remains of one of Bruges' original town gates, this off-the-beaten-track tavern is best known for its live blues and jazz sessions – check the website for dates. Bus 4 stops out the front. Serves up huge portions of couscous (and offers free bread, a rarity in Belgium).

Joey's bvba BAR
(Map p90; ☑ 050 34 12 64; Zuidzandstraat 16A; ⊗ 11.30am-late Mon-Sat) These days Joey's is run by Stevie, who performs with local band Cajun Moon; consequently, this dark, intimate bar is a gathering spot for Bruges' musos. You can sometimes catch live music here (call to check dates); chill out with a creamy Stevie cocktail or Joey's Tripel any time.

't Poatersgat PUB
(Map p90; ☑ 0495 22 68 50; Vlamingstraat 82; ⊗ 3pm-late) Look carefully for the concealed hole in the wall and follow the staircase down into this cross-vaulted cellar glowing with ethereal white lights and flickering candles. 't Poatersgat (which means 'the Monk's Hole') has 120 Belgian beers on the menu, including a smashing selection of Trappists.

Cafédraal BAR
(Map p90; ☑ 050 34 08 45; www.cafedraal.be; Zilverstraat 38; ⊗ 6pm-1am Tue-Thu, to 3am Fri & Sat) Attached to an upmarket seafood restaurant (mains €25 to €48), this remarkable cocktail bar is enclosed by beech hedges and red-brick gabled buildings. It displays bottles in gilt 'holy' niches. Suavely classy.

Uilenspiegel CAFE
(Map p90; ☑ 050 34 65 55; www.uilenspiegel brugge.be; Langestraat 2-4; ⊗ noon-10pm) For canal views it's hard to beat the seats outside Uilenspiegel.

De Windmolen PUB
(Map p86; ☑ 050 33 97 39; Carmersstraat 135; ⊗ 10am-10pm Mon-Thu, to 1am Fri-Sun) Quaint corner *café* with a sunny terrace overlooking one of the St-Anna windmills.

The Vintage PUB
(Map p90; ☑ 050 34 30 63; www.facebook.com/ TheVintageBrugge; Westmeers 13; ⊗ 11am-1am Thu-Tue) Unusually hip for Bruges, with a '60s/'70s vibe and a vintage Vespa hanging from the roof. The sunny terrace is a nice spot for a Jupiler, and the theme parties can be raucous.

Cambrinus PUB
(Map p90; ☑ 050 33 23 28; www.cambrinus.eu; Philipstockstraat 19; ⊗ 11am-11pm Sun-Thu, to late Fri & Sat) Hundreds of varieties of beer are available at this 17th-century sculpture-adorned brasserie-pub, as well as traditional Belgian and Italian-inspired snacks and meals.

☆ Entertainment

Bruges' nightlife area is centred just north of Markt (p87) on Kuipersstraat. **Cultuur-centrum Brugge** (Map p90; ☑ info 050 44 30 40, tickets 050 44 30 60; www.ccbrugge.be; Sint-Jakobsstraat 20) coordinates theatrical and concert events at several venues, including the 1869 theatre **Koninklijke Stadssc-houwburg** (Map p90; ☑ 050 44 30 60; www. ccbrugge.be; Vlamingstraat 29) and the out-of-centre **Magdalenazaal** (MaZ; ☑ 050 44 30 40; Magdalenastraat 27). Film buffs will enjoy **Cinema Lumière** (Map p90; ☑ 050 34 34 65; www.lumierecinema.be; St-Jakobsstraat 36b; ⊗ noon-11pm).

For the city's official event listings, visit www.visitbruges.be/events-2, or see what's on at youth culture centre Het Entrepot at www.hetentrepot.be.

★**Concertgebouw** CONCERT VENUE
(Map p90; ☑ 050 47 69 99; www.concertgebouw. be; Het Zand 34; ticket prices vary) Bruges' stunning 21st-century concert hall is the work of architects Paul Robbrecht and Hilde Daem. It takes its design cues from the city's three famous towers and red bricks. Theatre, classical music and dance performances are regularly staged. The tourist office (p102) is situated at street level.

Views from the 7th-floor Sound Factory are magnificent, though partly interrupted by vertical struts.

★**Cactus Muziekcentrum** LIVE MUSIC
(☑ 050 33 20 14; www.cactusmusic.be; Magdalenastraat 27) Though small, this is the city's top venue for contemporary and world music, hosting both live bands and international DJs. It also organises festivals including July's **Cactus Music Festival** (www.cactus festival.be; ☺ Jul), held in the Minnewater (p93) park at the southern edge of the old city.

🛍 **Shopping**

The main shopping thoroughfares are Steenstraat and Geldmuntstraat/Noordzandstraat, along with linking pedestrianised Zilverpand. There are morning markets on Wednesdays at Markt (p87) and Saturdays at **Het Zand** ('t Zand; Map p90).

Several shops offer a vast array of Belgian beers and their associated glasses to take away. Compare prices carefully and remember that 'standard' brews such as Leffe or Chimay will generally be far cheaper in supermarkets.

★**Chocolate Line** FOOD
(Map p90; ☑ 050 82 01 26; www.thechocolateline. be; Simon Stevinplein 19; per kg €50; ☺ 10am-6pm) Bruges has 50 chocolate shops, but just five where chocolates are handmade on the premises. Of those, the Chocolate Line is the brightest and best. Wildly experimental flavours by 'shock-o-latier' Dominique Persoone include bitter Coca-Cola, Cuban cigar, wasabi, and black olive, tomato and basil. It also sells pots of chocolate body paint, complete with a brush.

SATANIC SUNDAYS?

A former Masonic lodge, **Retsin's Lucifernum** (Map p90; ☑ 0476 35 06 51; www.lucifernum.be; Twijnstraat 6-8; admission incl drink €10; ☺ 8-11pm Sun) is owned by a self-proclaimed vampire. Ring the bell on a Sunday night, pass the voodoo temple and hope you're invited inside, where you might be serenaded with live Latin music and an otherworldly candlelit bar may be serving potent rum cocktails. It's always a surprise. Don't miss the graves in the tropical garden.

The permanent scaffolding is an artwork – and a thorn in the side of the local council.

★**De Striep** COMICS
(Map p90; ☑ 050 33 71 12; www.striepclub.be; Katelijnestraat 42; ☺ 10am-12.30pm & 1.30-7pm Tue-Sat, 2-6pm Sun) Look for Thibaut Vandorselaer's wonderful illustrated guides at this colourful comic shop. There's also a comprehensive collection of comics and graphic novels in Dutch, French and English. You'll find Bruges-set comics by the counter.

De Reyghere Reisboekhandel BOOKS
(Map p90; ☑ 050 33 34 03; www.reisboekhandel. be; Markt 13; ☺ 9.30am-noon Tue-Sat & 2-6pm Mon-Sat) This fabulously well-stocked travel bookshop is an extension of **De Reyghere Boekhandel** next door: it's been in the same family for generations. Past shoppers include Albert Einstein.

Bacchus Cornelius FOOD & DRINKS
(Map p90; ☑ 050 34 53 38; www.bacchuscornelius. com; Academiestraat 17; ☺ 1-6.30pm) There's a cornucopia of 450 beers and rare *gueuzes* (lambic beer), as well as *jenevers* (gins) and liqueurs flavoured with elderflower, cranberries and cherries. Ask the shop owner if you can try her home-brewed silky smooth *jenever*, made with real chocolate. The two pianos are there for shoppers to play; an open fire in winter adds to the cosy vibe.

Diksmuids Boterhuis FOOD
(Map p90; www.diksmuidsboterhuis.be; Geldmuntstraat 23; ☺ 10am-12.30pm & 2-6.30pm) This gorgeous traditional grocery is now surrounded by mainstream boutiques but has been here since 1933. Decked out with red-and-white gingham flounces and featuring a

ceiling hung with sausages, it sells cheeses, honey, cold meats and mustard.

't Apostelientje ARTS & CRAFTS

(Map p86; ☑ 050 33 78 60; www.apostelientje. be; Balstraat 11; ☺1-5pm Tue, 9.30am-12.15pm & 1.15-5pm Wed-Sat, 10am-1pm Sun) Bruges overflows with lace vendors, but this sweet little 'museum shop' is well off the normal tourist trail. The delicate garments and gifts on sale are made from beautiful authentic lace, handmade by two sisters and their mother; the husband of one of the sisters makes the wooden bobbins. An unusual opportunity to buy the real Bruges deal lace-wise.

2-Be FOOD & DRINKS

(Map p90; ☑ 050 61 12 22; www.2-be.biz; Wollestraat 53; ☺10am-7pm) Vast range of Belgian products from beers to biscuits in a snazzy, central location, but prices can be exorbitant. Their 'beer wall' is worth a look, as is the wonderfully located canal-side bar terrace, where 'monster' 3L draught beers (€19.50) are surely Belgium's biggest.

Mille-Fleurs HOMEWARES

(Map p90; ☑ 050 34 54 54; www.millefleurs tapestries.com; Wollestraat 33; ☺10am-6pm Mon-Sat) A cornucopia of Flemish tapestries made near Wetteren. Worth a browse if you want to take a piece of Belgium home with you. It also sells throws, tapestry cushions, runners and doilies, and bags and purses.

ⓘ Information

MONEY

For currency exchange, **Fintro** (www.fintro.be; Vlamingstraat 18; ☺8.30am-4.45pm Mon-Fri, 9am-12.30pm & 2-4pm Sat) offers better commission-free rates than most competitors.

MEDICAL SERVICES

Akademisch Ziekenhuis St-Jan (☑ 050 45 21 11; www.azsintjan.be; Ruddershove 10) The city's main hospital has a 24-hour emergency unit.

Apotheek Soetaert (☑ 050 33 25 93; Vlamingstraat 17; ☺9am-12.30pm & 2-6.30pm Mon-Sat, closed Wed afternoon) Charming olde-worlde pharmacy.

Doctors On Weekend Duty ☑ 050 36 40 10
Pharmacists On Weekend Duty ☑ 050 40 61 62

TOURIST INFORMATION

There are three main info-point locations. Ask for the excellent local Use-it map-guide (www. use-it.be) and/or browse a copy online.

Tourist Information Counter (Map p86; ☑ 050 44 46 46; www.visitbruges.be; Stationsplein; ☺10am-5pm Mon-Fri, to 2pm Sat & Sun)
Tourist Office (In&Uit Brugge) (Concertgebouw; Map p90; ☑ 050 44 46 46; www. visitbruges.be; Concertgebouw, 't Zand 34; ☺10am-5pm Mon-Sat, 10am-2pm Sun)
Markt (Historium) InfoKantoor (Map p90; ☑ 050 44 46 46; Markt 1; ☺10am-5pm)

ⓘ Getting There & Away

Bruge's **train station** (☑ 050 30 24 24; www. belgiantrain.be; Stationsplein 5) and main bus stations are 1.5km south of the Markt.

Eurolines (☑ 02-669 20 07; www.eurolines.eu) and **Flixbus** (www.flixbus.co.uk) have international bus services including nightly runs to London (from €30). Tickets are generally vastly cheaper booked online. When booking check which of two nearby departure points your service leaves from.

Trains run twice hourly to Kortrijk (€8.10, 40 minutes) and to Brussels (€14.50, one hour) via Ghent (€7, 23 minutes).

Hourly trains go to Antwerp (€15.40, 80 minutes), Knokke (€4.20, 20 minutes) and Ostend (€4.50, 13 minutes).

For Ypres (Ieper), take the train to Roeselare then bus 95 via Langemark or 94 via Passendale, Tyne Cot and Zonnebeke, all places you're likely to want to see anyway.

There's a **luggage room** (Stationsplein 5; per half-/full day €6.50/9.50, deposit €12.50; ☺7am-8pm) (must return same day) and **lockers** (Stationsplein 5; per 24hr small/large €3/4) at the station.

ⓘ Getting Around

BICYCLE

B-Bike (☑ 0479 97 12 80; 't Zand 8000; per hr/day €5/15; ☺10am-7pm Apr-Oct)
Blue Bike (www.bluebike.be; membership per year €12)
Rijwielhandel Erik Popelier (☑ 050 34 32 62; www.fietsenpopelier.be; Mariastraat 26; per hr/ half-/full day €5/10/15, tandem €10/20/30; ☺10am-6pm) Good bicycles for adults and kids; helmets for hire, free map, no deposit.

BUS

DeLijn (☑ 070 220 200; www.delijn.be/en) city buses run from 5.30am to 11pm. Single tickets cost €3 for a ride lasting up to an hour. A day pass is €8 bought on-board or €6 in advance.

Any bus marked 'Centrum' runs to **Markt** (p87). To return to the **station** (Map p86; Stationsplein 5), the most central stop to Markt is **Stadsschouwburg** (Map p90; Vlamingstraat 58).

CAR

Given central Bruges' nightmarish one-way system, the best idea is to use the large covered **car park** (☏ 050 33 90 30; www.interparking.be; Chantrellstraat 42-62; per hr/24hr €0.70/3.50) beside the **train station** (p102). Bargain fees here include a free return bus ticket to the centre for the car's driver and all passengers; just show your parking ticket when boarding the bus. If you park elsewhere, be aware that unmetered street parking still requires you to set your parking disc (maximum stay four hours). Traffic wardens are merciless.

TAXI

Taxis wait on the **Markt** (Map p90; Markt) and in front of the **train station** (p102). Otherwise phone 050 334 444 or 050 384 660.

Damme

POP 11,008

Charming Damme village is little more than a single street and a main square featuring a fine Gothic **stadhuis** (town hall). That is fronted by a statue of local 13th-century Flemish poet Jacob Van Maerlant who was buried in the then-new **Onze Lieve Vrouwekerk** (Our Lady's Church; Kerkstraat; church/tower €0.50/1; ⊙ 2-5.30pm Tue-Sun May-Sep). The church was vastly expanded in the village's heyday, only to be partially torn down in 1725 when it (and its maintenance bills) had become too big for the depopulating town. Opposite the stadhuis is a visitor centre and, in the same building, the **Uilenspiegel Museum** (☏ 050 28 86 10; www.visitdamme.be/uilenspiegelmuseum; Jacob van Maerlantstraat 3; adult/concession/family €2.50/1.50/5; ⊙ 9am-noon & 3-5pm Mon-Sat, 9am-noon & 2-5pm Sun), which recounts stories of a character who's a villain in German folklore but a jester and freedom fighter in Flemish literature.

Damme is linked directly to Bruges by 5km of perfectly straight canal with a road on one side and a cycle path on the other. Tall poplars create a canopy that attractively shades much of the route. Half the fun is getting there by bicycle, and continuing along quieter canal sides beyond, maybe seeking out rural taverns that are less busy than the cafes in central Damme. A classic alternative is to join the tourist throngs on the glacially slow Lamme Goedzak (p94) paddle steamer from Bruges.

BELGIAN COAST

After a period of stasis, Belgium's seaside region is fast regaining popularity among local, French and Dutch tourists as an 'it' destination. The 65km-long coastline is fronted by wide white-sand beaches, backed by dunes and dotted every few kilometres with resort towns.

Almost all resorts rent a selection of kids' buggies and go-kart-like *kwistax*.

Though many towns sport a concrete wall of midrise apartment blocks, these offer overnighters pretty beachfront views including sunrises and sunsets over the North Sea.

Despite a wide selection of accommodation, heavy bookings mean that finding a room can be difficult in midsummer. In contrast, out of season many towns can feel deserted. However, with its regular events and conventions, hub-town Ostend keeps a lively vibe year-round. Other top picks for coastal stays include De Haan, Bredene and wealthy Knokke-Heist.

❶ Information

Various discount passes are available. Check in with each town's tourist office when you arrive or ask at your accommodation to find out what's on offer.

Many local attractions have subscribed to the Kustpass (Coastpass; www.kustpas.be) program. Sign up online (it's free to join), pay for the attractions you're interested in at the discounted rate then print out your pass.

❶ Getting Around

DeLijn (p102) operates De Kusttram (coast tram) between Knokke-Heist and De Panne/Adinkerke. Serving every town on the Belgian Coast, it departs every 15 to 30 minutes between sunrise and midnight; the full route takes just over two hours. It's the longest tram line in the world.

Single tickets cost €3 for a ride lasting up to an hour. Buy a day pass on board for €8 or in advance for €6. See the website for other available discount passes.

Knokke-Heist

POP 34,063

A sprawling place renowned for its fancy dining and nightlife scene, Knokke (www.knokke-heist.info) is a popular summer destination for well-heeled Belgian and Dutch holidaymakers. Regular festivals include a major firework extraganza in late August and a summer-long beachfront pop-up **Cartoon Pavilion** (www.cartoonfestival.be; Cartoonpaviljoen Heldenplein Heist; ⊙ Jun-Sep; 🚊 Heist-Heldenplein). A highlight of diverse, changing exhibitions at the **Cultuur Centrum** (Maxim Willemspad 1; ⊙ 10am-5pm) is an annual selection of **world photojournalists' work** (www.worldpressphoto.org; ⊙ Jun-Jul). In October, historical motor cars tear around Knokke's Grand Prix circuit for an entire weekend in the **Zoute Grand Prix** (www.zoutegrandprix.be/en; ⊙ Oct).

Knokke's famous **casino** (☎ 050 63 05 05; www.grandcasinoknokke.be; Zeedijk-Albertstrand 509; ⊙ 11am-4am Sun-Thu, to 5am Fri-Sat) contains an incredible 72m circular mural by René Magritte and a superb 1974 Paul Delvaux lit by one of Europe's biggest glass chandeliers, yet oddly neither is usually on display to gamblers or visitors.

If you tire of window shopping, there's plenty of rubbernecking opportunities: take a drive around the scores of luxury low-rise mansions that extend beyond the main drag for several kilometres into neighbouring Duinburgen and De Zoute.

Focusing on the region's WWII history, the area's most appealing museum, **For Freedom** (☎ 050 68 71 30; www.forfreedommuseum. be; Ramskapellestraat 91-93; adult/child €10/6; ⊙ 10am-5pm May-Nov, 10am-5pm Sat & Sun Nov-May), is around 7km south. Or, for a sense of local nature, head for Het Zwin.

ⓘ BEST COASTAL TOWNS FOR...

Art De Panne; Ostend

Casinos Knokke; Ostend

Horseback fishermen Oostduinkerke

Medieval townscapes Nieuwpoort; Lissewege

Nudist beaches Bredene

Old-world elegance De Haan; De Zoute (Knokke)

Russian submarines Zeebrugge

Theme parks De Panne

Upmarket boutiques Knokke

Walking De Haan; Ostend

WWII sea defences Ostend

Yacht and boat trips Nieuwpoort

🛏 Sleeping & Eating

Hotel Du Soleil   BOUTIQUE HOTEL €€
(☎ 050 51 11 37; www.hoteldusoleil.be; Patriottenstraat 15; d from €115; 🐾) This popular hotel is one of the more down-to-earth options in Knokke, with well-trodden but well-maintained rooms and an excellent location just slightly back from the beach.

La Réserve   RESORT €€€
(☎ 050 61 06 06; http://la-reserve.be; Elizabethlaan 160; d from €295; P ❄ 🐾 ≋) Even though the property isn't directly on the beach, Knokke's fanciest digs are undoubtedly impressive, with opulent interiors, wide balconies, plenty of space and top-notch service.

★ **Cuines 33**   EUROPEAN €€€
(☎ 050 60 60 69; www.cuines33.be; Smedenstraat 33; lunch €46, tapas sets from €82; ⊙ noon-2pm & 7-9pm Fri-Sat & Mon-Tue) Leave it to the chef in this compact, airy bistro where the food is a work of art, crafted from the freshest ingredients of the day. Choose from set lunch or evening tapas menus, pick a cocktail and enjoy the experience as it unfolds.

Bistro Marie   BISTRO €€€
(☎ 050 62 25 61; https://bistromarie.be; Jozef Nellenslaan 229; mains €30-39) Lesser known than Knokke's other upmarket offerings, Bistro Marie serves beautifully prepared meals in equally classy surrounds, just a block back from the beach.

ⓘ Getting There & Away

Knokke has a number of stops on the Kusttram, which has its eastern terminus at Knokke station, 1km south of the beach on Knokkestraat. From the station, regular direct trains to Brussels (€18, 1½ hours) via Bruges.

Het Zwin

Around 5km northeast of Knokke, Het Zwin was once one of the world's busiest waterways, connecting Bruges with the sea. In medieval times the river silted up, devastating Bruges' economy. The marshy area is now this reserve, a tranquil region of polders (areas of drained land), ponds, scrub forest and mudflats that blush purple with *zwinnebloem* (sea lavender). Migrating swans, ducks and reed geese arrive here seasonally and there are populations of eagle owls and storks.

Sensitive areas are within the **Zwin Nature Park** (☎ 050 60 70 86; www.zwin.be; Graaf

Leon Lippensdreef 8; adult/child €2/1; ⊙9am-5.30pm Easter-Sep, to 4.30pm Oct-Easter, closed Mon Sep-Jun, closed Dec). Rubber boots might prove useful if you've come for more than the 3pm stork-feeding. Alternatively, to peruse the area from a distance (for free), walk (or cycle) a thoroughly upgraded 2.8km circular dune path that starts down the promenade from Knokke's Surfers' Paradise beach bar, accessed from the easternmost end of Zwinlaan then by walking up Appelzakstraat and turning right.

De Haan

POP 11,925

Prim and proper De Haan (Le Coq) is Belgium's most compact and engaging beach resort. Its most famous visitor, Albert Einstein, lived here for a few months after fleeing Hitler's Germany in 1933. Several fanciful half-timbered hotels and a scattering of tasteful eateries, bakeries and shops form an appealing knot around a cottage-style former tram station, from where Leopoldlaan leads 600m north to the beach passing a distinctive circular park, La Pontinière, that's perfect for picnicking and sunbathing.

De Haan's elevated promenade is raised high enough above the sands that sea views are not hidden by beach huts as they are at other Belgian resorts.

🛏 Sleeping

De Haan is one of the loveliest places to stay on the Belgian Coast, with many options catering for couples, seniors and the wealthy.

Apart!   APARTMENT €€
(📞059 43 00 43; www.apartmoment.be/en/sleep/apart-one-1; Koninklijke Baan 29; r/loft/apt from €120/165/185; P✳🔊) Formerly known as De Coqisserie, this almost beachfront property features four sleekly appointed guestrooms and five luxurious self-contained apartments above the stylish and popular coffee-house restaurant **Moment!** (www.apartmoment.be/en/eat; mains €8-18; ⊙8am-6.30pm). It's an excellent choice for couples and families.

ibis De Haan Hotel   HOTEL €€
(📞059 24 20 30; www.accorhotels.com/gb/hotel-8092-ibis-de-haan/index.shtml; Wenduinesteenweg 136; d from €69; P🚗✳🔊🏊) This popular chain hotel is set back from the beach, but has pleasant, quiet rooms and a lovely pool. Excellent value.

THE ROOSTER

According to local legend, De Haan (meaning 'The Rooster') got its name because it had no lighthouse and in fog fishermen used the sound of crowing cocks to work out where the shore was.

La Tourelle   B&B €€
(📞059 23 34 54; www.latourelle.be; Vondellaan 4; s/d/tr incl breakfast from €70/85/130; ⊙Feb-Nov; 🔊) Just behind the town hall, this lovely private house-hotel occupies a pale, turreted mansion dating back to around 1912. Rooms aren't large but they cram in contemporary four-poster beds, trestle tables and bow-tied lamps. There's a good free breakfast spread and day-round help-yourself coffee, plus a little roof-terrace sun deck.

Book well ahead to get the tower room (*torenkamer;* from €100).

★**Manoir Carpe Diem**   HOTEL €€€
(📞059 23 32 20; www.manoircarpediem.com; Prins Karellaan 12; s/d/ste from €160/180/200; ⊙Feb-Dec; P🔊✳) This cosy yet indulgent little hotel is set on top of a knoll amid the finest local villas on a quiet street. Classical music, oil paintings, aged silverware, log fires and hunting prints create a welcoming atmosphere in the bar and lounge. The private pool means you might not see much of the beach, though it's only 400m away.

🍴 Eating & Drinking

Bistro Villa Julia   BISTRO €€€
(📞059 44 93 42; http://villajulia.be; Van Eycklaan 2; mains €16-36; ⊙noon-2pm & 6-11pm Wed-Sun Apr-Nov, Thu-Sun Dec-Mar) Set in a beautiful historical villa and terrace, Bistro Villa Julia offers Flemish fine dining, with meals prepared from fresh local ingredients.

Strand Hotel   PUB
(📞059 23 34 25; Zeedijk-De Haan 19; ⊙noon-11pm) If it's too cold to stay outside, get a drink from the modest Strand Hotel and watch the sun set into the sea from its glassed-in terrace. Beer from €2.50.

ℹ Getting There & Rround

The main Kusttram stop is called De Haan An Zee. **Fietsen Andre** (📞059 23 37 89; www.fietsenandre.be; Leopoldlaan 9; rentals per day from €15; ⊙9am-6pm May-Oct, 9am-6pm Mon-Fri Nov-Apr) rents out bikes.

Bredene

📋 059 / POP 15,118

The only major seaside town where the beach isn't overshadowed by towering apartment blocks, Bredene (http://uitin bredene.be) is the coast's low-cost alternative for families and campers. Get off the Kusttram at the Bredene Campings stop for the main, white-sand beach area and **Duine-zwin Camping** (📋 059 32 13 68; www.duinezwin. be; Koningin Astridlaan 55b; sites €9-14 plus adult/child €3.50/2.75; ⊙ mid-Mar–mid-Nov; 🅿), or at Hippodrome for **Naktstrand** (Nudist Beach; http://uitinbredene.be; Koninklijke Baan 6; ⊙ Apr-Oct; 🄷 Hippodrom), Belgium's only officially sanctioned nudist beach.

Zeebrugge & Lissewege

POP 20,000

Coming to Belgium by ferry from Hull in England, you'll arrive in the enormous artificial harbour at Zeebrugge. It's a brutally functional place but you might stay long enough to visit **Seafront** (📋 050 55 14 15; www.seafront.be; Vismijnstraat 7; adult/child €13.50/9.50; ⊙ 10am-5pm) whose main attractions are a parked Russian submarine and a lightship. If you're driving on to Bruges, consider taking the back roads via Lissewege, 7km south. A contrastingly old-world village, Lissewege is a photogenic handful of whitewashed cottages scattered around an oversized brick church. Set in meadows 1.6km north of the village, **Hof Ter Doest** (📋 050 54 40 82; www.terdoest.be; Ter Doeststraat 4, Lissewege; s/d €110/130; 🅿 🛜) combines an excellent restaurant and small boutique hotel within a 17th-century farmhouse.

Ostend (Oostende)

POP 70,994

Ostend is the largest city on the Belgian Coast and its only truly year-round destination. Along its wide white-sand beach is a spacious promenade surveyed by an interesting mix of midrise architecture atop cosy seafront cafes with glassed-in terraces.

Always an important strategic port, Ostend has a rich history of fame, fortune, famine and hardship. It was ravaged by the Spanish between 1600 and 1604, before regrouping and reinventing itself as one of Europe's most stylish seaside resorts. Though bombing in WWII caused significant destruction to the city, Ostend has a wealth of beautiful belle époque and art deco architecture scattered around its residential streets.

Emerging from a period of economic decline that began when transcontinental ferry services ceased in the late 1990s, Ostend has again found its feet. It's worth spending a night or two here to explore.

◉ Sights

A number of Ostend attractions subscribe to the Kustpas (www.kustpas.be) program, a pay-as-you-use discount system.

◉ Central Ostend

The main promenade lies between the modern **pier** and the bold 1950s Kursaal convention centre, home to the popular **casino** (📋 059 70 51 11; www.partouchecasinos.be; Oosthelling 12; ⊙ slots/tables from 9am/3pm).

Random strolls into the suburbs can can be fruitful when stumbling on art nouveau and belle époque townhouse facades, eg on recently gentrified Oude Molenstraat, linking Tourhoutesteenweg and Prinsenlaan.

⭐ **St-Petrus-&-Pauluskerk**   CHURCH
(Prins Boudewijnstraat) Ostend's most striking historical building features beautifully ornate twin spires, a rose window and a gloomy neo-Gothic interior. It was consecrated on August 31 1908, though it appears eons older. It's a massive, magnificent building and quite a surprise the first time you come upon it: it's somewhat incongruous with its surrounds. A stone 'bridge' behind the altar leads into the tiny crown-topped Praalgraf Louise-Marie, the 1859 tomb-chapel of Belgium's first queen, whose sad tale is told at the Stadsmuseum.

Museumschip Amandine   MUSEUM
(📋 0494 51 43 35; www.zeilschipmercator.be/amandine/en; Vindictivelaan 35-Z; adult/child €4/2; ⊙ 10am-5pm Tue-Thu, Sat & Sun) The last Ostend trawler to have fished around Iceland (1970s) is brought to life with waxwork figures, videos and sound effects. Highlights include the fish-freezing room.

Mercator   MUSEUM
(📋 0494 51 43 35; www.zeilschip-mercator.be; Vindictivelaan; adult/child €4/2; ⊙ 10am-5pm) This fully rigged, three-masted 1932 sailing ship was once used for Belgian Navy training purposes and is now a nautical museum that hosts changing exhibitions.

Léopold II Statue
STATUE

(Zeedijk) Most of the beachfront is overshadowed by 10-storey concrete buildings, but beside the very '50s Thermae Palace Hotel (p109) there's some respite where a neoclassical arcade is topped by a striking equestrian statue of Léopold II. Below him stands a fawning gaggle of European and African subjects.

Stadsmuseum
MUSEUM

(☑059 51 67 21; Langestraat 69; adult/concession/child €4/2/free; ☺10am-12.30pm & 2-6pm Wed-Mon) One might expect this museum, occupying a house that hosted Napoleon in 1798 and Belgian royals from 1834–1850, to be a little more grandiose and exciting than it is. That said, it's the best place to get an introduction to the fascinating and, at times, troubled history of a city that has served as an important gateway to Europe for centuries. Multimedia displays, artefacts and models of 'lost' buildings recount the city's former glories.

Mu.Zee
GALLERY

(☑059 50 81 18; www.muzee.be; Romestraat 11; adult/concession €9/7.50; ☺10am-6pm Tue-Sun) Mu.Zee, Ostend's foremost gallery, features predominantly local artists. There's a significant collection by symbolist painter Léon Spilliaert (1881–1946) whose most brooding works are reminiscent of Munch.

◉ Oosterover

Oosterover is the east bank of Ostend harbour. From the town centre take the mini-ferry to Oosterover jetty (☑059 56 63 11; www.welkombijvloot.be/uurregeling-veerdienst-oostende) then walk 10 minutes to Fort Napoleon. Earth Explorer is 500m beyond that, near the Kusttram stop, Duin en Zee.

★ Fort Napoleon
FORTRESS

(☑059 32 00 48; www.fort-napoleon.be; Vuurtorenweg 13; adult/senior/child €8/7/4; ☺10am-6pm Wed-Sun Apr-Oct,1-5pm Wed, Sat & Sun Nov-May) The impenetrable, pentagon-shaped Fort Napoleon is an unusually intact fortress dating from 1812, though there's comparatively little to see inside. The audioguide covers many of the same topics you'll have heard at the Atlantikwall. Drinking at the fortress *café* gets you decent glimpses without paying the entrance fee.

Earth Explorer
MUSEUM

(☑059 70 59 59; www.explorado-oostende.be; Fortstraat 128b; adult/concession/child €15/13/12; ☺10am-6pm Apr-Aug; 🖼) Themed by the elements, this heavily interactive series of experiences is made to awe primary-school-age youngsters with the forces that shape the earth. The most dramatic attractions are a walk-through earthquake and a volcano ride. When quiet, some sections close on hourly rotation. Look for half-price vouchers at hotels.

◉ Domein Raverside

Around 6km west of Ostend, the dunes and marshes of this extensive provincial reserve create a rare green gap between all the coast's apartment towers. If visiting both of its main attractions, the Atlantikwall and Anno 1465, it's cheaper to buy the combination ticket (adult/child €10/5).

By public transport, take the Kusttram to 'Domein Raversijde'. Reach the Atlantikwall via wooden steps leading south up the duneside then follow the signs (around 150m). A footpath between the marshes takes around 10 minutes to Walraversijde, from which you can take bus 6 back to Ostend. By car the only parking is at Walraversijde.

Bring waterproofs and walking shoes.

Atlantikwall Raversyde
HISTORIC BUILDING

(☑059 70 22 85; www.raversyde.be/en/history; Duinenstraat 147, Domein Raversijde; adult/concession €8/6; ☺10am-5pm Apr-early Nov, last entry 4pm) The gripping Atlantikwall is a remarkably extensive complex of WWI and WWII bunkers, gun emplacements and linking brick tunnels created by occupying German forces. Most bunkers are furnished and 'manned' by waxwork figures, and there's a detailed audioguide explanation (albeit sometimes overly concerned with gun calibres). This is one of Belgium's best and most underrated war sites, but you'll need good weather, around two hours, and reasonable fitness to make the most of the 2km walking circuit.

Anno 1465
MUSEUM

(www.raversyde.be/en/anno-1465-0; Nieuwpoort-sesteenweg 636, Domein Raversijde; adult/concession €6/5; ☺2-5pm Mon-Fri, 10.30am-6pm Sat & Sun Apr-early Nov, 10am-6pm daily Jul & Aug, last entry 4pm) Once a vibrant fishing

Ostend (Oostende)

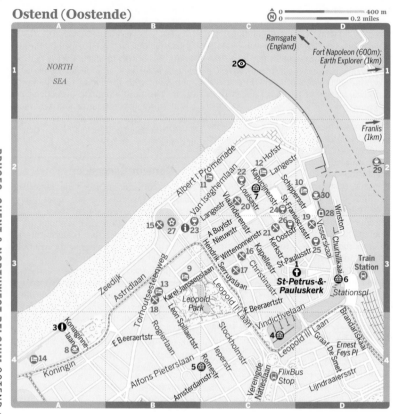

village, Walraversijde disappeared entirely following the strife of 1600 to 1604, leaving mere foundations. Today the archaeological site is enhanced by four convincingly rebuilt and furnished thatched houses. An audioguide tells the village's history through the voices of well-acted 1465-era characters. An interactive museum explains why the village died out.

🏃 Activities & Tours

Franlis　　　　　　　　　　BOATING
(☑ 059 70 62 94; www.franlis.be; Hendrik Baelskaai 36; 5-hr cruises from €40; ⏰ office 9am-noon & 2-5pm Mon-Fri) Offers a variety of out-and-back sea cruises.

Stedelijk Zwembad　　　　　SWIMMING
(☑ 059 50 38 38; www.oostende.be/zwembad; Koninginnelaan 1; adult/child €3.50/2.25; ⏰ 9am-5pm, longer hours in summer) A full-sized indoor swimming pool.

✨ Festivals & Events

Summer festivities include a **beer festival** (www.northseabeerfestival.com; Leopoldpark; ⏰ Aug), a **beach-music fest** (www.ostendbeach.be; ⏰ Jul) and Ostend's **film festival** (www.filmfestivaloostende.be; ⏰ early Sep).

⭐ **Disney Sand Magic**　　　　ART
(www.disneysandmagic.com; Ostend Beach; ⏰ Jul-Oct) The largest event of its kind in the world, Disney Sand Magic features more than 40 professional sand sculptors who create around 150 sculptures up to 6m high in a 10,000-sq-metre section of Ostend Beach.

🛏 Sleeping

Jeugdherberg de Ploate　　　HOSTEL €
(☑ 059 80 52 97; www.jeugdherbergen.be/en/ostend; Langestraat 72; dm from €29, d from €65; ⏰ closed Oct–mid-Mar; 🛜) This HI hostel is smart, modern and minimal, but the dorms, even with their vivid colours, lack that airy,

Ostend (Oostende)

bright feeling. But there's an elevator, no curfew, super-helpful and friendly staff, and a great location central to everything.

Thermae Palace Hotel   HISTORIC HOTEL €€
(📞 059 80 66 44; www.thermaepalace.be; Koningin Astridlaan 7; d from €99; 🅿🕸) Once Ostend's fanciest affair, the beautiful, beachfront Thermae Palace is ageing gracefully, but is no longer the best luxury accommodation on the increasingly popular Belgian Coast. That said, it retains appeal for history-lovers and folks seeking that old-school Euro-beach-resort vibe. It's a very photogenic place.

Leopold Hotel   HOTEL €€
(📞 059 70 08 06; https://leopoldhotelostend. com; Van Iseghemlaan 110; d incl breakfast from €69; 🅿🕸🕸) In a perfect location, the Leopold is a solid performer with a variety of room types in a range of layouts and sizes from tiny (and cheap) to something a bit more fancy. It's not a swanky hotel, but has a classy feel to it. There's a great lounge/bar with floor-to-ceiling street frontage in a pretty historical cloister. Good value.

De Hofkamers   HOTEL €€
(📞 059 70 63 49; www.dehofkamers.be; IJzerstraat 5; s/d incl breakfast from €70/99; 🕸) Model yachts and dozens of teddies create a welcoming reception and lounge. Rooms are all

different but play on romantic pseudo-antique themes; some have four-poster beds. All have a safe, fridge and kettle. There's a four-lounger roof terrace but be aware that any claims of 'sea view' mean craning your neck and looking north down a tunnel of other hotels.

Breakfast is relatively lavish.

Hotel Die Prince   HOTEL €€
(📞 059 70 65 07; www.hoteloostende.eu; Albert I Promenade 41; d incl breakfast without/with view from €90/110; 🕸) Die Prince is one of the rare hotels with a beach view. Prices here are modest and the public areas rather swish. Room decor is functional, but little two-seat desks allow you to wave-gaze from your window.

De Mangerie   GUESTHOUSE €€
(📞 059 70 18 27; www.mangerie.info/en/guest house.html; Visserskaai 36; r/ste from €90/130; 🕸) With dark-wood floors, fine linen and comfy sitting areas, the Mangerie's four spacious guest rooms continue the suave designer themes of their tempting fish restaurant downstairs (mains €20 to €25).

✖ Eating

For budget dining, loveable **Albrecht** (📞 0497 81 87 91; Christinastraat 81; light meals €4-14; ⊙9am-5pm) does good coffee and breakfast in an art nouveau corner shop, **Frituur Franky** (☑059 41 26 95; www.frituurfranky.be; Karel Janssenslaan 53; fast food €3-9; ☉noon-2pm & 5.30-11pm Tue-Sat, 5-10pm Sun; 🐾) is a great chip shop, and **Tea Room Benny** (☑059 50 82 65; Vlaanderenstraat 13; ☉9.30am-8pm Mon-Thu, till 9pm Fri-Sun) is a fabulously frozen-in-time booth cafe. For something a tad more contemporary, try **Belle de Jour** (☑0479 36 09 05; www.bistrobelledejour.be/over-ons; Aartshertoginnestraat 5; mains €14-28; ☉noon-9pm), a little cafe with pared-down decor, a mosaic floor, old-school furniture and Italian-influenced flavours.

★**Wijnbistro Di Vino**　　　BISTRO €€

(☑0473 87 12 97; www.wijnbistrodivino.be; Wittenonnenstraat 2; mains €13-20; ☉11.45am-2pm & 6.30-10pm Wed-Sun Sep-Jun, daily Jul & Aug) The product of one man's hard work, this intimate candlelit wine-bistro reflects its owner's passion for food and wine. The menu is simple (fish or meat), seasonal, well priced and executed, and paired expertly with one of the best wine lists in town.

't Zeezotje　　　BRASSERIE €€

(☑059 70 48 58; www.zeezotje.be; Bonenstraat 17; meals €12-26; ☉10am-midnight, kitchen noon-11.45pm) Floor-to-ceiling glass and masses of outdoor seating – including an easily missed upper-floor balcony – draw in tourist diners, as do the English-language menus, good prices and late-serving kitchen. Pizzas and pastas are supplemented by a selection of seafood options. Try the *Vispannetje*, a trio of different fish fillets topped with melted cheese, mini-shrimp and a creamy, light curry sauce.

Bistro Beau-Site　　　CAFE €€

(☑0486 77 45 74; www.galeriebeausite.com; Albert I Promenade 39; pasta €12-20; ☉11am-7pm Mon, Wed & Thu, noon-late Fri-Sun) Atmosphere-wise, this is a class apart from anything else on the seafront. This small arty cafe has art deco touches, a communal farmhouse table, jazz tinkling on the stereo and art books to peruse. Upstairs are window seats with great beach views.

Den Artiest　　　BRASSERIE €€

(☑059 80 88 89; www.artiest.be; Kapucijnenstraat 13; meals €14-25; ☉5pm-2am, kitchen 7pm-midnight) The tables of this casual brasserie are arranged on different levels within a spacious high-roofed hall to quite an effect. Long brass-tube lamps and fun knickknacks provide atmosphere, while ultra-generous meals are barbecued in front of you in the central fire hearth. Recommended for drinks only too. Occasional live music.

MARVIN GAYE IN OSTEND

'There are plenty of places I'd probably rather be, but I probably need to be here.' The story of how soul superstar and sex god Marvin Gaye came to Ostend in February 1981 is a curious one.

The tale of self-imposed exile in a one-horse seaside town is told in Richard Olivier's documentary *Marvin Gaye: Transit Ostend*. Promoter Freddy Cousaert met Gaye in London during a low in the singer's life – he was drugged, divorcing and losing it. Cousaert invited Gaye and his son for an open-ended visit to Belgium, partly so that Cousaert himself could stage a comeback concert for Gaye at the Kursaal. The visit ended up lasting two years.

Relocated to the somewhat bleak Belgian beaches, Gaye, who had attempted suicide by cocaine overdose in Hawaii two years earlier, spent time running along the sand, playing basketball and boxing in a briefly successful pitch at clean living. The singer also claimed to have eased up on the lovin' here – despite the fact that this is where the classic 'Sexual Healing' was written.

Gaye played his one-off comeback gig at the Kursaal in 1982; it was poorly attended but brilliant. The venue in turn commissioned an unflattering though glitzy bronze statue of the singer at his piano, which still sits in the lobby.

Within two years of Gaye leaving Ostend for Los Angeles he was dead. He was shot by his own father at the age of 44, having apparently goaded him into murder in a state of cocaine-fuelled paranoia. Unlikely as it seems, Ostend gave Gaye a last period of calm and creativity before the tragic storm that ended his life, and he gave the world 'Sexual Healing'.

Agua del Mar EUROPEAN €€€

(059 29 50 52; www.belvicci.com/restaurant/belgium/oostende/agua-del-mar; Kursaal Westhelling 12; mains €26-48; ⊗noon-9.30pm) This business-casual restaurant features imaginative mussel-shell-mosaics, and the arc of its raised terrace surveys the western beaches. The upmarket menu includes scallop risotto, lobster with asparagus, and duck in peanut sauce. Come between 3pm and 6pm for pancakes and coffee (from €3.50) or later for cocktails (€7 to €10).

Drinking & Nightlife

A series of great *cafés* and pubs leads north from the Kursaal on Langestraat and Van Iseghemlaan, and on several of the connecting lanes. **Mommy's Bastards** (059 80 73 10; www.mommysbastards.be; Dwarsstraat 10; ⊗11am-11pm) is the new hipster-kid on the cocktail block with Saturday DJ nights. **Lafayette** (Langestraat 12; ⊗2pm-2am; ⊗) has eclectic musical tastes and hits a fine balance between hip and friendly with the panelling of a traditional *café* and the backlit bottle racks of a cocktail bar. Refreshingly welcoming, friendly and fun, **Valentino** (059 80 54 11; Sint-Franciscusstraat 29; ⊗9pm-4am Fri-Wed) is the star of Ostend's compact gay scene. **Café Bottelje** (059 70 09 28; www.cafebotteltje.be; Louisastraat 19; ⊗11.30am-1am or later Tue-Sun, 4.30pm-1am Mon) features over 300 different Belgian beers, including a dozen on draught and serves beer-based meals. For brews at just €1 a *pintje*, head to merrily tatty, bric-a-brac filled **'t Kroegske** (059 80 81 91; St-Paulusstraat 80; ⊗11am-2pm & 6-11pm).

Shopping

Vistrap MARKET

(Visserskaai; ⊗9.30am-dusk, seasonal) Ostend's busy fish market is a briny bustling place and well worth a walk around its several wagon-stalls hawking smoked and cooked fish, pre-fried calamari rings, little tubs of grey shrimp and plastic bowls of steaming hot *wulloks* (whelks/sea snails) available *natuur* (in salty broth) or *pikant* (spicy).

⊙ Information

Tourist Office Oostende (059 70 11 99; www.visitoostende.be; Monacoplein 2-9; ⊗10am-6pm)

⊙ Getting There & Away

The most convenient Kusttram stop is Marie-Joséplein.

From Ostend's pretty train station, by the docks on Natiënkaai, trains to Bruges (€4.40, 16 minutes) continuing to Kortrijk, Antwerp via Ghent, or Liège via Brussels.

FlixBus coach services stop on **Mercatorlaan** (Mercatorlaan 17-19).

⊙ Getting Around

If you've driven to Ostend, you can park for free in Oosteroever (the east side of the harbour), then use the free passenger/bicycle **mini-ferry** (059 56 63 11; www.welkombijvloot.be/uurregeling-veerdienst-oostende) that shuttles several times an hour across to the aquarium jetty in the town centre.

There's free bicycle hire behind the train station.

Nieuwpoort

POP 11,062

Nieuwpoort is home to one of northern Europe's largest yachting **marinas** (058 23 52 32; www.vynieuwpoort.be; Watersportlaan 11; ⊗9am-5pm). Come here to gaze at the tall masts bobbing on the water, or to arrange charters or join local cruises. **Bon Vivant** (0477 35 18 10; www.zeilexcursies.be; Halvemaanstraat 2a; day charters from €400) runs two-hour sails for €20 per person (minimum six) at 12.30pm and 3.30pm, while **Seastar** (058 23 24 25; www.seastar.be; Robert Orlentpromenade 2) has river and sea trips plus dining cruises.

Historically the town is remembered for its key role in WWI; local partisans thwarted the German advance by opening the dykes and flooding surrounding low-lying land. Bombardments during the war devastated Nieuwpoort's historical townscape, but in the 1920s the medieval main square was rebuilt, including the former 1280 town hall, belfry and a sizeable church. Today, flanked by step-gabled houses, the scene looks lovely at dusk thanks to tasteful floodlighting. By day, however, the overly neat brickwork lacks the apparent authenticity of similar reconstructions in Ypres or Diksmuide.

Oostduinkerke

POP 8534

The archetypal vision of Belgium's rural North Sea coast is of *paardevissers:* shrimp fishermen riding their stocky Brabant horses into the sea, dragging triangular nets through the low-tide shallows. These days shrimp catches are minimal, but the age-old tradition can be witnessed at Oostduinkerke's Astridplein beach in a tourist-geared spectacle that's held about 30 times a year. For the low-down, see http://paardevissers.be.

Outside these times, the town is a quiet alternative to the larger resorts, with one or two attractions to pique your interest; consider visiting as a day trip.

⊙ Sights

★ **Navigo** MUSEUM
(Nationaal Visserijmuseum; ☑ 058 51 24 68; www.navigomuseum.be; Pastoor Schmitzstraat 5; adult/senior/youth €7/5/2; ⊙ 10am-6pm Tue-Fri, 2-6pm Sat & Sun) Visits walk you through a genuine 19th-century fisherman's cottage, teaching you about fish quotas and fishermen's superstitions, then send you and your audioguide beneath a 1930s fishing shack flanked by aquariums of fish. An accompanying soundtrack of waves and shrieking gulls builds up to a four-minute storm every half-hour. Veurne–Ostend bus 68 stops nearby.

Sint-Niklaaskerk CHURCH
(Leopold II Laan 85) Halfway between the village and coast, you'll find this extraordinary 1956 church whose bulky pale-brick tower has an almost medieval look, except for the massive 13m-high crucified Christ hanging on its east wall.

✦ Festivals & Events

Garnaalfeesten CULTURAL
(Shrimp Festival; ⊙ Jun) Folks come from far and wide in the last week of June to celebrate the humble shrimp in this festival that has both a culinary and cultural bent.

DON'T MISS

JULIA'S JOINT
....
Run by the fourth-generation, female-led fishmongers Mare Nostrum, **Julia Fish & Oyster Bar** (☑ 058 62 66 65; www.julia-baaldje.be; Arthur Vanhouttelaan 2; half-dozen oysters €15-22, mains €19-39; ⊙ noon-3pm & 6.30-10pm Thu-Mon) in De Panne is an acclaimed restaurant that secures its own supply of fresh seafood daily. If you love the humble bivalve, or are partial to ceviche or perch-and-chips, you simply must stop by.

🛏 Sleeping & Eating

De Peerdevisser HOSTEL €
(☑ 058 51 26 49; www.peerdevisser.be; Duinparklaan 41; dm/d from €26/52; P 🕾) This 34-room HI hostel has 138 beds, but outside the summer months it's blissfully quiet. It's situated near the dunes just a short walk to the ocean. Rooms are as basic as they come, but clean and comfortable. Sheeting packages are available, as are towels for purchase (€6). There's an excellent playground for the little ones.

★ **Estaminet de Peerdevisscher** CAFE
(☑ 058 51 32 57; www.facebook.com/paardevisser; Pastoor Schmitzstraat 4; ⊙ 10am-8pm Tue-Sun) Estaminet de Peerdevisscher is a wonderful old-time *café* with fishermen moonlighting as bar staff and a real seafaring vibe. It's 1.5km north of the beach in Oostduinkerke's second centre, Oostduinkerke-dorp, across the lawn from Navigo (p112).

Serves food: mains €12 to €20.

De Panne

POP 10,060

The westernmost resort-town on the Belgian coast, De Panne started life as a fishing village set in a *panne* (hollow) among the dunes. It was here that King Léopold I, arriving from London, first set foot on Belgian territory in 1831. For the beach use the De Panne Esplanade tram stop.

In a residential section of St-Idesbad, two tram-stops east of central De Panne, fans of surrealist art should seek out the superb **house-museum of Paul Delvaux** (☑ 058 52 12 29; www.delvauxmuseum.com; Paul Delvauxlaan 42; adult/concession €8/6; ⊙ 10.30am-5.30pm Tue-Sun Apr-Sep, Thu-Sun Oct-Dec, closed Jan-Mar),

West of De Panne's central strip, grassy-topped dunes provide a home for winter's migratory birds, though views in this direction are marred by the belching smokestacks of Dunkerque.

To the southwest, with its own Kusttram stop, **Plopsaland** (☑ 058 42 02 02; www.plopsa.be/plopsaland-de-panne/en; De Pannelaan 68; adult/child under 1m €36.50/11; ⊙ hours vary; P 🖫) is a kid-pleasing theme-park with roller coasters and other fun rides. The tram has its western terminus just beyond beside De Panne train station, a misomer as it's actually in Adinkerke, 3km southwest of central De Panne. Barely 1km off the E40 motorway, Adinkerke is utterly drab but its knot of tobacco and chocolate shops are ever-popular with motorists stocking up en route to the channel ports.

BEER COUNTRY

Veurne

📞 058 / POP 11,701

Delightful little Veurne, just south of the Belgian Coast, has a special architectural charm. Historical spires and towers peep above the picture-perfect Flemish gables that surround its quaint Grote Markt. The view is especially magical at dusk when partly floodlit.

◉ Sights

★ St-Walburgakerk   CHURCH

(Sint-Walburgapark 1) Veurne's main church is the delicately spired St-Walburgakerk, a spacious, heavily buttressed affair containing much-revered relics. The skull of St-Walburga is contained in a reliquary facing the entrance. A wooden fragment that was supposedly once part of Jesus' original cross is not displayed, but the story of its arrival here is the subject of local legends.

In an attractive small park behind, the **Citerne** is a strange crouched brick building that was converted into WWII barracks from the abandoned remnants of the 14th-century west portal.

Landhuis met Belfort   HISTORIC BUILDING

(Grote Markt) The 1628 octagonal *belfort* (belfry), a Unesco World Heritage site, rises behind the 17th-century former courthouse building. It now houses a helpful **tourist office** (📞 058 33 55 31; www.veurne.be; Grote Markt 29; ☉10am-noon & 1.30-5.30pm Apr-Sep, 10am-noon & 2-4pm Tue-Sun Oct-Mar, closed Sun mid-Nov–Mar) but is otherwise not accessible to the public.

Bakkerijmuseum   MUSEUM

(Bakery Museum; 📞 058 31 38 97; www.bakkerij museum.be; Albert I-laan 2; adult/senior/child €5/3.50/2; ☉10am-5pm Mon-Thu, 2-5pm Sat & Sun) A classical 17th-century farmstead houses this delightful museum that comprehensively examines baking from grain production to *speculaas* (a type of biscuit) moulding. There's also a chocolate statue and barns of milling machines. Come on

OFF THE BEATEN TRACK

BEAUVOORDE

Around 8km south of Veurne, the late-16th-century **Kasteel Beauvoorde** (📞 058 29 92 29; www.kasteelbeauvoorde. be; Wulveringemstraat 10, Beauvoorde; adult/child €8/6; ☉2-5.30pm Thu-Sun Mar-Oct, daily Jul & Aug) is an intact, picture-perfect (though tiny by castle standards), four-storey moated mansion with fully furnished interiors. It's free to wander around the pretty grassy area around the moat, and the surrounding village is a nice spot for a walk. The castle and church, opposite, provide a popular photo location for newlyweds.

Tuesdays in the summer holidays to see the baking demonstrations. It's located near the motorway junction 2km south of central Veurne.

Spaans Paviljoen   HISTORIC BUILDING

(Ooststraat 1) The 15th-century Spaans Paviljoen (Spanish Pavilion) was Veurne's town hall before being commandeered as a garrison for Spanish officers during Habsburg rule.

St-Niklaaskerk   CHURCH

(Appelmarkt 6; tower €1.50; ☉10-11.45am & 2-4.45pm mid-Jun–mid-Sep) Behind the Grote Markt's southeast corner, St-Niklaaskerk has a bulky 13th-century tower that you can climb for good summer views, plus a small exhibit on bell-ringing.

🛏 Sleeping & Eating

The local speciality *potjesvlees* is a cold mixture of rabbit, chicken and veal meat in jelly, often presented in a jar. Coffee in this region is very often served with a free thimble of thick local *advocaat* (a kind of eggnog). Use a spoon! Several inviting *cafés* ring the main square.

Auberge de Klasse   B&B €€

(📞 0479 76 55 13; www.aubergedeklasse.be; Astrid-laan 3; d from €135; 🛜) This comfortable three-room B&B retains more of its 18th-century structure than you'd guess from the outside. The interior is heaped with soft furnishings and frilly linens. It's set around an attractive courtyard garden. Check in from 4pm.

Old House
B&B €€

(☑ 058 31 19 31; Zwarte Nonnenstraat 8; s/d/q from €60/100/190; ℗ ✿) Creamy paintwork, indulgent oversized showers, splendid linen and gentle modernism turn this classically styled 1770 mansion into what's labelled a B&B but is more a beguiling boutique hotel. The salon-lounge features toy owls and a stuffed peacock, and there's an appealing front garden area. It's a short stroll through the park west of St-Walburgakerk. The very cheapest singles are narrow and cramped.

't Kasteel en 't Koetshuys
B&B €€

(☑ 058 31 53 72; www.kasteelenkoetshuys.be; Lindendreef 5; d from €120; ☎) This delightful 1907 red-brick mansion features high ceilings, old marble fireplaces and stripped floorboards, creating a lovely blend of classic and modern, all immaculately kept. Some rooms share one bathroom between two, and there's an extra charge for the sauna. It's three blocks south of Grote Markt.

't Hof van de Hemel
BISTRO €€

(☑ 0474 88 46 84; www.thofvandehemel.be; Noordstraat 13; mains €14-22; ◷ 11am-10pm Wed-Sun) This quaint teahouse-cafe with wooden beams and exposed brickwork was once a tiny alleyway. Over the generations it was gradually enclosed until it was finally encased in brick and annexed by the neighbouring house. Beer-wise, the highlight is St-Bernardus Tripel on tap. Its stews, soups, steaks and tarts are relatively inexpensive, if not especially refined.

Grill de Vette Os
STEAK €€

(☑ 058 31 31 10; www.grilldevetteos.be; Zuidstraat 1; mains €18-29; ◷ noon-2.30pm & 6pm-2am Fri-Tue) Old timbers, jugs, buckets, statues of saints and so much more are crammed into this atmospheric carnivore's lair.

❶ Getting There & Around

Veurne's extravagantly spired little train station is 600m east of Grote Markt via Ooststraat. Trains leave twice hourly for De Panne (€2.50, six minutes) and Ghent (€12.60, 65 minutes) via Diksmuide (€3.60, 11 minutes).

Hourly bus 68 goes to Oostduinkerke-dorp, Nieuwpoort and Ostend (€3, one hour). Bus 50 runs via Lo and Oostvleteren to Ypres (€3, 55 minutes) up to seven times daily.

Wim's Bike Center (☑ 058 31 22 09; www.wimsbikecenter.be; Pannestraat 35; per day from €9; ◷ 9am-noon & 1.30-6pm Tue-Sat) rents out bicycles.

Diksmuide

☑ 051 / POP 16,739

Diksmuide is a quiet and pretty town which, like Ypres, was painstakingly restored after total obliteration in WWI. Its resurrected Grote Markt (main square) offers a compact array of attractive traditionally styled buildings and a romantic city hall: it's hard to believe that almost everything in sight was rebuilt in the 20th century. West of the main square, there's a pretty little river port, behind which stands the town's main attraction, the very striking 1950 IJzertoren (☑ 051 50 02 86; www.ijzertoren.org; IJzerdijk 49; adult/senior/under 26yr €7/5/1; ◷ 10am-5pm, to 6pm Apr-Sep). Built of drab purple-brown brick and topped with power-station-style windows, this colossal 84m-high 'peace' tower is at once crushingly ugly and rather fascinating. It's set behind the shattered ruins of the 1930 original, the mysterious 1946 sabotage of which remains controversial. The tower is probably Flanders' foremost nationalist symbol: its 22 floors house a very expansive museum related to WWI and Flemish emancipation.

By road, Diksmuide is 28km south of Ostend and 23km north of Ypres.

Take bus 53 from Ostend's Kapellestraat (€6, one to 1¼ hours) or bus 20 from Ypres station (p120) (€3, 40 minutes).

Poperinge

☑ 057 / POP 20,010

For centuries the Poperinge area has produced the quality hops required for Belgium's beer industry. During WWI, Poperinge was just out of German artillery range, and it became a posting and R&R station for Allied soldiers heading to or from the Ypres Salient. English troops, remembering Poperinge for its many entertainments, referred to the town fondly as 'Pops'.

Today, it's one of the loveliest towns in Flanders Fields, with a pretty townscape and a number of historical WWI-related sites. Poperinge has less of the tourist crush and the heaviness that one can't help but feel when exploring nearby Ypres and the Salient.

◉ Sights

★ Talbot House
MUSEUM

(☑ 057333228; www.talbothouse.be; Gasthuisstraat 43; adult/senior/youth €8/7/5; ◷ 10am-5.30pm

Tue-Sun) This is an unusually light-hearted WWI attraction. Reverend Philip 'Tubby' Clayton set up the Everyman's Club here in 1915 to offer rest and recreation for WWI soldiers regardless of rank. The main 1790 townhouse has barely changed since; the garden is a charming oasis. Visits start with a modest exhibition (accessed from Pottestraat) where photos, quotes and videos remind visitors of Tubby's sharp gallows humour. End the visit with a free cup of English-style tea in the kitchen.

You can stay the night in one of the simple guest rooms (single/double from €45/80) with shared bathrooms; bookings advised.

National Hopmuseum
MUSEUM

(☑057 33 79 22; www.hopmuseum.be; Gasthuisstraat 71; adult/concession €6/2.50; ⊙10am-6pm Tue-Fri, 2-6pm Sat, 10am-noon & 2-6pm Sun, closed Dec-Feb) Once the municipal centre for weighing and storing hops, the 19th-century Stadsschaal now houses this distinctively scented museum, where you'll learn more about hops than you'd ever want to know. The simple attached *café* serves several local brews; the building was once home to Dirk Frimout, Belgium's first astronaut.

Sint-Janskerk
CHURCH

(Sint-Janskruisstraat; ⊙7.30am-7pm) The imposing Sint-Janskerk's 'miraculous' little Virgin-and-Child statuette reputedly brought a stillborn child to life in 1479.

Death Cell
MEMORIAL

(Guido Gezellestraat 1; ⊙9am-5pm) **FREE** Though English troops nicknamed it 'Good old Pops', Poperinge had a more sinister side – it was a place of execution for wartime deserters. Hidden behind a red door in the north side of the stadhuis you can still see the chilling original shooting post and the stone-walled death cell where deserters spent their last night. Brochures in the cell explain in some detail the era's injustices, accompanied by an audio recounting of the 1917 execution of 17-year-old soldier Herbert Morris.

🛏 Sleeping & Eating

Hotel Amfora
HOTEL €€

(☑057 33 94 05; www.hotelamfora.be; Grote Markt 36; d from €80; 🕸) While its step-gabled frontage and bar-restaurant are traditional in style, the rooms here have been upgraded with a muted modern look.

Hotel Recour
BOUTIQUE HOTEL €€€

(☑057 33 57 25; www.pegasusrecour.be; Guido Gezellestraat 7; d from €140; 🕸🕸) The main 18th-century house has a luxurious lounge and eight romantic individually themed rooms, most featuring nostalgic colour combinations, chandeliers, four-poster beds and hot tubs. A metal walkway above the garden lawn leads to seven contrastingly modern rooms, each adopting the style of a classic 20th-century designer.

Around 100m east in a separate building and approached by a doorless lift, the

---

BEER CYCLING

A network of quiet country lanes forms a circuit that starts and ends in Poperinge, offering both fine cycling and the chance to visit some of Belgium's best breweries. If you're fit and don't get stonkered, you can easily cover all of these in one day.

It's a 9km 30-minute flat cycle due west of Poperinge to the village of Watou, best known for its **Brouwerij Sint Bernardus** (Sint Bernardus Brewery; ☑057 38 80 21; www.sintbernardus.be; Trappistenweg 23; brewery tours €12.50; ⊙8.30am-noon & 1.30-4.30pm Mon-Thu, to noon Fri). The village has a pleasant central square dominated by a fine spired church. Here you'll find the little historical *café* **Het Wethuys** (☑057 20 60 02; www.wethuys.be; Watouplein 2; s/d €75/100), which serves St-Bernardus Tripel on tap, best consumed with its homey Belgian cooking such as *Hoppegaletten:* large cheese-filled pancakes.

From Watou, it's a 40-minute 12km ride northeast to Westvleteren to sample the coveted Westvleteren 12 Trappist beer from Abdij Sint-Sixtus (p116), at the In de Vrede (p116) pub. Then continue southeast for another 7km to Woesten for more tastings and potential takeaways at **Deca Brewery** (☑057 42 20 75; www.decabrouwerij.be; Elverdingestraat 4; ⊙2-6pm Tue-Fri, 1-4.30pm Sat). From here it's a 7km ride back to Poperinge.

Check in with the friendly folks at the National Hopmuseum (p115) for advice on the route.

WORTH A TRIP

WESTVLETEREN: TRAPPIST TREASURE

If you're driving from Veurne to Ypres, a post mill at Oostvleteren's main crossroads marks the turn to Westvleteren. The legendary Westvleteren Trappist beer actually comes from the isolated **Abdij Sint-Sixtus** (St Sixtus Abbey; ☑ beer sales 0702 100 45; https://sintsixtus.be/trial/bierverkoop; Donkerstraat 12, Westvleteren; ⊘ closed to visitors), some 4km further southwest via a web of tiny lanes. The architecturally unremarkable abbey is closed to visitors, but the abbey *café* **In de Vrede** (☑ 057 40 03 77; www.inde vrede.be; Donkerstraat 13; ⊘ 10am-8pm Sat-Wed) is the only place in the world where you can be (virtually) sure of tasting the incomparable Westvleteren 12, often cited as Belgium's greatest beer. That doesn't mean that you can take bottles away; purchasing a case is only possible by reserving an appointment using the abbey's infamously overloaded 'beerphone', preferably calling at 9am on the dot Monday morning. You'll need to give your car's number plate and agree on a pick-up time (weekday afternoons only, no credit cards).

somewhat cheaper *gastenkamers* (guest rooms) are excellent too, with exposed-brick walls and beams. One has a roof terrace.

★ **Restaurant Pegasus** FRENCH €€€
(☑ 057 33 57 25; www.pegasusrecour.be; Guido Gezellestraat 7; mains €32-39; ⊘ 8am-11pm Tue-Sat) Hotel Recour's (p115) Restaurant Pegasus is a very upmarket affair. Those under 60 might feel out of place, but the food is very creative. While mains are presented as nouvelle cuisine, extra sides are provided for those who secretly prefer old-cuisine Belgian-sized portions.

❶ Information

The office of **Visit Poperinge** (☑ 057 34 66 76; www.toerismepoperinge.be; Grote Markt 1; ⊘ 9am-noon & 1-5pm Mon-Fri, to 4pm Sat & Sun, closed Sun Oct-Mar) is on Grote Markt in the basement of the romantic neo-Gothic stadhuis, built in 1911.

❶ Getting There & Away

Poperinge is a short hop from Ypres by train (€2.80, eight minutes) or by bus 60 (€3, 18 minutes). The station is 750m west of Grote Markt on Ieperstraat.

Ypres (Ieper)

☑ 057 / POP 34,964

Once a bustling centre of industry ranking alongside Bruges and Ghent, it's now impossible to reference Ypres (Ieper in Dutch) without acknowledging the huge role it played in WWI. After its almost total annihilation, the town was rebuilt to its former specifications – a monumental task – to serve as a memorial to those who lost their

lives here in the Great War. Its restored Lakenhalle is one of Belgium's most spectacular buildings.

Ypres has become a place of pilgrimage for many. It's the gateway to the Salient (aka Flanders Fields), a bow-shaped bulge that formed the front line around town; some 300,000 Allied soldiers and up to 200,000 civilians and German troops lost their lives here.

In recent years visitor numbers from Commonwealth countries have soared; plan your visit well in advance to avoid disappointment.

⊙ Sights

★ **In Flanders Fields Museum** MUSEUM
(Map p118; ☑ 057 23 92 20; www.inflanders fields.be; Grote Markt 34; adult/under 26yr/child €9/5/4; ⊘ 10am-6pm Apr–mid-Nov, to 5pm Tue-Sun mid-Nov–Mar) No museum gives a more balanced yet moving and user-friendly introduction to WWI history. It's a multisensory experience combining soundscapes, videos, well-chosen exhibits and interactive learning stations at which you 'become' a character and follow his or her progress through the wartime period. An electronic 'identity' bracelet activates certain displays. Located in the historical Lakenhalle.

★ **Ramparts CWGC Cemetery** CEMETERY
(Lille Gate Cemetery; Map p118; Lille Gate) One of Ypres' most attractive military graveyards, this Commonwealth War Graves Commission site is found 1km south of the Grote Markt.

★ **Menin Gate** MEMORIAL
(Menenpoort; Map p118; Menenstraat) A block east of Grote Markt, the famous Menin Gate

is a huge stone gateway straddling the main road at the city moat. It's inscribed with the names of 54,896 lost WWI British and Commonwealth troops whose bodies were never found.

★ The Last Post
MEMORIAL

(Map p118; www.lastpost.be; ⊘8pm) FREE Every night at 8pm, traffic through the Menin Gate is halted while buglers sound the *Last Post* in remembrance of the WWI dead, a moving tradition started in 1928. Every evening the scene is different; buglers may be accompanied by pipers, troops of cadets or a military band. There's usually at least 100 or so visitors, most of whom have some connection to someone who was lost in Flanders Fields.

Lakenhalle
HISTORIC BUILDING

(Cloth Hall; Map p118; Grote Markt 34; €2; ⊘10am-6pm Apr–mid-Nov, to 5pm Tue-Sun mid-Nov–Mar) Dominating the Grote Markt, the enormous reconstructed Lakenhalle is one of Belgium's most impressive buildings. Its 70m-high belfry has the vague appearance of a medieval Big Ben. The original version was completed in 1304 beside the Ieperslee, a now covered-over river that once allowed ships to sail right up to the Lakenhalle to unload their cargoes of wool. These were stored beneath the high gables of the 1st floor, where you'll find the unmissable In Flanders Fields Museum.

To climb the Lakenhalle's tower, pay an extra €2 when entering the museum to have your electronic bracelet suitably charged to get you through the barrier.

Appended to the Lakenhalle's eastern end, the working stadhuis was reconstructed in 1969, partly to the original 1619 design.

Merghelynck Museum
MUSEUM

(Map p118; ☑ 057 23 92 20; www.merghelynckmuseum.be; Merghelynckstraat 2; €4) Unrelated to WWI, this museum faithfully reproduces a French manor house dating from 1774 and is filled with period antiques and artworks. The catch: it's only open to the public when (irregular) guided tours are being held: contact the tourist office (p120) to book a private tour or to find out if one is scheduled that you can join.

Gateway to Ypres
VISITOR CENTRE

(Commonwealth War Graves Commission; Map p118; Menenstraat 33; ⊘10am-4pm) This excellent visitors centre should be your first port of call if you're a Commonwealth citizen looking for information about a family member who died on the front.

St-Maarten en St-Niklasskerk
CHURCH

(Map p118; St-Maartensplein) Directly behind the Lakenhalle, this vast church was a cathedral until 1797 and was almost totally destroyed in WWI. Reconstruction has beautifully restored its soaring Gothic interior; it's hard to believe that the church was built in the 20th century.

Ramparts
HISTORIC SITE

(Map p118) Ypres is unusual in that it has retained extensive sections of its city fortifications. Designed by French military engineer Sébastien Le Prestre de Vauban, these sturdy brick-faced walls line the town's southeastern moat and are topped by pleasant gardens. The tourist office's (p120) free *Ramparts Route* leaflet introduces a dozen of the historical fortifications, but most visitors simply stroll from the Menin Gate to the medieval **Rijselpoort** (Lille Gate; Map p118; Rijselstraat), just beyond which is the Ramparts Cemetery.

ⓘ TICKET SAVVY YPRES

Consider keeping your In Flanders Fields Museum (p116) ticket stub. It also gets you free entry to two other pleasant if otherwise missable minor museums.

Stedelijk Museum (Map p118; Ieperleestraat 31; adult/student/child €15/7.50/free; ⊘10am-12.30pm & 2-5pm Tue-Sun Nov-Apr, to 6pm May-Oct) This decent little gallery is set in a three-storey 1555 almshouse complex. Exhibitions change regularly but usually feature 19th-century paintings.

Museum Godhuis Belle (Belle Almshouse; Map p118; ☑ 057 23 92 20; Rijselstraat 38; ⊘10am-12.30pm & 2-6pm Tue-Sun Apr-Oct) A single small chapel room featuring some unexpectedly high-quality medieval art, mostly religious.

Ypres (Ieper)

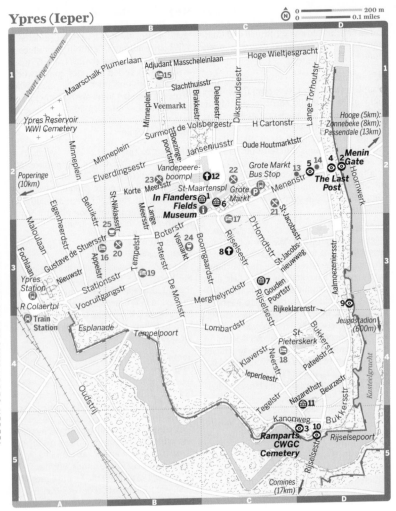

👉 Tours

Over the Top
BUS

(Map p118; ☑ 057 42 43 20; www.overthetoptours. be; Menenstraat 41; tours €40; ⊙ tours 9am-1.30pm & 2-5.30pm) Attached to a WWI specialist bookshop located towards the Menin Gate, Over the Top offers twice-daily half-day guided minibus tours of the Ypres Salient. The tour of the Salient's northern sector is run in the morning, the south is run in the afternoon.

British Grenadier
BUS

(Map p118; ☑ 057 21 46 57; www.salienttours.be; Menenstraat 5; tours from €40; ⊙ 10am-1.30pm) Offers three different Ypres tours, with morning and afternoon departures for sites on the Salient. It also offers full-day tours (€110) around the Somme and/or Vimy Ridge.

🎊 Festivals & Events

Kattenstoet
STREET CARNIVAL

(Cat Parade; www.kattenstoet.be) Every three years Ypres' classic feline fiesta features

Ypres (Ieper)

BRUGES, GHENT & NORTHWEST BELGIUM YPRES (IEPER)

parading giants and the throwing of cats from the Lakenhall tower. Toy cats these days, but before 1817 they were real. The next festival will be held in 2021.

Ypres Rally SPORTS
(www.ypresrally.com; ☉ Jun) This high-octane car rally rips and roars its way through town over a weekend in June.

🛏 Sleeping

Jeugdstadion CAMPGROUND €
(Map p121; ☏ 057 21 72 82; www.jeugdstadion.be; Bolwerkstraat 1; per tent/adult/child €3/4/2.50; ☉ mid-Mar–Oct; ℗) Campground and youth centre 900m southeast of the town centre.

Hotel New Regina HOTEL €€
(Map p118; ☏ 057 21 88 88; www.newregina.be; Grote Markt 45; r from €109; ❄ ⑤) Thoroughly refurbished and reopened in 2018, you cannot beat the location or the sparkling, swanky new rooms of this popular hotel on Grote Markt, overlooking the Lakenhalle (p117).

Ariane Hotel HOTEL €€
(Map p118; ☏ 057 21 82 18; www.ariane.be; Slachthuisstraat 58; d from €129; ℗ ⑤) This peaceful, professionally managed large hotel has a designer feel to its rooms and popular restaurant. Wartime memorabilia dots the spacious common areas.

Yoaké B&B B&B €€
(Map p118; ☏ 057 20 35 14; www.yoake-ieper.be/bedhome.htm; Tempelstraat 35; d from €90; ❄ ⑤) Smart two-room B&B attached to a hip wellness centre.

Kasteelhof 't Hooghe HOTEL €€
(Map p121; ☏ 057 46 87 58; www.hotelkasteelhofthooghe.be; Meenseweg 481, Hooghe; s/d from €65/85; ℗ ⑤) If you're driving, this out-of-town mock-Tudor-styled hotel is a great choice. It has genuine WWI trenches in the gardens and is ideally located for the kids to be first in at Park Bellewaerde (p123), directly behind. It is about 3km west of Ypres on the N8.

B&B Ter Thuyne B&B €€
(Map p118; ☏ 057 36 00 42; www.terthuyne.be; Gustave de Stuersstraat 19; s/d from €80/95; ⓐ) Three luminous, comfortable rooms that are scrupulously clean but not overly fashion-conscious.

★ Main Street Hotel GUESTHOUSE €€€
(Map p118; ☏ 057 46 96 33; www.mainstreet-hotel.be; Rijselstraat 136; d incl breakfast from €180; ⑤) Jumbling eccentricity with historical twists and luxurious comfort, this is a one-off that oozes character. The smallest room is designed like a mad professor's experiment. The breakfast room has a Tiffany glass ceiling.

🍴 Eating

Henk Bakery BAKERY €
(Map p118; ☏ 057 20 14 17; Sint-Jacobsstraat 2; breads & pastries from €2.50; ☉ 6.45am-6pm Tue-Fri, 5.45am-7pm Sat, 5.45am-4pm Sun) Fresh bread, pastries, croques and fancy patisserie goods to take away. Try the amazing and filling *broodpudding* (bread pudding) for just €0.40.

★ **De Ruyffelaer** FLEMISH €€

(Map p118; ☑ 057 36 60 06; www.deruyffelaer. be; Gustave de Stuersstraat 9; mains €15-26; ⊙ 11.30am-3.30pm Sun, 5.30-9.30pm Fri-Sun) Traditional local dishes are served in an adorable wood-panelled interior with old chequerboard floors and *brocante* (vintage) decor including dried flowers, old radios and antique biscuit tins.

't Leedvermaak BISTRO €€

(Map p118; ☑ 057 21 63 85; www.leetvermaak.be; Korte Meersstraat 2; mains €10-22; ⊙ 5-11pm Tue-Thu & Sat, 11am-2pm & 5-11pm Fri & Sun) Low-key theatre-themed bistro serving fair-priced pastas, veggie dishes and tapas.

In 't Klein Stadhuis PUB FOOD €€

(Map p118; ☑ 057 21 55 42; www.inhetkleinstadhuis.be; Grote Markt 32; mains €14-28; ⊙ 11am-midnight, kitchen to 10.30pm) Tucked away in a quirkily decorated historical guildhall beside the stadhuis, this split-level *café* serves gigantic good-value meals, including some beer-based recipes.

🍷 Drinking & Nightlife

't Binnenhuys CAFE

(Map p118; ☑ 057 35 97 06; Gustave de Stuersstraat 8; ⊙ 9.30am-6.30pm Mon & Wed-Sat, 2-6pm Sun; 🛜) One of Ypres' oldest houses, the 1772 Binnenhuys was rare in surviving WWI relatively intact. It's now an old-world home interiors shop, but tucked away in the rear sitting room and attractive back garden are tables for coffee and cake or a very relaxed beer.

De Vage Belofte PUB

(Map p118; ☑ 0495 53 24 12; www.facebook.com/devagebelofte; Vismarkt 3; ⊙ 4pm-late Tue-Sun) A piano hangs on the two-storey inner wall above a row of Champagne bottles. Summer tables spill out across appealing Vismarkt, and DJs turn the tables on weekend nights.

ℹ️ Information

Tourist Office (Map p118; ☑ 057 23 92 20; www.toerismeieper.be; Grote Markt 34, Lakenhalle; ⊙ 9am-6pm Mon-Fri, 10am-6pm Sat & Sun Apr–mid-Nov, to 5pm mid-Nov–Mar) Has an extensive bookshop.

ℹ️ Getting There & Around

Ypres Station (Map p118; Stationsstraat 1) is a 500m walk southwest of Grote Markt, on Stationsstraat. Many buses pick up both there and at the **Grote Markt bus stop** (Map p118)

(check the direction carefully). Route 20 to Diksmuide (€3, 50 minutes) runs five times daily.

Trains run to Brussels (€18.40, 1¾ hours), Poperinge (€2.80, eight minutes) and Kortrijk (€5.50, 30 minutes).

Bikes can be hired from **Hotel Ambrosia** (☑ 057 36 63 66; www.ambrosiahotel.be; D'Hondtstraat 54; bike per day €15; ⊙ 7.30am-7.30pm) or sign up to use the **Blue Bike** (p102) sharing service.

Ypres Salient

Flanders' WWI battlefields are famed for red poppies, both real and metaphorical. From 1914 the area suffered four years of senseless fighting during which hundreds of thousands of soldiers and whole towns disappeared into a muddy, bloody quagmire. The fighting was fiercest in the Ypres Salient, a bulge in the Western Front where the world first saw poison-gas attacks and where thousands of diggers valiantly tunnelled underground to dynamite enemy trenches.

These days many local museums have collections of WWI memorabilia, and dozens of painstakingly maintained war graveyards bear sad witness with regimented ranks of headstones. Concrete bunkers, bomb craters and trench sites can be visited; in 1917 these would have been infinitely muddier and unshaded as virtually every tree had been shredded into matchwood by artillery fire. A few non-war attractions lighten the mood.

👁 Sights

◉ North of Ypres

★ **Langemark Deutscher Soldatenfriedhof** CEMETERY

(Map p121; Klerkenstraat, Langemark) The Salient's largest German WWI cemetery is smaller than Tyne Cot but arguably more memorable, amid oak trees and trios of squat, mossy crosses. Some 44,000 corpses were grouped together here, up to 10 per granite grave slab; four eerie silhouette statues survey the site. Entering takes you through a black concrete tunnel that clanks and hisses with distant war sounds, while four short video montages commemorate the tragedy of war.

It's beyond the northern edge of Langemark on bus route 95.

Essex Farm CWGC Cemetery   CEMETERY
(Map p121; Diksmuidseweg, Ypres) The enduring image of poppies as a symbol of wartime sacrifice comes from the famous poem *In Flanders Fields*. It was written by Canadian doctor John McCrae in a concrete first-aid bunker that's now preserved at Essex Farm Cemetery. Rare bus 40 passes by.

Passendale & Zonnebeke

The 1917 battles around Passendale (then Passchendaele) left almost 500,000 casualties and made Passendale synonymous with wasted life. These days it's known much more positively for its cheese (p122). Ypres–Roeselare bus 94 (roughly twice-hourly weekdays, five daily weekends) goes through Zonnebeke, where you'll find one of the area's most comprehensive sites, Kasteelpark Zonnebeke. Bus 94 also passes within 600m of Tyne Cot.

⭐**Tyne Cot CWGC Cemetary**   CEMETERY
(Map p121; Vijfwegestraat, Zonnebeke; ⊙24hr, visitor centre 10am-6pm Feb-Nov; 🚌94) Probably the most-visited Salient site, this is the world's biggest British Commonwealth war cemetery, with 11,956 graves. A huge semicircular wall commemorates another 34,857 lost-in-action soldiers whose names wouldn't fit on Ypres' Menin Gate (p116). The name Tyne Cot was coined by the Northumberland Fusiliers who fancied that German bunkers on the hillside here looked like Tyneside cottages. Two such dumpy concrete bunkers sit amid the graves, with a third visible through the metal wreath beneath the white Cross of Sacrifice.

⭐**Memorial Museum
Passendale 1917**   MUSEUM
(Map p121; 📞051 77 04 41; www.passchendaele.be; Berten Pilstraat 5A, Zonnebeke; €10.50; ⊙9am-6pm Feb–mid-Dec; 🚌94) Within the grounds of Kasteelpark Zonnebeke you'll find this polished WWI museum charting local battle progressions with plenty of multilingual commentaries. The big attraction here is descending into its multiroom 'trench experience' with low-lit, wooden-clad subterranean bunk rooms and a soundtrack. Explanations are much more helpful here than in 'real' trenches elsewhere.

Kasteelpark Zonnebeke   CASTLE
(Map p121; Berten Pilstraat 5a, Zonnebeke; ⊙9am-6pm Feb–mid-Dec) FREE This lake-fronted

Ypres Salient

Ypres Salient

◎ **Top Sights**
1 Langemark Deutscher
   Soldatenfriedhof...............................A1
Memorial Museum
   Passendale 1917 ....(see 6)
2 Sanctuary Wood British Cemetery B2
3 Tyne Cot CWGC Cemetery................. B1

◎ **Sights**
4 Essex Farm CWGC Cemetery.............A2
5 Hooge Crater Museum......................B2
6 Kasteelpark Zonnebeke....................B2
7 Oude Kaasmakerij B1
8 Park Bellewaerde...............................B2
9 Sanctuary Wood (Hill 62) Museum....B2
10 St Juliaan Canadian War
   Memorial.. B1

🛏 **Sleeping**
11 Jeugdstadion.....................................A2
12 Kasteelhof 't Hooghe.........................B2

Normandy-chalet-style mansion and gardens are located in the centre of Zonnebeke village. The mansion was built in 1922 to replace a castle bombarded into rubble during WWI. Its stables host a stylish restaurant-cafe, while inside there's a tourist information booth and the Memorial Museum Passendale 1917 museum. The museum charges an admission fee, but it's free to wander the park grounds.

**Messines Ridge
(New Zealand) Memorial**   MONUMENT
(Hwy N314, Mesen) Located within the Messines Ridge British Cemetary is this tribute to New Zealand's war dead.

BRUGES, GHENT & NORTHWEST BELGIUM YPRES SALIENT

AT THE CROSSROADS OF WAR

The Ypres Salient was formed by Allied attempts to repel the invading German army before it reached the strategic North Sea ports in northern France. The area's line of barely visible undulations provided enough extra elevation to make good vantage points and were prized military objectives. Hundreds of thousands of lives were lost in numerous bids to take these very modest ridges. Years of deadlocked trench warfare obliterated local villages and created a barren landscape of mud and despair.

The first battle of Ypres (October and November 1914) set the lines of the Salient. After that, both sides dug in and gained relatively little ground for the remainder of the war, despite three valiant but suicidal battles that followed. The most infamous of these came in spring 1915 when Germans around Langemark launched WWI's first poison-gas attack. It had devastating effects on the advancing Allied soldiers, and on the Germans themselves. On 31 July 1917, British forces launched a three-month offensive commonly remembered as the Battle of Passchendaele (Passendale), or the 'battle of mud'. Fought in shocking weather on fields already liquidised by endless shelling, this horrifically futile episode killed or wounded more than half a million men, all for a few kilometres of ground; these modest Allied gains were lost again in April 1918.

The reconstruction of villages and replanting of trees took years, and even now farmers regularly plough up unexploded munitions. Today the pleasant farmland is patchworked with 170 cemeteries where rows of crosses stand in silent witness to wasted life.

Visiting The Memorials

The WWI sites are spread over a vast agricultural area of flat, pretty fields. It's important to first work out what it is you want to see or experience. Many are drawn to a place due to a family connection or affinity with the nation the site pertains to. Commonwealth residents are strongly advised to check in with the incredibly helpful staff at the Gateway to Ypres (p117) centre.

The books in the *Major & Mrs Holt's Concise Battlefield Guide* series (www.guide-books.co.uk/ypres-leper.html) are widely available in Ypres bookshops, which also organise guided tours.

For detailed information on the sites and history of the Salient, visit www.greatwar.co.uk/ypres-salient.

If you had relatives killed in the fighting you might want to locate their grave or memorial. Ypres bookshops offer a search service or you can look for yourself online:

American www.abmc.gov

British and Commonwealth graves www.cwgc.org

French www.memoiredeshommes.sga.defense.gouv.fr

German www.volksbund.de

St Juliaan Canadian War Memorial
MONUMENT

(The Brooding Soldier; Map p121; Brugseweg, Langemark-Poelkapelle) Memorial for Canadian war dead.

Oude Kaasmakerij
MUSEUM

(Map p121; ☑ 051 77 70 05; www.deoudekaasmakerij.be; 's Graventafelstraat 48a, Passendale; without/with cheese-tasting €6/9; ☺ 10am-5pm Mar-Oct, closed some Mon mornings) This interactive, mildly interesting cheese museum compares old and new cheesemaking techniques while a gratuitously naked Cleopatra figure takes

a bath in plastic asses' milk. It's 1.2km west of Tyne Cot.

HOOGE & AROUND

Ypres–Menen buses pass through Hooge, which during WWI was the eastern flank of the Salient. Of four CWGC cemeteries, the most significant is Sanctuary Wood.

Sanctuary Wood (Hill 62) Museum
MUSEUM

(Map p121; ☑ 057 46 63 73; Canadalaan 26, Ypres; adult/child €10/5; ☺ 9.30am-6pm Apr-Aug) This gnome-fronted, surreally ordinary house displays a chaotic hotchpotch of WWI helmets, shoes, guns and harrowing photos, some in antiquated wooden stereoscopic viewers. The main justification for the hefty entrance fee is a string of original trenches in the woodland garden and the cross-pinned relic of a bombarded tree. The museum is between **Sanctuary Wood British Cemetery** (Map p121; Canadalaan, Ypres) and the Canadian Hill 62 memorial, 2km down a dead-end lane from the Hooge bus stop.

Hooge Crater Museum
MUSEUM

(Map p121; ✆ 057 46 84 46; www.hoogecrater.com; Meenseweg 467, Hooge; adult/child €5/2; ☺ 10am-6pm Tue-Sat, to 9pm Sun) In a quaint repurposed chapel on the Ypres–Menen road (N8), this small but characterful two-room museum is entered between assorted WWI sandbags, rusty rail sections and field guns. Inside, uniformed mannequins, arms and assorted memorabilia are ranged in venerable display cases around a life-sized model of a red Fokker triplane. The attached *café* is appealing.

Massive explosions detonated beneath German defences by British engineers created the crater for which it's named. That crater now forms a pretty pond 100m east in the gardens of Kasteelhof 't Hooghe, which also has some re-excavated trenches.

Park Bellewaerde
AMUSEMENT PARK

(Map p121; ✆ 057 46 86 86; www.bellewaerdepark.be; Meenseweg 497; adult/child €31/26; ☺ 10am-6pm Jun-Aug, to 5pm Easter holidays & Wed-Sun May) This grand-scale high-adrenaline amusement park is the perfect place to give the kids a break from the histories of war.

❶ Getting There & Away

Buses do reach some WWI sites, but to see more than a couple in a day, you'll need a guided tours from Ypres, a well-planned cycle route or your own vehicle.

Kortrijk

✆ 056 / POP 76,265

Prosperous Kortrijk (Courtrai in French) was founded as the Roman settlement of Cortoriacum. It grew wealthy as a flax and linen centre, but was severely bombed by the Allies during WWII. It retains a gorgeous begijnhof and an important historical resonance as the venue for Flanders' defining medieval battle (p124).

Close to the French border and almost equidistant from Bruges, Ghent and Brussels, Kortrijk is a popular city for business travellers and trade expos.

◉ Sights

Broeltorens
TOWER

(Broelbrug) This iconic pair of three-storey fortress towers guards a picturesque arched stone bridge across the River Leie in central Kortrijk. Last reminders of a long-gone medieval city wall, their machicolations and conical roofs look magical in night-time floodlights when the backdrop of mediocre apartments is less obvious.

Grote Markt
SQUARE

Kortrijk's curved central square is scarred by insensitive 20th-century constructions, but the slightly leaning, multi-spired brick *belfort* (belfry) provides an attractive focus, and the restored 1421 Historisch Stadhuis (former town hall) building has a fine ornate facade dotted with stone mini-spires and niche statues.

St-Maartenskerk
CHURCH

(St-Maartenskerkstraat; ☺ 7am-5pm Mon-Fri, 10am-5pm Sat & Sun) The noble 83m tower that adds such finesse to the Kortrijk skyline belongs to this mostly 15th-century Gothic church, built on the site of St-Eloi's 7th-century chapel.

Broelmuseum
GALLERY

(✆ 056 27 77 80; Broelkaai 6; adult/concession/youth €3/2/free; ☺ 10am-noon & 2-5pm Tue-Fri, 11am-5pm Sat & Sun) Highlights of this fine art museum include Roelandt Savery's 1604 masterpiece *Plundering of a Village* and Emmanuel Viérin's semi-impressionist scenes of the begijnhof (p124). It occupies a classical river-facing 1785 mansion retaining Louis XVI gilt interiors and a notable orangery near the Broeltorens.

Kortrijk 1302
MUSEUM

(✆ 056 27 78 50; www.kortrijk1302.be; Begijnhofpark; adult/concession/youth €6/4/1; ☺ 10am-5pm Tue-Sun, to 6pm summer weekends) Promising seven centuries in one day, this modern multimedia 'experience' museum delves deep into the background events leading up to the Battle of the Golden Spurs (p124) and brings to life the significance and outcomes of the event from a Flemish perspective.

BRUGES, GHENT & NORTHWEST BELGIUM KORTRIJK

BATTLE OF THE GOLDEN SPURS

Flanders' French overlords were incensed by the Bruges Matins massacre of May 1302. Philip the Fair, the French king, promptly sent a well-equipped cavalry of aristocratic knights to seek retribution. Outside Kortrijk on 11 July this magnificent force met a ragged, lightly armed force of weavers, peasants and guild members from Bruges, Ypres, Ghent and Kortrijk. Expecting little from their lowly foes, the horseback knights failed to notice a cunningly laid trap: the Flemish townsfolk had previously disguised a boggy marsh with brushwood. Snared by the mud, the heavily armoured French were quickly immobilised and slaughtered, their golden spurs hacked off and displayed as trophies in Kortrijk's Onze Lieve Vrouwekerk. It was the first time professional knights had ever been defeated by an amateur infantry and the event became a potent symbol of Flemish resistance. At least that's the way it's remembered thanks to Flanders' first great novel, *De Leeuw van Vlaanderen* (The Lion of Flanders), and to this day 11 July is celebrated as Flanders' 'national' holiday.

The battlefield site is now Groeningheveld, a leafy park in relatively central Kortrijk marked by a 1906 pseudo-medieval gateway and the triumphant Groeninge Statue featuring a gilded woman unleashing the Flemish lion.

Begijnhof
NOTABLE BUILDING

(Begijnhofstraat; ⊙ 7am-9pm) **FREE** Small but utterly delightful, Kortrijk's enclosed *begijnhof* is as charming a cluster of whitewashed old terraced houses as you could hope to find. Enter through a portal that is tucked behind Café Rouge and admire the 1682 turreted mansion at Begijnhof 27.

Onze Lieve Vrouwekerk
CHURCH

(Deken Zegerplein 1; ⊙ 7am-7pm Mon-Sat, to 6pm Sun) Echoing with wistful music, this church has a gilt sunburst altarpiece, heraldic panels in the 1373 St-Catherinekapel and features Van Dyck's 1631 painting *Kruisoprichting* (Raising of the Cross) in the left transept. Poet-priest Guido Gezelle was once pastor here (1872–1889).

Texture
MUSEUM

(☑ 056 27 74 70; www.texturekortrijk.be; Noordstraat 28; adult/concession/child €6/4/2; ⊙ 10am-6pm Tue-Sun May-Sep, to 5pm Oct-Apr) The Texture museum is located in an 1902 flax factory and focuses on the town's flax and linen industry; you'll also see a lovely collection of damasks and laces. The history of flax is told through individual accounts and is surprisingly absorbing: you can touch and smell the fabric itself.

🛏 Sleeping

Kortrijk's accommodation prices rise during trade expos in September, October, February and March.

★ Hotel Messeyne
HOTEL €€

(☑ 056 21 21 66; www.hotelmesseyne.be; Groeningestraat 17; d from €135; @ 🖋) This grand 1662 townhouse's beamed high ceilings and original fireplaces meld with stylish contemporary decor, immaculate rooms and designer corridors imaginatively featuring cacti as art. There's a well-regarded restaurant (closed Sundays), free sauna, garden-facing fitness room and a darkly mysterious little bar-lounge.

Square Hotel
HOTEL €€

(☑ 056 28 89 50; www.squarehotel.be; Groeningestraat 39; d from €89; �️🖋) Suave minimalism aimed at businessmen with relatively limited budgets. Spooky doll faces survey the breakfast area. Weekend discounts are available.

Center Hotel
HOTEL €€

(☑ 056 21 97 21; www.centerhotel.be; Graanmarkt 6; d from €89; 🖋) Attractively modernised rooms at reasonable prices above a subtly fashionable bar with handy 24-hour reception. Breakfast €12.

Eating

Teater Kaffee
CAFE €

(☑ 056 20 23 89; Schouwburgplein 6; light meals from €4-14; ⊙ 11am-8pm Mon-Sat, to 2pm Thu) Classic wood-panelled *café* with tulip lamps, Rodenbach beer on draught and inexpensive pub meals (cheese croquettes, baguette sandwiches).

Brasserie de Heeren van Groeninghe
BRASSERIE €€

(📞 056 25 40 25; www.heerenvangroeninghe.be; Groeningestraat 36; mains €14-22; ⏰ 11.30am-2.30pm & 6-10pm Thu-Fri, 11.30am-10pm Sat-Sun) Excellent-value meals are served in twinkling candlelight in a grand old mansion with high ceilings and original gilt decor. Reservations are wise, especially at weekends. The outdoor terrace, sandwiched between dull brick walls, is bare by contrast but serves snacks and drinks all day, including bottled Quintine and draught Boon Kriek.

't Mouterijtje
BRASSERIE €€

(📞 056 20 14 14; www.mouterijtje.be; Kapucijnenstraat 25a; mains €14-26; ⏰ 5pm-midnight Fri-Tue) This spacious family-oriented brasserie features lots of old bare brickwork, red steel beams, convivial lighting and an undulating ceiling. There's a good range of beers, fish dishes and mussels and the signature dish *côte-à-l'os* (rib roast).

Café Rouge
BRASSERIE €€

(📞 056 25 86 03; www.caferouge.be; St-Maartenskerkhof 6a; mains €17-27; ⏰ 11am-9pm Tue-Sun, to 10pm Fri & Sat) This bistro's French-style shuttered facade contrasts with a bold semi-minimalist interior; the terrace fills a tree-lined pedestrianised square behind the *begijnhof*. Great for drinks, meals or afternoon pancakes (from €4).

B'thoven
STEAK €€

(📞 056 22 55 42; www.fonduehuisbeethoven.be; Onze-Lieve-Vrouwstraat 8; mains €17-25; ⏰ 6.30-10pm Tue-Sun) Amid the cracked paintwork of this recycled old *café*, Ludwig busts sniff enviously at the range of ribs, steaks and fondues.

★Restaurant Messeyne
EUROPEAN €€€

(📞 056 21 21 26; www.restaurantmesseyne.be; Groeningestraat 17; lunch with/without wine €53/38, dinner mains €18-43; ⏰ noon-2pm & 7-10pm Mon-Fri) Popular with the travelling business crowd, the restaurant of the fabulous Hotel Messeyne (p124) offers exquisitely presented lunchtime set menus and evening fine dining; the latter features the likes of foie gras, caviar and tuna tartare for starters and poached sole, wild duck or veal for the main event. Dress to impress.

🍷 Drinking & Nightlife

★Gainsbar
BAR

(📞 0497 45 10 04; Vlasmarkt 1; ⏰ noon-1am Tue-Thu, 2pm-2am Fri-Sun) Beer specialist bar with a youthful upbeat vibe. Organises occasional meet-the-brewer days and serves some rare gems, including occasional draught masterpieces from regional brewers Dupont and Struise.

Viva Sara
COFFEE

(📞 056 21 72 70; www.vivasara.be; Grote Markt 33; ⏰ 8am-6.30pm Mon-Fri, 9am-6pm Sat) Kortrijk's leading coffee house has become so beloved by locals that it now has branches in Bruges and Groeninge. It also has its own brand of chocolate (Viva Laura) and confectionary (Viva Lena).

Staminee den Boulevard
PUB

(📞 0474 99 39 76; https://stamineeboulevard.org; Groeningelaan 15; ⏰ 4.30pm-1am Thu-Mon) Flickering candles, soft jazz and more than 100 beers including draught Chimay Tripel (€3.50). Tables spill onto the park opposite.

ℹ Information

Centrale Bibliotheek (📞 056 27 75 00; Leiestraat 30; ⏰ 10am-6.30pm Mon-Fri, to 4pm Sat; 📶) Library with free internet computers and wi-fi.

Toerisme Kortrijk (📞 056 27 78 40; www.toerismekortrijk.be; Begijnhofpark (Parking Houtmarkt); ⏰ 10am-5pm) Offers maps, brochures and bicycle rental.

ℹ Getting There & Around

Kortrijk station is on Stationsplein, 500m south of Grote Markt. Regular trains run to Bruges (€8.10, from 40 minutes), Brussels (€13.40, one hour), Ghent (€7.20, 20 minutes) and Ypres (€5.50, 30 minutes).

At **Mobiel** (📞 056 24 99 10; www.mobiel.be; Pieter Tacklaan 57; bike rental from €12 per day; ⏰ 10am-6pm Mon-Sat) you can hire a wide range of wheels – everything from city bikes and electric bikes to rickshaws (with or without driver) – or consider signing up for the **Mobit** (📞 09-278 72 56; www.mobit.eu; from €0.45 per 20 min) bike-sharing service. With **Blue Bike** (p102) also in town, you're spoiled for choice.

Oudenaarde

POP 31,132

In the 16th and 17th centuries, Oudenaarde (Audenarde in French) was a wealthy rural town famed for its local weavers' elaborate, detailed tapestries. Today, it's brightly adorned cyclists that weave through the streets as the Tour of Flanders (p127) bike race finishes in the town.

Outside race times – when you'll be lucky to get near the place – Oudenaarde is an excellent gateway for explorations into the surrounding countryside. With a handful of niche museums, it's worth considering staying overnight at this very pretty and compact town.

◉ Sights

★ Centrum De Ronde van Vlaanderen
MUSEUM

(Tour of Flanders Centre; ☑ 055 33 99 33; www. crvv.be; Markt 43; adult/concession/child €8/6/4; ◐ 10am-6pm) Fans of the Tour of Flanders (De Ronde) – and lovers of cycling in general – shouldn't miss this state-of-the-art museum, featuring displays on the history of the race and cycling in general. Museum shop staff can help plan your own cycling tour of the Flemish Ardennes or Flanders Fields. Guided rides and packages are also available.

MOU Museum
MUSEUM

(☑ 055 31 72 51; www.mou-oudenaarde.be; Markt 1; adult/senior/student €6/5/1.50; ◐ 10am-5pm Tue-Sun Mar-Sep, 10am-5pm Mon-Fri, from 2pm Sat & Sun Oct-Feb) Occupying a significant chunk of the city's stunning **stadhuis** (Markt 1), the new-in-2012 MOU still feels fresh. It presents the visitor with an impressive multimedia presentation on a millennia of local history; there are also displays of silverware and a priceless collection of 16th-century Oudenaarde tapestries. The website has details on visiting exhibitions.

St-Walburgakerk
CHURCH

(☑ 055 31 72 51; Sint-Walburgastraat; ◐ 2.30-5pm Wed-Sun Apr-Sep, Tue & Sat only Oct-Mar) At the southwestern corner of Markt, this imposing church was cobbled together from a 13th-century chancel and a 15th-century Brabantine Gothic tower. Inside are numerous paintings and tapestries. There are carillon concerts at 8.30pm Thursdays in July and August.

PAM
MUSEUM

(Provincial Archaeological Museum; ☑ 055 30 90 40; www.pam-ov.be/ename; Lijnwaadmarkt 20, Ename; adult/concession €2.50/1.25; ◐ 9.30am-5pm Tue-Sun) This museum of archaeology and local history occupies a site that in AD 925 was one of three main defences along the border between pre-medieval France and Ottonian Germany. It later became a vast abbey that was destroyed in the French Revolution. That history is brought to life here with dioramas, video material and multilingual audioguides.

The museum is in a quiet back street in Ename village, on the outskirts of Oudenaarde, adjacent to a 1000-year-old stone church.

A network of walking trails take the inquisitive visitor on a journey over the land where these stories played out.

🛏 Sleeping & Eating

★ Beans and Dreams
B&B €€

(☑ 0494 15 05 09; www.beans-and-dreams.be; Hoogstraat 65; d from €90) This special little B&B is in an ideally located art nouveau townhouse atop an eponymous cafe. The design sensibilities of the owner-operators are as warm and wonderful as the barista-brewed coffee they serve below.

★ Steenhuyse
GUESTHOUSE €€

(☑ 055 23 23 73; www.steenhuyse.info; Markt 37; s/d incl breakfast from €95/120; 🐾) This splendidly restyled 16th-century mansion has 21st-century Nordic-styled rooms with sun-drenched interiors, top-quality Philippe Starck fittings and bath areas that are open to the room. Champagne breakfasts are provided in the cafe area (€20 for non-guests, reservation required). Rates rise on weekends.

Hotel Leopold
BOUTIQUE HOTEL €€

(☑ 055 69 99 65; https://leopoldhoteloudenaarde. com; De Ham 14; d incl breakfast from €109; 🅿🐾❄🐾) Oudenaarde's newest hotel, this 58-room boutique offering by the river is an excellent choice for the discerning traveller who'll appreciate the cool colour scheme, complimentary mineral water, dark woods, plush bedding and extras like in-room espresso machines. The property has an onsite bar-restaurant and a sun-drenched terrace.

Pasta Piccaso
ITALIAN €

(☑ 0487 47 20 75; www.facebook.com/pastapiccaso; Nederstraat 50; pasta €4-7; ◐ 11am-7pm Mon-Sat) For a quick bite, this joint doles out eight tasty sauces with the pasta of your choice in a jiffy. Food is mostly takeaway, but there's a handful of seats in the tiny shop.

De Mouterij
BISTRO €€

(☑ 055 30 48 10; www.facebook.com/DeMouterij; Meerspoortsteeg 2; mains €12-20; ◐ 10am-9pm

Thu-Sun) Tucked away on a side lane behind the Centrum De Ronde van Vlaanderen you'll find this homely Belgian affair. It offers al fresco dining in its spacious garden, which feels a bit like going to your favourite relatives' place for a family gathering in the back yard. The menu features grilled meats, seafood, salads and, of course, beer.

La Pomme d'Or BRASSERIE €€€

(☑055 31 19 00; www.pommedor.be; Markt 62; mains €12-28, set menu €46; ⊙noon-10pm; 🛜) Tiffany-glass windows, wrought-iron lamps and 1930s decor create a welcoming feel at one of East Flanders' better-value brasserie-cafes, where beautifully presented plates deliver Flemish cuisine prepared from fresh local ingredients. Set menus are good value, and the beer-and-wine list should hold your interest.

Tastefully upgraded guest rooms (single/double from €70/75) await upstairs, should you overindulge.

❶ Information

Toerisme Oudenaarde (☑055 31 72 51; www. oudenaarde.be/toerisme; Markt 1; ⊙9am-5.30pm Mon-Fri & 10am-5.30pm Sat & Sun Mar-Sep, 9am-5pm Mon-Fri & 2-5pm Sat & Sun Oct-Feb)

❶ Getting There & Away

The station, 900m north of Markt via Nederstraat and Stationstraat, has trains at least hourly to Kortrijk (€4.40, 20 minutes), Ghent's **Sint-Pieters station** (p141) (€4.80, 28 minutes) and Brussels (€9.40, 50 minutes).

Geraardsbergen

POP 32,477

Surrounded by vistas of the pretty, rolling terrain of the Flemish Ardennes, the 'free city' of Geraardsbergen has claimed this enviable hillside spot since 1068.

Though its medieval roots aren't apparent at first, trundle up steep, narrow Grotestraat to the hilltop Markt to uncover the city's historical gems.

Today Geraardsbergen (Grammont in French) is best known for its frequent role in cycling circles for its frequent role in the **Tour of Flanders** (De Ronde van Vlaanderen; www.rondevanvlaanderen.be; ⊙early Apr) bike race, and for its local speciality, the *Mattentaart* (a flaky almond curd tart).

◉ Sights

★Muur van Geraardsbergen STREET

(Wall of Geraardsbergen) For cycle-racing enthusiasts the name Geraardsbergen is inextricably linked with the 'Muur' (Mur de Grammont in French), a steep cobbled rise that frequently forms a major highlight of the Tour of Flanders, depending on the route chosen each year. Topped by a beautiful **chapel** (Chapel of our Lady of Oudenberg; Oudeberg) and offering wonderful views, the Muur is well signposted from the Markt and best approached on foot or by bike from Abdijstraat.

De Permanensje MUSEUM

(☑054 43 72 89; Markt 5-9; ⊙10am-5pm) FREE Combining the local tourist office (p128) and the former Manneken-Pismuseum, this compact museum has a variety of multimedia introductions to the trades and traditions of Geraardsbergen and the surrounding Flemish Ardennes. Highlights include push-and-sniff displays and a popular collection of antique costumes for the town's beloved Manneken Pis statue.

Manneken Pis STATUE

(Markt) Brussels isn't the only city in which a little boy statue relieves himself. Indeed, many locals insist that Geraardsbergen's Manneken Pis is the original. The gently dribbling fountain is in a corner of the main square fronting the turreted 1893 town hall, which adopts a medieval fantasy appearance when floodlit at night.

Geraardsbergse Musea MUSEUM

(☑054 43 72 89; Collegestraat 26; ⊙2-5pm Tue-Sun Apr-Sep, 2-5pm Sat & Sun Oct-Mar) FREE This simple, sweetly old-fashioned museum has no one distinct theme but features rooms with small collections of artefacts as diverse as matchboxes, cigars, smoking pipes, Geraardsbergen's signature Chantilly black lace, and, of course, local beer.

It's two blocks northeast of the train station.

🛏 Sleeping & Eating

★Hotel Geeraard BOUTIQUE HOTEL €€

(☑054 24 67 88; www.geeraard.be/en; Lessensestraat 36; s/d incl breakfast from €95/120; ℗❋🛜) Hotel Geeraard's recently renovated, chic, cream-coloured rooms have a splash of colour, plush bedding and comfy armchairs. Some rooms have deep soaking tubs. An excellent breakfast spread, on-site parking and fast wi-fi come with the package. It's less than a five-minute walk from Geraardsbergen station.

Casa Dodo
B&B €€

(☎054 58 02 59; www.casadodo.be; Nieuwstraat 12; s/d from €80/90; ⊜☎) Choose a colour-themed room at this swish B&B over the station-area hotels for its friendly English-speaking welcome and bean-bag recliners. Book ahead to rent one of the bikes. Casa Dodo is about 100m north of the tourist office, along Vredestraat: look for the rainbow-coloured building to your left.

Pasta Al Dente
ITALIAN €

(☎0489 77 70 61; www.aldente-geraardsbergen.be; Kaai 3; pasta €6-11.50; ⊙noon-6.30pm Tue-Thu, to 8pm Fri & Sat) This no-frills joint, located midway up the hill between the station and the Markt, offers great-value tasty and filling pastas. Takeaway is available, or sit at the restaurant's tables on the banks of the Dender just across the street.

★ 't Hemelrijck
TAVERNA €€

(☎054 41 05 77; www.taverne-hemelrijck.com; Oudeberg 2; mains €13-25; ⊙11am-10pm, closed Wed & Thu Oct-Mar) This usually bustling tavern has a pleasant outdoor patio, cold local beer and good-value pub food including plenty of seafood and local cuisine. For many, a meal here is the reward for making an ascent to the top of the Muur (p127). From September to June, the €15 *Dagmenu* (daily set lunch menu) offers excellent value.

🍷 Drinking & Nightlife

There's a handful of simple pubs and bars by the Markt and down the hill by the river.

Het Bruggenhuis
PUB

(☎054 24 48 89; www.bruggenhuis.be; Majoor Van Lierdelaan 50; ⊙3.30-10pm Wed-Thu, to midnight Fri & Sat, noon-10pm Sun) This picture-perfect rural tavern seems to have stepped straight out of an ethnographic museum. Seats spill out canal-side with rural views along the towpath. It's a 2km walk or cycle down the Dender's western bank to Van Lierdebrug bridge. Cold beer, limited light menu, live music Friday nights.

ℹ️ Information

Infokantoor Visit Geraardsbergen (☎054 43 72 89; www.visitgeraardsbergen.be; Markt; ⊙10am-5pm)

ℹ️ Getting There & Away

From Geraardsbergen station, 900m south of Markt on Stationsplein, frequent rail services operate to to Lessines (€2.40, seven minutes), Ath (€3.60, 23 minutes), Ghent (€6.40, 50 minutes) and Brussels (€7.80, 1⅓ hours).

GHENT

POP 248,358

Despite being one of Belgium's oldest cities, Ghent remains small enough to feel cosy but big enough to be a vibrant, relevant centre for trade and culture. There's a wealth of medieval and classical architecture here, contrasted by large post-industrial areas undergoing urban renewal that give Ghent a gritty-but-good industrial feel.

In the centre, tourists remain surprisingly thin on the ground, but Ghent's large student and youth population means there's always people about, enjoying the city's fabulous canal-side architecture, abundance of quirky bars and good-value restaurants, and some of Belgium's best museums.

History

The seat of the Counts of Flanders, medieval Ghent (Gent/Gand in Dutch/French) was a great cloth town that grew to become medieval Europe's largest city after Paris and Constantinople. The hard-working townsfolk fought hard for their civil liberties, but were finally cowed in 1540 having enraged Ghent-born Holy Roman Emperor Charles V ('Keizer Karel', 'Charles Quint') by refusing to pay taxes to fund his military forays into France. He came down swiftly and heavily, abolishing the town's privileges and humiliating the guildsmen by making them walk around town wearing nooses around their necks. Ghent-folk are still nicknamed 'Stroppendragers' (rope pullers) to this day. This episode signalled the beginning of a long decline as the Low Countries' centre of gravity moved to Antwerp.

In the early 19th century, Ghent was the first town in Flanders to harness the Industrial Revolution. Many of its historical buildings were converted into flax- and cotton-processing mills and the city became known as the 'Manchester of the Continent'. These days, Ghent is Flanders' biggest university town, while its vast docks stretching for miles to the north provide its economic life-blood. Older dock areas Achterdok, Handelsdok and Houtdok have begun a massive regeneration program which is set to continue for years to come.

Sights

⊙ Central Ghent

Ghent's magnificent medieval core comprises three interconnected squares – Vrijdagmarkt, Grote Markt and Korenmarkt – dominated by the towers and spires of the Belfort (p129) and two imposing churches. Directly west, the canal is lined with medieval-styled buildings curving around to the pretty Patershol district.

CityCard Gent (48-/72-hour €30/35) gives free entrance to all of Ghent's top museums and monuments and allows unlimited travel on trams and city buses, plus a boat trip. It's excellent value. Buy one at participating museums, major bus offices or the tourist office (p142). For the low down, hit https://visit.gent.be/en/good-know/good-know/citycard-gent.

★**Belfort** HISTORIC BUILDING
(Map p134; ☑ 09-375 31 61; www.belfortgent.be; Sint-Baafsplein; adult/concession €8/3; ☉10am-6pm) Ghent's Unesco-listed 14th-century belfry (91m) is topped by a large dragon weathervane: he's become something of a

city mascot. You'll meet two previous drag-on incarnations on the 350-stair climb to the top; there are elevators to help some of the way. Enter through the **Lakenhalle**, Ghent's cloth hall that was left half-built in 1445 and only completed in 1903. Hear the carillon at 11.30am Fridays and 11am on summer Sundays.

Other than some bell-making exhibits, the real attraction here is the view.

Check out the website for advance ticket purchasing, a free e-guide and smartphone app (Android only).

★**Gravensteen** CASTLE
(Map p134; ☑ 09-225 93 06; https://gravensteen.stad.gent/en; St-Veerleplein 11; adult/concession/child €10/6/free; ☉10am-6pm Apr-Oct, 9am-5pm Nov-Mar) Flanders' quintessential 12th-century stone castle comes complete with moat, turrets and arrow slits. It's all the more remarkable considering that during the 19th century the site was converted into a cotton mill. Meticulously restored since, the interior sports the odd suit of armour, a guillotine and torture devices. The relative lack of furnishings is compensated for with a handheld 45-minute movie guide, which sets a tongue-in-cheek historical costumed drama in the rooms, prison pit and battlements.

ADORING THE MYSTIC LAMB

Art enthusiasts swarm the Sint-Baafskathedraal (p131) to glimpse **The Adoration of the Mystic Lamb** (Het Lam Gods; Map p134; ☑ 09-269 20 45; www.sintbaafskathedraal.be; St-Baafskathedraal, Sint-Baafsplein; adult/child/audioguide €4/1.50/1; ☉9.30am-5pm Mon-Sat, 1-5pm Sun Apr-Oct, 10.30am-4pm Mon-Sat, 1-4pm Sun Nov-Mar), a lavish representation of medieval religious thinking that is one of the earliest-known oil paintings. Completed in 1432, it was painted as an altarpiece by Flemish Primitive artists the Van Eyck brothers, and has 20 panels.

The work represents an allegorical glorification of Christ's death: on the upper tier sits God the Father flanked by the Virgin and John the Baptist. On the outer panels are the nude Adam and Eve. The lower tier centres on the lamb, symbolising the sacrifice made by Christ, surrounded by all manner of religious figures and a landscape dotted with local church towers. The luminous colours and the rich, detailed crowd scenes are stunning.

The painting has had an illustrious history – the Calvinists nearly destroyed it; Austria's Emperor Joseph II was horrified by the nude Adam and Eve and had the panels replaced with clothed versions (the originals are now back in place); and the painting was marched off to Paris during the French Revolution and was later stolen by the Germans who concealed it in an Austrian salt mine during WWII. The panel De Rechtvaardige Rechters (The Fair Judges), stolen in 1934, is still missing, although in June 2018, engineer Gino Marchal and youth fiction author Marc de Bel created quite a stir by publicly declaring they had substantial evidence to suggest the missing panel was buried beneath the town's Kalandeberg square. At time of writing, Ghent officials were taking the claims quite seriously, but for many, the story reeks of a publicity stunt. Stay tuned as the mystery unfolds.

Ghent

Rabot

Museum Dr Guislain
(1.5km)

9

3

PATERSHOL

Geldmunt

Vrijdag
markt

Steendam

Ottogracht

Abrahamstr

St-Widostr

Kraanlei

Begijnhofdries
Proveniersterstr

Rabotstr

Burgstr

Hoogpoort

Belfortstr

St-Jacobsnieuwstr

Treck
Hostel
(800m)

Akkerstr

Ramen

St-Michielsplein

Nederpolder

St-Kwaadham

Hoogstr

12

Poel Drabstr

Rasphuisstr

Theresianenstr

Wispelbergstr

Holstraat

22 17

Oude Houtlei

Predikherenlei

Engelandgat

Limburgstr

Veldstr

Henegouwenstr Vlaanderenstr

Camping
Blaarmeersen
(2.5km)

Wellingstr

13

Zwartezustersstr

15

Gebr Vandeveldestr

See Ghent Centre Map (p134)

Papegaaistr

Anonciadenstr

Onderbergenstr

Zandpoortstr

Recollettenlei

Zonnestr Vogelmarkt

Kouter
Schouwburgstr

24 25

Ketelvaart

Coupure Rechts

Stoppelstr

Iependstr

Lindelei

Ketelvest

Savaanstr

21

Walpoortstr

29

14

Coupure Links

Bijlokevest

Coupure

Nederkouter

Guinardstr

Bagattenstr

Lammerstr

27

W

Wilsonplein

Martelaarslaan

Gr Brittannielaan

Offerlaan

Jozef Kluyskensstr

Apotheekstr

St-Kwintensberg

Gezusters
Lovelingstr

J Plateaustr

St-Pietersnieuwstr

23

Godshuizenlaan IJzerlaan

UNIVERSITY
QUARTER

St-Amandspl

St-Pieterspl

Abdisstr

5

Van Hulthemstr

Kattenberg

St-Amandstr

Muinkkaai

P Fredericqstr

Koning Albertlaan

Henleykaai

Eedverbondkaai

Verdedigingstr
de Grayerstr

Leopoldkaserne

Overpoortstr

2

6

19

Koning Leopold II laan

Kortrijksesteenweg

Meersstr

Baliestr

Smidsestr

28

Charles De Kerchovelaan

Eekhout

Kunstlaan

Kantienberg

20

Hertstr

Ter
Platen

Stalhof

18

Isabelkaai

Citadelpark

Citadellaan

Maria
Hendrikaplein

Kon Elisabethlaan

11

Fortlaan

Koning Leopold II laan

4

MSK

1

Hofbouwlaan

Nicholaas de Liemaerckeplein

Schoolstr

Gent-St-
Pieters

K. Lodewijk Ledeganckstr

7

Flanders
Expo (4km)

Ghent

◎ **Top Sights**

◎ **Sights**

▣ **Sleeping**

✕ **Eating**

◎ **Drinking & Nightlife**

◎ **Entertainment**

▣ **Shopping**

If you just want a photo of the castle, there's a great viewpoint on St-Widostraat.

Graslei   AREA
(Map p134) Ships have been docking on either side of the River Leie since the 11th century. The area on the east bank is known as Graslei; **Korenlei** (Map p134) is on the west. There are always people here milling about, wining, dining, or sitting on the stepped riverbank admiring the stunning architecture.

Sint-Baafskathedraal   CATHEDRAL
(Map p134; ☎ 09-269 20 45; www.sintbaafskathedraal.be; Sint-Baafsplein; ⊙ 8.30am-6pm Mon-Sat, 10am-6pm Sun Apr-Oct, to 5pm Nov-Mar) This

cathedral's towering interior has some fine stained glass and an unusual combination of brick vaulting with stone tracery. A €0.20 leaflet guides you round the cathedral's numerous art treasures, including a big original Rubens opposite the stairway that leads down into the partly muralled crypts. However, most visitors come to see just one magnificent work – the Van Eyck brothers' 1432 Flemish Primitive masterpiece, *The Adoration of the Mystic Lamb* (p129).

It's kept in a special temperature-controlled, half-darkened chapel near the west entrance. If you don't want to queue to see the original, a photographic copy is displayed for free in side-chapel 30, the sixth on the right beside the altar.

Stadhuis
NOTABLE BUILDING

(Map p134; ☎ 09-210 10 10; www.visitgent.be/en/town-hall; Bottermarkt 1; tour €5; ⏱ tours 2.30pm Mon-Thu May-Sep) Ghent's magnificent and flamboyant city hall was started in 1519 but not finished until 1600, by which time it had transformed into a Renaissance-style palazzo. It's a prime spot for weddings, but visitor access is limited to one-hour guided visits that can be booked online or through the tourist office (p142). Don't confuse the stadhuis with the controversial **Stadshal**, the modern barn-like construction located nearby.

Vrijdagmarkt
SQUARE

(Map p134) Once the city's forum for public meetings and executions, this large square is named for its Friday market (still held). Tempting *cafés* sit beneath step-gabled facades surveyed by a grand **statue of Jacob van Artevelde**, Ghent's 14th-century anti-French leader. A block west, you can see the 15th-century **Dulle Griet**, a red 5m-long super-cannon; its 660mm bore and 250kg cannonballs made it one of the five biggest siege guns of the entire Middle Ages.

Grasbrug
BRIDGE

(Map p134) To admire Ghent's towers and gables at their most photogenic, stand just west of the little Grasbrug bridge over the Leie at dusk. It's a truly gorgeous scene, though the appealing waterfront facades of Graslei (p131) aren't as old as they look – these 'medieval' warehouses and townhouses were largely rebuilt to make Ghent look good for the 1913 World Fair. Canal trips with **Rederij Dewaeler** (Map p134; ☎ 09-229 17 16; www.debootjesvangent.be; Steiger aan de Ko-

renlei 4A; adult/concession €7.50/4.50; ⏱ 10am-6pm Mar–mid Oct) depart from here.

Huis van Alijn
MUSEUM

(Museum of Daily Life; Map p134; ☎ 09-235 38 00; www.huisvanalijn.be; Kraanlei 65; adult/concession €6/2; ⏱ 10am-5pm Thu-Tue) Set in a restored 1363 children's hospice complex, this delightful museum examines everyday life from the 1890s to the present, with a fabulous emphasis on the 1960s to the '80s. Most of the exhibits are refreshingly self-explanatory, including quaint recreated shop interiors, photos of wedding fashions and a disarmingly moving collage of family home videos. There's always something new happening. The annexed *café* is a great spot to socialise and sample the local beers.

MIAT
MUSEUM

(Museum voor Industriële Archeologie en Textiel; Map p134; ☎ 09-269 42 00; www.miat.gent.be; Minnemeers 9; adult/youth €6/2; ⏱ 10am-5pm Thu-Tue) In a five-floor 19th-century mill-factory building, this thought-provoking museum celebrates Ghent's history of textile production and examines the social effects of 250 years of industrialisation. An extensive collection of heavy mechanical weaving equipment comes deafeningly alive on Tuesday or Thursday mornings around 10am; earplugs are provided. There are great city skyline views from the top floor.

Design Museum
MUSEUM

(Map p134; ☎ 09-267 99 99; www.designmuseumgent.be; Jan Breydelstraat 5; adult/under 26yr/child under 19 €8/2/free; ⏱ 10am-5.30pm Thu-Tue) A vast toilet-roll sculpture humorously marks the back side of this museum, which has a collection specialising in furnishings including baroque, art nouveau, '70s psychedelic and '90s furniture-as-art styles. It's hosted in an architecturally eclectic building that catapults you from the 18th century into the 21st, then drags you back again.

Prinsenhof
AREA

(Map p130) Originally the residence of the Count of Flanders and the birthplace of Charles V in 1500, the Prinsenhof was a walled castle with 300 rooms, a zoo and a pleasure garden. In the late 18th century the crumbling palace was repurposed as a sugar refinery, soap factory and cotton mill; little remains of the original compound. Today, it's a vibrant neighbourhood, home to the **Prinsenhoffeesten**, held each September.

Werregarenstraat
STREET

(Map p134; www.ghentizm.be; Werregarenstraat) Ghent's attachment to graffiti as an art form began in this central alley, known locally as Graffitistraatje. The website has a live map showing the locations of numerous graf sites around town.

⊙ Greater Ghent

★ MSK
GALLERY

(Museum voor Schone Kunsten, Museum of Fine Arts Ghent; Map p130; ☑ 09-323 67 00; www. mskgent.be; Fernand Scribedreef 1; adult/youth/child €8/2/free; ⊙ 9.30am-5.30pm Tue-Fri, 10am-6pm Sat & Sun) Styled like a Greek temple, this superb 1903 fine-art gallery introduces a veritable A–Z of great Belgian and other Low Countries' painters from the 14th to mid-20th centuries. Highlights include a happy family of coffins by Magritte, luminist canvases by Emile Claus, and Pieter Brueghel the Younger's 1621 *Dorpsadvocaat* – a brilliant portrait of a village lawyer oozing with arrogance. English-language explanation cards are available in each room.

The gallery also hosts visiting temporary exhibitions for which a supplemental admission fee is normally charged.

St-Pietersabdij
ABBEY

(St Peter's Abbey; Map p130; ☑ 09-266 85 00; www.sintpietersabdijgent.be; Sint Pietersplein 9; ⊙ 10am-6pm Tue-Sun) FREE Once the country's biggest abbey, St-Pieters was the original centre around which Ghent grew. Its fabulous wealth evaporated after French revolutionary armies confiscated all its properties, stripped its interiors and demolished the abbot's house. At the heart of the complex, its vast baroque-fronted church survived; the shell of the main monastery was later used as a military garrison. You can stroll among ruins, vines and apple trees in the abbey gardens.

Inside, the abbey's most impressive feature is the muralled roof of the former refectory; it's point 15 in 'Alison', a handheld video tour (€4) designed as 90 minutes of tangential musings by a ghost monk guide in a medieval love triangle. If you're rushed, the key tracks are 2 to 4 (history) and 10 (the garden).

STAM
MUSEUM

(Ghent City Museum; Map p130; ☑ 09-2671400; www.stamgent.be; Godshuizenlaan 2; adult/concession/ under 25yr €8/6/free; ⊙ 9am-5pm Mon-Fri, 10am-6pm Sat & Sun; ☑ 4) Shoehorned into a 17th-century former nunnery-hospital complex, this fabulous, architecturally striking, ultra-modern museum does a very thorough job of explaining Ghent's evolution from prehistoric times to the present. A giant satellite image vividly illustrates the vast extent of the docks; you could spend hours clicking between interactive map views of Ghent in different eras. City treaties and treasures are interspersed with choose-your-own film clips and a chance to peer into the future. Begin your city visit here. Audioguides (highly recommended) cost €3.

S.M.A.K.
GALLERY

(Museum of Contemporary Art; Map p130; ☑ 09-240 76 01; www.smak.be; Jan Hoetplein 1; adult/concession/child €8/2/free; ⊙ 9.30am-5.30pm Tue-Sun; ☑ 5) Ghent's highly regarded Museum of Contemporary Art is one of Belgium's largest. Works from its 3000-strong permanent collection (dating from 1939 to the present) are regularly curated to complement visiting temporary exhibitions of provocative, cutting-edge installations, which sometimes spill out right across the city.

Museum Dr Guislain
MUSEUM

(☑ 09-398 69 50; www.museumdrguislain.be; Jozef Guislainstraat 43; adult/concession €8/3; ⊙ 9am-5pm Tue-Fri, 1-5pm Sat & Sun; ☑ 1) Hidden away in an 1857 neo-Gothic psychiatric hospital, this enthralling mental-health museum takes visitors on a trilingual, multicultural journey through the history of psychiatry, from gruesome Neolithic trepanning to contemporary brain scans via cage beds, straightjackets, shackles and phrenology. Dr D'Arsonval's extraordinary 1909 radiographic apparatus looks like a Dr Frankenstein creation.

Universiteit Gent
Botanical Garden
GARDENS

(Ghent University Botanical Garden; Map p130; ☑ 09-264 50 73; www.ugent.be/we/en/services/garden; KL Ledeganckstraat 35; ⊙ 9am-4.30pm Mon-Sat, from noon Sun) FREE Home to more than 10,000 species, the pièce de résistance of Ghent's 2.75-hectare botanic gardens is its glasshouses, which contain an impressive collection of tropical plants, subtropical plants and succulents, and offer shivering winter travellers what's effectively a free sauna.

Ghent Centre

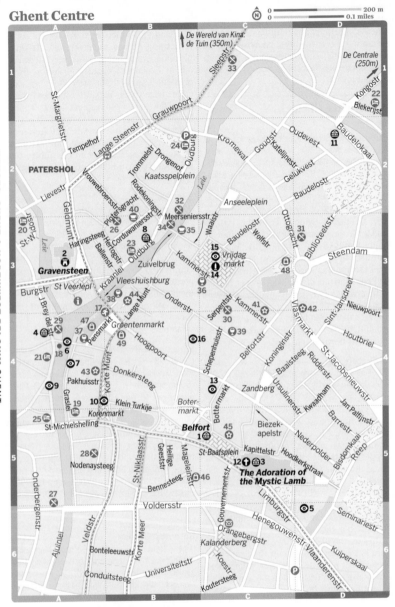

De Wereld van Kina: de Tuin GARDENS
(The World of Kina: the Garden; ☎ 09-225 05 42;
www.dewereldvankina.be; Berouw 55; adult/child
€3/1; ⏱ 9am-5pm Mon-Fri, Sun 2-5.30pm; 🖱)
This 7700-sq-metre garden and hot-garden
with more than 1500 plants has a broader

age appeal than its sister museum, the
House. It's somewhere the kids can come to
learn and have fun, while their custodians
can relax a little and enjoy the natural beauty of the plants and garden. The admission
fee grants entry to both complexes.

Ghent Centre

De Wereld van Kina: het Huis MUSEUM
(The World of Kina: the House; Map p130; ☑09-244 73 73; www.dewereldvankina.be; St-Pietersplein 14; adult/child €3/1; ☉9am-4.30pm Mon-Fri, 2-5.30pm Sun; ☝) This mishmash of a natural history museum is aimed primarily at school kids. Meet Pterygotus (a man-sized prehistoric lobster), walk through a human body with pounding heart, and get quizzed in the lively sex-education room. Press buttons to hear the songs of stuffed birds and find the model of Ghent as it looked in the 16th century. Admission grants access to Kina's sister complex, the Garden, located 3km to the north.

⊙ Around Ghent

On Ghent's outskirts, the upmarket suburban villages of **Deurle** and St-Martens-Latem peter out into woodlands. A century ago, this attractive area was home to several symbolist and expressionist artists, notably Gustave de Smet and Constant Permeke. Today the shady lanes are dotted with galleries and upmarket rural restaurants. Castle fans will love the moated **Kasteel Ooidonk** (☑09-282 26 38; www.ooidonk.be; Ooidonkdreef 7, Deinze; adult/concession/child €9/7/3, gardens only adult/child €2/0.50; ☉castle 2-5.30pm Sun Apr-Sep, grounds 10am-5pm Tue-Sun year-round; ℗), 3km beyond Deurle, still a family home and stunningly furnished.

🏃 Activities & Tours

Rederij De Gentenaer BOATING
(Map p134; ☑09-269 08 69; www.rederijdegentenaer.be; Groentenmarkt; adult/concession €7.50/4.50; ☉10am-6pm Mar–mid-Oct) Canal cruises are a great way to see some of the aspects of Ghent that you would otherwise miss. On fine days, this operator often adds an extra 10 minutes along Ketelvaart and then tunnels under Francois Laurentplein to emerge briefly outside the **Duivelsteen** (Castle of Gerard the Devil; Map p134; Geeraard de Duivelstraat 1) waterfront castle-house. Several other companies offer essentially similar 40-minute cruises for the same prices,

starting from Grasburg or Vleeshuisbrug bridges.

✨ Festivals & Events

Summer kicks off with a two week **Jazz Festival** (www.gentjazz.com/en; ☉late Jun–mid Jul) then the whole of Ghent turns into one giant raucous party during **Gentse Feesten** (Ghent Festivities; http://gentsefeesten.stad.gent; ☉mid-Jul) when many city squares become venues for music, street-theatre and more: a highlight of the year for some, an inconvenient logistical headache for others. Two months later the **Festival of Flanders** (www.gentfestival.be/en; ☉mid-Sep) is a mini-Gentse Feest of sorts featuring dozens of concerts and culminating in a big fireworks display. The season rounds off with **Film Fest Gent** (www.filmfestival.be/en; ☉early–mid-Oct), a 10-day carnival of celluloid with a particular focus on soundtracks.

🛏 Sleeping

Ghent offers innovative accommodation in all price ranges, including plenty for budget travellers, and plentiful B&Bs: see www.gent-accommodations.be and www.bedandbreakfast-gent.be.

★ Treck Hostel   HOSTEL €
(🖉09-310 76 20; www.treckhostel.be; Groendreef 51; dm/van from €19/35; 🛜) Treck earns bonus points for creativity and originality: indoor camping! Choose from nine seriously cool vintage vans, a large or small dorm, or pitch your own tent. Rest your weary head or get friendly at the bar.

Camping Blaarmeersen   CAMPGROUND €
(🖉09-266 81 60; www.gent.be/blaarmeersen; Zuiderlaan 12; campsite per adult/child/car/tent/caravan €6/3/3/6/6; ☉Mar–mid-Oct; P🛜) This simple campground is in a recreational park with a pretty pond that's perfect for swimming and aquatic sports. It's located about 4km west of Ghent's town centre. Simple huts are available (from €41; electricity and linen extra). Bus 8 will get you here.

Uppelink   HOSTEL €
(Map p134; 🖉09-279 44 77; www.hosteluppelink.com; Sint-Michielsplein 21; dm €19-35; 🛜) Within a classic step-gabled canal-side house, the showstopping attraction at this super-central hostel is the unbeatable view of Ghent's main towers as seen from the breakfast room (breakfast €5). It also has the biggest,

cheapest dorms. Smaller rooms have little view, if any.

Hostel 47   HOSTEL €
(Map p134; 🖉0478 71 28 27; www.hostel47.com; Blekerijstraat 47-51; dm/d incl breakfast from €27/72; 🛜) Unusually calm yet pretty central, this inviting hostel has revamped a high-ceilinged historical house with virginal white walls, spacious bunk rooms and designer fittings. Free lockers and cursory breakfast with Nespresso coffee; no bar.

De Draecke   HOSTEL €
(Map p134; 🖉09-233 70 50; www.jeugdherbergen.be/en/ghent; Sint-Widostraat 11; dm/tw from €26/30; @🛜) Behind a pseudo-medieval facade facing a picturesque willow-lined central canal lies this recently thoroughly renovated and spotless (though slightly institutional) HI hostel. Lockers cost €2 but the luggage room is free. No lockout.

★ Simon Says   GUESTHOUSE €€
(Map p134; 🖉09-233 03 43; www.simon-says.be; Sluizeken 8; d incl breakfast from €130; 🛜) Get in quick to snap up one of Simon and Christopher's two fashionably styled guest rooms located above their well-patronised, chilled-out coffee shop in a fabulous part of town. You can't miss it: it's the brightly coloured art nouveau house on the corner. Cheery hosts, excellent breakfasts and strong organic coffee.

Hotel Carlton   HOTEL €€
(Map p130; 🖉09-222 88 36; www.carltongent.be; Koningin Astridlaan 138; d/tw incl breakfast from €121/135; P🛜) Popular with both business and leisure travellers, this friendly family-run hotel in a prime position just east of Sint-Pieters station (p141) offers excellent value. Rooms are unaffected yet stylish, bright, comfortable and well maintained. An excellent fresh breakfast spread is prepared and served with care.

ApartGent
Apartments   APARTMENT €€
(Map p130; 🖉0497 51 75 25; www.apartgent.be; Zuidstationstraat 23; 3-night stay from €330; P🛜) Book in advance for these wildly popular fully self-contained apartments. They're spacious, stylish, central and aimed at the business or long-stay traveller. With great weekly and monthly rates, they offer superb value in at-times pricey Ghent. Three-night minimum stay.

Ghent Marriott
HOTEL €€

(Map p134; ☑ 09-233 93 93; www.marriottghent. be; Korenlei 10; d from €120; ⊛) On the inside, Ghent's Marriott is a standard international business/tourist hotel with stylish (if somewhat generic), comfortable, modern rooms and a glass and steel atrium. On the outside its handsome facade incorporates four medieval stone housefronts. Canal-view rooms (€50 extra) have wistful waterfront panoramas. Look online for some good deals.

Hotel Erasmus
HERITAGE HOTEL €€

(Map p130; ☑ 09-224 21 95; www.erasmushotel.be; Poel 25; s/d incl breakfast from €79/99; ⊙ reception 7am-10.30pm; ⊛) A suit of armour guards the breakfast in this creaky 16th-century building. Its 12 guest rooms have a mixture of old and antique furniture, giving it an atmospheric feeling of times gone by.

A Place To Be
B&B €€

(☑ 0495 15 47 42; Groot Begijnhof 91, Onze Lieve Vrouwstraat; s/d from €53/63; ⊛) A rare chance to sleep within the walls of a *begijnhof*. The nicest of three homely rooms has its own kitchenette. St-Amandsberg *begijnhof* is around 500m east of Gent-Dampoort (p141). Using the east gate off Schoolstraat, the B&B is the second doorway on the right, veering right near the little shrine-chapel. Check in before the *begijnhof* gates shut at night.

Big Sleep
B&B €€

(Map p130; ☑ 09-233 43 52; www.bigsleep.be; Hagelandkaai 38; s/d from €65/90; ⊛⊠) The three guestrooms of this friendly B&B in an attractive 1890s townhouse have high ceilings and private showers but shared toilets. The house is decorated with souvenirs of its owners' world travels, but perhaps its most notable features are that it is smoker friendly and has an attractive heated outdoor pool (summer months only). Handy for Gent-Dampoort (p141) station.

Atlas B&B
B&B €€

(Map p130; ☑ 09-233 49 91; www.atlasbenb.be; Rabotstraat 40; s/d from €69/84; ℗@⊛) This 1863 townhouse has attractive belle époque, art deco and art nouveau touches, a comfortable communal lounge area featuring maps, globes and an honesty bar, and four distinctive guest rooms themed by continent.

★ 1898 The Post
LUXURY HOTEL €€€

(Map p134; ☑ 09-277 09 60; www.zannierhotels. com/1898thepost/en; Graslei 16; d/ste €175/315; ⊛⊛) This beautiful boutique offering is housed in Ghent's spectacular twin-turreted former post office. The property's common areas, guestrooms and suites are dark and moody in a wonderful way, with elements of great design at every turn (though note the standard rooms are compact for the price). The hotel also offers fine dining and an ultra-atmospheric bar.

Hotel Verhaegen
B&B €€€

(Map p130; ☑ 09-265 07 60; www.hotelverhaegen. com; Oude Houtlei 110; d/ste from €210/265; ⊙ reception 2-6pm; ℗⊛) This sumptuous 1770s urban palace retains original sections of 18th-century Chinese wallpaper, a dining room with romantic Austrian-era murals, a dazzling salon and a neatly manicured parterre garden. The five guest rooms combine well-preserved modernist and retro touches. The lavish 'Paola's Room' is named for the young Italian princess who stayed here long before becoming Belgium's (now former) queen.

Hotel Harmony
BOUTIQUE HOTEL €€€

(Map p134; ☑ 09-324 26 80; www.hotel-harmony. be; Kraanlei 37; s/d from €140/155; ⊛⊠) Luxuriously heaped pillows, fine linen, Miró-esque art and swish modern colours lie beneath the 18th-century beams of this old-meets-new beauty. Even the smallest of the 25 rooms is amply sized, but shapes and views vary. Some have pastel nudes painted on the walls while others have hot tubs; rooms 30 and 31 share a wonderful panorama of Ghent's spires.

Check the hotel's Facebook page for promotional deals: www.facebook.com/hotel harmonygent.

✗ Eating

Cosy, half-hidden upmarket restaurants are dotted about the delightful cobbled alleyways of Patershol in old-world houses that were once home to leather tradesmen and to the Carmelite Fathers (Paters), hence the name. Several eateries jostle for summer terrace space on Graslei's (p131) gorgeous canal-side terrace; there's fast food around **Korenmarkt** (Map p134) and great-value Turkish options along Sleepstraat. Numerous vegetarian and organic choices feature on the tourist office's free *Veggieplan Gent* guide map.

Balls & Glory
BELGIAN €

(Map p134; ☑ 0486 67 87 76; www.ballsnglory.be; Jakobijnenstraat 6; balls €4.40-6; ⊙ 10am-9pm

Mon-Sat; ✐) This easy-going eatery is popular with students and hipsters for its classy interiors and good value. It serves big meaty or vegetarian balls (a bit like a hybrid of a traditional meatball and an arancini) that you can take away in a box or devour on-site.

Comida (by Palenque)
TEX-MEX €

(Map p134; ✆ 0472 83 42 85; https://palenque.gent; Serpentstraat 28; tacos from €4; ✐ 6-11pm Thu-Mon) Sister store of the neighbouring Palenque bar/boutique, Comida does tasty, cheap tacos and Tex-Mex.

Yaki Noodle
NOODLES €

(Map p130; ✆ 09-211 09 88; www.facebook.com/yakinoodlebar; Vlaanderenstraat 115; mains €6-14; ✐ noon-3pm & 5-10pm Thu-Tue) Cheap, tasty and with whopping portion sizes, Yaki Noodle is a student fave, best for big appetites or friends who like to share.

Pizza Gülhan
TURKISH €

(Map p134; ✆ 09-233 51 24; Sleepstraat 70; pide from €5, grills €9-14; ✐ 11.30am-midnight Wed-Mon) Want to (over) fill your stomach for €5? It's possible at Gülhan, a large, mildly garish modern diner that – despite the name – is *not* a pizzeria, unless you count the groaning plate-loads of excellent garnished fresh pide as 'pizza'. It's often crowded with appreciative locals, both Flemish and Turkish.

Soup Lounge
SOUP €

(Map p134; ✆ 09-223 62 03; www.souplounge.be; Zuivelbrug 4; small/large soup €5.50/6.50, sandwiches from €4; ✐ 10am-6pm) At this bright, central retro-'70s soup kitchen, each bowlful comes with add-your-own cheese and croutons, two rolls and a piece of fruit. Canal views are free.

Brooderie Jaffa
BAKERY €

(Map p134; ✆ 09-225 06 23; Jan Breydelstraat 8; light lunches €9-16; ✐ 9am-5.30pm Wed-Sun; ☎✐) This rustic bakery and tearoom looks a treat from the street, beckoning you inside for breakfasts, light lunches, soups, savouries and, of course, great coffee. If you find you want to stay longer, you can always check into one of the simple colourful B&B rooms with shared bathrooms (from €60).

★Holy Food Market
FOOD HALL €€

(Map p134; http://holyfoodmarket.be/en/home-en; Beverhoutplein 15; ✐ 11am-10pm Mon-Fri, to 11pm Sat & Sun, bar open till late) After transitioning from a church to a library, the 16th-century Baudelo Chapel has now morphed into Ghent's hottest dining destination – a glorified food court of the gourmet variety situated around a swanky central bar.

't Oud Clooster
CAFE €€

(Map p130; ✆ 09-233 78 02; www.toudclooster.be; Zwartezusterstraat 5; mains €16-22; ✐ 11.45am-2.30pm & 6-10.30pm Mon-Fri, 11.45am-2.30pm & 5.30-10.30pm Sat, 5.30-9.30pm Sun) Mostly candlelit at night, this atmospheric double-level cafe is built into sections of what was long ago a nunnery, hence the sprinkling of religious statues and cherub lamp-holders. Well-priced light meals are presented with unexpected style.

Amadeus
RIBS €€

(Map p134; ✆ 09-225 13 85; www.amadeusspareribrestaurant.be; Plotersgracht 8-10; mains €15-25; ✐ 6.30-11pm) Since 1987 this joint has been hardening the arteries of Gentiens with its knockout all-you-can-eat spare ribs (€17.95) at this and two other local addresses, all within ancient buildings that are full of atmosphere, bustle and cheerful conversation: see the website for the lowdown and other locations.

Panda
VEGETARIAN €€

(Map p134; ✆ 09-225 07 86; Oudburg 38; mains €17-22; ✐ noon-2pm & 6.15-8.45pm Mon-Sat; ✐) Good veggie food set to classical music and served on linen at tables with fresh orchids. Three windows have canal views. The daily changing lunch plate presents a truly artistic range of flavours, organic beers are available and there's a short wine list. By day enter through an organic food shop; at night seek out the side entrance passage.

★Carte Blanche
FLEMISH €€€

(Map p130; ✆ 09-233 28 08; www.carteblanchepw.be; Martelaarslaan 321; lunch menu €25, dinner menu €49; ✐ noon-2pm Mon-Thu, noon-2pm & 7-9.30pm Fri & Sat) Lobster is a big feature at this intimate, elegant restaurant. It's the brainchild of partners Walter Goderis and chef Paul Rapati, who've been receiving diners here for almost 25 years: Goderis serves and Rapati cooks. The dark-hued dining room feels very grown-up and the constantly evolving set menus, which focus on Rapati's take on traditional Flemish flavours, are beautifully presented.

Brasserie Pakhuis
EUROPEAN €€€

(Map p134; ✆ 09-223 55 55; www.pakhuis.be; Schuurkenstraat 4; mains €23-45; ✐ noon-2.30pm & 6.30pm-midnight Mon-Sat, bar 11am-1am) This hip, if mildly ostentatious, modern brasserie-bar-restaurant is set in a magnificently restored former textile warehouse. It retains the original century-old wrought ironwork and an incredible roof. It's well worth popping inside, even if you only stop for a drink.

🍷 Drinking & Nightlife

Ghent's fabulous bar scene is endlessly inspiring, with almost 300 watering holes to choose from in the city centre.

★ Dulle Griet   PUB
(Map p134; ☑09-224 24 55; www.dullegriet.be; Vrijdagmarkt 50; ⊙noon-1am Tue-Sat, to 7pm Sun, 4.30pm-1am Mon) Heavy beams, a heraldic ceiling, barrel tables, lacy lampshades and the odd boar's head all add character to one of Ghent's best-known beer pubs. It has more than 500 beers, including some of those hard-to-find ones you've heard all about.

★ Het Waterhuis
aan de Bierkant   PUB
(Map p134; ☑09-225 06 80; Groentenmarkt 9; ⊙11am-1am) Sporting a waterfront terrace, this photogenic classic beer-pub has an interior draped in dried hops, plus three exclusive house beers amid the wide selection.

In essentially the same building, 't Dreupelkot (Map p134; ☑09-224 21 20; www.dreupelkot. be; Groentenmarkt 12; ⊙11am-1.30am Mon-Thu, to 2am Fri-Sun) is a wonderful bar for tasting *jenever* (gin), with around 100 varieties.

Rococo   CAFE
(Map p134; ☑09-224 30 35; Corduwaniersstraat 5; ⊙9pm-late Tue-Sun) Lit only by candles, this classic late-night cafe-bar with carved wooden ceilings is an ideal place for cosy midnight conversations.

De Brouwzaele   BAR
(Map p130; ☑09-224 33 92; Ter Platen 17; ⊙11am-2am) Local gents unwind with newspapers, and grannies lunch on shrimp croquettes in this low-key classic *café* set in a triangular former brewery house. A giant copper brewstill is the focal point of its very original hop-decked central bar serving Westmalle among many classic draught beers.

Pink Flamingo's   BAR
(Map p134; ☑09-233 47 18; www.pinkflamingos. be; Onderstraat 55; ⊙noon-midnight Mon-Wed, to 3am Thu-Sat, 2pm-midnight Sun) Lively, kitsch cafe-bar with Barbie lamps, 1970s wallpaper and ample plastic fruit.

Het Spijker   PUB
(Map p134; ☑09-329 44 40; www.cafehetspijker. be; Pensmarkt 3; ⊙10am-5am) Built in the late 12th century, this heavy-beamed stone *café* is the oldest building on Graslei (p131) and was once the city grain store. Today it's a lively place that's usually the most central drinking spot to stay open really late.

De Planck   PUB
(Map p130; ☑0478 76 94 16; www.deplanck.be; Ter Platen; ⊙11.30am-11pm) Yes, palm trees grow in Ghent, albeit small ones on the deck of this appealing barge-*café*. Good-value snacks and meals supplement a choice of more than 200 beers, including its own, the pleasantly hoppy 6.8% Planckske house beer.

Gruut   BREWERY
(Map p130; ☑09-233 68 21; www.gruut.be; Grote Huidevettershoek 10; ⊙11am-1am) Ghent's uberpopular brewery-pub serves excellent herb-infused brews. Guided tours of the brewery (for a minimum of eight thirsty punters) are available by advance reservation.

De Geus van Gent   CAFE
(Map p130; ☑09-220 28 75; www.geuzenhuis.be; Kantienberg 9; ⊙4pm-late Mon-Thu, 7pm-late Fri-Sun) This congenial, multifaceted *café* with eclectic decor and at least 20 beers from the barrel hosts regular jam nights and live music.

Hotsy Totsy   BAR
(Map p130; ☑09-224 20 12; www.facebook.com/ Hotsy.Totsy.Gent; Hoogstraat 1; ⊙6pm-1am Mon-Fri, 8pm-2am Sat & Sun, from 8pm daily Jul & Aug) Silver-floral wallpaper, black-and-white photos from the glory days of celluloid and the occasional live jazz performance (9pm most Thursdays Oct-Apr) give this classic artists' *café* a real nostalgic vibe. It was founded by the brothers of famous Flemish author Hugo Claus.

Café Labath   COFFEE
(Map p130; ☑09-225 28 25; www.cafelabath.be; Oude Houtlei 1; ⊙8am-7pm Mon-Fri, 9am-7pm Sat, 10am-6pm Sun) Labath is a buzzing place for a fine coffee fix, organic Prosecco or a diverse selection of aromatic, tasty teas including Indian-style *masala chai* and *verse munt-thee* (fresh mint infusion).

Café Barista COFFEE
(Map p134; ☑0470 52 36 51; www.mybarista.be;
Meerseniersstraat 16; ⊘8am-6pm Tue-Fri, 9.30am-
6pm Sat & Sun; 🐾) Get your caffeine fix in this
central coffee specialist, brewing its beans in
a 14th-century riverside house.

☆ Entertainment

Dutch-language pamphlet-magazines *Week-
Up* and *Zone 09 Magazine* are free from
distribution boxes around town. Muziekclub
Democrazy (www.democrazy.be) details an
imaginative and varied network of clubs and
events at various venues.

Live Music

Most *cafés* don't charge entry fees for concerts, but might add a small supplement to
listed drink prices.

Hot Club Gent LIVE MUSIC
(Map p134; ☑09-256 71 99; www.hotclub.gent;
Schuddevisstraatje 2; ⊘3pm-late) Hidden down
the tiny alley behind 't Dreupelkot (p139)
jenever (gin) bar, this is a great place to seek
out live acoustic music. Be it jazz, gypsy,
blues or flamenco, there's likely to be a concert most term-time nights, when the venue
kicks on until late – sometimes very late.

Damberd LIVE MUSIC
(Map p134; ☑09-329 53 37; Korenmarkt 19;
⊘11am-1am) This local institution has been
a pub since the 18th century and a jazz club
of sorts for more than 30 years. There are
regular live performances across most musical genres.

Muzikantenhuis WORLD MUSIC
(Map p130; ☑0476 50 28 77; www.muzikanten
huis.be; Dampoortstraat 52; ⊘6pm-2am Tue-Sun,
concerts 9pm Thu-Sat) Ropes, horse harnesses
and the sayings of Rumi on the walls give
this very inexpensive *café* a slightly cheesy
atmosphere, but the free traditional Turkish
music concerts are the attraction here. You
might also find jazz and Latin styles.

De Centrale WORLD MUSIC
(☑09-265 98 28; www.decentrale.be;
Kraankindersstraat 2; ⊘2pm-midnight) Multicultural centre offering a range of world music
concerts and dance performances (flamenco, Turkish, North African, Asian).

Handelsbeurs CONCERT VENUE
(Map p130; ☑09-265 91 60; www.handelsbeurs.be;
Kouter 29) Historical central concert hall for

anything from classical music to Latin and
blues.

Café Trefpunt LIVE MUSIC
(Map p134; ☑09-233 58 48; www.trefpunt.be; Bij
St-Jacobs 18; ⊘bar 5pm-late, concerts 9pm Mon
Oct-Jul) On Monday evenings, when most
other places close, Trefpunt has jam sessions
or live concerts. Standards tend to be high
as performers want to impress the owners,
who also organise the Gentse Feesten (p136).

Charlatan LIVE MUSIC
(Map p134; ☑09-224 24 57; www.charlatan.be;
Vlasmarkt 9; ⊘7pm-late Tue-Sun) At perenni-
al favourite Charlatan you might find live
music in virtually any genre (from 10pm),
sometimes with a cover charge. It generally
opens long enough to leave you ready for
breakfast.

Performing Arts

★Vooruit ARTS CENTRE
(Map p130; ☑09-267 28 20; www.vooruit.be;
St-Pietersnieuwstraat 23; ⊘10am-1am; 🖵5)
A visionary architectural premonition of
art deco, the 1912 Vooruit building is a
prominent venue for dance, rock concerts,
film and visiting theatre companies. Its
lively *café* also hosts occasional low-key
free concerts and serves draught Moinette
bio-beer.

**★De Bijloke
Muziekcentrum** CLASSICAL MUSIC
(Map p130; ☑09-323 61 11; www.debijloke.be;
Jozef Kluyskensstraat 2) You'll find a wonderful
selection of classical music concerts (some
outdoors) at this repurposed historical site
that was once an abbey and then a hospital. Check the website for the low down on
what's coming up.

NT Gent Schouwburg THEATRE
(Map p134; ☑09-225 01 01; www.ntgent.be;
St-Baafsplein 17) Home to Ghent's premier
theatre company. It also offers interesting 'open rehearsals' and workshops, but
naturally almost everything's in Dutch. Its
cafe-restaurant has a great terrace overlooking the square.

De Vlaamse Opera OPERA
(Map p130; ☑070 22 02 02; www.vlaamseopera.be;
Schouwburgstraat 3) Ghent's 1840 opera hall
boasts horseshoe-shaped tiered balconies
and elegant salons.

🛍 Shopping

★ Sint-Jacob's Prondelmarkt　　MARKET
(Map p134; Bij Sint-Jacobs; ⊙8am-1pm Fri-Sun)
This extremely popular flea market is a must
for lovers of retro (especially the '70s). During the Gentse Feesten (p136) the market
runs for 10 days straight and attracts up to a
million visitors.

Supergoods Ghent　　CONCEPT STORE
(Map p130; ☑0468 31 63 20; www.supergoods.be;
Brabantdam 56b; ⊙10am-6pm Mon-Sat) Ecofriendly and fair-trade fashion for women
and men.

Fair Eco Fashion　　CLOTHING
(Map p134; ☑09-279 77 29; www.fairecofashion.
com; Mageleinstraat 11; ⊙10.30am-6.30pm Mon-
Sat) Ecofriendly, fair-trade fashion.

Groot Vleeshuis　　FOOD
(Great Abbatoir; Map p134; ☑09-223 23 24; www.
grootvleeshuis.be; Groentenmarkt 7; ⊙10am-6pm
Tue-Sun) This long medieval stone hall was
built as a meat market and now acts as a
promotion and tasting hall for regional agricultural produce. If you're passing by, consider strolling through beneath the hefty old
wooden beams and dangling smoked hams.

Atlas & Zanzibar　　BOOKS
(Map p130; ☑09-220 87 99; www.atlaszanzibar.be;
Kortrijksesteenweg 19; ⊙10am-1pm & 2-6pm Mon-
Sat) Ghent's best travel bookshop now has
two branches. This is the main and more
central; the other is at Kortrijksesteenweg
1036.

Tierenteyn-Verlent　　FOOD
(Map p134; ☑09-225 83 36; www.tierenteyn-
verlent.be; Groentenmarkt 3; ⊙9am-6pm Mon-
Sat) Mustard-makers since 1790, this museum-like shop also sells jams and spices.

ℹ️ Information

For free online and downloadable maps, check
out www.ghent.use-it.travel.

Ghent Tourist Office (Map p134; ☑09-266
56 60; https://visit.gent.be; St-Veerleplein 5;
⊙10am-6pm) Very helpful for free maps and
accommodation bookings.
Post Office (Map p134; ☑02-201 23 45; www.
bpost.be; Lange Kruisstraat 55; ⊙9am-6pm
Mon-Fri, to 3pm Sat)
Toerisme Oost-Vlaanderen (Tourism East
Flanders; Map p130; ☑09-269 26 00; www.
tov.be; Woodrow Wilsonplein 2; ⊙9am-noon &

1.15-4.45pm Mon-Fri) Useful for cycling-route
maps and information on the rural areas
around Ghent. It's in the historical Metselaar-
shuis, a medieval house with a stepped-stone
facade topped with 20th-century bronze jester
sculptures.

ℹ️ Getting There & Away

BUS

International buses with carriers **Eurolines**
(p102), **FlixBus** (☑ Netherlands +31 858 881
843; www.flixbus.be) and **DeinBus** (☑ Germany
+49 69 175 373 200; www.deinbus.de) depart
from **Gent-Dampoort Station** (p141).
　Some regional services start from **Gent-Zuid
Bus Station** (Map p130; Woodrow Wilsonplein),
and many more from various points around
Gent-Sint-Pieters Station.

TRAIN

Ghent has two main train stations.
Gent-Dampoort Station (☑ 02-528 28 28;
www.belgiantrain.be; Oktrooiplein 10) is the
closest to the centre of the old town and has
regular services to Antwerp (€9.90, fast/slow
42/64 minutes, three per hour), Bruges (€7,
36 minutes, hourly) and Kortrijk (€7.40, 35
minutes, hourly).
Gent-Sint-Pieters Station (☑ 02-528 28 28;
www.belgiantrain.be; Koningin Maria Hendrikaplein), 2.5km south of the centre, is Ghent's
main station and services more destinations,
including Brussels (€9.40, 36 minutes, twice
hourly), Ostend (€9.90, fast/slow 38/55 minutes) and Oudenaarde (€5, 30 minutes).

ℹ️ Getting Around

Biker (☑ 09-224 29 03; www.bikerfietsen.
be; Steendam 16; per day from €9; ⊙9am-
12.30pm & 1.30-6pm Tue-Sat) and **De Fiets
Ambassade** (The Bike Embassy; ☑ 09-242
80 40; https://fietsambassade.gent.be/
en; Voskenslaan 27; per half-day/day/week
€7/10/30; ⊙7am-7pm Mon-Fri) rent out
bicycles.
　Tickets on the **DeLijn** (p102) public transport
network are cheaper if prepurchased.
　Tram 1 runs through the centre from
Gent-Sint-Pieters Station, passing within close
proximity to most major sites.
　Local buses will take you further afield. Bus
lines 34, 35 and 36 go to St-Martens-Latem,
while the 16 will take you close to Ooidonk.
　Beware that much of the centre is essentially
off limits to cars: in the historic heart, don't
assume that you can necessarily drive up to
your hotel.

Antwerp & Northeast Belgium

LANGUAGE: DUTCH

Best Places to Eat

➡ The Jane (p158)

➡ Cachet de Cire (p166)

➡ Graspoort (p172)

➡ Infirmerie (p182)

➡ Life Is Art (p158)

Best Places to Stay

➡ Hotel Julien (p153)

➡ The Fourth (p177)

➡ Boutique Hotel Caelus VII (p182)

➡ Bed, Bad & Brood (p155)

➡ Carpe Diem (p180)

➡ Hof van Aragon (p168)

Why Go?

Design and diamonds, Rubens and techno, art nouveau and high fashion: in all its thrilling contradictions, the dynamic port city of Antwerp dominates northeastern Belgium. But it is by no means the only historic townscape that demands attention here. Were there no Bruges, Belgium might be celebrating Lier as one of its loveliest towns. Or maybe Mechelen, with its fascinating Brabantine history, remarkable churches and glorious central square. Like Lier, Diest and shamefully underappreciated Turnhout have some of Belgium's most romantically delightful *begijnhoven*. South of prosperous 'gin town' Hasselt lies lovable Tongeren, which claims to be Belgium's oldest settlement. Between here and buzzing university city Leuven is a charming region of undulating orchard-covered hills. This area is further dotted with easily accessible historic gems: the fairy-tale towers of Sint-Truiden, the unique church at Zoutleeuw and Tienen's trio of Roman tumuli (grave mounds).

Driving Distances (km)

	Antwerp	Tongeren	Turnhout	Mechelen
Tongeren	99			
Turnhout	40	82		
Mechelen	24	81	63	
Leuven	48	57	56	25

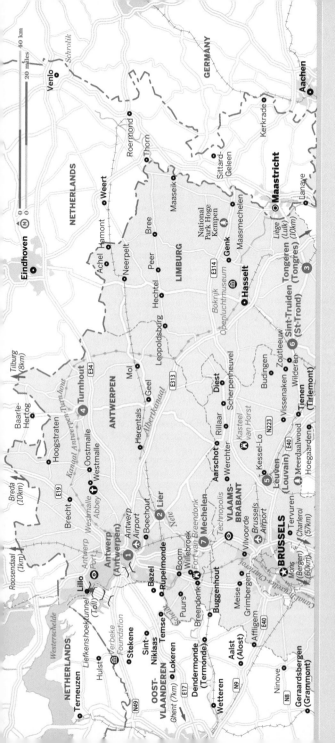

Antwerp & Northeast Belgium Highlights

1 Antwerp (p144) Revelling in Rubens and shopping for avant-garde design.

2 Lier (p167) Ambling around the super-quaint

historic city that once chose sheep over learning and has never lived it down.

3 Tongeren (p181) Getting beyond the antiques in Belgium's 'oldest town'.

4 Turnhout (p165) Strolling from the delightful *begijnhof*, past a courthouse in a moated castle to a unique museum of the town's playing-card production.

5 Leuven (p174) Admiring the superbly ornate town hall en route to 'Europe's longest bar', which gives this student city its ever-buzzing night-time heart.

6 Sint-Truiden (p180) Enjoying three magical towers for the price of one.

7 St-Romboutskathedraal (p169) Tackling the 97m cathedral tower in Mechelen.

ANTWERP (ANTWERPEN)

📱 03 / POP 521,700

Antwerp (Antwerpen/Anvers in Dutch/French) is Belgium's second city, biggest port and capital of cool. It has long been a powerful magnet for everyone from fashion moguls and club queens to art lovers and diamond dealers. In the mid-16th century it was one of Europe's most important cities and home to baroque superstar painter Pieter Paul Rubens – as many a museum will regularly remind you. Despite many historical travails thereafter, and severe WWII bombing, Antwerp retains an intriguing medieval heart with plenty of *café*-filled cobbled lanes, a riverside fortress and a truly impressive cathedral. Today, however, Antwerp's top drawcards are its vibrant fashion and entertainment scene, along with its startling architectural and cultural contrasts.

History

A fort built here during Charlemagne's time (768–814) was visited by such noted Christian missionaries as St Amand and St Bavo before being destroyed by Vikings in 836. Antwerp's well-protected port on the wide Scheldt River (Schelde in Dutch, Escaut in French) really came into its own once the Zwin waterway silted up, destroying Bruges' economy and forcing traders to move east. In 1531 the world's first specially built stock exchange opened here, and by 1555 Antwerp had become one of Europe's main trading,

cultural and intellectual centres, with a population of around 100,000.

But prosperity was ruthlessly cut short when Protestants smashed the city's cathedral in 1566 (a period known as the 'Iconoclastic Fury'). Fanatically Catholic Spanish ruler Philip II sent troops to restore order, but 10 years later the unpaid garrison mutinied, themselves ransacking the city and massacring 8000 people (the 'Spanish Fury'). After further battles and sieges, Antwerp was finally incorporated into the Spanish Netherlands and force-fed Catholicism. Thousands of skilled workers (notably Protestants, Jews and foreigners) headed north to the safety of the United Provinces (today's Netherlands).

By 1589 Antwerp's population had more than halved to 42,000. Affluence passed progressively to Amsterdam, although Antwerp revived somewhat after 1609 with the Twelve Years' Truce between the United Provinces and the Spanish Netherlands. Once the city was no longer cut off from the rest of the world, its trade and arts flourished and its printing houses became known throughout Europe. The world's first newspaper, *Nieuwe Tydinghen,* was produced here by Abraham Verhoeven in 1606.

Then the Treaty of Westphalia, which finally concluded the Dutch-Spanish wars in 1648, struck a massive blow by closing the Scheldt to all non-Dutch ships. Without its vital link to the sea, Antwerp was ruined. But Napoleon's arrival in 1797 changed all of that. The French rebuilt the docks, Antwerp got back on its feet, and by the late 19th century it had become the world's third-largest port after London and New York.

Antwerp was occupied by Germany in October 1914 after weeks of heavy bombardment including aerial Zeppelin attacks. Around a million refugees left for the UK, France and the Netherlands, although most returned after 1918 to rebuild the city. In 1920 Antwerp hosted the Olympic Games and in 1928 construction began on Europe's first skyscraper, the 27-storey Torengebouw (still standing, now called KBC Tower).

During WWII Antwerp's port again made it an obvious military target, and during German occupation around two-thirds of the Jewish population perished. The city's later 20th-century regeneration has been a sometimes contradictory mixture of modern multiculturalism and backlash, but few places seem so optimistic in forging ahead with 21st-century visions.

HANDS UP FOR A LEGEND

It's said the name Antwerpen derives from a riverside mound (*aanwerp*) where archaeologists found remnants of a Gallo-Roman settlement. But legend offers a colourful alternative starring a giant called Druon Antigoon. A fearsome extortionist, Druon controlled a bend of the Scheldt, forcing ship captains to pay a toll. However, the day was saved by Roman warrior Silvius Brabo, who killed the giant, chopped off his hand and chucked it in the river. The place of *hand werpen* (hand throwing) subsequently became Antwerpen. Today *Antwerpse handjes* (Antwerp hands) have become a virtual city trademark, turning up in all manner of guises, from De Koninck beer glasses to chocolates and souvenir jewellery.

⦿ Sights & Activities

Many parts of the city, including many museums, are undergoing a massive rebuild, which is due to continue till at least 2020.

Almost all major museums (except FOMU and M HKA) are free on the last Wednesday of each month. On other days except Mondays, the **Antwerp City Card** (one/two/three days €27/35/40) is worth considering. It allows free entry to almost all the classic attractions, including 17 museums, four churches and the De Koninck brewery, and also gives free use of public transport. Purchase it from Tourism Antwerp at the Grote Markt or Antwerpen-Centraal.

⊙ Old Antwerp & the Fashion District

As with every great Flemish city, Antwerp's medieval heart is a market square, the **Grote Markt**. Here the triangular, pedestrianised space features the voluptuous, baroque **Brabo Fountain** depicting the hero of Antwerp's giant-killing, hand-throwing foundation legend. Flanked on two sides by very photogenic guildhalls, the square is dominated by an impressive Italo-Flemish Renaissance-style **stadhuis** completed in 1565.

Currently being restored on a nearby riverside knoll, **Het Steen** is Antwerp's dinky but photogenic castle dating from 1200. A raised promenade running south along the **Scheldt Riverfront** (Map p150) from here offers strollers a pleasant way to reach the tree-shaded square of St-Jansvliet, south of which is the vibrant Fashion District.

★ Museum Plantin-Moretus   MUSEUM, HISTORIC BUILDING

(Map p150; ☑ 03-221 14 50; www.museumplantinmoretus.be; Vrijdagmarkt 22; adult/reduced/child €8/6/free; ⊙10am-5pm Tue-Sun, last entry 4.30pm) The medieval building and 1622 courtyard garden alone would be worth a visit, but it's the world's oldest printing press, priceless manuscripts and original type sets that justify this museum's Unesco World Heritage status. It's been a museum since 1876 and its other great highlights include a 1640 library, a bookshop dating from 1700 and rooms lined with gilt leather.

The valuable painting collection includes work by Rubens, a family friend of Jan Moretus, and there are fascinating examples of Moretus-published books by Rubens' brother Philip, illustrated by Pieter Paul.

★ Rubenshuis   MUSEUM

(Map p150; ☑ 03-201 15 55; www.rubenshuis.be; Wapper 9-11; adult/concession €8/6; ⊙10am-5pm Tue-Sun) This delightfully indulgent 1611 mansion was built as a home and studio for celebrated painter Pieter Paul Rubens. It was rescued from ruins in 1937 and has been very sensitively restored with furniture that dates from Rubens' era plus a priceless collection of 17th-century art. There are around a dozen Rubens canvases, most memorably his world-famous hatted self-portrait and a large-scale canvas of Eve glancing lustfully at Adam's fig leaf.

Notice also a Tintoretto from the late David Bowie's collection and a Van Dyck portrait study that was discovered on the BBC's *Antiques Roadshow* program. Period ephemera includes the metal frame used to support a ruff collar. A lovely baroque portico (under restoration at the time of research) leads into an exquisite formal garden. If you want more than the free 68-page highlights booklet (available in five languages), download the free app.

Note that it's worth paying the extra €2 for a combined ticket that also gets you into the excellent Museum Mayer van den Bergh.

★ Onze-Lieve-Vrouwekathedraal   CATHEDRAL

(Map p150; ☑ 03-213 99 51; www.dekathedraal.be; Handschoenmarkt; adult/reduced/under 12yr €6/4/free; ⊙10am-5pm Mon-Fri, to 3pm Sat, 1-5pm Sun) Belgium's finest Gothic cathedral was 169 years in the making (1352–1521). Wherever you wander in Antwerp, its gracious, 123m-high spire has a habit of popping unexpectedly into view and it rarely fails to prompt a gasp of awe. The sight is particularly well framed when looking up Pelgrimstraat in the afternoon light.

The cathedral's imposing interior sports late-baroque decorations, including four early Rubens canvases and also, while the KMSKA gallery (p149) is closed, some of that collection's religious masterpieces. Guided tours at 11am (Monday to Saturday) and 2.15pm (daily) are available in Dutch year-round, but often in English too (2.15pm during the summer).

★ Museum Mayer van den Bergh   MUSEUM

(Map p150; ☑ 03-232 42 37; www.museummayervandenbergh.be; Lange Gasthuisstraat 19; adult/reduced €8/6, with Rubenshuis €10/8; ⊙10am-5pm Tue-Sun) Styled as a 16th-century town house, this superb place was actually constructed in 1904 as one of the first museums in the

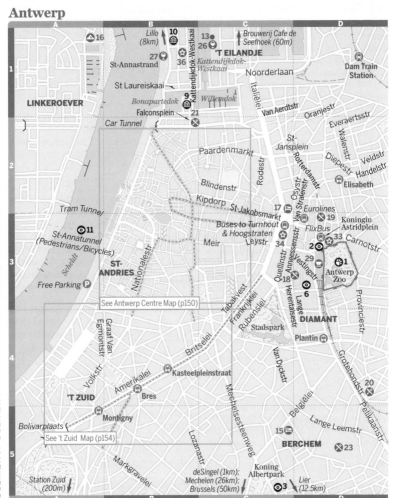

world built around a single collection. Fritz Mayer van den Bergh's collection is indeed as rich as that of many a national gallery with its notable paintings, sculptures, tapestries, drawings, jewellery and stained-glass windows. The undoubted highlight is the Brueghel Room, whose centrepiece is Pieter Brueghel the Elder's brilliantly grotesque *Dulle Griet* (Mad Meg), painted in 1561 and restored in 2018.

Snijder-Rockoxhuis MUSEUM
(Map p150; ☎03-201 92 50; www.snijdersrockox huis.be; Keizerstraat 10-12; adult/reduced €8/6;

⊘10am-5pm Tue-Sun) Combining the impressive 17th-century houses of artist Frans Snijders and of Antwerp lawyer, mayor and Rubens-patron Nicolaas Rockox, this recently revamped museum does a superb job of making accessible a fine collection of 16th- and 17th-century masterpieces with a very helpful tablet tour, headphones and two six-minute films.

Artists represented include Van Dyck, Brueghel, Van der Weyden and, yes, Rubens. The last of the 10 rooms allows you to choose which of three pieces of period music to play out with.

MoMu　　　　　　　　　　　　　　MUSEUM

(Map p150; www.momu.be; Nationalestraat 28)
Closed for renovation until late 2020, Antwerp's fashion museum has a rich avant-garde collection and typically produces exhibitions highlighting the broader inspiration and creative process behind local and international designer stars.

Het Ruihuis　　　　　　　　　　　WALKING

(Map p150; ☎03-344 07 55; www.deruien.be; Suikerrui 21; tablet tour adult/child €17/11, boat ride €5; ◷10am-5pm Tue-Fri, to 6pm Sat & Sun) Uncover a hidden side to the city's history from beneath, exploring what was originally the

city's 12th-century moat, later covered over to make sewers. Call ahead to find the day's departure times for 15-minute boat rides or 90-minute guided walks with information provided by tablet.

St-Jacobskerk　　　　　　　　　　CHURCH

(Map p150; www.sintjacobantwerpen.be; Lange Nieuwstraat 73a; adult/student/child €3/2/free; ◷2-5pm Apr-Oct, 9am-noon Mon-Sat Nov-Mar) The tomb of Rubens is the reason most visitors come to St-Jacobskerk. Located in a small chapel behind the high altar, the tomb is adorned with *Our Lady Surrounded by Saints,* a painting that Rubens executed specifically for his tomb.

It's actually a family portrait, with the master as St George. Other figures include his father and his wives, Helena and Isabella.

St-Carolus-Borromeuskerk CHURCH

(Map p150; www.mkaweb.be/site/english/062.mv; Hendrik Conscienceplein 6; ⊙10am-12.30pm & 2-5pm Mon-Sat) FREE Rubens turned interior designer as part of the team that created this superb 1621 baroque church, designed to give worshippers a very visceral foretaste of heaven's delights. A wonder of its era, the remarkable altarpiece allowed vast canvases to be changed using a series of wire pulleys.

Magnificently carved-angel confessionals were installed after a disastrous 1718 fire that ruined the original nave and destroyed 39 original Rubens' ceiling panels. In 1773 the church's surviving Rubens paintings were whisked off to Vienna after the Jesuits were disbanded locally.

St-Pauluskerk CHURCH

(St Paul's Church; Map p150; Veemarkt 13; ⊙2-5pm May-Oct, weekends only Nov-Mar) FREE Strangely easy to miss despite its towering bulk, this church was consecrated in 1571 as part of a Dominican monastery, and thoroughly rebuilt after a 1679 fire. It has retained elements of its resplendent baroque interior despite a further series of catastrophes, most notably a 1968 inferno after which restoration took more than 20 years.

◉ 't Eilandje

Around 800m north of Grote Markt, MAS museum is at the centre of a regenerated docklands area known as 't Eilandje.

MAS MUSEUM

(Museum aan de Stroom; Map p146; ☑03-338 44 00; www.mas.be; Hanzestedenplaats; viewpoint free, museum adult/reduced €10/8, btwn exhibitions €5/3; ⊙viewpoint 9.30am-11.30pm Tue-Sun, museum 10am-4.45pm Tue-Sun) Opened in 2011, MAS is a 10-storey complex that redefines the idea of a museum-gallery. Floors are designed around big-idea themes using a barrage of media, from old master paintings and tribal artefacts to video installations. But many people come just for the views over the city (no ticket required), which transform as you climb somewhat laboriously by a series of escalators and three flights of stairs (no public lifts).

Red Star Line Museum MUSEUM

(Map p146; ☑03-298 27 70; www.redstarline.be; Montevideostraat 3; adult/reduced €8/6; ⊙10am-5pm Tue-Sun, reservations required on weekends) Over two million passengers sailed from Antwerp on Red Star Line ships between 1873 and 1934, the great majority of these immigrants bound for America. This museum, housed in the very building where those many embarkations took place, is beautifully designed and extremely engaging, telling the story of individual journeys through photographs, recreations and objects, including some gorgeous period model ships.

PIETER PAUL RUBENS

Even if his signature plump nudes, muscular saints and gigantic ultra-Catholic religious canvases aren't your artistic cup of tea, it's hard to visit Antwerp without stumbling on at least a couple of attractions related to the city's superstar artist, Pieter Paul Rubens (1577–1640).

Rubens was born in Siegen, Germany, where his parents had temporarily fled to escape religious turmoil in Antwerp. They returned home a decade later, and by the age of 21 Rubens had become a master painter in Antwerp's Guild of St-Lukas. In 1600 he became court painter to the Duke of Mantua and travelled extensively in Italy and Spain, soaking up the rich Renaissance fashions in art and architecture. When his mother died in 1608, Rubens returned to Antwerp, built a city-centre house-studio (p145) and worked on huge religious canvases and portraits of European royalty. He was joined by contemporaries such as Anthony Van Dyck and Jacob Jordaens. The studio's output was staggering.

In the 1620s Rubens also took on diplomatic missions, including a visit to London, where he was knighted by Charles I.

Rubens' tomb is in a small chapel behind the high altar of the aristocratic, partly Gothic St-Jacobskerk (p147).

The observation tower has great views and is also a nod to the original chimney of the building, once a welcome landmark that guided passengers arriving at Antwerpen-Centraal station to the docks.

◉ Station Quarter & Diamant

Heading east from the old city area, Meir/Leystraat is Antwerp's major pedestrian shopping street, gloriously overendowed with statue-topped classical and rococo-style buildings, including the Stadsfeestzaal, an exuberant shopping mall within a 1908 neo-classical exhibition hall that's been restored to its full gilt-laden opulence since 2007. After around 1km you reach the magnificent Antwerpen-Centraal train station in a highly multicultural area with a different atmosphere every few blocks. Stretching further east is edgy Borgerhout.

Antwerpen-Centraal   LANDMARK
(Map p146; Koningin Astridplein 27; ⊘ ticket office 5.45am-10pm) With its neo-Gothic facade, vast main hall and splendidly proportioned dome, the 1905 Antwerpen-Centraal building has been rated as one of the five most beautiful train stations in the world.

Upstairs, enjoy the mirror-and-marble interiors over an inexpensive drink at the station buffet-cafe, Le Royal (Map p146; ☑ 03-225 58 80; www.brasserieroyal.be; ⊘ 8am-8pm).

Antwerp Zoo   ZOO
(Map p146; ☑ 03-202 45 40; www.zooantwerpen.be; Koningin Astridplein 26; adult/under 18yr/under 11yr €26.50/24.50/21.50; ⊘ 10am-4.45pm winter, to 7pm summer, last tickets 1hr before closing; ☑) Founded in 1843, Antwerp Zoo is one of the world's oldest and best-respected zoological parks. Enclosures in the 10-hectare site are state of the art and the breeding program has an international reputation.

There are a series of timed talks throughout the day. If you don't have time to visit properly, it's still worth walking into the entrance-yard area (no ticket required) for great views back towards the train station and for a good chance of spotting flamingos.

Diamant   AREA
(Diamond District; Map p146; www.awdc.be) An astounding 80% of the world's uncut diamonds are traded in Antwerp. Four dour exchange buildings lie along heavily guarded Hoveniersstraat and Schupstraat, pedestrianised streets that are also home to Indian banks, specialist transportation companies,

diamond 'boilers' and the industry's governing body, HRD Antwerp.

Though now Indian dominated, historically the diamond business was mainly the domain of Orthodox Jews, whose black coats, broad-rimmed hats and long hair-curls still remain a distinctive feature of the street scenes.

◉ 't Zuid & Zurenborg

As you head south, the Fashion District morphs into 't Zuid, a dining, drinking and museum zone interspersed by some areas of relatively grand urban residences. Further southeast is residential Zurenborg whose elegance stems from the fact that it was one of the few parts of Antwerp that were planned; virtually all of its rich concentration of belle époque, neoclassical and art nouveau house facades date from between 1894 and 1914.

KMSKA   GALLERY
(Map p154; www.kmska.be; Leopold de Waelplaats) In a neoclassical building topped with winged charioteer statues, KMSKA holds a world-class collection of artistic masterpieces. However, the gallery will be closed until at least 2019 while undergoing a total renovation. The website www.hetnieuwemuseum.be charts the restoration progress.

M HKA   GALLERY
(Map p154; ☑ 03-260 99 99; www.muhka.be; Leuvenstraat 32; some floors free, exhibitions adult/student/under 26yr/child €10/5/1/free; ⊘ 11am-6pm Tue-Sun, to 9pm Thu) M HKA is considered to be one of Belgium's best contemporary galleries. Its exhibitions focus on work produced since the 1970s by both Belgian and international artists. Shows change frequently and tend to be provocative. Access is free to three ground-floor displays, the library, the 4th-floor cafe and the 6th-floor 'Lodgers' exhibits. After 6pm on Thursdays, access to the whole gallery costs just €1.

FOMU   MUSEUM
(Fotomuseum; Map p154; ☑ 03-242 93 00; www.fotomuseum.be; Waalsekaai 47; adult/pensioner/under 26yr/child €10/5/3/free; ⊘ 10am-6pm Tue-Sun, last tickets 5.30pm) This excellent museum of photography has a regularly changing roster of exhibitions from historical themes to no-holds-barred work by contemporary photo-artists.

As well as a shop and cafe, there's a fantastic cinema screening many art-house films in their original languages.

Antwerp Centre

Lange Schipperskapelstr

Vinger-lingstr
Oude Manstr'lingstr
St-Pietersvliet
Orteliuskaai
38
Verversrui
Falconsplein
Kriekenstr
25
'T SCHIPPERSKWARTIER
Keistr
St-Paulusstr
Dries
Hulkstr
Klapdorp
Lange Noordstr
Lange Mutsaertstr

MAS Barge Collection
Jordaenskaai
Gorterstr
Saucier
Burchtgracht
Nosestr
14
Zwartzustersstr
Minderbroedersstr
Kl Goddaert
Minderbroedersstr
Ambtmanstr

Veemarkt
Zakstr
Vhouwerstr
Doornikstr
30
Stoelstr
Zirkstr
Hofstr
Lange Koepoortstr
36
Jeruzalemstr
44
34
Keizerstr
10

7
Steenplein
Palingburg
Kuipersstr
Repenstr
43
50
Oude Beurs
Wolstr
41
Hendrik Conscienceplein
Wijngaard
Wijngaardbrug
17
12

Cross-river Ferry
15
Gildek-amerstr
11 Grote Markt
5
Zilversmidstr
16
Kaasstr
9
Zuiderterras
Grote Pieter Potstr
Kl Pieter Potstr
Suikerrui
23
Haarstr
19
Blauwmoezelstr
Handschoenmarkt
28
Lijnwaadmarkt
46
Korte Nieuwstr
48
18
Vleminckstr

Tram Tunnel
Ernest Van Dijckkaai
Vlasmarkt
37
Zand
21
Stoofstr
Hoogstr
Reyndersstr
Heilige Geeststr
27
Pelgrimstr
Oude Koornmarkt
3 Onze-Lieve-Vrouwekathedraal
Melkmarkt
Groenplaats
49
Eiermarkt
Beddenstr
Meirbrug
6
St-Katelijnevest
Oudemanstr

Cruise Terminal
33
St-Jansvliet
55
31
Vrijdagmarkt
2 Museum Plantin-Moretus
Gier
52
53
Kammenstr
Karelstr
Groenplaats
Schoenmarkt
Lombardenvest
Schrijnwer-kersstraat
Wiegstr
Meir
Huidevettersstr

20
Scheldeken
Oever
Steenhouwersvest
8
Drukkerijstr
Lombardenstr
Korte Gasthuisstr
Everdijstr
Komedie-plaats
57

Plantinkaai
Kr Elleboogstr
Muntstr
Augustijnenstr
ST-ANDRIES
Vlaander-enstraat
47
Waal
St-Andriesstr
Sleutelstr
Kammenstr
Oudaan
Museum Mayer van den Bergh 1

St-Michielsstr
Lange Riddersstr
Pompstr
Nationalestr
St-Antoniusstr
22
Bogaardeplein
24
Happaertstr
Schoytestr
Bredestr
35
Vleminckveld

Arsenaalstr
26
Korte Vliersstr
St-Andriesplaats
Steenbergstr
54
Aalmoezenierstr
56
Rosier

Kloosterstr
Prekersstr
Mechelseplein

There's even an audition procedure for choosing the artists!

Justitiepaleis
NOTABLE BUILDING

(Law Court; Map p154; Bolivarplaats; 🚌12 to Bolivarplaats) Designed by Richard Rogers, famous for the Centre Pompidou in Paris, Antwerp's 21st-century law courts have a distinctive series of gleaming titanium 'sails' that glint like silver sharks when glimpsed down van Beerstraat from the Troonplaats cafes. However, there is nothing within for visitors.

Graffiti Streets
AREA

(Map p146; www.facebook.com/mosbelgium; Krugerstraat & Minckeleresstraat) Close to the art nouveau glories of Zurenborg, contrastingly forbidding Krugerstraat and Minckeleresstraat are so festooned in graffiti that they are essentially outdoor galleries of street art.

◎ Berchem

De Koninck
BREWERY

(Map p146; www.dekoninck.be; Mechelsesteenweg 291; adult/reduced €12/10; ⊙10am-6pm Tue-Sun, last ticket 4.30pm; 🚌15 to Berchem De Merode) Antwerp's historic brewery is both a temple to the city's favourite beer and an evocative example of early-20th-century industrial architecture. Self-guided tours, typically lasting over an hour, begin with interactive exhibitions on beer-making, then a 4m-high walkway that takes you over the working brewery hall.

☞ Tours

Antwerp Free Walking Tour
WALKING

(Map p150; www.vivastour.com; Grote Markt; tips accepted; ⊙English 2pm, Spanish 11am & 2pm) Two-hour walking tours start from the Brabo Fountain. Look for the orange umbrella.

Antwerp By Bike
CYCLING

(Map p150; www.antwerpbybike.be; with/without bike rental €20/15; ⊙11am Sat & Sun Mar-Oct) Two-hour weekend bicycle tours of Antwerp's highlights in English start from Steenplein at 11am.

🎊 Festivals & Events

Antwerp has a whole smorgasbord of summer events (www.zva.be) including the **Borgerwood** (www.borgerwood.be; Spoor Oost; ⊙late Jul) electronic-music festival held at Bourgerhout's Park Spoor Oost, the

ANTWERP & NORTHEAST BELGIUM ANTWERP (ANTWERPEN)

Antwerp Centre

two-night, bargain-value pop and indie fest of **Linkerwoofer** (www.linkerwoofer.be; Frederik van Eedenplein; ☉ early Aug), across the river in Linkeroever, and the amusing if kitschy **Rubens Market** (Grote Markt; ☉ 15 Aug) when stall vendors on the Grote Markt dress up in medieval costume for a day to celebrate Antwerp's favourite painter.

Museumnacht   ART
(www.museumnacht.be; adult/under 26yr/child €12/6/free; ☉ first Sat Aug) During Museumnacht over 20 museums stay open late, many staging original special events and performances. Bus transport between venues is free and there are late-night parties (€6 extra) once the museums close.

Tomorrowland   MUSIC
(Domein De Schorre, Boom; ☉ late Jul; ▭ 182 from Groenplaats) One of the world's largest electronic-music festivals, Tomorrowland is held over two weekends in Boom, 16km south of central Antwerp.

⊟ Sleeping

Antwerp offers a staggering range of stylish B&Bs, many listed on www.gasten kamersantwerpen.be. Central chain hotels include a Hilton with a lovely facade. Autograph-Marriott is expected to open a luxury hotel in the **Handelsbeurs building** (Map p150; Lange Nieuwstraat 20-24) once it's fully restored. An Ibis Budget beyond the southeastern corner of Antwerpen-Centraal makes a good standby if you missed the last train out, and the Park Inn beside the zoo shares use of the nearby Radisson's swimming pool.

Centre

Pulcinella   HOSTEL €

(Map p150; ☑ 03-234 03 14; www.jeugdherbergen.be; Bogaardeplein 1; dm/tw €29/64; 🛜) This giant, tailor-made HI hostel is hard to beat for its location on a quiet if unshaded square in the Fashion District.

The Ash   HOSTEL €

(Map p146; ☑ 03-500 88 17; www.antwerp studenthostel.com; Italiëlei 237; dm/tw from €15/49; ⊙ reception 8am-10.30pm) If you can put up with poor ventilation, some broken fittings and a few mosquitoes, the Ash's 12-bunk dorms are Antwerp's cheapest by a long way. Staying here would be far more congenial if they didn't lock the excellent kitchen and decent yard-seating so early.

Hotel O   BOUTIQUE HOTEL €€

(Map p150; ☑ 03-500 89 50; www.hotelokathedral. com; Handschoenmarkt 3; rear s/d from €79/89, with view d €99-154; ❇🛜) The immediate selling point of this excellent-value 39-room hotel is its unbeatable location, with oblique views across the square to the cathedral frontage. Expect moody decor with baths or showers in black-framed glass boxes and – in most rooms – giant 17th-century paintings reproduced as either headboards or covering whole walls. Enter via a little foyer bar lined with 1950s radios.

Yellow Submarine   B&B €€

(Map p150; ☑ 0474 50 82 11; www.yellowsub marine.be/bedandbreakfast.html; Falconplein 51; d with shower/bath €120/140; 🅿🛜) Advertising agency Yellow Submarine takes its job so seriously that they give their clients' products a real workout by furnishing three B&B rooms with them. The result is a stylish, high-design experience that includes espresso machines, stocked minibars and breakfast brought to your room. Free underground parking is a big bonus.

Matelote Hotel   BOUTIQUE HOTEL €€

(Map p150; ☑ 03-201 88 00; www.matelote.be; Haarstraat 11; d €95-160, ste €160-190; ⊙ 7am-10pm Mon-Sat, 7.30am-8.30pm Sun; ❇@🛜) In a partly 16th-century building on a pedestrianised old-city backstreet, the Matelote has 11 contemporary rooms in four categories, some rather small, others with original beams. There's air-conditioning in the upper rooms and free breakfast if you book directly.

Hotel Scheldezicht   HOTEL €€

(Map p150; ☑ 03-231 66 02; www.hotelschelde zicht.be; St-Jansvliet 12; s/tw/tr with bathroom €80/95/105, without bathroom €50/70/90; ⊙ reception noon-6pm Mon-Fri, 8am-8pm Sat & Sun; 🛜) Limited reception times, ragged stairways and irregular floors are well worth putting up with for the budget prices for rooms that have a certain old-world grandeur, most with gilded mirrors and views across the tree-shaded square. Many share toilets, but are spacious and have en suite showers. Breakfast (€7.50) is only available at weekends.

★**Hotel Julien**   BOUTIQUE HOTEL €€€

(Map p150; ☑ 03-229 06 00; www.hotel-julien. com; Korte Nieuwstraat 24; d €184-284, ste €334; ❇@🛜) In a grand old mansion with lots of designer detail, this discreet 21-room boutique hotel has a suave, understated

---

WORTH A TRIP

ANTWERP PORT

Beautiful it ain't. But its sheer jaw-dropping scale makes exploring the world's fourth-largest **port complex** (www.portofantwerp.com) an unforgettable experience. A surreal industrial-age maze of cranes, loading yards, container stacks, docks, pipes, rail lines, warehouses and petrochemical refineries stretches to the Dutch border, with everything neatly spaced amid the remnants of grassy polder fields.

In the 1960s, the space was created by largely bulldozing seven villages but one was spared: tile-roofed, two-street **Lillo** (www.lillo-krabbevanger.be), population 40, located within a former star-fort. Its little museum and two archetypal terraced cafes come alive on sunny Sunday afternoons.

A good way to get a sense of the port's extent is on a three-hour boat cruise on the **Flandria** (Map p146; ☑ 03-472 21 40 56; www.flandria.nu; Kattendijkdok; adult/child €19/3; ⊙ noon Thu, Sat & Sun Apr-Nov) starting from 't Eilandje and sailing past the new **Port Office building** designed by the late, great Anglo-Iraqi architect Zaha Hadid. Departures are daily except Monday in midsummer, and at least thrice weekly during shoulder seasons.

't Zuid (Antwerp)

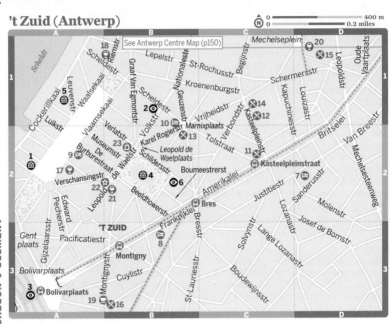

't Zuid (Antwerp)

◎ Sights

1 FOMU	A2
2 Help U Zelve	B1
3 Justitiepaleis	A3
4 KMSKA	B2
5 M HKA	A1
6 't Bootje	B2

🛏 Sleeping

7 Bed, Bad & Brood	D2
8 Hotel Rubenshof	B3
9 The Glorious	A2
10 The Soul	B1

✕ Eating

11 Ciro's	C2
12 De Broers van Julienne	C1
13 Fiskebar	B2

14 Le John	C1
L'Entrepôt du Congo	(see 9)
15 Life Is Art	D1
16 Mission Masala	B3

🍷 Drinking & Nightlife

17 Bar Zar	A2
Chatleroi	(see 21)
18 De Vismijn	B1
19 Kolonel Koffie	A3
20 Korsåkov	D1
21 Patine	B2

✦ Entertainment

22 Café Hopper	B2

🛍 Shopping

23 Ann Demeulemeester	B2

elegance, impressive lounge and bar spaces, and a staff attitude that hits the sweet spot between friendly and professional. Every room is different. Choose pricier versions for high ceilings, exposed beams, coffee maker etc. The breathtaking rooftop terrace view is a well-kept secret.

Hotel Franq　　　　BOUTIQUE HOTEL **€€€**
(Map p150; ☎ 03-555 31 80; www.hotelfranq.com; Kipdorp 10-12; r/ste from €170/340; ⓟ❄🛜) So

subtle as to be semi-invisible from the passing tram, 39-room Franq brings low-key elegance to a century-old bank building whose vault full of safety-deposit boxes now houses a wine cellar. The smallest rooms are a little tight at only 17 sq metres but all come with great beds, kettle, fridge and Nespresso machine.

Other delights include the atrium lounge, a 17th-century cottage in the yard-garden and remarkably refined food by a celebrity chef in the deceptively restrained restaurant. Parking costs €18.

Hotel 't Sandt
BOUTIQUE HOTEL €€€

(Map p150; ☑03-232 93 90; www.hotel-sandt. be; Zand 17; midweek s/d from €190/210, weekend from €160/180; [P][❋][☎]) This charming, 29-room boutique hotel was originally a 15th-century customs house then, from 1911, a banana warehouse. It's from that incarnation that big wooden pulley wheels have been retained in room 404 and penthouse 401. Many other rooms have period curiosities and exposed beams, and 'duplexes' have wrought-iron stairs up to bed.

Huis de Colvenier
APARTMENT €€€

(Map p150; ☑0477-23 26 50; www.colvenier.be; St-Antoniusstraat 8; apt €250; ⊙call ahead; [❋][☎]) Above a bistro in a house that you might swear was 18th century, four superb apartments have been installed by owner-chef Patrick Van Hereck. They have lots of revealed beamwork, super-comfy beds and a whole kitchen-lounge area with a sofa that can be used as an extra double.

Don't miss the unforgettable brick-floored wine bar in the genuinely old cellar. Rates include breakfast.

Borgerhout

★ABhostel
HOSTEL €

(Map p146; ☑0473-57 01 66; www.abhostel.com; Kattenberg 110; dm/tw €25/55; ⊙reception noon-3pm & 6-8pm; [☎]; [🚌]10, 24 to Drink) ⊘ This adorable, family-run hostel in Borgerhout is a great place to get to know fellow travellers while fixing breakfast from provided ingredients in the kitchen-bar, or relaxing in hammocks in the small yard-garden. Helpful traveller staff are a mine of information to help you make the most of the odd-ball location's opportunities and hot spots.

't Zuid & Zurenborg

Hotel Rubenshof
HOTEL €

(Map p154; ☑03-237 07 89; www.rubenshof. be; Amerikalei 115-117; s/tw/tr with bathroom €65/93/120, without bathroom €41/67/91; ⊙8am-11pm; [🚌]12 to Bresstraat) This large 1890s mansion has extraordinarily grand public spaces, with breakfast (free if you book directly) served in a fabulous art nouveau dining room adjoining a partly gilded neo-rococo salon. Rooms are contrastingly basic, budget affairs, if sometimes pleasingly quirky and

come with towels, soap and sink in even the small singles that share toilets.

★Bed, Bad & Brood
B&B €€

(Map p154; ☑03-248 15 39; www.bbantwerp.com; Justitiestraat 43; s/d/q from €62/76/135; ⊖@) In a 1910, belle époque–era town house near the vast Gerechtshof (former courthouse), this B&B impresses with authentic wooden floors, high ceilings and beautifully eclectic furniture. The three rooms are remarkably spacious and comfortable for the price and rates include a bountiful breakfast.

Prices assume a minimum two-night stay, though last-minute one-night stays are sometimes possible for an extra €10.

Boulevard Leopold
B&B €€

(Map p146; ☑0486-67 58 38; www.boulevard-leopold.be; Belgiëlei 135; d €115-130, ste €140-175) A fascinating evocation of Antwerp's 19th-century glory days in the heart of the Jewish district, this personable B&B mixes a collection of curiosities, museum-worthy antiques, claw-foot baths and open fires with modern coffee machines and flatscreen TVs.

As with most B&Bs it is important to pre-arrange arrival times. Cash payments only.

The Soul
APARTMENT €€

(Map p154; ☑0479-61 88 18; www.thesoul antwerp.com; Marnixplaats 15; ste/apt from €72/98; ⊙check-in 3-8pm Sun-Wed, 3-11.30pm Thu-Sat; [☎]) Above a pair of delightful cafes, these design-savvy units overlook Marnixplaats in 't Zuid, a drinking-dining hot spot that's always lively – if never oppressively so. At 40 sq metres, the five studios are each quite roomy, come with kitchenette and have many quirky features – the plastic bird perched near the ceiling is a disguised fire alarm.

The Glorious
BOUTIQUE HOTEL €€

(Map p154; ☑03-237 06 13; www.theglorious.be; De Burburestraat 4A; d €135-175) Up the stairs from an intimate Michelin-starred restaurant and wine bar, the Glorious' three wildly different rooms are decorated in romantic, maximalist styles with plenty of curious details and theatrical touches like birdcage lamps and a rainforest-effect shower space in the 'Stories' room.

Linkerover

Camping De Molen
CAMPGROUND €

(Map p146; ☑03-2198179; www.camping-de-molen. be; Jachthavenweg 6; tent/caravan/4-person hut €16/18/45, Jul-Aug €18/24/50; ⊙Apr-early Nov;

DON'T MISS

ART NOUVEAU & MORE: ANTWERP'S ARCHITECTURAL HERITAGE

't Zuid

While 't Zuid's streetscapes are far from cohesive, the area has some stunning stand-alone art nouveau masterpieces.

't Bootje (Map p154; Schildersstraat 2) Behind KMSKA, the eccentric 't Bootje has a corner balcony that resembles a boat's prow.

Help U Zelve (Map p154; www.steinerschoolantwerpen.be; Volkstraat 40) This is arguably the city's most arresting art nouveau building. Built in 1901 by architects Van Asperen and Van Averbeke as the Socialist Party headquarters, it's adorned with mosaics of rural workers – er, yes, naked workers – along with organic, sinuous wrought-ironwork and curved windows. It now houses a Rudolph Steiner school.

Zurenborg

Delightfully, Zurenborg's wrought-iron balconies, bay windows, slate tiles, stained glass and mosaic work are often in service of a theme.

De Vier Seizoenen (The Four Seasons; Map p146; cnr Waterloostraat & Generaal Van Merlenstraat; ☐ 15 to Cuperus) Four matching Joseph Bascourt houses on each corner of an intersection bear mosaics depicting the four seasons, with narrow windows that put style above practicality.

Sunflower House (Map p146; 50 Cogels Osylei; ☐ 15 to Cuperus) Perhaps the most striking of several side-by-side 'flower' houses, including 'Iris' at number 44, which is also an art nouveau delight.

Les Mouettes (The Seagulls; Map p146; Waterloostraat 39; ☐ 15 to Cuperus) Relatively modest by Zurenborg standards, but with a lovely central mosaic depicting seagulls and the Flemish coast.

De Twaalf Duivelkens (Map p146; Transvaalstraat 59-61) This 1900 gem isn't art nouveau but its 12-devil balcony is full of gentle humour.

☒; ☐ 36 to Gloriantlaan/Huygenstraat) A small, simple but pleasantly sited campground with 80 pitches across the Scheldt River, near Sint-Anna 'beach' and De Molen open-air swimming pool.

Visa or MasterCard payment only; no cash accepted. Add €5 for an electricity hook-up and €0.70 per person tourist tax.

✖ Eating

The choice is phenomenal in Antwerp, with 12 Michelin stars among the city's restaurants, not counting many more in suburban villages.

✖ Centre

Little Ethiopia　　　　　ETHIOPIAN €
(Map p150; ☎ 03-336 22 93; www.little-ethiopia.be; Zirkstraat 8; mains €9-19.50; ☉ noon-10pm Wed-Mon) Discover a veritable museum of African artefacts in a historic old Antwerp house while perusing the multilingual menu supplement that helpfully explains the intricacies of Ethiopian dining. Rather than using a knife and fork you scoop up mouthfuls of tasty food using strips of *injera* (pancake-like staple). Wash it down with a globular vial of *Tej* (honey wine). The magic hand towel is fun.

Nimmanhaemin　　　　　THAI €
(Map p150; ☎ 03-345 35 38; www.nimmanhaemin.be; Stadswaag 9; starters €6-10, mains €13-20; ☉ 6-10pm) Good-value, richly flavoured Thai food served in airy, paired-back, high-ceilinged rooms within a classic step-gabled old house. The mains dishes include rice. Summer seating spreads onto a pretty tree-shaded square amid a healthy scattering of small bars.

LOA　　　　　STREET FOOD €
(Map p150; ☎ 03-291 64 85; www.loa.be; Hoogstraat 77; dishes €7-13; ☉ 4-10.30pm Mon, Wed-Fri, noon-10.30pm Sat, noon-9pm Sun; ☏) Overlooking St-Jansvliet square, this tiny shop-cafe and takeaway peddles an interesting selection of good-value, international street food including veg- and non-veg *pad thai*

(Thai noodles), sweet-savoury Moroccan pancakes, tortillas and fried bananas. Don't miss sipping Moussa's Bissap, a locally made infusion of Senegalese hibiscus (€2.50).

De Groote Witte Arend   BELGIAN €€
(Map p150; ✆03-233 50 33; www.degrootewitte arend.be; Reyndersstraat 18; lunches €8-15, mains €16-26; ☺noon-9pm Sun-Thu, to 10pm Fri & Sat; ☎) Retaining the Tuscan stone arcade of a 15th-to-17th-century convent building, as well as a little family chapel, this place combines the joys of a good beer bar with the satisfaction of well-cooked, sensibly priced Flemish home cuisine.

As well as changing specials you'll find *stoofvlees/carbonade* (beef, beer and onion stew), eel in green sorrel, and huge portions of rabbit in a rich Westmalle sauce.

Chez Fred   BISTRO €€
(Map p150; ✆03-257 14 71; www.chezfred.be; Kloosterstraat 83; pasta €14.50-20, other meals €19-26; ☺10am-1am) Join the *brocante* dealers and local families for typical Belgian fare (croquettes, stews, chicken supreme) and bistro specials (steak, tuna with wasabi dressing) at this appealing, traditional-styled cafe-bistro with street terrace.

Elfde Gebod   BELGIAN €€
(Map p150; www.11gebod.com; Torfbrug 10; mains €14-24.50, sandwiches €8.50; ☺noon-11pm) In the heart of the tourist zone, this ivy-clad medieval masterpiece has an astounding interior decked with angels, saints, pulpits and several deliciously sacrilegious visual jokes.

Het Gebaar   BELGIAN €€€
(Map p150; ✆03-232 37 10; www.hetgebaar. be; Leopoldstraat 24; mains €34-48; ☺noon-5.30pm Mon-Fri) Celebrity TV chef Roger van Damme's Het Gebaar occupies the romantic former caretaker's house at the entrance to Antwerp's petite botanical gardens, within which some of the herbs are grown. It's an ideal setting to write off an afternoon over a Michelin-starred lunch. Don't miss the highly theatrical desserts, which are the true house specialities.

After 2.30pm you can drop in for pancakes (€8 to €12). There's no dinner nor any weekend service.

RAS   EUROPEAN €€€
(Map p150; ✆03-234 12 75; www.RAS.today; Ernest van Dijckkaai 37; mains €23-35; ☺11am-10pm, closed 3-5pm Mon-Fri) Whether in the upper-market glass box of a dining room or at one of the summer tables fanning out along the walkway, RAS is a superb place to be dazzled by sunset rays while dining on well-prepared fish, steak, artichoke couscous or lobster linguini. Dress up a little to fit in.

't Eilandje

Marcel   FRENCH €€€
(Map p146; ✆03-336 33 02; www.restaurant marcel.be; Van Schoonbekeplein 13; lunch €25, 3-/4-/5-course dinner €40/52.50/65; ☺noon-1.30pm Mon-Fri, 7-9.30pm Mon-Sat) In a delightful 1920s dining room with art nouveau touches, Marcel offers a classic French menu made with top-quality ingredients and a lot of love.

Station Quarter & Borgerhout

Cheap dining is the thing around Antwerpen-Centraal station: on the decidedly unglamorous Van Arteveldestraat alone you'll find African, Himalayan, Filipino, Thai and Indian *cafés* all within a block. Parallelling that one block east, the downmarket, one-street **Chinatown** (Map p146; Van Wesenbekestraat; meals from €7; ☺vary, daily) offers cheap, authentic East Asian food. Middle Eastern choices abound heading east on major through-road Turnhoutsebaan.

Aahaar   INDIAN €
(Map p146; ✆03-235 31 35; www.aahaar.com; Lange Herentalsestraat 23; buffet €10; ☺noon-3pm & 5.30-9.30pm Mon-Fri, 1-9.30pm Sat & Sun; ☻) An unpretentious little place that's well known for its basic vegan/vegetarian Jainist buffet with four mains, two sweets, simple salad and rice.

Miró   FLEMISH €€€
(Map p146; ✆03-235 03 25; www.bistrotmiro.be; Moorkensplein 28; 1/2/3 courses €26/34/39; ☺6-9pm Tue-Sat) If you're looking for something a little special in Borgerhout, try this excellent little family-run bistro, which gives local cuisine a fresh elegance without any undue pretention. Bookings are generally essential.

't Zuid & Zurenborg

Locals head to 't Zuid to dine. Traditionally the hot spots have been Leopold de Waelplaats, Vlaamsekaai and Marnixplaats but of late Troonplaats has been the up-and-coming place to be, while just one block away, contrastingly ungentrified Brederodestraat has excellent-value Turkish bakeries, kebab shops and East European groceries.

L'Entrepôt du Congo   BISTRO €
(Map p154; www.entrepotducongo.com; Vlaamse-kaai 42; meals €6-20; ⊙8am-midnight, kitchen to 10pm) Unsophisticated yet atmospheric, the interior here features marble tabletops, chequerboard floors, mirror panels and carved wooden beams, all surveyed by a portrait of a young King Baudouin. The menu is extensive, cheap and cheerful, and includes omelettes, basic pastas and steaks.

★**Life Is Art**   INTERNATIONAL €€
(Map p154; www.lifeisart.be; St-Jorispoort 21-23; lunch salads €15, starters/mains €13/22; ⊙11am-3pm & 7-10pm Thu & Fri, 10am-10pm Sat & Sun) Loose cushions on bench seats, *brocante* mirrors, an old piano and a dangling canoe-skeleton all conspire to create a casually quirky venue for super-fresh food that changes so regularly that you'll have to ask the waitstaff for details.

If it's available don't miss the sublime *tataki* (seared raw tuna) starter. With fresh ginger tea (€3) and inexpensive beer/wine options from €2/5, non-eaters will be tempted to linger on the sunny street terrace on weekend afternoons or in the bar section where there's live jazz on Fridays from 9pm.

Mission Masala   INDIAN €€
(Map p154; ☑03-501 60 10; www.missionmasala. be; Dendermondestraat 68; dishes €5-17; ⊙noon-11pm Tue-Sat) The look, the flavours, the punning menu and even the authentic *masala chai* (Indian-style tea) all buzz with the colourfully spicy verve of a Kolkata street-food stall, yet within the comfortable setting of a trendy 't Zuid location.

Tables spill out onto a super-sunny street terrace on Troonplaats.

De Broers van Julienne   VEGETARIAN €€
(Map p154; ☑03-232 02 03; www.debroersvan julienne.be; Kasteelpleinstraat 45; lunch from €11, dinner mains €14-20; ⊙noon-8.30pm Mon-Thu, to 9.30pm Fri & Sat, 5.30-8.30pm Sun; ☑) Serving all-vegetarian dishes apart from a couple of fish offerings, this enticing place opens with a deli section purveying huge takeaway quiche slices. Behind, candlelit tables stretch back through a vine-draped verandah into a narrow garden area.

For sensitive eaters there's an extensive menu addendum listing possible allergens.

Ciro's   BELGIAN €€
(Map p154; ☑03-238 11 47; www.ciros.be; Ameri-kalei 6; mains €19-29; ⊙11am-10pm Tue-Fri & Sun,

5-10pm Sat) Ciro's is an authentically nostalgic restaurant that dates back to 1962 and sports an almost untouched mid-century interior. The well-reputed cuisine features hearty steaks, great baked cod and some rarer Flemish classics.

However, certain menu items, like tongue with brain sauce, might strike foreigners as more of a dare than a treat. And yes, 'Black Beauty' really does mean horse fillet.

Fiskebar   SEAFOOD €€
(Map p154; ☑03-257 13 57; www.fiskebar.be; Marnixplaats 12; starters €14-19, mains €24-36; ⊙noon-2pm & 6-10pm Mon-Thu, noon-10pm Fri-Sun) For years, locals have sworn that this bustling, fashionably dishevelled former fishmongers' shop serves the best seafood in town. Finally the owners are responding to the ever-clamouring demand by enlarging the restaurant.

Le John   INTERNATIONAL €€
(Map p154; ☑0488-09 09 12; www.lejohn.be; Kasteelpleinstraat 23-25; pastas €12-16, other mains €18-26; ⊙6-10pm Tue-Sat) Sit at 1960s-style school chairs in a pair of artily sparse shopfronts while the chefs perform in a glass-fronted show kitchen. The short, monthly changing menu presents a variety of styles, often veering towards the Mediterranean.

For a post-prandial whisky from the extensive selection of malts, head upstairs to the very cool, intimate lounge and bar.

★**The Jane**   INTERNATIONAL €€€
(Map p146; ☑03-808 44 65; www.thejaneantwerp. com; Paradeplein 1; 12/14 courses €110/130, Upper Room lunch plates €7-22; ⊙7pm, 7.30pm or 8pm Tue-Sat, bar noon-2am; ☐9 to Zurenborg) In a stunningly repurposed old military-hospital chapel, the Jane's sublime two-Michelin-star dining is such an overwhelmingly fabulous experience that you'll need to book online exactly three months ahead...on the dot of 8am.

If you're not up for a full night of fine dining, it's just a little easier to get lunch reservations for the more casual upstairs bar space that stares down on the main restaurant through a gigantic 900kg starburst chandelier, but you'll probably still need to think weeks ahead. Alternatively, drop in any night after 10pm for cocktails (€16) or a glass of wine (from €8). The location is off the beaten track in a quiet if rather grand inner suburb.

Dôme sur Mer SEAFOOD €€€

(Map p146; ☑ 03-281 74 33; www.domeweb.be; Arendstraat 1; mains €24-34, platters per person €44-76; ⊙ noon-3pm Sun-Fri & 7-10.30pm daily; ☐ 9 to Zurenborg) In a classic Zurenborg building with an interior that's all white but for a mirror-topped blue stripe of an aquarium, this professional seafood outfit specialises in large, decadent sharing platters.

Next door there's a co-owned bakery-cafe ('Domestic') while Dome's more formal European restaurant, across the road, offers six-course tasting menus in a circular room beneath a talking-point chandelier.

🍷 Drinking & Nightlife

To sound like a local, ask for a *bolleke*. No, that's not an insult, but the nickname for a glass of De Koninck (p151), Antwerp's favourite brown ale (*bolleke* means 'little bowl'). Since 2017, Antwerp also has an exciting new local *pintje* with 't Eiland's Seef (p160), a carefully researched reincarnation of what had been one of Belgium's oldest brews till the recipe was 'lost' after WWII.

More associated with local grandmothers is *elixir d'Anvers*, a saccharin-sweet, bright-yellow liqueur made in Antwerp since 1863 and reputed to aid digestion – Louis Pasteur awarded it a diploma in 1887.

From May to September, a number of summer pop-up bars open, some at the riverside, others in parks. This Is Antwerp (www.thisisantwerp.be) lists the current crop.

At nightclubs, Thursdays tend to be cheaper (or free) for students.

🍷 Centre

Numerous old-world 'brown cafes' ooze atmosphere, including Grote Markt classic **Den Engel** (Map p150; www.cafedenengel.be; Grote Markt 3; ⊙ 9am-2am), calm, mirror-panelled **De Kat** (Map p150; ☑ 03-233 08 92; www.facebook.com/cafeDeKat; Wolstraat 22; ⊙ noon-2am Mon-Sat, 5pm-2am Sun), lively and inexpensive **Pelikaan** (Map p150; Melkmarkt 14; ⊙ 8am-late), and several options that spread summer seating onto the tree-shaded square at Graanmarkt, notably **De Duifkens** (Map p150; Graanmarkt 5; ⊙ 10am-late Mon-Thu, from noon Fri-Sun).

★ **Oud Arsenaal** BROWN CAFE

(Map p150; Pijpelincxstraat 4; ⊙ 10am-10pm Wed-Fri, 7.30am-7.30pm Sat & Sun) Little has changed since 1924 at this congenial *bruin café* (traditional pub) that attracts grizzled elderly locals with its exceptionally reasonable beer prices, brews of the month and guest ales.

Cafe Beveren PUB

(Map p150; ☑ 0495 81 81 34; www.facebook.com/cafebeverenantwerpen; Vlasmarkt 2; ⊙ 1pm-3am Fri & Sat, to midnight Sun) The very antithesis of Antwerp style, this unforgettable little *café chantant* is dominated by the city's last remaining 1930s Decap dance organ, a splendid creation that springs into action with a €1 coin in the slot.

Filling the musical gaps is a Wurlitzer jukebox pumping out sweetly unfashionable tunes that have all the boozy regulars singing, dancing and spilling beer in unison.

EXTRAVAGANT COFFEE & TEA

Normo (Map p150; www.normocoffee.com; Minderbroedersrui 30; ⊙ 8.30am-7pm Mon-Fri, 10am-6.30pm Sat) Distressed brick walls, merrily battered tiles and mismatched chairs provide the atmosphere while friendly, bearded baristas fix faultless coffees, including some pretty experimental brews.

On a hot summer day try the full-flavoured *nitro* (cold brewed coffee) or a deliciously sour iced *kambucha* (fermented tea-based drink) served with sprig of mint.

Biochi Tea Lounge (Map p150; ☑ 0495 82 68 35; www.biochi.be; Lange Koepoortstraat 43; ⊙ noon-6.30pm Tue-Wed, 10am-6.30pm Thu-Sat) If you just want a cuppa go elsewhere. This place is for tea connoisseurs who want to savour rare Chinese brews like Wild Purple or En Shuy Lu in an almost meditative setting (tea €7 to €15).

Three tea tastings cost from €25 per person, with explanations and ceremonially intricate preparation – allow a couple of hours. Tea leaves to take away cost €150 to €500 per kilogram.

Wijnbar Kloosterstraat 15　　　WINE BAR
(Map p150; Kloosterstraat 15; ☺1-6pm Sat & Sun)
It's only open 10 hours a week, but this
place is a ridiculously atmospheric spot for
an afternoon glass of wine, facing onto the
courtyard of the 16th-century Mercator-
Orteliushuis.

Baravin　　　WINE BAR
(Map p150; ☑0474 22 75 86; Minderbroedersrui
31; ☺noon-9pm Wed-Sun) This wonderful little
wine bar combines 19th-century plaster-
work, murals and parquetry with a gallery
space and a fine range of excellent French,
Spanish and Italian wines from €6 a glass.

Korsåkov　　　BAR
(Map p154; ☑0485 46 45 06; www.facebook.
com/vokasrov; Mechelseplein 21; ☺noon-4am
Mon-Thu, 2pm-5am Fri & Sat, noon-midnight Sun)
Scruffy-chic Korsåkov is one of the surest
places in central Antwerp to find the super-
late hipster crowd still getting served.

They serve their own 6% Korsåkov house
beer (€3.20), or keep downing standard Primus pils at a carefree €2.30 per *pintje*.

De Vagant　　　BROWN CAFE
(Map p150; www.devagant.be; Reyndersstraat
25; ☺11am-midnight Mon-Fri, noon-2am Sat,
noon-midnight Sun) More than 200 types of
jenever (gin; €3 to €20) are served in this
timeless, bare-boards local *café* decorated
with posters and enamel signs.

Bierhuis Kulminator　　　PUB
(Map p150; ☑03-232 45 38; Vleminckveld 32;
☺4-11.30pm Tue-Sat, from 8pm Mon) If the unpredictable and eccentric owner decides to
let you in, you'll discover a wonderfully chaotic old-world beer pub boasting hundreds
of brews, mostly Belgian, including some
notably rare 'vintage' bottles laid down to
mature for several years like fine wine.

Café d'Anvers　　　CLUB
(Map p150; www.cafedanvers.com; Verversrui 15;
☺11pm-7.30am Fri & Sat; ☒7) Dance till dawn
and beyond with highly rated guest DJs
setting abuzz what was once a 16th-century
church. The cover charge is typically €10.
The entrance is easy to miss between the
'pink windows' of the rather seedy red-light
district.

Cargo Club　　　CLUB
(Map p150; www.cargoclub.be; Lange Schipper-
skapelstraat 11; ☺11pm-7am Thu & Sat; ☒7) A
great dance venue with a decent-sized yet
still intimate dance floor. It's most famous for

its Saturday male-only gay night. There's also
Thursday student-only night (ID required).

🍺 't Eilandje

★Bar Paniek　　　BAR
(Map p146; Kattendijkdok-Oostkai 21B; ☺11am-
11pm) In a series of old warehouses transformed by an artists' collective, this magical
hang-out has concrete floors, barely hanging
together arrays of old windows, and a super-
sized rickshaw on the big dock-front terrace.
Add excellent cheap, well-chosen local beers
and it's no surprise that Paniek is the latest
Antwerp in-place.

Beers cost from €2, but it's well worth the
extra euro for a fascinating Bootjes Bier, with
its hints of apricot, ginger and coriander.

Brouwerij Cafe de Seefhoek　　　BREWERY
(www.seef.be/brouwerij-cafe-de-seefhoek; Indiestraat
21; ☺noon-11pm Sun-Thu, noon-1am Fri & Sat)
Antwerp's new kid on the beer block is re-
incarnated Seef. To taste their full range of
offerings (beers €3 to €3.50) head directly to
their fashionably dishevelled brewery cafe
where you can sit amid the Inox brew vessels or outside on an unsophisticated mass
of orange plastic chairs at the rough benches
that spill onto the post-industrial courtyard.

Bocadero　　　CLUB
(Map p146; ☑03-231 92 65; www.bocadero.be;
Rijnkaai 150; ☺noon-2am or later May-Sep) Amid
the cranes of the old harbour area, Bocadero
is an area of sand and deckchairs backed by
a series of bars and food stands (no cover
charge; beer from €3.30).

The result is a friendly spot that especially attracts a youthful crowd at weekends at
around midnight for drinks and perhaps an
early dance before heading on to a cluster
of more pretentious, later-night clubs some
300m further north.

🍺 Borgerhout

Much of multicultural Borgerhout feels very
run down so the area remains way off most
visitors' radars. However, the stirrings of a
future regeneration are showing through in
a scattering of truly excellent bars that have
managed to retain a local quality while offering an exciting sense of discovery for those
willing to go well beyond the tourist zone.

★Mombasa　　　PUB
(Map p146; ☑0498 52 11 94; Moorkensplein 37;
☺3pm-2am Tue-Sun) Overlooking one of

Antwerp's most underrated architectural glories (Borgerhout Town Hall) this superb beer bar stocks well over 100 choices (including excellent Saison Dupont on tap). It's doubly exciting for cycling fanatics.

The central portrait is of Stan Ockers, Eddy Merckx' inspiration and once the rider of the bike that hangs from the bar's ceiling. Mombasa's owner is himself the uncle of time-trial champion Victor Campenaerts, whose dad plays as drummer in the house band (gigs Sundays from 6pm in winter). There's even a selection of cycling-related beers ('Koersbieren') and when the Tour de France is on, expect all eyes to be glued to the draw-down screen.

Bakeliet
PUB

(Map p146; www.facebook.com/BarBakeliet; Laar 11; ☺ 9am-6pm Tue, to midnight Wed-Fri, noon-1am Sat, to 7pm Sun) Tucked away on the ungentrified central edge of Borgerhout, on a square facing a lumpsome brick church, this bar is a gem of a neighbourhood local with old enamel beer signs, a 1964 jukebox, Corsendonk among the brews on tap (beer from €2) and plenty of terrace seating. Plus there's live music on Friday nights from 9pm.

Bar Leon
BAR

(Map p146; www.barleon.be; Reuzenstraat 23; ☺ noon-2am Mon-Sat, 10am-2am Sun; ☐ 10 to De Roma) Backing onto a park and sandpit-playground, ever-busy Leon is the ultimate locals' local, shape-shifting its way from family afternoon haunt via early-evening catch-ups to late-night DJ-led party spot for the young Borgerhout crew.

Plaza Real
PUB

(Map p146; www.plazareal.be; Kattenberg 89; ☺ 8pm-late Wed-Sat, from 5pm Sun Sep-Jun; ☐ 10, 24 to Drink) On an otherwise typical Borgerhout street, this brilliantly unpretentious shop-room pub is owned by Klaas Janzoons of Antwerp indie-band dEUS.

Beers are cheap and Saturday nights can still see folks dancing at 4.30am. Next door, Klaas also owns a recording studio and the Pekfabrik occasional party/art space.

🍷 't Zuid

Lively drinking spots include Leopold de Waelplaats, Marnixplaats and Troonplaats. The southern section of Waalsekaai and Vlaamsekaai plus nearby roads have a crop of more upmarket cocktail bars.

De Vismijn
PUB

(Map p154; www.cafedevismijn.be; Riemstraat 20; ☺ 10am-1am Tue-Sun) This classic, high-ceilinged bar once provided after-sales refreshment to market fishmongers. Now it's the place to come for Antwerp's best-pulled *pintje* (beer from €2.20).

Like his father before him, Yves Van Roy stores his Stella Artois in 1000L tanks using a special vacuum-bag system to avoid the gassiness of keg beer. He has also won a 'golden tap' award for his carefully honed if deceptively simple pouring technique. A Stella never tasted so good.

Kolonel Koffie
COFFEE

(Map p154; www.kolonelkoffie.be; Montignystraat 51; ☺ 8am-6pm Mon-Fri, 9am-6pm Sat) Roasting their own beans for some of Antwerp's finest fresh coffee (from €2), this effortlessly hip cafe is the hub of the 'new Zuid', with a sunny roadside terrace, big central meet-and-chat table and lots of laptop action at window perches.

Chatleroi
BAR

(Map p154; Graaf van Hoornsestraat 2; ☺ 3pm-late; ☎) Grungier and friendlier than most bars in 't Zuid, Chatleroi has a deeply atmospheric interior and eclectic musical taste, whether piped or live.

Patine
WINE BAR

(Map p154; ☏ 03-257 09 19; www.gastro-by-mo. be/patine.html; Leopold de Waelstraat 1; ☺ 11am-late) This appealing wisteria-fronted street-terrace wine bistro and bar offers a good wine list along with an all-day menu of pastries, quiches, pastas, salads, tapas and Flemish favourites.

Monday happy hours offer beers from €1.50, and Wednesdays from 4pm there's wine from €2.75.

Bar Zar
COCKTAIL BAR

(Map p154; www.zarantwerpen.be; Pourbusstraat 8; ☺ 7pm-1am Wed-Sun) The decor is a mad mix of voodoo, Carribean, Pacific and Japanese elements and nine piranhas cruise in the centrepiece fish tank. The list of premium rums is impressive and there are home-infused fruit gins. But Bar Zar's party trick is excellent fresh cocktails (€10 to €14) swiftly served on draught.

🍷 Zurenborg

On warm weekend nights, terrace *cafés* heave with drinkers around Dageraadplats, over whose central basketball court a netting of lights twinkles like stars. Ever-busy local **Cafe Zeezicht** (Map p146; Dageraadplats 8; ⊙ noon-late) here has oodles of unaffected character, beers from €2.20, and live music on Sunday nights. There are more sedate *café* terraces on railway-bisected Draakplaats, nearby.

☆ Entertainment

Extensive, Dutch-language, *Week Up* (www.weekup.be) is available from tourist offices and many *cafés*.

Tickets for concerts, opera, theatre and dance performances can be bought from **FNAC** (Map p150; ☑ 0900 006 00; www.be. fnacspectacles.com/index.do; Grand Bazar, Beddenstraat 2/33; ⊙ 10am-6.30pm Mon-Sat) or **Info-Cultuur** (Map p150; ☑ 03-203 95 86; www. prospekta.be; Wisselstraat 12; ⊙ 10am-6pm Tue-Fri, noon-5pm Sat), which shares a guildhall with the tourist office.

☆ Live Music

De Roma   LIVE MUSIC
(Map p146; ☑ 03-235 04 90; www.deroma.be; Turnhoutsebaan 327; 🚊 10, 24 to Drink) This meticulously restored 1928 cinema in Borgerhout hosts wonderfully wide-ranging international musical acts as well as a fine program of alternative-film screenings.

De Muze   JAZZ
(Map p150; ☑ 03-226 01 26; http://jazzmuze.be; Melkmarkt 10; ⊙ noon-4am) Fascinating, intimate spaces fill this three-level gabled cafe, with good contemporary live jazz daily from October to May (9pm Monday to Thursday, 10pm Friday and Saturday, 4pm Sunday), and four days a week in summer.

There's no cover for gigs but drink prices rise by €0.50 (eg beer from €2.90).

Café Hopper   JAZZ
(Map p154; ☑ 03-248 49 33; www.cafehopper.be; Leopold De Waelstraat 2; ⊙ 11am-2am) An unpretentious, ever-popular bar with free live jazz sessions most Sunday afternoons (4pm) and Monday evenings (9pm).

Trix   LIVE MUSIC
(Map p146; www.trixonline.be; Noordersingel 28-30; 🚊 410-412 to Hof-ter-Lo) Great, slightly out-of-town venue with a calendar of alternative and up-and-coming bands, both international and local, plus DJ nights.

Sportpaleis/Lotto Arena   LIVE PERFORMANCE
(Map p146; www.sportpaleis.be/nl; Schijnpoortweg; Ⓜ 5) Sportpaleis is Belgium's foremost stadium-style performance arena, with events from P!nk to Plácido Domingo to the Harlem Globetrotters and celebrity tennis matches.

☆ Theatre, Dance & Opera

Opera House   OPERA
(Map p146; ☑ 03-202 10 11; www.operaballet. be; Frankrijklei 1) Don't be perturbed by the building-site setting – at the time of research work was underway to clean the grime off the once-beautiful 1907 neobaroque facade. Within, the opera house is a sumptuous feast of marble.

deSingel   PERFORMING ARTS
(☑ 03-248 28 28; www.desingel.be; Desguinlei 25; ⊙ Sep–mid-Jun) Near Antwerp's southern ring road, this multifaceted arts complex incorporates two theatre/concert halls that offer a highly innovative program of classical music, international theatre and modern dance.

Theater 't Eilandje   DANCE
(Map p146; ☑ 03-234 34 38; www.operaballet.be; Kattendijkdok-Westkaai 16; 🚊 1 to Londenstraat, 🚊 17 to Rijnkaai) Specialises in dance performances of the Ballet Vlaanderen company.

Koningin Elisabethzaal   CONCERT VENUE
(Map p146; www.koninginelisabethzaal.be; Koningin Astridplein 23-24) This venue is home to the Antwerp Symphony Orchestra, though it also showcases other classical concerts, visiting ballets and occasional popular music shows (in 2019 Joan Baez and 10cc).

🛍 Shopping

Meir is Antwerp's grand, pedestrianised shopping street, home to chain stores and the Belgian department store Inno. The diamond district is south of Antwerpen-Centraal, while fashion retailers cluster in the Fashion District, and 't Zuid specialises in homewares and furniture.

On Sundays the **Rommelmarkt** (Map p150; St-Jansvliet; ⊙ 7am-3pm Sun) flea market is an Antwerp institution.

Chocolate Line   CHOCOLATE
(Map p150; ☑ 0447-91 33 36; www.thechocolate line.be; Meir 50; ⊙ 9.30am-6.30pm Tue-Sat, 10.30am-6.30pm Sun & Mon) While you can find cheaper chocolate shops, the Chocolate Line

FASHION DISTRICT

Antwerp may seem far more sartorially laid-back than fashion heavyweights Paris or Milan, but it punches above its weight. In the space of just a few streets you'll find dozens of designer boutiques, along with a variety of streetwear, end-of-line discounters, upmarket vintage and designer consignment shops, and more mainstream labels. Few places in the world have such a convenient and covetable concentration.

The city's status as a global fashion leader dates from the late 1980s, when daring, provocative shows in London and Paris launched the reputations of half a dozen fashion graduates from Antwerp's Royal Academy. Now known as **The Antwerp Six**, the group's most commercially prominent figurehead is **Dries Van Noten**, whose beautiful Antwerp flagship store, **Het Modepaleis** (Map p150; www.driesvannoten.be; Nationalestraat 16; ☺10am-6.30pm Mon-Sat), occupies a distinctive 19th-century flatiron building in the heart of Sint-Andries, though his colourful bohemian clothes sell worldwide. Conceptual artist–designer **Walter Van Beirendonck** has created outfits for rock stars and ballerinas, and merges wild and futuristic clubwear with postmodern ideas about everything from biotechnology to aliens. **Ann Demeulemeester's** timeless designs favour monochromes – black, more often than not. Her **boutique** (Map p154; ☎03-216 01 33; www.anndemeulemeester.be; Verlatstraat 38, Leopold de Waelplaats; ☺10.30am-6.30pm Mon-Sat) is now in 't Zuid, but the main fashion area remains Sint-Andries, with outlets faning out from style museum MoMu (p147) – under reconstruction until 2020 – along Nationalestraat, Steenhouwersvest and Lombardenvest, plus, for streetwear, Kammenstraat.

offers you a unique combination of celebrity 'shocolatier'-creator, a workshop where you can watch production and a superb muralwalled shop that's a historic gem in its own right: a 1745 city palace adapted for use by Napoleon and later royals. Chocolate is €72 per kilogram.

Honest by. FASHION & ACCESSORIES
(Map p150; ☎03-485 87 35; www.honestby.com; Nationalestraat 91; ☺2-6pm Tue-Sat) 🍃 Bruno Pieters offers designer fashion that's 100% transparent – not like the Emperor's New Clothes, but with respect to cost breakdown and responsible sourcing of primary materials. Much of the clothing is 'vegan', avoiding all animal products.

Rosier 41 FASHION & ACCESSORIES
(Map p150; ☎03-225 53 03; www.rosier41.be; Rosier 41; ☺10.30am-6pm Mon-Sat) This is the place to come to find designer-label bargains, both overstock consignments and preloved items. The majority of items are for women, with a particularly large selection of Dries van Noten, but there are many other Belgian and French labels, plus a limited supply of menswear.

Fish & Chips FASHION & ACCESSORIES
(Map p150; www.fishandchips.be; Kammenstraat 18-22; ☺10am-6.30pm Mon-Sat, noon-6pm Sun) An ever-popular streetwear purveyor with humour-filled displays amid bare-concrete pillars. In-store DJs enliven proceedings on Saturday afternoons.

Verso FASHION & ACCESSORIES
(Map p150; ☎03-226 92 92; www.verso.com; Lange Gasthuisstraat 11; ☺10am-6pm Mon-Sat) In an old bank building with a gorgeous stained-glass ceiling, Verso offers designer wares, perfume and accessories. Attached is a dark and moody cocktail *café*, open until 6.30pm (8pm on Saturday).

ℹ Information

Tourism Antwerp (Map p150; ☎03-232 01 03; www.visitantwerpen.be; Grote Markt 13; ☺10am-5pm) Pick up maps, buy tram/bus passes and book tickets here. There's also a booth on the ground floor of Antwerpen-Centraal station (open 9am to 5pm). Ask for the excellent UseIt guide map (www.antwerp.use-it.travel) or download one yourself.

A great resource for events and offbeat visitor ideas is www.thisisantwerp.be.

ℹ Getting There & Away

AIR

Tiny **Antwerp Airport** (www.antwerpairport.be) is 4km southeast of the city, accessible via bus 14 from Antwerpen-Berchem. Most flights are to the UK or Germany with VLM or Flybe, plus there are some TUIfly holiday charters.

BUS

Eurolines (Map p146; ☎ 03-233 86 62; www.eurolines.eu; Van Stralenstraat 8; ◷9am-5pm Mon-Fri, to 3.15pm Sat) international buses depart from near their office. Most services with **FlixBus** (Map p146; www.flixbus.com; Koningin Astridplein) pick up on the square directly north of Antwerpen-Centraal but some use the Borsbeekbrug stop near Antwerpen-Berchem station.

De Lijn (☎ high toll 070-220200; www.delijn.be/en) regional buses 410 to Turnhout via Westmalle and buses 600/602 to Hoogstraten start from **Franklin Rooseveltplaats** (Map p146; Franklin Rooseveltplaats). Bus 90 for Lier (€3, 35 minutes) and many other services start from **Antwerpen-Berchem Bus Station** (Map p146; Guldenvliesstraat/Uitbreidingstraat), although trains are generally much faster. Bus 500 to Mechelen (€3, one hour) via Boom picks up at least hourly from **Station Zuid** (Kolonel Silvertopstraat) on the bridge above Antwerpen-Zuid train station.

CAR

Central Antwerp is a 'Low Emission Zone' (https://lez.antwerpen.be) so don't just drive in. If your car is neither Belgian nor Dutch, you must fill in details and upload scans of both the front and back of the vehicle's original registration document. Processing could take up to 10 days.

Limited **free parking** (Map p146; St-Michielskaai) is available on the southern riverside quay, entered opposite Fortuinstraat, 800m south of Grote Markt, and, until its redevelopment is finished, on the huge 't Zuid square between Vlaamsekaai and Waalsekaai.

TRAIN

The gorgeous main train station, **Antwerpen-Centraal** (p149), is an attraction in itself. Trains run frequently to many destinations including Lier (€3, 27 minutes), Leuven (€7.70, 45 to 65 minutes), and Brussels (€7.70, 46 to 60 minutes), plus twice hourly to Bruges (€15.50, 90 minutes) and Ghent-Dampoort (€9.90, 52 minutes). Trains to/from Ostend and De Panne stop additionally at Antwerpen-Zuid, which is handier for 't Zuid. Tickets marked 'Zone Antwerpen' are valid for any Antwerp station.

For Amsterdam, a high-speed Thalys (1st/2nd class from €98/73) takes 72 minutes via Rotterdam (32 minutes) and Schiphol Airport (54 minutes), with reservations required. Slower unreserved IC trains run hourly, taking almost two hours (from €37.40 booked online), adding stops in Breda (€15.20, 32 minutes) and the Hague (€27.40, 1½ hours).

Alternatively take the slow, hourly Antwerp–Essen–Roosendaal service (54 minutes). Adults pay €6.80 online or €12.80 from the ticket office. For those under 26, Go-Pass 1 gets you to Roosendaal from any Belgian station for just €8.20: a bargain. Roosendaal–Amsterdam trains (€22.50, two hours) run twice hourly via Rotterdam, Delft, the Hague and Leiden.

🛈 Getting Around

Check www.slimnaarantwerpen.be for plenty of ideas, tips and contacts for getting around in Antwerp.

BICYCLE

Velo-Antwerpen (☎ 03-206 50 30; www.velo-antwerpen.be; Kievitplein 7; day/week membership €4/10; ◷11am-5pm Mon-Thu, 9am-3pm Fri) is Antwerp's extensive short-hop bike-share system: sign up online. For longer-term bike hire there's **Cyclant** (☎ 03-232 01 09; www.cyclant.com; Pelikaanstraat 3/1050; 4/12/24hr €9/12/15; ◷10am-6pm Sun, Mon, Wed & Thu, to 7pm Fri & Sat) on the outer west side of Antwerpen-Centraal. To cross the river there's a **lift** (St-Jansvliet) down to the pedestrian/bicycle **Sint-Annatunnel** (Map p146) or, temporarily at least, a free **cross-river ferry** (Map p150; Steenplein; ◷7.15am-6.45pm Mon-Fri, 10.15am-9.45pm Sat & Sun) from Steenplein.

PUBLIC TRANSPORT

The same tickets (one ride/day pass €3/8) are valid for all buses, trams and *premetro* (underground trams), which mostly operate from about 5.30am to midnight. The day pass costs only €6 if prepurchased from De Lijn, where you can also buy three-/five-day passes (€12/17). The Antwerp City Card (p145) includes free public transport.

Premetro trams 3, 5, 9 and 15 run underground from Diamant to Groenplaats and beneath the Scheldt River to Linkeroever. For 't Zuid, tram 4 runs from Groenplaats. Tram 24 heads to Borgerhout.

TAXI

Taxis wait at Groenplaats, outside Antwerpen-Centraal station and on Koningin Astridplein, but are otherwise relatively hard to find. Instead, call or use the app for an **Antwerp Taxi** (☎ 03-238 38 38; www.antwerp-tax.be; €2.95, plus per km €2; ◷24hr). Between 10pm and 6am a €2.50 supplement is added to all fares.

AROUND ANTWERP

Westmalle

If you're on a Belgian beer pilgrimage, it's hard to resist seeking out the monastic complex that produces the famous West-malle Trappist brews. The brewery is hidden

VERBEKE FOUNDATION

Occupying a 12-hectare former industrial site, this **foundation** (☑03-789 22 07; www.verbekefoundation.com; 9190 Kemzeke, Stekene; adult/senior/student/under 14yr €12/11/10/free; ☺11am-6pm Thu-Sun) is one of Europe's largest private contemporary-art initiatives. The indoor-outdoor interactive gallery illuminates then blurs the boundaries between art and science, in the context of humanity's relationship to nature. The sheer volume and nature of the collection defies easy description; exhibits range from a larger-than-life fibreglass cat's anus, which you can sleep in for the night, to 'living' eco-art and commentaries on US presidents.

The gallery ethos celebrates recycling and repurposing, is working towards 100% sustainable power, and believes that 'copyright is for losers' – so you're free to photograph whatever you like and share on social media.

Access is awkward without a vehicle. It's 12km north of St Niklaas, just off the A11 Antwerp–Bruges highway on a parallel lane, accessed from exit 11 (Kemzeke).

behind high walls, and isn't open for visits, but you can cross the busy N12 main road to the monastery's own tavern, **Café Trappisten** (☑03-312 05 02; www.trappisten.be; Antwerpsesteenweg 487; mains €13.50-20; ☺10am-midnight, kitchen 11am-10pm, to 9pm winter) to sample their classic brews or have them mixed as a 'half and half' (€3.80).

The site is 2km southwest of Westmalle town, beside the Antwerp–Turnhout road. Bus 410 stops outside twice hourly at the Abdij stop.

Turnhout

POP 44,040

With a moated castle at its heart, an impossibly lovely *begijnhof,* an oversized Grote Markt and a whole slew of delightful traditional cafes, Turnhout ought to be a major draw. Yet for now it remains oddly undiscovered by most foreign visitors, perhaps because the **castle** (Kasteel van de Hertogen van Brabant; Kasteelplein 1) is still used as a functioning courthouse rather than a visitable sight.

◉ Sights

★ **Turnhout Begijnhof**   HISTORIC BUILDING
(Begijnstraat 61; ☺7am-10pm) **FREE** Hidden behind big wooden gates, one of Belgium's loveliest *begijnhoven* loops round a long, narrow garden set with a grotto, church and religious statues. Founded before 1340, it features tile-roofed brick houses with lanterns and matching shutters, and beside a sheep-mown lawn area, the excellent **Begijnhof Museum** (☑014 42 12 48; www.begijnhofmuseum.be; Begijnhof 56; adult/concession €5/3; ☺2-5pm Tue-Sat, 11am-5pm Sun).

Taxandria   MUSEUM
(www.taxandriamuseum.be; Begijnenstraat 28; adult/concession €5/3; ☺2-5pm Tue-Sat, 11am-5pm Sun) Guarded by a cannon, the spired, 16th-century Matten Thoren mansion hosts this lovable city history museum whose mishmash of art and artefacts range from a stuffed deer (the city mascot) to a measuring device that decided whether men were tall enough for the draft. As yet, relatively little explanation is in English. There's free entry on Tuesdays in July and August.

Speelkaartmuseum   MUSEUM
(☑014-41 56 21; www.speelkaartenmuseum.be; Duivenstraat 18; adult/concession/under 18yr €5/3/free; ☺10am-5pm Tue-Sat, 11am-5pm Sun) Celebrating Turnhout's role as one of the world's largest producers of playing cards (1.3 million packs per day), this extensive museum displays a range of antique industrial printing machines used in card creation, including a vast steam-powered drive wheel.

The guillotine draws attention to French revolutionary times when anti-royalist sentiment went as far as to remove kings and queens from the pack. The newest exhibits show 21st-century technological advances including UV-sensitive inks for low-light clarity.

🛌 Sleeping & Eating

Turnhout City Hotel   HOTEL €€
(☑014-82 02 02; www.turnhoutcity-hotel.be; Stationstraat 5; r weekend/weekday from €90/110; 🛜) Beside the bus station, this professionally run 38-room hotel was converted from a historic railway depot. Tidy, well-appointed rooms come with a bevvy of freebies including kettle, coffee, wine, chockies and (limited) bicycle hire.

A MEDIEVAL BAARLES-UP

A crazy, geopolitical jigsaw, Belgian **Baarle-Hertog** and Dutch Baarle-Nassau together form what appears to be one intermeshed town. Legally, however, the former consists of 22 miniature Belgian exclaves, within which are seven further enclaves of the Netherlands. The result is the world's messiest border. This bizarre arrangement can be traced back to an 1198 agreement in which the Duke of Breda (later Nassau) was given the village of Baarle but did not receive the surrounding farmland, which was jealously guarded by the Hertog (Duke) of Brabant for its valuable agricultural tax revenues.

Visit the exhibition room within the central **tourist office** (☑+31-13-507 99 21; www. toerismebaarle.com; Singel 1; ◷10am-4pm Tue-Sat, 11am-3pm Sun), which shows maps and explains more of the history. Then it's mildly entertaining to stroll the (otherwise unremarkable) streets looking for the metal studs and white crosses that show where roads are divided by otherwise invisible borders. Or order a beer at **Hotel Den Engel** (☑+31-13-507 93 30; www.hoteldenengel.nl; Singel 3; s/d €69.50/86) and sip it while sitting at the southernmost terrace table with one foot in Belgium and the other in the Netherlands.

Bus 460 runs hourly from Turnhout to Baarle (€3, 25 minutes). Dutch bus 132 (www. connexxion.nl) continues twice hourly to both Breda (€4.70, 40 minutes) and Tilburg (€4.30, 40 minutes). By car there's a pleasantly rural lane from Hoogstraten where it's worth stopping for 15 minutes to admire the **begijnhof** (www.hoogstraten.be/node/981; Vrijheit; ◷museum 2-5pm Wed-Sun) FREE and the superb 105m red-brick belfry of **St-Katherinakerk** (www.hoogstraten.be/node/979; Vrijheid; ◷1-4pm Sun Apr-Sep, plus 1-5pm Tue-Sat May-Sep) FREE. It was rebuilt in the 1950s after the 1556 original was cruelly dynamited by retreating WWII Nazi occupiers in 1944.

Hotel Terminus   HOTEL €€

(☑014-41 20 78; www.hotel-terminus.be; Grote Markt 72; s/d/tr from €67/89/116) Above a busy cafe-restaurant on the main square's southwestern corner, the Terminus' simple, cursorily redecorated rooms are some of the city's cheapest. Expect creaky, uneven floors and unrefined bathroom booths that can be pretty small.

Ter Driezen   BOUTIQUE HOTEL €€€

(☑014 41 87 57; www.ter-driezen.be; Herentalsstraat 18; r from €165) In the 220-year-old mansion of a former mayor, the highlights of this family-owned hotel are its ample communal spaces full of Chesterfield sofas and even a grand piano. The garden area is also delightful. The 16 well-equipped rooms are comfortable without any attempt at contemporary styling.

Cucina Marangon   ITALIAN €€€

(☑014 42 43 81; www.cucinamarangon.be; Patersstraat 9; starters/mains €25/30, 3-/4-/5-course menu €42/54/67; ◷11.30am-2pm & 6.30-9.30pm Tue-Fri, 7-9.30pm Sat) In an 1895 town house that oozes a restrained elegance, Cucina Marangon has been serving fine Italian cuisine for over 25 years.

★ Cachet de Cire   EUROPEAN €€€

(☑014-42 22 08; www.cachetdecire.be; Guldensporenlei 23; mains €24-29, 3-/4-course menu €39/49; ◷6-10pm Thu-Mon) Superb attention to detail is evident in every little touch here from the fresh market produce to the hand creams in the bathrooms. The cuisine and presentation are gourmet in quality, yet with generous portion sizes and at prices that are little more than those of a standard brasserie.

And if you want something less fancy, there are a few classic cafe options too (mussels, caesar salad etc), ideal for family dining. In summer the tables spill out into an unpretentious garden-yard shaded by espalier trees. The restaurant, which also has a few B&B rooms, is around 800m west of Grote Markt, just across the railway tracks.

🍷 Drinking & Nightlife

Bon Bon Jour & Nuit   CAFE

(☑0494 78 88 37; www.bonbonjournuit.be; Victoriestraat 10; ◷10am-5pm Thu-Mon) Imagine that you're the French painter Toulouse-Lautrec as you sip a range of absinthes (from €6.75) sitting between Mucha panels and an art nouveau frontage in this magical little chocolate-shop/cafe, which magically recreates the ambience of 1930s Paris.

There are four similarly atmospheric B&B rooms upstairs.

De Ranonkel BROWN CAFE
(Begijnenstraat 25; ⊙9am-3am Mon-Sat, 6.30am-3am Sun) It's hard to imagine a more archetypal street-corner local than De Ranonkel, with its panel-walled interior and ample outdoor seating in the Kasteelplein alley leading to the city's impressive moated castle-courthouse.

In den Spytighen Duvel PUB
(☑0486 41 52 59; www.spytighenduvel.be; Otterstraat 99; ⊙1pm-1am Tue-Thu, 3pm-2am Fri & Sat, 1am-11pm Sun) Sit beside a fireplace beneath historic beamed ceilings at this quiet pub and get stuck into a choice of over 200 brews including all the Trappists and 25 lesser-known local choices.

❶ Getting There & Away

The train and bus stations are located together, 700m west of the Grote Markt along Merodelai.

BUS

The following routes pick up at least hourly at both the bus station and either the Grote Markt and/or de Warende. All cost €3, which is usually significantly less than the train.

305 Leuven (1¾ hours)
410 Antwerp-Rooseveltplaats (85 minutes) via Westmalle (35 minutes)
416/417 Antwerp express (65 minutes)
430 Hoogstraten (30 minutes)
450 Tilburg (Netherlands, 55 minutes)
460 Baarle-Hertog (30 minutes)

TRAIN

Trains run hourly to Antwerpen-Centraal (€8.10, 55 minutes) via Lier (€6.40, 37 minutes). On weekdays there's also an hourly service to Brussels (€12, 75 minutes) via Mechelen (€8.50, 52 minutes).

Lier

POP 35,700

Far greater than the sum of its minor 'sights', Lier is one of Flanders' overlooked historical gems. The centre retains a satisfying architectural integrity and it's ringed by a circular waterway followed by a walkable green rampart where the city walls once stood.

◎ Sights & Activities

Archetypal pseudo-baroque facades line the Grote Markt, where an elfin-spired 1369 belfry gives an almost Disneyesque character to the refined **stadhuis**. Inside, a splendidly lavish **tourist office** (☑03-800 05 55; www.visitlier.be; Grote Markt 58; ⊙9am-4.30pm Mon-Fri, to 4pm Sat & Sun Apr-Oct, 9am-4.30pm Mon-Fri & closed weekends & lunchtimes Nov-Mar) features chandeliers, a ceiling mural and a portrait of Leopold I.

★**Lier Begijnhof** HISTORIC BUILDING
(Sint-Margaretastraat) Originally founded in 1258, this Unesco site is one of Belgium's prettiest 'street' *begijnhoven,* a picture-perfect grid of cobbled lanes lined with archetypal houses around the baroque-fronted 1671 St-Margaretakerk.

The Wenzenstraat entrance is two short blocks southwest of Zimmerplein. The southern door leads out onto the riverbank walk. Several houses have *kantkring* (lace-making clubs) whose members meet a few afternoons a week to work on their techniques, with visitors usually welcome to watch.

Zimmertoren TOWER
(☑03-800 03 95; www.zimmertoren.be; Zimmerplein; museum adult/child €4.50/2; ⊙10am-noon & 1-5pm Tue-Sun) Lier's most iconic monument is the photogenic Zimmertoren, a partly 14th-century tower incorporating a fanciful 1930 timepiece that's eccentrically overendowed with dials, zodiac signs, and a globe on which the Congo remains forever Belgian. At noon, a procession of figures – including Belgium's first kings – emerge from the south face. Paying the entrance fee allows horology fanatics to check out the mechanisms and an attached museum.

The museum includes a second 1935 astronomical Wonder Clock with 93 dials and representation of relative gravities: it wowed at the 1939 New York World's Fair but might not be so thrilling for nonspecialists; and the slow-moving half-hour video tends to clash with other push-button audio soundtracks if the museum isn't entirely empty.

Stads Museum Lier GALLERY
(☑03-800 03 96; www.stadsmuseumlier.be; Florent Van Cauwenberghstraat 14) Undergoing a total renovation at the time of research, this well-endowed provincial art gallery sits behind a classic step-gabled facade and, when finished, will set out the story of Lier through the works of local writers and artists.

The museum's collection includes pre-Raphaelite-style canvases by Isidore Opsomer (1878–1967), notably a 1900 painting of Jesus hanging out in Lier. Expect plenty of references to Felix Timmermans (1886–1947), whose 1916 novel *Pallieter* recast Lier folk as life-loving bohemians: they'd previously been dismissively nicknamed *schapekoppen* (sheep-heads) for their short-sighted medieval decision that the town should host a sheep market rather than Flanders' first great university.

St-Gummaruskerk
CHURCH

(www.topalier.be/bezoeken; Kardinaal Mercierplein; treasury €3; ⊙2-4.30pm daily & 10am-noon Tue-Fri, closed Nov-Easter) Stand amid the flower-boxes of the Aragonstraat bridge and look southeast for a beautiful perspective on this huge Gothic church with its distinctive clock tower.

It commemorates Lier's famously hen-pecked founder St-Gummarus, an 8th-century nobleman who saved a child from a python's mouth and made rain with a stroke of his staff. His remains are contained in a grand 1682 silver reliquary in the presbytery.

Bootjevaren
CRUISE

(☑03-480 80 75; www.bootjevareninlier.be; adult/child €3.50/2; ⊙departures 2-6pm Sat & Sun Apr-Oct, plus 2pm daily Jul & Aug) Jump aboard an unshaded open barge boat for a 40-minute cruise around Lier's canal ring. The jetty is near the northeast corner of the *begijnhof.*

🛏 Sleeping & Eating

The Grote Markt, Eikelstraat and Zimmerplein are lined with inviting places to eat and drink, with other characterful restaurants scattered in lanes near St-Gummaruskerk. Bakeries sell *Lierse vlaaike* (signature fat pastries made with syrup and cinnamon).

Bed Muzet
HOSTEL €

(☑03-488 60 36; www.vjh.be; Volmolenstraat 65; dm/d €27/62; ⊙check-in 4.30-7pm) This swish modern youth hostel occupies a repurposed monastery complex with great views of St-Gummaruskerk from some upper rooms.

Zimmerhof Hotel
BOUTIQUE HOTEL €€

(☑03-490 03 90; www.zimmerhof.be; Begijnhofstraat 2; s/d from €119/139) Very discreet in its pseudo-medieval 1902 almshouse location, Zimmerhof offers 25 comfortable rooms rebuilt in contemporary business style.

The misleadingly named 'lobby' is actually a semi-hidden bar-lounge within what was once a 14th-century gateway.

★ Hof van Aragon
HOTEL €€

(☑03-491 08 00; www.hofvanaragon.be; Mosdijk 6; small s/d €79/94, extra-large s/d/tr €109/124/157; 🐾) Quiet yet very central and overlooking the river, this obligingly run hotel combines several historic buildings, creating a minor maze between its 20 rooms, which are priced by four size categories.

Many include either moulded ceilings or elements of original beamwork. All but the smallest come with a kettle.

Annaloro
ITALIAN €€

(☑03-488 00 85; www.annaloro.be; Bril 17; mains €19-28; ⊙noon-1.30pm Wed-Fri & 7-9.30pm Wed-Sun) Named for the Sicilian chef whose open kitchen takes centre stage, this tiny upmarket Italian restaurant is so intimate that you'd easily mistake it for a cosy local house.

De Comeet
EUROPEAN €€

(☑03-297 27 24; www.decomeet.be; Florent Van Cauwenberghstraat 16; tapas €8-10, mains €19-32; ⊙5.30-10pm Tue-Sun) Gilt cherubs hold wooden beams, and a contemporary wrought-iron chandelier sits above the grand piano in this characterful place whose summer 'garden' retains the creeper-softened rubble of a demolished building. The menu is mostly Mediterranean and tapas but throws in the odd Belgian standard too.

In colder seasons a 'pop-up' winter bar covers the garden area.

ℹ Getting There & Away

Bus 90 runs from the Grote Markt to Antwerpen-Berchem (€3, 35 minutes). For Mechelen, slow buses 550 (one hour) and 560 (40 minutes) each run hourly (€3). The train station, 1km northeast of Grote Markt, is on the Turnhout–Mechelen–Brussels–Binche and Leuven–Aarschot–Antwerp lines. Trains run thrice hourly to Antwerp (€3, 20 minutes), and at least hourly to Leuven (€7.20, 40 minutes), Brussels (€7.20, 45 minutes) and Mechelen (€3.40, 16 minutes).

Mechelen

POP 86,140

With Belgium's foremost cathedral, a superb central square and a scattering of intriguing museums, Mechelen (Malines in French) is one of Flanders' most underrated historic cities. And, as the seat of Belgium's Catholic primate (the equivalent of an archbishop), it is overloaded with fine churches. While the canals aren't as pretty as Bruges', the city is appealingly calm and on summer weekends, when Bruges gets packed with tourists, Mechelen offers a very attractive alternative, along with slashed room rates.

History

Converted to Christianity by 8th-century Irish evangelist St-Rombout, Mechelen became and has remained the region's religious capital. In 1473 Charles the Bold chose Mechelen as the administrative capital of his Burgundian Low Countries, a role maintained after his death by his widow, Margaret of York. Margaret's step-granddaughter Margaret (Margriet) of Austria (1480–1530) later developed Mechelen's court into one of the most glamorous of its day. Science, literature and the arts thrived, and elaborate buildings rose. When Margaret died, her ultrapowerful nephew Charles Quint moved the capital to Brussels. Mechelen's star faded, though the city regained the historical spotlight very briefly in May 1835 when continental Europe's first train arrived here.

◉ Sights & Activities

At the heart of Mechelen is a splendid Grote Markt where the massive bulk of **St-Romboutskathedraal** is balanced by a contrastingly poetic **stadhuis** in all its devil-may-care stone flamboyance. Dotted around town are several superb churches, most opening afternoons only. The breathtakingly huge **OLV-over-de-Dijle** (www.onzelieve vrouwoverdedijle.be; ⊘1-5pm Thu-Tue Apr-Oct, to 4pm Nov-Mar) contains a 1619 tryptich by Rubens, who also made the altarpiece for **St-Janskerk** (Sint-Janstraat; ⊘1-5pm Thu-Tue Apr-Oct, to 4pm Nov-Mar). Other architectural curiosities include the double-spired 13th-century gatehouse **Brusselpoort** (Hoog-straat), the **Gerechtsgebouw** (Voochstraat 7; ⊘7.30am-6pm Mon-Fri, 9am-8pm Sat & Sun) **FREE**, Mechelen's step-gabled courthouse that was Margaret of Austria's palace from 1506, and the **Schepenhuis** (Steenweg 1), a small 1288 castle-style fantasy that's due to become the new tourist office. The unwalled *begijnhof* (www.groot-begijnhof-mechelen.be) area is especially photogenic around the junction of Schrijnstraat and Twaalf-Apostelenstraat.

★**St-Romboutskathedraal**   CATHEDRAL
(www.sintromboutstoren.mechelen.be; Grote Markt; church free, tower adult/under 26yr €8/3; ⊘church 9am-5.30pm, tower 1-4.40pm Sun-Fri, 10am-4.40pm Sat) This soaring, Gothic-vaulted cathedral features a 1723 monumen-

tal pulpit, a 1630 Van Dyck crucifixion scene in the south transept, and dozens more fine artworks below the stained-glasswork of the apse. But the most notable feature by far is the 15th-century tower, soaring 97m high and dominating the city skyline.

Climbing its 500-plus steps affords brilliant views but takes at least 40 minutes return, and capacity is limited to 25 people every 20 minutes. So during major holidays you might need to book ahead (through www.visitmechelen.be), though check the weather forecast first as the view platform is unsheltered. During the climb you'll see a human treadmill once used to bring up building materials, plus the impressive array of 49 bells that rings out across town during summertime hour-long carillon concerts.

★**Speelgoedmuseum**   MUSEUM
(☑015-55 70 75; www.speelgoedmuseum.be; Nek-kerstraat 21; adult/child €9.80/7.30; ⊘10am-5pm Tue-Sun; ◉) With 7000 sq metres of dolls, teddies, toys, games and other pastimes, the wonderful Speelgoedmuseum has lots to keep the kids busy. Meanwhile, adults can peruse the history of toys, walk inside a 'Bruegel' painting and get maudlin over the nostalgic range of playthings, from Mecca-no and Lego to toy soldiers, Airfix kits and working train sets. The museum backs onto Mechelen-Nekkerspoel train station.

Hof van Busleyden   MUSEUM
(☑015-29 40 30; www.hofvanbusleyden.be; Sint-Janstraat 2A; adult/under 26yr/child €11/5/ free) After years of preparation, Mechelen's historical museum should have reopened by the time you read this, offering state-of-the-art interactive exhibits and a multilingual audio guide to help bring context to the city's glory days of the 15th and 16th centuries. The setting is a splendid mansion dating from the period.

Het Zotte Kunstkabinet   MUSEUM
(www.vliegendpeert.be; Sint-Katelijnestraat 22; entry/audio guide €5/1; ⊘1.30-5pm Wed & Sat) This eccentric little shop-museum is great if you can catch it open, and has some fun with the 'crazy' hell scenes and frolicking odd folk of 16th-century paintings by artists such as Bruegel and Bosch.

Tongerlo Refuge   HOUSE
(Schoutestraat 7) In medieval times, abbots from wealthy monasteries would often travel to Mechelen to consult the primate

Mechelen

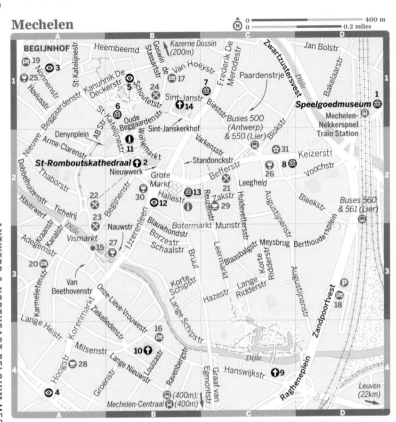

(archbishop) and thus required city residences. Known as 'refuges', some of these residences became grand affairs. One such example is the beautiful, 1484 Tongerlo Refuge. Since 1889 it has been home to the tapestry makers and repairers **De Wit Royal Manufacturers** (☑015-20 29 05; www.dewit. be; Schoutetstraat 7; adult/child €8/4; ⊙tours 10.30am Sat, closed Jul), who offer tours once a week.

OLV-Hanswijkbasiliek CHURCH
(Hanswijkstraat; ⊙1-4pm Tue-Sun) This dome-crowned three-wing basilica has an unusual circular interior, a superb *Paradise Lost* pulpit and brilliant 1690 carved confessionals. An octagonal floor stone commemorates the pope's 1985 visit. But its main treasure is the 'miraculous' Hanswijk Madonna statuette dating from 988, long an object of pilgrimage and still the centrepiece of Mechelen's greatest religious pageant.

Kazerne Dossin MUSEUM
(☑015 29 06 60; www.kazernedossin.eu; Goswin de Stassartstraat 153; memorial free, museum adult/reduced/under 21yr €10/8/4; ⊙museum 9.30am-5pm Thu-Tue, memorial from 10am) The 18th-century Dossin Barracks were used by the Nazis as a WWII deportation centre. Some 25,834 victims (mainly Jewish, 352 Roma) were sent in 28 convoys to Poland where most were gassed at Birkenau or died at labour camps. Only 1400 returned. The barracks' east portal has been preserved as a hushed and haunting memorial of 'relics and faces'. For much more detail and context, cross the road to the Museum of Deportation & Resistance.

The Museum of Deportation & Resistance is in a suitably austere building designed by celebrated Belgian architect bOb Van Reeth. There are extra charges to visit temporary exhibitions.

Mechelen

Boat Tours   CRUISE
(adult/child €6.50/4; ⊙ 1.30-5.30pm Apr-Oct)
Departing from Haverwerf at least hourly,
the open-topped boat *Malinska* takes passengers on interesting if somewhat tame
45-minute cruises along the Dijle River and
back.

◉ Around Mechelen

Fort Breendonk   HISTORIC SITE
(☑ 03-886 75 25; www.breendonk.be; Brandstraat
57; adult/reduced €10/9; ⊙ 9.30am-5.30pm Sep-
Jun, 10am-6pm Jul & Aug, last visit 1hr before close)
Some 12km northwest of Mechelen, this
haunting, moated prison-fort was built in
1906. However, its use as a notorious Nazi
internment camp in WWII is the main focus of the audio-guided visit, with over two
hours of detail including harrowing personal accounts: around 3500 victims were sub-
jected to its torture rooms, cells and dark,
dank corridors. An extra exhibition also
looks at later war-crimes trials.

Technopolis   MUSEUM
(☑ 015 34 20 00; www.technopolis.be; Technologie-
laan; adult/over 55yr/under 12yr €17/15.50/13.50;
⊙ 9.30am-5pm; P ♿) Designed for kids and
teenagers but fascinating for those of all
ages, Technopolis is one of Belgium's best
science museums, with dozens of hands-
on activities to entertain and engage. The
simulator rides are especially popular and a
series of new state-of the art digital experiences are being phased in.

It's 1.8km south of town at junction 10
(Mechelen-Zuid) of the E19 motorway, ideally located if you're driving from Brussels
to Antwerp. From Mechelen station take bus
282, which runs every half-hour on weekdays. There's free car and bike parking.

🎏 Festivals & Events

Hanswijk Procession   RELIGIOUS, FIESTA
(www.hanswijkprocessie.be; ⊙ May) Held on the
weekend before Ascension Day, Mechelen's
biggest festival is a curious mix of solemn
religious parade and fun-filled public party.

The core procession sees the 'miraculous'
Hanswijk Madonna statue carried around
town. Once every 25 years there is a full cav-
alcade involving many horses and the town's
collection of ceremonial giants.

🛏 Sleeping

Hostel De Zandpoort   HOSTEL €
(☑ 015 27 85 39; www.mechelen-hostel.com; Zand-
poortvest 70; dm €23-26, tw €55-58; ⊙ check-in
5-10pm; P ⬛ 🛜) A spick-and-span youth hostel
whose breeze-block-walled rooms all have
private bathrooms but a limited number of
powerpoints. Bring your own towel and a
padlock for the small safety lockers.

Dusk till Dawn B&B €€
(☑ 015 41 28 16; www.dusktilldawn.be; Onze-Lieve-Vrouwestraat 81; d €139-149; ⊘ usually closed Sun; 🛜) Turning the age-old silver handle rings the doorbell at this delightful two-room B&B in an 1870s town house once owned by the Lamot brewing barons. Subtle colours and discerning modern decor reign, while the bar-lounge adopts some art nouveau touches. Guests can use the peaceful garden.

Elisabeth Hotel HOTEL €€
(☑ 015 28 84 00; www.elisabeth-hotel.be; Goswin de Stassartstraat 28; r €71.40-202; 🛜) A giant, enigmatic O sits high on the road as you approach this quiet, central 69-room hotel. Superb value for staying on most Friday and Sunday nights, it is a super-stylishly repurposed former hospital using artistic lighting, black walls and white furniture to create something that's really just a bit too sexy for a business hotel.

Even the smaller rooms are very comfortable (kettle and fridge included) but forking out €20 extra for an 'Executive' version pays dividends in extra space – possibly over dual levels. A swimming pool was under construction at the time of research. Reception is open 24 hours.

Martin's Patershof BOUTIQUE HOTEL €€
(☑ 015 46 46 46; www.facebook.com/Martins Patershof; Karmelietenstraat 4; d €100-399; P✻🛜) 🖋 Fancy sleeping in a church? This one was originally part of an 1867 Franciscan monastery and it retains its rose window and religious mosaics. Of five categories of room, all but the least-expensive ones maintain original design elements, from column tops to stained-glass windows. The stylishly dark breakfast room features the heavily renovated altar.

Hotel Carolus HOTEL €€
(☑ 015 28 71 41; www.hetanker.be; Guido Gezellelaan 49; s/tw/d €99/109/119; P🛜) Motel-style rooms in a partly creeper-covered house whose main draws are the summer terrace overlooking stacked beer casks in the historic Brouwerij Het Anker. Weekend discounts average 20%. Parking costs €5.

🍴 Eating

There's a wide variety of dining styles on Grote Markt and a selection of lunch places and takeaway places along both IJzerenleen and Befferstraat. While most of the Vismarkt cafes are drinking holes, a couple of upper-market dining choices are mixed in. Brouwerij Het Anker has a good restaurant.

Sister Bean CAFE €
(☑ 015 65 86 65; www.sisterbean.be; Vismarkt 26; lunch mains €10-16, breakfast plates €7-9; ⊘ 8am-5pm, from 9pm some weekends; 🛜) This beautiful old corner building hosts a female-run cafe that's a great choice for breakfasts of smoothies and blueberry pancakes, or lunches including halloumi salads and quiche of the day. There's also a big weekend brunch buffet (€20) – assuming you can nab a table...

★ Graspoort FUSION €€
(www.graspoort.be; Begijnenstraat 28; pasta €16.50-23.50, mains €22.50-28; ⊘ 6-10pm Wed-Sat, closed mid-Aug–early Sep; 🖋) Despite her restaurant's improbable location down a dead-end residential alley, traveller-turned-chef Greet has a winning combination of Asian and Mediterranean flavours, market-fresh ingredients and lots of vegetables (some vegan options) that have made this place a locals' favourite for over a decade.

As everything is cooked from scratch by one person (no microwave, no fried food), don't be surprised if the food takes quite a time to arrive. Social interaction between courses is all part of the experience on the cosy, creeper-walled, vine-shaded terrace.

Stassart11 INTERNATIONAL €€€
(☑ 0468 11 11 68; www.stassart11.be; Goswin de Strassartstraat 11; lunch per person €27.50; ⊘ 11am-5pm Tue-Sat, kitchen to 3pm) Hidden away in the rear of the De Borght flower and interior design shop, this indulgent lunch spot has a menu of regularly changing sharing plates: select five dishes between each pair of diners. If you come alone, however, the chef will still make you something glorious.

Cosma Foodhouse INTERNATIONAL €€€
(☑ 015 67 00 70; www.cosma.be; Befferstraat 24; mains €20-30; ⊘ noon-1.45pm & 6-9pm Wed-Sat) At first glance it's easy to mistake this restaurant for a half-closed cooking-utensil shop. But the gorgeous aromas soon prove otherwise, drawing you through to the long verandah-room, behind which you'll find a delectable range of dishes inspired by the recipes of Yotam Ottolenghi.

Reservations are generally essential for dinner but easier to score at lunchtime (with the same menu).

BEER & HISTORY

All around town *cafés* serve beers produced by celebrated local brewery **Het Anker**, many named with Mechelen's curious history in mind. **Maneblusser** is a sneakily drinkable, well-built 5.8% blonde that literally means 'moon extinguisher'. That's been a self-mocking nickname for Mechelen townsfolk since 1687, when cloud-diffused moonlight above the cathedral tower was mistaken for a fire.

The famous **Gouden Carolus** range commemorates the golden coinage of Holy Roman Emperor Charles Quint. Gouden Carolus **Classic** is a rich 8.5% dark beer that has been declared the world's best on a few occasions. But there's also a sturdy 9% **Tripel** (cellar-aged blond) and the unique 8% **Ambrio** brown ale, loosely based on a 1433 recipe said to have been Charles' favourite tipple. Then there's the superbly rich **Gouden Carolus Cuvée van de Keizer Imperial Dark** (11%), as much of a mouthful to drink as to say.

Slightly cloudy, with a mildly spiced acidic edge, Gouden Carolus **Hopsinjoor** is a hoppy pun on Op-Sinjoorke, a lewdly cackling folkloric anti-mascot whose reputation for wife-beating was traditionally punished by tossing him in the air during annual parades. The theft of the original 1647 mannequin was once the cause of conflict between Mechelen and Antwerp. There's a large 'flying' **Op-Sinjoorke statue** (St-Romboutskerkhof) just north of the cathedral and a smaller, more artistic one outside the stadhuis.

🍷 Drinking & Nightlife

Brouwerij Het Anker
BREWERY

(www.hetanker.be; Guido Gezellelaan 49; ⊘tours 11am Tue-Sun & 1pm Fri-Sun, brasserie 10am-11pm, kitchen 11.30am-9pm) Operational since 1471, Het Anker is one of Belgium's oldest and most celebrated breweries. Most days there's at least one brewery tour (€8, two beers and a soft drink included). Or just head straight to the brasserie-bar to guzzle a range of classic Gouden Carolus beers. The beer-paired classic Belgian food is excellent too (mains €16 to €24).

Unwined
WINE BAR

(☑015 41 81 85; www.unwined.be; Steenweg 22; ⊘5pm-midnight Tue-Thu, noon-midnight Fri & Sat, 3-10pm Sun) This congenial, unthreateningly inclusive wine bar makes oenology accessible to novices by listing its ever-changing by-the-glass menu as a short series of quality categories: Wednesday (fresh and simple), Surprise, Friends, Gourmet and Spectacular. Wine from €3.90 per glass.

De Gouden Vis
PUB

(☑015 20 72 06; Nauwstraat 7; ⊘10am-1am or later) The bare boards of this youth favourite have a well-loved patina, the vine threatens to break chunks out of the verandah and the rear riverside terrace catches afternoon sunshine before the serious drinking gets going.

A representative selection of Mechelen beers is available.

Cafe Hanekeef
PUB

(Keizerstraat 8; ⊘9am-4am) Retaining its traditional patterned floor tiles and beamed ceiling, Mechelen's 'oldest pub' is ideal for low-key beery conversations with newspaper-reading locals. Beer/fruit *jenever* (gin) from €2.10/1.70. The place started life as the chicken-farmers' exchange, hence all the cocks on walls, windowsills and every spare ledge.

★ Peloton de Paris
CAFE

(☑015 64 48 26; www.pelotondeparis.be; Hoogstraat 49; ⊘9.30am-6.30pm Wed & Thu, noon-6.30pm Fri, 9.30am-5pm Sat; 🖝) At this cyclist's dream cafe, you can relax with a great coffee (from €2.30) or a specially bicycle-themed beer (from €2.90) microbrewed by Brouwerij Boelens, while a Belgian cycling aficionado looks over your bike (book ahead for a cycle-repair time slot).

SweetB
COFFEE

(www.SweetB.be; Zakstraat 2; ⊘9am-6pm Tue-Sat) Be it for top-quality flat whites, a slow- or cold-brew coffee, dirty chai or black mojitos, SweetB is Mechelen's magnet for quality caffeine fixes.

☆ Entertainment

Stadsschouwburg
THEATRE

(☑015 29 40 00; www.cultuurcentrummechelen. be; Keizerstraat 3; ⊘culture centre 1pm-4.30pm Tue-Fri) Mechelen's municipal theatre and cultural centre occupies the stone-fronted former palace of Margaret of York.

The diplomatically brilliant sister of English King Richard III, Margaret became the de facto dowager ruler of Burgundy's Low Countries, operating her court from this very building.

ⓘ Information

Visit Mechelen (☏ 070 22 00 08; www.visitmechelen.be; Hallestraat 2; ⊙10am-5pm Mon-Fri, 10am-4pm Sat, 12.30-4pm Sun Apr-Oct, to 4pm daily Nov-Mar) The city's helpful tourist office has a comprehensive website, gives away excellent free maps and rents out a few bicycles. A location move to the Schepenhuis is planned by 2019. Check out www.uitinmechelen.be for useful what's-on listings.

ⓘ Getting There & Away

The bus station and adjoining Mechelen-Centraal train station are 1.3km south of the Grote Markt.

BUS

From just outside Mechelen station, buses 284 or 285 are cheaper if slower than trains for reaching Leuven (€3) and run every 20 minutes (hourly on Sundays). **Buses** (Veemarkt) 500 to Antwerpen-Zuid (€3) and 550 to Lier pick up at Veemarkt. **Buses** 560 and 561 to Lier (€3, 35 minutes, twice hourly) pick up at Schuttersvest just south of Mechelen-Nekkerspoel station.

TRAIN

From Mechelen-Centraal, hourly trains run to Leuven (€4.70, 30 minutes), Amsterdam (€25 to €41.40, 2¼ hours), and to Turnhout (€8.50, 55 minutes) via Lier (€3.60, 17 minutes). Fast/slow trains take 15/28 minutes to Brussels (€4.70) and 17/33 minutes to Antwerp (€4.10). Each runs up to three times hourly. Some trains to Antwerp, Lier, Brussels and Nivelles (via Waterloo) also stop at slightly handier Mechelen-Nekkerspoel on the east edge of the city centre.

ⓘ Getting Around

Loop-bus 1 links Mechelen and Mechelen-Nekkerspoel stations via the town centre.

The tourist office has a few bicycles for rent, for €16 per day. This isn't for a 24-hour period, though if you just miss the return time you can take the bike back to the Novotel Hotel off Vismarkt instead.

Leuven

☏ 016 / POP 101.200

Lively Leuven (Louvain in French) is an ancient capital, a prominent brewing centre and Flanders' oldest university town. In term time, and even during the holidays, some 25,000 students give the city an upbeat, creative air. The picturesque core is small enough that you can easily see the sights in a short day trip, but characterful pubs and good-value dining could keep you here for weeks.

⊙ Sights

Much of Leuven's historic townscape was obliterated in the world wars, but a few eye-catching baroque churches survive, including **St-Michelskerk** (Naamsestraat; ⊙1.30-4.30pm Tue-Sun) and **OLV-Ter-Koorts** (www.kadoc.kuleuven.be; Vlamingenstraat 39). A €16 combi-ticket will save you money if you're visiting the KUL Carillon (p176) and M Van Museum, plus doing a tour of the Stadhuis.

★ Stadhuis   ARCHITECTURE
(Grote Markt 9; tours €4; ⊙tours 3pm) Far and away Leuven's most iconic sight, the incredible 15th-century stadhuis is a late-Gothic architectural wedding cake flamboyantly overloaded with terraced turrets, fancy stonework and colourful flags. Added in the mid-19th century, a phenomenal 236 statues smother the exterior, each representing a prominent local scholar, artist or noble from the city's history. Somehow the stadhuis survived the numerous wars that devastated the rest of the town. A WWII bomb that scoured part of the facade miraculously failed to explode.

The interior (by tour only) has several rooms outlandishly lavished with paintings and gilt-work ceilings, but the highlight is the pseudo-medieval 'Gothic Hall' council chamber with its splendid carved fireplace. Tour tickets are sold by the tourist office and should ideally be bought a day or two in advance.

★ Grote Begijnhof   AREA
This idyllic, village-like corner of Leuven would make an ideal film set for a medieval drama. The lantern-lit cobbled streets are lined with step-gabled brick houses with stone window frames. Semi-wild roses scent several green oases, which are richly serenaded with birdsong, and a couple of pretty footbridges cross the central stream.

M Van Museum   GALLERY
(☏ 016 27 29 29; www.mleuven.be; Leopold Vanderkelenstraat 28; adult/reduced €12/10; ⊙11am-6pm Fri-Tue, to 8pm Thu) This state-of-the-art

ANTWERP & NORTHEAST BELGIUM LEUVEN

Leuven

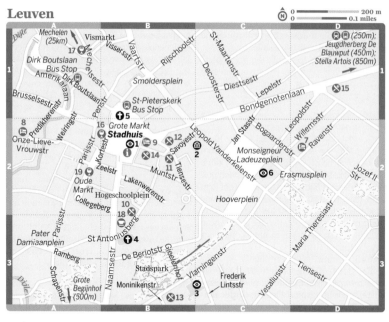

Leuven

gallery houses a priceless collection of 15th- to 18th-century religious works, fascinating Leuven-relevant historical objects and plenty of contemporary art displayed in thought-provoking if sometimes disorienting ways. Upper floors host high-profile temporary exhibitions.

Curiosities include a golden city key, playing 'spot the difference' in a room full of cruxified Christs, and learning about the 'photo-shopping' portraiture of Rogier van der Weyden's 1445 *Seven Sacraments* triptych. The follow these details you'll need to use the icon-activated audio guide (included) or download the M app for your phone.

Note that your ticket also allows free entrance to the *schatkamer* (treasury) of St-Pieterskerk (p176).

Stella Artois   BREWERY
(www.breweryvisits.com;   Aarschotsesteenweg 22; adult/concession €8.50/7.50; ⊘1pm & 3pm Sat & Sun) Just off the main inner ring road around 800m northwest of Leuven train station, this world-famous, highly automated brewery offers mostly group tours, though

individual visitors can join weekend visits at 1pm (in Dutch) and 3pm (in English). Buy tickets from the tourist office or through the website as far ahead as possible.

It's not unusual to find that a pre-booked group tour has extra space that you can sign up for via the website – choose according to the flagged language of the available tours.

St-Pieterskerk   CHURCH
(Grote Markt; church free, schatkamer adult/reduced €3/2, with M Van Museum 'M' ticket free; ⊙10am-4.30pm Mon, Tue & Thu-Sat, 11am-4.30pm Sun) At Leuven's heart is this Brabantine-Gothic church (1425) whose remarkable wooden pulpit is fashioned like twin palm trees that drip with cherubs. The elaborately carved stone rood screen is magnificent too. Tickets are required to go beyond here into the apse, whose *schatkamer* (treasury) most notably includes two priceless triptychs by Leuven-based Flemish Primitive artist Dirk Bouts.

The 1464–67 masterpiece *Het Laatste Avondmaal* is remarkable for placing Jesus' Last Supper in a typical Flemish Gothic dining hall. Its panels have been 'lost' several times, including during WWII, when Nazis carted them off and hid them in a salt mine.

Outside, if the church's northwest facade looks distinctly unfinished, that's because unstable subsoil forced builders to abandon a 170m-high tower that was originally planned here.

Universiteitsbibliotheek   ARCHITECTURE
(University Library; www.bib.kuleuven.be; Monseigneur Ladeuzeplein 21; library/library plus tower €2/7; ⊙library 9am-8pm Mon-Thu, to 7pm Fri, 10am-5pm Sat & Sun, tower 10am-7pm Mon-Fri, to 5pm Sat & Sun) Dominating Monseigneur Ladeuzeplein, this imposingly grand Flemish Renaissance–style palace features a soaring Scandinavian-style brick tower topped with a three-storey octagonal stone cupola.

The library was convincingly rebuilt after WWI with the financial aid of 400 American universities, having been infamously put to the torch in August 1914 during the *Schrecklichkeit* ('terror' or 'hard measures') of the German occupation. It was then rebuilt a second time after WWII. Tickets to access the library's impressive main reading room (occasionally closed) include a 10-point audio guide activated by somewhat hard-to-spot 'Podcatcher' points. Tickets often access additional changing exhibitions. The 300-step tower is worth climbing for the open-air balcony view, creaking clock room and 1928 seven-tonne Liberty Bell.

★KUL Carillon   MUSIC
(www.kuleuven.be; Monseigneur Ladeuzeplein 21; clock-room attendance €5; ⊙7pm Tue & Thu) The Katholieke Universiteit van Leuven (KUL) has a 63-bell carillon tower that rings out David Bowie's *Life on Mars*...among many other tunes. On Tuesday and Thursday evenings, except during exam periods (the poor studying students can't be disturbed), there are 45-minute concerts and, remarkably, visitors are allowed to watch first-hand from the tower-top clock room.

You might even get to request one of the tunes with which to serenade the city.

THE KUL

Within a century of its founding in 1425, the Katholieke Universiteit van Leuven (KUL) had become one of Europe's most highly regarded universities. It attracted famous academics and free thinkers, such as cartographer Mercator, Renaissance scholar Desiderius Erasmus and father of anatomy Andreas Vesalius.

In response to suppression by French and Dutch rulers during the 18th and 19th centuries, the university became a bastion of Flemish Catholicism, and it has continued to foster Flemish identity over the last century.

The destruction of the library in WWI by German troops caused an international outrage, and a massive post-war effort spearheaded by Herbert Hoover in the USA funded the building's reconstruction, led by Whitney Warren, architect of New York's Grand Central Station. In WWII the university was burnt down again, with the loss of 900,000 books.

In the 1960s, after a second reconstruction, KUL became a focal point of Flemish self-determination when student protests about the absence of lectures in their mother tongue led to violent riots. These eventually forced the French-speaking faculties to set up a separate Francophone campus in the purpose-built town of Louvain-la-Neuve, southeast of Brussels.

Booking ahead, through the KUL information desk or online, is highly advised.

🛌 Sleeping

Leuven City Hostel/
Hotel Ladeuze   HOSTEL €
(✆016 84 30 33; www.leuvencityhostel.com; Bogaardenstraat 27; s/d/tr/q with bathroom €70/80/ 95/120, dm/d/tr without bathroom €22/52/53; ⊙reception 4-8pm; @🛜) This small, 'grown-ups' hostel is appealingly low key with a comfy games lounge, a quality kitchen and a little smokers' courtyard area. Check in via the neat new Hotel Ladeuze (www. hotelladeuze.com), whose 16 well-appointed en suite rooms are well worth considering in their own right.

Reception for both closes at 8pm but the kitchen-lounge stays open with free tea and Senseo coffee. Wi-fi is patchy. The hostel's small dorms have a fair number of powerpoints but no reading lights. Linen (but not towels or soap) is provided. The simple buffet breakfast (€7.50) is included in some quoted rates.

Jeugdherbergen De Blauwput   HOSTEL €
(✆016 63 90 62; www.leuven-hostel.com; Martelarenlaan 11a; dm/s/d €26.70/46.60/60.60, under 30yr €24.20/46.60/55.70; ⊙reception 7am-11pm; 🛜) Relatively spacious four- and six-bed dorm rooms have reading lights and en suite bathrooms. There's a pleasant bar and maple-shaded yard seating but no kitchen for guests. Access from town is via the underpass that starts within the Leuven bus station.

Rates include breakfast and sheets but not towels (you can buy one for €6). HI members save €2.50.

Begijnhof Hotel   HOTEL €€
(✆016 29 10 10; www.bchotel.be; Tervursevest 70; d €95-170; P❄🛜) Serene gardens and the peaceful non-central location are the highlights of this three-winged bare-brick 1990s hotel, which is planning a gradual revamp of its rather dated rooms.

Air-conditioning is only in the upstairs rooms. Parking costs €12 per night, the sauna can be booked for €7.50 per person per hour, and reception is open 24 hours.

Martin's Klooster Hotel   HOTEL €€
(✆016 21 31 41; www.martinshotels.com; Onze-Lieve-Vrouwstraat 18; d €115-230, ste €299; @🛜) Central but peaceful, the Klooster is partly comprises a 16th-century building that was once home to Emperor Charles Quint's secretary and much later became an Augustinian convent. Some 39 of the rooms are in the historic building, typically with antique beams and simulated fires, while 103 more corporate versions are in the modern annexe linked by a glass-walled corridor.

All but the cheapest 'cosy' rooms have kettles. Room prices oscillate wildly but for the full-on Klooster experience you can choose one of the three 'Exceptional' options (notably Mother Superior's Room no 7), which include parking, breakfast, minibar and a half-bottle of champagne for a flat rate of €299.

Remarkably obliging reception staff work 24 hours.

⭐ The Fourth   HERITAGE HOTEL €€€
(✆016 22 75 54; www.th4th.com; Grote Markt 5; r from €107, peak times €245-295) Mirroring the ornate Gothic look of the nearby Stadhuis, is the photo-perfect building housing the Fourth is indeed a fourth incarnation of what had been a guildhouse in 1479. All but 15 of the 42 highly automated, luxury rooms are in the old building.

Light sleepers might prefer the rear, courtyard-facing rooms, most of which have a balcony. Breakfast is €20 per person.

🍴 Eating

Ma Hua   NOODLES €
(Eikstraat 2; noodles small/large €6/10; ⊙11am-7pm Tue-Sun; ❄) This bright, simple, six-stool counter cafe is named for a semisweet pastry twist (sold for €2 here), but it's the super-authentic noodles, freshly prepared by Shandong-born owner Zhen, that attracts a steady flow of appreciative Chinese students looking for a taste of home.

De Werf   CAFE €
(www.dewerf-leuven.be; Hogeschoolplein 5; snacks €5-7, pasta & salads €8-15; ⊙9am-midnight Mon-Fri, kitchen to 9pm) With an extensive tree-shaded terrace, this student classic uses road signs, lanterns and very rough walls dangling with builders' tools to add character. Remarkably low prices keep the crowds coming for back-to-basics fare including wraps, salads, pastas and 'chowders' (like vol-au-vents but with a crusty bread casing).

Small appetite? Then opt for a half-sized 'children's portion', as long as you're under 99 years old (if not don't worry, they rarely check IDs...). Cash only, no bookings, cheap beers, and yes, that kitchen roll on the table really is your serviette.

Domus
PUB FOOD €

(☑016 20 14 49; www.domusleuven.be; Tiensestraat 8; snacks €5-8, mains €11-18; ⊘10am-11pm Tue-Thu, 9am-1am Fri & Sat, 9am-11pm Sun, kitchen to 10.30pm; ☎) Reminiscent of a big old-English country pub, this brewery-*café* has heavy beams and rough-plastered part-brick walls generously adorned with photos, paintings and assorted knick-knacks. It's good for tavern fare, sandwiches and fairly priced Flemish dishes, with a meal of the day costing €10.50. Alternatively just sip one of Domus' own brews: try Ne Nostra (€2.40), a gentle but balanced 5.8% amber beer.

Lukemieke
VEGETARIAN €

(☑016 22 97 05; www.lukemieke.be; Vlamingenstraat 55; meals €15.50-16.50; ⊘noon-2pm & 6-8.30pm Mon-Fri; ☑) This friendly place has been serving vegetarian delights since 1967. Its high-ceilinged front room faces Stadspark from an otherwise residential street and there's a slightly overgrown little garden with further seating. The ever-changing menu offers a five-element taster plate, or a meal of the day, both with salad.

La Divina Commedia
MEDITERRANEAN €

(☑016 89 81 75; www.ladivinacommedia.be; Rector De Somerplein 15A; takeaway pasta cups small/large €3/5; ⊘9.30am-2.30pm & 5.30-9pm Mon-Sat) This place is two businesses in one. A bargain takeaway window serves homemade pasta in a cup, with nine choices of topping including pesto, four cheeses, and salmon and zucchini. Meanwhile the mirror-walled restaurant has an altogether more refined offering of elegantly presented dishes, including fish tempura and calf's liver with polenta chips (as well as the same pasta for around €21).

Zarza
EUROPEAN €€€

(☑016 20 50 05; www.zarza.be; Bondgenotenlaan 92; mains €24-32, lunch menus €24-35, 4-/5-/6-course dinner €58/65/75; ⊘11.45am-3pm & 6.30pm-midnight; ☑) Interesting combinations of high-quality, locally sourced ingredients, plenty of seafood and classy vegetarian alternatives feature at Zarza, and are best paired with matched wines (€24 to €36) or beers (€19 to €25).

While the front room feels a little formal, the verandah behind is more relaxed and the small garden is delightful, with potted herbs and dangling paper lanterns in the copper beech.

Drinking & Nightlife

Noir Koffiebar
COFFEE

(☑016 85 08 97; Naamsestraat 49; ⊘8.30am-6pm Mon-Fri, from 9am Sat & summertime) This gently bohemian barista-bar makes work-of-art espressos and flat whites on a La Marzocco machine.

★ Oude Markt
BEER GARDEN

(Oude Markt; ⊘8am-7am) The 30 bars that cram together on Oude Markt form one huge mass of happy drinkers whose chatter and midnight whoops reverberate around the baroque gables. This extraordinary array of pubs collectively has the local nickname 'Europe's Longest Bar'. It's one of Leuven's most remarkable sights and a must-see even if you rush away in terror to drink somewhere more sedate. It's most active in university term time (mid-September to June), when you'll generally find at least one place open at any hour. Many bars close in summer.

Beer Capital
BEER HALL

(www.thecapital.be; Grote Markt 14; ⊘noon-3am) When it opened, the Capital claimed to offer the world's widest beer range, with over 2000 brews. That has been trimmed a little since, but it's still so large that the requisite bottles are brought up from the cellar on a wonderful old pulley mechanism. Or you can choose from some 20 or so on tap.

De Blauwe Kater
BAR

(☑016 20 80 90; www.blauwekater.be; Mechelsestraat 51; ⊘11am-3am) Bringing a lively new vibe to Mechelsestraat, this old established jazz/blues bar serves a fine range of beers including eight on tap, but is best known for its free live performances, typically from 9pm most Monday nights in university term (mid-September to June).

Bar Stan
BAR

(☑016 88 90 83; www.barstan.be; Constantin Meunierstraat 2; ⊘8am-11.30pm Mon-Fri, 10am-4pm Sun) Coffeeshop, bar, restaurant and hip community meeting place all combine in the lovable little triangle of creativity that is Bar Stan, around 15 minutes' walk south from Leuven's centre.

Information

Leuven Leisure (☑016 43 81 44; www.leuvenleisure.com; Tiensestraat 5; ⊘10am-6pm Tue-Fri, to 7pm Sat) Share their infectious enthusiasm for the city via walks, beer tours, bike rides, raft and canoe trips and other activities.

Tourist Office (☑016 20 30 20; www.visit leuven.be; Naamsestraat 1; ⊘10am-5pm) Located around the side of the stadhuis, this office produces a handy app called Leuven Walk.

❶ Getting There & Away

The **Leuven Bus Station** (Martelarenplein) is beside the train station, 800m east of the Grote Markt, and is accessed by buses 1, 2 and many others. There are **luggage lockers** (small/large lockers €4.50/5.50) in the pedestrian underpass beneath.

Visit www.leuven.be for details on car-parking options, both free and paid.

BUS

For Mechelen, buses 284 or the much more direct 285 (€3) are significantly cheaper than the train, and helpfully pick up right in the city centre at a bus stop near **St-Pieterskerk**, plus at a stop on **Dirk Boutslaan**. The same stops are also for buses 317 to Tervuren and 351/358 to Brussels Nord.

From the bus station take Aarschot-bound bus 310 for Kasteel van Horst, and convoluted bus 6 (from platform 5) for Hoegaarden. Some 370 services run to Diest (€3, one hour).

TRAIN

For Antwerp (€7.70, fast/slow 46/65 minutes), dtrains go via either Lier (€7.20, 35 minutes) or Brussels Airport (€9.30, 15 minutes). Sometimes it's quicker to change at Mechelen (€4.70, fast/slow 26/33 minutes).

Other direct services include the following:

Brussels (€5.50, fast/slow 22/31 minutes, five times hourly)

Diest (€5.50, fast/slow 25/33 minutes)

Liège (€11.30, fast/slow 35/56 minutes). Slow trains go via Tienen (€3.70, 15 minutes).

HAGELAND

Between Leuven and the bustling city of Hasselt lies the largely agricultural area of Hageland. If driving, consider a short stop in **Scherpenheuvel** whose baroque, seven-sided **basilica** (www.scherpenheuvel.be; Albertusplein; ⊘7.30am-7.30pm May-Aug, to 6.30pm Sep-Apr) attracts a regular stream of Catholic pilgrims. Then continue via attractive Diest.

Diest

POP 23,810

The handsome town of Diest retains a considerable scattering of fine old architecture from its time (1499-1794) as a domain of the Orange-Nassau family, today's Dutch ruling family. But what really makes it worth a stop is its wonderful 1252 **St-Katharinabegijnhof** (Heilige Geeststraat), entered through a splendid baroque portal at the eastern end of Begijnenstraat. It's a 10-minute stroll east of the Grote Markt, starting out along Koning Albertstraat.

Hasselt

POP 77,600

Hasselt is a large, prosperous city which celebrates its fame as Belgium's unofficial *jenever* (gin) capital with a **gin festival** (www.jeneverfeesten.be; Maastrichterstraat; ⊘3rd weekend of Oct) and the **Nationaal Jenevermuseum** (☑011 23 98 60; www.jenevermuseum. be; Witte Nonnenstraat 19; adult/under 26/child €7/3/free; ⊘10am-5pm Tue-Sun, closed Jan), housed in a beautifully restored and still-active 19th-century distillery. **Free bicycle hire** (Groenplein; ⊘9am-6pm Mon-Fri, 10am-6pm Sat) from behind the attractive old town hall makes it easy to ride out using a well-organised web of cycle paths to an enticing series of provincial vast parks and woodlands at Bokrijk towards Genk.

These incorporate a splendid **arboretum** (Bokrijk; ⊘year-round) FREE and the 60-hectare **Bokrijk Openluchtmuseum** (☑011 26 53 00; www.bokrijk.be; adult/child €12.50/2; ⊘10am-6pm Tue-Sun Apr-early Oct, daily Jul & Aug), one of Europe's largest open-air museums with over 100 reassembled historic buildings. Hourly Hasselt–Genk trains (10 minutes) stop 500m south of the latter's southern entrance, but if you come by bicycle, don't miss **FDHW** (Fietsen door het water; www.dewijers.be/en-bokrijk-kiewit; Fietsknooppunt 91) where you can feel like Moses parting the waters as you cross 'through' a lake at eye level. Web search '#FDHW' for videos and more details.

As a business city, Hasselt has a wide range of mid-range accommodation. Hotel prices tend to climb midweek but conversely, B&B prices rise at weekends. There are two hostels, one is across the tracks from the train station, while the other, **De Roerdomp** (☑089 35 62 20; www.jeugdherbergen.be; Boekrakelaan 30; dm adult/under 26 €22.25/20; ⊘5-9pm mid-Feb–mid-Nov), is in a rustic location that's ideal for cyclists exploring the Bokrijk area.

For interesting dining options look on Zuivermarkt, northeast of the cathedral, and on several side streets leading west off the

ANTWERP & NORTHEAST BELGIUM DIEST

pedestrianised shopping street Hoogstraat/ Demerstraat. Grote Markt is jammed full of cafe-bars, with several more on Fruitmarkt and on Witte Nonnenstraat.

HASPENGOUW

The gently rolling Haspengouw region between Leuven and Tongeren is famed for its fruit orchards and even the odd vineyard. Landscapes are at their prettiest in the smaller lanes around Bogloon.

Tienen

POP 32,600

Once an important Roman centre for ceramics and glass-making, Tienen (Tirlemont in French) got rich in the 19th century as a centre of sugar processing. It retains a liberal scattering of older buildings, including two spectacularly vast churches: to see them both from one spot, stand at the bottom of Trapstraat. Learn more about the Roman Tienen at the fascinating little museum **Het Toreke** (Grote Markt; adult/under 26/child €4/2/ free; ⊘10am-5pm Tue-Sun), tucked into a yard off the huge Grote Markt behind the **tourist office** (⊘016 80 56 86; www.toerisme.tienen. be; Grote Markt 3-6; ⊘8.30am-12.30pm Mon-Fri). Some 3km towards Sint-Truiden you'll pass **Drie Tumuli** (Sint-Truidenssteenweg, Grimde; ⊘24hr; ⊑313 to Tumuli) **FREE**, a recently relandscaped trio of Roman grave mounds. A short walk away is **Grimde Necropolis** (Pastorijstraat; ⊘24hr; ⊑313 to Grimde Kerk) **FREE**, a church movingly turned into a WWI burial chamber.

🛏 Sleeping & Drinking

⭐**Carpe Diem**   B&B €€
(⊘0489 77 81 88; www.bbcarpediem.be; Wolmarkt 5; s €75-105, d €90-120) Carpe Diem B&B has been lovingly converted from an antique shop, with hand-painted floors, lots of church statuary, and bath foam that comes in wine bottles. The most expensive room has an antique oak bed and a view of the Sint-Germanuskerk tower.

The location is handily central, between Tienen's two main churches.

Ma Façon   COFFEE
(⊘016 41 50 41; Nieuwstraat 2; ⊘8.30am-6pm Tue-Sat Sep-Jun, noon-3pm Mon, 9am-4pm Tue-Fri, 11am-5pm Sat Jul & Aug) With artistically glazed earthenware cups and hefty unvarnished wooden bench tables, Ma Façon is part gin bar, part crockery store, but predominantly a comfortably hip place for superb coffee (€3 to €4.50).

From noon to 2pm a great selection of fresh lunches is also served, with the menu scrawled on hanging rolls of brown paper.

❶ Getting There & Away

Hourly bus 313 links Tienen to Sint-Truiden (€3, 40 minutes) via Grimde. Bus 22 heads for Diest (€3, one hour); change in Budingen for bus 23 to Zoutleeuw.

Tienen is a stop for trains running Mons–Liège (via Brussels and Leuven) and Ghent–Genk trains (via Brussels, Leuven, Sint-Truiden, Hasselt and Bokrijk), both hourly.

Zoutleeuw

POP 8490

If you're driving between Sint-Truiden and Tienen on a summer's afternoon, do stop briefly at historic little Zoutleeuw to visit the 13th-century **St-Leonarduskerk** (⊘011 78 12 88; Vleestraat; ⊘2-5pm Tue-Sun Apr-Sep, Sun only Oct). Topped with a fanciful tower reminiscent of a galleon's crow's nest, this Unesco-listed Gothic church is the only significant example in all of Belgium to have escaped essentially unscathed from the religious turmoil and invasions of the 16th to 18th centuries. Across the main square, also admire the **Stadhuis** (⊘011 94 90 46; www. zoutleeuw.be; Grote Markt 11; ⊘2-5pm Tue-Sun Apr-Sep) **FREE**, a 19th-century faux-medieval delight with majestic pre-Raphaelite murals in the ground-floor hall, exhibition spaces above, and a very appealing tavern.

Sint-Truiden

POP 40,400

A photogenic trio of historical towers gives the extensive Grote Markt of Sint-Truiden (St-Trond in French) a fairy-tale feel that easily justifies an hour or two of your time.

Thanks to a local saint named St-Trudo, Sint-Truiden became a major medieval pilgrimage centre from the 7th century. His relics are now housed in the treasury of the central, neo-Gothic **Onze Lieve Vrouwekerk** (Grote Markt; ⊘church 8.30am-5.30pm, treasury 10am-5pm Mon-Fri, 2-5pm Sat & Sun) **FREE**. All that remains of the older, 11th-century St-Trudo abbey church is the shell of its seven-storey bell-tower, the **Abdijtoren** (Diesterstraat 1, Kerkveld; adult/concession €4/2; ☺10am-6pm). You can climb that for fine views thanks to a series of 20th-century metal stairways. Getting in requires an access code that you get when buying Trudo-Pas (€4), available from the **tourist office** (☏011 70 18 18; www.toerisme-sint-truiden.be; Grote Markt; ☺9am-5pm) which you'll find inside the spired historic **stadhuis**.

It's also available, 1km northeast, from the **Begijnhofkerk** (Begijnhof; ☺10am-12.30pm Mon-Fri & 1.30-5pm daily, closed Nov-Mar) `FREE`, a fascinating barnlike church dating from 1258 and renowned for a gruesome medieval fresco depicting the torture of a topless St Agatha. You'll need the TrudoPas to visit the lovably slow-moving **Festraets Studio** (☏011 68 87 52; Begijnhof 24; ☺hourly 10.45am-3.45pm Tue-Fri except 12.45pm Tue-Fri, 2.45pm & 3.45pm only Sat & Sun, closed Oct-Mar) `FREE` nearby. It features a technologically remarkable working collection of pre-electronic clockwork mechanisms. It's charmingly dated and there's no English in the explanations but you can admire a 6m-high, 4-tonne astronomical clock, learn about the Foucault pendulum and get seasick watching a model of an ocean liner leaving New York.

Useful buses (all €3) include bus 313 to Tienen (40 minutes) via Grimde, bus 23a to Tongeren (35 minutes) and bus 23 to Zoutleeuw (10 minutes) via Wilderen.

Trains run hourly to Bokrijk (€4.70, 30 minutes) via Hasselt (€3.40, 15 minutes), and to Leuven (€7.20, 33 minutes) via Tienen (€4.40, 20 minutes).

Tongeren

POP 31,010

Proudly claiming to be Belgium's oldest town, Tongeren (Tongres in French) has a picturesque old core, is remarkable for retaining several sections of its Roman-era city walls and draws crowds to its Sunday antiques market. Great-value boutique accommodation plus an imaginative dining scene seal the deal and make for one of northeastern Belgium's most convivial touring bases.

Tongeren's sense of antiquity relies on its association with the Gallic Eburones tribe and their legendary leader **Ambiorix**. Loosely represented by Beefix in the classic Asterix comics, Ambiorix made a valiant if ultimately unsuccessful attempt to resist Roman rule in 54 BC. By the 2nd century, this was long forgotten and Tongeren had become a prosperous Roman settlement on the Cologne–Bavay road. By the 4th century it was one of the Low Countries' earliest Christian bishoprics. The city remained of great regional importance until 1677 when Louis XIV of France burnt it down. In the 1830s, with newly founded Belgium in need of national heroes, the Ambiorix legend was dusted off and the character's muscular, mustachioed **statue** (Grote Markt) now stares at the basilica from Tongeren's main square.

⦿ Sights

Gallo-Roman Museum   MUSEUM
(☏012 67 03 30; www.galloromeinsmuseum.be; Kielenstraat 15; adult/concession/youth €7/5/1; ☺9am-5pm Tue-Fri, 10am-6pm Sat & Sun) Sternly clad in battleship-grey stone, this very spacious modern museum devotes two well-crafted floors to the evolution of human culture then, after a drama-filled seven-minute film about local hero Ambiorix, there's another superb floor dealing with Roman Tongeren.

Onze Lieve Vrouwebasiliek   BASILICA
(Basilica of Our Lady; ☏012 21 33 24; www.basiliek tongeren.be; Kloosterstraat 1; ☺8am-5pm Mon-Fri, 9am-5pm Sat, 9am-6pm Sun) This central church mostly dates from the 14th to 16th centuries, with a finely proportioned stone tower that dominates Tongeren's neatly cafe-lined Grote Markt. The basilica marks the first place north of the Alps where the Virgin Mary is said to have been worshipped. Look in the north transept to see a much-venerated 1479 Madonna statue feeding baby Jesus with grapes. The basilica's rich treasury forms the core of the new museum **TeSeUm** (☏012 80 02 28; www.teseum.be; Onze Lieve Vrouwebasiliek, Graanmarkt; adult/senior/child €6/5/1; ☺10am-5pm Tue-Sun) whose state-of-the-art iPod-led tour guides visitors through Tongeren's post-Roman history.

Tongeren Begijnhof   AREA
(www.begijnhofmuseumtongeren.be; Onder de Linde 12; museum house €4; ☺2-5pm Tue-Sun) Three blocks south and west of Onze Lieve Vrouwebasiliek is a small web of very pretty backstreets that once formed Tongeren's *begijnhof*. One furnished 1660 house here now hosts the little Beghina Museum illustrating *begijn* lifestyles – cute but not a great draw.

A small canal leads towards Moerenpoort, the chunky 1379 city-gate tower.

Antiques Market MARKET

(www.antiekmarkt-tongeren.be; Veemarkt; ⊘7am-1pm Sun) This is one of Belgium's best flea markets, with a large number of *brocante* stalls and some serious antique dealers.

🛏 Sleeping & Eating

Tongeren's decent accommodation selection includes at least three boutique hotels in restored historical buildings, plus the functional but central youth hostel, **Begeinhof** (☑012 39 13 70; www.vjh.be; St-Ursulastraat 1; dm without/with bathroom €20.50/22; @🛜).

For such a modestly sized town, Tongeren has a superb dining scene, highlighted in the 86-page free booklet *#Foodies Tongeren*. There are two Michelin-starred restaurants and several other gourmet options, plus many simpler choices along Maastrichterstraat, the main shopping street. There's a concentration of pubs on Veemarkt. On Sundays some cafes open from 7am for the antique dealers.

★Boutique Hotel

Caelus VII BOUTIQUE HOTEL €€

(☑012 69 77 77; www.caelus.be; Kloosterstraat 7; d weekday/Sat/last minute €98/110/82; ❇🛜) Super-central, this seven-room hotel fills a former hat shop with antique and antique-style furniture, while offering all mod-cons including Nespresso machine, air-conditoning and thoroughly pampering beds. Upper-floor rooms are accessed by the steep, original spiral staircase, but there's a baggage lift so you needn't lug your bags up with you.

Reception times are limited so be sure to write down the door code you receive when booking. Near the station, around 600m east, even grander co-owned **Huys van Steyns** is a similarly good choice, with the bonus of private parking behind the rose garden.

Eburon Hotel HOTEL €€

(☑012 23 01 99; www.eburonhotel.be; de Schiervelstraat 10; d with shower/bath €109/139; ⊘reception 24hr; ❇🛜) The Eburon is within a repurposed historic convent, with a large, white lobby space that feels contrastingly contemporary – more like an art gallery than a hotel. Of the 51 stylish rooms, the 14 biggest come with show bath, coffee maker and beds that are like midroom sports pitches.

Puur Oogst CAFE €

(☑012 21 91 18; www.puuroogst.be; Maastrichterstraat 36; mains €7-10; ⊘9.30am-6pm Tue-Sat) With distressed walls, well-spaced seating and a street terrace, this organic grocery/salad bar is great for coffee, pancakes or especially for healthy lunches where you select five salads (also available by weight for takeaway) on a bed of lettuce (€9.95).

★Infirmerie BELGIAN €€

(☑012 44 10 44; www.infirmerie.be; St-Ursulastraat 11; mains €16-29; ⊘11.30am-10pm Wed-Sat, 9.30am-10pm Sun) Tucked away at the base of the *begijnhof*, Infirmerie is a relaxed brasserie incorporating elements of historical design from a 1701 building that had been a chapel before becoming the *begijns'* infirmary. The waterside terrace is especially appealing, ideal for drinks or afternoon coffee and cake (€5) when the main kitchen is closed between meals.

Bistro Bis INTERNATIONAL €€

(☑012 74 34 66; www.bistrobis.be; Hemelingenstraat 23; pizza €16, mains €20-25, 3/5 courses €37/52; ⊘6.30-10pm Fri-Mon, closed early Jul-Aug) For very fine bistro food with a rock-and-roll soundtrack, cosy up with fellow diners at a long rough-wooden table and choose from the day's three delectable choices of starter and main, created by bearded hipster Johan Haiverlain, former sous chef at the Michelin-starred Magis downstairs.

In summer when Bis itself is mostly closed, watch social media to catch Johan's pop-up pizza nights in the Magis garden.

ⓘ Information

Toerisme Tongeren (☑012 80 00 70; www.tongeren.be/toerisme; Via Julianus 2; ⊘8.30am-noon & 1-5pm Mon-Fri, 10am-4pm Sat, Sun & holidays) In the Julianus shopping centre, part of the redeveloped 1660 Gasthuis Kapel complex.

ⓘ Getting There & Around

The bus and train stations are 400m directly east of the centre via Maastrichterstraat. Hourly trains depart for Hasselt (€4.30, 20 minutes), Liège-Palais (€4.40, 27 minutes) and Sint-Truiden (via Hasselt, €6.60, 45 minutes).

Bus 23a runs directly to Sint-Truiden (€3, 35 minutes, hourly).

There's ample free parking in the new De Motten car park, just southwest of the Moerenpoort.

Bicycles are available for hire from **Marco's Véloshop** (☑012 39 39 66; Maastrichterstraat 99; per day standard/electric bicycle €10/20; ⊘9am-6pm Tue-Sat), helpfully close to the tourist office.

Wallonia

LANGUAGES: FRENCH (& GERMAN AROUND EUPEN)

Best Places to Eat

- ➜ La Petite Madeleine (p189)
- ➜ Hôtel Bonhomme (p238)
- ➜ L'O de Source (p237)
- ➜ La Bonne Auberge (p203)
- ➜ La Calèche (p216)
- ➜ La Table des Sépulcrines (p218)

Best Places to Stay

- ➜ La Malle Poste (p215)
- ➜ La Villa Sauvage (p234)
- ➜ Julévi (p242)
- ➜ Petit Chapitre (p204)
- ➜ Dream Hôtel (p193)
- ➜ Le Moulin des Ramiers (p211)

Why Go?

Wallonia (La Wallonie), Belgium's mostly French-speaking southern half, includes many a pretty rustic village in rolling green countryside, interspersed by a handful of postindustrial cities. The heavily wooded Ardennes is a major area for outdoors activities, a plateau land cut by rivers for kayaking, honeycombed with fabulous cave systems and offering just the tiniest hope of skiing in midwinter. Centuries of history are evident in the attractive cities of Mons and Tournai, in the unforgettable carnivals of Binche, Stavelot and Malmédy, and in a plentiful scattering of medieval castle ruins and grand châteaux. Sniffing out Liège's deep historical pedigree takes a little more delving beneath its rather disfigured surface. And then there's Waterloo, where Napoleon met his ABBA song. In many ways Wallonia feels like a different country from Flanders. Finding English speakers can't be so easily taken for granted and to reach the more rural highlights you'll appreciate having your own wheels.

Driving Distances (km)

	Waterloo	Mons	Tournai	Chimay
Mons	56			
Tournai	89	46		
Chimay	85	58	104	
Mariembourg	76	70	116	20

Wallonia Highlights

1 Mons (p191) Visiting fascinating museums, then unwinding over cocktails in the photogenic Grand Place.

2 Rochefort (p214) Cycling, caving or sipping Trappist

beers in this picturesque country getaway.

3 Bouillon (p216) Watching the falconry displays and marching the ramparts of its Crusader-era castle.

4 Namur (p204) Window-shopping, drinking and dining on the cobblestone lanes of Wallonia's vibrant capital.

5 Semois Valley (p219) Driving between charming

woodland viewpoints or kayaking on the river below.

6 Binche (p195) Bingeing with the orange-lobbing Gilles at the weirdest carnival you're ever likely to witness.

7 Tournai (p186) Observing architectural transformation in its cathedral.

8 Liège (p224) Revelling in the hospitable *joie de vivre* of this old city.

9 Bastogne War Museum (p220) Remembering the fallen of the Battle of the Bulge.

10 Chimay (p203) Exploring the lakes and forests of the Botte du Hainaut.

ⓘ Information

Wallonia Tourism (www.walloniabelgiumtourism
.co.uk) has lots of visitor ideas.

WESTERN WALLONIA

Tournai

POP 69,600

Enjoyable Tournai (tour-*nay;* Doornik in
Dutch) has a memorable Grand Place and
one of Belgium's finest cathedrals. Even
by local standards, the city has been in the
wars, occupied at various points by Romans,
Franks, Normans, French, English, Spanish,
Austrians, Dutch and Germans. Today it's a
lovely place for casual strolling, with a lively
bar and restaurant scene near the river.

History

Tournai grew to prominence as the Roman
trading settlement of Tornacum, and was the
original 5th-century capital of the Frankish
Merovingian dynasty. Autonomous from
France as of 1187, the city retains two towers
from the first 1202 city wall. In 1513 Tournai
was conquered by Henry VIII of England –
Thomas Wolsey, of *Wolf Hall* fame, was appointed bishop – before being sold back to
France in 1519. Just two years later it was
swallowed by the Habsburg Empire. Tournai
found renewed wealth as a centre for, succes-
sively, tapestries, textiles and porcelain, but it
was devastated by WWII bombing.

◉ Sights

As well as Tournai's main sights, notable
structures include a curiously fortified
bridge, **Pont des Trous,** two remnant towers
from the 1202 city wall – **Tour du Cygne** (Impasse de la Rue du Cygne) and **Tour St-Georges** (Rue St-Georges) – plus **Église St-Quentin**
(Grand Place 44; ⊙9am-4pm Nov-Mar, to 6pm Apr-
Oct), a hefty part-Romanesque church with a
12th-century nave.

★ **Cathédrale Notre Dame**   CATHEDRAL
(www.cathedrale-tournai.be; Place de l'Évêché;
⊙9am-6pm Mon-Fri, to noon & 1-6pm Sat & Sun
Apr-Oct, to 5pm Nov-Mar) FREE Dominating
Tournai's skyline are the five spires of its remarkable cathedral, which survived WWII
bombs only for a freak 1999 tornado to compromise its stability. It'll remain a vast building site for another decade; though work on

the five towers was completed in 2018. Despite the scaffolding, the interior remains a
fascinating example of evolving architectural
styles, from the magnificent Romanesque
nave through a curious bridging transept
into an early-Gothic choir whose soaring pillars bend disconcertingly.

The wood-panelled little Chapelle St-Louis
is under restoration and its large canvases
by Rubens and Jacob Jordaens are currently
hidden, but there are some impressive paintings, tapestries and relics in the **treasury**
(€2.50; ⊙10am-6pm Tue-Fri, 1-6pm Sat & Sun Apr-
Oct, 10am-5pm Tue-Fri, 1-5pm Sat & Sun Nov-Mar).
When viewed from near the latter,the cathedral's classic cluster of five grey-stone towers
seems to float ethereally above the Grand
Place.

★ **Grand Place**   SQUARE
Tournai's gorgeous triangular main square is
ringed with cafes in fine gable-fronted guild-
houses merrily flying guild banners. Kids
play in 'dare-you' fountains beneath an axe-
wielding statue of Princess d'Espinoy, the
doomed heroine who led Tournai's eventually
futile defence against a 1581 Spanish siege.

The Grand Place's finest building, the
Halle Aux Draps (Grand Place 57; ⊙exhibitions
only), is the old cloth hall whose 17th-century
Renaissance facade was painstakingly rebuilt after the original collapsed in 1881.

Beffroi   TOWER
(www.visittournai.be; Grand Place; adult/child
€2.50/free; ⊙9.30am-12.30pm & 1.30-5.30pm
Tue-Sun Apr-Oct, 9.30am-noon & 2-5pm Tue-Sat,
2-5pm Sun Nov-Mar) Belgium's oldest belfry is
72m high with a narrow 257-step spiral staircase that becomes even narrower higher up.
There's a good multilingual display on the
history and significance of belfries as symbols of civic liberties partway up, but otherwise the main attractions are the bells and
the views, described by faded signboards.
Ask at the tourist office about bell concerts,
during which you can climb the tower to see
the ringer at work.

Musée des Beaux-Arts   GALLERY
(☏069-33 24 31; www.tournai.be; Enclos St-Martin 3; adult/child €2.60/2.10; ⊙9.30am-12.30pm
& 1.30-5pm Wed-Mon Apr-Oct, 9.30am-noon &
2-5pm Mon & Wed-Sat, 2-5pm Sun Nov-Mar) This
airy gallery was designed by art nouveau
maestro Victor Horta. Though the interior
and display halls are in need of a pep-up,
it has a rich collection, including items by

Tournai

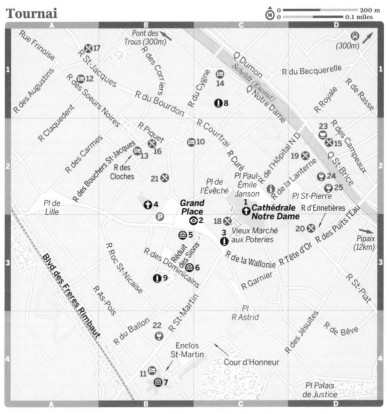

Tournai's best-known artist, the 15th-century Rogier Van der Weyden (Roger de la Pasture); works by Rubens, Jacob Jordaens, Manet and Monet; a beautiful Seurat seascape; and sketches by Van Gogh and Toulouse-Lautrec. In the central atrium, a flying purple hippo gazes benevolently down on more classical sculptural forms.

Musée de Folklore   MUSEUM
(☑069-22 40 69; www.tournai.be; Réduit des Sions 36; adult/child €2.60/2.10; ⊙9.30am-12.30pm & 1.30-5.30pm Wed-Mon Apr-Oct, reduced hours rest of year) This is a lovable and sizeable warren of fascinating city-relevant relics and ethnographic artefacts. It's all in French, but many of the cameo scenes are self-explanatory, and across the 'bridge-room' there's a great model of Tournai in its 18th-century heyday.

🛌 Sleeping

Auberge de Jeunesse   HOSTEL €
(☑069-21 61 36; www.lesaubergesdejeunesse. be; Rue St-Martin 64; dm/d/tr incl breakfast €25/58/75; 🛜) In a historic former music college, this friendly place is just five minutes' walk from the Grand Place. Dorms have showers, but the shared toilets can get overstretched when the hostel's full. Although the sleeping quarters are rather institutional looking, the elegant common areas – complete with 200-year-old tapestries, plus table football and a kitchen for guests – make up for its deficits.

★B&B Mme Daniel   B&B €€
(☑0472 38 69 72; fdaniel@skynet.be; Rue des Soeurs Noires 35; s/d €60/70; 🛜) Three art-filled rooms are available in this very homey 1673 stone house with flowerboxes and a charming little rear garden. Rooms are all very different in feel; the ground-floor room has garden access, the floral room is a dazzling visual overload, and the top-floor loft has a kitchenette and can sleep three. Homemade bread and jam make breakfast a treat.

The welcome is impeccable from Madame Daniel and two lovable collies (Dune and Angel), and this is a really authentic Belgian experience. There's no sign; book ahead.

★Hôtel d'Alcantara   HOTEL €€
(☑069-21 26 48; www.hotelalcantara.be; Rue des Bouchers St-Jacques 2; s €91-122, d €101-132, tr/q from €135/162; P@🛜) Tournai's most appealing hotel has a regal northern facade, behind which is a beautifully realised boutique hotel. Well-modernised rooms, often with bold colour schemes, come in a variety of shapes and sizes. Rooms themed for musical styles have better bathrooms than the 'artist' rooms. Some are tucked into old beam-eaves. Pretty garden terrace. Breakfast included.

Château Bagatelle   B&B €€
(☑069-66 33 35; www.chateau-bagatelle.com; Chaussée de Tournai 29, Arc-Wattripont; s/d/tr/q €90/100/110/120; P🛜) If you're driving, be tempted by this elegant yet homelike family castle offering two luxurious rooms in a building that's partly 12th century, albeit mainly 19th. Or rent the charming *gîte* cottage, which sleeps up to nine. It's on the N48, 20km northeast of Tournai. Often booked on weekends for weddings.

The owners also run the **Hôtel & Spa Bagatelle** (☑0497 65 89 97; Rue Beauvolers 7, Dergnau; s/d from €85/100; P🛜), located just over 2km southeast of the Château Bagatelle.

Appartement Studio Tournai   APARTMENT €€
(☑069-23 51 27; www.studio-spa-tournai.be; Rue Marché au Jambon 12; s €55, d €60-80; 🛜) An excellent central option, this offers great value and comfortable, sizeable apartments: don't be put off by the steep, narrow stairway. All apartments come with modern furnishings, big TV and excellent shower (some also have kitchens). Check in with the amiable boss in the attractive Tunisian restaurant downstairs.

La Chambre de Couvent   B&B €€
(☑0473 68 21 04; www.lachambreducouvent. be; 2nd fl, Quai Notre Dame 6B12; s/d/tr/q €90/100/150/160; 🛜) Comfortable homestay rooms are set in the stylishly appointed apartment of an English-speaking former guide and teacher. True to name, the guest rooms occupy a former convent next door to the Église des Rédemptoristes, and offer peaceful views over the Escaut River. The tiny roof terrace is a fine spot for a sundowner.

🍴 Eating

Corto Malté   TAPAS €
(☑069-22 34 00; Quai Saint-Brice 18; tapas €3.20-4.40, small plates €9-10; ⊙noon-3pm & 6.30-10pm Wed-Sat, 5.30-10pm Sun; 🖋) On the right bank of the Escaut, Corto Malté has a lovely tree-shaded terrace overlooking the river, with locals tucking into delicious tapas plates, creatively topped tartines and fresh salads. Among the temptations: tortilla (Spanish-style omelette), shrimp with garlic, and Maghreb salad with chickpeas and peppers, perhaps accompanied by a smoked trout and fresh goat's-cheese tartine.

Eva Cosy   CAFE €
(☑069-77 22 59; Rue Piquet 6; mains €11-16; ⊙noon-6pm Tue, 8.30am-6pm Wed & Thu, to

9.30pm Fri, 9am-6pm Sat; 🕿) This stylishly re-vived old-world bakery and teahouse offers not only a range of speciality teas but also wine, beer and excellent coffee accompanied by scrumptious 'traditional recipe' cakes. There's also a good selection of savoury dish-es, including Thai-style noodle dishes with sautéed vegetables, bretzel sandwiches and flavour-packed salads with shrimp, mango and avocado.

Le Pinacle BISTRO €
(🖉069-22 02 20; www.lepinacle.be; Vieux Marché aux Poteries 1; snacks €6-12; ⊘10am-11pm; 🕿) The interior is slightly bland, but Le Pinacle's enviable street terrace shares a quiet square with a breastfeeding Madonna and a view of the cathedral. The 'nonstop' kitchen pro-duces sizeable *croques*, salads, pastas and the Belgian classic *chicons au gratin* (ham-wrapped endives in white sauce).

Les Enfants Terribles FRENCH €€
(🖉069-84 48 22; www.enfants-terribles.be; Rue de l'Yser 35; mains €16-30; ⊘noon-3pm & 7-10pm Mon-Sat; 🕿🖉) In a sleek, modern space with red walls, upbeat jazz and a glass-fronted open kitchen out the back, this friendly restaurant serves excellent bistro cuisine. Standout dishes include scallops with sea-food risotto, grilled duck breast, and gnocchi with mushrooms and brie. Staff are friendly, and dole out whimsical touches (like pop-corn served as an *amuse-bouche*).

L'Écurie d'Ennetières FRENCH, BELGIAN €€
(🖉069-21 56 89; www.ecuriedennetieres.be; Ruel-le d'Ennetières; mains €17-25, 3-course menu €28; ⊘noon-2pm & 7-9.30pm Tue-Sun; 🕿) Affordable Belgo-French cuisine is served in this high-ceilinged room with exposed-brick walls and a tribe of marionettes hanging from hefty wooden beams. The menu choices are fair-ly straightforward – *entrecôte* (a thick pre-mium steak), roasted duck, and cod with *beurre blanc* – but the classic bistro ambi-ence, with gingham tablecloths and pitchers of wine, makes it a local favourite.

★**La Petite Madeleine** BELGIAN €€€
(🖉069-84 01 87; www.lapetitemadeleine.be; Rue de la Madeleine 19; menus lunch €39, dinner €59-69, mains €29-39; ⊘noon-2pm Tue-Fri, 7-9pm Tue & Thu-Sat) Petite indeed in size, but flexing grand culinary muscles, this place offers beautifully presented modern gastronomic fare, with more than a nod to the new Nor-dic cuisine's foraging ethos. The atmosphere is friendly and welcoming rather than intim-idating or formal, so the stage is set for a top dining experience. Reasonably priced wine flights are available for all menus.

Le Quai Gourmet FRENCH €€€
(🖉069-44 11 01; www.lequaigourmet.com; Quai du Marché au Poisson 8a; mains €25-30; ⊘noon-1.45pm Wed-Sun & 7-9.30pm Wed, Fri & Sat) The French food here is borne of a gourmet im-agination and served in an elegant setting: one of many revamped former shop-houses on the river quay. The menu is small but fea-tures standout dishes like house-made foie gras, *escargots de bourgogne*, lamb shank with honey and thyme, and fillet of bass with lemongrass cream.

🍷 Drinking & Nightlife

Humble Coffee CAFE
(www.facebook.com/humblecoffee; Quai St-Brice 19; ⊘8am-noon & 1-6pm Tue-Fri, 10am-6pm Sat) David Frere, the friendly and award-winning barista behind this small cafe, serves up some of the best coffee in Wallonia. It's well worth stopping in for a perfectly pulled flat white, a browse of the local papers and a chat with David, who speaks excellent Eng-lish (he studied for several years in the USA).

Le Bierodrome MICROBREWERY
(Quai Marché aux Poissons 21; ⊘noon-7pm Wed-Sat) Facing the waterfront, this buzzing new artisanal microbrewery makes its own per-fectly balanced brews, and also serves up quality seasonal beers from Belgium and beyond. On warm days, the outdoor tables make the perfect setting for a drink.

La Vie est Belge BAR
(Quai du Marché au Poisson 17; ⊘noon-midnight Mon-Thu, to 2am Fri, 2pm-2am Sat, 2pm-mid-night Sun; 🕿) On top of the usual beers and cocktails, this celebration of liquid Belgium pours Walloon *pékèts* (gin, sometimes fla-voured), fruit-wine tasters and Belgian nov-elty drinks, including mojitos with *jenever* (gin), Lambertus whisky, endive liqueur and *speculoos* (cinnamon-flavoured gingerbread) beer. You'll need long arms if you want to sit at the bar, though.

Aux Amis Réunis PUB
(Rue St-Martin 89; ⊘noon-last customer Mon-Sat) This archetypal old-time locals' pub dates from 1911. It retains its tiled floor, mirror-and-wood panelling, ceramic beer taps and pub game *jeu-de-fer,* in which players cue metal discs towards a series of pegs and gates. Decent-value food is also served.

❶ Information

Office du Tourisme (☑ 069-22 20 45; www.visit tournai.be; Place Paul-Émile Janson 1; ⊙ 9am-5pm Mon-Fri, 9.30am-12.30pm & 1.30-5pm Sat & Sun Apr-Oct, closed Sun morning Nov-Mar; 🛜) Facing the cathedral, this excellent office offers great information, a couple of audiovisual presentations, exhibitions in a medieval cellar, tablets for internet access, free wi-fi and a shop with cute Tournai souvenirs. It also organises a program of guided tours of the town.

❶ Getting There & Away

Tournai's **bus** and **train stations** (Gare du Tournai; Blvd des Nerviens) are around 1km northeast of the Grand Place. The following destinations have regular rail services:

Brussels (€13.40, 70 minutes)

Kortrijk (€5.50, 30 minutes) Via Mouscron.

Lille, France (€12.60, 30 minutes). Costs €6.60 bought online.

Mons (€7.70, 30 to 55 minutes)

Pipaix

POP 1530

The small village of Pipaix, 15km east of Tournai, has two very different breweries to experience, both reached by bus 95 (€3.50, 40 minutes), Monday to Friday only.

★**Brasserie à Vapeur**   BREWERY
(☑ 069-66 20 47; www.vapeur.com; Rue du Maréchal 1; tours €10, incl lunch €45; ⊙ 10am-6pm Sat & Sun, tours 11am Sun Apr-Oct, from 9am last Sat of month) Started in 1785, this tiny affair is Belgium's last traditional steam-operated brewery. This wonderfully authentic family enterprise is best known for its Vapeur Cochonne, whose bare-breasted cartoon-pig labels were 'censored' for the US market. Sunday brewery tours include beer tasters. But, ideally, come on the last Saturday of each month to observe the brewery's whizzing flywheels and experience the sauna-like heat of the brewing process. Before the tour, pig out on a beer-influenced buffet lunch with endless ale. Book visits ahead.

Brasserie Dubuisson   BREWERY
(Trolls & Bush; ☑ 069-67 22 22; www.dubuisson. com; Chaussée de Mons 32/N50; ⊙ 11am-11pm Tue-Sun, kitchen noon-3pm & 6-10pm; 🛜) Wallonia's oldest brewery, Dubuisson sits on the N50 2km outside Pipaix. Its bar-brasserie offers several of its tasty beers on tap, of which the best-known are fresh, aromatic 7% Cuvée des Trolls and sweet 12% Bush ambrée.

Good-value meals, including tasty salads and pastas, make this a great pit stop. Brewery tours (€7) are at 3pm Saturday.

Aubechies

Surrounded by verdant pastures, tiny Aubechies is a typical 19th-century village, with a barrel-vaulted 1077 church across the road from one Belgium's most authentic rural pubs, the **Taverne St-Géry** (☑ 069-67 12 74; www.taverne-saint-gery.be; Place 2; mains €9-16; ⊙ 6-11.30pm Fri & Sat, 10am-10pm Sun). On the edge of town, **Archéosite** (☑ 069-67 11 16; www.archeosite.be; Rue de l'Abbaye 1; adult/child €9.50/3.50; ⊙ 9am-5pm Mon-Fri mid-Oct–mid-Apr, shorter hours rest of year) is a recreated 'settlement' of ancient dwellings and workshops representing the Neolithic, Bronze Age, Iron Age and Gallo-Roman eras. It's an interesting visit and makes an effort to present Roman buildings as they actually might have been. Start off with a 20-minute video that gives an overview of the site (ask for English). On summer Sundays, volunteer craftspeople in period costume demonstrate cottage industries of times gone by.

From the nearest bus stop (Ellignies-Sainte-Anne, a 2km walk away), TEC bus 86a travels between Leuze-en-Hainaut (€3.50, 15 minutes) and Blaton (€3.50, 20 minutes) train stations several times a day on weekdays only.

Ath

POP 29,200

Ath's cobblestone centre and intriguing museums make for a rewarding half-day. Nicknamed the 'city of giants', it's famous across Wallonia for its spectacular **Ducasse** (festival) in August, when giant figures take over the streets. You can learn more at the **Maison des Géants** (☑ 068-68 13 00; www.maison desgeants.be; Rue de Pintamont 18; adult/child €6/5; ⊙ 10am-5pm Tue-Fri & 2-6pm Sat yr-round & 2-6pm Sun Feb-Nov), a museum showing how the giants are created and giving video tasters of the revelry. It's in a grand old mansion opposite the castle-style tower of **Église St-Julien**. Ath's other main draw is the **Espace Gallo-Romain**, a fascinating place to learn about the region's Roman roots. Among the highlights are two boats found in excavations at the nearby Pommeroeul site. Ath's train station, 400m south of the Grand Place, is on the Brussels–Tournai line.

Lessines

POP 18,600

Birthplace of surrealist artist René Magritte, Lessines would be largely forgettable but for two outstanding attractions. One is the spooky **penitents' procession** on the night of Good Friday: it's one of Belgium's most memorable parades. The other is **Hôpital Notre-Dame à la Rose** (☑068-33 24 03; www.notredamealarose.com; Place Alix de Rosoit; adult/child €10.50/5.50; ☺2-6pm Tue-Sun). Founded in 1242, this is Belgium's only medieval convent-farm-hospital complex to have survived reasonably intact. Audioguided visits demonstrate the development of medieval medicine, explaining a collection of historical medical implements: don't miss the bird-beaked plague doctor in his leather cape. Then there's the collection of religious art that includes a curious 16th-century painting showing Jesus with a female breast. The decent on-site restaurant opens from noon, and in central Lessines there's a charming, angel-filled family B&B, the **Maison des Anges** (☑068-28 09 04; www.maisondesanges.net; Rue de Grammont 4; s/d €90/105; ❀🛜). Hourly trains from Ath (€2.60) take 15 minutes.

Enghien

POP 13,700

Charming Enghien (Edingen in Dutch) has a small but picturesque old-town core with a soaring red-brick church, the **Église St-Nicolas**, at its epicentre. The real draw, however, is the lovely Parc d'Enghien, with its tree-lined promenades amid fountains, statuary, topiary, a mirror-like pond and a grand château (closed to the public). Views here are superb. The adjacent tourist office can provide an audioguide. Trains stop in Enghien between Brussels (€6, 30 minutes) and Kortrijk, Tournai and other destinations.

Mons

POP 95,300

With a characterful medieval centre climbing up a hill and a fine Grand Place, Mons (Bergen in Dutch) had a substantial facelift in 2015, when it was a European Capital of Culture. The legacy is a handful of entertaining modern museums, which make for an excellent visit and offer plenty to keep you busy for two or three days. One museum covers war in splendid fashion, while another

BELŒIL

Sitting in an artificial lake within a vast manicured park, the **Château de Belœil** (☑069-68 94 26; www.chateaudebeloeil.com; Rue du Château 11; adult/child €10/5, gardens only €4/2; ☺1-6pm daily Jul & Aug, 10am-6pm Sat & Sun Apr-Jun & Sep) is a regal country palace-house that's packed with classical furniture and portraiture relevant to the princes 'de Ligne'. English signage highlights unique pieces, such as 17th-century Brussels tapestries (by Judocus de Vos), a four-poster bed made for Queen Marie-Antoinette, and exquisite Meissen porcelain figures dedicated to Empress Catherine II of Russia. The extensive gardens contain reflective pools, bubbling springs and a grand mall lined with oak trees.

TEC bus 81 goes from the train station at Ath to Belœil (€3.50, 25 minutes) roughly hourly weekdays, five times a day on Saturday, and not at all on Sunday.

celebrates the riotous Doudou festival, which stars St George, a dragon, Ste-Waudru, devils and thousands of beery revellers.

Mons developed around the site of a Roman *castrum* (fortified camp). For centuries it was the capital of the powerful county of Hainaut, until 1436, when the country was incorporated into the Duchy of Burgundy. To some Brits, Mons is remembered for the Angels of Mons, a legend that arose in 1914 based around a host of heavenly archers. Since 1967 Mons has been home to NATO command-operations headquarters, based 5km north of town.

◉ Sights

★**Mons Memorial Museum**   MUSEUM
(☑065-40 53 20; www.monsmemorialmuseum.mons.be; Blvd Dolez 51; adult/child €9/2; ☺10am-6pm Tue-Sun) This superb museum mostly covers Mons' experience of the two world wars, though the constant sieges of this town's turbulent history are also mentioned. It gets the balance just right between military history, personal testimony of civilians and soldiers, and thought-provoking items on display. Some seriously good visuals make the to-and-fro (and the years spent stuck in

PAIRI DAIZA

Set on the grounds of a former Cistercian Abbey, the 65-hectare **Pairi Daiza** (☑068-25 08 50; www.pairidaiza.eu; Domaine de Cambron, Brugelette; adult/child €34/29, parking €7; ⏲10am-6pm daily Apr & Oct, 10am-6pm Mon-Fri & to 9pm Sat & Sun May-Sep; ♿) is home to more than 5000 animals (including pandas, koalas, gorillas and lemurs) living in beautifully designed settings with elements from every corner of the globe. You'll find a recreated African stilt village, the red desert outback of Australia, East Asian temples (plus the largest Chinese garden in Europe) and a spooky belfry where free-flying bats glide overhead. There are ample dining and drinking spots, including a charming canal-side brasserie with good Trappist beers.

Animal encounters include goat-feeding, elephant bathing and falconry demonstrations. Allow a full day and prebook online to save €2. Cambron-Casteau train station on the Mons–Ath line is a 10-minute walk from Pairi Daiza.

the mud) of WWI instantly comprehensible, and there's an animated 3D film on the legend of the Angels of Mons.

Collégiale Ste-Waudru CHURCH
(www.waudru.be; Place du Chapitre; ⏲9am-6pm) Within this lofty, airy, 15th-century Gothic church you'll find the golden reliquary of Ste-Waudru (hanging above the altar) and the fanciful 1782 Car d'Or, a gilded, cherub-adorned coach used to carry it during Ste-Waudru festival Le Doudou. The small **treasury** (www.tresorsaintewaudru.mons. be; adult/child €4/2; ⏲noon-6pm Tue-Sun) displays Ste-Waudru's shrouds and a sword-slashed skull in a reliquary – supposedly of sainted Merovingian king Dagobert II. Some conspiracy theorists consider that Dagobert's murder in 675 was an attempt to put an end to the 'Jesus bloodline'.

The stained-glass windows, dating from the 16th-century, are exceptional, as are the 16th-century sculptures and reliefs carved by the illustrious Renaissance artist Jacques du Broeucq.

Musée du Doudou MUSEUM
(☑065-40 53 18; www.museedudoudou.mons.be; Jardin du Mayeur; adult/child €9/6; ⏲10am-6pm Tue-Sun) Head through the Hôtel de Ville on the Grand Place to reach this museum, dedicated to Mons' riotous Doudou festival. All aspects of this curious event, as well as background on St George, Ste-Waudru and dragons, are covered in entertaining interactive fashion, and there are interesting cultural musings on the festival's changing nature over time. During the audiovisual, showing the climactic Lumeçon battle, you can almost smell the beer and sweat. There's audio content in French, Dutch and English.

Artothèque MUSEUM
(☑065-40 53 80; www.artotheque.mons.be; Rue Claude de Bettignies; adult/child €6/4; ⏲10am-4pm Thu-Sun) Ever thought it was a pity that all those items sat in museum storerooms, never seeing the light of day? Well, this innovative space in a former convent chapel lets you examine a wide range of objects from various museum basements, with interactive screens (in French, but staff can arrange translation) allowing you to locate them and inform yourself about them. Items range from soldiers' wartime rations and ceramics to clothing and fine art. Original and entertaining.

Hôtel de Ville HISTORIC BUILDING
(Grand Place 22) Mons' splendid 15th-century city hall is the most visually arresting building on the photogenic, *café*-lined Grand Place. It has become customary among visitors to score a wish by stroking the head of an iron monkey (Singe du Grand Gard) on the front left flank of the building's gateway portal, though traditionally it was only supposed to work for women hoping to get pregnant. The gateway leads to a pretty courtyard garden.

Beffroi TOWER
(www.beffroi.mons.be; Parc du Château; adult/child €9/6; ⏲10am-6pm Tue-Sun) The 87m-tall Unesco-listed baroque belfry is a 17th-century marvel topped by black-and-gold mini-domes. The lift takes you up to only 36m, though the panoramic views are still impressive (you can climb a further two flights of stairs for a look at the clock mechanism and bells). The surrounding garden (admission free) occupies the hilltop site of what was originally Mons' fortress.

Note that the entrance is up the steep ramp leading up from Rue des Clercs.

Musée François Duesberg MUSEUM
(⚏ 065-36 31 64; www.duesberg.mons.be; Sq Franklin Roosevelt; €8; ⊘2-7pm Tue, Thu, Sat & Sun) If you're a fan of exotic gilded clocks, dazzling porcelain and silver coffeepots from 1775 to 1825, check out the rich collection at this sumptuous three-room museum. It's in the former national-bank building between Collégiale Ste-Waudru and the train station.

BAM GALLERY
(Musée des Beaux-Arts; ⚏ 065-40 53 25; www.bam. mons.be; Rue Neuve 8; adult/child €9/6; ⊘10am-6pm Tue-Sun) This modernist glass cube of a gallery is the product of a rebuild for the city's tenure as a European Capital of Culture in 2015. It hosts temporary exhibitions, with at least one high-profile exhibition planned each year.

◉ Around Mons

Silex's MUSEUM
(www.silexs.mons.be; Rue du Point du Jour, Spiennes; museum adult/child €6/4, guided mine & museum visit €14; ⊘10am-4pm Tue-Sun Apr-Oct) Six kilometres southeast of Mons, a peaceful agricultural scene covers what was a major Neolithic flint-mining site. One of the most impressive shafts is covered by a small modern museum, which gives decent information on how the flint was knapped and made into durable tools. Three daily 90-minute visits descend to the mine – an atmospheric experience – but must be prebooked well in advance (around 15 days' notice) via Mons' tourist office (groupes@ville.mons.be). Children under age 10 aren't allowed in the mine.

There's access for travellers with disabilities, but otherwise you must park 1km away and stroll through pleasant farmland. There are buses to Spiennes from Mons.

**Cimetière Militaire de
Saint-Symphorien** CEMETERY
(Rue Nestor Dehon, St-Symphorien) Just 5.5km east of Mons, this small cemetery is one of the most peaceful and thought-provoking in Belgium. The resting place of roughly equal numbers of German and British soldiers from WWI, it includes the tombs of the first and last Commonwealth soldiers to die in the conflict.

✹✦ Festivals & Events

La Ducasse CULTURAL
(Le Doudou; www.doudou.mons.be) Known locally as Le Doudou, Unesco-listed festival La Ducasse sees the remains of Ste-Waudru (a 7th-century female miracle-worker and Mons' patron) raucously paraded around town on Trinity Sunday (eight weeks after Easter Sunday) in the Procession du Car d'Or. At lunchtime on the Grand Place, drums and chanting accompany the Lumeçon, a mock battle pitting St George against a wickerwork dragon.

Lesser characters include the Chinchins (18th-century soldiers and St George's sidekicks) and a gang of devils helping out the dragon. If you dare, join the boisterous crowd surging forward to grab hairs from the dragon's tail as it flails around. Purloining a dragon hair augurs well.

Get the full rundown at the Musée du Doudou.

🛏 Sleeping

Inexpensive, very central options include a well-equipped **HI hostel** (⚏065-87 55 70; www. lesaubergesdejeunesse.be; Rampe du Château 2; dm/d/q incl breakfast €26/56/104; 🅿@🛜) and the pleasant if boxy **Hotel Infotel** (⚏065-40 18 30; www.hotelinfotel.be; Rue d'Havré 32; d €90; 🅿🛜), where parking is a bargain €2 per day.

★ **Dream Hôtel** BOUTIQUE HOTEL €€
(⚏065-32 97 20; www.dream-mons.be; Rue de la Grand Triperie 17; s €94, d €113-130, ste €180-350; 🅿✴@🛜) Centrally located in a revamped 19th-century convent, Dream Hôtel combines a high level of comfort with more than a dash of Belgian eccentricity, including multilingual murals, bowler-hat lamps and side tables made from drums. Bathrooms, with separate toilet, are excellent, and noise insulation is relatively good. There's a lovely little spa to wallow in and free (valet) parking.

A good restaurant is on hand, as is a lounge-like bar. Other appealing eating and drinking spots are just a short stroll from the hotel.

Mons Dragon House GUESTHOUSE €€
(⚏0491 08 02 35; www.monsdragonhouse.be; Rue de la Grande Triperie 7; d €90; 🛜) In a great location in the old-town centre, this friendly five-room guesthouse boasts imaginatively designed rooms that don't lack for comfort. Among the favourites: the Golden Chariot room has gilded mirrors, vintage furnishings

WALLONIA MONS

and wall sconces à la 18th-century France, while the spacious Dragon's room comes with a clawfoot tub (perched near the window) and cowhide rugs. There's also a guest kitchen.

Appart Hôtel
Saint Georges   HOTEL €€

(☑065-65 20 14; http://hotelsaintgeorges.be; Place du Parc 32; r €100-160; 🐾) Set in a converted 18th-century mansion complete with a peaceful rear garden, the Saint Georges makes a great base for exploring Mons. The 15 rooms are spacious and comfortably furnished, and all come with small kitchens. The excellent service, however, is what really sets this place apart, as Baran, the hotel manager, and his staff go the extra mile to make guests feel at home.

Hôtel St James   HOTEL €€

(☑065-72 48 24; www.hotelstjames.be; Place de Flandre 8; s €85-105, d €90-120; 🅿🐾) This refined 18th-century brick-and-stone house has had a trendy two-tone makeover. Behind the main building, via a handkerchief of garden, a newer, equally fashionable rear section has less road noise. The bright, sunny rooms are elegantly designed with a colour scheme in blacks, whites and charcoals, and most are quite large.

It's just across the ring-boulevard, 10 minutes' walk east of the Grand Place: follow Rue d'Havré, then cross the big junction.

Eating

La Vie est Belle   BELGIAN €

(☑065-56 58 45; Rue d'Havré 39; mains €10-19; ⊙6-9pm Mon & Tue, noon-3pm & 6-9pm Wed-Sun) This family-style restaurant is superb value for home-style Belgian food that's filling rather than gourmet (think meatballs, mashed potatoes, rabbit or mussels). The naive puppet models adorning the decorative mirrors add character.

Henri   BELGIAN €

(☑065-35 23 06; Rue d'Havré 41; mains €11-19; ⊙noon-2.30pm & 6.30-9pm Tue-Sat, noon-2.30pm Sun & Mon; 🐾) A cheerful tavern-style restaurant, crammed with local diners. For an authentic Mons dish go for *côtes de porc à l'berdouille* (pork in brown sauce).

★Oscar   BRASSERIE €€

(☑065-95 96 12; www.brasserie-oscar.be; Rue de Nimy 14; mains €18-22; ⊙noon-2pm & 6-9.30pm Tue-Fri, 6-10pm Sat, noon-2pm Sun; 🍽) A few steps from the Grand Place, Oscar is a local favourite for its well-executed cooking that showcases high-quality seasonal produce. The creative menu features pork ribs à la

---

CANAL UPLIFT

The Canal Bruxelles–Charleroi was built in 1832 to carry coal to the capital, via 55 locks, two aqueducts and a tunnel – a journey of three days. It can now be done in one, thanks to various engineering marvels, which you can view, visit and appreciate by boat. Two are especially spectacular.

Strépy-Thieu Boat-Lift (Ascenseur Funiculaire Strépy-Thieu; ☑078-05 90 59; http://voiesdeau.hainaut.be; Rue Raymond Cordier, Thieu; lock adult/child €7.50/4, boat trip €15/10; ⊙9.30am-6.30pm Apr-Oct) The world's tallest ship lift (completed in 2002), raising or lowering gigantic 'baths' 73 vertical metres, is on a pharaonic scale, as was the €150 million it cost. Though you can watch the lift from outdoors, visits allow you to look down on the engine room, appreciate the construction via a multilingual video, watch the action from the cafe, or take part in a quiz on Belgian genius.

At 10am and 2pm daily (except Monday) from April through September, you can take a 2½-hour cruise passing through some photogenic 19th-century locks. For the vertical experience, you'll have to come on Sundays (May through August), with departures four times a day. Call ahead to reserve a spot.

Strépy-Thieu is just south of the Tournai–Brussels motorway, accessible on bus 30 from La Louvière.

Plan Incliné de Ronquières (http://voiesdeau.hainaut.be; Rte Baccara, Ronquières; adult/child €8/4.50; ⊙10am-6.30pm Apr-Oct) This 1.4km-long slope, or 'sliding lock', at Ronquières is a curious 1968 contraption that lowers boats down a steepish gradient in a giant bathtub. It's strangely mesmerising to watch it trundling oh-so-slowly into action. The two-hour visit includes a 3D film and views from the top.

Normande (with apples and camembert), Liege-style meatballs and Thai-style noodles with shrimp and scallops, as well as a few vegan choices (risotto with vegetables and saffron).

★ **L'Envers** BISTRO €€
(☑ 065-35 45 10; www.lenvers-mons.be; Rue de la Coupe 20; mains €15-29; ☺ noon-2.15pm & 6.15-10.15pm, closed Wed & Sun; 🛜 🍴) One of Mons' most popular restaurants, this lively spot deals out bistro favourites complemented by a list of daily dishes with innovative takes on traditional ingredients. Recent hits include gazpacho with goat's cheese and fennel, duck breast with mussels, or sea bass fillet with pesto. There's pleasant outdoor seating on the pedestrian lane. Reserve ahead. Meals can take a while on busy nights.

Le Pastissou FRENCH €€
(☑ 065-31 92 60; Rue des Fripiers 14; mains €16-22; ☺ noon-3pm & 7-10pm Tue-Sat) Warmly lit and cosy, this French-owned space brings flavours from southwestern France, with specialities like Auvergne-style tripe, duck breast with wild mushrooms, and cassoulet, which comes in a variety of delicious incarnations. First-rate wines add to the authentic feel.

Vilaine Fille, Mauvais Garçon FRENCH €€€
(Naughty Girl, Bad Boy; ☑ 065-66 67 62; www.vilainefillemauvaisgarcon.be; Rue de Nimy 55; mains €26-29, set meals lunch €27, dinner €45-57; ☺ noon-3pm & 7-10.30pm Tue-Fri, 7-10.30pm Sat) Artful gastronomic takes on traditional plates, with familiar ingredients appearing in surprising ways, are the hallmarks of this enjoyable restaurant. The smart contemporary interior in a historic building makes for relaxed, quality dining. The menu is short, and there are various set meals depending on which day it is.

 Drinking & Nightlife

Terrace *cafés* in the Grand Place are a grand place for a beer. Later, the bars on the Marché aux Herbes and adjacent Rue de la Clef get very lively.

★ **Hype Bar Lounge** BAR
(Rue des Chartriers 1; ☺ 11am-10pm; 🛜) Hype feels like a hidden retreat from the busy Grand Place, with a laid-back crowd gathered at outdoor tables on a peaceful square. The friendly staff whips up some fine cocktails, including a decent Aperol spritz, which goes down nicely on summer nights.

There are plenty of Belgian beers, though only Grimbergen on tap.

MoMA Coffee CAFE
(www.facebook.com/momacoffeemons; Rue de la Coupe 10; ☺ 7.45am-5pm Mon-Fri, 11am-5pm Sat; 🛜) The best espresso in town is served up at this buzzing cafe south of the Grand Place. MoMA (which stands for Mons Manhattan) takes its inspiration from NYC's third-wave coffee purveyors, and you can also order creatively topped bagel sandwiches (vegan option available) and munch on satisfying baked goods.

Ô Bar'Hik WINE BAR
(☑ 0479 73 52 41; www.facebook.com/Obarhic; Rue de la Clef 8; ☺ 5-10.3pm Tue-Thu, to 11.45pm Fri & Sat) For an alternative to the rowdy drinking holes on nearby Marché aux Herbes, this cosy wine bar is the perfect antidote. With a focus on France, Spain and Italy, the range of offerings is staggering. When in doubt, go with a wine flight (five 5cL pours for €14), and pair it with some delectable bruschette.

Citizen Fox PUB
(Rue de la Coupe; ☺ noon-2am) One of Mons' best-loved spots is this spacious drinking den a few paces from the Grand Place. It has an inviting terrace (though nonsmokers beware!), good weekday drink specials and live music on Thursdays.

🛈 **Information**

Maison du Tourisme (☑ 065-33 55 80; www.visitmons.be; Grand Place 27; ☺ 9.30am-5.30pm; 🛜) On the main square, with lots of booklets and information, and bike rental (two hours for €5).

🛈 **Getting There & Around**

Mons' **train station** (Gare de Mons; Place Léopold), which is provisional until the new Calatrava design is finally finished (slated for 2020), and neighbouring **TEC bus station** (☑ 065-38 88 15; Place Léopold) are 700m west of the Grand Place. There are very regular services to the following destinations.
Brussels (€9.90, 52 minutes)
Charleroi (€6.80, 35 minutes)
Tournai (€7.70, 30 to 50 minutes)
 Free public buses shuttle around, linking the train/bus station and the Grand Place.

Binche
POP 33,600
Historic Binche once sported an opulent palace-castle of Mary of Hungary, sister of mighty Charles Quint. That's long gone, but

WALLONIA BINCHE

the town still maintains sections of historical city walls, and has a scruffily attractive main square and a sizeable 17th-century church (Collégiale St-Ursmer). For most of the year the town has a rather grey and slightly forlorn look. But all that changes for a week of carnival festivities that are some of the world's most unusual. If you're anywhere near during Mardi Gras, Binche is an absolute must.

◉ Sights

Musée International du
Carnaval et du Masque MUSEUM
(☑064-33 57 41; www.museedumasque.be; Rue St-Moustier 10; adult/child €8/3.50; ⊙9.30am-5pm Tue-Fri, 10.30am-5pm Sat & Sun) For the low-down on the extraordinary Binche carnival, visit this museum just above the Grand Place. Aside from its Binche collections, this atmospherically lit museum has some exquisite masks and costumes from Africa, South America and Melanesia.

★ Festivals & Events

★ Carnaval de Binche CARNIVAL
(www.carnavaldebinche.be; ⊙Mardi Gras) Binche lives for its Unesco-listed carnival, which culminates on Shrove Tuesday. The undisputed stars are the Gilles: male figures dressed alike in clogs and straw-padded suits decorated with heraldic symbols. In the morning each 'brotherhood' of Gilles clomps to the town hall. Outside, they briefly don spooky green-eyed masks while shaking sticks to ward off evil spirits in a formalised stomp 'dance'.

After a lunchtime lull, up to 1000 Gilles march across town in one vast, shuffling, slow-motion parade, wearing their enormous ostrich-feather headdresses (weather permitting). Oranges are lobbed intermittently into the heaving crowd and at observers who cheer from those windows that haven't been protectively boarded up. Don't even think of hurling one back, however tempting it might be – the Gilles-thrown oranges are metaphorical blessings.

Despite appearances, the carnival is a serious celebration, taking months of preparation and involving strict rules of conduct. The rituals surrounding it date back hundreds of years and the Gilles' finery is thought to be an interpretation of the elaborate, Inca-inspired costumes worn by courtiers at a world-famous feast held here by Mary of Hungary to honour Emperor Charles V in 1549.

ⓘ Getting There & Away

Bus 22 (€3.50, 42 minutes) from Mons runs every 40 minutes or so, arriving two blocks north and 1½ blocks west of Binche's Grand Place. At carnival time you'd do better to take the train from to attractive **Gare de Binche** (Place Eugène Derbaix).

Nivelles
POP 28,500

Ancient Nivelles (Nijvel in Dutch) sports one of Belgium's most unusual and impressive churches, which looms powerfully over a photogenic town centre. Apart from this castle-like former abbey, the town makes a fine place for an afternoon wander, with local shops, cafes and patisseries tucked along the narrow lanes leading off the main square.

◉ Sights

★ Collégiale
Ste-Gertrude CHURCH
(www.collegiale.be; Grand Place; tours adult/child €6/2; ⊙9am-6pm Apr-Oct, to 5pm Nov-Mar, tours 2pm daily, plus 3.30pm Sat & Sun) FREE This 11th-century church was part of one of Europe's foremost abbeys, founded in 648. It's 102m long with a soaring multilevel western facade topped with a squat octagonal tower flanked by turrets. The interior's enormous Romanesque arches are unadorned, but notice the 15th-century chariot that's still used to carry Ste-Gertrude's silver *châsse* during Nivelles' principal procession. Fascinating and detailed 90-minute guided tours in French get you access to the crypt, the tower gallery and the pretty cloister for photogenic views.

The pleasant cloisters are another highlight. Outside, watch the southern turret to see a 350kg gilt statue strike the hour with a hefty hammer. Tours also take in archaeological excavations and the grave of Charlemagne's lofty first wife, Himeltrude, whose 1.85m skeleton can be seen reflected by a well-placed mirror.

The abbey's first abbess, Gertrude, was a great-great aunt of Charlemagne's, and was later sainted for her miraculous abilities, including rat catching (which warded off plague) and devil snaring (which saved the mythical Knight of Masseik from losing a Faustian bargain).

Eating

Le Chant du Pain BAKERY €
(Rue du Géant 1b; snacks €1.80-5; ⊘6am-7pm Mon-Sat) Nivelles' unique culinary speciality is *tarte al djote,* a creation that's somewhere between pizza and quiche but flavoured with fragrant green chard. Try a small takeaway one from this historic bakery-shop 150m east of the Grand Place via Rue de Namur.

❶ Information

Tourist Office (☑067-21 54 13; www.tourisme-nivelles.be; Rue de Saintes 48; ⊘9am-5pm Mon-Fri) This helpful office is 250m uphill from the Grand Place and can organise English-language tours of the Collégiale.

❶ Getting There & Away

The Grand Place is a 15-minute walk west from Nivelles' train station. Every hour a fast train stops here en route between Brussels (€6, 23 minutes) and Charleroi (€4.80, 22 minutes) and there's the slow S-train to Brussels via Waterloo (€3, 14 minutes).

Waterloo Battlefield

Tourists have been swarming to Waterloo ever since Napoleon's 1815 defeat, a seminal event in European history (sightseers were poking around as early as the morning after the battle). The bicentenary saw a new high-tech underground museum pep up the site of the battlefield, which is, in this case, many fields: a vast, attractive patchwork of gently undulating cropland dotted with memorials and historically meaningful buildings. Re-enactments are usually held on the weekend nearest the battle's anniversary (18 June).

The main battlefield site is known as Hameau du Lion (Lion Hamlet), some 5km south of central Waterloo town.

◉ Sights

◌ Hameau du Lion

★**Memorial 1815** MUSEUM
(☑02-385 19 12; www.waterloo1815.be; Rte du Lion, Hameau du Lion; adult/child €16/13, with Wellington & Napoleon HQ museums €20/16; ⊘9.30am-6.30pm Apr-Sep, to 5.30pm Oct-Mar) Inaugurated for the 2015 bicentenary, this showpiece underground museum and visitor centre at the battlefield gives some detail on the background to Napoleon's rise, fills in

information on key incidents, then describes the make-up of each side's forces. There's a detailed audioguide and some enjoyable technological effects. The climax is an impressive 3D film that sticks you right into the middle of the cavalry charges. Includes admission to Butte du Lion, Hougoumont and the loveably old-fashioned 1912 Panorama de la Bataille.

Butte du Lion HILL
(Lion Mound; www.waterloo1815.be; Rte du Lion; ⊘9.30am-6.30pm Apr-Sep, to 5.30pm Oct-Mar) Waterloo's most arresting sight is a steep, grassy cone topped by a massive bronze lion. It commemorates, incredibly, not victory nor the glorious dead but Prince William of Orange, wounded on this spot while co-commanding Allied troops. Building the mound took two years: women carted up soil in baskets. Climb 225 steps and survey the battlefield's deceptively minor undulations that so fooled Napoleon's infantry. Admission is included with entrance to Memorial 1815, through whose visitor centre the hill is accessed.

★**Hougoumont** HISTORIC SITE
(www.projecthougoumont.com; Chemin de Goumont 1; ⊘9.30am-6.30pm Apr-Sep, to 5.30pm Oct-Mar) This classic fortified farm is around 20 minutes' walk southwest of the Butte du Lion. Had Napoleon broken through here early in the battle, everything might have turned out very differently. Recently restored to its original appearance, this a peaceful rural spot: it's hard to imagine the desperate struggle of 1815, but a modern exhibition and impressive audiovisual display do their best to evoke it. Entry is included with Memorial 1815, from where free blue shuttle buses run to the farm.

A **cottage** (☑in UK +44 1628 825 925; www.landmarktrust.org.uk; Ferme d'Hougoumont; 4/7 nights summer £898/1777; ℗) in the complex houses a cosy apartment decorated in period style, which sleeps four and can be booked for stays of three days or more. Prices drop substantially in low season.

◌ Other Battlefield Sites

Ferme Brasserie Mont-Saint-Jean MUSEUM
(http://fermedemontsaintjean.be; Chaussée de Charleroi 591; adult/child €7.50/6.50; ⊘2.30-6pm Mon, 10.30am-6pm Tue-Sun) This fortified

THE BATTLE OF WATERLOO

After a disastrous invasion of Russia and the 1813 loss at Leipzig, Napoleon Bonaparte seemed defeated and was imprisoned on Elba. Yet on 1 March 1815 he escaped, landed in southern France and with remarkable speed managed to muster a huge army. The European powers promptly declared war and chose Brussels as the point at which to form a combined army. However, in those pre-rail days, that could take weeks. Napoleon knew that time was of the essence. If he could meet either army individually, Napoleon's 124,000 men would outnumber the roughly 106,000 Anglo-Dutch-Hanoverian troops or 117,000 Prussians. But he had to strike fast before the two combined.

On 16 June Napoleon struck the Prussians at Ligny, where Blücher, the Prussian commander, was wounded and the Prussian army appeared to have been put to flight. Napoleon then turned his attention to British commander Wellington, whose troops were assembling at Waterloo, a carefully chosen defensive position just south of Brussels.

At sunrise on Sunday 18 June the two armies faced off, but the start of the battle was delayed due to soggy ground. The French attack started midmorning with an assault on Hougoumont farm (p197), vital for the defence of Wellington's right. The doughty defence of it fatally slowed Napoleon's game plan. Meanwhile, by 1pm, the French had word that the Prussian army had regrouped and was moving in fast. Napoleon detached a force to meet it and for several hours battle raged at Plancenoit, depriving Napoleon of crucial manpower on the main battlefield.

At 2pm a massive wave of French infantry marched on Wellington's left flank. However, thousands of Allied musketeers, cleverly hidden in rows behind a ridge-top hedge, were invisible to the French infantry, slogging uphill through the mud – invisible, that is, until they rose row by row to unleash volleys of musket fire into the French ranks, whose close-knit formations compounded the difficulty of escape.

After this debacle, the French cavalry was sent in to charge Wellington's centre. However, the well-trained Allied infantrymen formed defensive squares in which their bayonets turned groups into impenetrable 'hedgehogs' of spikes. The musketeers couldn't reload and shoot, but the sabres of the cavalry were useless too: stalemate. For Napoleon the situation was becoming ever more urgent given the steady approach of the main Prussian force. Napoleon ordered his elite Imperial Guards to break through Wellington's centre. It was a desperate last-ditch effort through mud churned up by the cavalry's previous attempt; the soldiers were mown down by the opposing infantrymen from their protected high-ground position.

Around 8.15pm Wellington led a full-scale advance, the French fell into full retreat and Napoleon fled, abandoning his damaged carriage at Genappe with such haste that he left behind its cache of diamonds. He abdicated a week later and spent the rest of his life in exile on St Helena.

farmhouse was transformed into Wellington's field hospital during the 1815 battle, and was used to treat some 7000 men. A thought-provoking museum with audiovisual displays details the horrific medical practices of the time – namely amputation without anaesthetic. Primitive medicine aside, the site also houses a brewery where the excellent Waterloo beer is made. A small shop and cafe makes a fine spot for refreshment (though it's best not to imagine the piles of amputated limbs that once littered the courtyard).

Admission to the museum is included with the 1815 Pass. Brewery tours (€7.50) are available with seven days' notice.

Dernier Quartier
Général de Napoléon   MUSEUM
(Napoleon's Headquarters; ☑ 02-384 24 24; Chaussée de Bruxelles 66, Vieux-Genappe; adult/child €5/4; ☺ 9.30am-6pm Apr-Sep, 10am-5pm Oct-Mar) The farmhouse complex where Napoleon breakfasted the morning of the battle now forms a small museum, accessible on the combined Memorial 1815 (p197) ticket. It's 4km south of the Hameau du Lion on the Waterloo–Genappe road, accessible by hourly Charleroi-bound bus 365a (the bus runs every two hours on Sunday).

Among the objects on display are Napoleon's folding camp bed and furnishings owned by the farmer Boucquéau (such as the Tournai carpet) used by Bonaparte on the morning of 18 June. In the courtyard out the back is a rather macabre ossuary erected in 1912 that contains bones from dead soldiers found on the Waterloo battlefield.

Waterloo Town

Musée Wellington   MUSEUM
(Wellington's Headquarters; ☑ 02-357 28 60; www.museewellington.be; Chaussée de Bruxelles 147; adult/child €7.50/6.50; ☺ 9.30am-6pm Apr-Sep, 10am-5pm Oct-Mar; ☑ W) Opposite the church and tourist office on the main road in Waterloo itself, this former inn is where Wellington stayed before the battle. The museum, accessible on the combined Memorial 1815 (p197) ticket, is old-fashioned but well put together and has a decent summary of the battle as well as items and sketches from the period. An audioguide helps bring the past to life. Temporary exhibitions are presented in the annexe behind.

❶ Getting There & Around

TEC bus W runs every 30 minutes from Ave Fonsny at Brussels-Midi to Braine-l'Alleud train station, passing through Waterloo town and stopping near Hameau du Lion (€3.50) – disembark at at Braine-l'Alleud Route de Nivelles. If coming by train, get off at Braine-l'Alleud rather than awkwardly located Waterloo station, then switch to bus W to reach the battlefield.

In Waterloo town, the **tourist office** (☑ 02-352 09 10; www.waterloo-tourisme.be; Chaussée de Bruxelles 218; ☺ 9.30am-6pm Jun-Sep, 10am-5pm Oct-May; ☎) rents out bicycles.

Louvain-la-Neuve

POP 10,700

The youngest city in Belgium was created in the early 1970s when the Francophone university faculties split with Leuven and set up camp(us) near Ottignies, located in the French-speaking part of Brabant. Much of life revolves around collegiate life – indeed the entire town belongs to the university – though its brick pedestrian lanes, forested fringes and master-planned design make for an intriguing wander. The chief draw is the architecturally stunning Musée Hergé, dedicated to the famed creator of Tintin.

⊙ Sights

★ Musée Hergé   MUSEUM
(☑ 010-48 84 21; www.museeherge.com; Rue du Labrador 26; adult/child €9.50/5; ☺ 10.30am-5.30pm Tue-Fri, 10am-6pm Sat & Sun) The inventive and touchingly nostalgic Hergé Museum celebrates the multitalented creator of comic-strip hero Tintin with an engaging, inventive and extensive display. Highlights include numerous models, pictures and source materials assembled by the artist to ensure the accuracy of his sketches. There's an entertaining audioguide. Note the original triptych portrait of Hergé by Andy Warhol, for whom Tintin was a cited influence. The gift shop is worth a peek too.

❶ Getting There & Away

If driving, it's best to park (for free) on the N250 just above town. From there's it's a short downhill stroll to the Hergé museum, which is also a short walk from the bus and train stations. Trains to Brussels (€5.50, 50 minutes) generally require a change at Ottignies. TEC bus 3 runs six times on weekdays (€5.50, 35 minutes) to Braine-l'Alleud via Waterloo Mont-St-Jean, which is 1.5km from Waterloo's battlefield site. Bus 4 runs 10 times on weekdays to Nivelles (€5.50, 30 minutes).

Charleroi

☑ 071 / POP 201,800

Charleroi has seen dramatic transformations in the last few years. Alongside ambitious architectural projects, new galleries, restaurants and stores have opened, while

---

TINTIN

Quiff-headed boy-reporter Tintin is, dare we say it, the most famous Belgian. Charming young and old alike, Tintin's adventures involve a beloved team of misfits, including dog Snowy, crusty old salt Captain Haddock and diva-with-a-heart-of-gold Bianca Castafiore. Tintin books have been translated into more than 50 languages and still sell more than two million copies a year. Blistering barnacles! Creator Georges Remi's pen name, Hergé, came from his reversed initials, RG, pronounced in French. His initial efforts featured some crude racial stereotypes, later regretted by him as he took a genuine interest in portraying other cultures.

redesigned urban spaces have made the city centre more pedestrian friendly – all the better to see some of Charleroi's unsung art deco beauties. There are also a couple of great museums on the city's outskirts.

While things have improved, there's still a fair bit of industrial blight – remnants of hard times the city experienced after its steel and coal industries fell into decline in the 1970s.

◉ Sights & Activities

★ **Musée de la Photographie**   MUSEUM
(☑ 071-43 58 10; www.museephoto.be; Ave Paul Pastur 11; adult/child €7/free; ⊙ 10am-6pm Tue-Sun) One of Europe's biggest and most impressive photography museums, it has an engrossing collection of historic, contemporary and artistic prints. Don't miss the area upstairs dealing with airbrushing, tricks of the trade and optical illusions. Particularly intriguing is a little curtained room in which you effectively stand within a giant pinhole camera. Although most labels are in French, the ideas are generally self-explanatory. It occupies a 19th-century convent at the centre of dreary Mont-sur-Marchienne, 4km south of Charleroi by regular bus 70.

Le Bois du Cazier   MUSEUM
(☑ 071-88 08 56; www.leboisducazier.be; Rue du Cazier 80; adult/student €8/4.50; ⊙ 9am-5pm Tue-Fri, 10am-6pm Sat & Sun) This sizeable complex occupies a mine site where a horrific acci-

dent killed 262 miners in 1956. A gripping multilingual video commemorates that; admission also includes access to a museum celebrating Charleroi's heyday as a centre of steel, glass and coal industries. A glass collection has items dating back millennia, while workshops offer demonstrations of bronzeworking and glass-blowing. Allow at least two hours, or three if you include the landscaped walk up former slag heaps. Bus 52 runs hourly Monday to Saturday from Charleroi-Sud train station.

The audioguide (included with admission) gives a human dimension to the industrial site.

Tour Bleue   ARCHITECTURE
(Blvd Mayence) Rising some 75m above the city centre, the aptly named 'Blue Tower' is Charleroi's most eye-catching new building. Designed by celebrated French architect Jean Nouvel, the tapering blue-brick landmark houses the city's police headquarters. The adjoining buildings – redesigned by the same firm – house dance studios and artist residences for Charleroi/Danses, a rather surprising pas de deux between law enforcement and the performing arts.

Charleroi Adventure   OUTDOORS
(☑ 0494 98 26 43; http://charleroiadventure.com; tour €20-50) Nicolas Buissart leads urban safaris through forgotten corners of the city, climbing up old slag heaps, visiting the site where Magritte's mother committed suicide and wandering through an abandoned metal factory. The meeting point for tours is next to the Charleroi-Sud (p201) train station.

⌂ Sleeping

Most visitors don't spend the night, and options are rather limited. Apart from a new Novotel in the centre, there are B&Bs and chain hotels on the outskirts, as well as lodging near the airport.

✕ Eating & Drinking

2 Fenêtres   ITALIAN €€
(☑ 071-63 43 03; 27 Rue Basslé; mains €17-25; ⊙ noon-2pm & 6.30-9.30pm, closed Tue-Fri late Jul-late Aug; ☑) At this warmly lit space in the upper town, owner and head chef Caterina Cesari cooks up seasonally inspired dishes using recipes handed down through the generations. Vegetarians should stop in on *Jeudi Veggie* (Veggie Thursday) for a delectably meat-free menu.

ⓘ CHARLEROI ('BRUSSELS SOUTH') AIRPORT

Around 10km north of Charleroi, **Charleroi Airport** (www.brussels-charleroi-airport.com; Rue des Frères Wright 8; 🛜) is Belgium's main hub for budget airlines, notably Ryanair. Two or three **buses** (www.brussels-city-shuttle.com; around €15; ⊙ 7.50am-midnight) per hour take 55 minutes to get to Brussels. Flibco (www.flibco.com) offers connections to Luxembourg, Bruges and Ghent. Bus A runs to/from Charleroi-Sud train station (€6, 20 minutes, free with train ticket, purchase bus-plus-rail ticket at airport).

The nearest of the generic airport accommodation is Ibis Budget, which, while physically close to the terminal, is actually 1.4km away by road.

BlaBlah Wine   WINE BAR

(☑0493 74 91 94; 6 Rue de Marcinelle; ◷10am-6pm Mon-Wed & Sat, to 10pm Thu & Fri) Just off Place Verte, BlaBlah is an enticing spot for first-rate wines accompanied by charcuterie plates or flavour-packed sandwiches. On warm days, tables out on the quiet lane are the way to go.

☆ Entertainment

Charleroi/Danses   DANCE

(☑071-20 56 40; www.charleroi-danses.be; Les Écuries, Blvd Mayence 65c) Charleroi's cultural high point is its world-renowned avant-garde dance company, which performs here at Les Écuries theatre.

Tickets to most shows are around €15.

🛍 Shopping

Livre Ou Verre   BOOKS

(☑0470 70 62 99; Passage de la Bourse 6; ◷11am-7pm Tue-Sat) One of Wallonia's most atmospheric bookstores, Livre Ou Verre sells a beautiful selection of secondhand books. But even if you don't read French, it's worth stopping in for a drink (coffee, wine and ample beer choices) or a snack (cheese, desserts), followed by a wander through the lovely Passage de la Bourse – a neoclassical covered arcade dating from the late 19th century.

ℹ Information

Tourist Office (☑071-86 14 14; www.paysdecharleroi.be; Place Charles II 20; ◷9am-5pm Mon-Sat, 10am-2pm Sun; 🛜)

ℹ Getting There & Away

The main train station, **Charleroi-Sud**, is on the southern side of town, near the banks of the Sambre. Trains run around half-hourly to the following destinations:

Brussels (€9.90, 55 minutes)

Mons (€6.80, 35 minutes)

Nivelles (€4.80, 25 minutes)

Thuin

POP 14,700

One of central Wallonia's quainter towns, Thuin is a picturesque medieval huddle of ridge-top streets peering down on the wooded Sambre River. The centrepiece is its Unesco-listed 1639 **bell tower** (Place Albert Premier; adult/child €3/free; ◷10am-noon & 1-6pm Apr-Sep, 10am-noon & 1-5pm Tue-Sun Oct-Mar) topped with five slate spires and numerous

DISTILLERIE DE BIERCÉE

In Ragnies, around 6km south of Thuin, the **Distillerie de Biercée** (☑071-59 11 06; www.distilleriedebiercee.com; Rue de la Roquette 36, Ragnies; ◷shop 9am-4.30pm Mon-Fri year-round, plus noon-6pm Sat & Sun Apr-Nov) is a great opportunity to see inside one of Wallonia's classic fortified-farm complexes. This one is impressively renovated, the brick vaults hosting a spacious café decorated with historic enamel drink advertisements and winding copper piping. You can taste its local fruit brandies and gins, including classic P'tit Peket, or take a one-hour distillery tour (€7.50, 3pm Thursday to Sunday April to September, weekends only October and November) including samples. Ragnies itself is one of the region's most attractive hamlets but it's not reachable by public transport.

gilded baubles. Apart from the (loud!) bells and old/new clock mechanisms, the tower is empty, and one climbs up metal steps and steep ladders for the fine regional views. The adjacent tourist office has free town maps suggesting scenic walks in the area, with shorter strolls taking in the town's 'hanging' (ie steeply terraced) gardens.

Thuin train station is across the river far below the old city (a steep 1km walk up to the belfry). There are regular trains to Charleroi-Sud (€3, 20 minutes).

Aulne

Near a picturesque bend of the Sambre River, this small settlement is famed for its once-thriving Cistercian monastery, the **Abbaye d'Aulne** (www.abbayedaulne.be; Rue Vandervelde, Aulne; adult/child €4/free; ◷1-6pm Wed-Sun Apr-Sep, 1-6pm Sat & Sun Oct, daily Jul & Aug). With origins in the 7th century, but destroyed post–French Revolution in 1794, the complex is an atmospheric mixture of ruins, surviving 18th-century buildings and a later 19th-century convent church. Around the back, a timeless **brasserie** (☑071-56 20 73; http://abbayedaulne.com; Rue Vandervelde 273, Aulne; ◷1-8pm daily in summer, weekends only in winter) serves excellent high-fermentation beers. Consider staying overnight at the comfy, six-room **Auberge de**

WALLONIA THUIN

VILLERS LA VILLE

Nestled in a pretty wooded dell are the extensive, ivy-clad ruins of **Abbaye de Villers** (☑ 071-88 09 80; www.villers.be; Rue de l'Abbaye 55; adult/child €8/3; ⊘ 10am-6pm Apr-Oct, to 5pm Nov-Mar). Once one of Belgium's biggest monastic complexes, Villers was never rebuilt after the destructive onslaught of 1794, when, in the post–French Revolution fervour, virtually every such institution was sacked. It's an evocative, peaceful place with its gigantic, shattered church (an atmospheric venue for summer concerts and plays) grassy ruins and cute walled garden. An audioguide (included with admission) helps bring the past to life.

Kids will want to check out the tablet (€5) that transforms the wander through the abbey ruins into a mystery-solving scavenger hunt. Across the road, **La Cave du Moulin** (☑ 071-87 68 65; www.moulindevillers.be; Rue de l'Abbaye 55; mains €16-21; ⊘ 11am-7pm Wed-Sun Apr-Oct; ☏ ⏘) is mediocre food-wise but ideal for a drink in an old stone-vaulted mill house after you've visited the ruins.

Villers-la-Ville is on the Ottignies–Charleroi railway line. The train station is 1.6km south of the ruins.

l'Abbaye (☑ 0470 93 40 22; www.aubergede labbaye.be; Rue Vandervelde; d €80-105; ☏) and taking scenic forest-and-field walks along the River Sambre through a pretty landscape that justifies the nickname '*la vallée de la paix*' (the valley of peace).

On weekends in July and August, the ABBA special bus runs from Charleroi to Aulne (€3.50, 31 minutes). Otherwise, you'll need your own wheels.

BOTTE DE HAINAUT

This attractively undulating area of farms, woodlands and castle villages makes a relatively untouristed alternative to the holiday area of the Ardennes. Chimay or Mariembourg make good bases for exploration but accommodation is limited and although Philippeville and Mariembourg have train stations, you'll really need your own wheels to explore the area.

Philippeville

POP 9200

Between 1659 and 1815 Philippeville was an ultra-fortified enclave of France, completely encircled by the Holy Roman (and later Habsburg) Empire. At the eastern end of the pretty main square, the **tourist office** (☑ 071-66 23 00; www.tourismephilippeville.be; Rue de la Balance 2; ⊘ 9am-4.30pm Mon-Fri yr round, plus 10am-3pm Sat May-Sep) organises fascinating 90-minute guided walks through sections of the citadel's subterranean

passageways, the **souterrains** (adult/child €4/2, 1 person only €5; ⊘ tours 1.30pm or 3pm), of which more than 10km remains. Call ahead to reserve a spot.

Around a 10km drive west of Philippeville lies a cluster of five forest lakes, the **Lacs de l'Eau d'Heure**, where things are well set up for family-friendly outdoor activities: you can kayak, mountain bike, walk lakeside paths, skydive, sail, windsurf, waterski and visit a dam. Especially popular is **Natura Parc** (☑ 0478 09 16 72; www.naturaparc. be; Rte de la Plate Taille; adult/child from €25/20; ⊘ 10am-6pm Sat & Sun Apr-Oct, to 7pm daily Jul & Aug; ⏘), which has treetop walks along rope bridges and gangways, a cross-lake zip line and a 25m tower jump. Call ahead to reserve a time; otherwise waits can be long.

Mariembourg & Nismes

POP 2700/1850

Named after Mary of Hungary, little Mariembourg served as a key fortress guarding the region against the French, though nothing of its history remains, apart from the curious street plan of its town centre. Today it's primarily visited by railway buffs taking old-fashioned steam train rides through verdant valleys east of the city. It's also a good touring base for driving to lovely local villages like Lompret, Dourbes and Fagnolle, or somewhat bigger Nismes where a pretty river neatly divides the old church from a fanciful neo-Gothic castle (now the town hall).

◉ Sights & Activities

Les Jardins d'O   PARK

(off Rue Bassidaine; ⊞) Nismes' pride and joy is its lovely park with grassy lawns, tree-shaded paths and a scenic pond where you can hire boats. There's ample amusement for little ones, including a play space with giant water wheels, pumps and spurting fountains.

**Chemin de Fer à
Vapeur des 3 Vallées**   TRAIN RIDE

(☑ 060-31 24 40; www.cfv3v.eu; Chaussée de Givet 49; adult/child €12.50/8.50; ⊘ weekends Apr-Oct, Tue-Thu, Sat & Sun Jul & Aug) Mariembourg's principal attractions are these trains running through charming scenery to Treignes (40 minutes) from a station 800m southeast of the centre. Check the website's timetables for steam *(vapeur)* trains, which usually leave at 2.20pm (and sometimes at 5pm). These stop for about 20 minutes in Treignes (enough time for a Belgian brew at the station's terrace cafe) before returning. Total return journey time from start to finish is about 1¾ hours.

⊨ Sleeping & Eating

★**Château Tromcourt**   B&B €€

(☑ 060-31 18 70; www.tromcourt.com; Hameau de Géronsart 15, N939; s/d €70/80; ℙ ⊛) Around 3km northwest of Mariembourg, near the N5, is this welcoming, family-owned 1660 stone mansion with turret, banquet hall and lots of imitation old-master paintings. The lounges are packed with re-gilded classic furniture and ceramic fireplaces. The well-appointed rooms have soft beds, and breakfast is €10. A great attraction is the chance to hand feed the wallabies, llamas and deer.

★**La Bonne Auberge**   FRENCH €€

(☑ 060-31 10 90; www.bonneauberge.be; Rue Bassidaine 20; mains €16; ⊘ 11am-2.30pm & 6-9pm Fri-Wed; ⊛) Walking past the inviting terrace of this restaurant, it's hard not to salivate at the aromas of butter and garlic wafting from within. Despite the cosy country elegance, the delicious local food comes at unexpectedly affordable prices. Expect duck with fig and orange sauce, herb-crusted cod and other painstakingly made dishes, though service can be slow.

Brasserie des Fagnes   BREWERY

(☑ 060-31 15 70; www.brasseriedesfagnes.com; Rte de Nismes 26/N939; ⊘ 11am-8pm Tue-Thu, 10am-10pm Fri-Sun; ⊛ ⊞) Around 1km south of Mariembourg towards Nismes, this tourist-oriented microbrewery creates five well-balanced Fagnes beers (€3). Try them in a large part-timbered bar-bistro incorporating the working brewery equipment and a cute free museum of historic brewing paraphernalia. It offers pleasant outdoor seating and decent-value food (mussels, local trout, grilled meats, cheese and charcuterie plates).

It's also a great spot for kids – with indoor and outdoor playgrounds and video amusements.

Chimay

POP 9800

Globally celebrated for its Trappist beer, Chimay is a classic castle town, whose compact Grand Place is overshadowed by a looming, extravagantly spired 16th-century church. It's a good base for exploring the surrounding network of pretty lanes and rural villages.

◉ Sights

Château de Chimay   CASTLE

(☑ 060-21 45 31; www.chateaudechimay.be; Rue du Château 18; adult/child €9/7; ⊘ 2-5pm Tue-Fri, 11am-1.30pm & 2-5pm Sat & Sun late Mar–mid-Nov, 11am-1.30pm & 2-5pm daily Jul & Aug) Off the Grand Place, a stone archway leads to this 15th-century castle, which has been much damaged, altered and renovated over the years. It's the traditional home of the princes of Chimay and well worth a visit – self guided, with an iPad providing video and audio information. Don't miss the 3D film shown in the lavish 19th-century theatre – a miniature version of the theatre at the Château de Fontainebleau outside Paris.

Espace Chimay   MUSEUM

(Auberge de Poteaupré; www.chimay.com; Rte de Poteaupré 5; exhibition €6.50; ⊘ bar-restaurant 10am-6pm Tue-Thu, to 10pm Fri-Sun Nov-Mar, plus to 6pm Mon Apr-Jun, Sep & Oct, to 10pm daily Jul & Aug) Chimay's world-famous Trappist beers have been brewed since the 1860s at austere **Abbaye Notre-Dame de Scourmont** (www.scourmont.be; off Rue de la Trappe, Scourmont; ⊘ church 7am-8pm), 9km south of Chimay. There are no brewery visits, but 1km before the abbey, this visitor centre has a small interactive exhibition explaining the abbey's brewing, cheese-making and spiritual life. The entry fee gets you one 25cL beer, but you might feel it's money better spent to simply sit in the excellent *café*-restaurant reading the menu's potted history.

OFF THE BEATEN TRACK

HITLER'S BELGIAN BUNKER

For 22 days in 1940 the Nazi leader commanded Western Front operations from **Bunker d'Hitler 1940** (☑060-37 80 38; http://bunkerhitler.grottesdeneptune.be; Place St-Méen, Brûly-de-Pesche; adult/child €6/4; ☉10.30am-5pm Tue-Sun Apr-Aug, 12.30pm-4.30pm Tue-Sun Sep, to 4.30pm Sat & Sun Oct & Mar), in forest 8km south of Couvin. The chalet where he lived has been transformed into a small exhibition hall, where a film (English available) describes the events that preceded and followed his sojourn here. Another pavilion (the former dining hall) exhibits pieces related to the Belgian Resistance. You can also peek in the tiny concrete bunker, which was never used.

Afterwards, have a wander around tiny **Brûly-de-Pesche**. All residents were forcibly evicted by the Nazis when Hitler came to town, and signposted panels describe the transformation of the village (eg the church was used as a propaganda film hall). You'll need your own wheels to reach the village.

Various meals plus beer-and-cheese taster combinations are available, and it's the only place anywhere that serves the light Chimay Dorée on tap.

🛏 Sleeping

Reserve ahead as lodging choices are limited. As well as B&Bs, there's a cramped if central **campground** (☑060-51 12 57, 0476 99 85 80; www.chimaycamping.be; Allée des Princes 1; car, tent & 2 adults €14; ☉Apr-Oct; ℗) and the Espace Chimay (p203) has seven high-quality guest rooms (from €80 per double).

★**Petit Chapitre**   B&B **€€**
(☑060-21 10 42; www.lepetitchapitre.be; Place du Chapitre 5; r €85-115; ☉check-in 4.30-6.30pm; ℗☎) In Chimay's heart, this delightful place offers charming B&B in a turreted, wisteria-draped building full of antiques and flamboyant furnishings. Each room has a very distinct character (from the chambre Oiseaux with its gilt-framed bird prints and marble bath to the elegant chambre suite Coton with brass bed, vintage wallpaper and antique wooden furniture).

It's directly behind the church, with a tiny flower-decked front terrace.

❶ Information

Tourist Information (☑060-21 18 46; www.si-chimay.be; Rue de Noailles 6; ☉10am-4pm Mon-Fri, to 5pm Sat & Sun Sep-Jun, 9am-5pm daily Jul & Aug; ☎) Just east of the Grand Place.

❶ Getting There & Away

Buses arrive and depart from the **Gare de Chimay** on Places des Princes, about 500m southeast of the Château de Chimay.

Couvin Bus 60/1(€3.50, 50 minutes) runs five to seven times on weekdays, twice on Saturday, and once on Sunday.

Charleroi Bus 109a (€3.50, 1½ hours) runs via Beaumont six to 12 times daily.

THE ARDENNES

If you're looking for outdoor activities, fresh air and greenery, head for Belgium's southeastern corner. Here you'll find meandering rivers that are ideal for low-intensity kayaking. A whole series of dramatic cave systems have been sensitively equipped for visitors. Forested hills and deep valleys shelter appealing small towns topped by picture-perfect castle ruins. And in midwinter the slopes that edge the Hautes Fagnes fenlands might get enough snow to offer a weekend or two of skiing. As winter comes towards its end, the fabulous carnivals of Stavelot, Malmédy and Eupen burst with revelry. OK, so some of the Meuse Valley cities look dauntingly grimy, but scratch the surface and you'll find history, great hospitality and a wealth of attractions hiding history beneath the careworn exteriors.

Major towns are accessible by train and bus, but to really appreciate the rural highlights you'll need a car or strong cycling legs.

Namur

POP 111,000

Strategically located at the confluence of the Meuse and Sambre Rivers, Namur is crowned by vast citadel that was once one of Europe's mightiest fortresses. Below the citadel, Namur's gently picturesque old-town core has much to discover, including architectural treasures from centuries past and small but charming museums (covering everything from the medieval crafts of the Meuse Valley to 19th-century erotic paintings). The cobblestone lanes are dotted with sunny cafes, bookstores and vintage shops – catering in part to Namur's vibrant student population. You could easily spend a few days in the capital of Wallonia, with citadel exploring, old town walks and leisurely boat rides along the Meuse among the highlights.

History

Namur's history is interwoven with that of its fortress. Celts, and then Romans, had military camps here, and in the Middle Ages the Counts of Namur built a well-protected castle on craggy rocks overlooking the river junction. Strengthened under Spanish rule in the 1640s, the castle was captured by the French in 1692, then redesigned as a textbook fortress by Louis XIV's renowned military engineer Vauban. Razed and rebuilt again thereafter, by WWI the fortress was considered impregnable, yet it fell within three days of the German invasion. In WWII Namur suffered again, with heavy bombing causing extensive damage. The citadel continued in military use right up until 1977.

⊙ Sights

The citadel is directly across the Sambre from the town centre. Comparatively up-market Wépion straggles several kilometres southwest down the Meuse's western riverbank.

⊙ Citadel Area

A **Citadelle Pass** (adult/child €13/11) gives you entry to the Terra Nova visitor centre, and a tourist train visit to the Souterrains and medieval sections.

⭐**Citadelle de Namur**   FORTRESS
(🖉081-24 73 70; www.citadelle.namur.be; Rte Merveilleuse 64) Dominating the town, Namur's mighty fortress covers a whole hilltop with ramparts, tunnels and grey walls. What you see now is more 19th and 20th century than medieval, but is still compelling, great for strolling and offers terrific views. The best are from a section known as Château des Comtes and the *café* Le Panorama (p210), by the curious art deco sportsground Stade des Jeux. Most open areas, including the rampart footpaths, are accessible at any time.

Be careful not to get caught in the Terra Nova zone, whose main gates lock at 6.30pm. Citadel access for pedestrians is on the steep sloping Rampe Verte from Rue des Moulins or via a stairway from Place St-Hilaire. By car

use Rte Merveilleuse from behind the 1911 casino building.

Six shuttles (€2) run between the train station and Terra Nova on weekends. Alternatively take bus 3 (hourly) to the Château de Namur (p208) and stroll downhill from there.

Souterrains   FORTRESS
(Terra Nova; adult/child €8/7; ⊙3-5 tours daily Apr-Sep, Mon-Fri Oct-Mar) In its later guises, the fortress moved the majority of its key installations underground. Fascinating visits, by tour only, walk you through some 500m of the citadel's web of dripping tunnels showing you never-tested 1939 gas-proof bunkers and clever Vauban architectural tricks. Guides help bring the past to life using audiovisual displays and 3D projections on the wall. Be ready for temperatures of around 13°C (55.4°F).

There's always at least one English-language tour per day from April to September (two daily in July and August). Call ahead or check online for the latest schedule.

Terra Nova   MUSEUM
(Rte Merveilleuse 64; adult/child €4/3; ⊙10am-6pm Apr-Sep, to 5pm Oct-Mar) The citadel's central section is a 19th-century former barracks with a modern visitor centre exploring the history and architecture of this important military bastion. From here, subterranean tours depart, as well as tours on a **tourist train** (adult/child €6/5; ⊙10.30am-5.30pm Apr-Sep).

Casino Building   ARCHITECTURE
(www.casinodenamur.be; Ave Baron de Moreau) Namur's belle époque casino dominates the riverfront below the citadel.

⊙ City Centre

⭐**Église St-Loup**   CHURCH
(www.eglise-saint-loup.be; Rue du Collège 17; ⊙2-6pm Tue-Thu & Sun, 11am-6pm Sat) Baudelaire reputedly described this remarkable baroque church as a 'sinister and gallant marvel'. With purple marble columns, black stone arches, elaborately carved confessionals and complex ceiling tracery sculptured in white tufa, it's a curious and imposing sight.

Musée des Arts Anciens du Namurois   MUSEUM
(🖉081-77 67 54; www.museedesartsanciens.be; Rue de Fer 24; adult/child €3/free; ⊙10am-6pm Tue-Sun) In an 18th-century mansion, this

Namur

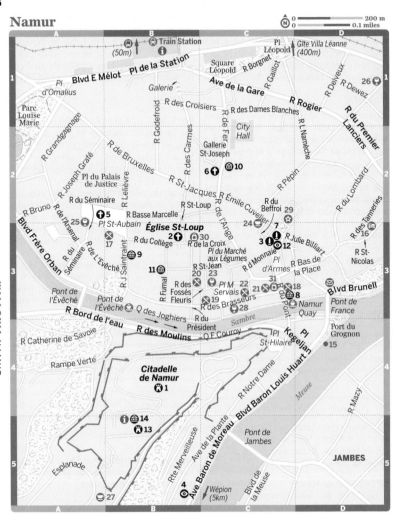

interesting museum displays old artworks from the local region, paintings by 16th-century artist Henri Blès and many religious pieces, including a hoard of priceless Mosan chalices, crosses and reliquaries with a very colourful history. Entry fees rise during temporary exhibitions. Enter opposite the tall, red baroque frontage of the 1655 **Église St-Joseph**.

Musée Félicien Rops   MUSEUM
(☑ 081-77 67 55; www.museerops.be; Rue Fumal 12; adult/child €3/free; ⊙ 10am-6pm Tue-Sun, daily Jul & Aug) Celebrated local artist Félicien Rops

(1833–98), born a few streets away at Rue du Président 33, had a penchant for illustrating erotic lifestyles and macabre scenes, as you'll rapidly discover at this eponymous museum.

Place d'Armes   SQUARE
Namur's central square has been marred by a 1980s department store yet still features the elegant stone-and-brick **Palais des Congrès** (www.namurcongres.be; Place d'Armes 1) conference centre, rebuilt in the 1930s with war reparations from Germany (the German army having torched the whole square in 1914). Behind lies the Unesco-listed **Beffroi**

Namur

⊚ Top Sights
1	Citadelle de Namur	B4
2	Église St-Loup	B3

⊚ Sights
3	Beffroi	C3
4	Casino Building	B5
5	Cathédrale St-Aubain	A2
6	Église St-Joseph	C2
	Halle al'Chair	(see 8)
7	'King of Liars' Seat	C3
8	Musée Archéologique de Namur	C3
9	Musée de Groesbeeck-de-Croix	B3
10	Musée des Arts Anciens du Namurois	C2
11	Musée Félicien Rops	B3
12	Palais des Congrès	C3
	Place d'Armes	(see 12)
13	Souterrains	B5
14	Terra Nova	B5

⊕ Activities, Courses & Tours
15	Croisières Namur	D4
	Tourist Train	(see 14)

⊜ Sleeping
16	Hôtel Les Tanneurs	D3

⊗ Eating
17	Brasserie François	B3
18	Délices du Grognon	C3
19	Entre Sambre et Mer	C3
20	Fenêtre Sur Cour	B3
21	Le Temps des Cerises	C3
22	Parfums de Cuisine	C3

⊖ Drinking & Nightlife
23	Boulevard du Rhum	C3
24	Coffee & More	C3
25	Le Chapître	A2
26	Le Merle	D1
27	Le Panorama	A5
28	Vino Vino	C3

⊕ Entertainment
29	Théâtre du Namur	C2

⊜ Shopping
30	Insolite N'Co	B3
31	Made In	C3

(Belfry; Rue du Beffroi), a medieval stone fortress tower with an 18th-century clock spire.

Just off the square, behind a statue of beloved local composer Nicolas Bosret, hides a tiny **stone seat** (Rue de Bavière). This is where the Roi des Menteurs (King of the Liars) is crowned during September's amusingly drunken Fêtes de Wallonie festivities.

Musée de Groesbeeck-de-Croix MUSEUM
(☑ 081-24 87 20; www.lasan.be; Rue J Saintraint 3; 👤) In a very fine 1753 former abbot's house are displays of decorative arts in 23 beautifully furnished rooms around a formal courtyard garden. Don't miss the 18th-century kitchen. At the time of research it was closed for long-term renovations, but is scheduled to reopen by mid-2019.

Halle al'Chair NOTABLE BUILDING
(Rue du Pont 21) Formerly the meat market, this 16th-century riverside building is one of few venerable structures to have survived Namur's history of continual wartime pummellings. Today it houses a small **archaeological museum** (☑ 081-23 16 31; www.lasan.be; ☉10am-5pm Tue-Sun) **FREE**.

Cathédrale St-Aubain CATHEDRAL
(www.cana.be; Place St-Aubain; ☉8.30am-4.45pm Tue-Fri, to 7.30pm Sat, 9.30am-7.30pm Sun) This vast Italianate neoclassical cathedral, finished in 1767, has an undeniably impressive exterior but a rather remote, mausoleum-like off-white interior.

⊙ Wépion

Early-20th-century turreted homes give a sedate grandeur to this riverside suburb 7km south of central Namur, that's synonymous with strawberries in any Belgian mind. During the summer, kiosks along the riverfront sell all kinds of strawberry products.

Musée de la Fraise MUSEUM
(☑ 081-46 20 07; www.museedelafraise.eu; Chaussée de Dinant 1037; adult/child €5/3.50; ☉11am-6pm Tue-Sun Apr-Sep, 1-5pm Tue-Fri Oct-Mar) This little museum-cum-store in the Wépion area sells strawberry beer, strawberry liqueurs and strawberry jams. The five-room museum delves into the local history of strawberry growing, touching on gastronomy, commerce, art and folklore.

A short stroll south of the museum is the city-owned *jardin des petits fruits* (berry garden), where you can freely wander and see (and discreetly nibble on) a variety of fresh temptations (blackberries, grapes and, of course, strawberries) growing in season.

🏃 Activities & Tours

Charlie's Capitainerie BOATING
(☑ 081-30 78 86; Blvd de la Meuse; SUP hire per hour €15; ☉10am-7pm Apr-Oct) On the edge of the Meuse 400m south of the Pont de Jambes, Charlie's hires out stand-up paddleboards

WALLONIA NAMUR

(SUPs) as well as motorised boats (from €80 for 90 minutes) that seat from four to 12 people. After a scenic paddle (or ride) on the water, you can recuperate with drinks on the appealing open-air deck at Charlie's. The cafe-bar also hosts occasional live music.

Croisières Namur BOATING
(☑ 082-22 23 15; www.croisieres-namur.be; Quai des Chasseurs Ardennais; ☺ Thu-Tue Apr-Sep) Offers three daily (except Wednesday) 50-minute river cruises around central Namur (adult/child €8/6) and, in July and August, a 3pm ride to Wépion, passing through the impressive lock of La Plante (adult/child return €13/11). Board at the jetty near the Walloon parliament building.

✯✯ Festivals & Events

Cap Estival STREET CARNIVAL
(www.capestival.be; ☺ Jun-early Sep) The open area at the confluence of the rivers Sambre and Meuse is transformed in summer into a sort of open-air Namur living room, centred on a casual outdoor brasserie, where people drop by to flirt, have a drink or meal, watch one of the regular arts performances or let their kids try out the sandpit or weekend bouncy castle.

🛌 Sleeping

Auberge de Jeunesse HOSTEL €
(☑ 081-22 36 88; www.lesaubergesdejeunesse.be; Ave Félicien Rops 8; dm from €23; ☺ 8am-11pm; @ 🛜) On a peaceful stretch of river happily away from the busy road, this modernised HI hostel partly occupies the attractive red-brick mansion that was once a studio of artist Félicien Rops. Good breakfast is included. It's 2.5km south of central Namur; bus 3 runs here from the train station and bus 4 stops nearby.

Gîte Villa Léanne GUESTHOUSE €€
(☑ 0495 84 40 53; www.leanne.be; Rue Léanne 82; d for 2 nights €180; P 🛜) In a peaceful neighbourhood a short walk from the centre, you'll find this adorable three-storey red-brick house built in the 1920s. The friendly hosts rent out the ground-floor apartment, which has comfy modern furnishings, good lighting and all the essentials (kitchen, wi-fi, garden access) for a fine pied-a-terre in Namur. Book well ahead. Two-night minimum stay.

Hôtel Les Tanneurs HOTEL €€
(☑ 081-24 00 24; www.tanneurs.com; Rue des Tanneries 13; s €55-200, d €70-215; P ✳ @ 🛜)

Fashioned out of a renovated 17th-century tannery, this hotel unites modern comfort with historical charm. It's a complex warren of rooms, with no two the same. Some are double-level affairs with hot tubs and saunas, while others have rooftop views. The cheapest rooms are very small and less atmospheric, but great value. Breakfast is €13.

Le Beau Vallon B&B €€
(☑ 081-41 15 91; www.lebeauvallonwepion.be; Chemin du Beau Vallon 38; d €70, s/d without bathroom €50/60; P 🛜) Set in well-kept lawns with a private chapel, these utterly charming rural *chambres d'hôtes* are within a 1650 stone farmstead maintaining original floorboards, banisters and fireplaces. Rooms have a cheerful cottagey decor and the host family is delightful. It's 11km south of central Namur, off the N92 beyond Wépion. Follow signs for Rougemont golf course.

★ **Ne5t** BOUTIQUE HOTEL €€€
(☑ 081-58 88 88; www.ne5t.com; Allée de Menton; r €260-400; P ✳ @ 🛜 ▣) Tucked away on the shoulders of the citadel hill in an upmarket residential district, this discreet, genteel hotel makes a great spot for relaxation. Located in a venerable farmhouse with extensive, manicured grounds, it offers the full range of spa treatments (not cheap) and feels like a rural retreat. Staff bend over backwards to be helpful.

Royal Snail BOUTIQUE HOTEL €€€
(☑ 081-57 00 23; www.theroyalsnail.com; Ave de la Plante 23; r €128-198, ste €278; P ✳ @ 🛜 ▣) Boasting bags of character and a good mix of business and leisure travellers, this sassy, offbeat hotel offers plenty of facilities – though the see-through plunge pool is more visual gag than leisure option – including an enticing on-site restaurant, nifty urban garden and relaxing bar deck. Rooms vary substantially, but all are cheerfully modern. Prices are usually lower than these rack rates.

Château de Namur HOTEL €€€
(☑ 081-72 99 00; www.chateaudenamur.com; Ave de l'Ermitage 1; r €120-220; P 🛜) Crowning lovely gardens at the top of the citadel park, this hotel looks, at first glance, like a Renaissance-era castle. In fact the building is a 1930s caprice with comfortable but decidedly modern rooms. You won't find baronial lounges or suits of armour, but the citadel-top location is peaceful and the on-site restaurant with fine terrace views is excellent.

Eating

Délices du Grognon
CRÊPES €

(Rue du Pont 15; light meals €9-13; ⊙11.30am-4.30pm Tue-Thu, to 9.30pm Fri & Sat; 🕿🍴) Much-loved locally, this cheery choice near the bridge offers a huge selection of crêpes and *croques* (toasted sandwiches), making it the perfect lunch or snack stop. Expect a genuine welcome.

★Entre Sambre et Mer
SEAFOOD €€

(☑081-83 55 04; www.entresambreetmer.be; Rue des Brasseurs 110; mains €15-23; ⊙noon-2pm & 6.30-9pm Tue-Sat) Offering great value for quality seafood, this is a family-run restaurant with a warm, unpretentious feel. Daily specials complement a fairly priced menu heavily weighted towards the sea; delicious oysters and other shellfish are highlights alongside full-of-flavour fish preparations. When the weather's fine, dining in the quiet courtyard alongside is a treat.

Le Temps des Cerises
BELGIAN €€

(☑081-22 53 26; www.cerises.be; Rue des Brasseurs 22; mains €21-24; ⊙noon-2.30pm Tue-Fri, 6-10.30pm Thu-Sat) The food is authentic Walloon and French, while the cosy restaurant lays on the charm in thick brush strokes with gingham tablecloths and scarlet-framed mirrors. The wall graffiti comes courtesy of star-thespian customers, including Charlotte Rampling and Benoît Poelvoorde.

Végétalicia
VEGETARIAN €€

(☑0471 56 87 31; Rue de la Gare Fleurie 16; mains €16; ⊙noon-2pm Wed-Sun, 6-10pm Thu-Sat; 🍴🚲) ✿ Namur's best vegetarian restaurant serves up beautifully prepared dishes made with high-quality organic ingredients. The selection isn't vast, but the culinary creativity ensures you're in for a treat. Located in the Jambes district, about 1km southeast of the Pont de Jambes it's a little tricky to find. Head into the Acinapolis cinema complex near Jambes train station. It's tucked in the back near a minigolf course.

Fenêtre Sur Cour
BELGIAN €€

(☑081-23 09 08; www.fenetresurcour.be; Rue du Président 35; mains €16-22; ⊙noon-2pm daily & 6-10pm Thu-Sat) In a high-ceilinged 1902 building with down-to-earth touches, Fenêtre Sur Cour serves reliable favourites including barramundi with saffron, rack of lamb and cheap weekday lunches (from €9). The restaurant interconnects with co-owned Exterieur Nuit bar: between the two hangs the world's most amusingly useless cable car.

Brasserie François
BRASSERIE €€

(☑081-22 11 23; www.brasseriefrancois.be; Pl St-Aubain 3; mains €19-33; ⊙10am-11pm Sun-Thu, to 11.30pm Fri & Sat; 🕿) This stately 200-year-old building has an interior full of polished brass and waistcoated waiters, and it serves up beautifully executed brasserie cooking (tender lamb chops, whole grilled bream, and steaming pots of mussels in season). Outside of meal times, the elegant bar or outdoor terrace at the back make fine spots for a drink. Weekday lunch specials (€15) are excellent value.

Parfums de Cuisine
FRENCH €€€

(☑081-22 70 10; www.parfumsdecuisine.net; Rue de Bailly 10; lunch/dinner menu from €26/39; ⊙noon-2pm & 7-9pm Tue-Sat) The homey candlelit interior here matches the fuss-free atmosphere and service. The cuisine, however, is rather more sophisticated, with plenty of innovation and subtle flavour combinations at a pretty generous price. Linger over mixed seafood paella, lobster with zucchini 'caviar', duckling with foie gras and delicate slices of smoked beef with anchovy cream. Be prepared to take some time over the meal and go with the flow.

L'O à la Bouche
FRENCH €€€

(☑081-58 34 83; www.restaurantloalabouche. be; Rue Armand de Wasseige 1, Wépion; mains €27-32, menu 3/4 courses €37/48; ⊙noon-2pm & 7-9pm Tue-Fri, 7-9pm Sat) Chef Olivier Vanden Branden calls his cuisine 'artisanal' rather than gourmet, but the standards are very high and some French-Belgian classics get an exotic twist. It's just off the main road in the heart of Wépion.

Two-course lunch service (€21) is a good way to sample the culinary wizardry without breaking the bank.

Drinking & Nightlife

★Vino Vino
WINE BAR

(www.vinovino.be; Rue des Brasseurs 61; ⊙5pm-midnight Tue-Wed, noon-midnight Thu-Sat) Marc Detraux, who is excellent value for a chat about wine, runs this little haven of pleasure. There's always something interesting available by the glass, and he rustles up plates of delicious deli products – with standout rabbit rillettes or Iberian ham with Manchego (plates €7 to €15).

Le Merle
BAR

(☑081-22 48 29; www.facebook.com/lemerlecafe; Rue Général Michel 31; ⊙4pm-midnight Mon-Fri)

Just off the beaten track, Le Merle has all the elements of a good neighbourhood pub: an easy-going crowd, a superb beer selection and, most importantly, live-music jams that go off regularly. Check the FB page to see what's on deck.

Le Panorama
CAFE

(☑081-65 58 71; www.lepanorama.be; Rte Merveilleuse 82; ⊙11am-last customer; 🐾) High in the citadel, this airy pavilion has eagle's-perch views across the Meuse and the woodlands that extend attractively into the distance. Vistas from the spacious terrace are even better. It does a varied menu ranging from snacks to brasserie-style dishes (mains €17 to €22).

Boulevard du Rhum
BAR

(☑0479 36 97 16; www.facebook.com/boulevard durhum; Rue des Fossés Fleuris 36; ⊙4pm-midnight Sun, Wed & Thu, to 2am Fri & Sat) This atmospheric, low-lit drinking space serves up some of Namur's best cocktails. The vibe is classy but not pretentious – just right for lingering over one of over 200 drink options (good mocktails too for the nondrinkers). On warm days, the front terrace is a fine place to start off the evening.

Coffee & More
CAFE

(☑081-41 14 16; Rue Émile Cuvelier 21; ⊙8am-6pm Tue-Fri, 9am-6pm Sat) Serving up Namur's best coffee, this charming little cafe is hard to resist. Expect latte art, tempting snacks, a welcoming vibe and at least one local toting a small, adorable dog. Grab a seat near the window and watch the city stroll past.

Le Chapître
PUB

(Rue du Séminaire 4; ⊙2pm-1am Mon-Sat, from 4pm Sun; 🐾) At this convivial and charmingly rustic pub, available brews are listed on a lengthy blackboard menu. The Chapître 'house beer' (€3.50) is a highly drinkable blonde. The outdoor tables get lively with students either side of the summer break.

☆ Entertainment

Théâtre du Namur
THEATRE

(☑081-22 60 26; www.theatredenamur.be; Pl du Théâtre 2; ⊙box office noon-5.30pm Mon-Fri) Namur's elegant main theatre sits just off the Grand Place. The wide-ranging repertoire features orchestras, ballet, modern dance, cabaret, jazz groups and experimental theatre. The season runs from September through May.

🛍 Shopping

★ Insolite N'Co
VINTAGE

(☑081-30 54 94; Rue du Collège 2; ⊙11am-6.30pm Mon-Sat) Spread across two floors, this giant cabinet of curiosities is a fun place to browse, with its array of old globes, antique maps, 1950s film posters, porcelain roosters, WWII helmets, vintage bikes, and tonnes of other bric-a-brac. Afterwards, head down to the cafe-bar to ebjoy a cappuccino or a refreshing Aperol spritz – best enjoyed on the peaceful front terrace on warm days.

Made In
CONCEPT STORE

(☑0472 21 12 28; Rue des Brasseurs 12; ⊙1.30-6pm Mon, 10am-6pm Wed-Sat, 3-6pm Sun) A delightful shop with a small, handsomely curated collection of handcrafted objects made by artisans from around the globe. You'll find architecturally inspired jewellery, artful paper products, delicate ceramics, handsewn purses made of vintage fabrics, and eye-catching kitchenware.

Details on the designers/creators (in French) ensure you're not getting any run-of-the-mill, mass-produced merchandise.

❶ Information

Post Office (www.bpost.be; Ave Fernand Golenvaux 43; ⊙9am-6pm Mon-Fri, to 1pm Sat)

Tourist Office (☑081-22 13 01; www.namurtourisme.be; Place de la Station; ⊙9.30am-6pm; 🐾) At the train station. Additional information booths at the **citadel** (Terra Nova; ⊙10am-6pm Apr-Sep, to 5pm Wed, Sat & Sun Oct-Mar).

❶ Getting There & Away

The **train station** (Place de la Station) is on the north edge of the centre. Just above it, will sit Namur's new bus station, scheduled to open in late 2019.

The following are fares for trains from Namur:

DESTINA-TION	FARE (€)	DURATION (MIN)	FREQUENCY (PER HOUR WEEKDAYS)
Brussels	9.30	65	2
Charleroi	6	37-50	2-3
Liège	9.30	50	2
Luxembourg City	39	120	1
Mons	12	65-75	2

ⓘ Getting Around

BICYCLE

For short-hop city rides use **Libiavelo** (www.libiavelo.be; membership per day/week/yr €1/3/30), Namur's city-bike scheme. For hires of over 30 minutes, visit **Pro Velo** (⏰ 081-81 38 48; www.provelo.org; Place de la Station 1; bike hire per 2hr/half-day/24hr €6/10/14, electric bikes per half-day/24hr €16/22; ⏱ 10am-7pm Mon-Wed & Fri, from 7am Thu, 9.30am-6pm Sat & Sun).

BOAT

In summer **Namourette** (www.ville.namur.be; ⏱ 10am-5.30pm Jul & Aug, weekends only Jun & Sep) riverboats link five central jetties, including **Pont de l'Évêché** and **Namur Quay**, two or three times an hour for €0.50 per stop.

BUS

From near the train station, bus routes 4, 21, 30 and Dinant-bound 34 pass through Wépion. Convoluted bus route 3 links the youth hostel and the Château de Namur. An all-day city-bus ticket costs €5.

Crupet

POP 440

One of the region's loveliest villages, little Crupet is set in gloriously verdant rolling countryside east of Yvoir. It's locally famous for its trout dishes, served in a handful of restaurants. Beside the stone church is an amusingly kitschy grotto shrine, and in the stream valley below is a moated 13th-century tower-house/château. It's private but very photogenic from the outside, especially in the morning light.

🛏 Sleeping

⭐ **Le Moulin des Ramiers**   B&B €€
(⏰ 083-69 02 40; www.lemoulindesramiers.be; Rue Basse 31; r from €85; 🛜) Beautifully set in the valley below town, this is an oasis of peace in what was once the village mill. It's caringly run, and the host pays genuine attention to guests' needs. Rooms are spacious and very comfortable. You'll generally need to pre-arrange arrivals.

You can explore the countryside by bicycle – available free for guests.

Château de la Poste   HOTEL €€€
(⏰ 081-41 14 05; www.chateaudelaposte.be; Ronchinne 25, Maillen; d €95-275; 🅿🛜) Contemporary colour and humorous twists bring life to this grand 19th-century castle-hotel set in 42 hectares of parkland. It's a spectacular sight, with postcard-perfect perspectives everywhere. Numerous activities are on offer, and there's a family-friendly atmosphere, though a personal touch is lacking. Be aware that some rooms aren't in the main building. Around 3km west of Crupet, near Ivoy.

Discounted pricing is usually available.

ⓘ Getting There & Away

Bus 128 heads from Yvoir train station to Crupet (€2.50, 15 minutes) five times on weekdays (morning and evening only) and twice on Saturdays.

Dinant

POP 13,500

Dinant has a striking setting, strung along a riverbank under spectacular cliffs. The village makes a pleasant outing for a day trip, highlighted by a visit to its clifftop citadel and a leisurely cruise (or more vigorous kayaking trip) along the Meuse. It also has great beer (Dinant is the birthplace of the famed Leffe abbey ale) and a fair amount of Sax – Adolphe Sax, that is. The creator of the saxophone grew up in Dinant, and sculptures dotting the city centre pay homage to his groundbreaking musical invention.

◎ Sights & Activities

Several boat companies including **Croisières Mosanes** (⏰ 082-22 36 70; www.croisieres-mosanes.be) offer short summer cruises along the Meuse, eg to Anseremme (adult/child €8/6.50, 45 minutes return) or Freÿr (adult/child €14/11, two hours return). Citadelle-cruise combination tickets are available (adult/child from €14/10).

Citadelle de Dinant   FORTRESS
(⏰ 082-22 36 70; www.citadellededinant.be; Le Prieuré 25; adult/child €8.50/6; ⏱ 10am-6pm Apr-Sep, to 4.30pm Oct-Mar, closed Fri mid-Nov–Mar, closed weekdays Jan; ♿) Though sparse on sights, this vast, unadorned 1818 citadel looms menacingly on its clifftop, offering toe-curling views high over town. The entrance price includes the cable car to the top, though you can take on the 408 steps if you need to work off lunch. Once there, it's worth taking a free one-hour tour through the fortress, with guides describing some of the key moments in Dinant's past.

Maison Leffe   MUSEUM
(⏰ 082-22 91 91; www.leffe.com/en/maisonleffe; Charreau des Capucins 23; adult/child €7/free;

WALLONIA CRUPET

⊙ 11am-6pm Tue-Sun Jun-Sep, Fri-Sun only Oct-May) Set in a former convent, this place tells the story of Dinant's most famous creation, Leffe beer, first brewed in the Abbaye de Leffe back in 1240. Although the original abbey no longer stands – and the brewing now takes place in Leuven – the museum is worth a visit for its intriguing multimedia exhibitions that relate the story of this well-known export. The visit ends with a beer tasting.

Maison Leffe is set inside La Merveilleuse hotel on the left bank of the Meuse, about a 10-minute walk south of the Église Notre-Dame.

Église Notre-Dame CHURCH
(Place Reine Astrid; ⊙ 9am-6pm Apr-Oct, to 5pm Nov-Mar) FREE Imparting gravitas and Gothic grandeur amid the tour coaches, this church sits right under the rock face. Indeed, the current church was built when part of the cliff fell away and destroyed the old one in 1227; only a beautiful Romanesque doorway (to the right as you enter) remains of the original. The distinctive bulbous spire was added in the 16th century.

Also of note are the gorgeous stained-glass windows, among the largest in Europe.

⊙ Around Dinant

Château de Freÿr CHATEAU
(☎ 082-22 22 00; www.freyr.be; Freÿr 12, Hastière; adult/child €8.50/free; ⊙ 11am-5pm Tue-Sun Jul & Aug, Sat & Sun only Sep–mid-Nov & Apr-Jun) Freÿr's riverside Renaissance château boasts very impressive formal gardens. It's located around 6km south of Dinant.

Jardins d'Annevoie GARDENS
(☎ 082-67 97 97; www.annevoie.be; Rue des Jardins 37, Annevoie; adult/child €8.20/5.50, parking €1.25; ⊙ 9.30am-5.30pm Apr-Oct, to 6.30pm Jul & Aug) Laid out in 1758 around the manor house of Charles-Alexis de Montpellier, these gardens are a delightful mix of French, Italian and English styles, incorporating plenty of fountains and tree-lined waterways. Annevoie is 12km north of Dinant.

Dinant Évasion OUTDOORS
(www.dinant-evasion.be; Rue du Vélodrome 15, Anseremme; kayak per person from €18, incl transport from €23; ⊙ 8.30am-5pm Apr-Oct) This outfit runs 12km (2½-hour) and 21km (five-hour) kayaking trips down the Lesse River – a scenic tributary of the Meuse. You can start in either Gendron (for the 12km trip) or Houyet (for the 21km trip). The trip ends in Anseremme, some 3.8km south of Dinant. Dinant Évasion has a ticket office at all three locations.

If coming by car, leave your vehicle in Anseremme. Shuttles are available travelling in either direction; there's also train service.

🛏 Sleeping & Eating

La Merveilleuse HOTEL €€€
(☎ 082-22 91 91; www.lamerveilleuse.be; Charreau des Capucins 23; d €150-325) Dinant's most dramatic place to overnight is this 19th-century neo-Gothic convent that was transformed into a hotel in 2008. Some rooms are small and rather basic (the nuns weren't ones for luxury), while others are bright and roomy with river views. It also has a spa, a restaurant and a museum dedicated to Leffe beer.

The hotel stands on a hill on the left bank of the Meuse – about 400m south of the Pont Charles de Gaulle.

Chez Bouboule BELGIAN €€
(☎ 082-22 22 39; www.chezbouboule.be; Rue Adolphe Sax 34; mains €19-27; ⊙ 11.30am-9pm Sun-Thu, to 9.30pm Fri & Sat) The self-described 'roi des moules' (king of mussels) is the best place in town to get your bivalve fix. Chez Bouboule serves generous (1.2kg) pots of mussels pre-

---

UNLUCKY DINANT

From the 12th century, Dinant was a major centre for a form of Mosan copper- and brasswork that's still known today as *dinanderie*. However, that ended in 1466, when the town was virtually destroyed by Burgundian King Charles the Bold. Why? Because some townsfolk had dared to call him a bastard. Naming the Bishop of Liège as Charles's illegitimate father certainly didn't help either. History repeated itself in WWI when around 10% of the population was executed and much of the town razed in retaliation for resisting the German occupation.

Adolphe Sax, born in Dinant in 1814, proved no luckier than his home town. He invented a wide range of musical instruments including the saxophone, which he patented in 1846. Yet he died penniless in 1894 after a decade of legal wrangles.

pared some 40 different ways, as well as various trout, salmon and grilled-meat dishes.

Go early to score a riverside table on sunny days.

ⓘ Information

Maison de Tourisme (☑082-22 28 70; www.valleedelameuse-tourisme.be; Ave Cadoux 8; ⊙9am-5pm Mon-Fri, 9.30am-5pm Sat, 10am-4pm Sun; 🛜) Just across the bridge from the church.

ⓘ Getting There & Away

Dinant is easily accessed by regular train (€5, 30 minutes) or bus (€3.50, 48 minutes) from Namur. Flat riverside bike paths trace much of the route (28km), albeit sometimes joining the busy main road.

Han-sur-Lesse

POP 920

At Han-sur-Lesse, the Lesse river tunnels underground, forming one of the most impressive cave systems in Belgium, before winding its way prettily out of town. The village itself is quite compact, with a walkable centre dotted with tourist-oriented shops and eateries. It also has an animal park and several other modest, historically themed museums.

⊙ Sights & Activities

PassHan (adult/child €30/21) offers three other attractions with the cave visit: the Parc Animalier; an archaeological museum displaying some astonishing pieces found in the River Lesse; and Han 1900, which has life-sized figures depicting rural life in the early 1900s.

Grottes de Han   CAVE

(☑084-37 72 13; www.grotte-de-han.be; Rue Joseph Lamotte 2, Han-sur-Lesse; adult/teen/child €16/14/10; ⊙daily Apr–mid-Nov, days vary rest of yr) The Lesse tunnels underground for some 8km to form a magnificent cave system that is the region's biggest tourist draw. Guided visits (English often available) start after a 10-minute ride in a charmingly rickety open-sided narrow-gauge train. Then you take a 2km guided stroll through a succession of impressive subterranean galleries, each well endowed with stalactites and especially fine draperies (beautiful translucent 'curtain' formations). The climax of the visit is a short sound-and-light show and a cave

whose stalactites reflect beautifully in the water.

Parc Animalier   ZOO

(www.grotte-de-han.be; Rue Joseph Lamotte 2, Han-sur-Lesse; adult/child €20/14; ⊙10am-5pm approx half-hourly) Sitting on partly covered truck wagons in this enjoyable 75-minute excursion, you're driven several kilometres past and through woodland and meadow enclosures stocked with wolf, lynx, bison, eagle owls, Przewalski's horses and other rare European fauna. The scenery is very pretty and viewpoint stops include one where the Lesse disappears into the hillside.

However, commentary is not in English and, in summer, pre-departure queues can be annoyingly long. A variant allows you to walk part of it and rejoin the truck wagon further along.

Gradients and steps aren't especially challenging, but dress appropriately (13°C) and allow around two hours. May to August departures are every half-hour, dropping to hourly in the off season. The ticket office is on the main square facing Han's grey-stone church and a **tourist office** (☑084-37 75 96; Place Théo Lannoy 2; mountain bikes 2hr/day €10/25; ⊙10am-4.30pm; 🛜) that rents out bicycles.

Parcours Speleo   CAVING

(☑084-37 72 13; www.grotte-de-han.be; Rue Joseph Lamotte 2, Han-sur-Lesse; adult/child €20/16; ⊙Sat, Sun & school holidays Apr-Oct; 🚶) For a down-and-dirty look at the caves, sign up for a self-guided walk through an underground tunnel. The passage, which runs for 600m, is quite narrow – good fun for those who aren't afraid of a little mud (and a lot of darkness). Protective overalls, helmets, headlamps and rubber boots are provided. Reserve in advance by phone or email.

🛏 Sleeping

Hotel Grenier des Grottes   HOTEL €€

(☑084-37 72 37; www.cocoonhotels.eu; Rue des Chasseurs Ardennais 1; d €98-126; 🅿🛜) If you want to make a full day of it in Han-sur-Lesse, this 41-room hotel makes a good base. Rooms are comfortably furnished, and it has a decent restaurant and bar (with flickering fire on cold nights).

It's right across the street from the village church, only a short stroll from the main ticketing office for the caves.

ARDENNES HIGHWAY STOPS

If you're driving the Brussels–Luxembourg highway, these attractions make easy part-way journey breaks.

Lavaux-Ste-Anne

The photogenic **Château de Lavaux-Sainte-Anne** (🖉 084-38 83 62; www.chateau-lavaux.com; Rue du Château 8; adult/child €8/5; ☉ 10am-6pm Wed-Sun, daily Jul & Aug) is a moated 1450 fortress that was converted into a lordly mansion in 1634. The four towers come with machicolations and bell-shaped domes, while rooms are relevantly furnished and display various exhibits from local crafts to hunting trophies. Tickets include entry to a three-pond wetland from which there are attractive views back to the castle. Just up the lane, a cute brasserie-B&B serves local beers and cheap snacks, while on the main village square, upmarket restaurant **Lemonnier** (🖉 084-38 88 83; www.lemonnier. be; Rue Lemonnier 82; mains €32-54, degustation €82; ☉ noon-2pm & 7-9pm Thu-Mon; 🕿) is a foodie delight.

Lavaux's junction is south-off, north-on so expect a small diversion to get back to the southbound highway.

Euro Space Centre

Right at Junction 23 of the E411, the solar-panel-wrapped **Euro Space Center** (🖉 061 65 64 65; www.eurospacecenter.be; Rue Devant les Hêtres, Transinne; adult/student/child €12/11/8; ☉ 10am-6pm Tue-Sun mid-Apr–Jun & Sep, daily Jul & Aug, last entry 4pm; 🖩; 🚌 61) is a family-oriented mix of fun and education. You'll need at least 90 minutes to do the full multilingual visit, which is audio-guided through a series of movies and gadgets, and culminates in a five-minute 5D cartoon-simulator experience. For €8 extra, don VR glasses and a bungee-style contraption to create the sensation of moon walking at one-sixth of earth's gravity. Outside (no ticket necessary) are a few space rockets, including an Ariane 4 launcher.

Redu

Though it's tiny, the sweet little 'book village' of Redu has several cafes, a mini-distillery and 15 bookshops, mostly secondhand and antiquarian, nestled close to its central church. These businesses tend to operate weekends and midsummer only but during the **Nuit-du-livre** (www.redu-villagedulivre.be; ☉ 1st Sat of Aug), shops and stalls open all evening, with fireworks going off at midnight.

🛈 Getting There & Away

Regular bus 29 runs seven to nine times daily from Han-sur-Lesse via Rochefort to the station at Jemelle (15 minutes, €3.50), which is on the Brussels–Luxembourg line.

Rochefort

POP 12,600

A very pleasant regional base for exploring this part of Belgium, Rochefort also has a lesser-known gem of a cave system. Almost everything is strung along the main street, known variously as Rue de Behogne, Place Roi Albert 1er and Rue Jacquet. This rises gently from an imposing statue-fronted church, passes the tourist office and continues to the private Château Comtal castle. Many shops and *cafés* sell Rochefort's famous Trappist beer, but the Abbaye de St-Rémy, where it's brewed (3km north), is closed to the public.

👁 Sights & Activities

⭐ **Grotte de Lorette**　　　　CAVE
(🖉 084-21 20 80; www.grotte-de-lorette.be; Drève de Lorette; adult/child €9/5.50; ☉ visits 10.30am, noon, 2pm & 3.30pm Sat & Sun Apr-Nov, every 45min 10.30am-4.15pm daily Jul & Aug) This cave system has fewer stalactites than nearby Han, and handling the 626 relatively steep steps is more physical. However, the small-group visits give a vastly more personal experience. Half-lit stairways give a magical hint of the main cave's great vertical depth (65m), and there's a memorable revelation of its full majesty at the end of a visit during an atmos-

pheric light show. It's 500m southeast of Rue Jacquet via Rue Beauregard.

Malagne RUINS
(Archéoparc de Rochefort; ☎084-22 21 03; www.malagne.be; Rue du Coirbois; adult/child €6.50/5; ⊙11am-6pm Sat, Sun & school holidays Apr-Oct) On the third Sunday of July, this Gallo-Roman archaeological site comes to life with a whole series of period demonstrations. At other times, the attractive rural ruins are less dynamic, and you'll probably value the free audioguide to make sense of the excavations, reconstructed mill, experimental archaeological projects and Roman vegetable gardens. It's 2km east of Rochefort.

Domaine Provincial
de Chevetogne PARK
(☎083-68 72 11; www.domainedechevetogne.be/contacts; Rue des Pirchamps 1; €10, free mid-Oct–Mar; ⊙9am-10pm; ☻) Around 12km north of Rochefort, this 550-hectare park is a wonderland for families. Chevetogne is set with forest trails, a natural-history museum, various thematic gardens, lakes, a petting zoo, and staggering playgrounds (creekside play areas, tree houses, and a massive slide inside a Trojan Horse). The admission fee gives access to everything inside the park – including a swimming pool, canoes and kayaks, minigolf and a train-like shuttle around the park. With so much on offer, plan to make a full day of it.

Chevetogne has a hotel, several on-site restaurants including a pretty waterfront brasserie, and great spots for a picnic if you come prepared. Bus 43/2 between Ciney and Mont-Gauthier stops here (weekdays only during school holidays).

🛏 Sleeping

Le Vieux Moulin HOSTEL €
(☎084-21 46 04; www.giterochefort.be; Rue du Hableau 25; over/under 26yr €36/31; P ☎) A pleasant riverside hostel. Zigzag down from the square beside the tourist office, cross the park and it's the orangey-red building directly across the footbridge to the right. Rates include simple breakfast. Regularly booked out by groups.

Le Briquemont B&B €€
(☎084-46 86 90; www.lebriquemont.be; Rue de Ciergnon 35, Briquemont; d €120-140; ☻) Overlooking peaceful countryside some 8km northwest of Rochefort, Le Briquemont delivers a winning combination of congen-

ial service, handsomely designed modern rooms and thoughtful extras (like an evening aperitif served fireside or on the terrace). Hosts Nadine and Alain make guests feel at home, and exquisite dinners are available by advance notice.

The small, heated indoor pool is open year-round.

Le Vieux Logis HOTEL €€
(☎084-21 10 24; www.levieuxlogis.be; Rue Jacquet 71; s/d/tr/q incl breakfast €85/95/140/170; ⊙check-in to 6pm; P ☎) Facing the château, with shutters and window-boxes on its stone facade, this atmospheric old place has lashings of antique furniture and wooden panelling, plus an almost medieval courtyard garden. Up creaky stairs, rooms have period furniture but dated bathrooms. Wi-fi doesn't reach most of them. If you love character rather than facilities, you'll love it here.

Margot'L GUESTHOUSE €€
(☎084-34 51 79; www.margotl.be; Place Roi Albert 1er 19; s/d from €55/70; ☎) On the main street, this modern bolthole is run by the excellent La Malle Poste hotel, which is also the place for checking in. It features six cute rooms with comfortable modern design, softened by a few touches in typically rustic French style.

★La Malle Poste HOTEL €€€
(☎084-21 09 86; www.malleposte.net; Rue de Behogne 46; s €80-160, d €110-200; P ☎ ☻) Enter through a 17th-century coaching inn that houses the indulgent restaurant, above which are two particularly impressive suites. A stone tunnel, complete with 8000-bottle wine collection, links to a subterranean swimming pool and sauna, as well as the steps up to a handful of large modern rooms complete with hot tubs. In the eaves, cheaper, smaller 'Maison du Cocher' rooms have Ardennaise decor.

The lovely garden and excellent service add to the appeal.

🍴 Eating

Samthaï THAI €€
(☎084-21 02 88; www.samthai.be; Place Roi Albert 1er 8; mains €11-15; ⊙6-10pm Wed-Sat, noon-3.30pm & 6-9pm Sun; ☻) A surprising find in tiny Rochefort, friendly Samthaï serves up steaming bowls of *tom ka* (coconut and lemongrass soup), flavour-packed red curries (try *pad phed ped* with duck), classic *pad taï* (noodles with sautéed shrimp) and lots

of other delectable dishes from Thailand. All go down nicely with a perfectly balanced Rochefort Trappist ale.

La Gourmandise
FRENCH €€

(☑084-22 21 81; www.la-gourmandise.be; Rue de Behogne 24; mains €14-28; ⊙10am-9pm; 🔊) With a cheery good vibe, expansive menu and outdoor seating on Rochefort's main street, La Gourmandise hits all the right notes. The space features a shop selling regional produce, a lounge bar and a restaurant area. You'll find plenty of temptations: think slabs of pâté, charcuterie and Ardennes fry-ups but also several salad choices.

Couleur Basilique
BISTRO €€

(☑084-46 85 36; www.couleurbasilic.be; Place Roi Albert 1er 25; mains €16-24; ⊙noon-2pm & 6-10pm Thu-Tue; 🔊) On Rochefort's restaurant-lined main drag, this fresh, youthful bistro has a fine front terrace for watching the city stroll past. The small but wide-ranging menu features hearty Thai- and North African–inspired salads, as well as grilled meats, mussel dishes, pastas, snacks (like shrimp croquettes) and a good drink selection.

★ La Calèche
FRENCH €€€

(☑084-21 09 86; www.malleposte.net; Rue de Behogne 46; menus €38-75, mains €25-45; ⊙7-10pm daily & noon-3pm Sun; 🔊) In the beautifully reappointed 17th-century building that forms the entrance to the Malle Poste Hotel, La Calèche offers elegant fine dining on pressed tablecloths, with an open kitchen, decent-sized portions and friendly staff. In season, the menu often features game. There's an excellent if pricey wine list; make sure you see the cellar.

❶ Getting There & Around

Regular bus 29 runs nine to 10 times daily from Rochefort to the nearby station at Jemelle (€2.50, seven minutes), on the Brussels–Luxembourg line. The bus makes several stops in Rochefort, including the **Sq Crépin** (off N86).

About 200m downhill from the church (Notre-Dame de la Visitation), **Cycle Sport** mends and rents out bicycles. The **tourist office** (☑084-34 51 72; www.rochefort.be; Rue de Behogne 5; ⊙8am-5pm Mon-Fri, 10am-5pm Sat, to 4pm Sun Oct-Mar, 8am-5pm Mon-Fri, 9.30am-5pm Sat & Sun Apr-Sep, to 6pm Mon-Fri Jul & Aug; 🔊) sells useful cycling maps.

St-Hubert

POP 5560

Dominated by the ancient basilica of a former abbey, the compact Ardennes town of St-Hubert is named for the patron saint of hunting. It plays on his image by hosting an early September festival full of red-coated huntsmen, dogs and curly hunting horns, which are blown again during a bizarre dog-blessing ceremony for **St Hubert's Day** (La Fête de Saint Hubert; Pl de l'Abbaye; ⊙3 Nov). Despite the human predators, the surrounding beech and pine forests remain rich in deer and wild boar. The area's one must-see sight is **Fourneau St-Michel** (☑084 21 08 90; www.fourneausaintmichel.be; Fourneau St-Michel 4; adult/concession/child €5/4/2; ⊙9.30am-5pm Tue-Sun Mar-Jun & Sep-Nov, to 5.30pm daily Jul & Aug; ♿), a fascinating open-air museum of historic rural buildings some 10km north towards attractive Nassogne village. If you don't have time to see the whole place, it's still worth having a drink or snack in the wonderful cafe-restaurant **L'Auberge du Prévost** (☑084 44 48 11; www.aubergeduprevost. be; Fourneau Saint-Michel 1; mains €12-30, pancakes €4-8, dinner menus €20-50, beer from €2; ⊙noon-9pm Tue-Sun Jul & Aug, noon-6pm Tue-Sun plus some Fri & Sat evenings Sep-Jun), occupying one of the complex's finest half-timbered farmhouses (no ticket needed).

Getting here requires wheels: bicycles are rented at **Cycles J Godefroid** (☑061 61 28 10; Rte de Poix 11b; per half-day/day/2 days mountain bike €13/19/25, electric bike €25/35/60; ⊙9am-7pm Tue-Sat, to noon Sun), 700m west of central St-Hubert. The town's best hotel-restaurant is the six-room **L'Ancien Hôpital** (☑061 41 69 65; www.ancienhopital.be; Rue de la Fontaine 23; s/d/ste €75/110/145; 🅿🔊).

Buses 51 and 162b from St-Hubert's Place de la Libération connect to Libramont station on the main Namur–Luxembourg railway line.

Bouillon

☑061 / POP 5350

Dreamily arrayed around a tight loop of the Semois River, Bouillon is dominated by the gnarled ridge-top ruins of a sturdy medieval castle. On a summer evening, limpid light and reflections in the shallow water can make this one of Belgium's prettiest towns.

⊙ Sights

If all goes to plan, by the time you read this a single **Bouillon Pass** ticket will have been introduced, allowing entry to the Château de Bouillon, Musée Ducal and Archéoscope Godefroid de Bouillon for a flat fee of adult/child €10/8. Opening times should also be simplified and aligned. At the time of research, however, **combination tickets** cost adult/child €14.50/10 for the three sites or €9.50/6 without the Archéoscope.

★**Château de Bouillon**   CASTLE
(☑061 46 62 57; www.bouillon-initiative.be; Rue du Château; adult/senior/student & child €7/6.50/5; ⊙10am-6.30pm Jul & Aug, 10am-5pm or 6pm Mar-Jun & Sep-Nov, see website for winter hrs; Ⓟ⛲) Slouching like a great grey dragon high on Bouillon's central rocky ridge, Belgium's finest feudal castle-ruin harks back to AD 988, but it's especially associated with Crusader knight Godefroid de Bouillon, the first 'Belgian' ruler of Jerusalem. The super-atmospheric site has everything you might wish for in a castle: dank dripping tunnel passages, musty half-lit cell rooms, falconry displays, rough-hewn stairwells and many an eerie nook and cranny to discover. Plus there are off-beat surprises like maturing cheeses and a caligraphy mini-museum.

Audio guides (€2.50) or guidebooks (€1.50) offer extra historical background in four languages. Access is across crag-spanning stone bridges from the car park at the castle's upper northeastern tip. Between March and October, time your visit to include the 45-minute open-air bird shows (11.30am, 2pm and 3.30pm; no extra charge), when trained 'wig-snatching' owls, hawks and eagles swoop low over spectators' heads. In July and August there's an extra 5pm show. To really get the heebie-jeebies prebook a night-time torchlight tour (adult/child/torch hire €10/7/2.50, 10pm Wednesday to Sunday in July and August).

Galerie Maurice Pirotte   GALLERY
(Ruelle de la Passage; ⊙2-6pm May-Sep) `FREE`
Even when it's closed, it's still worth seeking out this tiny gallery for its photogenic setting – an old stone house draped with flowers and creepers in a magical little corner of Bouillon that locals have dubbed the Quartier Bretagne.

Musée Ducal   MUSEUM
(☑061 46 41 89; www.museeducalbouillon. be; Rue du Petit 1; adult/senior/student/child €4/3.50/3/2.50; ⊙10am-6pm Easter-Sep, to 5pm Oct–mid-Nov) Between the town and Château de Bouillon's car park, this museum spreads over two historic houses and includes a small antique smithy (free access). Museum displays highlight Bouillon's history from the First Crusade through the local metallurgy industry, but also has works by celebrated local artist Albert Raty (1889–1970). The folklore section only opens in July and August.

In winter the museum is closed except during school holidays.

Archéoscope Godefroid de Bouillon   MUSEUM
(☑061 46 83 03; www.archeoscopebouillon.be; Quai des Saulx 14; adult/child €6.25/4.95; ⊙10am-5pm daily May-Aug, Tue-Sun Sep-Dec & Feb-Apr) Accessed via the tourist office, Bouillon's flashiest attraction is designed to bring the story of Godefroid to life. Visits start every 35 minutes with a multilingual film, after which

WALLONIA BOUILLON

GODEFROID DE BOUILLON

This crusader knight is seen as one of Belgium's oldest heroes, though the actions of his army would receive few medals today.

Born around 1058, Godefroid (Godfrey) sold his ducal castle at Bouillon to the prince-bishop of Liège in 1096 and used the money to lead one of three Crusader armies across Europe to the Holy Land. Well before meeting their Muslim foes, Godefroid's army seriously degenerated in both number and ethics, slaughtering thousands of Jews in towns across Germany soon after setting off.

It took three years to reach Jerusalem. The Crusader soldiers breached the city walls on 15 July 1099 and proceeded to massacre an estimated 40,000 Muslims and Jews. According to a contemporary account, six months after the orgy of slaughter, the streets still reeked of rotting bodies. Victorious Godefroid was offered the title 'King of Jerusalem' but settled instead for 'Defender of the Holy Sepulchre'. He died, perhaps poisoned, a year later, but his brother Baudouin reigned on, keeping the Holy Land 'Belgian' for several more years.

you walk through the screen into a darkened space moodily showing off a replica of Godefroid's Jerusalem tombstone.

🏃 Activities

The tourist office sells excellent walking and cycling maps that are great for exploring the extensive oak and beech forests surrounding Bouillon. The gentle meandering of the Semois River offers peaceful kayaking; as well as Bouillon-based operator **Les Epinoches** (☑ 0473 29 58 28; www.kayak-lesepinoches. be; Faubourg de France; ⊙ Easter-Oct), there are also several kayak outfits in the Semois Valley including the following:

Récréalle (☑ 061 50 03 81; www.recrealle.be; Rue Léon Henrard 16, Alle-sur-Semois; ⊙ 9.30am-4pm daily Apr-late Sep, Fri-Sun by arrangement Oct-Mar) At Alle.

Semois Kayaks (☑ 0475 24 74 23; www. semois-kayaks.be; Rue du Pont, Poupehan; ⊙ Easter-Sep) At Poupehan.

Cap Semois (☑ 0477 58 20 62; www.kayak-capsemois.be; Rue du Perré 79-80, Vresse-sur-Semois; half-/full-day bike rental €23/30, kayaking from €20; ⊙ Easter-Sep) At Vresse.

🛏 Sleeping

B&B Adam   B&B €
(☑ 061 46 71 56; guyadam10@skynet.be; Rue du Brutz 10; tw €35, breakfast €4) This B&B is in an utterly charming time-warp cottage backing onto the Quartier Bretagne art alley (a short-cut up to the castle). English-speaking Guy is a delightful host offering two homestay rooms, each with private (but not en suite) old bathrooms. The family kitchen, replete with homemade jams, is almost a museum of rustic style.

Guy particularly welcomes walkers and has two great-value, similarly antique *gîte* houses alongside.

Auberge de Jeunesse   HOSTEL €
(☑ 061 46 81 37; www.lesaubergesdejeunesse.be; Rte du Christ 16; dm €17-22, r from €40; ⊙ closed Jan & late Jun; P 🛜) Perched on a high ridge, this well-run HI hostel has breathtaking views over Bouillon's castle, the river and town from its terrace and breakfast room. If walking from central Bouillon there's a short-cut up a stairway from near Place St-Arnould.

Alternatively, from the bus station, follow Rue des Champs to the T-junction, turn right

and wind your way up. Call ahead to check that the hostel is staffed to avoid a needless, sweaty climb.

La Ferronnière   HOTEL €€
(☑ 061 23 07 50; www.laferronniere.be; Voie Jocquée 44; d/ste from €105/195; ⊙ restaurant closes Mon & lunchtime Tue & Sat; P 🛜) This ivy-clad, half-timbered mansion, 500m northeast of Bouillon's centre, is decorated in a lightly classical style, while newer duplex suites feel sleeker and include free access to the spa (€30 extra for other guests). There's a beautifully maintained little garden and the gourmet restaurant's flower-decked dining terrace has a perfectly framed if distant castle view (lunch €26, dinner menus €37 to €70).

Hôtel Panorama   HOTEL €€
(☑ 061 46 61 38; www.panoramahotel.be; Rue au Dessus de la Ville 25; r €100-130, ste €140; P 🛜) From the outside this hotel looks like a 1960s ski lodge, but the interior surprises with its attractive mix of russets and browns, art prints and the odd Indian cabinet. Nearly all of the 22 rooms have fine city views, and there's a gastronomic restaurant (menus €39 and €47) and three different 'flavours' of guest lounge.

🍴 Eating

⭐ **La Table des Sépulcrines**   FUSION €€
(☑ 061 32 07 63; www.latabledessepulcrines.be; Quai des Saulx 10; mains €21-28; ⊙ noon-1.30pm & 7-9.30pm Fri-Tue; 🛜) A comfortably contemporary bistro-style interior brings a gentle touch of modernism to the frontage of the 17th-century convent complex that also includes the tourist office. The chef creates some satisfyingly creative dishes, providing elements of Asian-fusion wizardry to hearty local recipes. It's great value for the quality on offer. Cash only.

BOM   INTERNATIONAL €€
(☑ 061 46 51 66; www.bomfoodanddrinks.be; Quai des Saulx; mains €15-25; ⊙ kitchen noon-2pm & 6-9pm; 🛜) BOM's riverside terrace has the best castle view of any Bouillon eating establishment. They serve great smoothies and offer the unusual luxury of an English-language menu. The wide-ranging food selection (tataki, falafels, quinoa-rhubarb crumble, garlic squid) is attractively presented, with several vegetarian options, though it's not quite as sophisticated as the hipster decor and waiters' garb might imply.

THE SEMOIS VALLEY

Northwest of Bouillon, the deep-cut Semois River Valley forms beautiful, eccentric loops flanked occasionally by vividly green waterside meadows at the base of high, steeply rising woodland banks. For kayaking or driving, the whole area is a delight, but don't expect to visit using public transport. By car, follow winding roads that roller-coaster between streamside and plateau-top villages. The famous **Tombeau du Géant** is the best known hoop of river valley, forming a lonely, forested peninsula that's best surveyed from way above at the **Tombeau viewpoint** (Rue Moulin du Rivage, Botassart) on a dead-end road around 10 circuitous kilometres north of Bouillon. Almost as lovely and more convenient to reach is the lovely view down from Rochehaut over another pretty river loop that enfolds tiny **Frahan-sur-Semois** hamlet.

In Rochehaut, well-organised **Auberge de la Ferme** (☑ 061 46 10 00; www.auberge delaferme.be; Rue de la Cense 12; s/d from €105/170; [P][⌂]) occupies a large proportion of the village's many traditionally styled buildings, and its excellent tavern is one of the area's few places to eat and drink that's open daily (and relatively late).

Continuing west you'll reach pleasant **Alle** where riverside **Récréalle** is a lively yet appealing activities centre with minigolf, winter skating, bike rental and a professional kayaking outlet.

Even smaller **Vresse-sur-Semois** has several more cafe-restaurants, family-style **B&B Del Campo** (☑ 0486 50 78 58; www.bbdelcampo.be; Rue Albert Raty 18; s/d/tr €70/80/105; [P][⌂]), the regional **tourist office** (☑ 061 29 28 27; www.ardenne-namuroise. be; Rue Albert Raty 83; ☺ 9am-6pm daily Jul & Aug, 8.30am-5pm Mon-Fri, 10am-5pm or 6pm Sat & Sun Mar-Jun & Sep-Dec, shorter hrs winter; [⌂]), a fortress-like 1786 stone church-tower and an incongruous reconstruction of Belgium's first steam locomotive. Historically, Vresse was a retreat for artists and thinkers, including surrealist poet Jean Cocteau; a recommended **gallery** (☑ 061 58 92 99; www.fondation-chaidron.com; Rue Albert Raty 112; adult/student/child €5/3/free; ☺ 1-5pm Mon-Fri & 2-6pm Sat & Sun Apr–mid-Nov) here exhibits some of the works of the 'Vresse School'.

Across the 18th-century bridge (Pont St-Lambert) from Vresse is the pretty stone hamlet of Lafôret. In midsummer walk 500m down an unpaved track from the Lafôret's church to find **Pont de Claies** (Lafôret; ☺ Jul & Aug), Belgium's last seasonal footbridge. Originally designed to let tobacco harvesters reach their crops, it's made by placing hazel-weave onto log stilts embedded in the river and is rebuilt each year in late June or early July.

La Vieille Ardenne   PUB FOOD €€
(☑ 061 46 62 77; Grand Rue 9; mains €12-18; ☺ 11am-11pm daily Jul & Aug, Fri-Tue Sep-Jun; [⌂]) Beer flagons dangle from the beams of this compact, traditional Ardennes-style *café*-eatery, and summer tables overflow onto neighbouring pavements. The menu includes a fair-priced fish of the-day (€14), old-world meatballs (€12) and, in October and November, seasonal *gibier* (game) dishes.

There's a decent choice of beers, including the deliciously refreshing IPA-style Septimus VII.

🛍 Shopping

Le Marché de Nathalie   ALCOHOL
(☑ 061 46 89 40; www.brasseriedebouillon.be; Grand Rue 22; ☺ 10am-noon & 2-6pm Thu-Tue)

Bouillon's best beer shop, with a wide selection including self-brewed local options.

ℹ Information

Maison du Tourisme (☑ 061 46 52 11; www. bouillon-tourisme.be; Quai des Saulx 12; ☺ 10am-5pm daily, to 6pm Fri & Sat Jul & Aug) The tourist office is by the river, on the other side of and opposite to the Château de Bouillon.

ℹ Getting There & Away

To reach Bouillon, take a train to Libramont, then bus 8 (45 minutes, roughly hourly weekdays, two-hourly weekends). It might seem quicker to use the Namur–Dinant–Bertrix line and get off the train at Paliseul, but other than one early-morning school bus 67, there is no easy connection from there to Bouillon.

Orval

None of Belgium's famous Trappist beer-abbeys is more photogenic than **Notre Dame d'Orval** (☑061 311 0 60; www.orval.be; adult/concession/child €6/5/3; ⊘9.30am-6pm Mar-Oct, 10.30am-5.30pm Nov-Feb), with afternoon light glowing off the sandstone of a giant Madonna and Child carved into its west wall. Beside it are the picturesque ruins of Cistertian Monastery dating back to 1132 but wrecked in 1793 by French Revolutionary soldiers. Rebuilding only started in the early 20th century, partly funded by the Trappist beers that have become its trademark. The brewery section is closed to visitors (except for two days in mid-September; book way ahead) but you can visit the old ruins along with an 18th-century pharmacy room, the grave of King Wenceslas (1337–83), a medicinal herb garden and an informative museum section that focuses on the beers and their advertising since 1931.

Around 150m south, the monastery pub-restaurant **À l'Ange Gardien** (☑061 31 18 86; www.alangegardien.be; Rte de Orval 3; ⊘10.30am-6pm Mon, Tue & Thu, to 9pm Fri-Sun Sep-Jun, plus to 6pm Wed Jul & Aug; 🛜) presents the chance to taste Orval Vert, a crisp, hoppy 4.5% draught beer served nowhere else.

Some 2km southwest, the nearest village is pretty, slow-moving Villers-devant-Orval.

❶ Getting There & Away

Three to five times on weekdays bus 24 from Florenville train station passes through Orval (13 minutes). The 11.56am train from Libramont arrives in time to connect at Florenville with the 12.30pm (sometimes 12.42pm or 12.57pm) bus, giving you time for an abbey visit and several beers before returning on the 4.50pm bus from the Orval crossroads and then the connecting 5.11pm train to Libramont.

Arlon

POP 29,700

First settled as a Roman trading post, Arlon is the south Ardennes' regional capital, with a selection of proud stone buildings on central **Place Léopold** and plenty more in the small central core, which retains a medieval street plan, though not a medieval appearance. The streets spiral up, almost imperceptibly, to **Knipchen**, a central church-crowned viewpoint, where a long-demolished fortress once stood. The town makes a pleasant pit

stop en route to Luxembourg, which is just 21/33 minutes away by regular fast/slow trains (home-printed e-ticket/at-station ticket €10.50/16.50).

Bastogne

POP 15,900

During WWII's Battle of the Bulge, Bastogne was encircled and heavily bombarded by German forces but refused to capitulate. More than 70 years later, the town's tourist industry still revolves around its valiant wartime history and it's a place where the US soldiers are unambiguously seen as heroes. Beside a large war memorial 1.5m northeast of the centre, the impressive museum of the conflict is well worth a trip.

◉ Sights & Activities

★**Bastogne War Museum**   MUSEUM
(☑061 21 02 20; www.bastognewarmuseum. be; Colline du Mardasson 5; adult/senior/child €14/12/8; ⊘9.30am-6pm Feb-Jun & Sep-Dec, to 7pm Jul & Aug, closed Jan & Mon mid-Nov–mid-Mar) This highly recommended modern museum takes you into the heart of WWII, with an audio guide featuring four imagined voices of civilian and military witnesses/participants. A usefully thorough summary of the war's context and key stages includes an engrossing 15-minute 3D film presenting Germany's early attacks as though to a press conference. Downstairs the focus is the Battle of the Bulge and defence of Bastogne. Two theatrical audiovisuals add impressively to well-displayed memorabilia.

For the full experience allow around two hours, ensure that the audioguide's black sensor faces forward and do click the buttons below several TV monitors to listen to moving civilian recollections of wartime atrocities. The museum is 1.5km northeast of Place St-Pièrre on the grounds of the **Mardasson American War Memorial**, which features a cave-like multifaith chapel-crypt with mosaics by Fernand Léger.

Bastogne Barracks   MUSEUM
(Camp Heinz; ☑061 24 21 24; www.bastogne-barracks.be; Rte de la Roche 40; ⊘10am & 2pm Wed-Sun Apr-Sep) **FREE** These active barracks were once the HQ of General McAuliffe's 101st Airborne Division. Excellent, enthusiastic two-hour guided visits peruse the reconstruction centre for WWII vehicles and the 'Nuts' room where mannequins add to

BATTLE OF THE BULGE

Widely nicknamed the Battle of the Bulge, the Battle of the Ardennes (not to be confused with the similarly named WWI battle) was one of the fiercest land confrontations of WWII. In September 1944, both Belgium and Luxembourg had been liberated by American troops after four years of German occupation. However, the Allies then pushed on into the Netherlands and France, leaving relatively few soldiers to defend the forested Ardennes. Hitler, sensing this weakness, ordered a counter-attack in the depths of winter. The offensive ploughed through the hills and valleys of northern Luxembourg and into Belgium, forming a 'bulge' in the Allied line. It was a desperate attempt to capture Antwerp and the Meuse River ports to block supplies and paralyse the Allied advance. Hitler's army got within sight of Dinant but failed to break through.

During this invasion, the town of Bastogne was surrounded, but its defenders, the American 101st Airborne Division, kept fighting. When offered an opportunity to surrender, their commander General Anthony McAuliffe gave the curt, much-quoted response: 'Nuts!' His troops held out until early January, when Allied reinforcements managed to drive Nazi forces back through snowy Luxembourg into Germany. By the end of the battle in January 1945, over 20,000 troops on each side had died, along with numerous civilians. Many Ardennes villages, including La Roche-en-Ardenne, Houffalize and St-Vith, had been bombed to rubble. Memorials to this tragic Christmas are numerous across the region. Bastogne and Luxembourg City have large military cemeteries and there are dozens of poignant museums, most memorably in Bastogne and Baugnez near Malmédy.

fascinating explanations of key parts of the Battle of the Bulge.

The barracks entrance is 500m north of Place St-Pièrre.

Reg Jans Battlefield Experience HISTORY
(www.regjans.com) Personalised, small-group English-language tours led by the grandson of a WWII veteran. Tours typically visit sites associated with the Battle of the Bulge, often seeking out extant bullet holes and bunkers. Book well ahead.

🛏 Sleeping & Drinking

Wagon Léo BRASSERIE €€
(☑061 21 14 41; www.wagon-leo.com; Rue du Vivier 4 & 8; mains €9.90-27; ⊙restaurant 11.30am-9.30pm, bistro 7.30am-10.30pm Tue-Sun; 🕸) Open since 1946, the genteel restaurant section of this spot is fronted by a 1940s tram carriage with wooden-inlay walls. Meals here can be quite elaborate French-style affairs, but for something lighter nip a couple of doors down to their more informal bistro section, which is a reliable, value-packed venue for standard family favourites.

Léo also offers 34 guest rooms in three Bastogne locations (s/d/tr €76/86/106, deluxe s/d €111/121).

Brasserie Lamborelle BAR
(☑061 21 80 55; www.brasserielamborelle.be; Rue Lamborelle 19; ⊙11am-11.30pm Wed & Thu, to midnight Fri & Sat, to 10pm Sun; 🕸) This small, cosy pub features elements of exposed brick and stonework amid cowhide wallpaper squares and enamel signboards. It serves a remarkable range of beers, including brown and blonde versions of the excellent house brew Airborne (9%, €4.50), served in novel helmet-shaped ceramic cups with a little dish of free snacks.

Food includes *raclette*, *pierrades* (hotstone on-the-table barbecues) and tasty, inexpensive bar meals.

ⓘ Information

Maison du Tourisme (☑061 21 27 11; www.paysdebastogne.be; ⊙9.30am-12.30pm & 1-5.30pm) By the WWII tank in Place McAuliffe. Rents out bicycles, both mountain bikes (€17/25 for a half-/full day) and electric ones (€25/35).

ⓘ Getting There & Away

From the 'Gare du Sud' **bus station** (Ave Matthieu), 400m southwest of centre, take bus 88 to Namur (6.25am, 7.25am and 10.25am Monday to Friday), bus 1011 to Liège (three to seven daily), or bus 163b to Libramont (€3.20, 45 minutes, several daily) for trains on the Brussels–Arlon–Luxembourg railway line.

Prebook online for the FlixBus (www.flixbus.co.uk) service to Luxembourg (65 minutes, 12.30pm).

Achouffe

POP 200

Set among trout ponds in what was for years a little-visited corner of the Ardennes, this tiny village is famed for its beer: named La Chouffe (the gnome) as a mild pun on Achouffe. Three cafe-restaurants offer *galopin* (120mL) taster glasses of several La Chouffe brews (best value at La Petite Fontaine), and the central Brasserie d'Achouffe offers brewery tours. Most are by appointment (book two weeks ahead) but there are also three weekly drop-in slots: sign in the same morning at the **Chouffe Shop** (Achouffe 8; ⊙ 9am-noon & 1-5pm Mon-Fri Sep-Jun, 9am-5pm Mon-Fri Jul & Aug, 10am-6pm Sat & Sun). You'll need your own wheels to get here.

La Roche-en-Ardenne

POP 4190

La Roche is known for smoked hams, kayaking and WWII decimation, with its most striking feature an evocative ancient fortress-ruin crowning the town's central knoll.

◉ Sights & Activities

Château Féodal   CASTLE

(☏ 084 41 13 42; www.chateaudelaroche.be; Rue du Vieux Château 4; adult/child €5.50/3.50; ⊙ 10am-6pm Jul & Aug, reduced hours rest of year) La Roche's picture-postcard 11th-century ruins look especially memorable floodlit on a foggy night when viewed from the Hotton road. There's not a great deal inside but the site makes for pleasant, steep strolls, and in July and August, looking up from the central bridge in town, you might apparently spot a ghost...at 10pm sharp!

In icy conditions the castle doesn't open and in heavy rain the ghost stays in her crypt.

Musée de la Bataille des Ardennes   MUSEUM

(☏ 084 41 17 25; www.batarden.be; Rue Châmont 5; adult/child €8/4; ⊙ 10am-6pm Tue-Sun Apr-Dec, plus Mon Jul & Aug, weekends only Jan-Mar, closed much of Nov) Waxwork scenes, maps and the odd video provide a competent, if unsophisticated, explanation of La Roche's involvement in the wintry WWII Battle of the Bulge (p221), when 114 villagers perished and 90% of La Roche's buildings were flattened.

Either side of La Roche, the winding Ourthe River passes through steep, wooded valleys with lovely meadows, making for appealing low-intensity kayaking.

Two main companies, **BrandSport** (☏ 084 41 10 84; www.brandsport.be; Pl du Maré 16) and **Ardenne Aventures** (☏ 084 41 19 00; www.ardenne-aventures.be; Rue de l'Eglise 35), both offer a smorgasbord of outdoor activities including rope-walk adventures, mountain biking and kayaking. See their websites for ideas. **Bike Zone** (☏ 0471 94 02 65; www.the-bike-zone.com; Rue Chamont 7C; per day €22-45; ⊙ 10am-1pm & 2-5pm Sep-Jun, to 6pm Jul & Aug) repairs and rents quality mountain bikes.

The tourist office sells maps detailing cycling and hiking routes.

🛏 Sleeping

Hôtel de Liège   HOTEL €

(☏ 0495 50 33 35, 084 41 11 64; www.hoteldeliege.be; Rue de la Gare 16; s/d without bathroom from €31.50/44; ☎) Simple but great value, this 12-room hotel is just two minutes' walk from La Roche's centre but has easy street parking. It makes no pretence at modern style but beds are comfy (pillows less so), the wi-fi works well and an OK breakfast costs just €5. Check-in time is limited so call ahead. No credit cards.

★**Moulin de la Strument**   HOTEL, CAMPGROUND €€

(☏ 084 41 15 07; www.strument.com; Petite Strument 62; s/d/ste from €93/105/121, sites per person/tent €3.50/10; ⊙ Fri-Sun Sep-Dec & Feb-Jun, daily Jul & Aug, camping Easter-early Oct; ℗ ☎) Except in July and August, you'll need to visit on weekends to enjoy Roche's most charming hotel, in an old stone mill nestled beside a babbling stream. The wooded valley is all a-twitter with birdsong yet is only 800m south of the town's Place du Bronze. The eight rooms are well appointed, the restaurant is enticing and the reception desk sits beside the original waterwheel.

Hidden discreetly behind there's also a well-tended campground.

Le Corumont   B&B €€

(☏ 084 84 41 14; www.le-corumont.webnode.be; Rue Corumont 13; d €85-100; ⊙ check-in 5-8pm; ℗ ☎) There is simply no better view of La Roche than the exceptional panorama that's all yours from the private balconies of this chalet-style B&B, which has four rooms named for different cityscapes (curiously, 'Hollywood' is the smallest). In fine weather,

HOTTON CAVES

Hidden beneath partly wooded hills 1.7km southwest of Hotton, the **Grottes de Hotton** (☑ 084 46 60 46; www.grottesdehotton.be; Chemin de Spéléoclub, Hotton sur Ourthe; adult/child €10/7; ⊙ 10am-4pm Apr-Jun, Sep & Oct, to 5pm Jul & Aug, Sat & Sun only Nov-Mar) are some of Belgium's most awesome caves. Sculpted grottoes sprout pretty stalagmites and weird 'eccentrics' – mini corkscrews or horizontal protrusions apparently defying geological logic. However, the real highlight is descending a former siphon through up-turned vertical strata into a dramatically narrow, 37m-high subterranean chasm.

Visits are only by relatively long guided tours (English often available) involving 580 steps. Tours start roughly hourly in summer, dropping to around five daily departures in shoulder season and only three (at 12.30pm, 2pm and 3.30pm) on Saturday and Sunday in winter. It's always worth calling ahead to check the day's departure times. Dress appropriately for spending between an hour and 90 minutes at 12°C (53.6°F). Access without your own vehicle is difficult.

take breakfast on a covered section of terrace that also features a swing seat.

Les Genêts HOTEL €€
(☑ 084 41 18 77; www.lesgenetshotel.com; Corniche de Deister 2; s/d €83/99; 🖥) This lovable family-style hotel boasts sweeping panoramas across the river to the sculpture park from its terrace, garden and cosily old-fashioned lounge, which has a grandfather clock and hunting trophies. The castle views from room 15 are particularly fine.

✕ Eating & Drinking

There's a fair choice of restaurants and cafes on and around Place du Bronze, including **Le Quai Son** (www.lequaison.be; Rue des Bateliers 7; ⊙ 10.30am-midnight daily Jul & Aug, 11am-7.30pm Tue-Sun Sep-Jun), a cosy bar whose big open terrace stares up at La Roche's castle across the river. On the main street, **Maison Bouillon et Fils** (☑ 084 41 18 80; www.maison-bouillon.be; Pl du Maré 9; light meals €3.45-12.95; ⊙ shop 8.30am-6.30pm Wed-Mon, salon 11.30am-3pm Wed-Sun) is a classic deli for Ardennes smoked meats.

Signé Jeanne EUROPEAN €€
(☑ 084 411 11 90; www.signejeanne.be; Pl du Bronze 17; mains €14-24, steaks €19.95-76; ⊙ 10am-10pm Fri-Wed) A step ahead of most La Roche offerings in terms of style and service, Signé Jeanne produces brasserie food with a lot of extra zest, delightful *amuse-bouches* and great house wine. It also has a wide range of steaks including locally reared bison (€40).

ℹ Information

Tourist Office (☑ 084 36 77 36; www.la-roche-tourisme.com; Pl du Maré 15; ⊙ 9am-5pm) On the main drag; sells maps detailing cycling and hiking routes (€1.50 to €7).

ℹ Getting There & Away

From Namur six possible train-bus combinations get you to La Roche in 1½ to two hours. All start with an Arlon-bound train to Marloie. There you either need to get bus 15 to La Roche, or take an additional train to Melreux then bus 13. From Liège there are seven viable combinations daily, with bus changes required in either Melreux or Marche-en-Famenne (around two hours total).

Durbuy

POP 1700

Sitting pretty in a green and pleasant valley, Durbuy sells itself somewhat contentiously as 'the world's smallest city'. Around a small, spired 1756 château (private), photogenic cobblestone alleys of solid grey-stone buildings are full of cute craft shops and charming restaurants, aimed squarely at the seasonal flood of tourists. While midsummer weekends can get unbearably crowded, things are usually pleasantly calm midweek in June or September.

✦ Activities

Adventure Valley ADVENTURE SPORTS
(☑ 086 21 28 15; www.adventure-valley.be; Rue de Rome 1; ⊙ 9am-6pm Apr-Oct; 🄿) Virtually all of Durbuy's countless family-oriented outdoor activites are organised under the umbrella of this slick outfit. Kayaking and a 'Challenge Park' (with a variety of rope walks) operate from near the Pré Georis car park west of town, and there's laser-paintball at Barvaux, but the biggest multi-activity area is here at Rome, between the two (parking €7).

Some activities are available separately but many more require you to buy a day-pass 'bracelet' (various colour-coded options). On weekends and during school holidays, customer shuttles link the sites.

🛏 Sleeping & Eating

Virtually every second building in central Durbuy is a hotel or rents out rooms, many tempting tourist restaurants double as cafes and there's a pair of small, fun seasonal cocktail bars at the western end of Rue des Récollectines. For a supermarket you'll need to drive 4km to Barvaux.

★ **La Petite Maison**   GUESTHOUSE €
(📞 086 21 49 00; www.durbuy-info.com; Rue des Récollectines 4; r €50; 🖥) Gregarious English-speaking owner Jacques offers three phenomenally good-value rooms in the loveliest quarter of town. The 'Petite Maison' itself is just that: a little cubic building that feels like an oversized doll's house, while the other two options are fair-sized studios around the corner in a historic cottage, one with its own grandfaher clock.

★ **Le Clos des Recollets**   BOUTIQUE HOTEL €€
(📞 086 21 29 69; www.closdesrecollets.be; Rue de la Prévôté 9; s/d/tr/q €108/135/180/225; 🖥) Harmoniously refurbished rooms are scattered around three delightful interconnecting half-timbered houses above a very well-reputed upmarket restaurant.

The restaurant is open Thursday to Monday (menus €37 to €75), and, in summer, it spreads tables onto an intimate triangular square here in the oldest part of town.

Aux 10 Clefs   BELGIAN €€
(www.aux10clefs.be; Rue Comte d'Ursel 41; mains €11-18; ⊙ 8.30am-9pm daily Easter-Dec, Thu-Sun only mid-Jan–Easter) This family-run, farmhouse-style place in a 300-year-old building serves inexpensive Belgian home cooking (meatballs, meat stew) along with trout, sandwiches and a good €8 breakfast spread.

B&B rooms are also available (from €65).

ℹ Getting There & Away

The nearest train station to Durbuy is 4km east at Barvaux, on the Liège–Jemelle line.

Daily in July and August plus weekends in June and September a TEC shuttle bus leaves Barvaux station at 11.05am, 12.05pm and 4.05pm for Durbuy and the Pré Georis kayak point, returning at 11.30am, 3.30pm and 5.30pm.

Pre-booked Adventure Valley guests can use regular shuttle buses that connect Barvaux, Durbuy, Pré Georis and their activities park at Rome up to three times an hour (depending on reservations).

Huy

POP 21,280

Straddling the Meuse River between Namur and Liège, Huy (pronounced 'wee'), was one of northern Europe's first chartered cities (1066) and later became a major metallurgical centre within the Prince-Bishopric of Liège. The outskirts can be off-putting but the centre retains a small, delightful warren of medieval cobbled lanes between the pretty little Grand Place and the town's quaint **museum** (📞 085 23 24 35; Rue Vankeerberghen 20; ⊙ 2-5pm Tue-Sun Apr-Jun, Sep & Oct, to 6pm Jul & Aug, Fri-Sun & holidays only Nov-Mar) 🆓, which occupies a very picturesque 1669 cloister.

Near the river, **Collégiale Notre-Dame de Huy** (www.tresordehuy.com; Parvis Théoduin de Bavière; ⊙ 10am-noon & 1-6pm Tue-Sun May-Oct, to 4pm Nov-Apr) is a brooding Gothic church with a 1066 crypt full of priceless medieval reliquaries. Towering above is the huge and inpenetrable if gloomy 19th-century **fortress** (www.huy.be; Chaussée Napoléon; adult/child €4/2; ⊙ 9.30am-5pm Mon-Fri, 10am-6pm Sat & Sun Apr-Jun, Sep & Oct, 10am-6pm daily Jul & Aug) in whose maze of dungeons PG Wodehouse was held prisoner by WWII Nazis in 1940.

Trains run to Namur (€5.50, 25 to 35 minutes) and to Liège-Palais (€4.90, 35 minutes) at least twice hourly. Bus 9 to Liège passes the Val St-Lambert glassworks-museum en route.

Liège

POP 196,300

Liège is like a living architectural onion with layer upon layer of history lying just beneath the surface. The proudly free-spirited citizens are disarmingly friendly and no Belgian city bubbles with more *joie de vivre*. The beer is cheap, the eating scene is authentically local and if you can cope with the grubby, downbeat facade you're likely to find Liège a quirkily compulsive discovery.

History

There had been a Roman villa here before the 4th century, but Liège's history really got going when St-Lambert, Bishop of

Tongeren-Maastricht, stopped to pray here in 705 and was murdered by enemies from an opposing clan. Miracles and pilgrimages ensued and donations from visitors such as Frankish Emperor Charlemagne allowed the development by 1015 of St-Lambert's Cathedral, which became one of the greatest in northern Europe.

Wielding both religious and secular powers, the prince-bishops of Liège ('mini-popes') managed to maintain their territory's independence for almost eight centuries, endowing the city with numerous religious architectural masterpieces. Initially the bishops' rule was remarkably enlightened. Personal liberties were enshrined here centuries before such freedoms were accepted in surrounding feudal Europe. Comparative broad-mindedness plus access to Crusader-purloined monastic translations of Arabic scientific texts gave the region a technological edge in the development of local industries, from metallurgy to distillation. However, by the late 18th century the prince-bishopric had become a clumsy anachronism and economic gripes led to the 1789 Révolution Liégeoise. Liège townsfolk ousted the prince-bishop and voted in 1793 to demolish the city's fabulous St-Lambert's Cathedral, a symbol of the hated rulers. Swiftly thereafter Liège was occupied and annexed by revolutionary France.

It wasn't long after the demolition of St-Lambert's that the monumental scale of the error was realised. St Pauls – one of seven ancient sub-churches – was then declared the new cathedral. After Waterloo (1815) the territory passed to the Dutch king, and English-influenced large-scale steel production swept Liège. By 1905 the city's industrial standing was such that it organised a World Fair.

WWI saw Liège become the world's first city to suffer a campaign of aerial bombing, courtesy of new-fangled Zeppelin airships. However, by holding out for 12 days, Liège's brave defenders gave the rest of Europe just enough time to prepare a defence against Germany's westward march. The city's fortunes declined greatly as the 20th century wore on and have never really recovered from the collapse of the steel industry that began in the 1970s.

◉ Sights

Entry to most city attractions is covered by a single €18 pass available from the tourist of-

MAGICAL MODAVE

Few of Belgium's numerous castles have an interior that beats the memorable **Château de Modave** (☑ 085 41 13 69; www.modave-castle.be; Rue du Parc 4, Modave; adult/senior/student/child €9/7/4/free; ☉ 10am-6pm Tue-Sun Apr–mid-Nov, daily Jul & Aug, last entry 5pm; ⓟ). The most arresting of the well-preserved 1673 stucco ceilings is the heraldic relief that covers the entrance hall. But doing the whole audio-guide visit (50 minutes) shows you another 20 majestically furnished rooms plus a lead-lined stone-cut bath, a remarkable bed-alcove and the balcony from which you can suddenly appreciate the castle's strategic perch on a 60m-high cliff above a pretty rural stream.

It's 13km south of Huy via the N641.

fice (valid 48 hours). As much closes on Mondays or Wednesdays and some minor sites open weekends only, it's best to start the pass on a Thursday or Friday. The first Sunday of the month, much is free.

While walking through the centre, notice the attractive 1719 city hall, peep inside the Gothic courtyard of the former Prince Bishops' Palace – now the appeal court – and wander up some of the fascinating little alley-stairways off rue Hors Château.

⭐ **Grand Curtius**   MUSEUM
(☑ 04-221 68 17; www.lesmuseesdeliege.be/grand-curtius; Féronstrée 136; adult/senior/child €9/5/free; ☉ 10am-6pm daily May-Oct, closed Tue Nov-Apr) Splendid Grand Curtius unites four disparate museum collections in the former mansion-warehouse of a 16th-century Liège arms dealer. The building's red outer walls had originally been painted with ox blood. The museum's ambitious aim is to explain the whole history of art, from prehistoric stone chippings to art nouveau pianos, while interweaving tales of Liège artists and industries.

The result is impressive, if sometimes overwhelming. There's an incredible wealth of treasures to discover and you'll need a couple of hours to do it justice, and more if you make full use of the detailed tablet guide (included) and temporary exhibitions (extra).

WALLONIA LIÈGE

Liège

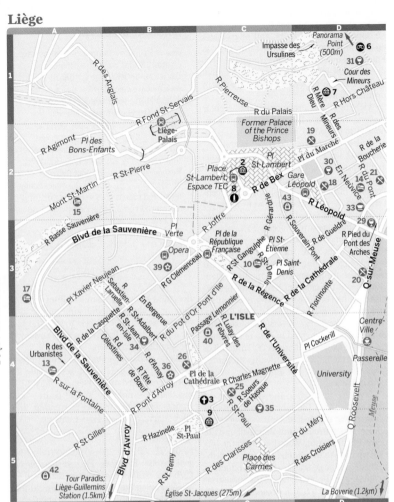

★ **Église St-Jacques**   CHURCH

(Pl Émile-Dupont; ⊙10.30am-12.30pm & 1.30-3.30pm Mon-Sat, 2.30-4.30pm Sun) Arguably Liège's most fascinating church, this architectural hotchpotch was founded in 1015 and retains a heavily patched-up 1170 west end whose Romanesque brown limestone and brick-filler clash discordantly with the 16th-century Gothic nave.

Inside, the colourful ceiling vaults are notable for over 150 carved bosses. Opening times can vary.

Musée de la Vie Wallonne   MUSEUM

(www.viewallonne.be; Cour des Mineurs; adult/student/child €5/4/3; ⊙9.30am-6pm Tue-Sun) In an adapted convent-cloister building, this curious museum takes visitors on an amble through the region's past, exploring everything from 12th-century Mosan metalwork to 1960s room interiors. Notable is the watercolour of the rooster that's now Wallonia's symbol, but the highlight for the ghoulish is an original guillotine and the embalmed head of the last man to feel her

WALLONIA LIÈGE

kiss. Stereoscope black-and-white photos of Liège are also intriguing. Temporary exhibitions, sometimes free, are housed in the attached former church. An audio guide is available.

Cathédrale St-Paul   CATHEDRAL
(www.cathedraledeliege.be; Pl de la Cathédrale; ⊘8am-5pm) FREE Cathédrale St-Paul's highlights include a big 19th-century painting depicting the legend of St-Lambert's assassination, and the saint's ornate silver coffin, a romantic 1893 creation for his 1200th anniversary. St-Lambert's skull, however, is

supposedly in the **Trésor** (Treasury; ☐ 04-232 61 32; www.tresordeliege.be; adult/child €6/free; ⊘2-5pm Tue-Sun), for which you'll need to pay (though admission is included with an Archéoforum ticket). In the late afternoon the cathedral's soaring grey-stone Gothic vaults are bathed in colourful light filtered through stained glass both old and new.

Archéoforum   MUSEUM
(☑04-250 93 70; www.archeoforumdeliege.be; Pl St-Lambert; adult/concession €6/5, includes cathedral Trésor; ☉9am-5pm Tue-Fri, 10am-5pm Sat during term time, 10am-5pm Tue-Fri school holidays) Once one of the greatest churches in northern Europe, St-Lambert's Cathedral was demolished from 1793 in the aftermath of the Révolution Liégeoise, very decidedly marking the end of the independent prince-bishopric of Liège. All that now remains is a mere scattering of foundation stones hidden beneath bleak Place St-Lambert. These archaeological diggings, along with remnants of an earlier Roman villa, can be seen in the atmospherically (if sometimes impractically) underlit Archéoforum.

Allow over an hour to do a visit justice.

Église Collégiale St-Barthélemy   CHURCH
(Pl St-Barthélemy; adult/child €2/free; ☉10am-noon & 2-5pm Mon-Sat, 2-5pm Sun) This large Rhenish-style church has twin Saxon-style towers and a cream-and-cerise exterior. It houses a famous 1118 baptismal font that's one of the world's most celebrated pieces of Mosan art.

To glimpse it for free, peer through the long, narrow slit window in the church's western end.

⊙ Guillemins & Around

La Navette Fluviale (p233), the city's inexpensive, multistop river ferry, makes it fun to sail 2km south to the Guillemins district. Alight at the **Guillemins Jetty** (Quai de Rome), admiring from outside the sleek, 118m glass tower **Tour Paradis** (SPF Finances; Rue de Fragnée; ☉visits 8 Sep only) and, from a distance, the remarkable architecture of Santiago Calatrava's 2009 **Liège-Guillemins Station**, its bold white sweeping curves creating the impression of a vast glass-and-concrete manta ray. Then cross the river on a pedestrian bridge into lovely gardens to find the superb art gallery **La Boverie** (www.laboverie.com; Parc de la Boverie; without/with temporary exhibitions €5/12; ☉10am-6pm; ☐26, 31) whose collection includes work by Magritte, Monet, Gauguin, Chagall and Picasso.

Returning towards the centre, consider hopping off the boat at **Pôle Fluviale** (Quai Edouard Van Beneden) and nipping inside the **Institut Zoologique** (aquarium/science museum/combi-ticket €7.50/3.50/9.90; ☉10am-5pm Mon-Fri, to 6pm Sat & Sun Sep-Jun, to 6pm daily Jul & Aug; ☞) to catch a glimpse of its Delvaux mural.

★☆ Festivals & Events

Festival Outremeuse   FIESTA
(☉mid-Aug) A week of raucously drunken celebrations in Outremeuse culminates on 15 August when sermons are read in Walloon dialect, then everyone gets tipsy on *pèkèt* (local gin). Expect firecrackers, puppets, traditional dances, a procession of giants and vast, unruly crowds. From 5pm the next day the surreal cremation and burial of a bone symbolically marks the end of festivities.

A 'mourning' parade shuffles around the Outremeuse district, its brass band interspersing up-tempo carnivalesque music with sombre dirges accompanied by hammy weeping. Hilarious. Dress in black and bring celery!

Nocturne des Coteaux   FIESTA
(www.lanocturnedescoteaux.eu; ☉1st Sat of Oct) Liège comes alive at dusk with 20,000 candles forming beautiful patterns on the vertiginous **Montagne de Bueren**. Some historic buildings open their doors, there are numerous free concerts and at 11.30pm fireworks cap things off.

🛏 Sleeping

Auberge de Jeunesse   HOSTEL €
(☑04-344 56 89; www.lesaubergesdejeunesse. be; Rue Georges Simenon 2; dm/s/d incl breakfast €28/46/68, 10% off for HI members; ☞) Apart from those pesky push-button taps, this is one of Belgium's best-designed HI hostels, a well-run place whose en suite dorms have large in-room lockers (bring your own padlock), plus lamps and USB phone-charging points above each bunk.

★N° 5 Bed & Breakfast   B&B €€
(☑0494-30 58 73; www.n5bednbreakfast.be; Pl St-Barthélemy 5; r €115-135; ☞) This super-elegant and highly original B&B is entered through the gorgeously appointed 18th-century home of the youthful, multilingual owners. This is where you'll get a generous, locally sourced breakfast. The five guest rooms and (free) sauna are in a separate building behind, totally rebuilt from

CRYSTAL CREATIONS

In much of Asia, Belgium's fame relies far less on its beer and chocolate than on its glassware. Nineteenth-century maharajahs loved the stuff, and barely an Indian palace exists that doesn't sport at least a couple of Belgian crystal chandeliers. The most famous name is Val St-Lambert from Seraing (www.val-saint-lambert.com), founded in 1826, with production peaking before WWI. Although some 90% of its lead crystal was sent for export, distinctive two-colour cut-glass pieces remain prized possessions in many a Belgian home. These days, Val St-Lambert still limps on with a **showroom and museum** (Cristal Discovery; ☑ 04-330 36 20; www.cristaldiscovery.be; Esplanade du Val; museum adult/senior/child €12/10/8; ⊙ museum 10am-5pm Tue-Sat, 1-5pm Sun, shop 11am-4.30pm Mon-Fri; 🚐9) at the former monastery site where it's made. However, most such manufacture has shifted to places with lower labour costs, while changing tastes have also posed a challenge for surviving designers. Should you want pieces of classic Belgian glassware, it's ironically often cheaper to buy antique items, especially if you don't need a full set. Some Brussels shops are Val St-Lambert specialists.

the still-visible remnants of a 16th-century half-timbered house.

In between there's ample space to sit outside in a courtyard that's astonishly large for the city-centre location.

Amosa Liège BOUTIQUE HOTEL €€
(☑ 04-331 93 35; www.amosaliege.be; Rue St-Denis 4-6; r €89-169; ❄ 🖥) This obliging, 18-room hotel sits behind a brick-and-stone facade that suggests a sedate town house. Yet you enter to a stylish bar backed by an expansive industrial-chic restaurant with an open kitchen and exposed metal vents in what was once a tram-repair works. In the wooden-floored rooms, curious bedside tap-lamps add to the subtly retro feel.

Hotel Neuvice BOUTIQUE HOTEL €€
(☑ 04-375 97 40; www.hotelneuvice.be; En Neuvice 45; r €99-170; 🖥) A superb conversion of a pair of historic houses, this stylish choice places you right on a characterful alleyway in the heart of central Liège. Service is personable, and rooms have a design quality while retaining the odd original element.

Hôtel Hors Château GUESTHOUSE €€
(☑ 04-250 60 68; www.hors-chateau.be; Rue Hors Château 62; s/d/ste €78/95/125; 🖥) Brilliantly located in the city's historical quarter, with nine rooms that combine contemporary design with bare antique brickwork and old beams. Call ahead to arrange arrival times as reception isn't permanently attended. Breakfast costs €12.

Hôtel Les Acteurs HOTEL €€
(☑ 04-223 00 80; www.lesacteurs.be; Rue des Urbanistes 10; s/d/tw/tr/q from €55/70/74/84/95; 🖥) This basic but personable 16-room hotel

has 24-hour reception in its congenial, inexpensive *café*. En suite toilet-shower booths are tiny in some rooms, very cramped singles lack natural light and 'double' beds are narrow. Nonetheless the triple rooms are generously sized and the overall atmosphere is pleasant. The location is relatively central; breakfast is included.

Pentahôtel Liège HOTEL €€
(☑ 04-221 77 11; www.pentahotels.com; Blvd de la Sauvenière 100; r €100-155; 🅿 ❄ 🖥) Penta have done a miraculous job transforming a ghastly 1960s office building into the city's most fashion-savvy hotel. Arrive at night for the full effect of the Vegas-ready cocktail-bar with Hollywood lamps, candlelit tables, bare-brick wall fragments and at least five disco balls. Bartenders double as receptionists.

Les Comptes de Méan BUSINESS HOTEL €€€
(☑ 04-222 94 94; www.lescomptesdemean.be; Mont St-Martin 9-11; s/d from €146/166, ste €345-470; 🅿 ❄ @ 🖥 ☒; 🚐 53, 61) Two of Liège's finest ridge-top historic town-house mansions combine to front this five-star business hotel. With a castle-like round tower and muralled interior, the Sélys Longchamps section contains eight 'historic suites' and the Selys Restaurant. Over 100 other rooms are discreetly hidden in a new six-storey block descending almost invisibly from a spectacular rooftop bar linked by a cafe-walkway to reception.

Upper rooms have great views but cheaper ones tend to be lower down and only look out at the cliff front.

LOCAL KNOWLEDGE

TCHANTCHÈS

Liège's mascot and oldest 'citizen' is a big-nosed wooden puppet called Tchantchès (pronounced *chan*-chay), supposedly born between cobblestones in the city's 'free' Outremeuse quarter on 15 August 760. His miraculous arrival is an oft-retold humorous tale that's a thinly disguised biblical satire. However, unlike the baby Jesus, Tchantchès has a penchant for getting riotously drunk on *pékèt* (Walloon gin) and head-butting people. Still, beneath such minor flaws, he's good-hearted and much loved, typifying the free spirit of the Liégeois. His 'life story' is retold in thickly accented Walloon-French through puppet shows at the **Musée Tchantchès** (☑04-342 75 75; www.tchantches.be; Rue Surlet 56; show €3.50; ☺shows 10.30am Sun & 2.30pm Wed Oct-Apr, museum 2-4pm Tue & Thu).

On Place St-Lambert kids merrily climb aboard a cartoonesque aeroplane statue piloted by Tchantchès.

Eating

Cafe Lequet
BELGIAN €

(Quay-sur-Meuse; mains €10-19, steak €21-23; ☺noon-2.30pm & 6-9.30 Thu-Tue, closed Sat lunch & Wed) Liège's mascot Tchantchès hangs from a ceiling moulding in this classic panel-walled cafe-restaurant, which remains an utterly authentic locals' place for Liégeois standards including veal kidneys in mustard and shrimp-filled tomatoes.

La Mouette
SANDWICHES €

(Féronstrée 131; meals €4.90-8; ☺10am-7.30pm) Shuttered mirror 'windows', blue-glaze seagulls and skeletal lamps create a surprisingly charming ambience, vaguely like a denuded English teashop but with Sufi-style music adding a mellifluous sense of calm. On paper the food seems forgettable; largely sandwiches, croques and omelettes. But these get a remarkable Turkish-inspired twist and it's the little extras that make any plate memorable.

Pollux
ICE CREAM €

(Pl de la Cathédrale 2; takeaway/eat-in waffles from €2.50/3; ☺10am-6.30pm Mon-Sat) Facing Liège's cathedral, Pollux is the city's classic choice for *gaufres liégeoises* – waffles freshly made while you wait.

★ Maccheroni
ITALIAN €€

(☑04-222 91 99; www.maccheroni.be; Rue St-Paul 5; mains €13-16, 3-course lunch €19, wine from €4.50; ☺10am-6.30pm Mon-Wed, Fri & Sat, to 9pm Thu, kitchen noon-4pm; ✷🎅) At lunchtime this delightfully welcoming little *traiteur* (deli-cafe) serves pasta and antipasto so good that they have customers clamouring for tables around the central open cook-station. Once lunch finishes it turns into a wine bar, with glasses served 'aperitivo' style with a delicious tapas-sized mini-dish included in the price.

★ Amon Nanesse
BELGIAN €€

(La Maison du Pékèt; ☑04-250 67 83; www.maison dupeket.be; Rue de l'Épée 4; mains €14-22.50; ☺noon-2pm & 6-10pm, bar 11am-2am; 🎅) Just behind Place du Marché, this rambling antique house with bare-brick walls and heavy beams combines a lively bar specialising in *pékèt* (gin) shots (€3.50) with a restaurant serving satisfying local pub meals including *boulettes a la liégeoise* (meatballs in raisin-sweetened gravy).

They have *café liégeois* (coffee and ice-cream sweet) for dessert.

Restaurant La Cène
BELGIAN €€

(☑04-343 10 38; www.lacene.be/en; Rue Henri de Dinant 17; mains €14-26; ☺11.30am-2pm Mon-Fri & 6-10pm Wed-Sat) Outremeuse's most appealing dining option, this classical-style bistro proudly displays its menu of Liégeois and Belgian classics across its windows in white handwriting. The plentiful terrace tables are partly shaded by trees.

Labo4
FRENCH €€

(☑0474 09 09 39; www.lelabo4.be/en; Quai Edouard Van Beneden 20; starters/mains €17/22, 3-course menu €38; ☺noon-2pm Sun-Fri & 7-10pm daily) Seeking some special chemistry at dinner? Here they take the idea quite literally, seating you between the test tubes and unchanged 1960s wooden workstations of a former university laboratory. French food comes in set menus and can be a little hit and miss, with service sometimes slow, but the setting is unforgettable.

It's tucked away in the grounds of the Institut Zoologique (p228), accessed from beside the building's south flank.

Como en Casa
VEGETARIAN €€

(http://comoencasa.be; Rue de la Poule; dishes €10-14; ☺7-10pm Tue-Sat & noon-2.30pm Thu & Fri; ☑) The concept in this spacious, slightly classroom-like space is to order around five small dishes to share between two. Menus change regularly to use the freshest local ingredients, of which much is vegan and all vegetarian – even their Liège *boulet* (meatball). The organic red house wine is excellent.

Chez Nathalie   FRENCH €€

(☑04-222 16 57; Rue de la Goffe 12; mains €13-25; ☺6.30-9.30pm Tue-Sat) Decorated with gilt-framed mirrors, copper pots and gingham tablecloths, this lovable spot could audition for the role of bistro in any mid-20th-century French movie. The food follows similar lines, including southern mainstays like cassoulet and scampi *fricassée*, all served with warm, motherly attention.

As Ouhès   BELGIAN €€

(☑04-223 32 25; www.as-ouhes.be; Pl du Marché 21; mains €15-25; ☺noon-2.30pm & 6-10.30pm) One of many jolly cafe-restaurants whose ever-busy terraces line Place du Marché, As Ouhès ('Aux Oisseaux' in Walloon) gives itself a slightly more upmarket feel by half-covering the zinc-topped tables with starched tablecloth strips. It offers authentic Walloon specialities including kidneys flambéed in *pékèt*, and delicious *lapin aux pruneaux* (thick beer-and-prune sauce on large pieces of rabbit). Mussels are available in season (€24).

🍷 Drinking & Nightlife

★ Le Pot au Lait   PUB

(www.potaulait.be; Rue Soeurs de Hasque; ☺10am-4am Mon-Fri, noon-4am Sat & Sun; 🛜) Liège's wackiest pub-*café* lurks down a private cul-de-sac decorated with psychedelic murals and lamps resembling radioactive triffids. Watch UFOs landing while lobsters wear dentures and mannequins show off their scars in a colour-overloaded masterpiece. There's regular live music too: it's an alternative classic.

Accattone   COFFEE

(☑04-340 03 63; www.accattonecaffe.be; Blvd Saucy 13; ☺9am-3pm Mon-Fri, 6-10pm Wed-Thu; 🛜) Outremeuse is the antithesis of all things hipster, right? Not if Accattone can help it, with great coffee (from €1.80), breakfasts and wine-and-pasta lunches (wine from €4.50, pasta €11) served in a converted cornershop with contemporary art on the back wall and a lamp fashioned from a newspapered mannequin.

Aux Olivettes   PUB

(☑0496 34 65 69; www.auxolivettes.be; Rue du Pont des Arches 6; ☺9pm-3am Fri & Sat, 11am-5pm Sun, lunchtime meals Tue-Sat) In the days of Jacques Brel *cafés chantants* were common – simple pubs where crooner, pianist and accordionist sang for their beer. Today Aux Olivettes is a very rare, authentic survivor, its *pékèt*-supping audience even more geriatric than the performers. No cover, expect plenty of interaction.

Fragrances   TEAHOUSE

(En Neuvice 56; ☺10am-6pm Mon-Fri, 10am-3pm Sun) The name of this gorgeous-smelling little shop-cafe is very apt, with its teapots, marmalades, strainers, tea cosies and around 350 types of tea. Little has changed since 1932, but it does now squeeze in four minuscule tables.

If you order a cup of coffee (€2), it comes with a veritable feast of extras: a mini side of Chantilly (with spoon), a choc-truffle and a handful of chocolate-coated coffee beans. Wow.

Brasserie {c}   BREWERY

(☑04-266 06 92; www.brasseriec.com; Impasse des Ursulines; ☺5pm-late Thu & Fri, from 2pm Sat, 2-8pm Sun) A tasting room for Liège's exciting new brewery whose products are already causing a stir, notably the refreshing Curtius wheat beer and the excellent IPA-style Smash.

La Cour St-Jean   PUB

(www.lacourstjean.be; Rue St-Jean-en-Isle 23; ☺11am-6am Mon-Fri, 2pm-6am Sat, 7pm-6am Sun; 🛜) In the heart of the youth-jammed nightlife zone, this popular little pub has genuinely ancient rough-stone walls painted lugubrious red and black, all a-flicker with candles as though in a medieval dungeon.

Beer Lovers   BAR

(www.beer-lovers.be; Rue de la Violette 9; ☺3pm-1am Tue, noon-1am Wed-Sat, to 11pm Sun) Brewery signs, high ceilings and the odd exposed beam contrast with a contemporary serving station, but the big draw here is the remarkable range of Belgian draught beers, which are served in 20cL taster glasses (€2.70) so you can work your way through a goodly selection.

Café Le Petit Bougnat   BAR

(Rue Roture 17; ☺5pm-late Tue-Sun) A wonderfully genuine local rustic *café* with rough floors, candles in bottles and the perfect

SUNDAY IN LIÈGE

To dig into down-to-earth Liégeois culture, head to Outremeuse. If you can't make it for the August mayhem of Festival Outremeuse (p228), come on a Sunday. Start at 10.30am (October to April only) with a folkloric puppet show at Musée Tchantchès (p230), snack your way round the big **La Batte Weekly Market** (Quay de la Ribuée; ⊘ 8am-2.30pm Sun), and catch the locals singing their hearts out at one-off *café chantant* Aux Olivettes (p231). Then ramp up the music with a live mini-gig at little **Lou's Bar** (Rue de la Boucherie 25; ⊘ noon-midnight Mon-Thu, noon-3am Fri, 4pm-3am Sat, 11am-8pm Sun) or utterly down-market Outremeuse haunt **Les Clémantines**, where crowd-watching can be as entertaining as the old-timer band's enthusiastic guitar squeals.

terrace on Outremeuse's sweetest square. Expect mayhem all around here during the Festival Outremeuse (p228).

☆ Entertainment

Le Forum CONCERT VENUE
(www.leforum.be; Rue Pont d'Avroy) Le Forum is a splendidly restored 1921 art deco masterpiece of a theatre that hosts larger-scale concerts, notably with French superstar singers from Sylvie Vartan and Étienne Daho to Francis Cabrel.

**Opéra Royal
de Wallonie** OPERA
(☑ 04-221 47 22; www.operaliege.be; Rue des Dominicains 1; ⊘ box office noon-6pm Mon-Sat) One of Liège's most prominent central buildings, the opera house contains a breathtaking, multilevelled classical-style auditorium.

🛍 Shopping

For interesting small shops and local workshops, look along the cute little medieval alley En Neuvice. Mainstream shops fill the big central Galeries Saint-Lambert.

★ Benoit Nihant CHOCOLATE
(www.benoitnihant.be; Passage Lemonnier 2; ⊘ 10am-6pm Mon-Sat) This Belgian family business makes fabulous chocolates from cocoa that they grow, roast and grind themselves on antique equipment (apparently newer machines aren't as good). Yes, they're expensive but a box of 20 pralines (€17.90) goes further than you'd expect.

Go next door to **Le Bar À Cacao** (Passage Lemonnier 40; ⊘ 8am-6pm Mon-Fri, to 6.30pm Sat) to order a coffee and you'll get two free mini-pralines as accompaniment.

Wattitude GIFTS & SOUVENIRS
(☑ 04-250 08 72; www.wattitude.be; Rue Souverain-Pont 19; ⊘ 10.30am-6pm Tue-Sat) A showcase for products made in Wallonia? *Non mais oui!* Local beers are included *bien sûre* but also honey-based cosmetics, chocolate moustaches, artisanal soaps, foodboards from recycled timber and numerous self-mockingly humorous badges – *trop is te veel!*

Vaudrée FOOD & DRINKS
(www.vaudree.be; Rue St-Gilles 79; ⊘ 10am-6pm Mon-Fri, to 7pm Sat, noon-6pm Sun) Vaudrée is one of the best-stocked beer shops in Liège (they also sell online through www.beerlovers.be).

ℹ Information

Visitez Liège (☑ 04-221 92 21; www.visitez liege.be; Quai de la Goffe 13; ⊘ 9am-6pm Jun-Sep, to 5pm Oct-May) Tourist office with bike rental, free maps and useful themed guide pamphlets.

There's a branch at Liège-Guillemins station.

In Dutch, website www.liegetown.be is a superb resource.

ℹ Getting There & Away

BUS

The **international bus stop** (Rue Bovy), where FlixBus, Eurolines and IC Bus services leave from, is a small parking area three minutes' walk southeast of Liège-Guillemins train station.

Buses to the surrounding area often serve Liège-Guillemins too, but it's generally more convenient to find the correct one of four main starting points in the centre:

Gare Léopold (Rue Léopold) Route 67 for Blégny Mine (though not all 67s go that far).

Opera Routes 9 to Huy, 27 to Seraing, 65 to Remouchamps and 377 to Esneux.

Place de la République Française Route 2 to Seraing.

Place St-Lambert Most other routes.

TRAIN

Long-distance trains arrive 2km south of the centre at dazzling Liège-Guillemins station. Switch onto a local train to reach Liège-Palais for the city centre.

From Liège-Guillemins, destinations include the following:

Aachen (€26 to €29, 22 minutes) High-speed trains. Or use local services (€9.60 to €15.60, 55 minutes) with a change in Welkenraedt.

Brussels (€15.50, one hour) Half-hourly via Leuven (€11.30, 30 minutes).

Cologne (Thalys/ICE €39/31, one hour, hourly) Prebook.

Frankfurt (€66 to €82, 2¼ hours, four direct daily) Prebook.

Luxembourg City (print-at-home/station ticket €33/39, 2½ hours, every second hour)

Maastricht (e-ticket/station ticket €5.80/11.80, 33 minutes, hourly)

Namur (€9.30, 45 to 55 minutes, twice hourly)

⊙ Getting Around

BICYCLE

Hourly/daily bike rental is possible through the tourist office (two hours/one day €6/12), and for longer periods from **Pro Velo** (☑ 04-222 99 54; www.provelo.org; Pl des Guillemins 2; per 24hr/week €14/56; ⊙ 1-6pm Mon, 7am-noon & 1-6pm Tue-Fri) at Liège-Guillemins train station: turn left as you exit at ground level. Both require €50 deposits.

BOAT

Transforming the Liège tourist experience, **La Navette Fluviale** (River Ferry; www.navette-fluviale.be; per stop €1; ⊙ 10am-5pm Tue-Sun May, Jun & Sep, daily Jul & Aug, Sat & Sun only Apr & Oct) is an hourly river-ferry that allows you to cruise delightfully between most of the main museums. It's most useful for accessing La Boverie, which is across a new footbridge from the **Guillemins Jetty** (p228). Getting here costs just €1 from either **Pôle Fluviale** (p228) beside Institut Zoologique or more central **Centre-Ville** (Quai Sur-Meuse) beside the impressive neo-Gothic former post office. You'll pay €2 from the **Cœur Historique Jetty** (Quai Godefroid Kurth), which is just across the river from Grand Curtius.

BUS

Bus 1 and bus 4 (which does a useful circuit) link the city with Liège-Guillemins (stop A). Tickets cost €2.50 or buy a €4.30 all-day travel pass from **Espace TEC** (☑ 04-361 94 44; www.infotec.be; Pl St-Lambert; ⊙ 8am-6.30pm Mon-Fri, 9am-1pm Sat) on central Place St-Lambert or at Liège-Guillemins (between platforms 3 and 4).

Verviers

☑ 087 / POP 55,070

Nestled in the steep-cut Vesdre River valley 20km east of Liège, the former wool-processing city of Verviers is a little off the tourist radar but has plenty of charm. There's a superb chocolate museum, the area's best blues-rock venue, lots of riverside dining and several patchily genteel neighbourhoods with some impressive B&Bs. These make Verviers a fine base for those with their own vehicle wishing to visit the Hautes Fagnes, Limbourg, Spa, Blégny Mine and the Val-Dieu abbey complex.

⊙ Sights

★**La Chocolaterie Darcis**   FACTORY
(Jean-Philippe Darcis; ☑ 087 71 72 73; www.darcis.com/chocolaterie; Esplanade de la Grâce 1; museum adult/child €8/6; ⊙ museum 9am-4.30pm Tue-Sat, 1-4.30pm Sun, cafe to 5.30pm, shop to 6pm) Playing a 21st-century Willy Wonka, one of Belgium's foremost *chocolatiers* has turned his modern factory into a superb interactive museum experience. Walk through a Mayan temple, get seasick on Hernán Cortés' galleon and visit a 19th-century cocoa parlour, before sniff tests, quizzes, a 10-minute video tour of Mexican plantations and explanations of modern chocolate making.

Allow at least an hour to do justice to all the information and complementary podcatcher audios. Wait until you're instructed before savouring the three sublime taster pralines. Even if you don't have time to visit the museum, the attached cafe is a place worth lingering over marvellous coffee, hot chocolate, cakes, pastries or one of Jean-Philippe Darcis' signature macarons.

**Centre Touristique de la
Laine et de la Mode**   MUSEUM
(☑ 087 30 79 20; www.aqualaine.be; Rue de la Chapelle 30; adult/concession/child €6/5/4; ⊙ 10am-5pm Tue-Sun) This impressive three-part museum occupies an 1803 former mill dating from Verviers' heyday as an international wool-processing centre. The 2nd floor displays well-preserved industrial equipment, and there's a history of cloth and clothing from neolithic furs via Crusader capes to 1930s garter belts, all extensively explained through a four-language audio guide.

Changing exhibitions in the beamed eaves are often excellent and relevant to the city's history.

WORTH A TRIP

RURAL DISCOVERIES AROUND LIÈGE

If you're driving, a very satisfying day trip from Liège or Verviers combines a visit to Blégny Mine with lunch at Val-Dieu abbey then continues to lovely Limbourg.

Blégny Mine (☑04-387 43 33; www.blegnymine.be; Rue Lambert Marlet 23, Trembleur; mine adult/senior/child €12.50/10.80/8.70; ⊘tours 11am, 11.30am, 1.30pm, 2pm, 3.30pm & 4pm Apr–early Sep, 6 extra tours Jul & Aug, Sat & Sun only mid-Feb–Mar & Sep-Nov) For one of the best industrial-experience tours you'll find anywhere, don a hard hat, jump in the cage lift and descend through a pitch-black moment into the underground life of a 20th-century Belgian miner at this Unesco-listed coal mine.

The two-hour guided subterranean tours run three to seven times daily in French, and almost as often in Dutch, but in English only by group reservation (minimum 15 people). A 20-minute film (English subtitles) and mining museum provide extra context.

Val-Dieu (☑087 69 28 28; www.abbaye-du-val-dieu.be/en; Val Dieu 227, Aubel; ⊘park 24hr) Iridescent dragonflies dart and hover over Monet-worthy lake scenes in the gloriously landscaped parkland of this historic rural abbey complex, dotted with inspirational Bible quotes in four languages. The complex is still an active Cistercian monastery with an excellent brewery whose beers you can taste in the popular cafe-restaurant.

Founded in 1216, the neo-Gothic basilica dates from an 1885 rebuild and is free to enter. The site is in very pretty rolling countryside around 15km north of Verviers.

Limbourg Well worth the 1km detour if you're driving between Eupen and Verviers (turn south at Dolhain), Limbourg is one of Belgium's most delightful historic villages.

It is raised on a promontory with a long, roughly cobbled central square lined by picturesque houses including a superb old-world brasserie-cafe facing the former town hall, which now hosts an art gallery featuring a model of medieval Limbourg as it looked when it was a fully fortified citadel.

Place du Marché ARCHITECTURE
Verviers's most attractive square is dominated by a stately town hall, with cobbled Mont du Moulin descending photogenically past ivy-draped and half-timbered buildings to the north. A road sign points incongruously to Bradford (775km) and other traditional textile towns. Markets are held here on Saturday mornings.

Musée des Beaux-Arts et de la Céramique GALLERY
(☑087 33 16 95; http://musees.verviers.be; Rue Renier 17; adult/concession/child €2/1/free; ⊘2-5pm Mon, Wed & Sat, 3-6pm Sun) If you can catch it open, pop in to see this small but high-quality collection of 14th- to 19th-century paintings and remarkable ceramics. Entry is free to all on weekends.

🛏 Sleeping

★**La Villa Sauvage** B&B €€
(☑0476 96 00 23, 087 63 22 57; www.lavillasauvage.be; Rue Francomont 2; d/ste €95/145; P⊛) In a tranquil if offbeat corner of outer Verviers, this palatially elegant yet unstuffy mansion is brimming with creativity and set in a large studio-garden with a giant 'tree nest'. Three regally spacious guest rooms offer a truly memorable B&B experience, where every detail has been carefully considered with philosophy and artistry yet a lightness of spirit.

Au Clair Obscur B&B €€
(☑087 23 22 21; www.auclairobscur.be; Pl Albert 1er 5; r €85-135; ☑706) In one of the most splendid mansions of Verviers' inner southern suburbs, four large, immaculate guest rooms with wooden floors and corner baths sit above a stylishly indulgent restaurant.

Hôtel des Ardennes HOTEL €€
(☑087 22 39 25; www.hotelverviers.com; Pl de la Victoire 15; d €70, s without bathroom €45; ⊘closed early Jul; P⊛) Handily close to Verviers-Central train station, this attractive little 1896 brasserie has nine inexpensive but tidily renovated rooms with coffee machines and slightly busy decor. Check in before 7pm.

🍴 Eating & Drinking

Verviers offers some excellent-value dining, though speaking some French will help a lot. For a good selection of reliable eateries, stroll the north bank of the Vesdre at Rue Jules Cerexhe, where many restaurants have wide terraces. Surrounded by terrace cafes, Place du Martyr is the epicentre of Vervier's bar scene. The cafe of La Choclaterie (p233) is an ideal place for superb coffee and a divine Darcis raspberry macaron.

★ **Le Patch**   BELGIAN €€
(📞 087 22 45 39; www.lepatch.be; Chaussée de Heusy 173; mains €13.50-25; ☉ noon-2.30pm Tue-Fri & 6.30-9.30pm Tue-Sat) Appetising aromas of fried garlic intermingle with jazzy music, dangling creepers and a ceiling hung with cookery utensils to create a multisensory treat in this inviting delight. The menu concentrates on beautifully prepared salads, pastas and Walloon classics: the sauce of their home-style *rognons* (veal kidneys) is as good as any you're likely to taste anywhere in Belgium.

The inner-garden seating is particularly popular on summer evenings.

Au Vieux Cerexhe   BELGIAN €€
(📞 087 33 78 49; www.auvieuxcerexhe.be; Rue Jules Cerexhe 84; mains €12.50-28.50; ☉ 11.30am-3pm Tue-Fri, 6-9.30pm Tue-Sun) One of the best in a strip of appealing brasserie-restaurants set just back from the Vesdre River's north bank, this atmospheric place covers the typical Belgian culinary bases along with standard steaks and various salads.

La Seigneurie   INTERNATIONAL €€
(📞 087 33 48 05; Pont St-Laurent 11; mains €15-24; ☉ noon-2pm & 6-10pm; 🖥) Like a culinary metaphor for Verviers population, La Seigneurie's menu is a slightly discordant mixture of Belgian, North African and Mediterranean. The dining room's daring monocoloured panels are set off by a jigglingly delicate centrepiece lamp to create a modish interior, and there's a very popular summer street terrace.

Georges Café   PUB
(Pl du Martyr; ☉ 10am-late) With 13 brews on tap, a quirky interior with seats that look like old tram benches, a large terrace and cosy rear garden-yard, Georges is the most appealing beer-pub in central Verviers.

☆ Entertainment

Spirit of 66   LIVE MUSIC
(📞 087 35 24 24; www.spiritof66.be; Pl du Martyr 16) One of Belgium's foremost venues for blues-rock gigs, Spirit of 66 also has a knack for

finding and re-presenting half-forgotten former greats whose star powers have waned.

From October to mid-June there's usually a concert every two or three days but things go quiet in summer.

ℹ Information

Maison du Tourisme (📞 087 30 79 26; www.paysdevesdre.be; Rue Jules Cerexhe 86; ☉ 9am-5pm Apr-Oct, closed Mon Nov-Mar; 🖥) In an attractive river-facing town house amid the restaurants of Rue Jules Cerexhe, the tourist office has some very useful free pamphlet-guides and numerous discount coupons for the region's attractions. There's free wi-fi and a video explaining why Verviers is the 'City of Water'.

ℹ Getting There & Away

Services from Verviers-Central train/bus station (500m west of central Place Verte) include the following:

Botrange Nature Centre Elsenborn/Rocherath-bound bus 390 (€3.50, 30 minutes, three to five daily).

Stavelot Bus 294 (€3.50, five to seven daily) via Malmédy.

Aachen, Germany Hourly stopping train (e-ticket/at-station ticket €6.20/12.20, 30 minutes).

Liège-Guillemins Fast trains twice hourly (€4.40, 18 to 24 minutes) plus one slow train (37 minutes), continuing to Liège-Palais (44 minutes).

Spa Hourly train (€3.30, 28 minutes).

Some local trains stop additionally at marginally more central Verviers-Palais.

Spa
POP 10,370

One of Europe's classic health resorts, Spa is *the* original spa from which the English word derives. The healing properties of Spa's spring waters were recognised as far back as the 1st century AD. Henry VIII of England, in need of a relaxing 16th-century bath after occupying Tournai, praised the waters' curative powers. By the 18th century, Spa had become a luxurious retreat for European royalty and intellectuals. Tsars, politicians and writers including Victor Hugo and Alexandre Dumas came to what became nicknamed the 'Café of Europe'. In the later 19th century its popularity waned, but it has seen a significant rejuvenation since the 2005 opening of the sparkling new Thermes de Spa complex on a hilltop directly above town.

WALLONIA SPA

SPA-FRANCORCHAMPS GRAND-PRIX CIRCUIT

Circuit Spa-Francorchamps (www.spa-francorchamps.be; Rte du Circuit 55; ☺mid-Mar–mid-Nov) is a world-class motor-racing circuit. It hosts Belgium's Formula 1 Grand Prix, and has been cited as many F1 drivers' favourite, but throughout the season there are also many lower-profile races and events, some of them free.

Set in hilly part-woodland, the contoured course includes a dramatic 150-degree bend near the main paddock, 500m west of Francorchamps village (between Spa and Stavelot). Be aware that hotels throughout the region book out way in advance for the Formula 1 race in August, when traffic can be gridlocked as far away as Liège.

The precious mineral water is still bottled on an industrial scale at **Spa Monopole** (☐087 79 41 11; www.spa.be/fr/eaudyssee; Rue Auge Laporte 34; adult/concession/child €5/4/2.50; ☺9.30am-12.30pm & 1.30-4.30pm Mon-Fri) behind the station.

⊙ Sights & Activities

★ Thermes de Spa   SPA
(☐087 77 25 60; www.thermesdespa.com; Colline d'Annette et Lubin; for 3hr adult/child €20/15; ☺10am-9pm Mon-Fri, to 10pm Sat, to 8pm Sun) Directly above the town centre and accessed by a short, steep €1.50 funicular ride, Spa's excellent main spa is a vast modern complex of well-designed spring-water pools, jet baths, saunas and hammams covering 800 sq metres. There are also fine views. The basic three-hour slot is timed on a waterproof smart-wristband on which you can charge any extras (snacks, drinks, towels etc).

Consider bringing your own towels unless you're having a massage or other treatment that costs extra but includes gowns, drinks and some snacks (eg apples). An hour's full-body massage costs €85. Among the more unusual speciality baths here is the *bain de tourbe* (€44) in which those suffering from arthritis are soothed by being immersed in hot, hydrated peat.

As well as funicular access there's a zigzag path through the woods from town, but by car the road is very circuitous and there's a minimum €2 parking charge at the site.

Casino   HISTORIC BUILDING
(☐087 77 20 52; www.casinodespa.be; Rue Royale 4; ☺11am-4am Sun-Thu, to 5am Fri & Sat) Spa had the 'world's first' casino in 1763, and the 19th-century incarnation here now forms part of a grand central trio of neoclassical buildings, along with the 1862 bathhouse (not currently in use) and the 1908 Exhibition Halls.

Entry is free to gamble or simply to admire the casino's muralled ceilings, but you'll need to be over 21 years of age and have your passport handy. The most elegant upstairs rooms are rarely in use but when they are, access is via a stairway passing a 1939 antique fruit machine.

Parc de Sept Heures   PARK
With a picturesque Léopold II–era pavilion and a wrought-iron marketplace hosting Sunday morning flea markets, this charming park also features minigolf, *pétanque* and €5 pony rides in summer.

Spa Story   MUSEUM
(Villa Royale Marie-Henriette; Ave Reine Astrid 77; adult/senior/child €4/3/1; ☺2-6pm Mar–mid-Nov) In a 1862 Napoleon III–style building 300m west of Spa's casino, the small but engaging Spa Story museum charts the town's history while looking at the evolution over time of *jolités* (the lacquered souvenir boxes of water-cure accoutrements once sold to spa-goers). Summaries are in English.

At weekends you can also visit the stables section containing a series of horsey exhibits and an old forge. The building itself is interesting: while Belgium's King Léopold II was playing colonial domination in Congo, his feisty Hungarian-born queen stayed here in what was then an exclusive hotel, avoiding the boredom of Brussels by riding her horses across the Ardennes.

Pouhon
Pierre-le-Grand   ARCHITECTURE
(☐087 79 53 53; www.spatourisme.be; Rue du Marché 1a; ☺10am-6pm Apr-Sep, to 5pm Oct-Mar) The restored, octagonal-fronted stone building hosting the tourist office was the site of Spa's original springs. It was renamed for Russian tsar Peter the Great, whose visit to Spa in 1717 helped popularise the resort. Buy a jetton for €1 to taste the waters from modernist fountain taps or pay €8 to enter a rich if somewhat spurious exhibition of Joan Miró lithographs in an attractive old hall.

Musée de la Lessive   MUSEUM
(📞 0494 17 14 61; Rue Hanster 10; adult/child €4/1; ⏱ 2-6pm Sun Sep-Jun, daily Jul & Aug) This lovably off-beat little museum fills the banal classrooms of a 1960s former primary school with a hotchpotch of old flat irons, linens, washing machines and soap-powder boxes in plotting an unsophisticated history of laundry.

🛏 Sleeping & Eating

Spa's numerous hotels are dotted around town and in the countryside nearby. They tend to be busiest in summer and on Saturday nights. Several better properties offer guest discounts (of around 10%) for the Thermes de Spa complex and lend special towels and dressing gowns.

Little Spa punches above its weight for upper-market dining choices but prices tend to be high for cafe food, making the central Carrefour Express mini-supermarket a useful standby for those on a budget.

⭐ **Villa des Fleurs**   BOUTIQUE HOTEL €€
(📞 087 79 50 50; www.villadesfleurs.be; Rue Albin Body 31; r €109-169; 🅿🛜) Glass doors glide open to reveal fine gilt-framed paintings and trickling wall fountains in this intimate Napoleon III-style villa. Complete with coffee machines and minibars, most of the 12 elegant rooms are very spacious, with original marble fireplaces and new, semi-classically styled furniture. There's a quiet guest lounge, mini-library and attractive garden with sun loungers and statuary.

Service is personal and highly obliging. Dressing gowns and towels are available for those heading to the Thermes de Spa, for which a discount entry ticket (€18) is available to guests. Sunday-night bargain rates can drop as low as €89, including breakfast.

Radisson Blu Palace Hôtel   HOTEL €€€
(📞 087 27 97 00; www.radissonblu.com; Pl Royale 39; midweek s/d/ste €129/149/199, weekend €179/199/269; 🅿🛜) Rendered stylishly contemporary by a 2017 refit, this immaculate 120-bed property is the obvious choice for spa-goers, with discounted day rates at the Thermes de Spa and a dedicated funicular car so you can get there in your dressing gown.

The on-site sauna and fitness facilities are free to guests; underground parking costs €18. Confusingly, Spa also has a second Radisson Blu, the manorial-style Balmoral 2km east.

A Table   SANDWICHES €
(📞 087 22 59 23; www.atablespa.be; Rue Delhasse 24; sandwiches €3.90-6.50, salads €8.50-10.50; ⏱ 11am-2.30pm Tue, Thu, Fri, to 5pm Wed & Sat) In summer, this central yet relatively peaceful, fountain-facing terrace is an ideal lunch spot for freshly made sandwiches and healthy plates of salad. The modern, smallish interior is behind a classic facade with half-timbered side walls.

It also opens Sundays until 5pm during holiday periods. Cakes and drinks only after 4pm.

⭐ **L'O de Source**   EUROPEAN €€€
(📞 087 22 11 39; www.lodesource.be; Pl Pierre Le Grand 2; 2-course lunch €26, 2/3/4/5 courses €33/37/48/55; ⏱ 7-9pm Tue, noon-2pm & 7-9pm Wed-Sat) Putting their energies into superb, refined food rather than fussy decor, L'O de Source offers a very short menu of gourmet offerings in a paired-back but modern interior within a 1775 mansion close to the tourist office.

ℹ Information

The tourist office is within the **Pouhon Pierre-le-Grand**.

ℹ Getting There & Away

Hourly trains run towards Aachen (Germany) via Verviers-Central (€3.30, 30 minutes) and Theux (€2.30, 10 minutes), which has a medieval castle. For Liège (€5.30, 55 minutes) change trains in Pepinster.

Coo

POP 300

In the 18th century, monks from nearby Stavelot's abbey created an oxbow lake on the Amblève by digging a short-cut river channel at the tiny hamlet of Coo (pronounced 'Koe'). Cascading 15m, this forms Belgium's tallest 'waterfall'. It's no Niagara, but cupped in a pretty woodland valley, the scene is charming at dusk once the hordes of amusement-park day trippers have gone home. Coo is also a usefully accessible starting point for all manner of outdoors activities.

🏂 Activities

Coo Adventure   ADVENTURE SPORTS
(📞 080 68 91 33; www.coo-adventure.com; Petit-Coo 4; ⏱ 9am-6pm) This multilingual outfit offers numerous activities including mountain-bike rental, kayaking, shooting, abseiling, archery,

BOATING UNDERGROUND AT REMOUCHAMPS

Between Aywaille and Coo, just off the E25 highway, the **Grottes du Remouchamps** (☏04-360 90 70; www.mondesauvage.be; Rue de Louveigné 3; adult/child €14/9; ☻10am-5.30pm Feb-Nov, holidays only Dec & Jan; ⌨65, 142) cave system might lack the dramatic depth of Rochefort's or the great stalactites of Han's. However, the 75-minute tours have the cachée of culminating in a remarkable 700m punt down a half-lit subterranean river: Europe's longest underground boat ride.

Mind your head and dress for 12°C (53.6°F) temperatures and dripping water: nothing too smart as you'll descend a narrow 1912 spiral staircase that can be a little muddy.

Tours run at least every hour at quiet times, and much more often at peak periods, though if there are big crowds there can be queues. If so, buy your ticket then repair for lunch to the tree-shaded terrace-restaurant of **Hôtel Bonhomme** (☏04-384 40 06; www.hotelbonhomme.be; Rue de la Reffe 26; lunch dishes €9-20, dinner mains €23-29, menus €37-56; ☻kitchen noon-2.30pm & 6.30-9pm; ☎), a nostalgically old-fashioned post hotel dating from 1768, for superb salads, croquettes, trout or seafood dishes.

Bus 65 from the Opera bus stop in Liège runs to Remouchamps (€3.50, one hour) 10 to 12 times daily. Bus 142 to Coo (€3.50, 30 minutes) is much less frequent.

zip-lining, caving, quad-biking and 'dropping', an orienteering exercise where you're dumped at a random location with a map (€10, minimum eight participants). An hourly tourist train visits a nearby game park (adult/child €7.50/4).

Plopsa Coo   AMUSEMENT PARK
(☏080 68 42 65; www.plopsacoo.be; Coo 4; per person over/under 1m €26/11, under 85cm free; ☻10.30am-5pm Thu-Sun May & Jun, daily Jul & Aug, Sat & Sun only Apr, Sep & Oct; ⓟ) Set amid pretty forests close to Coo's 'waterfall', this midsized amusement park has two roller coasters, a high spin-tower ('Mega-Mindy'), a dry bobsleigh and a labyrinth among around 20 attractions that are carefully graded for children and toddlers by height.

An advantage for families is that while grandma or grandad can watch the kids here (adults over 70 pay just €11), parents and teenagers can nip across the way to Coo Adventure (p237) for a whole series of adrenaline-filled activities.

🛏 Sleeping & Drinking

The's a basic hotel, campground and several rental houses in central Coo but better choices are at little La Gleize (4km) or in much bigger Stavelot (7km).

Le Coffee Ride   COFFEE
(www.lecoffeeride.cc; Ave Pierre Clerdent 14; ☻noon-8pm Fri, 10am-8pm Sat, 10am-6pm Sun, opens daily during holidays) Cool decor, great coffee (from €2) and suggestions for cycling fanatics; located just above Coo train station.

❶ Getting There & Around

Coo's train station is on the Liège–Luxembourg line with trains every two hours. Bus 142 runs to Remouchamps two to six times daily (€3.50, 30 minutes).

Parking costs €10 at Plopsaland's main car park but only €1/5 per hour/day in the village, from where you can easily walk to the amusement park in less than five minutes.

Stavelot
POP 7140

Set amid gentle slopes with appealing glimpses of surrounding lush green hills, little Stavelot is the Amblève Valley's most attractive and historic town. Its turbulent history long revolved around the scheming prince-abbots, rulers of the territory of Stavelot-Malmédy, which enjoyed long periods of virtual independence – much like Liège. Architecturally, Stavelot offers a lovable mix of grey-stone, tile-fronted and half-timbered 18th-century houses on the narrow lanes around its cobblestoned central square.

⊙ Sights

Abbaye de Stavelot   MUSEUM
(☏080 88 08 78; www.abbayedestavelot.be; Cour de l'Abbaye 1; incl temporary exhibition adult/concession €9.50/8; ☻10am-6pm) The once-gigantic church of the Stavelot-Malmédy prince-abbots was destroyed in the aftermath of the French Revolution. But behind the archaeological fragments that remain is

a similarly large abbey building painted a vibrant crab-red. Its museums, videos and audio guide introduce the historical intrigues of the former principality. There's also an interesting series of temporary exhibitions and an impressive collection of racing cars and motorbikes illustrating 100 years of motor racing – not so strange, given the proximity of the Circuit Spa-Francorchamps (p236).

Upstairs, a sub-museum celebrates (though with somewhat insufficient explanation) Guillaume Apollinaire (1880–1919), the French poet, art critic and champion of Picasso. Youthful Apollinaire summered in Stavelot one year while his mum gambled in Spa. Presumably she lost, as they slipped away without paying their hotel bill.

Led by a detailed audio guide (English available) the overall experience is pleasant, if a little disjointed. There's a fine gift shop and cafe with extra seating in the open courtyard.

Eglise Saint-Sébastien CHURCH
(📞0474 08 65 25; Pl du Vinâve 16; ⏰2-6pm Thu-Sun Jul-Sep) Behind a slightly shabby facade, this 1754 baroque church contains the truly magnificent sarcophagus of St-Remacle, a 1268 masterpiece of gilded metalwork containing the relics of Stavelot Abbey's founder, who had already been dead for 600 years before the casket's fabrication.

✰✰ Festivals & Events

Laetare CARNIVAL
(www.laetare-stavelot.be) One of eastern Wallonia's most celebrated pageants, Laetare is one of the last festivals in Belgium's busy Lenten calendar, and is held three Sundays before Easter. The stars of the show are the eerie 'Blancs Moussis', who wear distinctive masks like sneering, blank-eyed Pinocchios.

These disguises reputedly date back to the 16th century when the prince-abbot forbade local monks from taking part in the town's festivities.

🛏 Sleeping

Camping de Challes CAMPGROUND €
(📞080 86 23 31, 0476 33 91 34; Rte de Challes 5; sites per adult/child/tent/car/caravan €6/2.50/2.50/2.50/5; ⏰Apr-Oct; 🅿) About 1.5km east of Stavelot in a lovely meadow by the river, this simple, family-run campground feels like a private garden, with plenty of trees providing shade.

★Bel Natura B&B €€
(📞0476 49 37 40; www.belnatura.be; Ave Ferdinand Nicolay 18; s/d €72/80; 🅿🖥) Behind an upmarket Italian grocery, this fabulous 1869 tannery-owner's mansion has six vast, fully equipped rooms. The fine breakfast is blessed by a wooden Buddha in a grand drawing room with a baronial-style ceiling and an alluring terrace facing trees and hills. It's remarkable value.

Pre-organise your arrival time as the charming English-speaking owners don't live on-site.

★Dufays B&B €€
(📞080 54 80 08; www.hoteldufays.be; Rue Neuve 115; standard/comfort d €130/140; ⏰check-in 2.30-10pm; 🖥) This exquisitely restored 200-year-old stone building offers six lavish rooms, each with a special character. All are delightful but the art deco decadence of 'Années 30' and the tasteful on-safari brilliance of the 'Africa Room' (great balcony views, huge bathroom) are particularly memorable.

La Maison/L'Espion BOUTIQUE HOTEL €€
(📞080 88 08 91; www.hotellamaison.info; Pl St-Remacle 19; s/d from €75/110; 🖥) Combining two distinguished town houses dating from around 1801, this family-run hotel on Stavelot's main square retains antique floorboards, staircases and a particularly lavish, chandelier-lit breakfast room. Much of the period furniture is original, the art less so. Some rooms have rather dated bathroms.

There's a good restaurant (dinner only), a pleasant bar and a rear-yard terrace with plenty of seating.

🍴 Eating

Auberge St-Remacle CAFE €
(📞080 86 20 47; www.stavelot-auberge.be; Ave Ferdinand Nicolay 9; mains €10.50-21, beer from €2; ⏰11am-11pm, kitchen noon-2.30pm & 6-10pm; 🖥) At first glance this pub-restaurant might not look like the most impressive of Stavelot's eating establishments, but service is friendlier than most and the unpretentious local food is consistently well cooked. There are additional lunchtime snacks (€6 to €9) and dinner options include fondues, raclette and *pierrade* (meat self-cooked on hot stones; €18.50 to €26.50).

The terrace continues over the road to a shaded area facing Stavelot's abbey.

Five simple but well-renovated rooms above the bar-restaurant are available (double/quad from €85/130).

Le Table de Figaro   ITALIAN €€
(☑ 080 86 42 86; www.restaurant-figaro.be; Pl du Vinâve 4; mains €13.50-24; ☺ noon-2pm & 5-9.30pm or later) With a slightly off-line terrace poking onto Place St-Remacle, this super-friendly place serves handmade pasta, thin-crust pizza and, in summer, a good range of salads and local fare – their *boulettes* (meatballs) are as good as the Liège originals.

Unusually, it opens seven days a week.

★ **Ô Mal-Aimé**   BELGIAN €€€
(☑ 080 86 20 01; www.omalaime.be; Rue Neuve 12; meals €35; ☺ 7-9.30pm Fri & Sat, noon-3pm & 7-9.30pm Sun) If you're in Stavelot on a weekend, don't miss this eccentric delight. The dining room is smothered in bohemian quotes, poems and massed pictorials relevant to the French poet and art critic Guillaume Apollinaire, who did a runner from this very place in 1909. The three-course set dinners are imaginative and remarkably good quality, and Sunday meals are four-course 'surprises'.

No credit cards and no mobile phones at the table.

❶ Information

The abbey's cash desk doubles as a **tourist office** (☑ 080 86 27 06; www.stavelot.be/tourisme; ☺ 10am-1pm & 1.30-5pm). A useful selection of maps and guides for cycling and hiking is sold from the abbey's gift shop.

❶ Getting There & Away

The nearest train stations are Coo and Trois Ponts on the Liège–Gouvy–Luxembourg line. From Trois Ponts, bus 745 runs roughly hourly (every two hours on Sunday) to Stavelot (€2.50, 10 minutes), continuing to Malmédy. Bus 294 runs the Trois Ponts–Stavelot–Verviers route (€3.50, 70 minutes, five to seven daily) via Francorchamps and Tiège, where you can change for Spa.

The Eastern Cantons

For Belgium's finest area of walkable wilderness, numerous little-known castles and even a couple of ski slopes, head to the 854-sq-km Eastern Cantons. Known in French as the 'Cantons de l'Est', or in German as 'Ost Kantonen' (www.eastbelgium.com), this area is also a historico-cultural quirk – Belgium's officially German-speaking area, with its own Germanophone parliament in Eupen,

though two of the region's 11 communes are actually Francophone, most notably the town of Malmédy. The greatest attraction here is the Hautes Fagnes area of moorlands between Eupen and Malmédy, edged by beautiful areas of deep-cut forested valleys. Both towns hold excellent carnivals and make good bases for regional exploration.

Malmédy

POP 12,600

Lively Malmédy makes a great base for visiting the Hautes Fagnes region – as long as you are driving. A former tanning centre, much of the city was tragically destroyed in a trio of WWII 'friendly fire' bombing raids in 1944. However, the centre has retained a core of historical buildings, notably a 1784 cathedral, from whose doorstep you can survey a grand series of spired, century-old mansions that reveal the remnants of a very wealthy past that's recalled next door in the **Malmundarium Museum** (www.malmundarium.be; Pl du Châtelet 9; adult/child €6/3; ☺ 10am-6pm Tue-Sun Apr-Jun, Sep & Oct, daily Jul & Aug, to 5pm Tue-Sun Nov-Mar).

◉ Sights

Baugnez 44   MUSEUM
(☑ 080 44 04 82; www.baugnez44.be; Rte du Luxembourg 10, Baugnez; ☺ 10am-6pm Wed-Sun Sep-Jun, daily Jul & Aug, last entry 5.15pm) On 17 December 1944, American and SS troop columns met fatefully at the Baugnez crossroads, 4km southeast of Malmédy. Some 84 captured GIs were shot on the spot in what became known as the 'Malmédy Massacre'. The site now hosts a fascinating, high-tech museum full of WWII uniforms, models and hardware plus the balaclava worn by the perpetrating German commander, Joachim Peiper, during his war crimes trial.

☆ Festivals & Events

Cwarmê   CARNIVAL
(☺ 7 weeks before Easter) Malmédy's big annual event is this four-day series of carnival festivities, whose high point is on the Sunday before Mardi Gras – handy if you want to head to Eupen's Rosenmontag (p242) the next day. Amid a confusing cast of characters, the luridly colourful *Haguètes* dance with *hapetchâr* (flesh-snatcher) articulated tongs. If grabbed, the correct response is to kneel and mutter a special Walloon 'apology'.

THE HAUTE FAGNES

The Hautes Fagnes ('High Fens') constitute Belgium's largest nationally protected re-serve, an environmentally unique upland plateau of swampy heath and sphagnum peat bogs surrounded by considerable stands of woodland. The region is often wet, misty and shrouded in low cloud. But if you're suitably prepared, this can add to its mesmerising quality. The 40-sq-km reserve is a haven for wild boar, roe deer, hen harriers and black grouse, though you're far from certain to see any. Indeed, some trails close to protect the grouse during nesting periods (April to July). Hard to spot botanical curiosities include *Drosera rotundifolia* (a carnivorous sundew plant) and *Trientales europaea* (wintergreen chickweed), a rare seven-petalled flowering plant.

The area is criss-crossed with trails for bracing hikes, some with boardwalk sections, allowing you to observe the boggy environment without causing damage or sinking into it. There are four main trailheads on the N676, each around 1.5km apart. Best known is the **Signal de Botrange**, marked by restaurant and a stone tower that has all the charm of a fire-station lookout. It's Belgium's highest point, though at 694m that's not saying much. A better place to start a short walk is **Baraque Michel** (☑ 080 44 48 01; www.labaraquemichel.be; ⊘ restaurant 9.30am-9pm), a lonely, atmospherically typical Ar-dennes-style restaurant in the heart of the moorlands. Directly east across the road, the footpath signposted to Eupen quickly passes two smaller grey-stone pillars that once marked the Belgian–Prussian border. Continue a little further then veer left away from the treeline to find a stretch of over-bog boardwalk that's ideal for a short return stroll (though a section of boarding is missing for the first 200m, which can get boggy if wet). Good for something a little longer is the well-signed **Fagne de la Polleûr loop**, a partly boardwalked 4km circuit with useful interpretive panels (in French, Dutch and German). The nearest approach is from the charred ruins of Mt Rigi restaurant but an access spur-path starts just south of the Baraque Michel car park, behind the tiny 1830 **Chapel Fis-chbach** which is unusually topped with a lantern window. In pre-road days, that offered a landmark for those crossing the dangerously featureless moors.

Buses across the Fagnes are very limited. Route 390 (Verviers towards Rocherath; three to five daily) takes 30 minutes to Ovifat, with route 394 (Eupen to St-Vith) running three to eight times daily. If you're driving (recommended), do stop at the **Botrange Nature Centre** (☑ 080 44 03 00; www.botrange.be; Rte de Botrange 31; visitor centre free, museum adult/child €6/3; ⊘ 9-5pm Mon-Fri, 10am-6pm Sat & Sun), an impressive informa-tion centre 200m west of the Bütenbach–Eupen road between Ofivat and the Signal Botrange. It includes a museum section with an interesting experiential walk-through of darkened environments, runs Char-a-Banc **wagon tours** (adult/senior/child €6/5/3.50; ⊘ 11am & 2pm Wed, Sat & Sun Apr-Oct, plus Mon & Fri Jul & Aug) and rents electric bicycles (half-/full day €22/30) and skis (in season) for a cross-country trail that starts outside. There are still wagon tours of the nearby forests and lanes. The centre is 1.4km south of Signal de Botrange, 2.5km north of Ovifat, which has resort hotel, a decent **Gîte d'Étape hostel** (☑ 080 44 46 77; www.giteovifat.org; Rue des Charmilles 69; dm incl breakfast €21, under 26 €17, plus €3 per person per stay; ᴘ 🛜), a modest downhill **ski slope** (☑ 080 44 63 54; www.skialpin-ovifat.com; Rue de la Piste, Ovifat; access/lift/parking/ski-set rental €2/1.50/4/15; ⊘ 9.30am-4.30pm when snow allows), and – via a tiny back lane – the very picturesque 1354 **Château de Reinhardstein** (☑ 080 44 68 68; www.reinhardstein.net; Chemin du Cheneux 50; grounds free, tour adult/child €8.50/6.50; ⊘ grounds 9am-6pm, visits 2.30pm Wed & hourly Sat & Sun, daily Jul, Aug & Christmas holidays) half hidden in a forested valley. For food as well as fine beer produced in situ, don't miss the flashy new glass-walled brewery-restaurant **Peak Beer** (☑ 080 21 48 76; www.peakbeer.be; Rue de Botrange 123; ⊘ 11am-7pm Wed-Sun), whose open terrace offers sweeping forest-framed views.

🛏 Sleeping & Eating

The area has a good selection of holiday rent-als and small hotels, including several cen-tral properties with rooms above restaurants.

The **HI Hostel** (☑ 080 33 83 86; www.lesauberges dejeunesse.be; Route d'Eupen 36, Bévercé; dm/ tw €24/52, under 26 €2 less, HI members 10% off; ⊘ reception 4-10pm; ᴘ 🛜) is 2km towards

Eupen on (rare) bus 397. There are plenty of dining and drinking options around the two main squares, Place du Rome and Place Albert 1er.

★ Manufacture de Malmedy

BOUTIQUE HOTEL €€

(☑ 0471 44 04 03; www.manufacturedemalmedy.be; Rte de Waimes 19b, Géromont; s/d/f €85/90/120; P 🛜 🌊) The kind of place James Bond might stop at for a romatic interlude, this vaguely Scandinavian-styled lodge attatched to a rural recording studio is the region's most contemporary accommodation. Rooms are well designed but small, encouraging use of the ample public spaces, including a mini-cinema operated from iPads that are provided instead of in-room TVs.

The swimming pool is open to guests until 7.30pm, after which you can book it for a four-person wellness evening (€75 extra including one treatment, fruit, juices and a bottle of bubbles). Or you can simply rent the whole lodge for a few thousand euros while you're recording your next album. It's around 2km southeast of central Malmédy towards Baugnez.

L'Espirit Sain

HOTEL €€

(☑ 080 33 03 14; www.espritsain.be; Chemin-Rue 46; s/d/tr from €98/118/148; 🛜) Bright splashes of colour enliven 11 suitably stylish rooms here, while there's also a pair of apartments and two new deluxe rooms with garden access, both in separate nearby buildings. Most quoted prices include breakfast. It's above a contemporary design restaurant that serves straightforward honest food – salads, trout and meat dishes at sensible prices.

❶ Getting There & Away

From Trois Ponts station on the Liège–Luxembourg railway line, bus 745 runs roughly hourly to Malmédy (€3.50, 20 minutes). For the Hautes Fagnes you'll need your own wheels but for Ovifat, the rare 845 bus does run once or twice daily.

Eupen

POP 19,500

Eupen has been part of Belgium for a century but still retains a distinctively Germanic feel and hosts the **parliament** (www.pdg.be; Platz des Parlaments 1; ⊙ 9am-5.30pm Mon-Thu, to 4pm Fri) of Belgium's German-speaking region. It's the most vibrant town of the Eastern Cantons, with an active cultural life and a particularly joyful if satirical **Rosenmontag**

(⊙ Mon before Mardi Gras) carnival full of colour and music. With its copper-cladded twin spires, the 1726 church of St Nicholas is Eupen's visual centrepiece.

🛏 Sleeping & Eating

There's good dining on central Kirchstrasse and along the easterly section of Gospertstrasse. Marktplatz buzzes with street cafes.

Gîte d'Étape

HOSTEL €

(Eupener Jugendherberge; ☑ 087 55 31 26; www.gitesdetape.be/eupen; Judenstrasse 79; dm/s/d/tr/q €24/40/61/87/103; ⊙ reception 5-8pm; P 🛜) Completely rebuilt in 2016, this modern hostel's hilltop location at the southern edge of town provides some lovely sweeping views over rolling forested hills.

★ Julévi

B&B €€

(☑ 0478 49 32 36; www.julevi.be; Heidberg 4; s/d/f €80/100/180; 🛜) Charming English-speaking owners have transformed this 1869 linen-merchant's house into a stylishly comfortable retreat featuring quality box-spring mattresses, fluffy monogrammed towels and a delightful guest lounge with honesty bar. It trumps most hotels and there's even a little verandah, garden and library. Breakfast is superb.

Ratskeller

EUROPEAN €€

(☑ 087 30 16 01; www.ratskeller-eupen.be; Klötzerbahn 2; mains €15.50-27, pastas €11.50-16.50; ⊙ 9am-late, kitchen to 10pm) Dating from 1714, this historic pub has had a recent facelift but remains one of the most archetypal places for a hearty local meal or an Eupener beer.

★ Au Couleur Rouge

FUSION €€€

(☑ 087 64 79 51; www.couleurrouge.be; Gospertstrasse 22; mains €27-34; ⊙ noon-2pm & 6.30-9.30pm Thu-Mon, closed Sat lunch) Accessed through a stone archway behind a grand patrician villa, this excellent restaurant does everything right, from the exquisite floral details on the beautifully artistic starters to perfectly balanced mains with subtle Asian twists. Even the coffee is excellent, and the €29 lunch deal is superb.

❶ Getting There & Away

Hourly trains from Eupen's *bahnhof* (station) head for Ostend (€22.20, three hours) via Verviers (€3.70, 20 minutes), Liège-Guillemins (€7.20, 40 minutes), Leuven, Brussels, Ghent and Bruges.

Bus 294 runs to Stavelot via Malmédy.

Luxembourg

LANGUAGES: LUXEMBOURGISH, FRENCH & GERMAN

Best Places to Eat

➡ Restaurant Mathes (p256)

➡ Le Sud (p252)

➡ La Cristallerie (p252)

➡ La Distillerie (p258)

➡ Bistro Quai (p256)

Best Places to Stay

➡ Château d'Urspelt (p263)

➡ Maho (p250)

➡ Hôtel Le Place d'Armes (p250)

➡ La Pipistrelle (p250)

➡ Auberge Aal Veinen (p262)

Why Go?

Stretching just 82km and 57km at its longest and widest points respectively, Luxembourg is a charming slice of northern Europe that consistently ranks among the world's top three nations in both wealth and wine consumption.

The Grand Duchy's capital, Luxembourg City, has a fairytale quality to its Unesco-listed historic core, perched on a dramatic clifftop. Beyond in the rolling forested hills, a string of beguiling villages clusters beneath stunning medieval castles. Then there's superb wine tasting in the Moselle Valley and invigorating hiking in the rugged, rocky gorges of the Müllerthal region.

Luxembourg has recovered impressively from widespread destruction during WWII, a sad history remembered in war museums across the country. Today, 49% of the population are foreigners, drawn here by the high standards of living, glorious landscapes and an ideal location at the crossroads of Europe.

Driving Distances (km)

	Luxembourg City	Clervaux	Vianden	Echternach
Clervaux	64			
Viaden	45	37		
Echternach	33	54	32	
Bastogne (Belgium)	63	27	43	72

Luxembourg Highlights

1 Chemin de la Corniche
(p245) Promenading along
Europe's 'most beautiful
balcony' in Luxembourg City.

2 Vianden (p261) Riding a
chairlift to the hilltop above
this picturesque village, then
strolling to its castle.

3 Echternach (p257)
Hiking into the enchanting

Müllerthal's woodlands and
rocky micro-canyons.

4 Beaufort (p259)
Exploring Beaufort's medieval
and Renaissance castles and
tasting the local Cassero.

5 US Military Cemetery
(p249) Paying homage to
General Patton outside
Luxembourg City.

6 Moselle Valley (p255)
Sipping sparkling wines amid
the Moselle Valley's hillside
vineyards.

7 Esch-sur-Sûre (p263)
Strolling through this pretty
riverside village and its
adjacent nature park.

ℹ Information

Visit Luxembourg (www.visitluxembourg.com)

ℹ Getting Around

Public transport within Luxembourg (www.mobiliteit.lu) costs a flat €2/4 for up to two hours/all day, however far you go.

With the Luxembourg Card (1-/2-/3-day adult €13/20/28, family €28/48/68) it's entirely free, as is entry to many sights countrywide.

LUXEMBOURG CITY

POP 116,323

Majestically set across the deep gorges of the Alzette and Pétrusse rivers, Luxembourg City is one of Europe's most scenic capitals. Its Unesco-listed Old Town is a warren of tunnels, nooks and crannies sheltering some outstanding museums, as well as lively drinking and dining scenes. The city is famed for its financial and EU centres, making weekends an ideal time to visit, as hotel prices drop dramatically.

History

The foundations of today's city took root in AD 963 when Sigefroi (Siegfried), Count of the Ardennes, built a castle. From 1354 the region was an independent duchy; conquered by Burgundy in 1443, it was later incorporated into the Habsburg empire. The city's remarkable fortifications proved particularly impressive during the French revolutionary wars, although not quite good enough to survive a seven-month French siege in 1792–93. After the Battle of Waterloo in 1815, Luxembourg was declared a Grand Duchy under the Dutch king, though it eventually split in two after Belgian independence.

When the Dutch King William III died in 1890, his daughter Wilhelmina became queen of the Netherlands. However, by Luxembourg's then-current rules of succession, only males could rule the Grand Duchy. This quirk resulted in Luxembourg's previously nominal independence becoming a reality, and thus Luxembourg City emerged as a fully fledged European capital.

Germany occupied the city during both world wars, and despite shelling in WWII, the city remained largely intact. In the second half of the 20th century, Luxembourg City's shiny glass Kirchberg area became host to several major EU organisations, including the European Investment Bank and European Court of Justice.

⊙ Sights

The Old Town counterpoints ancient fortifications and palatial historic buildings with modern museums. The picturesque Grund area lies riverside, way below, at the base of a dramatic fortified escarpment.

◉ Old Town

Luxembourg City's charm is best appreciated by strolling the Chemin de la Corniche and Old Town. Buzzing Place Guillaume II, surveyed by the neoclassical Hôtel de Ville, is the city's heart.

★**Chemin de la Corniche** STREET
Hailed as 'Europe's most beautiful balcony', this pedestrian promenade winds along the course of the 17th-century city ramparts with views across the river canyon towards the fortifications of the Wenzelsmauer (Wenceslas Wall). The rampart-top walk continues along Blvd Victor Thorn to the Dräi Tier (Triple Gate) tower, stretching 600m in total.

★**Bock Casemates** FORTRESS
(www.luxembourg-city.com; Montée de Clausen; adult/child €6/3; ⊙10am-5.30pm mid-Feb–Mar & Oct-early Nov, 10am-8.30pm Apr-Sep) Beneath the Montée de Clausen, the clifftop site of Count Sigefroi's once-mighty fort, the Bock Casemates are an atmospheric honeycomb of rock galleries and passages initially carved by the Spaniards from 1644 onwards. They were extended by French engineer Vauban in the 1680s, and again by the Austrians in the mid-18th century. Over the years the casemates have housed everything from garrisons to bakeries to slaughterhouses; during WWI and WWII they sheltered 35,000 locals. Kids will adore exploring the passageways.

Palais Grand-Ducal PALACE
(Royal Palace; ☑22 28 09; www.luxembourg-city.com; 17 Rue du Marché-aux-Herbes; tours adult/child €12/6; ⊙tours mid-Jul–early Sep) Luxembourg's turreted palace was built in 1572 and has been greatly extended over the years. It now houses the Grand Duke's office, with parliament using its 1860 Chamber of Deputies. In summer the palace opens for 50-minute guided tours (English available), mostly concentrating on family history. From the medieval-Gothic dining room, the palace's interior style morphs into sumptuous gilded

Luxembourg City

200 m
0.1 miles

Bock Casemates 1

Musée d'Histoire de la Ville de Luxembourg

Chemin de la Corniche

PFAFFENTHAL

GRUND

OLD TOWN

Pont Adolphe

Montée de Clausen

R de la Tour Jacob (6.3km)

Stairway to Fort Thüngen (250m);
Mudam (350m);
Philharmonie (550m)

R du Fort Olizy

R Vauban

R Mohrfels

R Sosthène Weis

Blvd Victor Thorn

R Sigefroi

R Large

R d Rost

R Wilthelm

Marché-aux-Poissons

Drai Tier

Blvd J Ulveling

R du Nord

Côte d'Eich

Pl du Théâtre

R Génistre

R du Curé

R du Fossé

R des Capucins

Grand Rue

Pl d'Armes

R de la Porte-Neuve

R des Bains

R Beaumont

R de la Poste

R Louvigny

R Aldringen

Blvd Royal

Ave Monterey

Grand Théâtre (500m)

Av Marie-Thérèse

Hôtel Parc-Belleye (200m)

Blvd de la Pétrusse

Am Tunnel (200m)

Place de Metz

Citadel Gardens

Pl de la Constitution

Blvd Roosevelt

R Chimay

R Notre-Dame

Pl Guillaume II

R du Marché-aux-Herbes

R de la Congrégation

R du St-Esprit

Montée du Grund

R de la Corniche

Chemin de la Corniche

R Plaetis

R Münster

GRUND

R St-Ulric

Bisserweg

Blvd Général Patton

R de Trèves

R Émile Mousel

R des Trèves

Gare Centrale (800m);
Musée-Mémorial de la Déportation (2.1km)

29

14

30

32

42

43

45

36

27

40

9

16

34

25 21

39

12

35

18

23

17

26 20

22

15

28

41

5

13

7

6

8

3

33

44

2

31

19

4

37

11

24

38

Luxembourg City

romanticism upstairs. Tours must be prebooked online or via Luxembourg City Tourist Office (p254), where you're required to pick up your ticket.

MNHA
MUSEUM

(Musée National d'Histoire et d'Art; ☑ 47 93 301; www.mnha.lu; Marché-aux-Poissons; permanent exhibition free, temporary exhibitions €7/free, both free after 5pm Thu; ⊙ 10am-6pm Tue, Wed & Fri-Sun, to 8pm Thu) Startlingly modern for its Old Town setting, the national art and history museum starts deep in an excavated rocky basement with exhibits of Neolithic flints, then sweeps you through Gallic tomb chambers, Roman mosaics and Napoleonic medals to an excellent if small art gallery. Cézanne and Picasso get a look-in while Luxembourg's Expressionist artist Joseph Kutter (1894–1941) gets a whole floor.

★ Musée d'Histoire de la Ville de Luxembourg
MUSEUM

(Luxembourg City History Museum; ☑ 47 96 45 00; www.citymuseum.lu; 14 Rue du St-Esprit; adult/child €5/free, after 6pm Thu free; ⊙ 10am-6pm Tue, Wed & Fri-Sun, to 8pm Thu) Hidden within a series of 17th- to 19th-century houses, including a former 'holiday home' of the Bishop of Orval, the city's history museum is engrossing. Permanent collections on its lower levels cover the city's industrial, handicraft and commercial heritage, with models, plans and engravings, textiles, ceramics, posters, photographs and household items. Upper floors host temporary exhibitions. Its enormous glass elevator provides views of the rock foundations, the Grund valley and Rham plateau; there's also a lovely garden and panoramic terrace.

Cathédrale Notre-Dame
CATHEDRAL

(www.cathol.lu; Rue Notre-Dame; ⊙ 10am-noon & 2-5.30pm) FREE Built between 1613 and 1621, and enlarged between 1935 and 1938, Luxembourg's cathedral is most memorable for its distinctively elongated black spires, ornately carved Renaissance portal inside the main doorway, and 19th- and 20th-century stained glass. Interior highlights include a tiny but highly revered Madonna-and-child idol above the altar and the graves of the royal family in the crypt.

Casino Luxembourg GALLERY
(Forum d'Art Contemporain; ☑ 22 50 45; www.casino-luxembourg.lu; 41 Rue Notre-Dame; ⊙ 11am-7pm Wed & Fri-Mon, to 11pm Thu) FREE Hungarian composer-virtuoso Franz Liszt gave his last concert at this grand one-time society mansion. Today, the building hosts regularly changing contemporary art exhibitions.

Place de la Constitution SQUARE
Towering above this leafy triangular 'square' is a WWI memorial, Gëlle Fra. Beyond, the valley falls away to the Pétrusse River.

Hôtel de Ville ARCHITECTURE
(City Hall; Place Guillaume II) Completed in 1838, the city's neoclassical town hall was largely constructed from the stones of a Franciscan monastery that previously occupied the site. The interior is closed to the public.

◎ Grund

Many visitors find that this idyllically pretty waterside district down in the valley is their favourite part of the city. The main attraction is cafe-hopping while strolling the pedestrian lanes down from the Old Town and over to the Clausen area.

Abbaye de Neumünster ARTS CENTRE
(☑ 26 20 52 1; www.neimenster.lu; 28 Rue Münster; ⊙ 8am-6pm Mon-Fri, from 10am Sat & Sun) Dominating the Grund riverbank, this 17th-century Benedictine abbey has been transformed into a cultural centre. Around the cloister are bronze sculptures by local artist Lucien Wercollier, who in 1942 refused to create Aryan artworks and was imprisoned by the Nazis in this building. Several other exhibition spaces surround a central atrium and a large river-facing courtyard, a venue for outdoor performances. Prices vary depending on the exhibition or event. The brasserie opens to a table-lined terrace.

Natur Musée MUSEUM
(☑ 46 22 33 1; www.mnhn.lu; 25 Rue Münster; adult/child €5/free, from 6pm Tue free; ⊙ 10am-8pm Tue, to 6pm Wed-Sun) Ranging over 10 exhibition halls, this family-oriented, interactive museum covers all the natural history bases with stuffed animals, preserved insects and life-size dinosaurs. Most interpretive information is in French and German.

◎ Kirchberg Plateau

EU institutions sit on a hilltop new-town area in modern steel-strutted, blue-glass towers. The plateau is edged with chunky fortification remnants and cultural attractions including art galleries, museums and concert halls.

★ Mudam GALLERY
(Musée d'Art Moderne; ☑ 45 37 85 1; www.mudam.lu; 3 Parc Dräi Eechelen; adult/child €8/free; ⊙ 10am-6pm Thu-Mon, to 9pm Wed) Groundbreaking exhibitions of modern, installation and experiential art take place in this airy architectural icon designed by Pritzker-winning architect IM Pei (best known for his glass pyramid entrance to Paris' Louvre museum). The collection includes everything from photography to fashion, design and multimedia. Regional products are used in local specialities at its glass-roofed cafe, which hosts free concerts on Wednesday evenings.

Fort Thüngen MUSEUM
(Musée Dräi Eechelen; ☑ 26 43 35; www.m3e.public.lu; 5 Park Dräi Eechelen; adult/child €5/free, from 5pm Wed free; ⊙ 10am-8pm Wed, to 6pm Thu-Sun) FREE A 1730 twin-towered extension of the plateau's vast complex of Vauban fortifications, Fort Thüngen has an intruiging museum about Luxembourg's historic defences and also hosts changing exhibitions. Sweeping views over the city unfurl from the rooftop viewing deck.

◎ South of the Centre

Musée de la Banque MUSEUM
(☑ 40 15 24 50; www.bcee.lu; 1 Place de Metz; ⊙ 9am-5.30pm Mon-Fri) FREE Where better than the financial hub of Luxembourg to spend an hour browsing through a bank museum? It's housed in the dramatic, century-old, castle-style headquarters of the Banque et Caisse d'Épargne de l'État, and traces over 150 years of tradition and innovation in banking, from piggy banks to ATMs and bank robbers.

Am Tunnel GALLERY
(☑ 40 15 24 50; www.bcee.lu; 16 Rue Ste-Zithe; ⊙ 9am-5.30pm Mon-Fri, 2-6pm Sun) FREE Deep beneath the Spuerkeess bank is a permanent exhibition on photographer Edward Steichen, who put together Clervaux' Unesco-listed Family of Man (p264) photographic exhibition. Access is via the separate building Bâtiment Rousegaertchen and a tunnel

carved 350m through the Bourbon plateau. The tunnel walls display rotating photography exhibits.

Musée-Mémorial de la Déportation   MUSEUM
(☑ 24 78 81 91; www.luxembourg-city.com; Gare de Hollerich, 3a Rue de la Déportation; ⊙ 9-11.30am & 2-4.30pm Tue-Thu) FREE Prior to WWII, Luxembourg had a Jewish community of approximately 3500 people. Of them, some 2500 fled, most to France, before emigration was halted in 1941. During the Nazi Occupation, some 800 Jews were deported to concentration camps in Poland and then-Czechoslovakia. The train station where their harrowing journey began is now a small museum. Take bus 18 or the RB train from Gare Centrale.

⊙ Hamm

US Military Cemetery   CEMETERY
(☑ 43 17 27; www.abmc.gov; 50 Val du Scheid; ⊙ 9am-5pm) In a beautifully maintained graveyard 6km east of the city near the airport, lie 5075 US WWII war dead, including the general of the US Third Army George Patton, who played a key role in Luxembourg's 1944 liberation. It's a humbling sight, with long rows of white crosses and Stars of David. At the entrance, a white-stone chapel has a stained-glass window with the insignia of US commands that operated in Luxembourg. You'll need your own wheels or a taxi.

⚐ Tours

Wenzel Walk   WALKING
(www.visitluxembourg.com; adult/child €18/9; ⊙ 2.30pm Sat) Departing from the tourist office (p254), this three-hour, English-language walking tour winds through the upper and lower towns, past fortifications and along nature trails. If you miss the weekly guided walk, you can download a self-guided tour from the website.

✯✯ Festivals & Events

Luxembourg National Day   CULTURAL
(Grand Duke's Birthday; ⊙ 22–23 Jun) Luxembourg City is the place to celebrate the country's national day, aka the Grand Duke's Birthday (although no Grand Duke has been born on 23 June). Festivities begin the day before with a changing of the guard in front of the Palais Grand-Ducal at 4pm, followed by the Fakelzuch torchlight procession and 11pm fireworks launched from Fort Thüngen.

Concerts and parties continue all over the city throughout the night. On the day itself, an official ceremony takes place at the Philharmonie, followed by a 21-gun salute. The Grand Duke then inspects his troops and attends a military parade through the capital.

Christmas Markets   CHRISTMAS MARKET
(www.luxembourg.public.lu; ⊙ 11am-9pm Sun-Thu, to 10pm Fri & Sat 23 Nov-24 Dec) In the month leading up to Christmas, enchanting Christmas markets set up on Place de la Constitution and Place d'Armes in the city centre, and Place de Paris, close to Gare Centrale. Wooden huts sell handcrafted toys, Christmas decorations, candles, sweets and local delicacies, along with *Glühwäin* (mulled wine), *Gromperekichelcher* (shredded potato pancakes) and *Mettwurscht* (Luxembourg sausages).

Fête de la Musique   MUSIC
(www.fetedelamusique.lu; ⊙ 15-21 Jun) Hip-hop, electropop, classical, experimental, jazz, blues and rock concerts take place across the country during this free week-long music festival, with the greatest concentration held in Luxembourg City.

Luxembourg Light Festival   LIGHT SHOW
(www.luxembourg.public.lu; ⊙ 6-11pm 15-17 Dec) Interactive light shows, video projections and audiovisual installations illuminate monumental buildings in Luxembourg's Old Town over three evenings in mid-December.

Blues and Jazz Rallye   MUSIC
(www.luxembourg-city.com; ⊙ mid-Jul) Jazz and blues musicians perform free concerts on open-air stages in the streets of Grund, Clausen and Pfaffenthal during this two-day festival.

🛏 Sleeping

Many (though by no means all) accommodation options range from dated to distinctly dowdy. Midweek, many seem dauntingly overpriced, but prices drop substantially at weekends by up to 50%. Accommodation is marginally cheaper around the train station, a slightly sleazy area by Luxembourg's high standards.

There is only one city youth hostel, but rural HI hostels are relatively accessible, including at Larochette (☑ 26 27 66 550; www.youthhostels.lu; 45 Rue Osterbour; dm/s/d €24.70/39.70/60.40; [P] [☎]), 25km away on Luxembourg–Diekirch bus route 100.

Auberge de Jeunesse
HOSTEL €

(☑26 27 66 65 0; www.youthhostels.lu; 5 Rue du Fort Olisy; dm €25.15-26.15; P ✳ @ 🛜) Luxembourg City's state-of-the-art hostel has 240 beds in 50 very comfortable, single-sex dorms with electronic entry. En suite dorms cost €1 more. There are good-sized lockers (bring a padlock), laundry facilities and loads of space including a great terrace with views to the Old Town. Rates include a basic breakfast. HI members receive a discount.

It's a short but steep walk down from the Casemates area via stairs near 'Clausen Plateau Altmunster' bus stop. The hostel's cafe serves a decent two-course dinner for €10.90.

Hôtel Bristol
HOTEL €€

(☑48 58 30; www.hotel-bristol.lu; 11 Rue de Strasbourg; s/d/studio incl breakfast from €75/120/130, d without bathroom incl breakfast from €85; 🛜) Handy for the train station, located a 300m stroll southeast of the hotel, the Bristol's bright, contemporary rooms are great value at prices that are a relative bargain. The cheapest doubles share bathrooms and have two single beds that can be pushed together. Kitchenette-equipped studios sleep up to three people. Reception stays open 24 hours and there's a bar downstairs.

★Maho
BOUTIQUE HOTEL €€€

(☑28 99 80 00; www.maho.lu; 2 Place Ste-Cunégonde; s/d from €150/180; P ✳ 🛜) Behind an ivy-clad facade, Maho's seven rooms spread over two floors, served by an lift. Each has an individual theme, such as sunflower-yellow Provence, Bibliothéque ('library'), with a wooden bookcase framing the tartan-quilted bed, and pink-accented Roses with wrought-iron furniture. Its glass-paned restaurant opens to a magical garden with a pond and a gazebo.

★La Pipistrelle
B&B €€€

(☑621 300 351; www.lapipistrelle.lu; 26 Montée du Grund; s/d from €185/220; 🛜) Just four sumptuous suites and a charming location mean you'll have to book early to enjoy this intimate B&B-style hotel. Carved into the rock face, the 18th-century property retains period features but the spacious rooms are stylishly rendered with designer fabrics and open bathrooms. Breakfast is an extra €16; bars and restaurants abound close by. The nearby lift (p255) can zip you up to the Old Town, saving your legs.

★Hôtel Le Place d'Armes
BOUTIQUE HOTEL €€€

(☑27 47 37; www.hotel-leplacedarmes.com; 18 Place d'Armes; d incl breakfast from €295; ✳ 🛜) On the city's busiest central square, seven 18th-century buildings have been combined into an enchanting labyrinth incorporating part-cave meeting rooms with stone walls, light-touch modern lounges and inner courtyards. Each of the 28 luxurious rooms is different, with details including fireplaces, beams or timber ceilings. One of its two restaurants, La Cristallerie (p252), has a Michelin star; the other is a rotisserie. There's also an elegant cafe.

Hôtel Parc Beaux-Arts
BOUTIQUE HOTEL €€€

(☑44 23 23; www.goereshotels.com; 1 Rue Sigefroi; ste from €269; @ 🛜) A trio of 18th-century houses contains 11 gorgeous suites featuring original contemporary artworks, oak floors, Murano glass lamps and fresh flowers. Seek out the 'secret' lounge hidden away in the original timber eaves. It's in the heart of the bar and restaurant zone, but double glazing minimises street noise. Breakfast costs €20.

Hôtel Simoncini
BOUTIQUE HOTEL €€€

(☑22 28 44; www.hotelsimoncini.lu; 6 Rue Notre-Dame; d incl breakfast from €160; ✳ 🛜) Modern and contemporary art fills the gallery-style foyer at the Simoncini. Its 36 light-filled, streamlined rooms have all-white decor and a retro-cool edge. As prices are low by Luxembourg City standards for the central location, it gets booked up quickly, so book well ahead.

Hôtel Vauban
HOTEL €€€

(☑22 04 93; www.hotelvauban.lu; 10 Place Guillaume II; s/d/apt incl breakfast from €120/155/210; 🛜) The Vauban's location is fabulously central – the city's markets set up on Place Guillaume II on Wednesday and Saturday mornings, and Christmas markets also take place here. The 16 rooms have contemporary whitewashed walls and blond timbers, though smaller singles can feel claustrophobic. Apartments sleep up to four, with a double bed and pull-out sofa.

Hôtel Français
HOTEL €€€

(☑47 45 34; www.hotelfrancais.lu; 14 Place d'Armes; s/d incl breakfast from €120/140; 🛜) Bang in the middle of the pedestrian zone on cafe-clad Place d'Armes, above a popular brasserie serving Luxembourgish and French cuisine, the Hôtel Français has 24 somewhat small but light, brightly painted rooms with tangerine tones and pine furniture. The trade-off for epicentral location is that it can be noisy at night.

Hôtel Carlton
HOTEL €€€

(☑29 96 60; www.carlton.lu; 9 Rue de Strasbourg; s/d/tr incl breakfast €145/180/190; 🛜) With geranium-filled window boxes gracing its grand facade, this 1932 building retains its original staircases and floral stained glass in the old-fashioned foyer. Hallways lined with striking conical torch-style lamps lead to spacious modern rooms. It's 300m northwest of the train station.

✖ Eating

Eating is expensive in Luxembourg City, but there's a lively dining scene. For atmospheric options, hunt around in the alleys and passages collectively nicknamed 'Îlot Gourmand' directly behind the Palais Grand-Ducal (Royal Palace). There are interesting alternatives in Grund and the Clausen area. Cafe and restaurant tables spill on to city squares such as leafy Place d'Armes daily in summer.

To fill up cheaply on soups, baguettes or wraps, try local mini-chain **Á la Soupe** (www.alasoupe.net; 9 Rue Chimay; soup €5.50-7.10, salads €6.40-8.90, sandwiches €3.90; ⊙10am-7pm Mon-Fri, to 6pm Sat; ☑).

Beet
VEGAN €

(☑26 20 13 75; www.beet.lu; 32 Place Guillaume II; mains €9.80-18.80; ⊙noon-9.30pm Tue-Thu, noon-10.30pm Fri & Sat, 11.30am-3pm Sun; 🛜☑🚼) 🌿 Minimalist Beet, with bare-brick walls and timber tables, sizzles up eight different vegan burgers (such as the 'Vietnamese', with a chickpea and sprout patty, spicy mango chutney and pickled daikon) served on organic buns. Other all-vegan dishes include quinoa salad with vegan feta. Along with fresh-squeezed juices and infusions, there are local wines and beers. Kids get a choice of felafel or a mini burger with fries and chocolate cake.

Cathy Goedert
CAFE, BAKERY €

(www.cathygoedert.lu; 8 Rue Chimay; cakes & pastries €2.50-4.80, salads & sandwiches €6.50-8.50, Sunday brunch €27.50; ⊙8am-6pm Tue-Sat, from 9am Sun) Chic cafe/*pâtisserie*/*boulangerie* Cathy Goedert is an especially good option on a Sunday for a smorgasbord of sweet and savoury hot and cold dishes at brunch. Throughout the week, stop by for filled home-baked baguettes and intricate pastries, along with a wide variety of coffees and loose-leaf teas.

Am Tiirmschen
BISTRO €€

(☑26 27 07 33; www.amtiirmschen.lu; 32 Rue de l'Eau; mains €19-29; ⊙noon-2pm Tue-Fri, 7-10.30pm Mon-Sat) At this cosy restaurant with exposed-stone walls and heavy bowed beams, Luxembourg specialities include *Judd mat Gaardebounen* (smoked pork with broad beans), *Gromperekichelcher* (a spiced potato pancake), *Rieslingspaschtéit* (a loaf-shaped meat pie made with Riesling) and *Kniddelen mam Speck* (flour-based dumplings topped with bacon and served with apple sauce). Wines are predominately from Luxembourg's Moselle Valley.

Chiggeri
FUSION €€

(☑22 99 36; www.chiggeri.lu; 15 Rue du Nord; mains €20-32; ⊙noon-11pm Mon-Sat, to 6pm Sun; 🛜) Views extend across the valley to Fort Thüngen from the terrace of this lemon-yellow painted mansion with a succession of interior dining spaces including a lantern-filled, glass-roofed winter garden. The wildly experimental menu swings from salmon gravlax with fresh mango to beetroot and coconut risotto, and grilled chicken with honey-infused beer sauce. There is regular live acoustic music in summer.

On Tuesday and Thursday evenings, you also have the option of a 'dine-in-the-dark' experience in pitch-black surrounds (four-course menu €75, by reservation).

Mamacita
MEXICAN €€

(☑26 26 23 96; www.mamacita.lu; 9 Rue des Bains; mains €15-26; ⊙kitchen 11.30am-2.30pm, 6.30-8pm & 9-10.30pm, bar 11.30am-1am Mon-Sat; 🛜☑) Feisty dishes like Baja spice–marinated pike tacos with beetroot slaw and avocado croquettes with smoked chipotle mayo are complemented by eight Mexican beers and over 60 different tequilas at this buzzing bar/restaurant. Book ahead for the first dinner sitting at 6.30pm; the later 9pm sitting generally has room for walk-ins.

L'Adresse
FRENCH €€

(☑27 85 84 68; www.ladresse-restaurant.com; 32 Rue Notre-Dame; mains €17.50-29.50; ⊙noon-2.30pm Mon, noon-2.30pm & 7-9.30pm Tue-Sat) With its little wooden tables and classic French posters, this cosy place evokes a Parisian bistro. The intimate atmosphere is backed up by the daily changing blackboard menu featuring classics such as *steak-frites*,

Burgundy snails, and confit duck with spiced honey sauce.

Basta Così   ITALIAN €€

(☑26 26 85 85; www.bastacosi.lu; 10 Rue Louvigny; mains €13-29; ☺noon-2.30pm & 7-10.30pm Mon & Wed-Sat, noon-2.30pm Tue; 🐟) Old beams and wall drapes create a romantic ambience at this inviting restaurant. Pizzas (21 different varieties) and fresh house-made pastas are excellent but it really comes into its own for classic *secondi* (mains) such as *osso buco* (veal shanks braised in white wine) and *scaloppine alla milanese* (Milanese-style breaded cutlets with butter sauce).

Bosso   ALSATIAN €€

(www.bosso.lu; 7 Bisserweg; mains €10-29; ☺kitchen 5.30-11.30pm Tue-Thu, from 11am Fri-Sun, bar to 1am daily; 🐟) In summer, the biggest attraction of this good-value Grund restaurant is its hidden courtyard garden with tree-shaded seating. Try the *flammeküeche* (wafer-thin Alsatian 'pizzas') or various takes on potato rösti, or just linger over a drink.

★La Cristallerie   GASTRONOMY €€€

(☑27 47 37 42 1; www.la-cristallerie.com; 1st fl, Hôtel Le Place d'Armes, 18 Place d'Armes; 3-course lunch menu €58, 3-/4-/6-/9-course dinner menus €98/138/178/228; ☺noon-2pm & 7-9.30pm Tue-Fri, 7-9.30pm Sat, closed mid-Jul–mid-Aug) Art nouveau stained glass, gilded timbers, chandeliers and white tablecloths set the stage for one of Luxembourg City's finest dining experiences at this Michelin-starred address. Artistically presented multicourse menus are accompanied by wines selected by award-winning sommeliers from the 400-strong list featuring vintages from as far afield as the French Polynesia atoll of Rangiroa.

★Le Sud   FRENCH €€€

(☑26 47 87 50; www.le-sud.lu; 8 Rives de Clausen; mains €37-42, 2-/3-course lunch menu €28/32, 5-course dinner menu €78; ☺kitchen noon-3pm & 7.30-10pm Tue-Fri, 7.30-10pm Sat, noon-3pm Sun, bar 6pm-1am Tue-Thu, 6pm-3am Fri & Sat, 2-6pm Sun; 🐟) *Crémant*-poached lobster, brioche-crumbed garlic snails, line-caught John Dory with artichoke mousseline and Grand Marnier soufflé are among the refined French dishes at this stone-walled restaurant in the historic Rives de Clausen neighbourhood. Stupendous views extend over the area's rooftops and wooded hillsides from the bar's panoramic rooftop terrace.

Bouquet Garni   FRENCH €€€

(☑26 20 06 20; www.lebouquetgarni.lu; 32 Rue de l'Eau; 3-course lunch/dinner menus €32/55; ☺noon-2pm & 7-10pm Tue-Sat, closed Aug; 🐟) Opposite the Palais Grand-Ducal, Bouquet Garni occupies an 18th-century house with weathered masonry, exposed wooden beams and a small covered terrace. Three-course menus (no à la carte), such as lobster ravioli in langoustine broth, Morello cherry–marinated duck with potato mousse, and salted caramel *mille-feuille* (layered pastry) with chocolate and redcurrant ice cream, are excellent value for Luxembourg City.

🍶 Drinking & Nightlife

Luxembourg City's Old Town, Grund and Clausen are the top drinking spots. Nightlife centres on the repurposed former Mousel brewery at Rives de Clausen, with numerous bar-resto-clubs. A handy night bus runs back to the centre. There are more clubs and late-night bars along the Old Town's Rue des Bains and southwest of the train station on Rue de Hollerich.

★Dipso   WINE BAR

(☑26 20 14 14; 4 Rue de la Loge; ☺5pm-1am Tue-Thu, 5pm-3am Fri, 3pm-1am Sat; 🐟) Dating from 1453, this stone building with leaded glass windows incorporates part of the old city walls. Its wines, including 20-plus available by the glass, are accompanied by cheese and charcuterie platters. DJs hit the decks on Friday nights year-round; umbrella-shaded tables set up on its tiny, fight-for-a-seat cobbled terrace in summer.

Vinoteca   WINE BAR

(www.barvinoteca.lu; 6 Rue Wiltheim; ☺noon-3pm & 6pm-1am Mon-Fri; 🐟) Try dozens of Luxembourg Moselle Valley wines by the glass or bottle in Vinoteca's contemporary ground-floor tasting room, in its ancient vaulted cellar carved out of the rock, or out on its charming terrace looking out over the ramparts of the Old Town.

Café des Artistes   PUB

(22 Montée du Grund; ☺5pm-1am Wed & Thu, to 3am Fri & Sat) Every inch of wall and ceiling space is plastered with old and new posters at this lovable *café* (pub). The convivial atmosphere peaks when musicians knock out folk tunes on the candlelit vintage piano from around 10pm most nights.

Brauerei BREWERY
(www.bigbeercompany.lu; 12 Rives de Clausen; ⊘4.30pm-1am Mon-Thu, to 3am Fri & Sat; 🕿) Dating from 1511, this vast brick brewery complex retains its copper boilers and steam engines. Beers now brewed at its latest incarnation include blonde, amber and bruin varieties. Soak them up with Bavarian specialities such as sausages, pretzels, *Spätzle* (hand-rolled noodles) and sauerkraut. The huge main brewhall reverberates when DJs spin tunes on weekends.

Go Ten BAR
(www.goten.lu; 10 Rue du Marché-aux-Herbes; ⊘noon-1am Mon-Thu, noon-3am Fri, 2pm-3am Sat, 5pm-midnight Sun; 🕿) In central Luxembourg's pedestrian zone, with crowds spilling right across the street, Asian-inspired Go Ten has a vertical garden 'living wall' and serves Thai cuisine during the day and bite-sized Japanese dishes at night. It's as a cocktail bar that it excels though, with over 30 different gins and nine different tonics.

Zanzen BAR
(www.zanzen.lu; 27-29 Rue Notre-Dame; ⊘noon-1am Mon-Fri, from 4pm Sat) With timber-panelled walls, lamp-lit tables and seasonal cocktails, this well-established spot is central but tucked away from the more boisterous action. Adjoining the bar, its restaurant serves contemporary French fare.

Konrad Cafe BAR
(☏26 20 18 94; www.facebook.com/Konradcafe; 7 Rue du Nord; ⊘5pm-1am Mon-Thu, from 3pm Fri, from 11am Sat & Sun; 🕿) Bohemian Konrad feels like a sociable share house with its wallpaper, mismatched vintage furniture, and vaulted cellar hosting open-mic and jam sessions, live-music gigs, comedy nights and DJs. During the day on weekends it doubles as an organic cafe.

Liquid PUB
(www.liquid.lu; 15-17 Rue Münster; ⊘5pm-1am Mon-Fri, from 1pm Sat & Sun; 🕿) Two rough-walled antique houses have been knocked together to create this cosy Grund *café* with fringed sepia-toned lamps on the horseshoe bar, and craft beers (on tap and in bottles) from Luxembourg and neighbouring countries chalked on the blackboard. Live jazz plays on Tuesdays; blues gigs take place on Thursdays.

Scott's PUB
(www.scotts-pub.com; 4 Bisserweg; ⊘noon-1am Mon-Fri, from 11am Sat & Sun; 🕿) Scott's has a superb location in the heart of Grund. Inside, it's a British-style pub with cherry-red-painted walls, comfy couches and a crackling open fire but in warm weather its biggest draw is the table-covered terrace perched right above the river. It's one of the few places in Luxembourg with Guinness on tap.

Café Interview PUB
(21 Rue Aldringen; ⊘7am-1am Mon-Fri, 10am-1am Sat, 3pm-midnight Sun; 🕿) Mirrors and wood panelling make this wonderfully unpretentious *café* look like an old-timers' hang-out. All ages stop in for a quiet coffee during the day; evenings are pumping, when some of the city's cheapest beer and well-chosen music attracts a pre-party, student-age crowd.

Urban Bar BAR
(www.urban.lu; 2 Rue de la Boucherie; ⊘11am-1am Sun-Thu, to 3am Fri & Sat; 🕿) Waves of 1970s-retro foam panelling at this stylish lounge-style bar look like ceilings for a *Star Trek* space pod, while the picnic tables on the pavement are where the action is in summer.

De Gudde Wëllen CLUB
(www.deguddewellen.lu; 17 Rue du St-Esprit; ⊘5pm-1am Tue-Thu, to 3am Fri & Sat; 🕿) This small, stone-walled bar in the Old Town has a varying program of DJ nights, parties and live music (predominantly rock, pop, folk and indie) as well as occasional film screenings and comedy nights. Ticket prices vary but are generally cheaper online than at the door.

⭐ Entertainment

Concerts bring the city alive on summer weekends, which blur into what feels like one long festival (www.summerinthecity.lu); the Blues & Jazz Rallye (p249) is a highlight. Tickets for a vast range of other concerts and events are available through **Luxembourg Ticket** (☏47 08 95 1; www.luxembourg-ticket.lu).

Cinema

Check cinema listings online at www.cinema.luxweb.lu.

Cinémathèque CINEMA
(☏47 96 26 44; www.vdl.lu; 17 Place du Théâtre; tickets adult/child €3.70/2.40) Golden oldies, cult classics and world movies play at this single-screen art-house cinema. In July and August there are evening open-air screenings in the courtyard of nearby Théâtre des Capucins and in the forecourt of the Palais Grand-Ducal (Royal Palace; p245). The box

office for all sessions opens 30 minutes prior to screenings.

Live Music

Many big-name acts perform at either Kulturfabrik (www.kulturfabrik.lu) or Rockhal (www.rockhal.lu), both in Esch-sur-Alzette, 18km southwest of Luxembourg City (25 minutes by train).

Den Atelier   LIVE MUSIC

(⏲49 54 85 1; www.atelier.lu; 54 Rue de Hollerich) Big names regularly perform at this industrial 1200-capacity venue (a former Renault truck garage) 750m west of Gare Centrale. Past acts have included Queens of the Stone Age, Smashing Pumpkins, Motörhead and Arctic Monkeys.

Theatre, Opera & Dance

Philharmonie   CONCERT VENUE

(⏲26 32 26 32; www.philharmonie.lu; 1 Place de l'Europe) French architect Christian de Portzamparc conceived this stunning modernist glass oval with 823 white steel columns as a 'natural filter' to enter the world of music. Opened in 2005, its 1500-capacity Grand Auditorium, 313-seat Salle de Musique de Chambre and 180-seat Espace Découverte ('discovery space') host orchestras, chamber music, recitals, world music, jazz, blues and experimental performances. It's across the Pont-Grande-Duchesse Charlotte in Kirchberg.

Théâtre des Capucins   THEATRE

(⏲47 96 39 00; www.theatres.lu; 9 Place du Théâtre) A former monastery dating from 1623, and later a garrison during the French Revolution, this historic building was first used as a theatre between 1869 and 1964, and has been again since 1985. Seating just 269 people, it presents mainly local theatre productions in French, German and Luxembourgish. Summer film screenings take place in its courtyard.

🛍 Shopping

Luxembourg House (www.luxembourghouse.lu; 2 Rue de l'Eau; ⊙10am-6.30pm Tue-Fri & Sun, from 9am Sat) 🖊 is a one-stop-shop for a very wide range of products made or designed in the Grand Dutchy. **Vinoteca** (www.vinoteca.lu; 14 Côte d'Eich; ⊙10am-7pm Mon-Fri, to 6pm Sat) stocks over 200 Luxembourg wines.

ℹ Information

HotCity (www.hotcity.lu) public wi-fi provides free access through much of the city.

Luxembourg City Tourist Office (LCTO; ⏲22 28 09; www.luxembourg-city.com; 30 Place Guillaume II; ⊙8.30am-7pm Mon-Sat, to 6pm Sun mid-Jul–Aug, reduced hours rest of the year) Has maps, walking-tour leaflets and event guides.

ℹ Getting There & Away

AIR

Luxembourg Airport (LUX; www.lux-airport.lu; Rue de Treves) is 8km northeast of the city centre via the N1. There are car-hire desks, free wi-fi, currency-exchange counters, tourist info and ATMs. Until the tram line is finished (2021), access is by bus from Gare Centrale. Direct route 29 (15 minutes) runs every 15/30 minutes weekdays/weekends. Route 16 (30 minutes via Kirchberg) runs every 10/25/30 minutes weekdays/Saturdays/Sundays. Taxis cost around €50.

Flibco (www.flibco.com) buses connect Luxembourg to Frankfurt, Hahn and Charlwroi airports.

BUS

Long-distance – the term is relative – buses pick up from a variety of central points. Several routes head into Germany and France, where you can connect with local networks. Consult timetables at www.mobiliteit.lu. Useful connections include the following:

Bitburg (€2, bus 401, 1¼ hours, up to two per hour) via Echternach (45 minutes)

Diekirch (€2, bus 100, 1¼ hours, hourly Monday to Saturday, every 90 minutes Sunday) via Larochette (50 minutes)

Echternach (€2, buses 110 and 111, one hour, every 30 minutes)

Saarlouis (€2, bus 155, 1½ hours, 11 per day Monday to Friday, one Saturday, none Sunday)

Trier (€2, buses 117 and 118, one hour, four per hour Monday to Friday, four per day Saturday and Sunday)

TRAIN

Gare Centrale is 1km south of the Old City. Routes include the following:

Brussels (€43.60, 3¼ hours, hourly) A few services require changing in Arlon or Liège (€50.40, 3¾ hours).

Diekirch (€2, 45 minutes, every 30 minutes) via Ettelbrück (35 minutes).

Liège (€33 to €41, 2½ hours, every two hours) Some direct; others changing in Namur or Marloie.

Paris (€92 to €110, 2¼ hours) Direct six times daily via Metz (€18.40, 40 minutes).

Trier (€19.90 to €24.60, one hour, hourly) Some continue to Koblenz (€42.70, two hours, every two hours).

ℹ Getting Around

Free, handy elevators link the valleys with the city centre, one between **Plateau St-Esprit and Grund**, and the other between **Montée du Pfaffenthal and Pfaffenthal**.

BICYCLE

Velóh (☎ 800 611 00; www.en.veloh.lu; subscription per week €1, 1st 30min free/subsequent hr €1; ⊙ 24hr) Short-hop shared bike-hire scheme with 683 bikes across 75 docking stations. The initial subscription is payable by credit card at one of 25 special stands; locations are listed online.

Vélo en Ville (☎ 47 96 42 71; www.vdl.lu; 8 Bisserweg; per day/week bike hire from €20/75, helmet €3.50/10; ⊙ 8am-noon & 1-8pm Mon-Fri, 10am-noon & 1-8pm Sat & Sun Apr-Sep, 7am-3pm Mon-Fri Oct-Mar) Hires out city bikes and tandems.

BUS & TRAM

➜ For detailed route maps see www.vdl.lu.

➜ Tickets (€2/4 for two hours/whole day) are good for all city and national transport. Purchase tickets from the driver, from vending machines at major stops, or from at the Gare Centrale.

➜ Most routes operate from 5.30am to 10pm; on Friday and Saturday nights there's also a limited night bus service.

➜ On Saturdays during the day, most buses are free.

➜ Luxembourg's tram line links Place de l'Étoile with Kirchberg (6.30am to midnight Monday to Friday, 8.15am to midnight Saturday and 5.30am to midnight Sunday).

➜ By 2021, the tram line should extend to Luxembourg Airport (northeast) and Cloche d'Or (southwest).

CAR

➜ The city's pedestrian zone is ringed by underground parking garages, with rates typically starting at €2 per hour (€0.80 per hour overnight).

➜ Street parking is limited with many areas catering to residents only. Where available it costs €2 per hour and is free on Sundays, with a maximum stay of two hours.

MOSELLE VALLEY

Forming the border with Germany, the Moselle River is flanked by steeply rising banks ribboned with vineyards. Along the scenic stretch from Schengen to Wasserbillig are a succession of villages and wineries, while a variety of fruit orchards hides in the hinterland. The area's transport hub is hotel-packed

Remich, from which one-hour river cruises are operated by **Navitours** (☎ 75 84 89; www.navitours.lu; Quai de la Moselle; adult/child 1hr tours €10/5, 20min one-way trip to Schengen €7.50/4; ⊙ 3-7 departures daily Mar-Oct).

ℹ Getting There & Around

BOAT

Princess Marie-Astrid (☎ 75 82 75; www.marie-astrid.lu; ⊙ Apr-Sep) This river boat cruises various Moselle routes on different summer days (see website), with on-board dining options. Sample fares: Schengen–Remich €6.50, Schengen–Grevenmacher €14 and Schengen–Trier €23.

BUS

Single/day tickets cost €2/4. Frequency on all routes drops to once hourly on Sundays.

Useful routes include the following:

160, 175 Luxembourg City–Remich (50 minutes, every 10 minutes)

185 Remich–Schengen (15 minutes, up to three per hour)

450 Remich–Grevenmacher (30 minutes) via Wormelange (15 minutes), twice hourly

474, 475, 485 Grevenmacher–Echternach (50 minutes, up to three per hour)

BICYCLE

A good option for exploring the wine route is hiring a bicycle with **Rentabike Miselerland** (www.entente-moselle.lu/en/rentabike/presentation; standard/mountain/electric-bike hire per day €12/15/20). Standard bikes are free if you have a Luxembourg Card, with discounts for mountain and electric bikes. Pick a bike up at one of 11 stations and drop off at another: just make sure that you check closing times and take ID.

Schengen & Remerschen

POP 4220

If the name Schengen sounds familiar it's likely due to the 1985 and 1990 treaties signed here that led to the border-free travel regime across large parts of Europe – the Schengen Area. Actually the signing took place in a boat moored off Schengen at a midriver point where, symbolically, France, Germany and Benelux meet.

This is commemmorated by a small **European Museum** (www.visitschengen.lu/musee-europeen; 6 Rue Robert Goebbels; ⊙ 10am-6pm Apr-Oct, to 5pm Nov-Mar) FREE whose displays including hats from customs officers of all the EU's member states. It's next to Schengen's ivy-draped 1779 castle-tower in which both Goethe and Victor Hugo once stayed.

DON'T MISS

MOSELLE WINE TASTING

Excellent *crémants* (sparkling wines) from the Moselle vineyards give Luxembourg the fizz and pop that keeps it buzzing throughout the summer. The region also produces whites – fruity Rivaners, lush Pinot Blancs and balanced Rieslings, not to mention El-bling, Chardonnay, Pinot Gris, Gewürztraminer, Auxerrois and Pinot Noir.

You can taste many of these along Luxembourg's 'Wine Route', though be aware that wineries are generally large companies and cooperatives rather than family châteaux. Typically a video of production techniques precedes a walk through the vast stain-less-steel fermentation and storage tanks with explainions of the *méthode traditionelle* of creating Champagne-style bubbles. Visits end with tastings. Alternatively forgo the tour altogether and head straight to the wineries' tasting rooms.

The most famous of all the Luxembourg *crémants* come from **Caves Bernard-Massard** (☑ 75 05 45 1; www.bernard-massard.lu; 8 Rue du Pont, Grevenmacher; tour incl 1 glass of wine €6; ☺ tours 9.30am-6pm Tue-Sun Apr-Oct, by reservation Nov-Mar, shop 10am-noon & 1.30-6pm Mon-Fri, 10am-1pm Sat) on the riverside just by the border bridge in work-aday **Grevenmacher**. Smartly dressed guides here lead slick, humorously presented tours lasting just 20 minutes with frequent departures, and the genteel tasting cafe has an open summer terrace with river views.

Most other wineries have less frequent departures and tours that last an hour or more. One-such is **Crémant Poll-Fabaire** (☑ 76 82 11; www.vinsmoselle.lu; 115 Route du Vin, Grevenmacher; tour €5.50, wine tasting €8, tour & wine-tasting €10.50; ☺ tours by reservation Oct-Aug, tasting room 8am-8pm Mon-Fri, 9am-8pm Sat, 9am-9pm Sun May-Oct, reduced hours rest of year), a large art deco block at pretty **Wormeldange**'s northern edge. The tastings here offer five glasses of still or sparkling wine, presented on a wrought-iron 'vine'.

Some 1.5km north of Remich by bus 450, the **Caves St-Martin** (☑ 23 69 97 74; www.cavesstmartin.lu; 53 Rte de Stadtbredimus; tour incl 1 glass of wine €6; ☺ tours 1.30-5pm Tue, 10-11.30am & 1.30-5pm Wed-Sun Apr-Oct) really are caves – time blackened and hewn directly into a riverside cliff. Their excellent *crémant* is actually produced elsewhere but the creation process (new and historic) is explained during 40-minute tours inside the cool, tunnels (always 12°C so bring a sweater). Advance reservations are recommended.

The wine route is also excellent for top-notch dining. Glass-box dining room **Bistro Quai** (☑ 24 55 87 75; www.quai.lu; 3 Rte du Vin; mains €16.50-29, platters €11-18.50; ☺ kitchen 11.30am-2pm & 6-10pm, bar to midnight; 🔊🕹) in Grevenmacher uses local wines in its rich sauces, while **Restaurant Mathes** (☑ 76 01 06; www.restaurant-mathes.lu; 37 Rte du Vin; mains €29.50-42, 6-course tasting menu €72; ☺ noon-2pm & 6-9.30pm Wed-Sun May-Oct, closed Sun Nov-Apr) in Han offers full-on gastronomy overlooking its own vineyards.

Around 3km northwest in Schengen's sister town of Remerschen you'll find a wetlands nature centre and a remarkable architectural museum as well as a fine **HI hostel** (☑ 26 27 66 700; www.youthhostels.lu; 31 Rte du Vin; dm/s/d €24.70/39.70/60.40; ☺ check-in 5-10pm; 🅿@🛜) opposite a big 1940s winery with boat-shaped tasting-bar.

◉ Sights

Valentiny Foundation   MUSEUM
(www.valentiny-foundation.com; 34 Rte du Vin, Remerschen; ☺ 2-6pm Tue-Sun) **FREE** World-renowned Remich-born architect François Valentiny built this extraordinary Arctic-white building with lattice-like cut-out win-dows in 2016 as an exhibition space for his and his Viennese business partner Hubert

Hermann's designs. On display are 3260 piec-es including architectural plans, drawings, sculptures and scale models; it also hosts temporary exhibitions by other architects.

Le Centre Nature et Forêt Biodiversum   NATURE CENTRE
(☑ 23 60 90 61; www.environnement.public.lu; 5 Bréicherwee, Remerschen; ☺ 10am-6pm Tue-Sun Apr-Oct, to 5pm Nov-Mar) 🖋 **FREE** Built in nat-ural timbers by star Luxembourg architect François Valentiny, this truncated pyra-mid-shaped nature centre features inter-active exhibitions on the evolution of the surrounding Haff Réimech wetlands. From the centre, a signposted 2.5km 'discovery trail' leads visitors through the biodiverse ecosystem, with birdwatching hides along

the boardwalk circuit. Over 250 bird species have been recorded here, including the grey woodpecker, melodious warbler, crested grebe, purple heron and great white egret.

MÜLLERTHAL REGION

Nicknamed Little Switzerland for its patchwork of forests and grassy fields (if not Alpine peaks), the Müllerthal is Luxembourg's best region for outdoor activities. A great network of hiking trails leads to narrow, mossy ravines, crystal-clear creeks and strange rock formations, particularly west of Echternach. Pedal here through castle villages or paddle down the Sûre.

Larochette

POP 2094

In a deep-cut valley on the banks of the Ernz Blanche river, little Larochette's sturdy slate-roofed houses cluster beneath the dramatic clifftop ruins of its medieval **château** (☑83 74 97; www.visitlarochette.lu; Rte de Mersch; adult/child €4/1; ⊘10am-6pm Apr-Oct). Accessed by steep paths or by a longer, gentler 2km road (start off towards Mersch then double back), the castle site is less complete than it appears from below, but exploring its lawns, wall stubs and stairways is nonetheless compelling. The four-storey 1385 keep is especially worth climbing for the vertiginous view from its box window. The surrounding forest has fantastic hiking.

On a wooded hillside 750m north of the village centre there's a handy HI hostel (p249). Bus 100 on the Diekirch–Luxembourg City route stops in Larochette.

Echternach

POP 5614

One of Luxembourg's prettiest towns, with a beautiful central square, Echternach has a long history as a monastery settlement. It makes a great base for hiking and cycling or just an afternoon's stroll on a sunny day.

History

Site of a 1st-century Roman villa, Echternach passed to the Merovingian kings, who in turn presented the area to Northumbrian missionary St-Willibrord who, as Bishop of Utrecht, founded a church here in AD 698. Among Ripon-born Willibrord's many miracles was the fact he wasn't beaten to death by the angry guardians of pagan temples that he vandalised in the name of his God.

By the time of Willibrord's death in 739, Echternach had become a thriving monastery. Its scriptorium became one of northern Europe's most influential and its basilica-church was rebuilt in fine Romanesque style in 1031. A vast Benedictine abbey developed around the basilica and a town around that. After the French invasion of 1794, however, the church was sacked and the abbey used as a porcelain factory.

⊙ Sights

St-Willibrord Basilica　　　　CHURCH
(www.willibrord.lu; Parvis de la Basilique; ⊘9.30am-6.30pm) St-Willibrord Basilica is part of the Abbaye d'Echternach complex. First raised around AD 700, it was rebuilt in 1862 but bombed to rubble during WWII, when much of the town was severely damaged. Nonetheless, Willibrord's relics slept peacefully in the 8th-century crypt, and while the reconstructed basilica is a dark and sombre affair with 1950s stained-glass windows, the vaulted crypt still contains the highly venerated relics of St Willibrord in a stone coffin covered by an elaborate white-marble canopy.

★**Abbaye d'Echternach**　　　MONASTERY
(☑72 74 72; https://web.cathol.lu; 11 Parvis de la Basilique; adult/child €3/free; ⊘museum 10am-5pm Jul & Aug, 10am-noon & 2-5pm Apr-Jun, Sep & Oct) Just north of the basilica, 19th-century Benedictine abbey buildings spread towards the tree-lined banks of the Sûre. Most of the complex is now a school and closed to the public, but its famous scriptorium the vaulted basement houses an atmospheric museum. You'll see facsimiles of beautiful pages from classic illuminated manuscripts, the stunning cover of the *Codex Aureus*, a copy of a Celtic high cross, Merovingian sarcophagi and a video of the Sprinprozession (St-Willibrord Pageant) through the ages. Admission includes an audioguide.

Stroll through the gateway in the Abbey's north arcade to peek through wrought-iron gates at the splendid 1736 Orangery in formal French-style gardens, or head east between tennis courts to find a 1761 rococo pavilion.

Villa Romaine　　　　　　　RUINS
(☑47 93 30 214; www.mnha.lu; 47 Rue des Romains; ⊘10am-noon & 1-5pm Tue-Sun Easter-Sep) FREE Excavated during the creation of the reservoir lake, today a popular boating and

DON'T MISS

DINE AT BOURGLINSTER CASTLE

Spectacularly set inside the turreted, story-book castle Château de Bourglinster, parts of which date from the 11th century, Michelin-starred **La Distillerie** (☑78 78 78 1; www.bourglinster.lu; 8 Rue du Château, Bourglinster; degustation menus €90-150, with wine €140-225; ☺noon-3pm Wed, noon-3pm & 7-9.30pm Thu-Sun; ☑) is a full-blown gastronomic extravaganza. Vegetables are the star of chef René Mathieu's intricate tasting menus (there's no à la carte); all-vegetarian menus are available at both lunch and dinner. Mathieu forages for wild herbs in the castle's grounds.

Part of the same set-up but in a separate wing, the more casual **Brasserie Côté Cour** (☑7-9.30pm Wed, noon-3pm & 7-9.30pm Thu to Sun; mains €28, menus €35-65) is excellent value.

recreation area, this Roman villa has sparse, over-neatened remains but was obviously an impressively large, peristyle set-up. Free 30-minute guided tours in English take place at 3pm on Sundays. Its ornamental garden is planted with medicinal species used during Roman times and has a grapevine-draped pergola. It's set in parkland 1km southwest of the town centre.

Dënzelt ARCHITECTURE

(Place du Marché) The most distinctive building on Echternach's delightful town square is this stone-fronted former law court. Its origins date back to the 14th century, though the arcade, statues and corner turrets that give it its current neo-Gothic appearance date from an 1895 rebuild. The interior is closed to the public.

🏃 Activities

Marked hiking trails start near Echternach's bus station. Flat riverside bicycle paths trace the Sûre River all the way to Diekirch (27km), south into the Moselle Valley and along a former railway line to Luxembourg City. The youth hostel rents out bicycles and has an indoor **climbing wall** (☑26 27 66 400; www.youthhostels.lu; Chemin vers Rodenhof; adult/child €8/5.50, 1hr lesson €20/13, equipment hire €2; ☺7-10pm Tue & Fri, 2.30-4.30pm Wed & Thu, 2.30-7pm Sat & Sun Jul–mid-Sep, reduced hrs mid-Sep–Jun). Kayakers can take bus 500 to Dillingen and

paddle back with **Outdoor Freizeit** (☑86 91 39; www.outdoorfreizeit.lu; 10 Rue de la Sûre, Dillingen; 1-/2-person canoe or kayak hire €15/30, 6-person raft €150, mountain bike per half-/full day €15/20; ☺9am-4pm Apr-Sep).

🎉 Festivals & Events

Sprinprozession CULTURAL

(https://web.cathol.lu; ☺May/Jun) On Whit Tuesday, 51 days after Easter Sunday, the Sprinprozession sees many townsfolk and pilgrims whipping out their handkerchiefs as thousands dance in formation through the streets of Echternach. It's the culmination of the St-Willibrord pilgrimage, and some suggest that the dance was originally designed to mimic the writhing of plague-sufferers and in so doing provide protection.

🛏️ Sleeping

Echternach has the Müllerthal's widest range of accommodation, including a lakeside **HI hostel** (Auberge de Jeunesse; ☑26 27 66 400; www.youthhostels.lu; Chemin vers Rodenhof; dm/s/d €24.70/39.70/60.40; ☺check-in 5-10pm; P@🎧) with an activities centre 1.5km south of the centre.

Hostellerie de la Basilique HOTEL €€

(☑72 94 83; www.hotel-basilique.lu; 7 Place du Marché; s/d incl breakfast from €106/126; ☺late Mar-early Nov; P🌡🎧) With a perfect location right on the central square, Hostellerie de la Basilique makes a great base for exploring the Müllerthal, with spacious rooms with bold accent colours such as lime or plum, and the bonus of on-site parking. Children aren't permitted. Its cafe-restaurant downstairs has a table-filled terrace. Enter via 3 Rue de la Montagne.

Hôtel Le Pavillon HOTEL €€

(☑72 98 09; www.lepavillon.lu; 2 Rue de la Gare; s/d/q incl breakfast €72/88/146; 🎧) Just off Echternach's main square on pedestrianised Rue de la Gare, the Pavillon's public areas and guest rooms have warm colours, lantern-style lamps and prints by German expressionist painter August Macke. On the ground floor is a popular French-Luxembourgish brasserie. Bike hire costs €10 per day.

Tours Medievales APARTMENT €€€

(☑72 02 30; www.visitechternach.lu; per 3 nights/week from €480/750; 🎧) Small sections of Echternach's former city walls are still visible amid suburban houses. Three of the wall's medieval towers have been imaginatively converted into modern, upmarket accommodation, each sleeping four to six. However, they're only available for stays of three nights or more and should be booked well ahead via the tourist office.

✗ Eating & Drinking

Restaurants and cafes line Rue de la Gare.

GriMouGi   MEDITERRANEAN €€
(☑ 72 00 26; www.grimougi.com; 34 Rue du Pont; mains €16-29.50; ⊙ 11.30am-2pm & 6-10pm Mon, Wed-Fri & Sun, 6-10pm Sat, closed mid-Aug–mid-Sep) Away from the tourist beat, 400m east of the central square by the bridge to Germany, contemporary GriMouGi serves innovative salads, such as seared duck with roast plums, and artistically presented mains like mussel and octopus *bouillabaisse*, wild boar tortellini, or asparagus, walnut and blue cheese risotto. It's essential to book at weekends, when locals pack it out.

Oktav Amadeus   ITALIAN €€
(☑ 26 72 15 18; www.oktav-amadeus.lu; 56 Rue de la Gare; pizza & pasta €10.50-19.50, mains €17.50-31.50; ⊙ 11.30am-4.30pm & 6-10.30pm) Framed by a wrap-around street terrace, this sleek spot has black-and-white decor and waist-coated waiters serving classic Italian pasta, thin-crust pizza and more substantial mains (such as scampi sautéed in garlic, Cotechino Modena sausage with polenta or veal Milanese). Finish off with ricotta-filled *cannoli* pastries or an icy Tartufo (chocolate-coated ice cream) for dessert.

ℹ Information

Tourist Office (☑ 72 02 30; www.visitechternach.lu; 10 Parvis de la Basilique; ⊙ 10am-6pm Mon-Sat, to noon Sun) Very helpful office facing the basilica, with comprehensive information on hiking the area. The website has a useful town map you can download.

ℹ Getting There & Away

Bitburg (bus 401, €2, 30 minutes, hourly Monday to Saturday)

Larochette (bus 414, €2, 45 minutes, eight to nine per day Monday to Saturday) via Beaufort (20 minutes)

Luxembourg City (buses 110 and 111, €2, one hour, two per hour)

Beaufort

POP 2412

On a plateau surrounded by large rock formations, forests and waterfalls, Beaufort makes an excellent base for hiking the Müllerthal's trails, which fan out from the town.

◎ Sights

★ **Beaufort Castles**   CASTLE
(☑ 83 66 01; www.beaufortcastles.com; 24 Rue du Château; adult/child medieval castle €5/free, Renaissance castle €10/5; ⊙ medieval castle 9am-6pm daily Easter-early Nov, Renaissance castle by reservation Thu-Sun Easter-early Nov) Beaufort's two castles sit across a wooded valley on the town's western edge. Built from sandstone on the site of a Roman camp, the five-storey

---

OFF THE BEATEN TRACK

HIKING THE MÜLLERTHAL TRAILS

West of Echternach, hikers can squeeze through shoulder-wide micro-gorges, cross trickling streams with mossy banks and pass eroded sandstone formations along the **Müllerthal trails** (www.mullerthal.lu).

Three distinct but connected loop trails (37km to 38km each) form the backbone of the network, but various connected local walks, designated as 'Extra Tours', mean that you could happily spend a week or more hiking the whole circuit. Echternach is a trailhead for trails 1 and 2, while trail 3 passes through both Beaufort and Larochette. Trail 2 is the prettiest, has the most rock formations and is also the most up-and-down. The website suggests a six-day grand circuit of the three loops, which is easily accomplished either overnighting along the trail, or taking the bus back to Echternach each day. The trails are very well signposted.

Shorter walks include the E1 (11.7km), a marked circular path that starts up Rue Charly from Echternach bus station and winds past the Gorge du Loup (Wolfsschlucht), meaning 'wolves' canyon' (though no wolves have inhabited the area since the early 1800s), where a stone staircase leads to a viewpoint overlooking Echternach and the Sûre. Further on, the trail traverses the Labyrinthe, a succession of otherworldly cliffs and tight ravines. You'll come to a small cave system, Hohllayust, just before reaching the village of Berdorf.

medieval castle expanded from 11th-century origins but never recovered from WWII bombing during the Battle of the Ardennes. You're free to explore its many levels. In the 17th century, a Renaissance-style castle was constructed alongside it – compulsory guided tours last 50 minutes. Admission to either castle includes a tasting of locally made Cassero fruit liqueur.

🛏 Sleeping & Eating

Beaufort has a year-round campground (☑83 60 99 300; www.campingplage.lu; 87 Grand-Rue; camp site for 2 people & small tent €12, with car €20, tipi/chalet from €45/50; P 🕹) 600m north of centre, a modern HI hostel (☑26 27 66 300; www.youthhostels.lu; 55 Rte de Dillngen; dm/s/d €24.70/30.70/60.80; check-in 5-10pm; P @) 500m northeast, and a couple of small, central hotels with pleasaent dining.

Half way between Beaufort and Echternach, Berdorfer Keis (www.berdorfer.lu; 2 Rue de Consdorf, Berdorf; 8.30am-noon & 1-4pm Mon, Wed, Fri & Sat) 🌾 is a great farm shop selling its own cheeses.

Auberge Rustique   INN €€
(☑83 60 86; www.aubergerustique.lu; 55 Rue du Château; s/d/tr from €44/80/108; kitchen noon-8.30pm; P) Vine-draped Auberge Rustique would overlook the castle except for a curtain of trees. Receiving guests since 1790, its eight cosy rooms with contemporary white-tiled bathrooms sit above a lovable country pub-restaurant serving French and Luxembourgish cuisine (mains €13.50 to €22) using fruit, vegetables and herbs from its own organic garden. In summer, the best seats are on the shaded terrace.

ℹ Getting There & Away

Ettelbrück (bus 502, 15 minutes) via Diekirch (10 minutes), hourly Monday to Saturday, every two hours Sunday

Larochette (bus 414, 25 minutes) via Echternach (20 minutes), no Sunday service.

ÉISLEK

Winding, fast-flowing rivers cut deep through green tablelands in Luxembourg's section of the rugged, wooded Ardennes region. Website www.visit-eislek.lu is packed with information on the region whose highlights include pretty Esch-sur-Sûre, Bourscheid's dramatic castle ruins and charming Vianden. Contrastingly workaday, the main transport hubs are Diekirch and forgettable Ettelbrück, whose one minor attraction is the General Patton Museum (☑81 03 22; www.patton.lu; 5 Rue Dr Klein; adult/child €5/3; 10am-5pm Tue-Sun) commemorating the achievements of US Third Army general George S Patton who led a liberating US force into town on Christmas Day 1944.

Bourscheid
POP 266

Especially when seen from afar, the splendid ruin of the Château de Bourscheid (☑99 05 70; http://chateau.bourscheid.lu; Rue du Château; adult/child €5/3; 9.30am-6pm Apr–mid-Oct, 11am-4pm mid-Oct–Mar) is surely Luxembourg's most dramatic. Occupying the site of a former Roman watchtower, its construction began around AD 1000 and the original belfry and inner walls still survive. Outer walls were added in 1350 and the dungeons in 1498. Restoration is ongoing but the castle remains open for audioguided visits. Climbing the squat, 12th-century, square keep you're rewarded with turret-framed views over the forested river bend far below, an area known as Buurschter Plage, home to rural hideaway accommodation at Cocoon Hôtel Belair (☑26 30 351; www.cocoonhotels.eu; Buurschter Plage; s/d/ste incl breakfast from €100/120/160; P). To get there follow the steeply descending road that winds 2km down to Bourscheid-Moulin, where the Brasserie de Vieux Moulin (☑90 80 88; www.amkeller.lu; Rue du Château; snacks €3-9, mains €16-24; kitchen 11am-2pm & 6-10pm Tue-Sun, bar to midnight Tue-Thu & Sun, to 1am Fri & Sat;) is a good bet for a beer and a snack. The hotel is around 500m west of that.

From Ettelbrück bus 545 runs hourly to tiny Bourscheid village, 1.8km above the castle, while route 550 passes Bourscheid-Moulin after around 15 minutes. However, no bus takes the road between Bourscheid and Bourscheid-Moulin that passes the castle.

Diekirch
POP 6756

Diekirch is synonymous with the nation's most famous beer, but it also played a pivotal role during WWII: US troops crossed the river here on January 18 1945 at the culmination of the bloody Battle of the Ardennes (aka the Battle of the Bulge). Today Diekirch is the Grand Duchy's military headquarters and home to the country's most important war museum, the **Musée National d'Histoire Militaire** (📞 80 89 08; www.mnhm.net; 10 Rue Bamertal; adult/child €5/3; ⊘ 10am-6pm Tue-Sun). Packed full of WWII equipment, vehicles and memorabilia, the museum has numerous well-executed mannequin scenes that powerfully illustrate the suffering and hardships of the battles fought in the thick snows of Christmas 1944. It's 300m north of the compact, pedestrianised old-town core, which has two other minor museums and a **tourist office** (📞 80 30 23; http://tourisme.diekirch.lu; 3 Place de la Libération; ⊘ 10am-12.30pm & 1-6pm Mon-Fri, 10am-12.30pm & 1-5pm Sat, 10am-2pm Sun mid-Jul–mid-Aug, reduced hours rest of year). The train and bus stations are a further 850m southwest.

ℹ️ Getting There & Around

To Luxembourg City, half-hourly trains take 45 minutes via Ettelbrück (10 minutes). Hourly bus 100 takes 75 minutes via Larochette (25 minutes).

Just west of the pedestrian zone, **Nordstad** (📞 26 80 33 76; www.rentabike.lu; 27 Rue Jean l'Aveugle; standard/mountain/electric-bike hire per day €12/15/20; ⊘ 10am-5pm Apr-Sep, by arrangement Oct-Mar) rents out bicycles.

Vianden

POP 1811

Towering amid the mists and wooded hills above Vianden is a vast slate-roofed castle complex whose impregnable white-stone walls glow golden in the evening's floodlights, creating one of Luxembourg's most photogenic scenes. Vianden's appealing Old Town is essentially one road, cobbled Grand-Rue, which rises 700m to the castle gates from a bridge across the Our river. Newer sections of town follow the riverbanks in either direction.

On weekend afternoons in summer, Vianden can get overloaded with tourists and traffic. But get up early and you'll have the whole town largely to yourself.

History

First mentioned in AD 698 but dating back to Roman times, when the valley was used for viticulture, Vianden (Veianen in Luxembourgish) gained its charter way back in 1308 and developed as a major leather and crafts centre. Its craftspeople had formed their own guilds by the late 15th century, by

which stage the county of Vianden had become part of the greater Nassau lands.

In the 1790s, like the rest of Luxembourg, Vianden was swallowed by revolutionary France, but after 1815 when the French withdrew, a large part of the county was given to Prussia. Vianden itself was left an impoverished backwater cut off from its traditional hinterland. Trade died off and many townsfolk were forced to seek work as travelling minstrels. Meanwhile, the Dutch king who'd been handed the town saw little use in its gigantic, hard-to-heat castle. In 1820 he sold it to a scrap merchant who stripped out and flogged any marketable building materials. What remained of the castle fell into ruin despite occasional attempts to shore up the walls. French writer Victor Hugo visited in 1862 and 1865, before living here for three months in 1871; the town has a literary museum dedicated to him.

It wasn't until 1977, when the Grand Ducal family formally gave the castle to the Luxembourg state, that long-term restoration finally went ahead. The result was spectacular and the castle has since been not only a tourist magnet but also the backdrop set for several movies.

⊙ Sights & Activities

★ **Château de Vianden**   CASTLE
(📞 83 41 08; www.castle-vianden.lu; Montée du Château; adult/child €7/2; ⊘ 10am-4pm Nov-Feb, to 5pm Mar & Oct, to 6pm Apr-Sep) This château's extraordinary outline is the result of an almost-total 20th-century restoration after the original, built from the 11th to 14th centuries, had fallen into complete ruin. Walkways in the lower levels display different layers of occupation, from the Roman era onwards. The open-air Byzantine Hall is a marvellous space, while the Gothic polygonal chapel is built around a central well. Plusher halls display fine Flanders tapestries, while photo galleries show the reconstruction process and famous visitors. A worthwhile audioguide costs €2. The vaulted, barrel-strewn Keller bar opens occasionally for jazz concerts.

Grand-Rue   STREET
Grand-Rue's most attractive section is around Place Victor Abens, where the town hall straddles a small spring. The Église des Trinitaires church was built in 1248 and reconstructed after a fire in 1498; behind it the pretty cloister that was once the heart of the monastery remains. Both the stairway between Grand-Rue 58/60 (opposite

the church) and the alley Montée du Beffroi (just west of Musée de la Ville de Vianden) take you towards an isolated 1603 belfry on a ridge outcrop. It's closed to visitors, but there are beautiful views over the town and river.

Télésiège
CABLE CAR

(www.vianden-info.lu; 39 Rue du Sanatorium; adult/child return €4.80/2.50, one way €3.50/2; ⊙10am-5pm Easter–mid-Oct) The *télésiège* (chairlift) takes 11 minutes to swing across the river and up through oak woods to a snack bar whose terrace offers far-reaching views across town and oblique glimpses of the castle, a 250m downhill forest walk to the south. It closes in adverse weather. Photos of you with the town as a backdrop are snapped as you come up, which you can then purchase.

Parc d'Aventure Tree Climber Vianden
ADVENTURE SPORTS

(www.vianden-info.lu; Montée du Château; adult/child €20/16; ⊙10am-6pm Apr-Oct) North of the castle, this hillside adventure park has routes through the forest using zip lines (including Luxembourg's longest, at 375m) and rope courses. The easiest way to reach it is to take the chairlift to the top and walk down 150m.

Musée d'Histoire de la Ville de Vianden
MUSEUM

(☑83 45 91; www.vianden-info.lu; 96-98 Grand-Rue; adult/child €3/1.50; ⊙11am-5pm daily Jun-Aug, 11am-5pm Tue-Sun Easter-May & Sep–mid-Oct) Vianden's local history museum is formed from two houses knocked together. One maintains its full 19th-century decor; the other partly retains equipment from its 1950s incarnation as a bakery. Upstairs, historical and cultural exhibits are brought to life by human cut-out mannequins and push-button music. It's all in German, but a well-presented English-language accompanying text is available on request at the ticket desk.

Musée Littéraire Victor Hugo
MUSEUM

(☑26 87 40 88; www.victor-hugo.lu; 37 Rue de la Gare; adult/child €5/free; ⊙noon-6pm Tue-Sun mid-Apr–Oct, 11am-5pm Tue-Sun Nov–mid-Apr) Across a stone bridge from Grand-Rue is a replica Rodin bust of French writer Victor Hugo. In 1871 Hugo stayed for three months in the house facing this point, part of his 19-year exile from France. Those three months were long enough for him to get the Vianden castle architect fired for substandard reconstruction work. Along with Hugo's manuscripts and sketches, highlights of the

house-turned-musem include stupendous castle views from its windows.

Piscine Vianden
SWIMMING

(www.vianden.lu; Rue du Sanatorium; adult/child €5/2.50; ⊙1-7pm Mon & Tue, from 10am Wed-Sun Jun-Aug) In summer, this outdoor swimming complex is the most scenic place to cool off. Set high up in the forest, a steep 1.5km walk north of the town centre (or a five-minute drive), it has an Olympic-sized pool and a smaller play pool with a water slide, along with a kiosk selling refreshments. Valley-and-town views from here are sublime too.

★ Festivals & Events

Festival Médiéval
CULTURAL

(www.castle-vianden.lu; Château de Vianden; ⊙late Jul–early Aug) Held at the Château de Vianden (p261) over seven days each summer, this is Luxembourg's largest medieval festival, with jousting, jugglers, minstrels, birds-of-prey shows, and a medieval market with food and drink stalls serving mead (honey wine). A free shuttle bus serves the town centre each day from noon to 7pm.

⭐ Sleeping & Eating

Plentiful accommodation includes summer campgrounds south of the centre and an HI hostel (☑26 27 66 80 0; www.youthhostels.lu; 3 Montée du Château; dm/s/d €24.70/39.70/60.40; ☐) 650m up Grand Rue near the castle base: don't lug your bags up here before 5pm when reception opens.

There's ample dining choice along both Grand-Rue and the riverbanks, but when it's quiet, restaurants tend to close very early.

★ Auberge Aal Veinen
INN €€

(☑83 43 68; http://vianden.beimhunn.lu; 114 Grand-Rue; s/d €60/90; ⊙closed mid-Dec–mid-Jan; ☐) Painted a pretty rose-pink, this charming inn has nine stylish, well-appointed rooms seamlessly inserted into an ultra-quaint barrage of ancient dark-wooden beamwork, plus a good German **restaurant** (Beim Hunn; mains €16-34.50; ⊙noon-3pm & 6-10pm Thu-Tue; ☐☐). A public car park is located across the street.

Hôtel-Restaurant Petry
HOTEL €€

(☑83 41 22; www.hotel-petry.com; 15 Rue de la Gare; s/d incl breakfast from €66/86; ☐☐☐☐) Situated just across the Our river from the town centre, the Petry's rooms are comfy if fairly spartan; superior rooms are worth the small upgrade. South-facing rooms have river views. Guests get free use of the pool and

CASTLE SLEEPS

Château d'Urspelt (☑26 90 56 10; www.chateau-urspelt.lu; Am Schlass, Urspelt; s/d/ste incl breakfast from €139/146/189; P ⊙ ⚍) A vision of conical turrets and grand gates, this romantic castle wraps around a central courtyard overlooked by an elevated swimming pool and sun terrace. It's worth upgrading to a superior room or palatial suite for the full fairy-tale experience; suites come with sofa beds and sleep up to four people. Its gourmet restaurant serves exquisitely presented modern European cuisine.

There's a hot tub and steam room. It's 4km northeast of Clervaux in a château that was rebuilt in 1860 and has been a hotel since 2008.

Auberge de Jeunesse Hollenfels (☑26 27 66 500; www.youthhostels.lu; 2 Rue du Château, Hollenfels; dm/s/d €24.70/39.70/60.40; ⊙check-in 5-10pm; P ⊙) Hollenfels' hostel lies across the moat bridge of the mighty medieval castle of the same name. The main tower was built in 1380 but is closed to the public. Within an adjacent 1729-constructed building, there are 68 beds in brightly painted, modern dorms with timber bunks (plus another 56 beds reserved for groups). HI members receive discounts.

It's around 5km southwest of Mersch towards Ansembourg where the grand **château** (www.gcansembourg.eu; 8 Rue de la Vallée; ⊙gardens 9am-sunset) FREE is closed to the public but has an 18th-century Baroque garden that's free to explore.

---

spa complex 160m to the east. Opening to an terrace, its on-site restaurant (mains €16 to €28) specialises in wood-fired pizza.

Hôtel Heintz HOTEL €€
(☑83 41 55; www.hotel-heintz.lu; 55 Grand-Rue; d/tr/f from €75/110/145; ⊙Easter-Sep; P ⊙) Adjacent to the monastery, old-fashioned Hôtel Heintz occupies what was once the brewery-inn of the Trinitarian monks. Grandfather clocks, top hats and other knick-knacks decorate landings flanking the staircase (there's also a lift). Guest rooms at the rear open to honeysuckle- and wisteria-draped balconies overlooking the gardens, courtyard and car park (spaces are limited, so reserve one when you book).

❶ Getting There & Away

Buses stop outside the **tourist office** (☑83 42 57; www.vianden-info.lu; 1a Rue du Vieux Marché; ⊙10am-noon & 1-6pm Mon-Fri, 10am-3pm Sat & Sun) hourly for Clervaux (40 minutes), and once or twice hourly for Ettelbrück (25 minutes) via Diekirch (20 minutes).

Esch-sur-Sûre

POP 314
One of Luxembourg's prettiest scenes, Esch-sur-Sûre wraps around a knoll surrounded by an emerald-green loop of the Sûre river. It's topped by a ruined 10th–13th-century **castle tower** (off Rue de l'Église; ⊙sunrise-sunset) FREE that's illuminated at night. West of the village is the Parc

Naturel de la Haute Sûre, a nature park with beautiful scenery as well as hiking and lake-swimming on part of the Lac de la Haute Sûre, which supplies 70% of Luxembourg's water. The park's visitor centre is 600m southwest of Esch at **Duch vum Séi** (Musée de Draperie; ☑89 93 31 1; www.vumsei.lu; 15 Rte de Lultzhausen; adult/child €3/free; ⊙10am-6pm Jul & Aug, 10am-noon & 2-6pm Mon, Tue, Thu & Fri, 2-6pm Sat & Sun Sep-Jun), an interesting museum of textile looms in a former cloth factory.

🛏 Sleeping & Eating

There's a scattering of small hotels in the village, a **campground** (☑83 95 14; www.campingaal.lu; 1 Rue Camping Aal; camp site €7 plus per adult/child €7/4, cabins per week from €400; ⊙Feb-Dec; P ⊙) 900m east and a contemporary **HI hostel** (☑26 27 66 600; www.youthhostels.lu; 20 An der Driicht, Lultzhausen; dm/s/d €24.70/39.70/60.40; ⊙check-in 5-10pm; P ⊙) with its own beach, 6km west on the Lac de la Haute Sûre where kayaks and paddleboards are available to guests.

Hôtel de la Sûre HOTEL €€
(☑83 91 10; www.hotel-de-la-sure.lu; 1 Rue du Pont; d/studio incl breakfast from €109/282; P ⊙) In the village centre, this hotel's 23 guest rooms spread across several adjacent cottages. While some have quainter settings than others, they're all well kept and relatively modern, and a couple of rooms have hot tubs. Studio apartments are equipped with kitchenettes. The central building has a gourmet **restaurant**

(mains €19-31; ⊙ noon-3pm & 6.30-10pm Feb–mid-Dec) 🚲 ; services include bike hire.

ⓘ Getting There & Away

Monday to Saturday, buses run hourly to Ettelbrück (30 minutes) and seven times daily to Wiltz (20 minutes). On Sundays there are just three Esch–Ettelbrück services.

Wiltz

POP 5469

Sweeping up a partly wooded hill, Wiltz's historic centre is largely hidden behind trees, which conceal a Renaissance town hall and a stately château containing a trio of museums. In the valley, the lower town is a modern residential and service hub with amenities including petrol stations and supermarkets.

◉ Sights & Events

★ Château de Wiltz   CASTLE

(☑ 95 74 44; www.wiltz.lu; Rue du Château; adult/child €3.50/free, brewery tastings extra €4; ⊙ 9am-6pm daily Jul & Aug, 9am-noon & 2-5pm Mon-Sat Sep-Jun) Wiltz's castle was originally built in the 13th century but destroyed several times; the present château was constructed between 1631 and 1720 in the Renaissance style. Admission includes an audioguide and entry to its three museums: a tannery; an exhibition on the Battle of the Ardennes; and a brewing museum in the stables, with a bottle collection, an authentic if relocated classic bar, and a working microbrewery.

Wiltz Festival   PERFORMING ARTS

(www.festivalwiltz.lu; Château de Wiltz; ⊙ Jul) Running for a month in July, this excellent arts festival featuring jazz, orchestras, theatre, dance, acrobats and street performers takes place largely in the open-air theatre in the town's château.

🍴 Sleeping & Eating

★ Restaurant Beim Schlass   FRENCH €€

(☑ 95 80 18; www.beimschlass.lu; 1 Grand-Rue; mains €18-32, 2-/3-course lunch menus €15/18.50, 6-course dinner menu €37; ⊙ noon-2pm & 6-9pm Wed-Sun; 🅿) Spilling on to a tree-shaded garden terrace by the château, Beim Schlass serves gourmet French fare: beef tartare with confit tomato sorbet, Cognac-flambéed sweetbreads with pigeon sauce, dry-aged Sal-ers fillet steak with wild-mushroom mousse, and chocolate soufflé with caramelised pistachio dust and fresh raspberries for dessert. Reislings and sparkling *crémants* from Luxembourg's Moselle Valley dominate the wine list.

Super-handy for the castle, it's in a modernised 19th-century mansion that's also an eight-room hotel renovated in 2018 (doubles from €79). Superior rooms have balconies or terraces with castle views.

ⓘ Getting There & Away

Trains to Ettelbrück (30 minutes) and Luxembourg City (one hour) require a change in Kautenbach. Buses to Clervaux (35 minutes) run hourly but not on Sundays.

Clervaux

POP 1309

Wrapped into a wooded curl of the Clerve river, pretty Clervaux is dominated by its distinctive whitewashed castle, a fully rebuilt replica of the 1129 original that was razed in WWII. Inside are three museums, the standout of which is Edward Steichen's Unesco World Heritage–listed photography exhibition **Family of Man** (☑ 92 96 57; www.clervaux.lu; Montée du Château; adult/child Family of Man exhibition €6/free, other museums €5/free; ⊙ Family of Man exhibition noon-6pm Wed-Sun Mar-Dec, other museums 10am-6pm Tue-Sun May-Oct, 10am-6pm Sat & Sun Nov-Apr). Gifted to Clervaux in 1964, this 'mirror of the essential oneness of mankind' comprises 503 black-and-white, mid-20th-century photos by 273 photographers from 68 countries interspersed with thought-provoking quotations. Free 90-minute tours in English are held at 4pm on Sundays.

There's also a 1909 neo-Romanesque **abbey** (www.abbaye-clervaux.lu) with exhibition space and Gregorian chants at 3pm on Sundays.

Clervaux has a string of traditional and contemporary hotels in the town centre and along the Clerve river. For restaurants and cafes with heated outdoor terraces, look along pedestrianised Grand-Rue.

Buses run to Vianden (50 minutes, four daily) and Wiltz (40 minutes, not Sundays). Trains link to Luxembourg City (one hour) hourly via Ettelbrück (30 minutes) and Liège (€25.40, 1¾ hours) every two hours.

Understand Belgium & Luxembourg

Belgium & Luxembourg Today

The tumults of history mean that both countries are multilingual states. However, while little Luxembourg, one of the world's richest countries per capita, seems to take its status as cultural-linguistic melting pot in its stride, in Belgium a more defined linguistic divide is the cause of frequent tensions and political rifts. So while the economy remains remarkably resilient despite years of EU austerity, the question of whether Belgium will one day split in half is never far from the surface.

Best on Film

The Brand New Testament (2015) God exists, and lives in Belgium.
Two Days, One Night (2014) Factory life in Wallonia's industrial heartland.
Rust and Bone (2012) A gritty tale set on the Côte d'Azur and Belgium.
Les Barons (2009) Comedy set in Brussels' North African community.
In Bruges (2008) Black comedy with a *Pulp Fiction*–style code of gangster honour, filmed in Bruges.
Girl with a Pearl Earring (2003) Belgian cityscapes stand in for Vermeer's Delft.

Best in Print

A Tall Man in a Low Land (Harry Pearson; 1998) Still the funniest, most insightful Belgian travelogue.
King Leopold's Ghost (Adam Hochschild; 1998) Both a biography and an account of Belgium's Congo history.
Flanders: A Cultural History (Andre de Vries; 2007) An anecdote-packed cultural history of Flanders.
War and Turpentine (Stefan Hertmans; 2013) A century's memories of war and art with Ghent as a backdrop.
The Belgians: An Unexpected Fashion Story (Oscar van den Boogaard et al; 2015) From the 2015 exhibition of the same name, the ultimate overview of the country's fashion industry.

Let's Stay Together?

In May 2019 Belgium goes to the polls. As ever, the key question of Belgium's continued existence as a single country is likely to remain a major background theme. However, much work has been done to reduce nationalist pressure over the last few years. State reforms pushed through in 2012 gave so much autonomy to the regions that Belgium is one of the most decentralised countries in Europe. Since 2014, when the parliamentary term was extended to five years, the Flemish nationalist N-VA has been the biggest single party in the federal parliament. During these years, it has seemingly put any more radical separatist ideas pragmatically on hold while playing a more mainstream role as part of the centre-right ruling government. Though Charles Michel from the French-speaking MR party has been prime minister since 2014, N-VA leader Bart de Wever has been widely seen as the power behind the throne. His rapid rise to prominence over the last decade has been as astonishing as his physical transformation: his loss of over 60kg (in less than a year), along with his running of marathons, was applauded by his fans, discussed by TV diet programs, and eyed with suspicion as a kind of Putinesque show of machismo by his critics. He certainly remains the man to watch, and most believe that longer-term, moves towards confederalism or beyond are part of his plan.

Marching Ahead

Economically, while there remains much talk of decline, Belgium hardly seems in the grip of austerity. Certainly heavy industry has continued to be battered despite extremely high productivity: car-production facilities at Antwerp (Opel) and Genk (Ford) that were once state of the art closed in 2010 and 2014 respectively. But industrial production recovered strongly in 2016 and 2017, with unemployment falling markedly and GDP climbing steadily. Antwerp's vast port and related chemical industries remain a major motor of growth, with Ghent's port a success story too. Falling corporate taxation has encouraged start-ups and tech companies, and very slowly the country is chipping away at a heavy fiscal deficit.

Meanwhile cultural life appears to be as healthy as ever. Mons celebrated 2015 as a European City of Culture, long-neglected Charleroi has seen valiant attempts at regeneration, and Antwerp's gentrification of the once-ragged docklands area continues, pushed on by Zaha Hadid's ambitious Port Authority Building, museum refurbishments and the new Noorderlijn tramway, which is due to start operation in 2019.

Red Devil Magic

Terror attacks in Paris (2014), at Brussels' Jewish Museum (2014) and Brussels Airport and Metro (2016; Belgium's worst ever), along with a thwarted 'jihadist' plot to kill police in Verviers (2015), were all linked to returning Belgian fighters who had gone to Syria and Iraq to fight with ISIS. Some of the international press extrapolated this discovery into suggestions that Belgium was becoming a 'hotbed of terror', linking the attacks to statistics showing the rapid growth of Islamic populations in Brussels and other cities. Research reported in March 2018, however, suggests that Belgium has done relatively well in recent years in preempting terror attacks, even postulating that the Brussels 2016 attack was a rapidly hatched last-ditch reflex from a debilitated group whose leader had already been apprehended four days earlier. In January 2018, Belgium was the first country in Western Europe to reduce its terror threat level a notch, and among the population there is little discernible sense of unease.

Indeed, in June and July 2018, Belgium's highly multiracial football team, nicknamed the Red Devils, brought the country to a recently unparalleled sense of togetherness. All across the land, the red-gold-black national tricolour fluttered from windows (often with little horns attached) as the team advanced to the World Cup semi-finals. There's more to life than football, of course, but for at least one parched, heat-wave summer, Belgium was filled with a sense of delirious joy and unity. While it that's unlikely to last with the 2019 elections approaching, it was a refreshing sense of national togetherness to savour.

POPULATION:
**11.4 MILLION/602,000
(BELGIUM/LUXEMBOURG)**

AREA: **30,528/2586 SQ KM**

GDP: **€424 BILLION/
55.1 BILLION**

INFLATION: **2.17%/2.0%**

UNEMPLOYMENT:
6.1%/5.5%

if Belgium & Luxembourg were 100 people

52 would be Dutch-speaking
38 would be French-speaking
1 would be German-speaking
9 other

belief systems
(% of population)

Catholic   non-religious

Non-Catholic   Islam   other
Christian

population per sq km

BELGIUM   LUXEMBOURG   USA

 = 30 people

History

The current nation states of Belgium and Luxembourg first appeared on the political map of Europe rather haphazardly in the 19th century. Little Luxembourg only emerged from under the Dutch umbrella due to a quirk in royal inheritance rules. And when an opera kick-started Belgium's independence in 1830, nobody thought that the country would last. Some still doubt that it will. However, the fascinatingly tangled history of the 'Low Countries' goes back way before such shenanigans.

Overview

The region had a rich Roman history but really came to prominence in the 13th and 14th centuries, when the cloth trade brought Bruges, Ghent and Ypres international stature. When Protestantism swept Europe in the 16th century, the Low Countries (present-day Belgium, the Netherlands and Luxembourg) initially embraced it, mainly in the form of Calvinism, much to the chagrin of their ruler, who was, by this stage, the fanatically Catholic Spanish king Philip II. From 1568 a series of wars lasting 80 years resulted in Holland and its allied provinces claiming independence under Protestantism, while Belgium and Luxembourg stayed under Catholic rule – first Spanish, then Austrian Habsburg. A short but destructive period of French rule following the French Revolution resulted in the desecration of the great monasteries, which had long been major players in the rural economy, and notably in Liège, which had been ruled by prince-bishops for over 800 years. After Napoleon's defeat in 1815 (at Waterloo, near Brussels), the Dutch took over for 15 years. Catholic Belgium split from the Protestant Netherlands in 1830, grabbing half of Luxembourg, the other half staying Dutch until 1890.

By this time Belgium was growing rapidly wealthy through impressive industrialisation, helped by King Léopold II's brutal asset-stripping from his 'personal' colony – the Congo.

In WWI Belgium was officially neutral, but the Germans invaded anyway. Western Flanders became a blood-soaked killing field, and whole towns, including historic Ypres, were bombarded into the mud. In WWII the countries took another pasting as Allied bombing raids tried to dislodge Nazi German occupiers. The Ardennes (including Luxembourg)

Belgian talent for industry and trade was already apparent 6000 years ago, when neolithic miners dug extensively to create high-quality flint tools at Spiennes near Mons. Aubechies' Archeosite is a recreated village showing how these and later eras of early 'Belgians' might have lived.

TIMELINE	57–50 BC	AD 466	980
	Julius Caesar's invading Roman legions find unexpectedly stiff resistance from brave Belgae warriors around Tongeren.	Clovis, the uniting king of the Frankish clans, is born near Tournai. His conversion to Catholicism has lasting effects throughout the region.	Liège becomes an independent prince-bishopric, a status it will keep for over 800 years.

were the scene of Hitler's last-gasp offensive around Christmas 1944. After two such devastating wars, Benelux countries understandably became prominent in the drive for European security and integration: Brussels now hosts the headquarters of both the EU and NATO.

Romans, Vikings & Bishops

As any Belgian schoolkid will proudly tell you, Belgae warriors were the 'bravest' opponents of Julius Caesar during the Roman conquests of Gaul (57–50 BC). Students elsewhere might be less familiar with these Germano-Celtic heroes and their leader Ambiorix, who was essentially resurrected as a national icon once Belgium became independent in 1830. Of course, this being Belgium, he soon gained a slightly self-mocking Asterix-style comic-book persona.

Having shrugged off the Belgae, the Romans stayed in Gallia Belgica for 500 years. Perhaps they liked the beer. They founded Tournai and Tongeren and built many a *castrum* (military camp) and villa, notably at Arlon and Echternach. In the 5th century, with the Roman Empire collapsing, Germanic Franks took control of Flanders, while in the south, Merovingian kings set up a kingdom based around Tournai that eventually controlled much of northern France. The south thus moved into a Latin linguistic orbit, creating a division with the Germanic north that remains to this day.

In the 9th and early 10th centuries, parties of raiding Vikings wreaked havoc, looting churches and pillaging villages. In reaction, a jigsaw of feudal domains developed, with locals offered the protection of increasingly powerful counts and dukes in exchange for funding. In the middle of all this was a curious patchwork of church territories ruled autonomously by the prince-abbots of Stavelot-Malmédy and the prince-bishops of Liège, entities that would retain autonomy right through to the late 18th century. Among other factors, tax advantages in the prince-bishopric led to the flourishing of metal crafts at Huy and brewing in Hoegaarden.

Flanders Gains Its Spurs

Flanders lacked much in the way of natural resources, but once Viking threats had receded, its citizens grew rich turning imported wool into top-quality textiles. As the cloth cities of Ypres, Bruges and Ghent bloomed over the 12th to 14th centuries, merchants exchanged not just goods but also cosmopolitan ideas. Craftsmen and traders joined forces to form guilds, setting standards for their craft and establishing local trade monopolies. But the aspirations of these burghers – a historically significant manifestation of non-aristocratic, non-clerical power – often clashed with those of their overlord counts in terms of rights, privileges and taxes. To confuse matters further, there were also conflicts between the lords and their kings.

HISTORY ROMANS, VIKINGS & BISHOPS

Top Gallo-Roman Sites

Malagne
(Rochefort)

Gallo-Roman Museum
(Tongeren)

Villa Romaine
(Echternach)

Het Toreke & Drie Tumuli (Tienen)

Musée Archéologique
(Arlon)

Archéoforum
(Liège)

Archeosite
(Aubechies)

A statue in Brussels' Place Royale depicts Crusader knight Godefroid (Godefroy) de Bouillon, who sold up his Ardennes estates at Bouillon to lead an army in the First Crusade in 1096. While their men were away crusading, many women of the Low Countries joined religious-based self-help communities called *begijnhoven/ beguinages* in Dutch/French.

1196	1302	Early 14th century	1339–41
The counties of Namur and Hainaut go to war in one of many regional battles over inheritance rights.	Flemish guildsmen defeat a far superior French cavalry force. They celebrate by hacking off defeated knights' gilded spurs and displaying them in Kortrijk's main church.	Ghent becomes one of Europe's biggest cities.	Plague kills huge numbers of people. Those who survive often turn to superstitious religion, the distant basis for several odd Belgian folkloric parades.

Medieval cities each needed a royal charter before they could build belfries, which thus became a symbol of civil freedoms. The trend started in Tournai (1188); Aalst was not permitted one until 1460.

Flanders was in a particularly tricky situation. The Count of Flanders was vassal to the French king. However, Flanders' weaving economy relied on a steady supply of high-quality wool from England. So when Flanders sided with its English trading partners during Anglo-French conflicts, the French army showed up to teach it a lesson. In 1302, bloody confrontations known as the Bruges Matins kicked off a famous anti-French revolt that culminated at the Battle of the Golden Spurs at Kortrijk/Courtrai, where the French knights were dramatically (if temporarily) defeated. Since 1830 the battle has become romanticised as a symbol of Belgian (and more recently Flemish) pride. However, the revolt actually resulted in a humiliating 1305 treaty that forced Flanders to pay huge indemnities and give France a large tract of its territory.

The Burgundian Empire

The region's political landscape changed significantly under Philip the Bold (r 1363–1404), who had been 'given' Burgundy by his father the French king and went on to acquire Flanders by tactical marriage. His grandson, the extraordinary Philip the Good (Phillipe-le-Bon, Philip III) of Burgundy (r 1419–67), continued playing off France and England while collecting counties much as a philatelist collects stamps. By the end of his reign most of proto-Belgium (except Liège) had joined northeastern France and the Netherlands in what would be remembered as the Valois Burgundian Empire. Remarkable prosperity saw Ghent become northern Europe's largest city after Paris, and many Flemish towns built magnificently ornate belfries, market houses and town halls as symbols of wealth and hard-won civil liberties. Bruges-born Philip was the richest man in Europe and his Brussels court the height of culture and fashion. The arts flourished, particularly tapestry-making and painting, with the emergence of the artists known now as the Flemish Primitives.

Habsburg Rule

In Mechelen, Margaret of York's palace is now a theatre, while Margaret of Austria's palace has become the courthouse. Of the Hof ten Walle in Ghent where Charles V was born, only a gatehouse now remains, though the area is still called Prinsenhof in his honour.

When Philip's successor died in battle in 1477, his only offspring was the as-yet-unmarried 19-year-old Mary of Burgundy. Guided by her wily British-born stepmother, Margaret of York, Mary married Maximilian of Austria, yanking the Burgundian lands into a rapidly expanding Habsburg empire. Her son became Philip I (the Fair), the first Habsburg king of Castile (Spain). But her daughter, Margaret of Austria, remained in Mechelen as the de-facto ruler of the Low Countries. Her rule ushered in Mechelen's massive cultural blossoming, while Margaret also acted as guardian to her nephew, Philip I's son, the future Holy Roman Emperor Charles Quint (aka Keizer Karel V).

Charles ruled an empire on which the sun never set three centuries before Britain's Queen Victoria could claim the same. Born in Ghent,

1346–60	15th century	1420s onwards	1425
The continuing Anglo-French war leads England's Edward III to cut off wool exports. Numerous Flemish weavers who are forced out of work emigrate to Britain.	The progressive silting up of the Zwin undermines Bruges' role as a leading international port.	Duke Philip the Good of Burgundy sponsors classic Flemish Primitive artists, including Jan van Eyck and Hans Memling.	Belgium's first university is established at Leuven. It will later educate the famous map-maker Gerardus Mercator, born in 1512.

CHARLES QUINT OR KEIZER KAREL?

What do Charles Quint, Keizer Karel, Charles V, Carlos I and Kaiser Karl all have in common? Answer: they were all the same person. Born in Ghent in 1500, Charles was arguably the most powerful teenager in human history. Once you've learnt the various possible alternative renderings, you'll notice his name turning up in all sorts of Belgian contexts, from beer labels to the Brussels Ommegang festival.

By the age of 15 Charles already ruled the Low Countries (as Charles II of Burgundy). The next year he also became king of Spain (as Carlos I), a position of extraordinary wealth in the 16th century given Spain's brutal seizure of the New World (ie Mexico, Peru and the Caribbean) and its hoards of Inca and Aztec gold. Then in 1519 he was crowned king of Habsburg Austria and the Germanic 'Holy Roman Empire' as Emperor Charles/Karel/Karl V. He wasn't yet 20. As if that weren't enough, his good fortune (briefly) continued in 1522 when his tutor, advisor and closest friend, Adrian of Utrecht, was elected Pope.

Charles grew up in Mechelen and, before moving to Spain, ruled from the splendid Coudenberg Palace in Brussels, where he was advised by the great humanist Desiderius Erasmus.

Suffering increasing competition from manufacturers in England, the great Flemish cloth towns were feeling an economic pinch. So when Charles imposed a series of taxes to finance his foreign wars, the burghers of Ghent planned an uprising. Charles returned to suppress the revolt in 1540, making the defeated ringleaders walk around town wearing nooses, the source of a nickname for Ghent folk that's used even today. Thereafter Charles made conscious efforts to encourage Antwerp's growth rather than rely on the troublesome West Flemish towns. In 1555 Charles abdicated, leaving his Germanic territories to one son (Ferdinand) and his western empire, including the Low Countries, to another son (Philip II), whose conservative Catholic Spanish education would prove very significant.

Religious Revolt

From the mid-15th century, the development of semi-mechanised printing caused a blooming of education, with humanist thinkers including Erasmus and Thomas More attracted to the vibrant intellectual centres of Mechelen and Brussels. However, printing also made it easier for literate 'ordinary' people to read the Bible. Suddenly priests who had grown wealthy by 'selling' indulgences (reduced punishments for sins) could no longer claim such practices were God's will. The result was a wave of revolutionary Protestantism, the Reformation. The staunchly Catholic Philip II tried the techniques of the Spanish Inquisition to stifle dissent, but in further raising taxes to pay his Spanish mercenaries he stirred up

The 'glorious entry' of Philip II into Brussels in 1549 was so grand that it is now recreated every July as the Ommegang.

1429–67	1500	1513	1562
The formerly antagonistic duchies and counties of proto-Benelux are brought together within the Burgundian empire.	The future Holy Roman Emperor Charles V, who will become one of the most powerful rulers in European history, is born in Ghent.	Henry VIII of England conquers Tournai; he will sell it back to France in 1519.	Although faithful servants of the Spanish crown, Counts Egmont and Hoorn vocally oppose the introduction of the Inquisition in the Low Countries.

Ransacked Religious Sites

....
Abbaye d'Aulne (near Charleroi)
....
Abbaye de Villers (Villers-la-Ville)
....
Abbaye Notre Dame (Orval)
....
Archéoforum (Liège)

local resentment all the more. In 1566 many Protestants ran riot, ransacking churches in an 'Iconoclastic Fury' – destroying religious icons, which they considered idolatrous. Philip retaliated with a force of over 10,000 troops led by the Duke of Alba (Alva). Alba's tenure as governor of the Low Countries, infamous for its cruelty, kicked off 80 years of turbulence known variously as the Dutch Revolt, the Wars of Religion and the Eighty Years' War. British involvement was blatant, with England's Protestant Elizabeth I actively supporting the revolutionaries against Philip, her brother-in-law. It was to punish English meddling in Flanders that Spain sent the ill-fated Armada in 1588.

The 'Spanish Netherlands'

After decades of destruction, the Netherlands expelled the Spaniards and emerged as an independent Protestant entity. However, Spain recaptured Belgium and Luxembourg (the 'Spanish Netherlands'). In the regained territories, the population was fed a heavy dose of Catholicism. Many Protestants and anti-Spanish free thinkers (including much of the merchant class) moved to the Netherlands or England. The economy thus stagnated, though Liège, as a large independent prince-bishopric, was spared the worst convulsions and its businessmen prospered around this time.

In 1598 Philip II handed the Spanish Netherlands to his daughter Infanta Isabella and her husband (and cousin), Archduke Albert of Austria. While wars rumbled on sporadically, their flamboyant court sponsored new industries such as lace making and diamond processing. Bombastic baroque churches were built to underline the Catholic Church's power and were filled with magnificent artworks stressing a religion where the faithful were offered the hope of magical redemption.

In 1648 the Peace of Westphalia treaties finally recognised the independence of the Netherlands from both Spain and the Holy Roman Empire. However, this newly confirmed 'peace' was an economic disaster for the Spanish Netherlands, as a clause of the treaty demanded that part of the Scheldt River be closed to all non-Dutch ships. As a result, Antwerp's trade collapsed while a golden age dawned for Amsterdam, the region's new premier port. The 'peace' proved very short lived. France had already helped itself to parts of Flanders and southern Wallonia in the 1650s. Then in 1667, with Spain fighting Portugal and Holland battling England, the way lay open for Louis XIV to grab much more. The Dutch and British patched things up to prevent further French advances. Indeed the countries became strong allies after England's return to Protestantism, with Dutchman William of Orange becoming England's William III (as co-monarch with Mary II). Nonetheless, Franco-Dutch wars continued to sweep proto-Belgium for much of the following decades, reaching a climax in 1695, when Louis XIV bombarded Brussels

The only church whose interior has remained intact from before the Iconoclastic Fury is the splendid St-Leonarduskerk at Zoutleeuw.

1566	1604	1609	1659
Iconoclastic riots and Protestant idealism set off decades of fighting, leading to the 'Dutch Revolts' against the rule of Catholic Spain.	After a devastating four-year siege, Ostend becomes the last major Benelux town to be recaptured by the Spaniards.	Rubens' arrival in Antwerp coincides with a 12-year ceasefire in the Eighty Years' War between Spain and the proto-Netherlands.	The Treaty of the Pyrenees makes Philippeville a French fort within the Spanish lowlands and also formalises Flanders' loss of Artois.

to splinters. Once again France occupied much of the area, sending in military engineer Vauban to fortify military strongholds such as Namur, Ypres, Philippeville and Luxembourg.

Austrian Rule & French Occupation

When Charles II of Spain died childless in 1700, his will passed the Spanish Netherlands to a French prince. This implied that the French and Spanish empires would eventually be joined into one superpower. The prospect horrified Britain and Holland and resulted in the War of Spanish Succession (1701–13). French and English forces skirmished for a decade until the Treaty of Utrecht forced a curious compromise in which Spain handed over proto-Belgium (as well as much of Italy) to the Habsburg Austrians, who ruled the area from 1713 to 1794. Influenced by the Enlightenment, the Austrians relaxed censorship and encouraged significant development.

In 1789 the French Revolution threw European politics into a new maelstrom. Anti-religious and anti-monarchic events in Paris reverberated in proto-Belgium, where the Brabantine Revolution created the short-lived United States of Belgium and the Révolution Liégeoise ousted the prince-bishops of Liège. The Austrians swiftly restored the old order, but in 1794 French armies marched into the Austrian Netherlands and introduced French revolutionary laws, including the repression of the Catholic Church. The independence of Liège's prince-bishopric was definitively ended, many churches were ransacked, and Belgium's once-magnificent monasteries were looted and their lands were nationalised. Many abbey churches were demolished as a source of building stone.

Napoleon Bonaparte's brief new French Empire came crashing down with his ill-advised 1812 attempt to conquer Russia. But 'Boney' made a remarkable last-gasp return in 1815, during which the whole future of Europe was decided in mud, rain and a few hours of fighting near Brussels at the pivotal Battle of Waterloo. After Napoleon's defeat, the Congress of Vienna created the United Kingdom of the Netherlands. This incorporated what are today the Netherlands and Belgium. Meanwhile, the newly restored Grand Duchy of Luxembourg (then twice its current size) was declared the personal property of the Dutch king, who concurrently became Grand Duke.

The United Kingdom of the Netherlands

The United Kingdom of the Netherlands was created largely to preserve the balance of power in Europe and to create a buffer state should France have any northward ambitions. That people of different religions and customs were being forced together was of little consequence. William of Orange-Nassau, crowned William I in Brussels, made enemies quickly after refusing to give the south fair political representation and trying

Among Catholic Brits who joined anti-Protestant Spanish forces in the Low Countries was one Guy Fawkes, later infamous for his botched British gunpowder plot (1605).

HISTORY AUSTRIAN RULE & FRENCH OCCUPATION

Great Museums for Regional History

Grand Curtius (Liège)

Musée BELvue (Brussels)

Musée d'Histoire de la Ville de Luxembourg

Abbaye de Stavelot

STAM (Ghent)

1695	1713–14	1717	1789–96
Louis XIV's French troops bombard and largely destroy Brussels. Miraculously the magnificent city hall survives.	After decades of war with France, a Europe-wide peace deal splits the Spanish Empire, with its Southern Netherlands given to the Austrian Habsburgs.	Spa, south of Liège, becomes synonymous with 'taking the waters' after Peter the Great of Russia credits a stay here with curing his liver problems.	Proto-Belgium is swallowed up by the ideas and then the troops of revolutionary France, resulting in the looting, destruction and privatisation of its once-magnificent abbeys.

to impose Dutch as the national language. The latter angered not only Francophones but also Flemish speakers, who regarded their language as distinct from Dutch. Few would have imagined a Brussels opera performance would be the spark to set off a revolution, yet that's what happened on 25 August 1830.

A monument on Brussels' Place des Martyrs commemorates the 467 people who died in the 1830 revolution. Meanwhile, a statue at De Panne marks the spot where Léopold I came ashore to become the new country's king.

Independence

The January 1831 Conference of London recognised the independence of Belgium (initially incorporating Luxembourg), and the country was declared a neutral state. Unemployed royal wannabe Léopold of Saxe-Coburg Gotha, who had been moping around London following the death of his wife, the Princess of Wales, was bundled out of the British court to be crowned Léopold I of Belgium. However, Belgium's independence was only accepted by the Netherlands in 1839, once Belgium agreed to 'give back' the eastern half of Luxembourg (the section that's now independent Luxembourg) over which the Dutch king was recognised as Grand Duke.

The Industrial Revolution got off to a roaring start, with coal mines around Mons and Charleroi and iron making in Liège and Luxembourg. But Luxembourg's membership of a German customs union led to tensions between France and Prussia. To stop a war breaking out, the 1867 Second Treaty of London enforced Luxembourg's neutrality by tearing down Luxembourg City's main fortifications. The Grand Duchy nonetheless remained under the Dutch crown until 1890, when a quirk in the rules of royal succession meant that its previously notional independence suddenly became a reality.

Léopold II

Coming to the Belgian throne in 1865, Léopold II was committed to transforming his father's little kingdom into a world-class nation. He put

REVOLUTIONARY PERFORMANCE

An enchanting if highly simplified story of Belgium's foundation starts on 25 August 1830, with the Brussels premiere of French composer Daniel Auber's then-new opera, *La Muette de Portici*, at La Monnaie in Brussels. The story, sung in French, centres on a 1647 Naples uprising against the Spanish, featuring large crowd scenes and dramatic effects. Fired up by the duet *Amour sacré de la patrie* (Sacred Love of the Homeland, now the French national anthem), the mainly bourgeois Francophone audience poured into the streets to join workers already demonstrating outside the theatre against their Dutch rulers. Together they stormed the Palais de Justice, chased out the Dutch troops and, in a glorious crowning moment, raised the flag of Brabant over Brussels' City Hall. Belgium was born.

1794	1815	1830	1885
The prince-bishops of Liège reach the end of the line, and the city's great cathedral is ceremonially demolished by popular demand.	Napoleon's surprise comeback is quashed at Waterloo, just south of Brussels. Luxembourg is designated a Grand Dutchy under the Dutch Crown.	An opera in Brussels sparks revolution against 15-year-old Dutch rule. Belgium is born, much to its own surprise.	Belgium's Léopold II personally acquires the Congo, ultimately leading to the fabulous regeneration of Brussels but the death of millions of Africans.

great effort into bolstering Brussels, commissioning the construction of monumental buildings such as the daunting Palais de Justice.

Then in 1885, mainly through a series of dubious treaties and contracts, Léopold personally acquired a huge slice of central Africa that was 70 times larger than Belgium. This he disingenuously named the 'Congo Free State'. While he appeared to be setting up schemes to 'protest' the slave trade, 'his' Congolese people were anything but free. The rubber plantations proved extremely lucrative for Léopold (tyres had been developed in the mid-1890s), but Congo army manuals from that time describe women and children kept hostage to force men to fulfil rubber quotas. Reports suggest that, over the next 25 years, huge numbers – perhaps up to half of the Congolese population – perished, directly or indirectly, due to Léopold's rule. Writers including Mark Twain and Sir Arthur Conan Doyle were vocal campaigners for Congolese reforms, and Joseph Conrad's novel *Heart of Darkness,* the inspiration for the movie *Apocalypse Now,* was set in Léopold's Congo. Finally in 1908 the king was stripped of his possession by the Belgian state, embarrassed by the terrible reputation it had brought the nation. Congo nonetheless remained an important Belgian colony until 1960.

It is unknown how many Congolese people died in Léopold II's 'private garden'. According to Adam Hochschild's fascinating book *King Leopold's Ghost,* the furnaces in the Congo offices in Brussels burnt for over a week to destroy the archives after he forfeited the territory.

HISTORY WWI

WWI

When Léopold II died in 1909 he was succeeded by his 21-year-old nephew Albert I (r 1909–34). Five years later the whole world changed as WWI broke out and Germany occupied neutral Belgium. However, fast as it was, the German advance was crucially slowed by the plucky defence of Liège. And in the far north at Nieuwpoort, it was halted altogether by the old defensive trick of flooding low-lying fields. This required the opening of the canal sluice gates, a dicey operation undertaken by brave volunteers under daily fire. Thus protected, a tiny remnant triangle of Belgian land around Veurne remained unoccupied, and Albert took up residence here to personally lead the Belgian army. Further German advances towards the strategic French coastal towns were prevented. 'Brave Little Belgium' was born, and 'Remember Belgium' was used on recruitment posters in Great Britain. But Allied counter-attacks proved futile. The armies dug trenches and became bogged down for four years of futile sorties that killed hundreds of thousands and devastated Western Flanders.

After WWI the Treaty of Versailles abolished Belgium's neutral status, and the country was given reparations from Germany, including an area known today as the Eastern Cantons, along with Germany's former colonies of Burundi and Rwanda in central Africa. In 1934 much-loved Albert I died in a mysterious rock-climbing accident and was succeeded by his son, Léopold III.

To follow the Belgian royals check out www.monarchie.be or their official twitter feed at #monarchiebe. For Luxembourg's Grand Duke it's www.monarchie.lu.

Early 20th century	1905–14	1914–18	1939–44
Wallonia's steel and glass manufacturers put Belgium at the forefront of modern technology.	Booming Belgian cities embrace the sinuous aesthetics of art nouveau. Brussels (1911) and Ghent (1913) host major World Fairs.	WWI makes Flanders' fields synonymous with mud, blood and poppies. Ypres, Nieuwpoort and Diksmuide are wiped off the map, though they're eventually reconstructed.	Germany invades again. Belgium and Luxembourg remain occupied for most of WWII, and Jewish and Roma populations are decimated.

WWII

On 10 May 1940 the Germans launched a surprise attack and rapidly occupied the Netherlands, Belgium and Luxembourg. Unlike his father, Belgian king Léopold III put up little resistance and quickly surrendered to the Germans, leaving the Allies in a precarious state. This appearance of appeasement would eventually force Léopold's abdication in 1951. The Belgian government, opposing the king's decision, fled to London, where it operated in exile throughout WWII. A strong resistance movement developed during the Nazi occupation, but there was also collaboration from fascist elements of Belgian society, notably Léon Degrelle's Francophone Rexists and parts of the Flemish nationalist movement. The German occupation regime deliberately played up long-festering tensions between the linguistic groups for divide-and-rule purposes, Belgium's Jewish population fared terribly, and the small Roma (gypsy) minority was all but wiped out.

When Belgium was liberated in 1944, Léopold's brother Charles was appointed as regent, a duty he carried out until Léopold's abdication.

After WWII

Despite the serious wartime beating, Belgium rebounded rapidly, fuelled by the coal and iron industries. In 1958, Brussels' World Fair showcased Belgium's great industrial advances, a message driven home by the unique architecture of the Atomium. The same year Brussels became the provisional seat of the European Commission, and in 1967 NATO moved its headquarters to Brussels from France, the French having withdrawn from NATO's military wing.

But linguistic tensions remained and a 'language frontier' was officially delineated in 1963, creating four language areas (Dutch-, French- and German-speaking communities plus bilingual Brussels). As in many Western nations, the peace-and-love attitude of the Flower Power era was shaken in 1968 by violent student-led demonstrations. In Belgium these riots took a particular intercommunal turn at Leuven, where the Francophone part of the city's world-famous university was effectively forced to leave the stridently Flemish city, decamping eventually to Louvain-la-Neuve.

During the 1970s the global economy was hard hit by an overnight quadrupling of oil prices. The 'old' heavy industries (mining, glass and iron) slumped, and with them the formerly prosperous steel and mining cities of Wallonia and Luxembourg. Luxembourg circumvented these economic woes by introducing favourable banking and taxation laws that encouraged a new raft of investors and financial institutions. For bigger Belgium such solutions were not possible, and well-intentioned attempts to shore up its moribund factories with subsidies and socialist rhetoric

---

WWII Commemoration Sites

Battle of the Bulge Museums (Bastogne, Baugnez and La Roche)

Atlantikwall (Ostend)

Mons Memorial Museum (Mons)

Kazerne Dossin (Mechelen)

US Military Cemetery, Luxembourg

Fort de Huy (Huy)

Fort Breendonk (Mechelen)

Christmas 1944	1951	1958	1968
A last-gasp German counter-offensive, the 'Battle of the Bulge', devastates many towns and villages across Luxembourg and the Ardennes.	King Léopold III abdicates following the complex 'Royal Question' over his supposed wartime collaboration with the Nazi occupation regime.	The Atomium is built as the centrepiece for the last Brussels World Fair, celebrating the nation's remarkable postwar economic resurgence.	The Western world is rocked by student-led popular civil disobedience, most famously in Paris. In Leuven the troubles turn violently intercommunal.

BELGIUM'S ROYALS

Léopold I (r 1831–65) Belgium's first king had narrowly missed out on the British throne when his wife, British heir apparent Princess Charlotte, died in childbirth. He then turned down the throne of newly reborn Greece, thinking Greek independence had little future.

Léopold II (r 1865–1909) Bearded 'brute' with controversies in Congo.

Albert I (r 1909–34) Brave, tin-hatted 'soldier king' of WWI.

Léopold III (r 1934–51) Questions over his dealings with Hitler caused the 'Royal Question'; he abdicated. His brother Charles, who had been regent during Léopold III's Swiss exile (1944–50), later retired to Ostend where he became an artist.

Baudouin (r 1951–93) Popular, bespectacled 'priestly' king.

Albert II (r 1993–2013) Baudouin's younger brother who abdicated in favour of his son.

Philippe/Filip (r 2013–) Belgium's current monarch.

proved futile. But while the post-industrial Walloon economy stagnated, the more diversified, smaller-scale industries of Flanders were less affected, and in later years the Flemish economy surged ahead as investment in newer technologies bore fruit. Increasingly an economic angle was added to the disputes between linguistic communities. State reforms of the 1980s and '90s gave parliaments to both the linguistic communities and the three regions (Flanders, Wallonia and Brussels-Capital), overlaid within a newly federalised state.

Into the 21st Century

Towards the end of the 20th century Belgium was rocked by infamous paedophile scandals and rising racism. The 1999 elections booted out the Christian Democrat party after 40 years in power. The decade that followed was characterised by party-political gridlock, reflecting an increasing polarisation of politics along linguistic lines. A series of uncomfortable coalitions would take months to form, and fully 1½ years in the case of the 2010 election. Government that was traditionally based on multiparty compromise had become a tense, tetchy affair. However, Belgium muddled through the 2008 financial crisis and, in a nail-biting episode, managed to save the banking sector when a major Belgo-Dutch bank was teetering over the abyss. In 2012, the worst rumblings of a potential north–south split were, at least temporarily, resolved by the devolution to regional level of numerous powers. And in 2018, Belgium's success in reaching the World Cup semifinals saw a wave of national feeling unprecedented in the preceding decades.

For those born into a world of Spotify and on-demand downloads, it's hard to conceive just how much 1960s teenagers relied on Radio Luxembourg as the only non-pirate radio station broadcasting new 'pop' music into the UK, years before Radio 1 and way before MTV.

1970s	1993	2010–11	2018
Economic stagnation sets in as heavy industry becomes uncompetitive in Wallonia and Luxembourg.	Belgium becomes a three-part federal state comprising Flanders, Wallonia and Brussels-Capital. Further regional autonomy is granted in 2012.	Elections leave Belgian politicians unable to form a coalition government for nearly 18 months.	Belgium's soccer dream team reaches the semifinals of the World Cup.

The Belgian People

Unlike many European countries, Belgium has existed as a nation state for less than two centuries, so the idea of Belgian-ness is not a source of enormous patriotism – except perhaps during football matches. There's a deep linguistic split between Dutch-speaking Flemish and French-speaking Belgians (not all of whom self-identify as Walloon), but most have in common a background of low-key cultural Catholicism, self-deprecating straightforwardness and a sharp-witted love for the surreal.

The Linguistic Divide

The historically vibrant Jewish community was decimated in WWII during occupation by German forces. Many were sent to concentration camps from Mechelen barracks, which have been restored as a sombre memorial. Today Antwerp has a small but visible Orthodox Jewish community concentrated on the diamond district.

For Luxembourgers, French-Letzeburgesch bilingualism is a day-to-day necessity that's worn very lightly. But in Belgium, language is a defining issue. Belgium's population is basically split in two, a split that can, broadly speaking, be traced back to the break-up of Europe after the decline of the Roman empire. Dutch-speaking Flemish make up about 60% of the population, mostly in the country's north – predominantly flat Flanders (Vlaanderen). In southern Belgium – Wallonia (La Wallonie) – the population mostly speaks French, albeit a variant that sounds slightly comical to Parisians. To complicate matters, in Wallonia's Eastern Cantons (Ost Kantonen) live around 70,000 German speakers. And then there's Brussels: officially bilingual but predominantly French speaking and geographically surrounded by Flanders.

French-speaking locals describe themselves as Belgians and only rarely as 'Walloons', which would imply speaking one of the almost-folkloric Walloon languages now mainly used in festivals (see www.fgfw.be). However, most people in Flanders consider themselves primarily Flemish in a way that is equivalent psychologically, though not linguistically, to the self-image of Scots within the UK. Everything from the media to political parties is divided along language lines. And the result is a remarkable and growing lack of communication between Wallonia and Flanders. Francophones tend to stereotype the Flemish as arrogant and humourless; the Flemish see Francophone Belgians as corrupt, lazy or feckless, an exaggerated image jocularly accepted by some southerners.

SPORT IN BELGIUM

After football (soccer), cycling is Belgium's great sporting passion, with champions such as Tom Boonen and especially Eddy Merckx seen as national heroes. Two of the five 'Monument' one-day classic road races are held in Belgium: the part-cobbled Tour of Flanders (www.rondevanvlaanderen.be) has its finish line in Oudenaarde, where there's a major cycling museum, and the Liège-Bastogne-Liège (www.letour.fr/liege-bastogne-liege) takes in some glorious Ardennes scenery.

Curious local sports include pigeon racing, finch sitting (vinkenzettingen) and balle-pelotte (aka kaatsen, jeu-de-balle or jeu-de-paume). The last is a team game batting a hard ball using gloved hands, often played on village squares accompanied by the boozy oompah of local trumpeters, though there are also leagues.

A century ago, Wallonia was Belgium's wealthiest half, but its heavy industries slumped in the 1970s. Meanwhile, Flanders invested in 'new' businesses and its massive ports boomed from increasing global trade. Many in Flanders resent financially propping up the now poorer south, a tendency only increased by global economic woes. For decades, Flemish nationalists have been calling for greater autonomy or even Flemish independence, though the major devolution of powers to the regions in 2012 has somewhat satisfied such demands. Contrastingly, Walloon nationalism is virtually unknown, and while TV immerses most Francophone Belgians in French popular culture, very few would actually consider joining France in the event of a national split. Indeed Francophone Belgians are far more disparaging of the French than of their Flemish cousins.

Multiculturalism

Curiously, on paper, Luxembourg is by far the EU's most multicultural country, with over 40% of the population having been born elsewhere. However, as such foreigners are mostly Italian, Portuguese and other predominantly Catholic Western Europeans, you shouldn't expect a radical ethnic melting pot.

Statistically, Belgium's main immigrant communities are Moroccan, French, Turkish and Italian. There's also a sizeable population originating from Belgium's former African colonies (Congo, Rwanda and Burundi). The first major wave of post-WWII immigrants arrived to work in the mines.

As in many European countries, attitudes to immigration seem to have hardened over the past decade or so, and the Vlaams Belang far-right party has won votes actively opposing it. Perceptions of Islamic extremism haven't helped the cause either. The 2016 bombings of Brussels Airport and Maalbeek Metro Station led some newspapers to describe Belgium as 'Europe's terror hotbed', citing a figure of around 400 'radicalised' Belgians as having joined ISIS in the Syrian civil war. Post-industrial cities like Verviers have often been noted by Western intelligence sources as particularly vulnerable to such radicalism. As always, however, behind the sensational headlines is an overwhelming majority of peacefully coexisting citizens.

Religion

Christianity was established early in the Low Countries, with powerful abbeys and monasteries the main politico-administrative force in some areas (notably Liège) for centuries. A wave of Protestantism hit during the 16th century, and when the Low Countries were divided, Holland adopted a predominantly Protestant faith while proto-Belgium was force fed a heavy dose of Roman Catholicism. Despite a wave of anti-religious desecration in the wake of the French Revolution, Catholicism remains a defining strand of national identity in both Belgium and Luxembourg. However, church attendance has plummeted since the 1970s, with only 3% of the Flemish population now going to church weekly. Nonetheless, roughly 75% of Belgians (and 87% of Luxembourgers) still consider themselves Catholic, at least as a badge of social status and politically enlightened conservatism.

Belgium's strong Catholic background once kept women's issues on the back burner; when abortion was legalised in Belgium in 1990, it caused a national drama as the pious King Baudouin I temporarily stood down rather than sign the law. However, over the last decades attitudes have changed radically; Belgium was the second European country after the Netherlands to legally recognise both same-sex unions (2003) and euthanasia (2002).

Dutch spoken in Flanders is similar to that spoken in the Netherlands. Belgian and French French are as close as American and British English. Some Walloon dialects, though little spoken nowadays, are essentially distinct languages. Bruxellois is a unique Brussels pidgin, mixing words from Dutch, French, Walloon, Spanish and Yiddish.

Islam is Belgium's fastest-growing religion and is by some estimates likely to become the majority faith in Brussels within a decade or so. Many of the faithful are immigrants from Morocco, Turkey, Algeria and Pakistan, plus their descendants. If you want to find a nearby mosque, a useful website is www.embnet.be.

THE BELGIAN PEOPLE MULTICULTURALISM

Creative Cuisine

Belgium is justifiably known for great mussels, double-fried chips and superb chocolate. Belgian chefs were once famed for offering French cuisine in Germanic portions, but these days a new wave of globally influenced gastronomy often references flavours from world cuisines, notably Spanish, Thai and Japanese. At the same time, old Belgian home-cooking favourites, from meatballs to rabbit stews, have been increasingly resurrected and given new zest, while seasonal game dishes remain popular in the Ardennes.

The Basics

There is plenty that is distinctively Belgian.

Don't be too shy to order *chèvre chaud*. While the direct translation means 'hot goat', what should actually arrive is a delicious starter plate of salad topped with warm goat's cheese.

Mussels and chips The most iconic Belgian meal is a hearty portion of *moules-frites* (in Dutch, *mosselen-friet*). Succulent Zeeland mussels are conspicuously larger than French equivalents. Forget forks – eat them local-style using an empty mussel shell as a pair of tweezers and remember that fresh mussels open spontaneously during cooking, so if you find one that hasn't opened, don't force it as it might be off.

Waterzooi Cream-based, soupy stew made with chicken or fish plus potatoes and vegetables. It's a whole meal-in-a-bowl so you won't need a side dish.

Eel *Paling in 't groen/anguilles-au-vert* is eel in a bright-green sorrel or spinach sauce: typical of Flanders.

Rabbit *Konijn met pruimen/lapin aux pruneaux* is rabbit meat cooked until tender in a sauce that's sweetened with prunes.

Carbonade The rich meaty stew known in French as *carbonade flamande* is variously called *stoverij, stoofvlees* or *Vlaamse stoofkarbonade* in Dutch. Recipes vary, but essentially you'll get a thick beer-based hotpot using chunks of tasty but usually low-quality stewing steak (usually beef, sometimes horse).

Meatballs Until the 1990s, *ballekes/boulettes* (Belgian meatballs in tomato sauce) were sneered at as something a 1950s homemaker might have served when the pantry was bare. However, a resurgence of traditional food has seen them reappear, with a gourmet twist, on menus. In Liège, the larger (tennis ball–sized) *boulette Liègoise* version served in fruity gravy has never gone out of fashion.

Stoemp Another home-cooking classic, *stoemp* is essentially boiled potatoes mashed together with vegetables and served as a side dish or turned into a basic main meal by being topped with sausage or ham plus gravy.

Endives You might expect Brussels sprouts to be common here. But a far more archetypically Belgian vegetable is the endive, commonly served in local homes wrapped in ham and smothered in cheesy white sauce as *gegratineerde witloof/chicons au gratin*.

A *boudin* can be any of several forms of sausage incorporating so much milk and breadcrumb filler that they can be eaten raw. But used as a mild Francophone insult, the word means 'fatso'.

Gibier (game) The Ardennes is famed for hams, pâtés and – especially in autumn – seasonal game meats, including *marcossain* (wild boar).

Meanwhile Luxembourg has many distinctive specialities of its own:

F'rell am Rèisleck Trout in Riesling sauce.

Huesenziwwi 'Jugged hare' cooked in lard, flambéed in brandy and served in a blood-thickened stew.

Hiecht mat Kraiderzooss Pike in a herb-based green sauce.

Bouneschlupp Green bean soup with potatoes, onion and bacon.

Träipen Luxembourg's version of black pudding prepared from hog's head and served with apple sauce.

Frites – Non-French Fries

The Belgians swear they invented *frieten/frites*, so don't think of calling them French fries here. At a proper *frituur/friture* (chip stand), *frieten/frites* are given a to-order second crisping before being served in a paper cone, usually smothered with large blobs of thick mayonnaise or another sauce (extra charge). There are dozens of sauces – if you're overwhelmed by the choice, try Andalouse, which tastes like a mildly spiced thousand-island dressing.

Seasonal Foods

In spring it's time for white asparagus *(asperges),* most famously hailing from Mechelen but liable to dominate menus anywhere in May and June. The official mussels season is usually September to February, although you can increasingly find them year-round. In the Ardennes, autumn menus will be full of *gibier* – a general term for seasonal game meats (pheasant, wild boar etc).

Vegetarians & Vegans

Bigger cities have growing numbers of vegetarian restaurants, and organic *(bio)* ingredients can be found in many shops and eateries. However, in rural areas vegetarians will find relatively slim pickings. Salads appear on most standard menus, but many contain some form of cheese or meat. If you're stuck for dinner, a useful standby is the sensibly priced nonmeat fare at one of the ubiquitous Chinese, Vietnamese or Thai restaurants.

For extensive listings of vegetarian and organic options (in local languages) consult EVA (www.evavzw.be) for Flanders and Vegetik (www.vegetik.org) for Wallonia. Both cover Brussels.

Chocolate

Chocolate is fundamentally a mix of cocoa paste, sugar and cocoa butter in varying proportions. Dark chocolate uses the most cocoa paste, milk chocolate mixes in milk powder, and white chocolate uses cocoa butter but no cocoa paste at all. Belgian chocolate is arguably the world's best because it sticks religiously to these pure ingredients, while other countries allow cheaper vegetable fats to replace some of the cocoa butter (EU regulations allow up to 5%).

Most essentially Belgian are pralines and creamy *manons:* bite-sized filled chocolates sold from an astonishing range of specialist *chocolaterie* shops. Here glove-clad assistants patiently wrap whatever you select from the enchanting display – it's perfectly fine to buy a single chocolate. Or you can opt for a packaged selection (125g to 1kg) in a ribbon-wrapped *ballotin* (top-folded cardboard box). Either way, the price per kilogram stays the same.

In the last 20 years, hip, experimental choc-artists have appeared. Pierre Marcolini pioneered smaller praline sizes, black-box presentation and innovative flavours (think oolong tea). Chocolate Line's 'shock-latier' Dominic Persoone made headlines by creating nasally ingested chocoshots for the Rolling Stones. Jean-Philippe Darcis, Belgium's *macaron* king, became known for his use of pure-origin cocoa beans and is the force behind Vervier's superb chocolate museum. One of the most

On French-language menus don't confuse a *cassolette* with a *cassoulet* (silent 't'). The former refers to a little cooking pot holding virtually anything the chef might have dreamt up; a *cassoulet* is a rich bean-and-meat casserole originally from southern France.

GETTING RAW

If you see the term *filet* on a menu it generally implies a steak of some type. But *filet américain* is quite different: it's Belgium's equivalent of steak tartare, ie a blob of high-grade, raw minced beef, prepared with small quantities of onion, seasoning and a raw egg yolk. Meanwhile *carpaccio*, originally an Italian import, is a popular starter dish of raw meat strips served with olive oil, lemon and Parmesan.

In most European Catholic countries, the scallop shell is instantly recognised as the symbol of pilgrims making the ancient cross-continent trek to Santiago di Compostela – so much so, in fact, that the words in both Dutch and French for the scallop incorporate the name of St James *(St-Jacobss-chelpen/coquilles St-Jacques).*

exciting craft-*chocolatiers* at present is Liège's Benoit Nihant, who carefully sources some beans from his family's own Peru plantation then roasts and grinds them on antique machines.

Waffles

The waffle *(wafel/gaufre) is* Belgium's signature semisweet snack. For tourists waffles are often heaped with cream, fruit or chocolate sauce, but traditionally they should be just lightly dusted with icing sugar and eaten hot off the griddle. Brussels' waffles are light, crispy, rectangular and deeply indented. The *gaufre de Liège* has rounder edges and a breadier dough made with a hint of cinnamon. Recipes for several lesser-known versions are on www.gaufresbelges.com.

Luxembourg Desserts

Beyond the Moselle's grapes, Luxembourg produces a whole range of stone fruits (apricots, nectarines, peaches, cherries and plums), plus pears and apples, strawberries, rhubarb and walnuts. Many of these are used in *quetschentaarten* (fruit tarts) while *äppelklatzen* take cooked apples, spiced with cinnamon and nutmeg, and wrap them in pastry.

Coffee & Tea

Order a coffee in a traditional Belgian *café*-pub and you'll generally get something approximating an Americano in strength and style. It will generally come accompanied by a biscuit or chocolate, and unlike in France, you don't normally pay extra for milk (real or evaporated). Meanwhile, over the last decade, global coffee culture has well and truly arrived. The bigger cities are now full of enticing coffee houses where specialist baristas really know their stuff, using high-quality roasts and sometimes supplementing the standard choices (espresso, *macchiato,* flat white, *cortardo* etc) with specialist options like slow-drip and nitro cold-brew coffees. Even tea is being treated with a newfound respect, with some places providing an egg-timer to ensure the perfect brewing time, and others offering iced *kambucha* (a fermented tea-based drink). Biochi Tea Lounge in Antwerp is a veritable temple to Chinese tea, selling and serving some of the world's rarest varieties.

If you want eel *(anguille)* be careful not to order *andouille* by mistake. The latter is a super-strongly flavoured sausage made with intestines and stomach parts that rarely suits the squeamish.

Wine & Spirits

Beer may be king in Belgium, but wine *(wijn/vin)* – typically French – is the standard accompaniment to a more formal meal. Belgium's Haspengouw region does produce a few minor vintages, however, and Luxembourg's Moselle Valley is far more prolific, producing some fine whites, and specialising particularly in sparkling *crémants.*

Jenever (*genièvre* in French, *pékèt* in Walloon) is an archetypal local spirit, classically flavoured with juniper berries. It's the historical precursor to modern gin, but it's sipped straight not diluted with tonic. Beginners often prefer sweetened fruit versions, but ask for a *witteke* (literally a 'little white one') and you'll get a classic *jenever,* whether almost colourless *(jonge)* or yellow-tinged *(oude)*. Hasselt boasts a *jenever* museum and an annual *jenever* festival, while seemingly endless mini-shots of *pékèt* are *de rigueur* during Liège's chaotic mid-August Outremeuse celebrations.

Belgian Beer

Belgium is beer paradise. Standard lagers, notably Jupiler, Maes and Stella Artois, are what you'll get at any *café* **(ie pub/bar) if you just ask for a** *pintje/bière*. **Then there are wine-like Flemish reds and sour self-fermenting lambics. But it's the 'angels and demons' that draw most attention: big, bold brews that might have diabolical monickers like Forbidden Fruit, Judas or Duvel (devil) or, contrastingly, be named for an abbey, as with the famous Trappist beers, still brewed in monasteries.**

First Sips

When the Black Death came to the low lands in the 11th century, Arnold, the abbot of Oudenburg, convinced his parishioners to drink beer instead of water. Part of the process of medieval beer making involved boiling the water, so this trick proved rather, well, miraculous. Arnold became patron saint of brewers, and beer became an everyday drink. Early beer may have been little more than spontaneously fermented barley soup but over the next few centuries beer-mad monks developed sophisticated brewing methods, as well as ways to enhance the flavour, adding honey and spices.

The great era of abbey beer production did not, in fact, begin until the early 19th century. Monasteries that had been ravaged in the anti-religious convulsions of the French Revolution were in need of funds to rebuild their shattered communities, and their numbers swelled with those from French orders. Old monastic beer recipes were revived and improved upon, and the monks realised they were onto a nice little earner.

Trappist & Abbey Beers

Today many top Belgian brews remain 'abbey beers' in name only, the monks having outsourced the brewing in return for royalties. Examples include excellent Corsendonk, Grimbergen, Maredsous and Leffe. The latter was originally linked with a monastery in Dinant but is now brewed by the giant multinational AB-InBev. Some local producers have named brews for ruined abbeys, as with Oudenaarde's recommended Ename and Val de Sambre's Abbaye d'Aulne, created in a microbrewery beside the ruins of Aulne Abbey. Almost all the abbey beers are available in at least two styles, Bruin/Dubbel/Double beers are usually dark, Blonde/Tripel/Triple usually golden.

Six Belgian abbeys of the strict Cistercian order still brew within the monastery walls, and these rich, smooth and intriguingly complex Trappist beers are considered the epitome of the Belgian beer experience. 'Trappist' is a controlled term of origin, rather than a style, and come in varying colours and strengths. Chimay, Orval and Westmalle are now ubiquitous, and each has a beer-tasting *café* near the respective abbey. It takes a little more effort to seek out excellent Rochefort or relative newcomer Achel from the rural Sint Benedictus Monastery (www. achelsekluis.org), where brewing was only revived in 1999. But the Holy Grail for Belgian beer fans is Westvleteren, whose beers have no labels and can only be identified by the colour of their caps. The yellow cap

Beer Resources

Belgian Brewers Association (www. belgianbrewers.be)

Confederation of Belgian Beer-tasters (www. zythos.be)

International beer-drinkers' opinions (www. ratebeer.com)

Beer Tourism (http://belgium. beertourism.com)

Podge's Beer Tours (www.podgebeer. co.uk)

Belgian Smaak (www.belgian smaak.com)

Westvleteren 12 (10.8% alcohol) is a dark, unfiltered, malty beer whose intense complexity sees it regularly voted among the world's very best. But with supply incredibly limited, your best hope of tasting it is to visit the abbey *café* in person. Even there, if you want to buy more than a six pack, you'll need an appointment. It all adds to the thrill and mystique. If you can't find a bar serving Westvleteren, consider sipping St-Bernardus from nearby Watou, based on recipes and techniques originally guided by a Westvleteren master brewer.

Based in Leuven, AB.InBev (www.ab-inbev.com) is the world's biggest brewer with a 28% global market share. It owns brands from Budweiser to Boddingtons, Labatt to Löwenbräu as well as Belgian trademarks Stella Artois, Leffe, Hoegaarden and Jupiler. Its Belgian origins stretch back to the Artois/Den Hoorn brewery founded in 1366.

White Beers

Known as *witbier*/*bière blanche* in Dutch/French, white beers are thirst-quenching wheat beers, typically cloudy, flavoured with hints of orange peel and cardamom and drunk ice cold with a twist of lemon on summer afternoons. The best known is from Hoegaarden, which has an interesting brewery museum. Brugs Tarwebier (from Bruges) is also a good choice.

Lambics & Fruit Beers

Airborne micro-organisms allow the spontaneous fermentation of archetypal lambic beers (*lambiek* in Dutch). The idea is magical. However, the taste of pure lambic is uncomfortably sharp and acidic. It's rendered more palatable by barrel-maturing for up to three years, then blending (to make *gueuze*), sweetening with sugar/caramel (for *faro*) or by adding fresh soft fruit, notably cherries (for *kriek*) and raspberries (for *framboise*). You can discover a whole range of *gueuze*, *kriek* and lambic flavours and learn more about their production at De Lambiek in Alsemberg near Brussels. Some commercial fruit beers are over-sweetened, but Boon Kriek is better than most, richly fruity and tart without heavy acidity.

Category Busters

Not all beers fit into neat categories, and not all abbey-style brews are abbey beers. Mechelen produces the splendid Gouden Carolus range. Refreshing, golden ales are brewed by La Chouffe, Brasserie des Fagnes and many more. Antwerp's trademark beer, de Koninck, is a distinctive brown ale. And then there is the recent explosion of craft beers. Far from getting left behind in this movement, Belgian brewers have proved ever more inventive, experimenting with curious vegetable additions, historic

CHARGE YOUR GLASSES

One of the adjunct pleasures of drinking beer in Belgium is the branded glass that each beer is served in. You'll find them for sale at specialist beer shops as well as at flea markets, where you can pick them up for around €4 each, with some dealers also stocking vintage versions and special editions. Each style of beer has a particular shaped glass, which supposed highlights its flavour and other characteristics.

Bowls The archetypal Belgian bowls are large stemmed vessels designed especially for sipping heavy ales. Some are solidly goblet like, while others can be as dainty as a wine glass. Dating back to the 1930s, Orval's chunky faceted glass chalice evokes a far longer monastic past.

Tulip A bulbous body and gently flaring lip makes the most of aromatic beers and is also designed to enhance the head. The best known is Duvel's, which also has yearly artist editions and a high-tech unbreakable version designed to take the punishment that Belgium's many summer festivals can dish out. La Chouffe's gnomes also grace a pretty tulip.

Flutes The wine-like fruit beers and lambics are, fittingly, often served in what looks like a bloated champagne flute, which aides the retention of carbonation.

UNUSUAL BREWS

Pannepot Experimental Struise Brewers' signature beer tastes something like liquid, alcoholised black chocolate.

Garre A floral-headed 11% marvel unique to the eponymous bar in Bruges.

Ichtegem's Grand Cru An oak-aged red 'sour' ale that tastes almost like wine and pairs well with traditional pickled herring.

Airman Served in a helmet at Bastogne.

Alpaïde stout Proves that Hoegaarden can go beyond white beer.

Lupulus Excellent range of hop-rich ales from the eastern Ardennes.

La Chouffe Achouffe's blond, elf-branded beer.

Vaudrée Blonde Powerful but great-tasting.

Liefmans Goudenband Strong Flemish sour brown, care of Belgium's first female brewmaster.

Tits Great beer meets breathtaking political incorrectness in a hilarious glass.

Luvanium A range of beers inspired by a historic university recipe rediscovered by a historian in the Leuven archives.

recipes or 'seasonal' beers. The historic steam-brewery at Pipaix somehow manages almost all of the above. Meanwhile the exploding popularity of American IPA styles has spurred the extra hopping of a range of classic brews most notably with La Chouffe Houblon and Duvel Triple Hop. Even Leffe has caught on with a range of differently hopped 'Royale' brews, most successfully with the green-label Cascade Royale.

Brewery Tours

The Trappist monasteries remain closed to visitors beyond their tasting cafes. However, many other breweries offer visits by arrangement for groups. Drop-in opportunities are possible at Bruges' De Halve Maan (p89), the brilliantly old-fashioned Cantillon Brewery (p58) in Brussels and the monthly mash at Pipaix's steam brewery (p190). With a little planning, it's easy to join group tours of Stella Artois (p175) in Leuven or La Chouffe in Achouffe (p222). Drop-in visits are generally possible at De Koninck (p151) in Antwerp and the historic Het Anker (p173) in Mechelen, while Chimay (p204) offers 'beer experience' visits and Antwerp's hip new Seef brewery (p160), like those at **Wilderen** (☑011 58 06 80; www.brouwerijwilderen.be; Zootleeuwsesteenweg, Wilderen; ⊙1-10pm Tue-Sun Jul-Aug, to 7pm Apr-Jun & Sep, weekends only Oct-Mar; 🖈) and Mariembourg (p203), doubles as a bar.

Arts & Architecture

Although Belgium has only been Belgium since 1830, the region's cities have been at the forefront of the arts for much of the last seven centuries. Bruges was the centre for the 'Flemish Primitives', Antwerp the base of superstar Pieter Paul Rubens, and Brussels an early centre for both art nouveau and surrealism. The country continues to have a vibrant cultural life, with globally recognised contemporary-art stars, a flourishing electronic-music scene, great modern dance and a devotion to the ninth art: the comic strip.

Art

Primitives & Hellraisers

Blossoming in 15th-century Bruges was a group of groundbreaking painters who pioneered a technique of painting in oil on oak boards, adding thin layers of paint to produce jewel-bright colours and exquisite detail.

They became known collectively as the Flemish Primitives. Not all were Flemish and their work was anything but primitive: the name derives from the Latin *primus,* meaning first – an indication of their innovative and experimental approach. Perhaps the greatest such work still extant is the world-famous *Adoration of the Mystic Lamb,* a multipanelled altarpiece in Ghent's cathedral by one or both of the Van Eyck brothers.

Gain an appreciation for Jan van Eyck's intricate masterpieces from the comfort of home at www.jan-van-eyck.org.

Particularly significant was the decision to use oil-painting techniques to achieve a new degree of realism and to then use this realism to depict secular subjects in place of religious themes. Bruges' Groeningemuseum has some superb works, including an intimate portrait of his wife by Jan van Eyck (c 1390–1441). In his wake came Tournai-born Rogier van der Weyden (c 1400–64), who at one time was even considered to outshine the master. Judge for yourself at Tournai's main gallery.

Possibly trained in Brussels under van der Weyden, German-born Hans Memling (c 1440–94) arrived in Bruges aged around 25 and swiftly became a favourite among the city's merchant patrons. His association with St John's Hospital resulted in the commissioning of the glowing religious works now displayed in the Memlingmuseum, where his St Ursula reliquary counts among Bruges' most important treasures.

Another significant Flemish Primitive figure was Leuven's Quentin Matsys (1466–1529), who painted a set of grotesque portraits so timeless that they could have jumped out of a Lewis Carroll fairy tale. These hinted at the chaotic horrors to follow in the works of Dutchman Hieronymus Bosch (c 1450–1516). Bosch's most fascinating paintings are nightmarish scenes, visual parables filled with gruesome beasts and devilish creatures often devouring or torturing agonised humans. Bosch's work had obvious influences on the great 16th-century Flemish painter Pieter Brueghel the Elder, whose studies of peasant life remain as collectable as Bosch's apocalyptic canvases. Antwerp's Museum Mayer van den Bergh holds his classically grotesque painting *Dulle Griet* (Mad Meg), there's more of his work in Lier and you can visit his grave in Brussels' Kapellekerk. Brueghel's sons continued the family craft, though Jan Brueghel would turn away from his father's depiction of crowd scenes towards an obsession with the floral still life. The world was changing.

Baroque Counter-Reformation

Styles changed dramatically following the Counter-Reformation of the 17th century. Suddenly huge, powerful canvases full of chubby cherubs and ecstatic biblical figures were just the thing to remind a wavering population of a Catholic God's mystical power. Few artists proved so good at delivering such a dazzling, seductive spectacle as Antwerp-based Pieter Paul Rubens (1577–1640). His most celebrated altarpieces were painted for Antwerp's Onze-Lieve-Vrouwekathedraal. Rubens was so prolific that after you've spent some time in Antwerp it's almost a relief to find a museum that *doesn't* feature his works.

Rubens' studio nurtured artists such as Anthony van Dyck (1599–1641), who focused on religious and mythical subjects, as well as portraits of European aristocrats wearing shimmering silks and velvets. In 1632 Van Dyck became court painter to Charles I of England, and was knighted. His contemporary Jacob Jordaens (1593–1678) specialised in depicting everyday Flemish life and merrymaking.

If you believe Karl Hammer's 2010 art-detective mystery thriller *The Secret of the Sacred Panel,* the Van Eyck Ghent altarpiece is not just a glorious example of 1420s art but the key to unravelling sacred mysteries surrounding Jesus' crucifixion that held occult significance for WWII Nazi Heinrich Himmler.

Modern Movements

Three Belgian names dominate in the latter 19th century, each taking art in notably different directions. In mid-career Constantin Meunier (1831–1905), Belgium's most famous sculptor, took the morally brave step of giving up lucrative bourgeois commissions to concentrate on painting social-realist scenes depicting the lives and difficulties of workers in industrial Belgium. James Ensor (1860–1949), especially celebrated in his home town of Ostend, pioneered expressionism way ahead of its time. And Fernand Khnopff (1858–1921) developed a beguiling 'symbolist' style reminiscent of contemporary pre-Raphaelites Gabriel Rossetti and Edward Burne-Jones. Khnopff's work decorates part of the St-Gilles town hall, and his (largely rebuilt) childhood home is now the Hotel Ter Reien in Bruges.

As Argenteuil was to French impressionism, rural St-Martens-Latem was to Belgian expressionism after 1904, with two formative groups of painters setting up home there. Best-known of the set was Constant Permeke (1886–1952), whose bold portraits of rural Flemish life blended cubism, expressionism and social realism. Meanwhile Mechelen-born Rik Wouters (1882–1916), a prime figure of Brabant Fauvism, sought the vibration of light in sun-drenched landscapes, bright interiors and still-life canvases. Antwerp's KMSKA holds a major collection of his work.

Emerging in Paris in the 1920s as a response to the horror of WWI and to the technological changes of the early 20th century, surrealism worked with the neglected associations and omnipotent dream world of the subconscious. It found fertile ground in Belgium: artists had grown up with the likes of Bosch and Brueghel, and the country had a front-row seat to the carnage of the trenches. Best known of Belgium's surrealists were René Magritte, now celebrated with his own Brussels gallery-museum, and Paul Delvaux, whose St-Idesbald house-studio gives a curious set of insights.

Contemporary Scene

Belgium's contemporary-art scene is booming, with a strong base of local collectors, proximity to art-fair hubs Cologne and Basel, and a network of respected art schools and museums.

One of Europe's best known, and often most controversial, painters, is Luc Tuymans (1958–), who lives and works in Antwerp. Based on photographic source material, his washed-out, haunting canvases toggle between historical events – the Holocaust, Belgian Congo controversies, child-abuse scandals – and the absolutely banal, acknowledging the long Belgian realist tradition while displaying a dark mistrust of the image itself. Tuymans' work was among the first to be exhibited in Brussels' cutting-edge Wiels gallery after its 2007 inauguration.

Major Writers

Guido Gezelle
(1830–99)

Hendrik
Conscience
(1812–83)

Georges Simenon
(1903–1989)

Hugo Claus
(1929–2008)

Amélie Nothomb
(1967–)

Like Tuymans, Ghent-based Michaël Borremans also works from photographic images, although his work is far more invested in the technique of oil painting. His precise but ever-elusive work is known for its emotional, but far from romantic, depiction of human subjects.

Back in Antwerp, the now (supposedly) retired 'assemblagist' Henri Van Herwegen (1940–), aka Panamarenko, a pseudonym conjured from a bastardised abbreviation of 'Pan American Airlines Company', spent much of his career creating installations that fuse authentic and imaginary flying contraptions. Also from Antwerp, Jan Fabre is a huge creative and intellectual presence in his home town. A stage designer and playwright as well as an artist, he is best known for using the wing cases of exotic beetles as a medium for creating images and transforming room interiors, including a church and the Africa Room in Brussels' Royal Palace.

Every country needs at least one arch-provocateur, and neo-conceptual Wim Delvoye gleefully fulfills this role in Belgium. A penchant for tattooing pigs and making stained glass from X-rated X-rays has made him famous, but his creation of *Cloaca,* an installation that's a gustatory production line, turning food into faeces, has also made him wealthy.

The late Jan Hoet (1936–2014) was perhaps the Belgian art world's most influential figure of recent years. A charismatic character often dubbed Belgium's 'sexiest man', his most lasting achievement was the establishment of the SMAK gallery in his adopted home of Ghent.

Film

Belgium's best-known film star is martial-arts expert Jean-Claude Van Damme. While Van Damme is hardly known for his high-brow performances, the local movie scene tends to be contrastingly thought-provoking. Its hard-hitting classics include *L'Enfant,* about a petty crook coming to grips with fatherhood, and *Rosetta,* about a girl searching for work and meaning in her life. Both are gritty affairs filmed in miserable suburbs of Liège. Neither does much for that city's tourism image.

In 1929, *My Fair Lady* screen superstar Audrey Hepburn was born to a Dutch mother in Brussels. Their home at Rue Keyenveld 46 has a commemorative plaque.

Other memorable offerings include *Les Barons* (2009), a look at attitudes in Brussels' North African community, and *Man Bites Dog* (1992), a cult crime mockumentary written, produced and directed by Rémy Belvaux, André Bonzel and Benoît Poelvoorde, the film's co-editor, cinematographer and lead actor respectively. The film helped cement Belgium's reputation for black comedy and led Poelvoorde to stardom in the French film industry. Indeed by 2015 he had become God, at least for the sake of the black comedy *Le Tout Nouveau Testament,* whose tagline in English read: 'God Exists: He Lives in Belgium'. The director, fellow Belgian Jaco Van Dormael, had risen to prominence with the French comedy drama *Le Huitième Jour* (The Eighth Day; 1996), not to be confused with *De Achtste Dag* (On Day Eight; 2018), a Belgo-Dutch docu-film that charts the nail-biting last-minute salvage of Fortis Bank during the 2008 financial crisis.

Dance

Until the 1980s, Belgian ballet was dominated by Swiss choreographer Maurice Béjart and his Mudra school in Brussels. Mechelen-born Anne Teresa De Keersmaeker changed that, with her experimental dance school PARTS and her group Rosas (www.rosas.be) putting Belgium back on the international dance map. In her elegant, if sometimes extreme, wake have come a number of Belgian experimentalists, including Wim Vandekeybus, Jan Fabre, Alain Platel and current international darling Sidi Larbi Cherkaoui. Belgian dance companies, including the venerable Antwerp-based Flemish Royal Ballet (www.operaballet.be), enjoy fruitful relationships with the fashion scene: the likes of Dries van Noten and Walter Van Beirendonck are regular costume designers.

Music

Proto-Belgium produced fine if little-noticed classical musicians for hundreds of years, of whom the best known is probably Liège-born composer César Franck (1822–90). You might recognise his intense symphony in D-minor even if you haven't heard of Franck himself.

During the 20th century, the country's global impact grew through popular music. Romani guitarist Django Reinhardt (1910–53), known as the first European-born jazz musician, became one of the world's most-loved guitarists. His fame is possibly matched only by thoughtful Brussels-born *chansonnier* Jacques Brel (1929–78), who was of Flemish background but sang almost exclusively in French. Other Belgians are household names in the world of *chanson* and French pop, including Adamo, Lio, Annie Cordy, Lara Fabien, Maurane and Axelle Red, along with 1970s one-off Plastic Bertrand and popular Elvis-impersonator-turned-tenor Helmut Loti.

Belgium has been a huge if rather self-deprecating player in the world of electronic music, and is known throughout Europe for being a hotbed of experimentation. With no legislation limiting club hours, the scene went wild with newbeat and EBM (electronic body music) in the late '80s (Technotronic's *Pump Up the Jam* foreshadowing what was to come). From the early '90s onwards, Ghent's R&S label unleashed a stream of 'cutting-edge techno gold'. As well as signing and mixing the likes of international stars Aphex Twin and Derrick May, it also championed local acts such as CJ Bolland. Another Ghent export, Soulwax and its later incarnation 2manydjs, shot to global fame in the mid-2000s, while Brussels-based The Magician, best known for his 2014 single 'Sunlight' as well as his famous remixes for Norwegian Lykke Li, is a recent star.

Jozef Devillé's 2012 film *The Sound of Belgium* (www.tsob.be) explores the scene in loving detail and proposes that its roots can be found in the electronic organ–fuelled country dance halls of the '50s, the slowed-down-soul 'Popcorn' dance nights of the '70s and the region's far more ancient but no less exuberant carnival traditions.

DJ mad as Belgium might be, the last few years have seen a growing indie scene as well, with bands such as Intergalactic Lovers, Goose and Amatorski being firm festival-circuit favourites. Classical music thrives too, and the country has opera houses in Brussels (www.lamonnaie.be), Antwerp, Ghent (https://operaballet.be) and Liège (www.operaliege.be).

Comic Strips

Belgian comic series and characters will more than likely have played a part in your childhood, no matter where you grew up. The country's consuming passion for comic strips is such that they are considered the 'ninth art' and spawned a major 20th-century publishing industry. Les Schtroumpfs, De Smurfen or, yes, *The Smurfs* began life as an in-joke by comic artist Peyo (the pen name of Pierre Culliford) in 1958 and are now a worldwide franchise. Asterix may have been drawn and written by the French duo René Goscinny and Albert Uderzo, but it was first published and made famous by the Franco-Belgian magazine *Pilote*.

Before them, though, was Tintin, first created by the great Hergé (the pseudonym of Georges Remi) in the late 1920s as a pullout section in a newspaper. Tintin books have been translated into dozens of languages and have sold hundreds of millions of copies. The series has also survived long enough to encounter charges of colonialism and racism, although it's defended by most fans as simply a product of its time. Hergé is celebrated at a fine museum in Louvain-la-Neuve. Other cartoon stars include Philippe Geluck's thought-provoking fat cat Le Chat, Willy Vandersteen's Suske and Wiske (Bob and Bobette in French) and Morris' Lucky Luke.

In Brussels, Belgium's love of comic-strip art takes to the streets, with many house ends painted with cartoon-character scenes. Every August Antwerp invites top graffiti artists from around the world to re-tag Krugerstraat with giant street-paintings. Ghent also has places where graffiti artists can express themselves, including central 'graffiti alley', Werregarensteeg.

Architecture

Despite a seemingly endless succession of wars over the centuries, Unesco's World Heritage list includes a large selection of Belgian buildings, plus the whole old-town centres of Bruges and Luxembourg City.

Some of the countries' finest cathedrals and most of the great abbey churches were ripped down during the antireligious turmoil of the 1790s; the abbeys at Aulne and Villers-la-Ville still lie in ruins from that time. However, many religious structures did survive, including the Collégiale Ste-Gertrude in Nivelles. Romanesque architecture, characterised by hefty columns and semicircular arches, disappeared over the 12th and 13th centuries once new building techniques allowed the introduction of pointed arches and the development of Gothic vaulting. Tournai's cathedral, built in three sections, offers a vivid example of that architectural progression.

In the cloth-trading towns of the medieval Low Countries, wealth and education led to ideas about personal rights. These notions are embodied in the guildhouses on market squares and, particularly, in the construction of secular belfries and city halls, most memorably in Brussels and Leuven. Another architectural innovation unique to the Low Countries was the *begijnhof/béguinage,* a protected, semi-religious enclosed village-settlement for women. There are many delightful, well-preserved examples of these oases.

The Counter-Reformation's Italian influence can be seen in Antwerp's St-Carolus-Borromeuskerk, although the church's baroque style, incorporating Rubens' sculptural and painterly decoration, is uniquely Flemish.

For most of the 18th century, under Austrian rule, architecture took on a colder, neoclassical style, typified by Brussels' Place Royale. After independence, but especially under its second king, Léopold II, Belgium focused on urban redevelopment. Léopold realised that making Brussels more aesthetically appealing could boost its economic potential. Partly using personal riches he'd gained through exploitation of the Congo, he funded gigantic public buildings including the Palais de Justice, created the monumental Cinquantenaire, and laid out vast suburban parks linked to the city by splendidly wide thoroughfares such as Ave Louise and Ave Tervuren. Much of this expansion coincided with a late-19th-century industrial boom that saw Belgian architects experimenting with materials such as glass and iron.

From the early 1890s, Brussels was at the forefront of art nouveau design, using sinuous lines, organic tendrils and floral motifs to create a genuinely new architectural aesthetic. One of the best examples, the Old England Building, combines wrought-iron frames, round windows, frescoes and *sgraffito,* a distinctive incised-mural technique of which a stunning example graces the facade of Brussels' Maison Cauchie. Antwerp also has some excellent art nouveau facades, especially in the Zurenborg suburb.

After WWI, the rectilinear lines of art deco came to dominate, presaged by buildings such as Ghent's 1912 Vooruit and Brussels' 1911 Palais Stoclet.

Tragically, earlier-20th-century styles were largely unvalued during the 1960s and 1970s and some of Belgium's finest art nouveau buildings were torn down. Worldwide protests over the 1965 destruction of Victor Horta's Maison du Peuple helped bring about laws protecting Brussels' heritage, and the Atelier de Recherche et d'Action Urbaines (ARAU) was formed to save and renovate city treasures. The former Belgian radio and TV building, Flagey, was one art deco landmark to be rescued, but swaths of cityscape have gone under the demolition ball, notably in Brussels to make way for the bland glass buildings that typify the EU quarter.

Despite some public acclaim, Belgium's 21st-century architecture has mostly proved less than majestic, with Luxembourg's EU zone similarly uninspired. Antwerp's Justitiepaleis is memorable but fails to offer much wow factor and Bruges' Concertgebouw feels like a modernist token. That said, Santiago Calatrava's Guillemins train station in Liège is astonishing.

Between Durbuy and Liège, peeping through trees on a ridgetop in Esneux is the remarkable 1904 Château de Fy. Some locals believe that a photo of Fy was the inspiration for Walt Disney's Sleeping Beauty Castle. However, most mainstream reports cite Neuschwanstein in Germany as a likelier candidate.

Survival Guide

Directory A–Z

Accessible Travel

Progressive tourism management bodies have produced a wealth of information to help those with a disability to plan and enjoy a stay. Naturally, all those cobblestones are a literal pain in the derrière for wheelchair users, but the country is well endowed with kerb cuts, tactile paving, audible signals at pedestrian crossings and wheelchair-accessible taxis. Most major museums are accessible, particularly in Flanders, but the caves and castle ruins of rural Wallonia and Luxembourg are never likely to be.

Accommodation

Accommodation availability varies markedly by season and area. From May to September occupancy is very high (especially at weekends) along the Belgian coast and in Bruges, with the Ardennes also packed during July and August and on sunny weekends. However, those same weekends you'll find business-centred hotels cutting prices in cities like Brussels, Luxembourg, Liège and Mechelen. Many options include breakfast. National taxes are invariably included in quoted prices, but several towns add a small additional *stadsbelasting/taxe de séjour* (city tourist tax), which might add a euro or three per head to the tally.

Camping, Caravan Parks & Hikers' Huts

Camping and caravan facilities are plentiful, especially in the Ardennes. Typical rates are compounded from per-person, per-car and per-site fees. For those with small tents, it is sometimes cheaper to arrive without a reservation, assuming space remains. But for those with a caravan, booking ahead is wise, especially in summer. Many sites close from October to April.

Simple wood-cabin accommodation for walkers is available in much of the region; they're known as *wanderhütten* in Luxembourg and *trekkershutten* (www.trekkershutten.nl) in Flanders. They're often attached to campgrounds or provincial recreation parks. Most have basic cooking facilities, charge an extra fee for electricity/heating and limit stays to a maximum of four nights.

Gîtes & Apartments

A great family option, particularly in rural areas, is to rent an apartment or especially a holiday home, with some options on farms or in castles, converted stables or historic buildings. In Flanders such places are often known as *landelijk verblijf;* in Wallonia as *gîtes rurals*.

Rentals are typically, but not always, by the week and for the whole building, with prices varying by season, number of occupants and house standards. There is often an extra cleaning cost that's charged per stay. Don't confuse a *gîte rural* with a *gîte d'étape,* which in Belgium is essentially a hostel, albeit sometimes limited to group bookings.

Paid homestays and rentals are available through the usual home-sharing services.

Hostels

Hostels (*jeugdherbergen* in Dutch; *auberges de jeunesse* in French) generally charge from €18 to €28 for a dorm bed, including sheets and basic breakfast. Neither towels nor soap are usually included. Lockers are often included, but you'll frequently need your own padlock to use them. A few of the cheapest private hostels charge extra for sheets. At Hostelling International (HI) affiliated hostels, rates are cheaper for under-30s in Flanders, or for under-26s in Wallonia. HI members also save €2 to €3 per night – so if planning to stay at a few hostels, you can save money by joining your country's HI association before leaving home.

Gîtes d'étape are aimed primarily at school kids and youth groups (typically a minimum of 20 people), but eight of them operate exactly like youth hostels with bunk beds at bargain prices. In lieu of membership there's a €3-per-stay fee in addition to quoted costs.

Hostels an be unstaffed at night, have limited check-in times and might close in midwinter (or longer).

Hotels

Belgium's hotel classification system awards stars for facilities (lifts, room service, dogs allowed etc), so it doesn't necessarily reflect overall quality. Prices for a room (*kamer/chambre* in Dutch/French) often vary to fit demand, sometimes as much as 300%. Check-in time is rarely before 2pm. Smaller hotels seldom have 24-hour reception, so if you plan to arrive late, be sure to note key-codes or make necessary alternative arrangements.

Motels

If you're driving and don't mind drearily banal locations in outer suburbs, Campanile (www.campanile.com) has simple motels off motorways near Ghent, Liège, Brussels and Brussels Airport. Ibis Budget (www.accorhotels.com) has nine simple, low-cost Belgian properties, most of them close to train stations and airports.

Booking Services

It's worth booking accommodation ahead, especially B&Bs and smaller hotels, which don't always have receptions.

Hostels (www.lesaubergesdejeunesse.be, www.youthhostels.be, https://youthhostels.lu) Hostelling International–affiliated sites for Wallonia, Flanders and Luxembourg respectively.

Gîtes d'Étape (www.gitesdetape.be) Hostel-style accommodation in Belgium.

Bed&Breakfast BeNeLux (http://bedandbreakfast.be) Official B&B listings.

Gîtes (www.gitesdewallonie.be, www.gites.lu) For rural holiday lettings in Wallonia and Luxembourg respectively.

Logeren in Vlaanderen (www.logereninvlaanderen.be) Apartments and holiday homes in rural Flanders.

Camping.be (https://www.camping.be) Campground finder.

Camping Wallonia (https://campingbelgique.be) Wallonian campgrounds listed by commune.

Camping Luxembourg (www.camping.lu) Campgrounds in the Grand Dutchy.

Activities

Belgium, and to a lesser extent Luxembourg, are delightful for cyclists, an unexpected discovery for long-distance walkers and a charming place for beginner kayakers to put gentle beauty above high-adrenaline white water. Most activities are well set up for families with children.

Cycling

As the homeland of the world's first cycling superstar, Eddy Merckx, it's no surprise that Belgium is a place that's passionate about cycling whether as a spectator sport, as a functional means of low-impact transport, or as an activity for both fitness and touring.

Belgium has excellent networks of well-signed bicycle paths and minor lanes linked together to maximise the possibilities for cyclists. Keyed maps and booklets are almost always available in local tourist offices.

In Flanders consult incredibly extensive www.fietsroute.org or buy the multilingual book *Topogids Vlaanderen Fietsroute*, which compiles over 60 detailed 1:50,000 route maps and relevant accommodation options. There are downloadable versions.

Wallonia's networks of cycle paths, RAVeL (Réseau Autonome de Voies Lentes; http://ravel.wallonie.be) and Rando-Vélo (www.randovelo.org) often use canal or river towpaths and former railway tracks rebuilt with hard surfaces. Rando-Vélo sells a range of guide maps.

CYCLE-PATH SIGNAGE

Flanders, along with the Netherlands, shares a single system of LF cycle routes that are assiduously marked. Most helpfully, the routes use a series of numbered turn points (*knooppunten* – literally 'intersections', sometimes translated as 'nodes'), reassuring cyclists that they are at the right place on a planned route. A cyclist can then remember a '*knooppuntroute*' as a simple string of two-digit numbers.

Signs are typically green-on-white or white-on-blue, with the number of the specific *knooppunt* plus those others nearby and ringed with arrows to show direction.

In the Germanophone Eastern Cantons, *knooppunten* are known as *knotenpunkten*, and over 180 are marked with VeloTour signage using orange arrows on white backgrounds.

Golf

To find one of Belgium's numerous golf courses, use the website www.golfbelgium.be and select *Cherchez un club* / *Zoek een golfclub* in the French/Dutch version.

Hiking

Crossing southern Belgium, you'll find various long-distance footpaths called Sentiers de Grande Randonnée (www.grsentiers.org), along with countless shorter trails for afternoon rambles. Most are well signposted and keyed to topographical hiking maps sold by tourist offices, which can offer plenty of advice to walkers. In flat Flanders, hiking routes typically follow countryside bicycle paths where you must be careful to give way to cyclists. Though mostly located in the Netherlands, some *trekker-shutten* (www.trekkershutten.nl) are located within Flanders offering simple accommodation to walkers.

Rock Climbing

BelClimb (http://en.belclimb.be) is a superb resource for climbers, offering exhaustive links to climbing guides, a searchable map of Belgium's indoor-climbing practice gyms and details of local competitions.

Skiing

Belgium might be the last country that springs to mind for skiers, but when the white stuff does fall, the E411 highway road rapidly fills up with wannabe skiers hurrying to the Ardennes area before it all melts again. Most such skiing is cross-country (*langlaufen*) on woodland tracks, but there are also a handful of modest downhill pistes, notably near Ofivat on the edge of the Haute Fagnes. Dutch-language site Ardennen Sneeuw (www.ardennen-sneeuw.be) gives snow conditions at all the major Ardennes ski areas.

Customs Regulations

For goods purchased outside the EU, the following duty-free allowances apply:

Tobacco 200 cigarettes, 50 cigars or 250g of loose tobacco
Alcohol 1L of spirits (more than 22% alcohol by volume) or 2L light liquor (less than 22% abv); 4L of wine; 16L of beer
Perfume 50g of perfume and 0.25L of eau de toilette

Crossing an EU border, you can carry unlimited quantities as long as it's for personal use: expect questions if you are found to be carrying more than 800 cigarettes, 200 cigars or 1kg of loose tobacco; 10L of spirits, 20L of fortified wine or aperitif, 90L of wine or 110L of beer.

Discount Cards

Museums and sights typically offer small discounts to seniors (those over 65, sometimes over 60) and often give bigger discounts to those under 26. Accompanied children (typically under 12, sometimes under 18) generally pay even less or go free. Students with an ISIC (International Student Identity Card) might, but won't always, qualify for the 'concession rate' (usually the same as seniors). Bigger Belgian cities offer discounted passes to a selection of municipally owned sights, and many have one day a month when key museums are free.

The highly worthwhile Luxembourg Card (www.visitluxembourg.com; 1-/2-/3-day adult €13/20/28, family €28/48/68) gives

Climate

Brussels

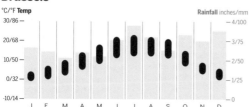

Luxembourg City

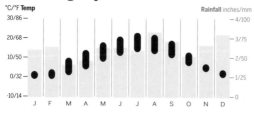

Ostend

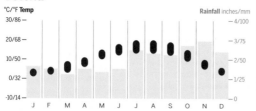

free admission to 76 of the country's top attractions, discounts on several others, plus unlimited use of public transport countrywide. Family tickets cover two adults and three children. You'll save money if visiting more than two museums or castles a day. Purchase it online, from tourist offices, museums, campgrounds and hotels.

Electricity

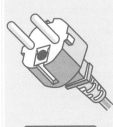

Type E
220V/50Hz

Type C
220V/50Hz

Food

For more on food see the Creative Cuisine chapter (p280).

Health

Travel in Belgium and Luxembourg presents very few health problems. The standard of care is extremely high; English is widely spoken by doctors and medical clinic staff.

Pharmacies

For minor self-limiting illnesses you might save a doctor's fee by asking advice at a pharmacy (*apotheek/pharmacie* in Dutch/French). Most are open from about 8.30am to 7pm Monday to Friday, plus Saturday mornings.

At night or on weekends special 'duty' pharmacies charge higher prices. Use these websites to find which one is open when:

Belgian Pharmacies (www.pharmacie.be; search *Apotheek van Wacht* in Dutch or *Pharmacie de Garde* in French)

Luxembourg Pharmacies (www.pharmacie.lu/service_de_garde)

Insurance

Paying for your airline ticket with a credit card often provides limited travel accident insurance, and you may be able to reclaim the payment if the operator doesn't deliver. However, a fuller travel insurance policy is recommended to cover theft, personal liability, loss and medical problems. Many policies also cover cancellation or delays in travel arrangements; eg, if you fall seriously ill two days before departure. Buy such insurance as early as possible: if you buy it the week before you are due to fly, you might find that you're not covered for delays caused, for example, by strikes that had been

planned before you took out the insurance.

Browse extensively online to find the best rates, ensuring that all sports and activities are covered and comparing excesses as well as just the premiums. Be sure to check the small print. Multi-trip policies are often good value if you're making more than one annual trip.

Although EU nationals qualify for reciprocal health care in Belgium and Luxembourg, doctors and hospitals generally expect payment up front, so medical cover remains important. Make sure you get a policy that covers you for the worst possible scenario, and check whether your insurance plan will make payments directly to providers or reimburse you later for overseas health expenditures.

Worldwide travel insurance is available at www.lonelyplanet.com/travel-insurance. You can buy, extend and claim online anytime – even if you're already on the road.

Internet Access

Wi-fi access is widespread; nearly all hotels, as well as many restaurants, cafes and bars, offer free customer access.

If you've got an unlocked smartphone, you can pick up a local SIM card for a few euros and charge it with a month's worth of data at a decent speed for under €20.

Internet cafes – often doubling as call-shops – do still exist but are increasingly rare; ask at the local tourist office.

Legal Matters

You are legally required to carry either a passport or a national identity card at all times, though a photocopy should suffice.

Should you be arrested you have the right to ask for your consul to be immediately notified.

For extensive information on the Belgian legal system (in French), see www. belgium.be/fr/justice. For Luxembourg, www.police. public.lu is informative, while website www.barreau.lu lists lawyers who speak multiple languages.

LGBT+ Travellers

Attitudes are pretty laid-back. Same-sex couples have been able to wed legally in Belgium since 2003, and since 2006 have had the same rights enjoyed by heterosexual couples, including inheritance and adoption. Luxembourg legalised same-sex marriage in 2015, and prime minister Xavier Bettel soon took advantage to tie the knot himself.

Money

Credit cards are widely accepted. ATMs are very prevalent but currency-exchange offices are rare.

Opening Hours

Many sights close on Monday. Restaurants normally close one or two full days per week. Opening hours for shops, bars and cafes vary widely.

Banks 8.30am–3.30pm or later Monday to Friday, some also Saturday morning

Bars 10am–1am, but hours very flexible

Restaurants noon–2pm and 7pm–9.30pm

Shops 10am–6.30pm Monday to Saturday, sometimes closed for an hour at lunchtime

Post

Websites of the postal agencies in Belgium (www. bpost.be) and Luxembourg (www.post.lu) list post office locations and postal rates. In Belgium there are small discounts if you buy stamps in multiples of five. Post offices are usually counters within other shops.

Public Holidays

New Year's Day 1 January

Easter Monday March/April

Labour Day 1 May

Iris Day 8 May (Brussels region only)

Ascension Day 39 days after Easter Sunday (always a Thursday)

Pentecost (Whit Monday) 50 days after Easter Sunday

Luxembourg National Day 23 June (Luxembourg)

Flemish Community Day 11 July (Flanders only)

Belgium National Day 21 July (Belgium)

Assumption Day 15 August

Francophone Community Day 27 September (Wallonia only)

All Saints' Day 1 November

Armistice Day 11 November (Belgium)

Christmas Day 25 December

Safe Travel

Belgium's traffic jams, poorly maintained roads and bad driving practices combine to make motoring taxing by European standards.

According to a 2015 EU report, the country is statistically the most dangerous place in Western Europe in terms of road deaths per million citizens.

Telephone

When calling from abroad, dial the country code (+32 Belgium, +352 Luxembourg) and the full number without an extra area code, dropping the initial 0 for Belgian numbers. The international dial-out code is 00.

Mobile Phones

There are no roaming charges within the EU. If you're travelling from outside the EU, the cheapest and most practical solution for making calls and using data is usually to purchase a chealply available local SIM card but check before departure that your home network has unlocked your phone.

Time

Clocks run on Central European Time (GMT/UTC plus one hour), moving forward one hour for daylight-saving time on the last Sunday in March, and reverting on the last Sunday in October. That makes Brussels an

---

PRACTICALITIES

Media Keep up to date with English-language news weekly *The Bulletin* (www.thebulletin.be), or bimonthly *The Word* (http://thewordmagazine.com), which is especially helpful with arts and culture listings.

Weights & Measures Both countries use the metric system. Decimals are indicated with commas, while thousands are separated with dots (full stops).

hour ahead of London and (usually) six hours ahead of New York.

The 24-hour clock is used.

Toilets

Museums and restaurants are well provided for, but cafe toilets sometimes leave a lot to be desired, and stand-alone public toilets can be infuriatingly hard to find. Facilities at train stations and motorway service areas often incur a charge.

Tourist Information

Marked with an easily identifiable white-on-green 'i' symbol, almost every town and village has its own tourist office known as *dienst voor toerisme, toeristische dienst* or simply *toerisme*

in Flanders; and *maison du tourisme, office du tourisme* or *syndicat d'initiative* in Wallonia and Luxembourg.

Most give away brochures and accommodation listings, sell detailed walking/cycling maps and local products, and can often arrange guided tours on your behalf.

Useful contacts:

Visit Brussels (https://visit.brussels/en)

Visit Flanders (www.visit flanders.com)

Visit Wallonia (http://wallonia belgiumtourism.co.uk)

Visit Luxembourg (www.visit luxembourg.com)

Visas

EU citizens can stay indefinitely; many other nationals can enter visa-free for up to 90 days.

Work

Foreigners other than EU, EEA and Swiss nationals generally require a permit to work in Belgium or Luxembourg. These are issued by the regional authorities. For more information search www.werk.be for Flanders, http://emploi.wallonie.be for Wallonia, http://werk-economie-emploi.brussels for Brussels and www.luxembourg.public.lu for Luxembourg.

Self-employed individuals or employers sending staff on short-term contracts in Belgium need to register through www.limosa.be.

A high percentage of Luxembourg's workforce is made up of cross-border workers (www.lesfrontaliers.lu) who live in neighbouring countries.

Transport

GETTING THERE & AWAY

Belgium and Luxembourg are easily accessed from Europe and beyond. There are direct flights and international buses from numerous destinations and a comprehensive rail network connecting to locations across the continent.

Flights, car hire and tours can be booked online at lonelyplanet.com/bookings.

Entering the Region

As part of the Schengen group of countries, there are no passport checks on any of the nations' land borders. If you fly in or arrive by ferry from the UK, passports (and visas, if required) need to be shown, but there is rarely any great delay if all paperwork is in order.

Air

Brussels is Belgium's most globally connected airport and the hub for the country's biggest carrier Brussels Airlines (www.brusselsairlines. com). Charleroi airport, sometimes misleadingly described as Brussels-South, attracts budget airlines. Luxembourg Airport, home to Luxair (www.luxair.lu), Luxembourg's national carrier, has many connections to major destinations across Europe. Antwerp's small airport offers mostly business shuttle flights to the UK and Germany, while Liège and Ostend airports focus mainly on cargo plus summer charter flights.

For long-haul flights it can be worth comparing costs with flying into neighbouring countries via Frankfurt, Amsterdam or Paris, for example, then continuing on by land.

Land

Trains are generally faster but more expensive than buses, though price depends greatly on how early you book. If driving from the southeast, fill your petrol tank in Luxembourg for low prices. Only in exceptional circumstances are there border controls at crossings between neighbouring countries.

Bus

LONG DISTANCE

Long-distance international buses almost always require advance booking. Book as far ahead as possible for the best fares, which can be remarkable bargains. The two biggest players are Eurolines (www.eurolines.eu) and Flixbus (www.flixbus.be), both with wide networks from Brussels and other cities, including links to Amsterdam (via Antwerp), Berlin, Paris and London (via Bruges and/or Ghent). Ecolines (www.

CLIMATE CHANGE & TRAVEL

Every form of transport that relies on carbon-based fuel generates CO_2, the main cause of human-induced climate change. Modern travel is dependent on aeroplanes, which might use less fuel per kilometre per person than most cars but travel much greater distances. The altitude at which aircraft emit gases (including CO_2) and particles also contributes to their climate change impact. Many websites offer 'carbon calculators' that allow people to estimate the carbon emissions generated by their journey and, for those who wish to do so, to offset the impact of the greenhouse gases emitted with contributions to portfolios of climate-friendly initiatives throughout the world. Lonely Planet offsets the carbon footprint of all staff and author travel.

ecolines.net) specialises in mostly Baltic and Eastern European destinations. IC Bus (www.bahn.com) has a two-hour Liège–Maastricht–Düsseldorf service. Flibco (www.flibco.com) runs long-distance airport shuttles between Charleroi and Luxembourg airports with handy stops in Namur, Bastogne and Arlon.

REGIONAL

A few local and city bus companies operate cross-border services, such as De Panne/Adinkerke-Dunkerque and Tilburg-Turnhout. Used mostly by locals, these are rarely well publicised to visitors.

Car & Motorcycle

➡ Northern Europe is one vast web of motorways, so Belgium is easily accessed from anywhere.

➡ There's no problem bringing foreign vehicles into Belgium, provided you have registration papers and valid insurance ('Green Card').

➡ Most car-hire companies in other EU nations won't have a problem with you taking their car into Belgium, but check rental conditions before you do so.

➡ Be aware that, as in France, the *priorité à droite* rule gives right of way to vehicles emerging from the right even from a small side lane, unless otherwise indicated.

➡ City centres in most larger Flemish cities are increasingly pedestrianised and can be awkward if not inaccessible for motorists. Ideally park outside and shuttle in.

Train

Useful resources include the following:

www.b-europe.com Belgian Railways' international site.

www.cfl.lu Luxembourg's joint railway-bus network.

www.seat61.com An invaluable compendium of advice when planning European train trips.

www.loco2.com A useful website for comparing routes and times and buying tickets.

HIGH-SPEED TRAINS

High-speed trains offer fast, easy connections between Brussels and London, and to the broader French, Dutch and German networks, but such trains require seat reservations and can prove expensive if demand is high. Advance-purchase discounts can be massive, though you'll usually forfeit the right to changes.

ORDINARY TRAINS

Less-publicised ordinary IC trains do still run, most usefully on routes Antwerp–Amsterdam, Antwerp–Roosendaal, Kortrijk/Tournai-Lille, Spa–Aachen and Liège–Maastricht. Using these routes combined with domestic tickets is slower but usually far cheaper than high-speed services for last-minute journeys. There are no assigned seats, but if purchasing ex-Belgium, it's still worth booking online and printing your own ticket (or using the e-ticket app when available) to save the cheeky €6 in-station international ticketing fee.

Sea

At the time of research, there was only one ferry service operating from Belgium: the twice-weekly P&O (www.po ferries.com) Zeebrugge–Hull service (14 hours, overnight).

Quicker ways to reach the UK use the French Channel ports. From Calais, around an hour's drive west of Ostend, the drive-on tunnel trains of Eurotunnel (www.eurotunnel.com) take 35 minutes to Folkestone, departing about twice an hour. Usually less expensive but taking around 90 minutes are the ferry services to Dover run by P&O and DFDS (www.dfdssea ways.co.uk). DFDS also sails to Dover from Dunkerque (two hours), but though

Dunkerque is nearer Belgium, the port is awkwardly located, so going via Calais can prove faster overall.
Tips:

➡ Same-day returns, sometimes valid for one night and two days, can be vastly cheaper than one-way tickets. However, you MUST use the return section as planned or else you become liable for a hefty supplement that gets charged to your credit card.

➡ Fares can vary enormously but usually include up to five passengers per car.

➡ The cheapest ferry deals insist on you sticking to a specific sailing time.

➡ Arrive around an hour before your booked departure to allow time for security clearance.

GETTING AROUND

In Belgium, most trains are run by a single national company NMBS/SNCB (www.b-rail.be) but buses have three regional operators plus a few long distance private companies. Luxembourg has a single one-price domestic ticket system: wherever you go by public transport within the country, the price is the same – €2 for up to two hours or €4 for the day. Mobilitéit (www.mobiliteit.lu) has a handy Luxembourg journey planner.

Air

Speedy trains and short distances mean that there are no domestic scheduled flights.

Bicycle

Bicycle on train In Belgium pay €5/8 for one journey/whole day. In Luxembourg bikes travel free if space permits.

MOBIB

The MOBIB card is an electronic purse akin to the OysterCard in London or the OV-Chipkaart in the Netherlands, allowing contactless payment for public transport. There are two types:

➡ A personalised MOBIB is valid on all three of Belgium's bus-tram networks and on Belgian trains. Soon all season tickets will require one.

➡ Anonymous MOBIB Basic cards (€5, valid five years) are worth buying if you'll make more than 10 rides on STIB transport (in Brussels) or TEC buses (Wallonia).

Bike helmets Not a legal requirement for cyclists and generally not worn by adults.

Rental City bikes and electric bikes can easily be hired in many cities: for Belgium, www.fietspunten.be gives many useful contacts.

Belgium's Blue Bikes

While some train stations rent bicycles 'manually', around 50 in Belgium (plus some park-and-ride car parks) use the good-value, members-only Blue Bike scheme (www.blue-bike.be). Online membership costs €12 per year and you should ideally sign up well in advance, though if you can't, it's possible to join at around 20 major station outlets during working hours for €18.30. As a member you can make 24-hour hires for €1.15 at most outlets, or €3.15 in a few bigger city stations (two bicycles per member is possible). Return the bike(s) to the same station.

Short-Hop Bicycle Hire

Several cities including Brussels, Luxembourg and Antwerp operate bike-hop schemes. Grab a bicycle from the nearest automated stand, ride towards your destination then drop it off at the nearest empty stand. As long as you return it within 30 minutes, hire charges are minimal or nil, but if you keep the bike longer, fees accrue rapidly on your credit card: so keep changing bikes if you want to ride around town all day.

➡ To start, use a credit card to buy a membership or day pass, usually online.

➡ You'll receive a swipe card or PIN code that releases a bike when you need one.

➡ When returning a bike, double-check that the return has been registered to avoid charges. If there is a hitch when returning, phone the helpline immediately.

➡ Download the app, which gives real-time info as to which stands are full or empty.

➡ If you arrive at a full stand and so can't drop off the bike (not uncommon on Saturday nights in popular nightlife areas), enter your code and you should get an extra five minutes to find an alternative.

In Hasselt, Mechelen and Kortrijk, **Mobit** (www.mobit.eu; 1/2/3/4hr hires €1.35/3.30/5.70/8.70) short-hop bikes use a QR-coded key-release system activated by smartphone using the app. Your account is debited per 20 minutes of usage.

Boat

Antwerp, Namur and Liège have short-hop passenger services on limited stretches of river. Other boat trips, like the Bruges–Damme run, tend to be taken as a tour rather than as transport.

Bus

Longer-distance bus journeys tend to be slow and circuitous. Where bus and train options link the same two cities, the bus is usually cheaper but far slower. In Belgium a single ticket is valid for transfers for up to an hour after the ticket's validation (or 90 minutes for TEC Horizon), plus however long the final leg of your ride takes. In some rural areas buses are on-demand only, so you must phone ahead (details vary).

Bus frequency is highest on school days. Fewer operate on Saturday, while Sunday services can be scant or nonexistent. Some rural buses don't operate at all during school holidays (including the whole of July and August).

Flanders

Bus and tram networks are operated by **De Lijn** (☑high toll 070-220200; www.delijn.be/en). When purchased aboard, virtually any single ticket costs €3 (notes of €20 or above are not accepted; express buses 68, 178 and 179 cost more). Tickets are cheaper if purchased by smartphone: €1.80 using the De Lijn app or €2.15 by texting 'DL' to 4884 (from a Belgian SIM card).

Passes offering unlimited bus and tram travel anywhere in Flanders cost €6/12/17 for one/three/five calendar days. The one-day pass can be purchased on board (adult/child €8/4), or you can get a 24-hour M-Pass by smartphone: €6 through the app, or €6.15 by texting DLD to 4884.

Wallonia

TEC (www.infotec.be) buses have three basic single-ticket types:

Next (€2.50) allows travel within a two-zone area (https://tinyurl.com/TEC-Zone), allowing transfers within 60 minutes.

Horizon (€3.50) allows transfers within 90 minutes on the whole TEC network, except for express buses.

Horizon+ (€5.50) is for express buses. You'll save €0.50 per ticket if you use a MOBIB Card (p300), payable online through https://eshop.infotec.be. One-day go-anywhere passes cost €10/8 without/with MOBIB. Three-day passes cost €16 for MOBIB-holders.

Car & Motorcycle

For visiting rural Belgium, especially in the hills of Wallonia, having your own wheels will transform your experience, as many attractions are awkward to reach by public transport. However, in Bruges, Ghent, Brussels and Antwerp (which requires LEZ registration (p164)), a car will generally prove an encumbrance: you'll spend more time finding parking than actually driving anywhere.

While Belgium's motorway system is extensive and toll-free, traffic often grinds to a halt, especially on the ring roads around Brussels and Antwerp (at rush hour, September to June), on the Brussels–Ghent–Ostend highway (sunny weekends) and on the Ardennes-bound E411 (holidays and snowy weekends). Seemingly interminable repairs also result in frequent diversions and long traffic jams.

Hitching & Ride Sharing

Hitching can be a good way of meeting locals but is never entirely safe, and Lonely Planet does not recommend it. Travellers who hitch should understand that they are taking a small but potentially serious risk.

Long-distance ride sharing is widespread in Northern Europe: Blablacar (www. blablacar.com) is probably the most popular app/website for posting and searching for rides.

Local Transport

Major cities have efficient public transport – mostly buses but also metro and trams in Brussels and Antwerp. Services don't run all night.

Train

Belgium's trains are run by NMBS/SNCB (www. belgianrail.be), and Luxembourg's by **CFL** (www.cfl.lu).

Ticket Tips

➡ Tickets should be pre-purchased at ticket offices or ticket machines, or online (website or app). Buying once aboard will incur a €7 surcharge.

➡ Check online first for advance-purchase specials.

➡ Single tickets are priced by kilometre, but there's a higher fee for Thalys trains, which must be pre-reserved.

➡ For under-26s, a Go-Pass 1 costs €6.40 and allows any one-way trip within Belgium. Pay €52 for 10 tickets or €8.20 for one that adds Roosendaal or Maastricht in the Netherlands. Return tickets are normally twice the price of singles except:

➡ on weekends from 7pm Friday, when a return ticket getting back by Sunday night costs 75% of the price of two singles or less.

➡ for seniors (over 65), who pay just €6 for a return

PLACE NAMES

Frequently, road signs in Belgium give only the Dutch or French rendering of town names. This can be very confusing for foreigners. Some key ones to be aware of:

ENGLISH OR OTHER	DUTCH	FRENCH
Aachen* (G)	Aken	Aix-la-Chapelle
Antwerp	Antwerpen*	Anvers
Bruges	Brugge*	Bruges
Brussels	Brussel*	Bruxelles*
Courtrai	Kortrijk*	Courtrai
Jodoigne	Geldenaken	Jodoigne*
Köln*/Cologne (G)	Keulen	Cologne
Leuven/Louvain	Leuven*	Louvain
Lille* (F)	Rijsel	Lille
Mechelen/Mechlin	Mechelen*	Malines
Namur	Namen	Namur*
Nivelles	Nijvel	Nivelles*
Mons	Bergen	Mons*
Paris* (F)	Parijs	Paris
Roeselare	Roeselare*	Roulers
The Hague (N)	Den Haag*	La Haye
Tournai	Doornik	Tournai*
Trier* (G)	Trier	Trèves
Veurne	Veurne*	Furnes
Ypres	Ieper*	Ypres

* Name as used locally; (F) place is in France; (G) place is in Germany; (N) place is in the Netherlands

Train Routes

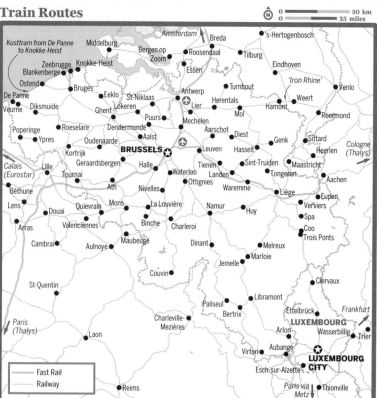

2nd-class day trip anywhere in Belgium. Valid for travel after 9am weekdays or any weekend except mid-July to mid-August.

CHILDREN & YOUTH FARES

In Luxembourg, anyone under 20 travels free. In Belgium, children under 12 travel free when accompanied by an adult. Families travelling with three kids or more pay half price for over-12s (including adults) too. For student fare passes in Belgium you'll generally need a MOBIB card (p300).

Train Passes

Various passes, notably InterRail (www.interrail.eu) for Europeans and Eurail (www.

eurail.com) for non-Europeans have options including Benelux (Belgium, Luxembourg and the Netherlands), but you'll still need to pay supplements and reservation costs for high-speed services. Just to visit Belgium, the Go Pass and Rail Pass options are generally a much better deal, while in school holidays Go Unlimited is an utter bargain for the under-26s.

GO PASS & RAIL PASS

Rail Pass Ten one-way trips anywhere in Belgium (except to/from border stations) for those over 26 years cost €118/77 for 1st/2nd class. Transfers en route are permitted, but not stopovers (ie you're supposed to take the first feasible connection). Before

getting aboard you must write into the space provided the start and end stations plus the date. Valid for one year, the pass is not limited to one person, so you could, for example, write in the same details four times over and use the ticket for a group of four people.

Go Pass 10 Essentially the same as the Rail Pass but for under-26s and costing just €52. Or buy single-day one-way **Go Pass 1** tickets for €6.40 if 10 journeys are too many.

Go Unlimited For those under 26, during school holidays a week's unlimited travel costs just €15, or get a whole month in July or August for €25. You'll need either a MOBIB card or a Facebook Messenger account to sign up.

Language

Belgium's population is split between Dutch-speaking Flanders in the north, French-speaking Wallonia in the south, and the small German-speaking region, known as the Eastern Cantons, based around the towns of Eupen and St Vith in the east. Brussels is officially bilingual though French has long been the city's dominant language.

The Dutch spoken in Belgium is also called 'Flemish', underlining the cultural identity of the Flemish people. The grammar and spelling rules of Dutch in Belgium and in the Netherlands are the same, and 'Flemish'*(Vlaams)* is not a separate language in itself.

Visitors' attempts to speak French in Flanders are generally considered culturally insensitive and ill-informed, especially in less tourist-oriented cities such as Leuven and Hasselt. English, on the other hand, is considered neutral and quite acceptable – many Flemish speak English fluently.

Luxembourg has three official languages: French, German and Letzeburgesch. Most people are fluent in all three as well as in English, which is widely spoken in the capital and by younger people around the countryside.

Letzeburgesch is most closely related to German and was proclaimed the national tongue in 1984. Luxembourgers speak Letzeburgesch to each other but generally switch to French when talking to foreigners. A couple of Letzeburgesch words often overheard are *moien* (good morning/hello), *äddi* (goodbye) and *wann ech gelifft* (please). Like French speakers, Luxembourgers say *merci* for 'thank you'. A phrase that might come in useful is *Schwatzt dir Englesch?* (pronounced 'schwetz dear anglish') meaning 'Do you speak English?'

DUTCH

The pronunciation of Dutch is fairly straightforward. The language does distinguish between long and short vowels, which can affect the meaning of words; for example, man (man) and maan (moon). Also note that aw is pronounced as in 'law', eu as the 'u' in 'nurse', ew as the 'ee' in 'see' (with rounded lips), oh as the 'o' in 'note', öy as the 'er y' (without the 'r') in 'her year', and uh as in 'ago'.

The consonants are pretty simple to pronounce too. Note that kh is a throaty sound, similar to the 'ch' in the Scottish loch, r is trilled – both may require a bit of practice – and zh is pronounced as the 's' in 'pleasure'.

If you read our coloured pronunciation guides as if they were English, you'll be understood just fine. The stressed syllables are indicated with italics.

Where relevant, both polite and informal options in Dutch are included, indicated with 'pol' and 'inf' respectively.

Basics

Hello.	Dag./Hallo.	dakh/ha·*loh*
Goodbye.	Dag.	dakh
Yes.	Ja.	yaa
No.	Nee.	ney
Please.	Alstublieft. (pol)	al·stew·*bleeft*
	Alsjeblieft. (inf)	a·shuh·*bleeft*
Thank you.	Dank u/je. (pol/inf)	dangk ew/yuh
You're welcome.	Graag gedaan.	khraakh khuh·*daan*
Excuse me.	Excuseer mij.	eks·kew·*zeyr* mey
How are you?		
Hoe gaat het met u/jou? (pol/inf)		hoo khaat huht met ew/yaw

WANT MORE?

For in-depth language information and handy phrases, check out Lonely Planet's *Western Europe Phrasebook*. You'll find it at **shop.lonelyplanet.com**, or you can buy Lonely Planet's Fast Talk app at the Apple App Store.

Fine. And you?
Goed. — khoot
En met u/jou? (pol/inf) — en met ew/yaw

What's your name?
Hoe heet u/je? (pol/inf) — hoo heyt ew/yuh

My name is ...
Ik heet ... — ik heyt ...

Do you speak English?
Spreekt u Engels? — spreykt ew eng·uhls

I don't understand.
Ik begrijp het niet. — ik buh·khreyp huht neet

Accommodation

Do you have a ... room?	*Heeft u een ...?*	heyft ew uhn ...
double	*tweepersoons-kamer met een dubbel bed*	twey·puhr·sohns·kaa·muhr met uhn du·buhl bet
single	*éénpersoons-kamer*	eyn·puhr·sohns·kaa·muhr
twin	*tweepersoons-kamer met lits jumeaux*	twey·puhr·sohns·kaa·muhr met lee zhew·moh

How much is it per ...?	*Hoeveel kost het per ...?*	hoo·veyl kost huht puhr ...
night	*nacht*	nakht
person	*persoon*	puhr·sohn

Is breakfast included?
Is het ontbijt inbegrepen? — is huht ont·beyt in·buh·khrey·puhn

bathroom	*badkamer*	bat·kaa·muhr
bed and breakfast	*gasten-kamer*	khas·tuhn·kaa·muhr
campsite	*camping*	kem·ping
guesthouse	*pension*	pen·syon
hotel	*hotel*	hoh·tel
window	*raam*	raam
youth hostel	*jeugdherberg*	yeukht·her·berkh

Directions

Where's the ...?
Waar is ...? — waar is ...

How far is it?
Hoe ver is het? — hoo ver is huht

What's the address?
Wat is het adres? — wat is huht a·dres

Can you please write it down?
Kunt u dat alstublieft opschrijven? — kunt ew dat al·stew·bleeft op·skhrey·vuhn

Can you show me (on the map)?
Kunt u het mij tonen (op de kaart)? — kunt ew huht mey toh·nuhn (op duh kaart)

Eating & Drinking

What would you recommend?
Wat kan u aanbevelen? — wat kan ew aan·buh·vey·luhn

What's in that dish?
Wat zit er in dat gerecht? — wat zit uhr in dat khuh·rekht

I'd like the menu, please.
Ik wil graag een menu. — ik wil khraakh uhn me·new

Delicious!
Heerlijk!/Lekker! — heyr·luhk/le·kuhr

Cheers!
Proost! — prohst

Please bring the bill.
Mag ik de rekening alstublieft? — makh ik duh rey·kuh·ning al·stew·bleeft

I'd like to reserve a table for ...	*Ik wil graag een tafel voor ... reserveren.*	ik wil khraakh uhn taa·fuhl vohr ... rey·ser·vey·ruhn
(eight) o'clock	*(acht) uur*	(akht) ewr
(two) people	*(twee) personen*	(twey) puhr·soh·nuhn

I don't eat ...	*Ik eet geen ...*	ik eyt kheyn ...
eggs	*eieren*	ey·yuh·ruhn
fish	*vis*	vis
(red) meat	*(rood) vlees*	(roht) vleys
nuts	*noten*	noh·tuhn

bar	*bar*	bar
beer	*bier*	beer
bottle	*fles*	fles
bread	*brood*	broht
breakfast	*ontbijt*	ont·beyt
cafe	*café*	ka·fey
cheese	*kaas*	kaas

Question Words – Dutch

How?	*Hoe?*	hoo
What?	*Wat?*	wat
When?	*Wanneer?*	wa·neyr
Where?	*Waar?*	waar
Who?	*Wie?*	wee
Why?	*Waarom?*	waa·rom

Numbers – Dutch

1	*één*	eyn
2	*twee*	twey
3	*drie*	dree
4	*vier*	veer
5	*vijf*	veyf
6	*zes*	zes
7	*zeven*	*zey*·vuhn
8	*acht*	akht
9	*negen*	*ney*·khuhn
10	*tien*	teen
20	*twintig*	*twin*·tikh
30	*dertig*	*der*·tikh
40	*veertig*	*feyr*·tikh
50	*vijftig*	*feyf*·tikh
60	*zestig*	*ses*·tikh
70	*zeventig*	*sey*·vuhn·tikh
80	*tachtig*	*takh*·tikh
90	*negentig*	*ney*·khuhn·tikh
100	*honderd*	*hon*·duhrt
1000	*duizend*	*döy*·zuhnt

coffee	*koffie*	*ko*·fee
cold	*koud*	kawt
dinner	*avondmaal*	*aa*·vont·maal
drink list	*drankkaart*	*drang*·kaart
eggs	*eieren*	*ey*·yuh·ruhn
fish	*vis*	vis
fork	*vork*	vork
fruit	*fruit*	fröyt
glass	*glas*	khlas
grocery store	*kruidenier*	*kröy*·duh·*neer*
hot	*heet*	heyt
juice	*sap*	sap
knife	*mes*	mes
lunch	*middagmaal*	*mi*·dakh·maal
market	*markt*	markt
meat	*vlees*	vleys
menu	*menu*	me·*new*
milk	*melk*	melk
plate	*bord*	bort
pub	*kroeg*	krookh
restaurant	*restaurant*	res·toh·*rant*
rice	*rijst*	reyst
salt	*zout*	zawt
spicy	*pikant*	pee·*kant*
spoon	*lepel*	*ley*·puhl

sugar	*suiker*	*söy*·kuhr
tea	*thee*	tey
vegetables	*groenten*	*khroon*·tuhn
vegetarian	*vegetarisch*	vey·khey·*taa*·ris
water	*water*	*waa*·tuhr
wine	*wijn*	weyn
with	*met*	met
without	*zonder*	*zon*·duhr

Emergencies

Help!
Help! — help

Leave me alone!
Laat me met rust! — laat muh met rust

I'm lost.
Ik ben verdwaald. — ik ben vuhr·*dwaalt*

There's been an accident.
Er is een ongeluk gebeurd. — uhr is uhn *on*·khuh·luk khuh·*beurt*

Call a doctor!
Bel een dokter! — bel uhn *dok*·tuhr

Call the police!
Bel de politie! — bel duh poh·*leet*·see

I'm sick.
Ik ben ziek. — ik ben zeek

Where are the toilets?
Waar zijn de toiletten? — waar zeyn duh twa·*le*·tuhn

I'm allergic to (antibiotics).
Ik ben allergisch voor (antibiotica). — ik ben a·*ler*·khees vohr (an·tee·bee·*yoh*·tee·ka)

Shopping & Services

I'd like to buy ...
Ik wil graag ... kopen. — ik wil khraakh ... *koh*·puhn

I'm just looking.
Ik kijk alleen maar. — ik keyk a·*leyn* maar

Can I look at it?
Kan ik het even zien? — kan ik huht *ey*·vuhn zeen

Do you have any others?
Heeft u nog andere? — heyft ew nokh *an*·duh·ruh

How much is it?
Hoeveel kost het? — hoo·*veyl* kost huht

That's too expensive.
Dat is te duur. — dat is tuh dewr

Can you lower the price?
Kunt u wat van de prijs afdoen? — kunt ew wat van duh preys *af*·doon

There's a mistake in the bill.
Er zit een fout in de rekening. — uhr zit uhn fawt in duh *rey*·kuh·ning

| **ATM** | *pin-automaat* | *pin*·aw·toh·maat |

foreign exchange	*wisselkantoor*	*wi*·suhl·kan·tohr
post office	*postkantoor*	*post*·kan·tohr
shopping centre	*winkel-centrum*	*wing*·kuhl·sen·trum
tourist office	*VVV*	vey·vey·vey

Time & Dates

What time is it?
Hoe laat is het?   hoo laat is huht

It's (10) o'clock.
Het is (tien) uur.   huht is (teen) ewr

Half past (10).
Half (elf). (lit: half eleven)   half (elf)

am (morning)	*'s ochtends*	*sokh*·tuhns
pm (afternoon)	*'s middags*	*smi*·dakhs
pm (evening)	*'s avonds*	*saa*·vonts
yesterday	*gisteren*	*khis*·tuh·ruhn
today	*vandaag*	van·*daakh*
tomorrow	*morgen*	*mor*·khuhn
Monday	*maandag*	*maan*·dakh
Tuesday	*dinsdag*	*dins*·dakh
Wednesday	*woensdag*	*woons*·dakh
Thursday	*donderdag*	*don*·duhr·dakh
Friday	*vrijdag*	*vrey*·dakh
Saturday	*zaterdag*	*zaa*·tuhr·dakh
Sunday	*zondag*	*zon*·dakh

Transport

Is this the ... to (the left bank)?
Is dit de ... naar (de linker-oever)?   is dit duh ... naar (duh *ling*·kuhr·oo·vuhr)

ferry	*veerboot*	*veyr*·boht
metro	*metro*	*mey*·troh
tram	*tram*	trem
platform	*perron*	pe·*ron*
timetable	*dienst-regeling*	*deenst*·rey·khuh·ling

When's the ... (bus)?
Hoe laat gaat de ... (bus)?   hoo laat khaat duh ... (bus)

first	*eerste*	*eyr*·stuh
last	*laatste*	*laat*·stuh
next	*volgende*	*vol*·khun·duh

A ticket to ..., please.
Een kaartje naar ... graag.   uhn *kaar*·chuh naar ... khraakh

Signs – Dutch

Dames	Women
Gesloten	Closed
Heren	Men
Ingang	Entrance
Inlichtingen	Information
Open	Open
Toiletten	Toilets
Uitgang	Exit
Verboden	Prohibited

What time does it leave?
Hoe laat vertrekt het?   hoo laat vuhr·*trekt* huht

Does it stop at ...?
Stopt het in ...?   stopt huht in ...

What's the next stop?
Welk is de volgende halte?   welk is duh *vol*·khuhn·duh *hal*·tuh

I'd like to get off at ...
Ik wil graag in ... uitstappen.   ik wil khraak in ... *öyt*·sta·puhn

Is this taxi available?
Is deze taxi vrij?   is *dey*·zuh *tak*·see vrey

Please take me to ...
Breng me alstublieft naar ...   breng muh al·stew·*bleeft* naar ...

I'd like ...	*Ik wil graag ...*	ik wil khraakh ...
my bicycle repaired	*mijn fiets laten herstellen*	meyn feets *laa*·tuhn her·*ste*·luhn
to hire a bicycle	*een fiets huren*	uhn feets *hew*·ruhn

I'd like to hire a ...	*Ik wil graag een ... huren.*	ik wil khraakh uhn ... *hew*·ruhn
basket	*mandje*	*man*·chuh
child seat	*kinderzitje*	*kin*·duhr·zi·chuh
helmet	*helm*	helm

Do you have bicycle parking?
Heeft u parking voor fietsen?   heyft ew *par*·king vohr *feet*·suhn

Can we get there by bike?
Kunnen we er met de fiets heen?   *ku*·nuhn wuh uhr met duh feets heyn

I have a puncture.
Ik heb een lekke band.   ik hep uhn *le*·kuh bant

bicycle path	*fietspad*	*feets*·pat
bicycle repairman	*fietsen-maker*	*feet*·suhn·*maa*·kuhr
bicycle stand	*fietsenrek*	*feet*·suhn·*rek*

FRENCH

The sounds used in spoken French can almost all be found in English. There are a couple of exceptions: nasal vowels (represented in our pronunciation guides by o or u followed by an almost inaudible nasal consonant sound m, n or ng), the 'funny' u (ew in our guides) and the deep-in-the-throat r. Bearing these few points in mind and reading our pronunciation guides below as if they were English, you won't have problems being understood. Note that syllables are for the most part equally stressed in French.

In this chapter both masculine and femine forms are provided where necessary, separated by a slash and indicated with 'm/f'.

Basics

Hello.	Bonjour.	bon·zhoor
Goodbye.	Au revoir.	o·rer·vwa
Excuse me.	Excusez-moi.	ek·skew·zay·mwa
Sorry.	Pardon.	par·don
Yes.	Oui.	wee
No.	Non.	non
Please.	S'il vous plaît.	seel voo play
Thank you.	Merci.	mair·see
You're welcome.	De rien.	der ree·en

How are you?
Comment allez-vous? ko·mon ta·lay·voo

Fine, and you?
Bien, merci. Et vous? byun mair·see ay voo

You're welcome.
De rien. der ree·en

My name is ...
Je m'appelle ... zher ma·pel ...

What's your name?
Comment vous appelez-vous? ko·mon voo· za·play voo

Do you speak English?
Parlez-vous anglais? par·lay·voo ong·glay

Question Words – French

How?	Comment?	ko·mon
What?	Quoi?	kwa
When?	Quand?	kon
Where?	Où?	oo
Who?	Qui?	kee
Why?	Pourquoi?	poor·kwa

I don't understand.
Je ne comprends pas. zher ner kom·pron pa

Accommodation

Do you have any rooms available?
Est-ce que vous avez des chambres libres? es·ker voo za·vay day shom·brer lee·brer

How much is it per night/person?
Quel est le prix par nuit/personne? kel ay ler pree par nwee/per·son

Is breakfast included?
Est-ce que le petit déjeuner est inclus? es·ker ler per·tee day·zher·nay ayt en·klew

campsite	camping	kom·peeng
dorm	dortoir	dor·twar
guesthouse	pension	pon·syon
hotel	hôtel	o·tel
youth hostel	auberge de jeunesse	o·berzh der zher·nes

a ... room	une chambre ...	ewn shom·brer ...
double	avec un grand lit	a·vek un gron lee
single	à un lit	a un lee
twin	avec des lits jumeaux	a·vek day lee zhew·mo

with (a)...	avec ...	a·vek ...
air-con	climatiseur	klee·ma·tee·zer
bathroom	une salle de bains	ewn sal der bun
window	fenêtre	fer·nay·trer

Directions

Where's ...?
Où est ...? oo ay ...

What's the address?
Quelle est l'adresse? kel ay la·dres

Could you write the address, please?
Est-ce que vous pourriez écrire l'adresse, s'il vous plaît? es·ker voo poo·ryay ay·kreer la·dres seel voo play

Can you show me (on the map)?
Pouvez-vous m'indiquer (sur la carte)? poo·vay·voo mun·dee·kay (sewr la kart)

Eating & Drinking

What would you recommend?
Qu'est-ce que vous conseillez? kes·ker voo kon·say·yay

What's in that dish?
Quels sont les ingrédients?	kel son lay zun·gray·dyon

I'm a vegetarian.
Je suis végétarien/ végétarienne. (m/f)	zher swee vay·zhay·ta·ryun/ vay·zhay·ta·ryen

I don't eat ...
Je ne mange pas ...	zher ner monzh pa ...'

Cheers!
Santé!	son·tay

That was delicious.
C'était délicieux!	say·tay day·lee·syer

Please bring the bill.
Apportez-moi l'addition, s'il vous plaît.	a·por·tay·mwa la·dee·syon seel voo play

I'd like to reserve a table for ...	*Je voudrais réserver une table pour ...*	zher voo·dray ray·zair·vay ewn ta·bler poor ...
(eight) o'clock	*(vingt) heures*	(vungt) er
(two) people	*(deux) personnes*	(der) pair·son

appetiser	*entrée*	on·tray
beer	*bière*	bee·yair
bottle	*bouteille*	boo·tay
bread	*pain*	pun
breakfast	*petit déjeuner*	per·tee day·zher·nay
cheese	*fromage*	fro·mazh
children's menu	*menu pour enfants*	mer·new poor on·fon
coffee	*café*	ka·fay
cold	*froid*	frwa
delicatessen	*traiteur*	tray·ter
dinner	*dîner*	dee·nay
dish	*plat*	pla
egg	*œuf*	erf
food	*nourriture*	noo·ree·tewr
fork	*fourchette*	foor·shet
glass	*verre*	vair
grocery store	*épicerie*	ay·pees·ree
highchair	*chaise haute*	shay zot
hot	*chaud*	sho
(orange) juice	*jus (d'orange)*	zhew (do·ronzh)
knife	*couteau*	koo·to
local speciality	*spécialité locale*	spay·sya·lee·tay lo·kal
lunch	*déjeuner*	day·zher·nay
main course	*plat principal*	pla prun·see·pal

Numbers – French

1	*un*	un
2	*deux*	der
3	*trois*	trwa
4	*quatre*	ka·trer
5	*cinq*	sungk
6	*six*	sees
7	*sept*	set
8	*huit*	weet
9	*neuf*	nerf
10	*dix*	dees
20	*vingt*	vung
30	*trente*	tront
40	*quarante*	ka·ront
50	*cinquante*	sung·kont
60	*soixante*	swa·sont
70	*soixante-dix*	swa·son·dees
80	*quatre-vingts*	ka·trer·vung
90	*quatre-vingt-dix*	ka·trer·vung·dees
100	*cent*	son
1000	*mille*	meel

In Francophone Belgium, though not in Luxembourg, the numbers 70 and 90 are *septante* and *nonante* respectively.

market	*marché*	mar·shay
menu (in English)	*carte (en anglais)*	kart (on ong·glay)
milk	*lait*	lay
plate	*assiette*	a·syet
red wine	*vin rouge*	vun roozh
rice	*riz*	ree
salt	*sel*	sel
spoon	*cuillère*	kwee·yair
sugar	*sucre*	sew·krer
tea	*thé*	tay
vegetable	*légume*	lay·gewm
(mineral) water	*eau (minérale)*	o (mee·nay·ral)
white wine	*vin blanc*	vun blong
wine list	*carte des vins*	kart day vun
with	*avec*	a·vek
without	*sans*	son

Emergencies

Help!
Au secours!	o skoor

I'm lost.
Je suis perdu/   zhe swee·pair·dew
perdue. (m/f)

Leave me alone!
Fichez-moi la paix!   fee·shay·mwa la pay

There's been an accident.
Il y a eu un accident.   eel ya ew un ak·see·don

Call a doctor.
Appelez un médecin.   a·play un mayd·sun

Call the police.
Appelez la police.   a·play la po·lees

I'm ill.
Je suis malade.   zher swee ma·lad

It hurts here.
J'ai une douleur ici.   zhay ewn doo·ler ee·see

I'm allergic to ...
Je suis   zher swee
allergique à ...   za·lair·zheek a ...

Shopping & Services

I'd like to buy ...
Je voudrais acheter ...   zher voo·dray ash·tay ...

May I look at it?
Est-ce que je   es·ker zher
peux le voir?   per ler vwar

I'm just looking.
Je regarde.   zher rer·gard

I don't like it.
Cela ne me plaît pas.   ser·la ner mer play pa

How much is it?
C'est combien?   say kom·byun

It's too expensive.
C'est trop cher.   say tro shair

Can you lower the price?
Vous pouvez baisser   voo poo·vay bay·say
le prix?   ler pree

There's a mistake in the bill.
Il y a une erreur dans   eel ya ewn ay·rer don
la note.   la not

ATM   *guichet*   gee·shay
    automatique   o·to·ma·teek
    de banque   der bonk

Signs – French

Entrée	Entrance
Femmes	Women
Fermé	Closed
Hommes	Men
Interdit	Prohibited
Ouvert	Open
Renseignements	Information
Sortie	Exit
Toilettes/WC	Toilets

credit card	*carte de crédit*	kart der kray·dee
internet cafe	*cybercafé*	see·bair·ka·fay
post office	*bureau de poste*	bew·ro der post
tourist office	*office de tourisme*	o·fees der too·rees·mer

Time & Dates

What time is it?
Quelle heure est-il?   kel er ay til

It's (eight) o'clock.
Il est (huit) heures.   il ay (weet) er

It's half past (10).
Il est (dix) heures   il ay (deez) er
et demie.   ay day·mee

morning	*matin*	ma·tun
afternoon	*après-midi*	a·pray·mee·dee
evening	*soir*	swar
yesterday	*hier*	yair
today	*aujourd'hui*	o·zhoor·dwee
tomorrow	*demain*	der·mun

Monday	*lundi*	lun·dee
Tuesday	*mardi*	mar·dee
Wednesday	*mercredi*	mair·krer·dee
Thursday	*jeudi*	zher·dee
Friday	*vendredi*	von·drer·dee
Saturday	*samedi*	sam·dee
Sunday	*dimanche*	dee·monsh

Transport

boat	*bateau*	ba·to
bus	*bus*	bews
plane	*avion*	a·vyon
train	*train*	trun

I want to go to ...
Je voudrais aller à ...   zher voo·dray a·lay a ...

Does it stop at ...?
Est-ce qu'il s'arrête   es·kil sa·ret
à ...?   a ...

At what time does it leave/arrive?
À quelle heure est-ce   a kel er es
qu'il part/arrive?   kil par/a·reev

Can you tell me when we get to ...?
Pouvez-vous me   poo·vay·voo mer
dire quand   deer kon
nous arrivons à ...?   noo za·ree·von a ...

I want to get off here.
Je veux descendre   zher ver day·son·drer
ici.   ee·see

first	*premier*	prer·myay
last	*dernier*	dair·nyay
next	*prochain*	pro·shun
a ... ticket	*un billet ...*	un bee·yay ...
1st-class	*de première classe*	der prem·yair klas
2nd-class	*de deuxième classe*	der der·zyem las
one-way	*simple*	sum·pler
return	*aller et retour*	a·lay ay rer·toor
aisle seat	*côté couloir*	ko·tay kool·war
cancelled	*annulé*	a·new·lay
delayed	*en retard*	on rer·tar
platform	*quai*	kay
ticket office	*guichet*	gee·shay
timetable	*horaire*	o·rair
train station	*gare*	gar
window seat	*côté fenêtre*	ko·tay fe·ne·trer
I'd like to hire a ...	*Je voudrais louer ...*	zher voo·dray loo·way ...
4WD	*un quatre-quatre*	un kat·kat
bicycle	*un vélo*	un vay·lo

car	*une voiture*	ewn vwa·tewr
motorcycle	*une moto*	ewn mo·to
child seat	*siège-enfant*	syezh·on·fon
diesel	*diesel*	dyay·zel
helmet	*casque*	kask
mechanic	*mécanicien*	may·ka·nee·syun
petrol	*essence*	ay·sons
service station	*station-service*	sta·syon·ser·vees

Is this the road to ...?
C'est la route pour ...? say la root poor ...

(How long) Can I park here?
(Combien de temps) (kom·byun der tom)
Est-ce que je peux es·ker zher per
stationner ici? sta·syo·nay ee·see

The car/motorbike has broken down (at ...).
La voiture/moto est la vwa·tewr/mo·to ay
tombée en panne (à ...). tom·bay on pan (a ...)

I have a flat tyre.
Mon pneu est à plat. mom pner ay ta pla

I've run out of petrol.
Je suis en panne zher swee zon pan
d'essence. day·sons

I've lost my car keys.
J'ai perdu les clés de zhay per·dew lay klay der
ma voiture. ma vwa·tewr

GLOSSARY

Nl/Fr after a term signifies Dutch/French.

abdij/abbaye (Nl/Fr) – abbey
apotheek (Nl) – pharmacy
ARAU (Fr) – Atelier de Recherche et d'Action Urbaine (Urban Research & Action Group)
auberge de jeunesse (Fr) – youth hostel

bakker/bakkerij (Nl) – baker/bakery
balle-pelotte – Belgian ball game
begijn/béguine (Nl/Fr) – inhabitant of a *begijnhof*
begijnhof/béguinage (Nl/Fr) – community of *begijnen/béguines*; cluster of cottages, often around a central garden
Belasting Toegevoegde Waarde (BTW) (Nl) – value-added tax, VAT
Belgische Spoorwegen (Nl) – Belgian Railways
Benelux – Belgium, the Netherlands and Luxembourg
benzine (Nl) – petrol
betalend parkeren (Nl) – paid street parking
biljart/billard (Nl/Fr) – billiards
billet (Fr) – ticket
boulangerie (Fr) – bakery
BP (boîte postale) (Fr) – post office box
brasserie (Fr) – brewery; café/restaurant often serving food all day
brocante (Fr) – bric-a-brac
brouwerij (Nl) – brewery
brown café – small, old-fashioned pub with wooden-panelled interior
bruine kroeg (Nl) – *brown café*
Brusselaar (Nl) – inhabitant of Brussels
Bruxellois (Fr) – inhabitant of Brussels; name of the city's old dialect
bureau d'échange (Fr) – foreign-exchange bureau

café – pub, bar
carte (Fr) – menu

centrum (Nl) – centre
chambre (Fr) – room
chambre d'hôte (Fr) – B&B guesthouse
Charles Quint – Holy Roman Emperor Charles V
château (Fr) – castle, country mansion
chocolatier (Fr) – chocolate-maker
commune (Fr) – municipality
couvent (Fr) – convent
cuistax – see *kwistax*

dagschotel (Nl) – dish of the day
demi-pension (Fr) – half board (ie accommodation, breakfast and dinner)
dentelle (Fr) – lace
dienst voor toerisme (Nl) – tourist office

église (Fr) – church
entrée (Fr) – entry
estaminet (Fr) – tavern
étang (Fr) – pond
EU – European Union
Eurocrat – EU administrative official
Europese Instellingen (Nl) – EU Institutions

fiets (Nl) – bicycle
frieten/frites (Nl/Fr) – chips or fries
frituur/friture/friterie (Nl/Fr/Fr) – chip shop

galerij/galerie (Nl/Fr) – covered shopping centre/arcade
gare (Fr) – train station
gastenkamer (Nl) – B&B/guesthouse
gaufres (Fr) – waffles
gemeente (Nl) – municipality
Gille (Fr) – folkloric character typical of the Binche carnival
gîtes d'étapes (Fr) – rural group accommodation, sometimes also a hostel
gîtes ruraux (Fr) – countryside guesthouses
godshuis (Nl) – almshouse

GR (Fr) – long-distance footpaths
grand café (Fr) – opulent historic *café*
gratis/gratuit (Nl/Fr) – free
grotte (Fr) – cave, grotto

hallen/halles (Nl/Fr) – covered market
herberg (Nl) – old-style Flemish pub
hof (Nl) – garden
holebi – LGBT (*ho*mosexual-*le*sbian-*bi*sexual)
Holy Roman Empire – Germanic empire (962–1806) that was confusingly neither theocratic nor predominantly Italian/Roman for most of its history
hôpital (Fr) – hospital
horeca (Fr/Nl) – the hospitality (*ho*tel-*re*staurant-*ca*fe) industry
hôtel (Fr) – hotel, historic town house
hôtel de ville (Fr) – town hall

Institutions Européennes (Fr) – EU Institutions
ISIC – International Student Identity Card

jardin (Fr) – garden
jenever – (Nl) Flemish/Dutch gin
jeu-de-balle (F) – see *balle-pelotte*
jeugdherberg (Nl) – youth hostel

kaartje (Nl) – ticket
kamer (Nl) – room
kant (Nl) – lace
kasteel (Nl) – castle
kerk (Nl) – church
kwistax – pedal-carts popular on Belgian beaches

magasin de nuit (Fr) – 24-hour shop
marché aux puces (Fr) – flea market
markt/marché (Nl/Fr) – market
menu (Nl & Fr) – fixed-price meal with two or more courses (what is called the menu in English is the *kaart/la carte*)

menu du jour (Fr) – fixed-price, multicourse meal of the day

molen/moulin (Nl/Fr) – windmill

Mosan – from the Meuse River valley

musée (Fr) – museum

nachtwinkel (Nl) – 24-hour shop

NATO – North Atlantic Treaty Organisation military alliance headquartered in Brussels (NAVO/OTAN in Dutch/French)

NMBS (Nl) – Belgian National Railways

office de tourisme (Fr) – tourist office

oude (Nl) – old

OV (originele versie) (Nl) – nondubbed (ie movie shown in its original language)

pâtisserie (Fr) – cakes and pastries; shop selling them

pékèt – Walloon for *jenever*

pension complète (Fr) – full board

pharmacie (Fr) – pharmacy

pitas (Fr) – stuffed pitta bread

place (Fr) – square

plat du jour (Fr) – dish of the day

plein (Nl) – square

poort/porte (Nl/Fr) – gate in city wall

premetro – trams that go underground for part of their journey (found in Brussels and Antwerp)

prior[itaire] (Fr) – priority mail

priorité à droite (Fr) – priority-to-the-right traffic rule

RACB (Fr) – Royal Automobile Club de Belgique

routier (Fr) – trucker (also truckers' restaurant)

SHAPE – NATO's 'Supreme HQ Allied Powers Europe' near Mons

slijterij (Nl) – shop selling strong alcohol

SNCB (Fr) – Belgian National Railways

sortie (Fr) – exit

stad (Nl) – town

stadhuis (Nl) – town hall

stadsbelasting (Nl) – city tax

stationnement payant (Fr) – paid parking

STIB (Fr) – Société des Transports Intercommunaux de Bruxelles (Brussels Public Transport Company)

syndicat d'initiative (Fr) – tourist office

taxe de séjour (Fr) – visitors' tax

terreinfiets (Nl) – mountain bike

toeristische dienst (Nl) – tourist office

toneel/théâtre (Nl/Fr) – theatre

toren/tour (Nl/Fr) – tower

trekkershut (Nl) – hikers' hut

tuin (Nl) – garden

TVA (Fr) – value-added tax, VAT

vélo (Fr) – bicycle

VO (version originale) (Fr) – nondubbed film

voorrang van rechts (Nl) – priority-to-the-right traffic rule

VTT (vélo tout-terrain) (Fr) – mountain bike

wassalon (Nl) – laundrette

weekend gastronomique (Fr) – accommodation plus breakfast and some meals

ziekenhuis (Nl) – hospital

Behind the Scenes

SEND US YOUR FEEDBACK

We love to hear from travellers – your comments keep us on our toes and help make our books better. Our well-travelled team reads every word on what you loved or loathed about this book. Although we cannot reply individually to your submissions, we always guarantee that your feedback goes straight to the appropriate authors, in time for the next edition. Each person who sends us information is thanked in the next edition – the most useful submissions are rewarded with a selection of digital PDF chapters.

Visit **lonelyplanet.com/contact** to submit your updates and suggestions or to ask for help. Our award-winning website also features inspirational travel stories, news and discussions.

Note: We may edit, reproduce and incorporate your comments in Lonely Planet products such as guidebooks, websites and digital products, so let us know if you don't want your comments reproduced or your name acknowledged. For a copy of our privacy policy visit lonelyplanet.com/privacy.

OUR READERS

Many thanks to the travellers who used the last edition and wrote to us with helpful hints, useful advice and interesting anecdotes: Anna Richardson, Beth Kriebel, Gabriella Sonnifero, Gaetano Lapenta, Manuel Francisco Rodriguez Góme, Richard Lemon, Steve Douglas, William Ballantine

WRITER THANKS

Mark Elliott

Endless thanks to ever-inspiring Sally Cobham for love, company and great insights. Many thanks also to old Belgian friends Wieland, Guy and Danielle and new friends Rosamund, Martin and family. On the road, thank yous are due to more people than I can fairly start to name here, but a particular shout goes to Jamie in Mechelen – may your new life bring you joy.

Catherine Le Nevez

Merci/Vielen Dank first and foremost to Julian, and to everyone in Luxembourg and beyond who provided insights, inspiration and good times during this update and over the years. Huge thanks too to Destination Editor Daniel Fahey and my co-authors, and everyone at Lonely Planet. As ever, *merci encore* to my parents, brother, *belle-sœur, neveu* and *nièce*.

Helena Smith

Sincere thanks to Pierre Massart and Gary Divito for the lowdown on all that is hip and happening in Brussels, and to EU expert Andrew Gray. Plus all my friends in Brussels for their advice, ideas and support.

Regis St Louis

I'm grateful to many people who offered insight into one of Belgium's most fascinating regions. I'd like to thank Myriam and Yves in Havelange, Laura in Waterloo, Anna in Mons, Ariane at Frasnes-lez-Anvaing and Paule at the Lac de l'Eau d'Heure. Warm thanks to Cassandra and our daughters, Magdalena and Genevieve, who joined me on the great south Belgium road trip.

Benedict Walker

A huge shout out to Daniel Fahey and Tamara Sheward at Lonely Planet for their patience, trust and guidance. My special thanks to Stefano Marin and my friends in Berlin, Matti, Anna, Robert and Kira for your support; to Maarten Masscheleyn for being an excellent Ghentian-guide; to my brother Andy, to Mum (as always) and the rest of the Walker and Cook clans for your continued encouragement. Dedicated to Warner Cook, Kevin Hennessy and James Ham.

ACKNOWLEDGEMENTS

Climate map data adapted from Peel MC, Finlayson BL & McMahon TA (2007) 'Updated World Map of the Köppen-Geiger Climate Classification', Hydrology and Earth System Sciences, 11, 1633–44.

Cover photograph: Bruges, Belgium, Rudy Balasko/ Getty Images ©

THIS BOOK

This 7th edition of Lonely Planet's *Belgium & Luxembourg* guidebook was researched and written by Mark Elliott, Catherine Le Nevez, Helena Smith, Regis St Louis and Benedict Walker. The previous edition was written by Helena Smith, Andy Symington and Donna Wheeler. This guidebook was produced by the following:

Destination Editor
Daniel Fahey

Senior Product Editors
Genna Patterson, Grace Dobell

Regional Senior Cartographer Mark Griffiths

Product Editor
Alison Ridgway

Book Designer Fergal Condon

Assisting Editors Imogen Bannister, Nigel Chin, Lucy Cowie, Pete Cruttenden,

Melanie Dankel, Andrea Dobbin, Tamara Sheward, Simon Williamson

Assisting Cartographers
Anita Banh, Katerina Pavkova, Anthony Phelan

Cover Researcher
Naomi Parker

Thanks to Jennifer Carey, Sandie Kestell, Kirsten Rawlings, Jessica Ryan, Dianne Schallmeiner, James Smart, John Taufa, Juan Winata

Index

Map Pages **000**
Photo Pages 000

Map Legend

Sights
- Beach
- Bird Sanctuary
- Buddhist
- Castle/Palace
- Christian
- Confucian
- Hindu
- Islamic
- Jain
- Jewish
- Monument
- Museum/Gallery/Historic Building
- Ruin
- Shinto
- Sikh
- Taoist
- Winery/Vineyard
- Zoo/Wildlife Sanctuary
- Other Sight

Activities, Courses & Tours
- Bodysurfing
- Diving
- Canoeing/Kayaking
- Course/Tour
- Sento Hot Baths/Onsen
- Skiing
- Snorkelling
- Surfing
- Swimming/Pool
- Walking
- Windsurfing
- Other Activity

Sleeping
- Sleeping
- Camping
- Hut/Shelter

Eating
- Eating

Drinking & Nightlife
- Drinking & Nightlife
- Cafe

Entertainment
- Entertainment

Shopping
- Shopping

Information
- Bank
- Embassy/Consulate
- Hospital/Medical
- Internet
- Police
- Post Office
- Telephone
- Toilet
- Tourist Information
- Other Information

Geographic
- Beach
- Gate
- Hut/Shelter
- Lighthouse
- Lookout
- Mountain/Volcano
- Oasis
- Park
- Pass
- Picnic Area
- Waterfall

Population
- Capital (National)
- Capital (State/Province)
- City/Large Town
- Town/Village

Transport
- Airport
- Border crossing
- Bus
- Cable car/Funicular
- Cycling
- Ferry
- Metro station
- Monorail
- Parking
- Petrol station
- S-Bahn/Subway station
- Taxi
- T-bane/Tunnelbana station
- Train station/Railway
- Tram
- Tube station
- U-Bahn/Underground station
- Other Transport

Routes
- Tollway
- Freeway
- Primary
- Secondary
- Tertiary
- Lane
- Unsealed road
- Road under construction
- Plaza/Mall
- Steps
- Tunnel
- Pedestrian overpass
- Walking Tour
- Walking Tour detour
- Path/Walking Trail

Boundaries
- International
- State/Province
- Disputed
- Regional/Suburb
- Marine Park
- Cliff
- Wall

Hydrography
- River, Creek
- Intermittent River
- Canal
- Water
- Dry/Salt/Intermittent Lake
- Reef

Areas
- Airport/Runway
- Beach/Desert
- Cemetery (Christian)
- Cemetery (Other)
- Glacier
- Mudflat
- Park/Forest
- Sight (Building)
- Sportsground
- Swamp/Mangrove

Note: Not all symbols displayed above appear on the maps in this book

OUR STORY

A beat-up old car, a few dollars in the pocket and a sense of adventure. In 1972 that's all Tony and Maureen Wheeler needed for the trip of a lifetime – across Europe and Asia overland to Australia. It took several months, and at the end – broke but inspired – they sat at their kitchen table writing and stapling together their first travel guide, *Across Asia on the Cheap*. Within a week they'd sold 1500 copies. Lonely Planet was born.

Today, Lonely Planet has offices in Franklin, London, Melbourne, Oakland, Dublin, Beijing and Delhi, with more than 600 staff and writers. We share Tony's belief that 'a great guidebook should do three things: inform, educate and amuse'.

OUR WRITERS

Mark Elliott

As a small child, Mark was dragged up a conical hill to meet a giant lion (at Waterloo) then let loose inside an enormous chemistry set (the Atomium). To a baby Brit, Belgium already looked pretty weird. But that was just the start. Having been based there for half of the last three decades, he has long since discovered that the country's surrealism runs even deeper – from art to countless crazy carnivals. He is the (co)writer of more than 60 travel books and guides.

Catherine Le Nevez

Catherine's wanderlust kicked in when she roadtripped across Europe from her Parisian base aged four, and she's been hitting the road at every opportunity since, travelling to around 60 countries and completing her Doctorate of Creative Arts in Writing, Masters in Professional Writing, and postgrad qualifications in Editing and Publishing along the way. Over the past dozen-plus years she's written scores of Lonely Planet guides and articles covering Paris, France, Europe and far beyond.

Helena Smith

Helena is an award-winning writer and photographer covering travel, outdoors and food – she has written guidebooks on destinations from Fiji to northern Norway. Helena is from Scotland but was partly brought up in Malawi, so Africa always feels like home.

Regis St Louis

Regis grew up in a small town in the American Midwest – the kind of place that fuels big dreams of travel – and he developed an early fascination with foreign dialects and world cultures. He spent his formative years learning Russian and a handful of Romance languages, which served him well on journeys across much of the globe. Regis has contributed to more than 50 Lonely Planet titles, covering destinations across six continents.

Benedict Walker

A beach baby from Newcastle (Australia), Benedict turned 40 in 2017 and decided to start a new life in Leipzig (Germany). Writing for Lonely Planet was a childhood dream for him. He's thrilled to have covered big chunks of Australia, Canada, Germany, Japan, USA (including Las Vegas), Switzerland, Sweden and Japan.

Published by Lonely Planet Global Limited
CRN 554153
7th edition – April 2019
ISBN 978 1 78657 381 0
© Lonely Planet 2019   Photographs © as indicated 2019
10 9 8 7 6 5 4 3 2 1
Printed in China